NOTE:✝ CAPT. ROSS' WHARE.

TURI TURI MOKAI.

THE DEFENDERS

OF

NEW ZEALAND

BEING

A SHORT BIOGRAPHY

OF COLONISTS WHO DISTINGUISHED THEMSELVES IN UPHOLDING

HER MAJESTY'S SUPREMACY IN THESE ISLANDS

BY

THOS. WAYTH GUDGEON

AUTHOR OF

"THE REMINISCENCES OF THE WAR IN NEW ZEALAND"
"THE DOINGS OF THE MAORIS FROM 1820 TO THE SIGNING OF THE TREATY
OF WAITANGI IN 1840," ETC., ETC.

The Naval & Military Press Ltd

Published by

The Naval & Military Press Ltd

Unit 10, Ridgewood Industrial Park,

Uckfield, East Sussex,

TN22 5QE England

Tel: +44 (0) 1825 749494

Fax: +44 (0) 1825 765701

www.naval-military-press.com

www.military-genealogy.com

*In reprinting in facsimile from the original, any imperfections are inevitably reproduced
and the quality may fall short of modern type and cartographic standards.*

Printed and bound by Lightning Source

DEDICATION.

TO THE MOVING SPIRITS, WHO TOOK SO ACTIVE A PART IN THE

VARIOUS INCIDENTS OF

THE LATE WAR

WHICH PROSTRATED FOR A PERIOD

THE DISTRICTS OF TARANAKI, WAIKATO, WANGANUI, AND

THE EAST COAST OF THE NORTH ISLAND,

ENTAILING MUCH LOSS AND SUFFERING UPON THE SETTLERS IN

THEIR PROTRACTED STRUGGLES

WITH THE NATIVES,

I DEDICATE WITH PLEASURE THIS MY FEEBLE ATTEMPT

TO CHRONICLE THEIR SERVICES,

SO THAT AFTER-GENERATIONS MAY LOOK BACK WITH

PRIDE ON THE DOINGS OF THEIR FOREFATHERS

(THE PIONEERS OF NEW ZEALAND),

IN QUELLING THE REBELLION AGAINST BRITISH AUTHORITY.

THOS. WAYTH GUDGEON,

LIEUTENANT AND QUARTERMASTER OF

WANGANUI MILITIA AND VOLUNTEERS.

AUCKLAND, 1887.

CONTENTS.

PLANS, VIEWS, ETC.

INTRODUCTION.

TRADITION tells us that the Maori race has not occupied New Zealand more than five hundred years. They describe themselves as a race that came to these islands at different periods in canoes from the north east, landing first in the neighbourhood of Auckland, whence they have gradually spread throughout the length and breadth of the land. Both mentally and physically they are a fine and noble race; but although interested writers have brought conspicuously forward their best qualities, nothing can be said of them that is not equally applicable to many other savage tribes.

No one can doubt the mental capacity of the Maori, and had it been possible to educate them and inculcate habits of sustained industry, they might by this time have altogether cast aside their savage habits and associations. It is true the missionaries have effected much good, but the unfortunate divisions amongst ourselves have not only prevented the gradually-awakening mind of the Maori from receiving fixed and decided principles, but have nearly rendered it impossible to convert any heathen nation to Christianity.

The Maori, like most of the primitive races, possesses an ardent love for his fatherland, and, startled at the gradual increase of the white population, he conceived the idea of preventing any more territory from passing under British rule; and from feelings of jealousy at the success of the Anglo-Saxon in the tillage of the land, the tribes combined to check our progress. Had they been better instructed in the facts of history, they would have understood how impossible it was to stay the progress of civilisation; and that the only way left to savage nations of escaping the doom of extinction and living in enjoyment, is by floating with the current instead of battling against it.

Perhaps the truest description of Maori character ever written was given by Dr. Thomson in his work on New Zealand. He says: " The New Zealanders have the minds of children and the passions of men. They respect ancient laws and customs, but are ready to embrace new opinions given out by men in authority. So constituted are their minds that it is impossible to decide how certain circumstances will affect them. Futurity is seldom looked into, although, like all mankind, they long for what is unknown, and regret what is lost.

" Fondness for novelty is a passion, but it is almost impossible to excite wonder. Vanity, arrogance, and independence are universal, but they are more vain than proud. In all their actions they are alive to their own interest and in seeking this, are not overburdened with conscientiousness.

"A New Zealander could not brook in word or deed an insult when witnessed by others. Wounded vanity caused much strife and cruelty, and cannibalism was occasionally produced by love of notoriety. They value life, but die with indifference when death is inevitable. They have little benevolence towards others; long absent friends are greeted with a profusion of tears, but as with children this grief is destitute of impression.

"Gratitude is unknown, no word expressive of this feeling being found in their language. Theft is rare amongst them, revenge being their strongest passion, and this feeling is kept alive for generations.

"They are jealous of each other, and love to excite terror. When excited they derive pleasure from cruelty and bloodshed. Tried by the European standard their conversations are sensual and their ideas unclean. Secrets are kept with difficulty. Of their deeds they are boastful. They accost their equals without levity, and their superiors without awe; and it is reckoned disgraceful to give way to anger. Cheerfulness more than laughter predominates.

"They are liberal in giving presents, but presents are merely modes of trade, as returns are always expected. They possess a great flow of words, and are fond of eloquence and oratory. They are dirty and indolent; strong against the weak, but weak against the strong. When mastered, either physically or mentally, they become as manageable as children; but this power must be exerted in the right way, for, like their own forest supple-jack, they are more easily overcome by gentle and skilful management, than by ill-directed force."

The Maoris appear to be a very mixed race, many being possessed of such strong Jewish features that one could easily imagine the Lost Tribes had visited New Zealand in times past—not to mention the woolly, the curly, and the straight-haired generations amongst them.

But I myself was once asked by an Irishman the nationality of my own children, and for the moment was so puzzled that without answering his question I referred it back to him, observing that my father was a Suffolk man, my mother a Dorsetshire lady, and being myself born in Hampshire, I was purely English. But I married the daughter of a Capt. Johnson, a Highlander by birth, and whose mother was a French lady, while my wife herself was born on board her father's vessel as she lay in the Bay of Naples.

"Now," said I, "what are they?" He mused for awhile, and exclaimed, "They are everything but Irish."

And so it is; as the world moves on, the intermarriages will bring us so closely allied with other nations that a few centuries hence we shall be so nearly related to each other as to make our quarrels family quarrels, and our wars civil wars.

SIR GEORGE GREY.

SIR GEO. GREY, K.C.B.

SIR GEORGE GREY was born at Lisbon, in 1812, three days after the death of his father, Colonel Grey, who fell while bravely leading his regiment at Badajoz; consequently, having imbibed the spirit of war at his very birth, it is not so much to be wondered at that he should still be found in the thick of the fight. Politically, Sir George Grey's career has been an eventful one. Too able and intractable to be led, and too much feared ever to be a strong leader, he has won staunch supporters and provoked bitter opponents; as with all men of pronounced character, his friends are as enthusiastic as his enemies are bitter. There are those who believe Sir George to be only one remove from the angelic, while others associate him with angels of a darker hue. Sir George started upon his public career in a rather remarkable way. A successful military course at Sandhurst gained him a captaincy in Her Majesty's 83rd Regiment before he was twenty-four years old. Two years later, his services were accepted by the Colonial Office, to explore North-Western Australia, and, in 1836, he landed at Hanover Bay, with Lieut. Lushington and twelve men, and had only penetrated about 70 miles inland, along the course of the Glenelg River, when his party were attacked by natives, and he received a spear-wound, from which he suffers to this day. Under these trying circumstances, further progress became impracticable, and, returning to Hanover Bay, the party were taken on board H.M.S. *Beagle*. After two years' recruiting at the Mauritius, Sir George prepared for a second attempt, and a whaler conveyed him to Shark's Bay, in Western Australia, where he was left, with three whaleboats and six months' provisions. Disaster again followed; the stores were washed away in a storm, and the party had to set out for Perth, a distance of 600 miles, in whaleboats, now in a leaky condition. They suffered such terrible privations, that all his party becoming exhausted, Captain Grey had to proceed ahead, and eventually succeeded in not only reaching his destination, but in sending back timely succour to his men. He was accompanied in this perilous journey by two non-commissioned officers of the Royal Sappers and Miners, John Cole and Richard Auger—two resolute and noble-minded men—and by a faithful native named Kaiber. His conduct on this occasion found such favour in the eyes of the Colonial Office that they rewarded him with the Governorship of South Australia; and some time after, when news of the native disturbances in New Zealand, under Captain Fitzroy's Government, reached England, Captain Grey was appointed to the head of affairs in this colony. He arrived here in November, 1845, and finding that the operations against the rebellious chief Heke were proceeding slowly and unsatisfactorily, he soon infused such spirit into the campaign, that within two months, not only had the Ruapekapeka Pa fallen, but Heke's power was completely broken. Matters were also in a very disturbed state in the southern part of the North Island, owing to the lawless behaviour of the chiefs Rauparaha and Rangehaeate, and the new Governor lost no time in punishing them. Having on the 23rd July, 1846, landed at Rauparaha's settlement before daylight with 130 men, he seized the old chief and carried him a prisoner on board ship, which act completely restored peace to the island. For these services Captain Grey was made a K.C.B.

The Home Government, having by this time formed a good opinion of Sir George Grey's administrative abilities, he was raised to the Governorship of the Cape Colony, and appointed High Commissioner for South Africa. The Kaffirs being in a state of insubordination, he took the reins of government at a most critical period, but was so successful in pacifying the natives, that in 1861, after the outbreak of the Maori War, he was once more dispatched to this colony, and continued to administer its affairs up to February, 1868, when his appointment ceased by effluxion of time.

During this period he came to an open rupture with General Cameron, who returned to England some two years before Sir George. Upon the latter's arrival, the Imperial Government who had throughout the correspondence apparently favoured the General against the Governor, instead of offering His Excellency another appointment, quietly pensioned him off. Sir George soon afterwards came back to New Zealand, and gave his valuable services for the good of the colony, by accepting various offices, such as the Superintendency of the Province of Auckland, the Leadership of the Opposition, and Premiership of the colony, which latter position he held for two years. In his quarrel with General Cameron, he vigorously refuted the charge brought by the General against the colonists, of desiring to use Her Majesty's forces in support of an iniquitous job, viz., to wrest land from the natives, and perpetuate large military expenditure. Sir George Grey was a man without fear, and his perseverance and courage were often called into play, particularly in his explorations, and during the Kaffir and Maori Wars. At Wereroa, after General Cameron had declined to attack the pa, on the ground that it could not be taken, and communications kept open, with less than 2000 soldiers, and then at a great sacrifice of life, Sir George assembled 309 friendly natives, 139 Forest Rangers, and 25 of the Wanganui Cavalry, and while 200 Imperial troops looked on as spectators, he personally, at the risk of his life, directed the operations against the pa, which he eventually succeeded in taking, capturing fifty natives who were hurrying to the relief.

The following correspondence took place between the Governor and the General upon the subject. The General wrote to the Governor on the 28th January, 1865, as follows :—

" I consider my force insufficient to attack so formidable a work as the Wereroa Pa. It would be necessary to establish two posts to keep our communication open with Wanganui, and we should have to furnish escorts daily for convoys. This would reduce my force to 700 or 800 men, which would not be sufficient to provide for the protection of the camp in such a country, and at the same time to carry on all the laborious operations of the siege. Instead of 1100 men, my present available force, I should require 2000. Besides, I should not have a single soldier left in reserve, and if anything should happen in any other part of the settlement, it would take a week or ten days to remove all the stores and raise the siege. For these reasons I do not intend to attack the pa, but to cross the Waitotara, and see what can be done on that side."

As the General would not attack the pa, the Governor proposed to let the friendly natives do it. He writes to General Cameron—

" The natives of this place and their friends, about 500 strong in all, wish to be allowed to attack the Wereroa Pa at Waitotara. Will their doing so interfere with your operations? If not, I will give them permission to do it. I am satisfied if they enter upon this that they will not commit any acts of cruelty, but will proceed in entire conformity with the rules of civilised nations."

The General, who had no faith in friendly natives, replies—

" So far from interfering with my operations, the friendly natives will materially facilitate them by attacking the Wereroa Pa, which Mr. Mantell affirms they will take ' in little more time than they will require to march thither.' I am quite sure that we could not take it in that off-hand manner, nor take it in any manner without considerable loss—that is, supposing the natives defend it in earnest, which there is no reason to think they will not do."

And a few days after—

" I was anxious to hear what the friendly natives are about. I expect to hear that their supposed desire to attack the Wereroa Pa was all bounce, though both you and Mr. Mantell seemed to have believed in it. However, if our operations should have the effect of drawing the greater part of the garrison

B*

out of the pa, which I expect they will, the friendly natives may have an opportunity of attacking it with some prospect of success."

The Governor replies—

" Mr. Mantell tells me that when the natives arrived at Wanganui, elated with their late victory over Pehi, they were anxious at once to have proceeded against the place, but he did not feel justified on his own responsibility in allowing them to do so. Since that time many of them have dispersed, and although they have repeatedly pressed me on the point of their going there I have thought it better for a little time to watch the course of events, and see what opportunities presented themselves, and what your movements may be, and what results flowed from these."

The General rejoins—

" I was very confident that the desire stated to have been entertained by the friendly natives to be allowed to attack the Wereroa Pa was mere bounce ; and I was astonished that you should have believed in it, that is to say, if you really did believe in it; and yet you could hardly have proposed that 500 natives should attempt what I told you I would not undertake at that time with fewer than 2000 soldiers, if you did not really believe that they would succeed. As to Mr. Mantell, he appears to me an excitable person, entirely devoid of common sense, and I shall pay no attention whatever in future to his opinions."

A few days afterwards, however, he writes more soberly—

" The country north of Wanganui to the Patea cannot be subdued without taking possession of the Wereroa Pa ; indeed, I believe that the capture of that position is all that is necessary to give us possession of the whole country between the Kai-Iwi and the Patea, for between the Waitotara and the Patea the country is perfectly open, and not likely to be defended. I wish, therefore, you would inform me whether you consider the immediate possession of the Waitotara block of such consequence that you wish me to attack the Wereroa Pa at once, notwithstanding the risk to which I have referred, or whether you wish me to continue my advance towards Taranaki."

The Governor answers—

" You have in your own correspondence answered the question whether or not I can wish you attack the Wereroa Pa at once. However necessary I might think the capture of the pa to be, to prevent wrong impressions in the native mind, or to attain the important objects, which you have pointed out in your letter of the 17th instant would follow from the capture of that pa, it is quite impossible for me to request you to attack it at once, when you have told me that you consider your force insufficient to attack so formidable a work, and that to enter upon this task you would require an available force of 2000 men ; that the natives have rendered the pa so formidable a position, and have at the same time occupied it in such strength, that it could not be taken without serious loss, uncompensated by any corresponding loss on the side of the rebels, who could at any time escape into the bush with impunity. The other alternative presented to me, must, therefore, necessarily be the one that I choose, viz.—that you should continue your advance towards Taranaki, so far as the means at your disposal will admit."

The General now left the coast and retired to Auckland, without

having attempted to take the pa. Then the controversy was renewed, the Governor writing on the 19th May—

"I have said that I have not taken so gloomy a view of the state of affairs as you appear to have recently done. I believe that large numbers of natives were prepared to submit to the Government. I think that they have in some measure been led to pause in this intention from what has taken place in regard to the Wereroa Pa, and the rumours which have for the last two months been circulated of the intended withdrawal of the troops; but I still think much may shortly be done to bring about the submission of many of their leading men.

"My own view of the course which ought to be taken in the present circumstances of the country, is that a sufficient force should be collected with the least delay practicable, to take the Wereroa Pa in such a manner as, if possible, to secure a marked and decided success on our part; that the local government should then, occupying as it would an advantageous position, attempt to come to terms with the leading rebel chiefs, which I believe it could speedily do; and that then, as a consequence naturally and properly following the pacification of the country, the proposed reduction of the troops should be promptly carried out. The colony having in the interim made such arrangements as it thinks necessary for raising additional local forces to take the place of the troops which are to be sent home. In this way I think effect might safely be given to the instructions of Her Majesty's Government."

To this, General Cameron replies —

"In regard to your Excellency's proposal to collect, with as little delay as possible, a sufficient force to take the Wereroa Pa, I must inform your Excellency that I consider it impossible to take that position by any formal operation in such a manner as your Excellency wishes, viz., so as to secure a marked and decided success, inflicting a large loss on the enemy, and sustaining but a trifling loss ourselves. I believe that in any formal attack on this position (which, it must be remembered, cannot be surrounded, and from which the natives can effect their escape at any moment), our loss would most probably be heavier, much heavier, perhaps, than that of the enemy; and that, under such circumstances, the mere possession of the place would not be followed by the important advantages which it is your Excellency's desire to attain.

"On the contrary, it is possible that its capture, with a loss on our side exceeding that of the enemy, might have an injurious moral effect on the natives, and, instead of hastening their submission, encourage them in postponing it.

"It is, indeed, a matter of surprise to me, that any one with a knowledge of the country between Wanganui and Taranaki, can entertain a hope of striking a decisive blow there. The nature of the country forbids the idea, and if Her Majesty's troops are to be detained in the colony until one is struck, I confess I see no prospect of their leaving New Zealand."

And again—

"With reference to your remarks as to the expediency of now attacking the Wereroa Pa, I would observe that the numerous army which you state to be at present in the colony (and which, I may remark, is distributed in posts on lines amounting to some hundreds of miles in length, with the finest artillery in the world, and abundance of scientific appliances), is not wanted for such an operation as an attack on the Wereroa Pa ; and were the army in the country much more numerous than it is, I should consider it unadvisable, at the present time, to assemble a large force for a formal attack on this position, by which there is, in my opinion, no reasonable grounds for expecting that the advantages your Excellency desires could be obtained. I stated my opinions fully on this subject in my last letter, and expressed my readiness to attack the position if, after the expression of those opinions, you thought proper to instruct me to undertake the operation.

" As your Excellency, however, still confines yonrself to the expression of opinions in which I find it impossible to concur, and leaves the decision of the question to me, I must exercise my own judgment as to the time and manner of getting possession of the place ; and I shall not allow myself to be influenced by remarks, however disparaging, to undertake an operation for the success of which I alone am responsible, in a manner which I do not fully approve.

" Under any circumstances, I consider that the capture of the Wereroa Pa, at the present moment, is not of sufficient importance to justify the detention of the whole force in the colony, after the instructions received from Her Majesty's Government."

As already stated, the issue of this correspondence was that Sir George Grey himself took the field, exposing himself to great danger, and with the colonial troops and native contingent, captured the pa. Some interesting facts in connection with this operation are given in the biographies of Colonel Rookes and Lieut.-Colonel McDonnell, who were in command of the attacking forces.

In the appendix to " Sir Gilbert Leigh," the author thus speaks of Sir George Grey, under the title of the Great Pro-Consul :—

" Few English or American children have failed to hear of Sir George Grey. In the religious periodicals, in the stories of missionaries, both in New Zealand, South Africa, and the Islands of the South Pacific, that name continuously occurs. He was the friend of Ellis, the Madagascar Missionary ; of Moffat and Livingstone of South Africa ; and of Selwyn in New Zealand. In the colonial wars of the last thirty years, Sir George Grey continually appears. He was, as it were, born and bred for a soldier. His father, at Alexandria, first turned the tide of victory against the soldiers of the Republic, leading his regiment in a bayonet charge against the French. But Sir George Grey never saw that father, as Colonel Grey fell at the storming of Badajos, three days before his son was born.

" Sir George was educated at Sandhurst, but enjoyed through the days of his youth the teaching and guidance of Dr Whately, afterwards Archbishop of Dublin. Thus trained, the student also meets his name in the treasuries of art, science, and philosophy ; yet few men are aware of his public labours, while still fewer attach to his life the notice which it merits. He started in the race with a definite purpose—that of opening a new future for Anglo-Saxondom in the boundless colonies of England. In those vast territories, washed by the waves of every sea, and canopied by every constellation, trusting to see communities arise free in the fullest sense—

communities in which the facilities for success in life should be vastly increased, and where talent, virtue, and worth should have free play and a fair field; where the crowded hives of the United Kingdom, from the fields of Norfolk and Devonshire, from the hills of Scotland, and from the 'Green Isle of the West,' a continued exodus of the over-populated nation could wander forth to till the mighty solitudes, and gather the harvests of the world. With a prophetic eye he saw the continents and islands of distant seas peopled with settlers, rich and prosperous, virtuous and free, great and powerful.

" It was in this way he formed the lofty ideas which filled him with the future dominance of his kindred, and revealed to him their future destiny. As years rolled on, he saw them anchoring deeper and deeper in every quarter of the earth, claiming and holding nearly all the habitable globe, every sea whitened by the sails of their commerce, every land ringing with their tongue; and, judging from mortal arguments and human logic, he believed that eventually the united Anglo-Saxon power would be strong enough to quell, by its mere existence, all warlike opposition, and restrain mankind to decide their quarrels by a Congress of the Nations. He looked forward to times and states in which these nations should govern themselves by the most perfect and equal laws.

" He went to the colonies, therefore, as to a most delightful field of labour, and undertook the duties of a Colonial Governorship as a congenial task, firmly believing that directly a nation ceased to grow and expand it began to decay.

" Sir George Grey had been appointed Governor of the Cape of Good Hope two or three years before the Indian Mutiny, and after the campaign in which General Cathcart had done so much to destroy the Kaffir power, there still continued a series of alarms and outbreaks, occasioned by certain Hottentot troops, who, having been disbanded, were receiving less pension than they had been led to expect. Sir George Grey, finding this to be correct, issued a proclamation, in the Queen's name, stating that the Hottentot forces should receive the same pension as their English comrades, and all arrears should be paid up, which settled the discontent then and there, as far as the Hottentots were concerned. This act made the War Office furious; but their fury was unavailing, as it was done beyond recall, in the Queen's name, and by the Queen's High Commissioner.

" A more terrible peril now menaced the Cape. The Governor learned that the Kaffir chiefs were leaguing together to invade the colony at various points. He also discovered that the chiefs had induced their people to destroy their own crops and cattle before starting, so that behind them was nothing but a barren desert, whereas before them lay the land of promise—the crops, bread, and cattle of the English, which they must either take or starve; and, as they numbered 200,000 strong, a most appalling tragedy was imminent.

" Sir George Grey at once proceeded to the Kaffir country, while

General Michel, who commanded the British troops, had received orders to take up a certain series of positions along the frontier.

"As Sir George Grey was passing through Kaffraria, with about fifty men, he was aroused from his sleep one night by messengers from the General. The missive was evidently drawn out of a brave officer by the weight and extent of the danger which threatened his forces, and the community they had to guard, as he set out the perilous condition in which his army would be placed by continuing to hold so extended a position, which rendered his line liable to be attacked at an awful disadvantage. He then continued, that, having well considered the position, he had determined to draw back to another line of defence on the Fish River, which his troops could hold against all-comers. But Sir George Grey, knowing well that the first step of retreat, the first receding standard of an English regiment, would be a certain signal for the onslaught of an almost innumerable host, without a moment's hesitation sat up and wrote the answer. Acknowledging the receipt of the letter, and the force of the General's reasoning, he said, that in his own opinion it was absolutely necessary to hold the advanced line. He reminded the General, that by the Queen's High Commission, he was in supreme command, and stated the line must be held, even if it became necessary for him to remove General Michel, and place in command some officer who would do it.

"The next day brought back the General's reply. 'He would obey and do what man could, and Sir George Grey might depend upon it, that no man would carry out his orders with greater skill or determination.' Sir George consequently passed on, and saw the Kaffir chiefs, satisfying himself that the tidings were too true. He pointed out to them the fact that they were only injuring themselves, and committing veritable suicide; but his arguments were useless, as one of their prophetesses, a woman reputed amongst the Kaffirs, as knowing the mind of the Fates, had said that it was the will of the deities that this sacrifice should be made, and that in return they would obtain tenfold from the English, in the day of victory. So Sir George returned, but in doing so, struck an efficacious blow. By a clever combination of secret movements, skilfully executed, and with great daring, he captured all the principal chiefs, and thus broke the neck of the confederacy, for now, the Kaffirs having destroyed their crops and cattle, had no one to lead them, and the people began to starve. Pale death reigned there, in dreadful silence, 50,000 Kaffirs dying of starvation, so that their villages became vast charnel houses, and stank with unburied corpses. Then the wisdom and humanity of Sir George came into full play, for, as Governor, he dispatched relief parties far and wide, rescuing the remnants from destruction. 34,000 of them he brought to the Cape, and distributed them amongst the colonists as servants, for a specified time. The remainder he built villages for, and, providing food, implements, seed, etc., settled them in British Kaffraria. So the dreaded tempest passed away, and history affords few parallels to these circumstances, and to the wisdom, determination, and mercy which marked the whole proceedings of the great Pro-Consul in this matter.

"In 1857, while Governor of the Cape Colony, he was called upon by Lord Elphinstone, then Governor of Bombay, to assist in the defence of the British Empire in India, and it so happened that just at this time a part of Lord Elgin's army, on their way to Canton to punish the Chinese, touched at Cape Town. These, Sir George Grey, on his own authority, directed to Calcutta, two days only after receiving Lord Elphinstone's letters, together with a part of the Artillery stationed there, fully horsed, and transmitted from the Cape Treasury £60,000 in specie; continuing to forward both men and horses. Knowing the Cavalry and Artillery must be supplied, he dismounted his own Cavalry and Artillery, even taking the horses from his own carriage, to keep up the supply. Vast stores of food for men and horses he also provided, and sent on with a quantity of ammunition. All this Sir George Grey did without any authority from the Imperial Government, and so quickly that the troops which enabled Lord Elphinstone to hold the mutineers in check at Bombay, and Sir Colin Campbell to relieve Lucknow, on the 17th November, 1857, were largely drawn from the forces sent by Sir George from the Cape.

"Yet all this time the great Pro-Consul was training a mixed community of Dutch, English, and natives to use the forms and substance of free representative political institutions, and laying the broad foundation of a great nation; while at the same time, he was contending and struggling against Downing Street, which did its best to hamper him in his great work.

"To sit down calmly and read the official correspondence is enough to make a man's cheeks glow with surprise and indignation. As I write, with the papers spread out before me, I wonder at the perverseness of the swiftly changing Secretaries of State, and with the patience with which Sir George marched on—not to fame, emolument, or distinction, but what is infinitely nobler, to the accomplishment of a great purpose—that of preserving peace and good government at home, and, at the same time, giving all possible assistance to Canning and Elphinstone in their tremendous conflict in the East.

"In one despatch Lord Stanley tells the Governor that the Parliamentary annual grant for 1858, for British Kaffraria, would be reduced from £40,000 to £20,000. Now British Kaffraria was a portion of the British Empire, in it 50,000 people, subjects of the Queen, were almost on the point of starvation. The cost of civil government, gaols, police, hospitals, justice, education, etc., demanded the whole of this £40,000, and yet, when half of the year was gone, during which the expenditure had been on the same scale as formerly, the High Commissioner is told, without warning, that only half the former amount will be given. At that time, owing to the judicious management of Sir George Grey, all affairs of British Kaffraria had been brought to a peaceable condition, and most of the native inhabitants located in regular villages, and another two or three years would have seen a great amount of prosperity; but had this reduction been carried out, all things would again have been thrown into confusion, and a fierce and bloody Kaffir war must have resulted. The authority of the Governor and High Commissioner would have been weakened. Deep offence would have been given in many dangerous quarters. Many of the most useful departments of Government would have been crippled or forsaken, and the common instincts of humanity outraged by the abandonment of thousands of starving Kaffirs to a miserable death. Meanwhile the 34,000 Kaffirs employed at the Cape would have filled the whole colony with bloodshed and destruction. Nor must it be forgotten by the public, although it seemed altogether forgotten by the Government, that Sir George Grey had, by the time the despatch reached the Cape, well nigh stripped South Africa of troops to send to India, 5000 veteran troops, with about 3000 horses and nearly all the Royal Artillery stationed at the Cape, having been sent on, while it was well known that some of the Kaffir chiefs, pretending to sympathise with the Sepoys, were intriguing against the English power. So Sir George Grey at once paid into the public account of British Kaffraria the sum of £6000 of his own private money. Then using as much economy as was consistent with safety, he carried on the government of British Kaffraria partly out of his own pocket.

" It is to be hoped that the British Government will never again place itself in the humiliating position which it then occupied. The most powerful and incomparably the most wealthy empire the world has seen was indebted to the private moneys of its servant for the lives and safety of tens of thousands of its subjects; on the other hand, long may the British people possess servants so true-hearted as to offer of their own for the public safety. It is satisfactory to know that the Imperial Government, after some considerable time, repaid this money to Sir George Grey, much to the credit of Sir Edward Bulwer Lytton.

" It was about this time that, stung by the continued and unmerited censures heaped upon him by the War Office, he wrote to Downing Street thus :—

" ' If virtual censures are continually recorded against me by one department of the State when I am right, what hope is there for me if, in the difficulties with which I am daily beset, I commit some error ? And how can those who are not acquainted with the real state of the case think otherwise, even when I am right, but that I must have acted wrongly to be so censured ? '

" In 1858-59 Sir George Grey, in accordance with the evident desire of the Home Government, invited the different legislatures in South Africa to express their willingness or objection to bring about a federation of all the States, which they were unanimous in wishing him to do. For this, in conjunction with the German immigration and his management of British Kaffraria, he was in 1859 recalled, —in effect dismissed from Her Majesty's service. This confederation in itself was the wisest step possible in relation to South Africa, and would have made those colonies and states a great and powerful confederation. The everlasting wisdom of Downing Street, however, thought otherwise, and he was harshly recalled. He broke up his establishments, suffered all the loss of such a step, and went home to find some in England who thought he was not deserving of censure. Among these were Her Most Gracious Majesty and the Prince Consort. When the steamer reached England, the first person whom Sir George Grey saw was a *Times* reporter. The ex-Governor asked the gentleman if he could tell him who had been appointed as the new Governor of the Cape.

" ' Oh,' said the roporter, ' there has been a fuss over that matter. There has been a change of Ministry, no new Governor has been sent up, Sir George Grey has been re-appointed, and a steamer has been despatched to stop him from coming home.'

" This was so far satisfactory, as while straining every nerve to aid in the suppression of the Indian mutiny he was by the Minister of the day misunderstood and misrepresented, he was gladdened and supported by the love of the people whom he governed, and by the generous gratitude which Canning and Elphinstone, with their councils, expressed for the wise and noble assistance he was continually affording them in the great crisis. Yet no adequate public recognition of his services had been made. Indeed, when we remember that he was almost always at war with the Colonial and War Offices, this is not wonderful.

" The English Government, some time before Sir George Grey became Governor of the Cape, had abandoned to their fate certain portions of South Africa and the communities therein living. This, we suppose, was the first step in the plan so favourably regarded by some modern politicians known as ' Economists,' of dismembering the Empire and allowing the colonies to shift for themselves. One of the said communities erected itself into a Republic by the name of the Orange Free State, and the Colonial Office made a species of treaty with this State, allowing it, in case of war with the native tribes, to purchase all munitions of war in the British colonies, and at the same time bound the English people and Government not to sell or allow its people to sell any such to the natives.

" In 1857 a desperate and sanguinary war broke out between the Orange Free State and the Basutos, a powerful native tribe, under the chief Moshesh. At first the Free State gained ground, having such facilities for getting arms and ammunition, but ultimately the natives obtained the upper hand. While, therefore, Sir George was denuding South Africa of English troops, there was a constant danger upon the frontier of a war arising with the Basutos and other tribes, who bitterly resented the treaty which compelled us to sell powder, arms, and bullets to the Free State men, and made us deny the same to them. At the very height of this savage and bloodthirsty conflict, Sir George assumed the position of mediator, and so well was he loved and trusted, that he succeeded in averting all fear of an expensive and dangerous war, and in restoring perfect and complete peace between the contending parties, a peace so complete that he was enabled to send off, at once, 3000 more men to India, out of the 5000 then remaining in the colony.

" Yet, for all this he was severely reproved by the home authorities, and his accounts disallowed. Again, he had hardly received the despatches thus condemning him, when there appeared in the public press of the colony, letters which showed that some person in authority at home had communicated their contents to persons in South Africa, for the communications published in the colony stated that Sir George Grey's Kaffir policy was viewed so unfavourably by the Ministry at home, that he would be obliged to resign his commission and retire. Sir George, being at this time well nigh overwhelmed with toil and anxiety—anxious as he was to serve his country, yet possessed of a proud sensitiveness which was keenly touched by the idea so publicly set forth as to his probable conduct—wrote thus to Lord Stanley, then Secretary of State for the Colonies :—

CAPE TOWN, *23rd June, 1858.*

" ' MY LORD,—In reference to some of the despatches which I have recently received, and which it appears to be thought here, and which (as you will find from my despatch No. 91) it is stated here, it was believed in England when they were written to me, were of such a nature that they would render it imperative on me to resign my office, I think it right to state that my life has been one of such constant active duty in remote parts of the world, and I have been so little mixed up in ordinary political affairs, that I am quite ignorant of what may be the conventional rules amongst public men on such subjects.

" ' I simply believe, in so far as your Lordship is concerned, that if you thought it would be for the advantage of the public service that I should vacate my office, you would, in a very straightforward, although courteous manner, tell me so.

" ' Yet, lest I should be violating any conventional rules which I do not understand, I beg to tell your Lordship that nothing but a sense of duty has made me hold my present office so long as I have done. My life is one of ceaseless toil and anxiety—of long separation from much which makes life valuable to man. I have only remained here because I thought I was useful to Her Majesty and to my country, from an attachment I feel for any duty which I am set to do, and from a personal regard to the very great number of persons in the colony who have helped me in my many difficulties. But when it is thought to be for the advantage of the public service to send me back to private life, I shall cheerfully and gladly make way for my successor.

" ' If, therefore, Her Majesty's Government desire to remove me, the slightest intimation to that effect from your Lordship shall lead to my immediate retirement.—I have the honour to be, your Lordship's most humble servant,

" ' G. GREY.'

" On another occasion, when he was severely galled by one of these despatches, he wrote to Downing Street :—

" I am here beset by cares and difficulties which occupy my mind incessantly and wear out my health. I feel I have conducted Her Majesty's affairs for the advantage of her service and the welfare of her subjects whose love, gratitude, and loyalty I have secured for the Queen, and I certainly feel it hard that the reward I should receive should be to have my spirits broken by accounts which I feel are entitled to the approval of Her Majesty's Government, disallowed, thus throwing me into new difficulties, and that this should be done in the uncourteous manner it is and in letters which as an old and loyal Government servant sorely wound my feelings is still worse."

" This was in relation to the non-payment for 2000 pairs of boots used for the German Legion, which force was clearly entitled to them.

" When will the farce of attempting to govern the colonies from the Home Office by men who cannot know anything of the colonies or of the people dwelling in them be played out?

" Here was a man governing a great satrapy or consulate with wonderful ability and patience, healing the wounds left by long years of war, mediating between fierce and hostile nations, tiding quietly over a tremendous crisis, inaugurating a system of free government, caring for the wants of his people down even to the desires of the meanest peasant, rectifying the mistakes of his predecessors, and amid all this, sending well nigh 10,000 veteran troops in strength and efficiency to aid the Empire in India, taking upon himself a responsibility so vast that if it had been unwisely or improperly taken, or if one single step had miscarried, it would have brought upon him ruin utter and absolute. Yet we see him in the midst of these congregated cares and perils suggesting to the Ministry at home new schemes for the welfare of the people and the glory of the Queen's Empire, fostering science, aiding religion, promoting education, art and settlement, binding the affections of the community to the Queen, and so ruling that the people refused absolutely to take the power from his hands and rule themselves. With one Minister he was strongly at variance in relation to the federation of the colonies of the South African Group. With a wise forethought he saw that all the colonies belonging to Great Britain in South Africa, together with the free territories upon our border, should be, before the safety and true greatness of that country were accomplished, drawn together into a federal union, which would give them unity of council and strength, unity of wealth and all resources. In a word, he in 1859 desired to accomplish what in 1875 the British Government sent Mr. Froude to the Cape to attempt. For this he was recalled in disgrace, but subsequently, when the Duke of Newcastle became Secretary for the Colonies, reinstated in his command, and it is, to say the least, wonderful that the same minister (Lord Carnarvon) who was so strongly averse to federation in 1859 should be the Colonial Minister who tried to achieve it in 1875.

" Sir George Grey was essentially a man of original ideas and determination. When a great crisis arose the Ministry sent him to the spot confident in his powers although the very exercise of that power alarmed them. When Colonel Gawler, the Governor of Adelaide, got into a mess the Ministry sent Sir George Grey to Adelaide and he soon settled matters. Then when Governor Fitzroy had embroiled the Government of New Zealand with the Maoris Captain Grey was sent there and succeeded. Then affairs at the Cape of Good Hope brought upon England a disastrous Kaffir War, Sir George Grey was sent there again to be successful, and there it was that the Indian Mutiny found him. It is questionable whether another man could have been found in the Queen's dominions to do the work done by him as well or as surely as he did it. Swift to read the signs of the times, fruitful in expedients to achieve victory and to avert defeat, wielding marvellous influence over the minds of those, whether civilised or barbarian, with whom he came in contact, Sir George Grey took steps which surprised and discomfited both the officials in Downing Street and at the War Office in Pall Mall. They were willing enough to accept the happy results, but they grumbled and chafed at the means by which those results were obtained."

SIR THOMAS GORE BROWNE.

SIR T. GORE BROWNE.

*Incidents of the Afghan War—Appointment as Governor of New Zealand—
Origin of the war—History of the Waitara land purchase—The discovery and early settlement of Taranaki—Governor Browne's firmness
with the natives—The rival claimants, William King and Te Teira—
Dilatory action of Imperial troops.*

COLONEL SIR THOMAS GORE BROWNE, K.C.M.G.,
son of Robert Browne, Esq., of Morton House, Buckinghamshire, and brother of the Bishop of Winchester,
was born in 1807. He entered the army when very
young, and served many years in the 28th Regiment; acted as
Aide-de-Camp to Lord Nugent, Lord High Commissioner of the
Ionian Islands, and was for some time Colonial Secretary. In
1836 Major Gore Browne exchanged into the 41st Regiment, and
was engaged in the occupation of Afghanistan. After the massacre
of our troops at the Khyber Pass the 41st joined General England,
and advanced to the rescue of General Nott and his troops. At
this time Major Browne held the command of his regiment, and was
also in command of the reserve at the disastrous battle of
Hykulzie, where by forming his men into a square, when the van
of the army had been broken, he was enabled to repulse the enemy
and cover the retreat. He held command of the regiment also at
the battles of Candahar, Ghuznee, Cabul, and during the march
through the Khyber Pass, where he commanded the rear, as he did
also under General McGaskett at the storming of the Nik Fort at
Issaliff—the most daring action during the war. Major Gore
Browne's gallantry and humanity were praised in the General's
despatches, which were quoted in both Houses of Parliament, and
for his services he obtained a lieutenant-colonelcy and was made a
C.B. On his return with his regiment from India he exchanged
into the 21st, which he commanded until made Governor of St.
Helena in 1851. From St. Helena he was promoted to the
Governorship of New Zealand, and in 1861, having completed his
term of office, he took the place of Sir Henry Young as Governor
of Tasmania; on resigning this last-mentioned appointment in
January, 1869, he was created a Knight Commander of the Order
of St. Michael and St. George, and appointed Governor of
Bermuda.

It was in the month of September, 1855, that Colonel Gore

Browne succeeded Sir George Grey as Governor of New Zealand, Sir George having left to assume the direction of affairs at the Cape. I was residing at Taranaki at the time of the new Governor's first visit to that part of the colony, and from the unassuming and unostentatious manner of the Colonel's landing, he had nearly passed through the guard of honour drawn up to receive him before the settlers were aware of his presence. He was a soldier in every sense of the word, a man of prompt and decided action, and not easily turned from the strict path of duty by any fear of consequences. He was the first and only Governor who treated the natives in a blunt John Bull manner, a treatment which the Maoris, having hitherto been used to the flour-and-sugar policy, could not for a time understand. His policy began by impressing on the natives that his word was law; that he was here to dispense justice and defend the rights of Her Majesty, as well as to listen to and redress Maori grievances, and, as there was but one law for the two races, he would, in obedience to that law, respect and defend the individual rights of any native having land of his own and willing to sell. This declaration fell like a bombshell into the camp of the Maori King Land League, and caused the new Governor many enemies, not only amongst those who had hitherto existed on the peace-at-any-price policy, but also of many missionaries, who could see nothing wrong or extravagant in anything the natives did or demanded, and who were mainly instrumental in delaying, if not in preventing, the settlement of the great question at issue between the two races, viz., who were to be the future masters of New Zealand, for it was soon evident to Colonel Gore Browne that the policy hitherto pursued had not only lost us the prestige usually accorded to Englishmen, but had gained us the contempt of the whole Maori race, as up to this time they had actually dictated to the Government, bouncing them with the most extravagant demands, and defying the law whenever it suited them , and were supported in their rebellion by those who should have known better. To these false sympathisers may be attributed most of the troubles that have befallen the natives.

The new Governor's first attention was directed to the land question, the source and origin of all disputes in a new colony, particularly when the sovereignty of the same is vested in the hands of the natives, for they never will understand that land is of little or no value until rendered so either by population or cultivation, by labour bestowed upon it, or by roads made towards it, and it is only when so improved that, jealous of its increased value, they become dissatisfied, and, setting up some frivolous excuse, either demand the land back again or double the amount already paid for it. Many a settler who, by the labour of his hands, has carved from the wilderness a really comfortable homestead, sooner than leave it has, for the mere sake of peace, submitted to be robbed times out of number. This was the case of the Waitara settlers, who were dispossessed of their farms after a long occupation, the Government, to save a conflict, giving way, and removing the settlers to the site of the present township of New Plymouth. The dispute over this block was the legacy left by his predecessors to Colonel Gore Browne, to be fought out between the two races, and his determination to master the difficulty, by taking forcible possession of the land he had purchased, was not only endorsed by the authorities, but fully approved of by the settlers generally.

Taranaki, the seat of the war, takes its name from the lofty, snow-clad mountain, called by us Egmont, and by the natives Taranaki. The first European who beheld Taranaki was the Dutch navigator, Tasman, in December, 1642, and on the 10th January, 1772, Captain Cook sighted Mount Egmont, just one month before the French navigator, M. Marion du Fresne, made the land. From that time to 1839 Taranaki was only visited by whalers. In 1839 a company was formed in England, called the Plymouth Company, to establish a colony in New Zealand, and this company invested £10,000 in the purchase of 50,000 acres from the New Zealand Company at the Waitara, Colonel Wakefield acting as agent for them in negotiating the purchase. He first arranged for the purchase with the fugitives residing on the shores of Cook's Straits, who had been driven from off the lands in question, and were afraid to return. About the end of the same year, the company's naturalist, Ernst Duffenbach, found a handful of wretched natives living at Taranaki, on obscure plantations, hidden deep in the recesses of the forest, and succeeded in purchasing their right to the soil. After this, the head chief of Waikato who had conquered these tribes, sent a subordinate named Te Kaka, with 200 men, to demand payment for the Waitara land, it being his by conquest, and to satisfy him Governor Hobson gave him £150 in cash, two horses and saddles, two bridles, and 100 red blankets, and further, entered into an agreement, that for the future one-tenth of the land purchased should be reserved to the natives, and so as to expedite their civilization, these reserves should be in the midst of the lands selected by the Europeans. Consequently, a village was soon formed about eight miles from the present township of Taranaki, on a beautiful and level tract of land on the banks of the Waitara, and the settlers had hardly taken possession of the dwellings they had erected, when a number of returned slaves, the original owners of the district, who had been set at liberty through the influence of the Rev. John Whiteley, became in their turn most insolent and tyrannical, demanding the land back again. And to settle this question, the Home Government sent out a Commissioner, by the name of Spain, who having heard all the pros and cons, gave his decision against the returned slaves, and confirmed the purchase : but as this decision rather increased the feeling of discontent, Governor Fitzroy, to avert unpleasantness, reversed the award of the Imperial Commissioner, declared the settlers trespassers, and abandoned the settlement (already twice purchased) to the returned slaves, with this proviso, that the dispossessed settlers should re-enter on their original selections whenever the native title should be extinguished. It was this imprudent act of Governor Fitzroy that first gave the natives a knowledge of their power over us, which they never forgot from that moment to exercise, and laid the foundation of a future war of races, which was staved off from year to year only by expensive gifts and repeated acts of humiliation on the part of the Government up to the arrival of Governor Browne. It was also a death-blow to the new settlement, inasmuch as many emigrants immediately left for Australia, others were induced by the Government to go up to Auckland and work a newly-discovered copper and manganese mine, while those who remained were compelled to go into the heavily-timbered land at Taranaki and hew out for themselves farms with the axe.

The new Governor had hardly set his foot in Taranaki before a deputation of the settlers waited upon him to describe the straits they were in ever since their removal from the banks of the Waitara on to a block of land far from sufficient in area to give to each sufficient acreage, with all their ingenuity, to carry their increase, while all around them were millions of acres of wild, uncultivated land lying idle, belonging to natives, who refused to cultivate it themselves, or dispose of it to those who would, the Taranaki tribes having joined the Land League initiated (through the suggestions of the pakeha-Maori) by the so-called Maori King, to put a stop to any further sale of land to the Government of the country. These representations it was that caused the Governor to take the first step towards counteracting and breaking up this compact, by declaring, at his first interview with the natives, that, for the future, it was his intention that if any native had land, of which he could give an undisputed title, and was willing to sell, he would respect such a one's wish, and make good his purchase; inasmuch as he would not allow any third person to interfere or forbid the sale of land he had no real interest in. On hearing this, a native by the name of Teira immediately arose and offered to the Governor a small block, belonging to himself and friends, at the Waitara, and asked him if he would purchase it. The Governor replied, " Yes, if you can show you are really the owners; but I will have nothing to do with any land where any of the parties interested are unwilling to sell. I do not wish anyone to sell against his will." This was the death-blow to the League, and William King as chief, saw that his only chance lay in his disputing Teira's right to sell, in which step he would be supported by all the King natives, and the League in every part of the island; for on the question being put to William King, " Is the land in question Teira's?" he, before a large assembly of pakehas and Maoris, replied, " Yes, the land belongs to Teira, but I, as chief, will not allow him to sell it." Notwithstanding this reply of William King, the Governor, to be further satisfied that Teira's title was good, took the greatest trouble to ascertain, by referring the question to the Chief Land Purchase Commissioners, Mr. McLean, Mr. Parris, and Mr.

Stephenson Smith, for their report thereon, before he would entertain the purchase, as the following memorandum will show :—

[MEMORANDUM BY HIS EXCELLENCY THE GOVERNOR.]

"GOVERNMENT HOUSE, *20th July, 1860.*

"In order to complete the documents about to be printed for both Houses of Assembly, the Governor requests the Chief Land Purchase Commissioner to answer the following questions :—

"First : Had Tamata Rara, Rawiri Rauponga, and their people such a title to the block of land recently purchased at the Waitara as justified them in selling it to the Queen?

"Secondly : Had William King any right to interfere to prevent the sale of the above block of land at the Waitara to the Queen?"

[CHIEF LAND PURCHASE COMMISSIONER'S REPLY.]

"AUCKLAND, *23rd July, 1860.*

"SIR,—In reply to your Excellency's memorandum of the 20th inst., I have the honour to state, with reference to the first-mentioned question, that I believe the above-mentioned chiefs, conjointly with others at the South, associated with them in the sale, had an undoubted right of disposal to the land in question. With reference to the second inquiry, William King's question of title has been carefully investigated. All the evidence that has come before me, including William King's own testimony, that the land belonged to the above parties, goes to prove that he had no right to interfere ; the interference assumed by him has been obviously based upon opposition to land sales in the Taranaki province generally as a prominent member of an anti-land-selling league.—I have, etc.,

"DONALD McLEAN,
"Chief Land Purchasing Commissioner.

"To His Excellency
"Colonel GORE BROWNE, C.B., etc."

Mr. Parris' answer was equally condemnatory of William King's action in trying to stop the sale.

So anxious was the Governor to get at every information on the subject from both sides that he allowed nine months to elapse before he was completely satisfied, and paid over the deposit, he having during this time obtained the opinion of all those who were competent to judge on Maori matters, and who all declared Teira's title good. William King, in the meantime, had not been idle. He knew full well that if he once allowed the purchase of Teira's land to go unchallenged, all the resolutions of the Land League were useless ; consequently he fought for the mana—the right of a chief to control his tribe and keep them slaves to his will—which Teira naturally objected to, and the Governor would not sanction while one law existed for both races. During the time the purchase was under consideration, Teira's party got tired of waiting, and wrote the following curious letter, showing the figurative language of the Maoris in their communications :—

"WAITOKI, *19th January, 1860.*

"Go this loving letter to Governor Browne and to Mr. Smith. Friends, salutations to you. This is our word to you. Hearken. Why do you delay?

You say that Mr. Parris has the arrangement of the matter. Mr. Parris says that it lies with the Governor to consummate our marriage with the beautiful woman, Waitara—with the land which we have given up to you. Give your consent at my request. You said that it was deceit on my part. Agree that Mr Parris shall complete it; do not delay the matter. If you are willing to do so, write to me; and if you are not, write to me. Write speedily, that it may come straight to your children who are residing with Mr. Parris. We are sad because of our marriage with this woman being deferred so long. This woman that we gave to you in the face of day is now lying cold. You had better turn her towards you and warm her, that she may sleep comfortably in the middle of the bed. Come also yourself, that I may know your intentions, and that you may hear my word to you. Come my father the Governor. This is our letter to you.

"From Te Teira, Hemi, Tamati, Weterini, Eruera, Paranihi,

"Te Retimana, Rawhiri, Matiu, Hori.

"To His Excellency Governor Browne, Auckland."

On Thursday, March 1st, 1860, the *Airedale* arrived from Auckland with Governor Browne and suite, accompanied by Colonel Gold, an extensive military staff, and 200 rank and file of the 65th. The same day Her Majesty's steamship *Niger* dropped her anchor in the roadstead. The first step of the Governor was to issue the following proclamation in Maori, a translation of which is given in full, as it tends to explain both the origin and justness of the war :—

[TRANSLATION.]

" 1. When the Pakehas first came to Taranaki there were no natives at the Waitara. The Ngatiwa had been dispossessed by the Waikato. 2. The Waikato transferred their rights to the Government and received a payment for the land. 3. Afterwards the Ngatiawa returned and occupied the land: the Government acquiesced in this occupation. 4. In March, 1859, some of these occupants, Te Teira and others, openly offered to sell to the Government their claims to a portion of the land at the Waitara. 5. William King opposed this offer, and said that no land at the Waitara should be sold. But the ' mana ' of the land was not with William King, and he had no right to forbid the sale of any land which did not belong to him personally. 6. The Queen has said that all the natives shall be free to sell their lands to her, or to keep them—as they may think best. None may compel the Maori people to sell their lands, nor may any forbid their doing so. 7. William King sets his word above the Queen's, and says, though the rightful owners of the land may wish to sell, he will not allow them to do so. 8. The Governor cannot allow William King's word to set aside the words of the Queen. 9. The Governor has said that he will not allow land to be bought, the title to which is disputed. He has also said that he will not allow interference with the rightful owners in the sale of their lands. When land is offered, the title to which is clear, the Governor will use his own discretion in accepting or declining the offer. 10. The Governor accepted Te Teira's offer conditionally on its being shown that he had an indisputable title. 11. Te Teira's title has been carefully investigated and found to be good. It is not disputed by any one. The Governor cannot, therefore, allow William King to interfere with Te Teira in the sale of his own land. 12. Payment for the land has been received by Te Teira. It now belongs to the Queen. 13. William King has interfered to prevent the survey of the Queen's land by her own surveyors. This interference will not be permitted. 14. The Governor has given his word to Te Teira and he will not go back from it. The land has been bought and must be surveyed. The Queen's soldiers will protect the surveyors. If William King interferes again and mischief follow, the evil will be of his own seeking. 15. The Governor desires peace. It depends upon William King whether there shall be peace or not. If he ceases to interfere with what is not his own he will be treated as a friend, and there will be peace.

Closely following this, a meeting took place between the Maoris and the Governor, who after stating how anxious he was to see the natives become a happy and civilised people, told them boldly and determinedly that had he been in New Zealand when Katatore slew Rawiri, he would have had him arrested and brought before the judge, and, if the judge had sentenced him to be hanged, he would have caused him to be hanged. The Governor also stated that the Maoris would be wise to sell the land they could not use themselves, as it would make what they could use more valuable than the whole.

Governor Browne, seeing that the undecided and pusillanimous manner with which Government had hitherto met these difficulties had done much towards giving the Maoris an exaggerated confidence of their own prowess, gave instructions over and over again, in the early days of the rebellion, to officers commanding troops, to show the natives, by a decided demonstration, our superiority in arms, so as to convince them how futile it would be to attempt to compete with us and hope for success. Had the Governor's wishes been met, there is every reason to believe that the rebellion might have soon ended in a confirmed peace throughout the island. Instead of which, no one who has made himself acquainted with the proceedings of the Imperial forces in the conflict, but must see that in no one instance was an advantage gained that was followed up. At the very commencement of hostilities we allowed an inferior number of savages to evince their superiority in strategy, by escaping from their besieged pa, on an open flat, in the face of a very superior European force. After the Battle of Waireka, the beaten rebels were permitted, unmolested, to retire to their own country laden with plunder. The same at Kaihihi, and Mahoetahi, and in no instance were the beaten Maoris, by judicious and rapid movements on our part, prevented from occupying fresh, and in many cases, more advantageous positions. This it was that gave the Maoris such false hopes, and which tended to prolong the war for so many years.

The war, in consequence of the increasing disaffection of the natives, extended throughout the North Island, and on the termination of Colonel Gore Browne's term of office the Home Government recalled him, and re-established Sir George Grey as Governor, hoping that his previous knowledge and influence among the Maori chiefs would assist him in putting down the rebellion. News having reached the colony of the appointment of Sir George Grey as successor to Colonel Gore Browne in the Governorship of

New Zealand, a valedictory address was presented to the retiring Governor, signed by the entire male adult population of Taranaki. Sir George Grey arrived in Auckland, from the Cape of Good Hope, on the 26th of September, and was welcomed on shore by Colonel Gore Browne, and on the 1st of October, Colonel Browne and family left Auckland, for Sydney, in the *Henry Fernie*, amidst the warmest expressions of respect and esteem from the inhabitants.

TROOPER A. RODRIQUEZ.

A brave Foreigner.

ANTONIO RODRIQUEZ was one of the earliest settlers at Taranaki, and was suddenly called upon to defend his life and property from the assaults of the disaffected natives of the district. He joined the mounted force under Captain Mace, and did such good service all through the war that he was recommended for and received the New Zealand Cross for noble and daring conduct in assisting and carrying wounded men from the field, under fire, on several occasions, notably on the 2nd October, 1863, at Poutoko, and 11th March, 1864, at Kaitaki, upon which latter occasion he was particularly mentioned in garrison orders after the engagement. Rodriquez's conduct was repeatedly mentioned by Colonel Warre and other officers in their despatches.

MAJOR ATKINSON.

MAJOR ATKINSON.

His life as a bush settler—Growth of Maori discontent—Company of Bush Rangers formed—A series of spirited engagements—A devoted and brave company—Political success.

MAJOR ATKINSON and his brother (the late Decimus Atkinson) arrived in the colony about the year 1855, and settled down at Taranaki, where they purchased a quantity of bush land, and set to work with a will to carve out of the forests of New Zealand their future homesteads. Prior to their arrival some uncertainty existed as to the peaceful character of the natives of the district. Their constant demands on the Government, and the visible change in their behaviour towards the pakeha, induced the settlers to accept the offer of an old Indian officer (Major Lloyd) to give them lessons in drill, so that, in case of an outbreak, they might be able to work together, under their officers, for the protection of their wives and children. Major Lloyd constantly warned the young men to miss no opportunity, but to learn all they could, and as quick as they could, as the question of supremacy might arise at any moment, and would have to be fought out before any lasting peace could be established.

On my arrival in 1850, and for a few years afterwards, the natives of the Taranaki district were the best behaved and the most civilized of the North Island, vieing with each other as to who should possess the best farm implements, the best bullocks and carts; bringing in every Saturday (the market day) their produce, and laying out the proceeds in European clothing and provisions. But at last, quarrelling among themselves over the boundary of land claimed by one of their most influential men, a native magistrate named Rawiri, they shot him down. From that moment all was changed; the European clothing was discarded for the blanket, and the farm implements were seized and burnt. Although the settlers were not mixed up with these disputes at first, they were gradually drawn in by their sympathies.

When the war began in earnest, the colonists of Taranaki found the value of the drill they had received, and, having something to fight for, were always to be found where danger threatened. Amongst the foremost of these was Major Atkinson. The young men of the district were as thoroughly used to bush life, and as much at home in the forests of New Zealand as the natives themselves. Forming themselves into a company of bushrangers, they chose Mr. Atkinson as their captain. It was this sort of fighting the Imperial British soldier dreaded—a guerilla warfare in every sense of the word—which the newly-arrived regular was neither fitted for either in dress, nor in the way he was armed.

The first action fought by the colonial troops was at Waireka, on the 28th March, 1860, where their behaviour elicited the admiration of the whole colony, being the first under fire, and the last to leave the field. After this, Major Atkinson was present at the taking of several pas at Kaihihi in October, 1860; the battle of Mahoetahi, on November 6th of the same year; and the battle of Matarikoriko, in the following month. He also assisted in the capture of Kaitake, on the 24th March, 1864; the several skirmishes at Sentry Hill; the recovery of the wounded and killed at Ahu-Ahu, after the defeat of the Imperial troops; the battle of Allen's Hill at Potokou; and the taking of the pas and strongholds at Manutahi and Mataitawa. Having 150 men under his command, who would follow him anywhere, his company were effectively employed in clearing the bush and district of rebel natives. For his gallant services in the field, he was promoted to the rank of major, was repeatedly mentioned in despatches, and on several occasions received the thanks of the Government of the day. Colonel Warre, in his despatches, said that Major Atkinson possessed the energy and perseverance requisite to make him a first-rate guerilla leader.

Major Atkinson was soon afterwards chosen to represent a Taranaki constituency in the House of Representatives, and on a change of Ministry taking place, he accepted the portfolio of Defence Minister; and eventually rose to the highest office in the public service—the Premiership of New Zealand. Whatever the Major undertook, he gave his whole attention to; and, although many may have differed with him in his politics, all must admit and admire his earnestness in promoting the welfare of the colony.

CAPTAIN R. BROWN.

Early troubles with the Natives—Shot by a former Maori servant—His competition with the New Zealand Company.

RICHARD BROWN was born in Dublin, in 1804, and was brought up and educated in that city by an uncle. In his youth, he was employed in a mercantile house in Hobart, and at the age of twenty paid a visit to the Bay of Islands, and to the islands of the Pacific Ocean, in a Tasmanian whale ship. Shortly after the occupation of Taranaki, he settled in New Zealand, and, after conducting a coasting trade for some time, ultimately became a merchant in New Plymouth, having for his place of business, a long, low warehouse near to the boat-sheds. In 1847, he had a quarrel with the natives about a horse, and striking one on the head with a heavy whip handle, nearly paid for his temerity with his life. The natives came into town in large numbers, danced the war dance, and demanded that he should be given up to them. For safety, the authorities confined him in the town prison, around which the natives kept watch all night. In the morning, the natives were pacified by Mr Brown consenting to give up the horse, as utu for the injury he had done. For some time after this, Mr Brown engaged in whaling, employing a shore party at Moturoa, under the management of Robert Sinclair, and at the same time added to his business the profession of land agent. He was also believed, about this time, to have been the editor of the *Taranaki Herald.*

When the war broke out, Mr. Brown received a commission as captain of the native contingent, and proved himself to be an intrepid officer. On Saturday, 26th May, 1860, Captain Brown left the camp, at Waitara, for the purpose of seeking a straying horse. When riding along the beach towards the township, he was surprised at the ford of the Waiongona River by three of William King's natives, one of them a young man whom the Captain had employed in his store. This man sprang out from behind a bush, where he was lying concealed, and fired at his master. The first shot struck Captain Brown's revolver cartouch-box and glanced off, the next penetrated his thigh, and the third passed through his left side, and lodged in his body. At the first shot, Captain Brown's horse swerved, and the succeeding shots struck him as he was turning. Captain Brown galloped back to the Waitara camp, and being observed to drop out of the saddle, was carried to the camp in a fainting state. Here he lingered till the 21st of August, bearing his sufferings with great patience and resignation, until death brought him a release. Captain Brown was a man of education and polite manners, a clever improvisatore, and convivial, but sober in his habits. He was singularly reticent regarding his antecedents and business transactions, strictly just and pleasant in his dealings; but there was an inner intrenchment in his nature that was impenetrable, and a fire in his eye that forbade too close an acquaintance. To a certain extent he lived and died a mystery. Dying intestate, and without legal heirs, his estate was escheated.

The above statement I have taken from Well's "History of Taranaki," but knowing Richard Brown personally as early as January, 1850, I am enabled to say something more of this very extraordinary energetic settler. His first appearance at Taranaki was on board a vessel which had anchored in the roadstead, having quantity of merchandise belonging to him, and on his applying for the surf boats to land his cargo he was refused, the New Zealand Company at that time usurping the whole of the trade Richard Brown, I fancy, must have had some inkling of this as he was evidently prepared for the emergency. He had packed all his merchandise in hogsheads and coolly waiting for the turn of the tide, put them over the ship's side, floated them ashore, rolled them up on the beach, knocked in the heads and commenced selling his cargo there and then at prices not to be refused. He soon arrived with another cargo, and, building premises, settled down as a merchant and completely upset the monopoly of the company.

Richard Brown was a strictly honourable and upright man, a good and firm friend, but an unforgiving enemy. He took the part of Ihaia against Katatore, and often risked his life to assist him. Daring to a degree and brave as a lion, this extraordinary man died about the time the war began, being, as I before said, shot by a Maori he had befriended for years. He left a half-caste son and daughter behind him. His son George was until lately in the Native Office in Auckland.

MAJOR BROWN.

Major Brown.

MAJOR CHARLES BROWN arrived in Taranaki in the
year 1841, and in 1853 was elected the first Superintendent of the province. In 1855 he received his commission
as Captain of the Taranaki Militia, and held that post
up to 1860, the year of the outbreak of the Maori Rebellion. On
martial law being proclaimed, Major Herbert, of Her Majesty's
58th Regiment, who had seen some service and who had been
wounded in previous Maori rebellions, was appointed to the
command of the district, Captain Brown, from his knowledge of
engineering, acting as engineer officer under him. After a
consultation with the Governor (Colonel Gore Browne), respecting
the danger the Omata out-settlers were exposed to, a council of war
was held, and the result of the deliberation was, that a force of fifty
militia and 100 volunteers, under Captain Brown, supported by a
company of Her Majesty's 65th Regiment, under Colonel Murray,
to which were subsequently added some sailors and marines from
Her Majesty's ship *Niger*, under Lieutenant Blake, were ordered to
their relief. The plan of operations agreed upon was that Captain
Brown, in command of the militia and volunteers, should proceed
by the beach, keeping the sea coast, and try to pass in rear of the
natives, who had built a pa on the Waireka Hill, while the Imperial
forces should proceed by the main road and dislodge the rebels
reported to have taken up a position near the Whalers' Gate, thereby
cutting off communication between the village of Omata and the
town. The militia and volunteers marched out about noon, taking
the coast track, and on approaching the Waireka, the rebels
showed in force. The volunteers, under Captain Atkinson, were
then thrown forward, and all parties were soon warmly engaged,
many casualties occurring on both sides, when, a reinforcement of
the enemy appearing on their flanks, Captain Stapp joined with his
force, and took command of the volunteers, occupying Jury's farm
buildings, while Captain Atkinson, with his company, defended the
sea face of the hill and shot many natives who attempted to get
in rear. Colonel Murray, hearing the firing some two miles in

advance, marched his force to the town side of the Waireka gully, sending the Naval Brigade, under Lieutenant Blake, R.N., and a section of the 65th Regiment, under Lieutenant Urquhart, to their assistance, who by that time had been joined by some of the garrison of the Omata Stockade, under Lieutenant Armstrong, and by some Royal Artillery, under Lieutenant McNaughton. With their assistance the militia and volunteers drove the natives under cover, but being reinforced by natives from Ratapihipihi, they endeavoured to intercept the line of communication between the Imperial and colonial forces, when Lieutenant Urquhart returned and occupied the opposite side of the gully, thus keeping open the communication. He had not, however, taken up the position long, when "the recall" was sounded, Lieutenant Blake being then severely wounded, and Colonel Murray marched the Imperial forces home. Colonel Murray's explanation is at follows :—
" Considering my force too small to keep our communication open should the enemy attack us in force, I recalled Lieutenants Blake and Urquhart's party, particularly as the day was far advanced, and my orders were to return by dark." No sooner had Lieutenant Urquhart retired, than the rebel natives took up a position in rear of the militia and succeeded in killing and wounding several of the volunteers. The natives were now rampant, shouting out, "Kahoro, kahoro!" ("They are beaten, they are beaten !") Captain Brown, finding his present position untenable, moved his force forward, carrying the killed and wounded across the gully to the advanced volunteer position, where the wounded were placed in Jury's house, which had been strengthened with a rough breast-work and converted into an hospital. The wounded were attended to by Mr. Grayling, in the absence of a medical officer. A gentleman named Pitcairn here greatly distinguished himself by his gallantry in riding through the rebel position with his haversack full of cartridges, he having heard that the volunteers were short of ammunition. His daring was all the more apparent, as, at the time, he was suffering with a dislocated shoulder, and carried his arm in a sling.

At this critical moment, Captain Cracroft, of the *Niger*, hearing the firing, landed some of his men, and proceeding to the battlefield, ascertained from some of the settlers the position of the enemy's pa, and guided by them made an onslaught on their stronghold, carrying all before him, which attack was no sooner made known to the other rebels, when they ceased firing and decamped, leaving the militia and volunteers to retire in peace. Nothing but this gallant attack of Captain Cracroft saved them, by diverting the attention of the enemy to another part of the field. Captain Brown on retiring left all his killed and wounded at the Omata Stockade, and was there met by a force of militia and volunteers, under Major Herbert, hurrying to their assistance from the township of New Plymouth. The natives, who numbered between three and four hundred, suffered severely, as several cart-loads of killed and wounded were taken by them down the coast on the following day.

The chief Taurua and seventeen of their principal men bit the dust, and the whole of the rebels were so panic-stricken that on meeting a body of natives coming up to their assistance, they endeavoured to persuade them to return, and actually took their arms from them in their sleep to save them, as they said, from destruction.

Captain Brown was afterwards appointed second in command at Mahoetahi, and was in charge of the advanced line of skirmishers at Omata on the 23rd February, 1861, his conduct on that occasion being brought under the notice of the general commanding. A coolness existing between Major Herbert and himself caused Captain Brown to accept the paymastership of militia and volunteers, and when the Major retired, Captain Brown again assumed the command, performing field officer's duty for some time. On the 7th November, 1864, he was gazetted Major, and was in command of the local forces when the Rev. Mr. Whiteley and Lieutenant Gascoigne were murdered. He had been ordered to hunt up the rebel Titokowaru when a change of ministry put an end to further military operations. Major Brown then resumed his seat in the House of Representatives and when called upon by Mr. Fox to resign the command or his seat in the House he sent in his resignation as commanding officer.

The fight at Waireka was the first occasion of the settlers meeting the natives in fair combat, and they acquitted themselves most creditably, although many were youths under twenty years of age.

Cols. Butler and Hassard.

GENERAL CHUTE having determined to attack the Hauhau position at Otapawa, the troops stood to their arms three hou s before daybreak. The plan of attack was that the troops and Forest Rangers should follow the track previously taken by the reconnoitring party, and attack on the comparatively open front of the pa, while the contingent and kupapas marched through the bush to the rear of the position, with the view of cutting off retreat. The plan was a good one. Had it been carried out few of the enemy would have escaped; but when the General arrived in front of the pa, he ordered an Armstrong gun to be brought up, and fired several shells into the place, to make the enemy show their strength. Some whares were set on fire, and, as we afterwards heard, a man's head blown off his shoulders; but the garrison made no sign. All was still as death; not a sound could be heard, and the General would not believe that the enemy were there. Under these circumstances he declined to wait for the contingent to get in rear, they having a long and difficult road to travel, and ordered the detachment of the 57th Regiment, under Lieut.-Colonels Butler and Hassard, to storm the stockade, supported by the 14th. Well the old Crimean veterans maintained their reputation. On advancing they found that the enemy had carefully levelled the ground in front of the pa to prevent the attacking party finding cover, and when within fifty yards of the palisades, the hitherto perfect silence was broken by a volley from at least 200 Hauhaus, who, hidden in their rifle-pits behind the strong palisades, rained death and destruction upon the gallant 57th. For a moment the storming party halted, but Colonel Butler's voice, calling out, "Go on, Die Hards!" steadied them, and rushing to the palisade, they tore it down with hands and tomahawks, and entered the pa, killed all who had the presumption to stop, or had not time to escape. Meanwhile, Major Von Tempsky, with his Forest Rangers, had been engaged with a party of the enemy, who were in the bush on the right flank of the pa, and had driven them back, with a loss to himself of two men wounded. The enemy lost 29 men killed, and our casualties were equally heavy, being eleven killed and twenty wounded, among the latter the gallant Colonel Hassard, mortally, and Lieutenant Swanson, of the 14th Regiment, slightly.

CAPTAIN MORRISON.

CAPTAIN MORRISON.

The first engagements in the Taranai War—The attac on Turi-turi Mokai—Pursuit of Titokowaru—Expeditions against Te Kooti.

CAPTAIN HENRY CHARLES MORRISON arrived in Taranaki a day or two after the first Waireka fight, in March, 1860. He was enrolled as a volunteer, and at once sent on outpost duty to Bell Blockhouse, at that time garrisoned by both regular and colonial troops. He was under fire for the first time at General Pratt's attack on Huirangi (known as the Retreat of the Fifteen Hundred). Whilst at Bell Block, he was placed in charge of the signal department at that post. During the fight at Mahoetahi against the Waikatos, a message was received at Bell Block, by signal, from Puketekaurere to the effect that a large body of natives were on the march from Huirangi to reinforce the Waikatos at Mahoetahi, and Captain Morrison immediately volunteered to carry the message to General Pratt, which he was permitted to do by his commanding officer (Captain Strange, afterwards killed at Matarikoriko). He succeeded in delivering the despatch to the General just as the Waikatos were being driven out of their works under a heavy fire. He afterwards joined the Bush Rangers under Major Atkinson, and took part in most of the skirmishes so frequent around New Plymouth at that time. He subsequently served in the Taranaki Mounted Volunteers under Captain Mace, and accompanied the various expeditions conducted by Colonel Warre, doing despatch duty from the military camps. In 1866 he received a commission in the Taranaki Military Settlers, and was posted to No. 5 company, commanded by his brother (Captain W. J. Morrison). Was stationed in command of the Mataitawa Redoubt with a part of the company, and eventually proceeded to the Patea district with the company, in 1867, where they built and occupied the Turi-turi Mokai Redoubt.

When the military settlers where placed on their land, he took up and occupied an officer's grant of 200 acres, until the murders of Squires, Cahill, and others compelled the occupants to abandon their holdings. Upon the re-occupation of the Turi-turi Mokai Redoubt by Captain Frederick Ross and a party of Armed Constabulary, Captain Morrison, whilst engaged in looking after stock and property, was invited by Captain Ross to share his whare, and probably only missed sharing that gallant officer's fate by having gone into Patea late on the afternoon prior to the attack on the redoubt. When the news of the disaster reached Lieut.-Colonel McDonnell, Captain Morrison was ordered on active service again, and proceeded with the Colonel at once to Turi-turi Mokai, where he was placed as second in command, Captain (now Colonel) Roberts being his superior officer. When the latter was ordered to headquarters at Waihi, Captain Morrison assumed command of the redoubt, and upon the withdrawal of the forces to Patea, he was left as second in command of Kakaramea Redoubt, under Captain Harvey Spiller, the only outpost in the district at that time.

In January 1869, Captain Morrison was made Sub-Inspector of Armed Constabulary, and was posted to No. 6 division, under Major Roberts. He accompanied Colonel Whitmore's expedition up the coast in pursuit of Titokowaru, and was present at the engagements at Taurangaika, Karaka Flats, Otauto, and Whakamaru. Prior to the column under Colonel Whitmore marching through the bush, in rear of Mount Egmont, to Waitara, he was ordered, with fifty of the Armed Constabulary, to march by the coast to Opunake, to embark on board the *Sturt* (Government steamship), for Waitara; but on their arrival at Opunake, the sea being very rough, they had to continue their march towards Taranaki, and could not embark before arriving at Tataraiwaka, having made a raid of upwards of fifty miles through the enemy's country.

Upon the removal of operations to the East Coast, Captain Morrison accompanied No. 6 division to Tauranga, and throughout the Uriwera campaign, under Colonel Whitmore, returning to Tauranga for a few months prior to his company being ordered to Taupo (the Government having decided to occupy that district by establishing posts between Lake Taupo and Napier). He was placed in command of Tapuaeharuru, and soon afterwards accompanied the expedition under Colonel McDonnell to Tapapa. Upon that column being divided, he was ordered to accompany Major Kepa's party, with fifty of the Armed Constabulary, marching through the bush to Oropi, where Colonel Fraser had checked Te Kooti. Te Kooti having got through to the Uriwera country, Captain Morrison proceeded, with part of the column, to Taupo and again took up the command at Tapuaeharuru, participating in the several expeditions to prevent Te Kooti from entering the King country.

In October, 1871, he was ordered to Tokanu, at the south end of Lake Taupo, to organise a party of natives for the purpose of watching and scouting the tracks along the Kaimanawa Ranges. In 1872 he was sent to the Waikato district, and in 1878 to Taranaki, where Te Whiti, the prophet, began to be troublesome, and was stationed at Opunake, Pukehinau, and Cape Egmont. At the Parihaka demonstration he commanded No. 7 company.

In October, 1883, on the Government deciding to occupy the Kawhia district, Captain Morrison proceeded there with the party under Major Tuke, and in May, 1885, was appointed to the command of the batteries at the North Head, Auckland.

LIEUT.-COLONEL STAPP.

LIEUT.-COLONEL STAPP.

Bravery displayed in Heke's War—Services in Crimea—The murders of Volkner, Fulloon, and Rev. Mr. Whiteley.

LIEUT.-COLONEL STAPP joined Her Majesty's 58th Regiment in April, 1842, and came out to New South Wales the following year. When Heke's war broke out in the North, the 58th Regiment was ordered to New Zealand, and the Colonel was present at the attack on the Okaihau Pa, on the 8th May, 1845. Forming one of the forlorn hope that stormed the Ohaeawae Pa, he particularly distinguished himself on that occasion by carrying a wounded man off the field under a heavy fire. He was afterwards at the night attack up the Waikare River, and was engaged at the recapture of a hill on the 1st July, 1845; was present at the assault and capture of Kawiti's Pa, at Ruapekapeka, on the 11th January, 1846, which event terminated the war. Returning to England, he volunteered for service in the Crimea, and received the appointment of Staff Officer to Lord William Paulett, who commanded in the Bosphorus, where he remained until the breaking up of the military establishment at Scutari, on the 31st July, 1856.

Returned to New Zealand in 1857, and, on his regiment being ordered home the following year, he retired from the Imperial service, and was appointed Adjutant of the Taranaki Militia. In March, 1860, he greatly distinguished himself at the battle of Waireka, by the judgment and coolness he displayed during the day, and in drawing off his wounded at night, after the Imperial forces had retired. In 1865, he was appointed to the expeditionary force sent to Opotiki, to avenge the murders of Volkner and Fulloon, and was several times engaged with the enemy. After relinquishing the command, he again returned to Taranaki, and was placed in charge of the force that recovered the bodies of the Rev. Mr. Whiteley, Lieutenant and Mrs. Gascoigne and children, and the two settlers who were murdered by the natives. His name has been continually mentioned in despatches, and he has received the thanks of the Government on several occasions. On the 21st March, 1872, Major Atkinson, on behalf of the officers of the district, presented him with a field officer's sword, in appreciation of his services, and the Government has placed him at present in command of the militia and volunteer district extending from the White Cliffs to Rangitikei.

Bishop Williams.

BISHOP WILLIAMS was at Whaerenga-a-Hika in March, 1868, when Kereopa made his first appearance in the Bay. His advent caused the greatest excitement among the Bishop's people. Nearly 500 of them rushed to arms, and insisted upon proceeding to the village of Taureka, where Kereopa was, announcing their intention of either expelling him from the district, or handing him over to the pakehas as a murderer. Bishop Williams evidently did not place much reliance on these valiant words ; he feared the effect of the prophet's influence on the fickle Maori mind, and determined to accompany them. His men remonstrated, but to no purpose, for his lordship was firm. When they arrived at the village of Taureka, Kereopa was surrounded by the people of the place, who had evidently fallen under his influence. This was so patent to the Bishop's party that they forgot all about the expelling and capturing, and contented themselves with sitting down quietly and speechifying. The usual amount of talk ensued, and the result was that these rabid churchmen welcomed the murderer by rubbing noses with him. This concluded, Kereopa walked up and offered his hand to the bishop, who refused it. Kereopa demanded the reason, and his lordship replied, " I see blood dripping from your fingers." This was a sufficient answer. The prophet walked off somewhat crest-fallen, and the bishop seeing that a large majority of his people would join the new religion, left them and returned to his own home. Things now went rapidly from bad to worse, Kereopa openly urging the murder of the bishop ; but the tribes had hardly reached the pitch of fanaticism which was necessary before they could kill a man from whom they had received nothing but kindness ; and the faithful few mounted guard every night at Waerenga-a-Hika.

By this time the Government had received information as to the state of affairs in the Bay, and fearing that the Rev. Mr. Volkner's fate might overtake the bishop, despatched a steamer to bring him and his family to Napier. His lordship handed his property over to the old catechist and left. Scarcely had they reached the steamer when Kereopa and his converts arrived to loot and burn his house, but old Haronga seated himself on a pile of valuables and declared that nothing should move him. The house was not burnt, and old Haronga saved the property.

COLONEL HAULTAIN.

COLONEL HAULTAIN

Colonel Haultain's antecedents—Indian services—Organisation of the Auckland Militia—Political career.

COLONEL HAULTAIN was born at Stoney Stratford, in Buckinghamshire, his ancestors being of Dutch extraction, having come over with William of Orange, in 1688. They were a race of soldiers, and from that date to the present have had their representatives in the Imperial service. At the age of fourteen the Colonel entered the Royal Military College at Sandhurst, and obtained his commission in 1834, when he was ordered on foreign service, ten years of which were spent in India. He was placed on the Quartermaster-General's staff, with the Army of Reserve, then assembled at Ferozepore, with a view of covering the return of the army operating in Afghanistan. The Gwalior campaign succeeding, he took part in the same, serving with his regiment, the 39th, at the battle of Maharajpoor.

Some four years later he returned to England with his regiment. He was then adjutant, but soon after gaining his company was appointed Staff Officer of Pensioners, and in 1849 brought out to New Zealand the eighth division of Fencibles.

This detachment was first located at Onehunga, but on the retirement of Lieut.-Colonel Grey he was removed to Panmure. On the completion of his term of service with the Pensioners, namely, seven years, the Colonel retired from the army, and in 1856 settled down to farming pursuits at Mangere in company with the late lamented Colonel Nixon. On the outbreak of the war in 1860 Colonel Haultain's military services were availed of by the Government in organising the Auckland Militia, he becoming Lieut.-Colonel of the first battalion. Shortly after the opening of the Waikato campaign of 1863 the Government enrolled a large force of military settlers, in order to occupy the confiscated lands, and guard the frontier. This force was formed into four regiments, Lieut.-Colonel Haultain having the command of one of them, the 2nd Waikato Regiment, then stationed at Alexandra. He was present at the engagement at Orakau, and here he gained the rank of Colonel for his services on the field on that day, and was afterwards promoted Colonel-Commandant of the four Waikato regiments.

In 1865 he resigned his military post to attend the session of the General Assembly. Here he was in opposition to the Weld

F

Ministry with respect to the policy of the removal of the Imperial forces. Colonel Haultain entered the Assembly in 1859 as member for the Southern Division of Auckland, having defeated Mr. David Graham by a majority of one. At the general election of 1861 he was defeated by Mr. Charles Taylor, but was again returned in 1864 as the representative of Franklin consequent on the death of Colonel Nixon.

In October, 1865, the Weld Ministry were defeated and resigned office, and on Mr. Stafford forming a new cabinet the Colonel was offered and accepted the portfolio of Defence Minister. In this capacity, from 1865 to 1869, he supervised the location of the military settlers, and directed the operations of the colonial forces on both the east and west coasts of the North Island, a period which included the Wanganui Campaign, opening with Turi-turi Mokai, the crossing over the great Ngaire swamp after Titokowaru, the siege and capture of Ngatapa, and finishing with the expeditions into the Uriwera country. The operations of the Whakamarama expedition in the vicinity of Tauranga were conducted by Colonel Haultain in person until stricken down with rheumatic fever, which compelled him to retire from active service.

Colonel Haultain went out of office with his colleagues in June, 1869, and received the title of Honourable on the recommendation of His Excellency the Governor, having served the colony as Defence Minister over three years. At the general election in 1870, the Colonel declined to stand for re-election, retiring from that date from active political life. In 1871 he was made a member of the Flax Commission, drew up a report on the workings of the Native Lands Act, took charge of the payment of the Imperial pensioners, became Trust Commissioner under the Native Lands Frauds Preventive Act, and, on the death of Colonel Balneavis, succeeded to the office of sheriff, the duties of which he fulfilled until it was united with that of registrar. He was trustee of St. John's College and Grammar School, member of the Board of Education, joint secretary of the Howe-street Industrial Home, and was selected by the present Government to represent the Colony of New Zealand in the reception given in Sydney to the New South Wales contingent on their return from the Egyptian campaign. The Colonel's bearing as Defence Minister was, although firm, most gracious. A strict disciplinarian himself, giving his whole mind to any duty he undertook, he naturally expected all under him to do the same.

MAJOR NEILL.

Major S. Neill.

---

*Twenty years' army life in New Zealand—The attack on Kai-taka-turia Pa—
The first brush in the Waikato—Fighting at Razorback—The shelling
of Meremere.*

SAMUEL NEILL enlisted in Ireland in Her Majesty's
65th Regiment, or Royal Bengal Tigers (as they were
always called), when quite a young man, and after a few
years of home service was despatched with his regiment
to New Zealand, where they remained until the rebellion was
nearly over, a period of twenty years. His diary, which I give
verbatim, shows the vicissitudes the regiment passed through, and
how a steady, sensible soldier can rise from the lowest ranks of the
service to one of the highest, in a short space of time, if he only
takes advantage of the opportunities that offer in the daily routine
of life. He left the regiment on the expiration of his term of
service as Colour-sergeant to join the colonial force as the
author's Quartermaster-sergeant and has now retired a Major of
Militia, a rank which his steady conduct and constant attention to
his duties fully entitled him to.

THE ROYAL BENGAL TIGERS.

DIARY OF AN OLD 65TH MAN.

" Her Majesty's 65th Regiment landed in Auckland on the 26th
of March, 1847, and on the following January my company with
others were drafted to Wellington. During the year 1849 I was
sent into the commissariat department, where I remained until the
issue of ration rum to the troops was discontinued. In September, 1853, I was sent on detachment to Porirua until that post
was broken up when I again returned to Wellington, acting as
Commissariat-sergeant on board the *Shepherdess* while shifting
troops to Wanganui. The war having in the meantime broken out
in Taranaki, and the volunteers and militia of the colony called out,
I was sent to Turakina to assist in drilling this portion of the
newly-raised force ; but the rebellion spreading I was called upon
to join my company and we landed at Taranaki in July, 1861, and
immediately marched for the Waitara, occupying a redoubt until
recalled to garrison the town so as to enable the 57th Regiment
quartered there to take the field, which they did on the following

E*

morning by marching southwards and occupying the country by building three redoubts, variously named St. Patrick's, St. Andrew's, and St. George's. They were just finished and manned when the Governor and General Cameron arrived. This was in April, 1863, and preparations for the winter campaign commenced, urged on by the massacre of Lieutenant Tragett, Dr. Hope and nine non-commissioned officers and men, who were ambuscaded by the natives at the Wairoa Stream on their way to town; one man alone escaped by running for his life. On his reaching St. Andrew's Redoubt a relief party was sent out, who found nothing but the dead and mutilated bodies of their comrades.

" The news of the massacre caused a fearful commotion in town, the volunteers and militia clamouring to be allowed to avenge their deaths, while the whole of the Imperial force involuntarily got under arms, expecting orders to march immediately, and were greatly disappointed when the only orders given were that three hundred men proceed to meet and assist the party bringing in the bodies. No further steps were taken until the 3rd of June, when orders were issued that the militia and volunteers should garri on the town, and that the whole of the Imperial force parade at sundown in light marching order, with ninety rounds of ammunition per man; the artillery and baggage waggons to start one hour before the troops, under proper escort. On arrival at St. Patrick's Redoubt, the 57th were relieved by 200 of the 70th, and, on reaching St. Andrew's Redoubt, the 70th replaced the 57th there also, while the 40th, 200 strong, relieved the headquarters of the 57th at St. George's. We then formed in column by regiments—mounted and foot artillery on the right, Royal Engineers next, the 57th and 65th, and 100 men of the 70th on the left.

" General Cameron then addressed us, saying that he was about to attack and carry by assault the Kai-taka-turia Pa on the hill in front, to avenge the loss of the officers and men who fell at the Wairoa Stream, and he knew well we would uphold the prestige of the British army. The 57th immediately begged the honour of the storming party, and that their old friends, the Tigers, should support them, which was immediately granted; and the whole force piled arms and laid down to rest until daybreak. All was profound stillness, when, as the first streaks of dawn appeared, the quiet was broken by a shell on its flight from a man-of-war in the offing opening the ball. The force sprang to their feet as one man, fell in by companies, and moved off by divisions from the right. The 57th and 65th, extended in skirmishing order, doubled up the hill, and the attack commenced. The natives reserved their fire until the 57th was close up to the pa, when the dogs of war were let loose in earnest. Nothing daunted, the 57th made straight for the pa, and, despite the Maori fire and tomahawk, threw themselves over the pallisades in every conceivable manner, and, with the old Tigers at their heels, were soon in possession of the pa. In fact, the 57th had fairly taken it before the reserve got properly up. Many of the natives in the pa took refuge in their whares, and could only be got out by setting fire to them. The loss on our side was four killed and twelve wounded, while 54 dead bodies of the enemy were visible, besides three consumed in the whares. A few escaped, and, after our dead and wounded were collected, we started in pursuit, and had just found their where-abouts, when from all parts of the field the bugle sounded the halt, retire, and double, while orders were issued to leave all behind, and make for the beach to embark on board the man-of-war, as the town had been attacked during our absence. And it was not until after we had rounded the Sugar Loaf Rocks, we could see that it was an Exeter Hall or a political dodge to save the natives. The killed and wounded had been got on board, as well as the 57th and 65th, while the 70th and baggage were to return by the road.

"A few days after the attack, the Governor and General both left for Auckland, as affairs began to look very 'pouri' in the Waikato, and on the morning of the 28th June, just as another expedition was about to start from Taranaki, under Colonel Warre of the 57th Regiment, to make a second attack on the Kai-taka-turia Pa, the natives having returned and taken possession of it in our absence, a man-of-war steamer was seen in the distance, evidently coming from Auckland, and our expedition was postponed until after her arrival in the roadstead. Captain Sullivan, the officer in command of the vessel, came on shore, having despatches for Colonel Warre, to embark without delay the men of the 40th, 65th, and 70th Regiments, as they were required in Auckland. Consequently the second expedition fell through. The natives, remaining in comfortable possession of their fortifications, and verily believing we dared not again attack them, acquired boldness in their future operations against us.

"The men and baggage were soon on board, and we left the same evening for Auckland, arriving on the night of the 29th. As the 2nd battalion of the 18th Royal Irish were daily expected, being under orders to relieve the 65th, ordered home, every prepa-ration was made by the men for embarking on their arrival, and great were the rejoicings of the old Tigers when, on the 4th July, the 18th Royal Irish arrived. But, alas! they were doomed to disappointment by orders received on the 9th to proceed to Drury, and not to take with them anything further than a change, their great-coats, and one blanket each, as they would not be away more than nine days. We arrived in Drury on the 10th, and, having pitched camp, the whole regiment assembled together for the first time since leaving Dublin in 1845, a period of eighteen years. After the men had dined the whole regiment fell in, and were each served with a tomahawk, haversack, and ninety rounds of ammunition, when some artillery and the right wing of the 65th, under Colonel Wyatt, started for Tuakau; 100 artillery, some of the 18th Royal Irish, and the left wing of the 65th, under the command of Lieut.-Colonel Murray, left for Kirikiriroa, to warn all the natives who were disloyal to the Queen to cross the Waikato river within fourteen days, or they would be treated as rebels, and taken prisoners. After performing this duty the Captain of my company applied and obtained permission for his men to do duty as bush rangers, so that we were out nearly every night, scouring the bush and forming convoys to protect the commissariat drays that left Drury every morning for the Queen's Redoubt. On the 17th of July, while the grog was being served out, a volley was heard from the direction of Shepherd's Bush, and, at the call for the bush rangers, we did not even wait to fall in, but each one ran as fast as he could in the direction of the firing. It turned out to be an attack made by the Maoris on a small convoy returning from the Queen's Redoubt to Drury, in command of Captain Ring, of Her Majesty's second battalion of the 18th, on a very dangerous part of the road. Captain Ring had retired with some of his men to Martin's Farm. On arrival we found the Maoris so busy plundering the commissariat drays that they did not notice our approach, and the first volley made them scatter away into the bush, where we followed them, until we got abreast of Martin's Farm, where we were joined by some men from Williamson's Clearing, who had also heard the firing; and as we started back again to look for Captain Ring we picked up four men of the 18th Regiment and one of the 70th killed, besides twelve of the 18th wounded, and carried them back to Drury.

"During the running skirmish there was a man of the 65th Regiment named Gallagher, who, annoyed at seeing a huge Maori urging on the rest to stand and fight the pakeha, ran after him and shot him down, and on examining him found he had on three shirts and a large Hauhau flag wrapped round his chest, measuring nine feet in length. Having buried him decently we cut and planted a flagstaff near him, on which we hoisted the Maori flag with the Union Jack over it. This was the first brush in the Waikato district.

"The fourteen days having expired, the Artillery (under Lieutenant Rate), the 18th Regiment (under Major Inman), with 300 of the 65th Regiment, the whole under the command of Colonel Murray, started to pay another visit to Kirikiri to see if the Maoris had obeyed orders and cleared out of the district. On our arrival at Papakura we fell in with Colonel Nixon's two troops of volunteer cavalry, and at daylight the following morning the force was divided. One part, under Major Inman, started for Wairoa; the other part, under Colonel Murray, for Kirikiri. We advanced in light skirmishing order and took two pas without firing a shot. Fulloon, the Maori interpreter who was with Colonel Murray's party, found out from an old Maori in the pa that all the fighting men were in the bush, and would soon be returning; he consequently advised Colonel Murray to plant his prisoners under guard in the whares, and get his men under cover in the bush around the pa. He had hardly done so when about a dozen women came in with swags on their back, followed by the men walking in Indian file, armed with guns, tomahawks and spears. They had just formed up inside the pa when, at a signal given, the troops made a rush and took them prisoners, while the interpreter shouted out to them in Maori that the soldiers would not harm them if they laid down their arms. Major Inman was also successful in taking a pa, so that the first lot of Maori prisoners taken in the Waikato war were sent down to Otahuhu, while Captain Ring and two hundred of the 18th Regiment were left in charge of the district, with orders to erect redoubts and keep it clear of Maori rebels.

"Soon after this, a settler went into the bush for a load of firewood, and was waylaid and shot, the natives taking his bullocks and dray. No sooner was this known than Colonel Wyatt, of the 65th, ordered out some of the 18th and 65th men to search for the murdered man, and they found him in a Maori clearing near the bush, and on the way to Hay's farm, hearing heavy firing towards Kirikiri, Colonel Wyatt started off in that direction. On arrival the only occupant of the pa was found to be an old decrepit woman who told us the Maoris were all in the bush and pointed out a road which she stated they had taken, but the Colonel, not deeming it necessary to go further, returned with the dead body to Drury, where he was overtaken by the bugler of the Royal Artillery, who informed Colonel Wyatt that Captain Ring was surrounded in the bush, and had already one man killed and four wounded. 'Right-about-turn' was the order given, and back again to Kirikiri we marched, taking the track the Maori woman had pointed out, and we had not proceeded far when we came upon the unfortunate man's bullocks, and a little further on we saw a scout perched up in a tree, who gave the alarm; but a corporal of ours, who was leading, soon brought him down, and we all made for the clearing, where we found some of the rebels sitting quietly around their fires cooking, while the rest kept up a brisk fire on Captain Ring and the 18th. Our first fire dispersed them like magic as they rolled themselves down the hill and disappeared in the bush. Colonel Wyatt, fancying he had got between two fires, ordered the 65th regimental call to be sounded, when a cheer to the left showed the position of the 18th, whom we hastened to relieve. We then followed up the Maoris, knocking over nine of them in the skirmish. At this moment we were joined by Lieutenant Rate and his artillerymen, whom he had dismounted, and were armed with revolvers and swords. We only lost one man, private Meade, of No. 1 Company, and I succeeded in taking a first-class double-barrel gun, tomahawk and spear. I handed the spear over to Dr. White, while the gun and tomahawk I had to give up on our return to camp. We remained on the ground until Captain Ring took off his detachment and returned to Drury.

"Soon afterwards we were relieved by the 70th Regiment and shifted to Queen's Redoubt, where we were broken up into small detachments and sent to Razorback, Williamson's Clearing, Martin's Farm, and other places along the old South Road, where the convoys had to pass. One of our sentries noticing a body of Maoris crossing the road between Razorback and our redoubt, I increased the guard that night, in case of an attack. All was quiet until day dawn, when a volley was heard away to the left, a post occupied by the 1st Waikatos. Fifty of our men, under Colonel Murray, started as quick as possible, guided by the firing, and arrived only in time to have a parting shot. Here Captain Saltmarch was wounded, and we lost one man, Private John McKay; the Maoris lost heavily. We had hardly got back to breakfast, when the alarm was again sounded, firing being heard in the neighbourhood of Razorback, and away we started again, the Maoris having this time attacked the convoy close to the redoubt. Only two men were wounded. One a young man, or rather lad, was wounded in the hand, the ball passing between two of his fingers without breaking any bones. Nevertheless it caused the young soldier to cry out so lustily, 'Oh mother, dear, I am kilt!' as to amuse the whole of his company.

"The next skirmish we had was on the day the Maoris killed the two sentries placed over the arms of the 40th while the men were felling bush between Razorback and Williamson's Clearing. The advanced guard of the convoy saw the Maoris crossing the road into the bush, carrying the captured rifles, and two of the convoy fired at them, and one man was seen to fall, but he rose again, when Captain Clark, who was in charge of the convoy, jumping off his horse, asked the man what distance he had sighted his rifle. He replied 600 yards; and Captain Clark, taking a loaded rifle from another man, sighted it and fired at the same Maori, who was limping behind the others, and brought him down a second time. He again tried to rise, when a large black dog belonging to one of the men caught him and held him until we got up. The remainder got clear away with the fifty stand of new rifles.

"A few days after, the Maoris attacked Razorback Redoubt, where two companies of the 65th were stationed. One of the sentries noticed a bush that seemingly got nearer and nearer to him. He thought it so strange that he told the next sentry to look out, and pass the word into the redoubt to hold themselves in readiness. The bush still advanced, and, just as the sentry was about to fire, a Maori darted out with rifle levelled, but the sentry was too quick for him, and shot him dead before he could get his weapon to his shoulder. The next moment a regular volley was fired from the surrounding bush, riddling the tents and wounding three of the men. The Maori killed turned out to be a chief who had adopted that method of leading his men. We gave him a burial suited to his rank, some of the men erecting a slab to his memory.

"Soon after, we were shifted to the Queen's Redoubt, and from there were sent one night to strengthen the Whangamarino Redoubt, overlooking Meremere, which was threatened with an attack. While here, an outlying picket, a young lad of the 12th Regiment, seeing something resembling a pig moving about in the dark, hesitated to fire for fear of being laughed at by his comrades;

when suddenly this supposed pig sprang upon him, making a desperate blow at his head with a long-handled tomahawk, but struck his rifle just where the sentry had his left thumb ready to fire. The force of the blow severed the thumb from his hand, and the yell he gave was heard all over the camp, but the Maori got away clear. The lad was in the hospital for two months.

"Subsequently, Lieutenant Pickard was sent up the Waikato River with two guns to shell Meremere. This pa was situated about nine miles from the Queen's Redoubt, on the bank of the river. General Cameron ordered up two gunboats, the *Avon* and *Pioneer*. Their bulwarks were iron-plated to withstand bullets, and all the best marksmen were collected and sent on board, as the General wished to reconnoitre the enemy's stronghold. On the steamer arriving opposite the place the Maoris opened fire from some old ships' guns they had fixed in the forks of some trees. One of the shots penetrated the bulwarks and lodged in a cask of beef which was on deck. The cask was quickly opened and the missile was found to be the weight taken from a pair of steelyards. Taking no notice of their fire we proceeded up the river nearly to Rangiriri; when, on returning, the General ordered the artillery to get ready for action, as he was going to give the natives a volley when he arrived off Meremere. The consequence of our not returning their fire on going up the river was apparent by the confident manner in which they had assembled to annihilate us on our return. The word was now passed along to man the portholes and load, which we did quickly, and the General ordered the forty-pounders to open fire with shell, and the artillery poured in a volley which made them scamper under cover in every direction, so that a minute later not a Maori was to be seen. About twenty or thirty shells were thrown into the pa, but as no one landed the effect could not be ascertained. The General was only too anxious to be at them, but he had to wait the Governor's orders and the Governor was waiting for nobody knows who, the result being that, a day or two after, the Maoris actually came down and opened fire upon us while in the midst of divine service outside the Queen's Redoubt. After the service was over Colonel Havelock and Major Blythe, of the 40th, took out a party of men and drove them back into the bush without loss on either side. In the evening I received orders to issue a large quantity of picks, spades and shovels for the use of the troops, when word came down from Lieutenant Pickard that the Maoris were evacuating Meremere. Every man was now put in motion —steamers, vessels and every craft that would carry a man was brought into use—but the place was deserted before we arrived. They had left their big guns behind, being too heavy to remove, which we afterwards sent down to Auckland as trophies. General Cameron, after leaving a strong detachment at Meremere, returned to the Queen's Redoubt, and I again joined the store department and saw no more fighting in the Waikato.

"On the 9th of April I received my discharge and proceeded to Wanganui, and on the 29th joined the staff of militia and volunteers of the district, was promoted Captain on the 19th April, 1873, and commanded the volunteers in the Patea, Rangitiki, and Wanganui districts from 1st July, 1883, to the 31st, and was further promoted to Major unattached on the 3rd April, 1883."

Sergeant S. Austin.

Heroic conduct at Putaki Pa—Narrow escape of Captain W. McDonnell.

SERGEANT SAMUEL AUSTIN received the New Zealand Cross for gallant and distinguished conduct on the 7th January, 1866, when at the capture of the Putahi Pa, Lieut.-Colonel McDonnell was severely wounded, and Sergeant Austin carried him during a great part of the engagement, under a raking fire, and finally off the field, which action was witnessed by General Chute, who then thanked him for his fearless and heroic conduct, not only in this instance, but on all occasions during the campaign on the West Coast. Also, on the 17th October, 1866, at the capture of the village of Keteoneta. Captain William McDonnell, leading a small advance guard of Maoris, came upon an ambush, and fell severely wounded. His men, leaving him, retired on the main body, who commenced to retreat, when Sergeant Austin, assisted by another man (since dead), returned to where Captain McDonnell lay on the point of being tomahawked by the enemy, and at all risks carried him off.

JOHN WHITE.

John White.

___

JOHN WHITE, for many years Resident Magistrate at Wanganui, came out to this colony in its very earliest days, and took up his residence at Hokianga until Heke's war compelled him to move to Auckland. He was present with Colonel Wynyard, the then Deputy-Governor, at a meeting of the chiefs at Coromandel, when that district was first proclaimed a goldfield, and received his appointment as Gold Commissioner, under Major Heaphy, V.C. Soon afterwards, he was appointed interpreter and land purchaser, under Surveyor-General Ligar, and purchased for the Government the district now known as Waitakerei, and obtained from the natives a deed of gift of two chains in width, from the head of the Waitemata River to Helensville, for the present Helensville railway. He also succeeded in extinguishing the native title over most of the land in the Auckland district. Being appointed Resident Magistrate of Central Wanganui, he soon made himself acquainted with the native chiefs, attending all their meetings and instructing them in English laws, etc., opening his court, and deciding their disputes so satisfactorily that even Hemi Hape, the rebel chief, who had headed the natives in the former raid on Wanganui, gave in his adherence to the Government. General Cameron had now arrived at Wanganui, and having taken up his quarters at Waitotara, gave Mr. White orders to inform the rebel natives up the river that if they made their appearance below the island of Moutoa they would be fired upon by the friendly natives who were protecting the river. But Epanaia and his party, taking no notice of the warning, came down the river and, firing on the friendly Maoris, killed Nape. A regular fight ensued, in which the rebels were beaten back, many of them being killed, and the remainder taken prisoners. As Resident Native Magistrate, Mr. White was instructed to discover, and report to the General commanding, the movements and intentions of the rebel natives, which he did very successfully.

Mr. White was also present at the attack on Puketekauere, at Taranaki, and his report of this battle being the best given, I quote it *verbatim*. He says:—"We had been stationed at Waitara for some time when Mr. Richard Brown, in passing on his way to town, was waylaid by a Maori servant of his, and mortally wounded. The camp was situated on the south bank of the river, about a thousand yards from its mouth, on rising ground, while Puketekauere lay about half a mile inland on a sugar-loaf shaped hill. The pa was about an acre in extent, surrounded with an embankment, and a fence about ten feet in height. The hill all around was covered with high fern. On the south was a deep, swampy valley, covered with soft grass and fern, and on the south-east a narrow strip of dry land, connecting the pa with the mainland, also covered with high fern. The day before we made the attack on the pa, we noticed that the natives had, in a valley between us and the pa, built up some fences. While in the act of destroying these, one of our men's rifle burst, in consequence of a Maori bullet entering the barrel, just as he had pulled the trigger. A council of war was held, and it was determined to attack the position. Colonel Gold was to leave the township, marching overland, so as to join us by five o'clock in the morning. One half of our force was to take up a position on the river bank side of the pa, whilst the other half were to attack on the inland side. This party consisted of 175 soldiers and sailors, under command of Captain Seymour and Captain Nelson, of the 40th Regiment. We left camp about two o'clock in the morning on a miserable drizzling day, Sergeant Margorem having charge of our one gun—the twelve-pounder. About a quarter of a mile from the camp our party divided— one half going off to the left, the other half continuing on the main road to the pa. Having taken up our position on the south side of the valley, we there waited for daylight and for the force under Colonel Gold, which was expected to join us. We had been seen from the pa, and had been fired upon, and we found our men on the north side of the pa returning the fire. The shots fell thick amongst us, as we held a position on a hill about three hundred and fifty yards from the pa, the only position from which the pa could be seen. As the fire from the pa became hot, we returned it, when an old chief left the pa, walking down the narrow strip of land described as joining the swamp to the mainland, and although some of our shots fell close to him, he did not seem to take the slightest notice. Reaching the valley, we soon found the fern alive with the rebels intending to attack our right. The twelve-pounder opened on them with canister and grape, which soon dispersed them. I was standing near to Captain Seymour when a rifle ball cut a piece off a bullock's horn which was attached to the gun, and one of the artillerymen was shot in the stomach, and dropped dead within a few yards of me. Soon afterwards, Captain Seymour was hit in the thigh, and taking off his neck-tie bound up the wound. In doing so he said, 'By all that's good, do not let it be known that I am wounded,' and took no further notice of his injury, save that now and then he bit his lip in silence as he moved about to give his orders. Just then, we perceived, in the direction of the Hui range, a large body of natives coming to the support of the rebels, and as our men on the bank of the river were not able to get near the pa, and could not see the enemy coming, they were soon surrounded and cut off from us. Some of them fell fighting to the last, while others were driven up the river and killed or drowned. The wounded with our party included a midshipman, whose hand was smashed, and a soldier, who had a ball in his left breast. They were taken charge of by me and another soldier, and taken to the camp. On the way we met another wounded man, who had his ankle broken, and after reaching the camp we went back to assist him. For thirty-six hours before the battle, I had not time to eat, and I had no sooner seen the wounded safe in the hospital than I swooned away, and was laid up for ten days."

Since the war, the New Zealand Government has entrusted Mr. White with the onerous duty of writing a complete history of the Maori race, and from his knowledge of the native customs and language, it will probably become a standard work.

Sergeant R. Shepherd.

How he won the New Zealand Cross—The siege of Ngatapa—Hair-breadth escapes.

ERGEANT RICHARD SHEPHERD, of the Armed Constabulary, obtained the New Zealand Cross for distinguished bravery at Otauto, the 13th March, 1869, while holding the ground close to the encampment, and enabling a close reconnaissance to be made by Major Kepa and the colonel commanding. Sergeant Shepherd was dangerously wounded on this occasion. The bullet entered at the left side of the jaw, passing under the tongue and out of the right side of neck, within a hairbreadth of the jugular vein. Sergeant Shepherd was entrusted with this important duty by Colonel G. S. Whitmore (now Sir George), and told to hold the narrow path leading to the Maori encampment until relieved by Colonel Lyon, who was expected up in a short time with a portion of the field force. Of the six volunteers who were along with him, three of them were shot through the head. Corporal Guthrie was struck in the mouth by a spent bullet, knocking out two of his teeth, and he coolly put his fingers into his mouth and pulled out the bullet. A young man named Langford was in the act of firing when a bullet passed through the wrist of his left hand, then cutting off two fingers of his right hand, and finally entering his right breast and passing out under the shoulder-blade. It was all but a hand-to-hand conflict. There were three killed and four wounded out of the seven.

When Te Kooti made his escape from the Chatham Islands, and landed at Poverty Bay, Sergeant Shepherd was along with No. 1 Division in their long chase after him; and when the arch-rebel and his followers entrenched themselves in the Ngatapa Pa, Sergeant Shepherd was selected as the officer to take charge of ten men who were appointed to hold a narrow ridge at the back of the pa, it being the only place where there was a possibility of the Maoris making their escape. The position this party occupied was on a hill at the back of the pa, and situated about twenty yards from the enclosure. Amongst the party was Solomon Black, Whaponga (a Maori), and Barry Reid, who also got the New Zealand Cross for gallant services. This party had their work cut out, as they were constantly exposed to a galling fire from the Maoris. The only cover they had was a small breast-work of stones, and about a foot deep of a trench they dug out with bayonets and tomahawks. They held this position from the 1st of January to the morning of the 5th, when the pa was taken by the besieging forces. On the fourth day, the men were worn out with their long watch, and some of them left the trench to get refreshed by having a good wash. The Maoris, taking advantage of the weakened state of the place, to the number of about twenty, made a sortie, and killed two of the party and wounded one. Sergeant Shepherd had a very narrow escape on this occasion, as the shoulder-knot was shot off his coat, and a bullet tore the skin off his forefinger and thumb. During the fight he reached out his hand to prevent a wounded man from falling down the cliff, and when he looked up a big Maori was standing with his rifle to his shoulder and the muzzle within about three feet of the Sergeant's body. He fully expected his time had come, as he could plainly see a line from the fore-sight along the barrel and over the back-sight to the rebel's eye, and if the Maori had fired a period would have been put to his existence; but Sergeant Flowers, of the Poverty Bay Scouts, had come upon the scene just at the critical moment, and, by a shot from his revolver, laid the Maori low.

The following letter and memorandum show that Sergeant Shepherd did good service during the war, and also that the training he received in Her Majesty's 68th Light Infantry was not lost upon him :—

"NATIVE AND DEFENCE OFFICE, WELLINGTON, *15th May, 1876.*

"SIR,—Under instructions from the Honourable Native Minister, I have the honour to inform you that His Excellency the Governor has been pleased to award you the New Zealand Cross for gallant services rendered by you during the late war.

"W. MOULE, Lieut.-Colonel.

"Mr. R. SHEPHERD, late Sergeant
   "Armed Constabulary Force."

"WELLINGTON, *14th August, 1870.*

"Sergeant Shepherd served under my command in the Armed Constabulary from the first raising of No. 1 division, and was only discharged on account of a very severe and painful wound, which he received at Otauto, near Patea, on the 13th March, 1869. The Sergeant was always a steady, civil, well-conducted man, and a brave, smart, and willing soldier. I have seen him on several occasions under fire, and have known him to distinguish himself upon many occasions.

"G. S. WHITMORE, Colonel, late Commanding Field Force."

MAJOR HERFORD.

Herford's bravery at Orakau—He is shot in the head while assaulting the pa—Remarkable recovery and sudden death.

MAJOR HERFORD, in 1863, when the New Zealand Government sent officers to Australia to raise men to serve in the Waikato, was practising as a barrister, in South Australia, and being full of the love of adventure, threw up his practice and, raising a company, joined the 3rd Waikato Regiment, in which he was gazetted captain. He subsequently joined the Transport service and was sent to the front within a week of his arrival at Te Awamutu. The Maoris, under Rewi Maniapoto, were discovered entrenching themselves at Orakau. Captain Herford at once applied for, and received from the general in command, permission to join the storming party. The pa was much stronger than was anticipated, the consequence being that most of the officers and a number of the men comprising the storming party fell under the withering fire of an unseen enemy, and the first rush of our men was beaten off by the rebels. Major Herford, however, with Lieutenant Harrison and a few of the Transport men, would not give way, and bursting through the light outer palisading surrounding the pa, rushed into the great inner trench and endeavoured to scramble up the embankment. It was an act of splendid but unavailing bravery; for while vainly struggling to clamber up the steep sides of the trench, Major Herford was shot by a Maori who, for a moment, stood on the top of the parapet just above him. The bullet entered his skull, just above the eyebrow, and he fell apparently dead. His comrades carried his body to the rear, out of the enemy's fire, and the surgeon proceeded to examine him, but, upon seeing an apparently lifeless body with a bullet-hole in the forehead, naturally concluded that it was a case beyond his skill, and did not hesitate to say so. Very soon after, however, Herford showed signs of life, and opening his uninjured eye, recognised some of those around him. He subsequently, to all appearance, recovered, was promoted to the rank of major, when he suffered a sudden relapse, and died in great suffering. A *post mortem* disclosed the remarkable fact that the bullet was still in his head, having traversed round to the back of the skull, where its irritating presence had caused a fatal abscess to form.

CAPTAIN MESSENGER.

CAPTAIN MESSENGER.

Taranaki settlers summoned to arms—The battle of Waireka—Attack on Mimi Pa—Battle of Mahoetahi—Engagement at Allen's Hill—Amusing incident at Stoney River--Wreck of the steamer Alexandra—The White Cliffs massacre.

CAPTAIN MESSENGER, with most of the younger settlers of Taranaki, perceiving the warlike disposition of the natives around them, had formed themselves into a company of volunteers years before the outbreak, determined to prepare themselves for the defence of their homes in the fight for supremacy which had only been delayed by the Government of the day acceding to the demands of the natives and bribing them with costly presents. When the threatened outbreak did take place, therefore, William Messenger, who had done duty as full private and sergeant, was made ensign of the Taranaki Militia, promoted to the rank of lieutenant on the 4th December, 1862, made captain on 27th July, 1863, and sub-inspector of Armed Constabulary on the 2nd December, 1877, when he was placed in command of the post at White Cliffs, where he has been stationed ever since. His own account of the events as they occurred at Taranaki is so lucid that I give it *verbatim.*

He says that he joined the volunteer force in consequence of the uneasy feeling of the settlers with regard to native matters, about June, 1858, as a private, was elected sergeant in 1859, and at the outbreak of hostilities in 1860 received a commission as ensign in the Taranaki Militia. After assisting in building the stockade at Omata, a village about three miles out of New Plymouth, he was ordered into town to assist in putting it into a state of defence. He marched with the militia and volunteers, under Major Stapp, to the relief of the Rev. H. H. Brown, on the 28th March, 1860, which led to the first battle (Waireka). In this engagement he was under the immediate command of Captain Charles Brown. It is a fact, perhaps not generally known, that the militia in that engagement were armed only with the old Brown Bess muskets; the volunteers had rifles, but many of the members having just joined, were ignorant of the sighting of the weapons placed in their hands. Messenger was near Lieutenant Urquhart, of the 65th, about four o'clock in the afternoon, when the "retire" sounded. The fire was very heavy at the time, and not until it had sounded three times and an order arrived for Lieutenant Urquhart to retire at once, did this brave officer leave the field. On leaving he said to the volunteers, " Well, I suppose I must go," and he took his men back across the gully to where the main body of his regiment were. Only a few minutes elapsed before the natives swarmed down the gully, cutting off the retreat of the militia and volunteers, and Captain Brown sent a messenger to warn a party under Captain Webster, who were carrying wounded to the rear, that the road was blocked, consequently a position was taken up round a house and some low hills and held until long after dark. Some of the men had only two or three rounds of ammunition left and had to husband it with great care, only firing when a native came too near. Just after dark they heard shouting and saw flashes in the direction of the pa on Waireka Hill, where the main body of natives were. Captain Messenger continues : " Major Stapp had a portion of our rough defences pulled down and preparations were made for going to assist in the assault (it turned out afterwards that it was an attack on the pa by the sailors from Her Majesty's ship *Niger*, guided by my two brothers, Charles and Edward, and F. Mace), but as the firing suddenly ceased, Major Stapp was, I believe, doubtful whether it might not be a *ruse* to draw us out. Volunteer Coad offered to go by himself and find out what was going on, but was not allowed to do so. As soon as we had completed stretchers to carry the wounded we marched by the beach road, which the natives had left unguarded when the pa was attacked by the blue jackets. We reached the stockade at Omata without any other incident than an alarm, which turned out on closer inspection to be caused by some dead bodies of natives lying in the flax. We then marched back to town, meeting a body of troops who had been sent out to try and discover our whereabouts."

After this, Captain Messenger was stationed in town and at one or other of the small blockhouses in its vicinity, also at Bell Block stockade with a detachment of the 12th Regiment. Constant skirmishing went on. On one occasion he formed one of a small scouting party, Captain Queade and Dr. Lynch, of 12th Regiment, and Lieutenant Hammerton, Taranaki Volunteers, being with them ; returning to camp, they were suddenly greeted with a sharp volley from a detachment of the 12th Regiment, who, surprised by their appearance, had mistaken them for a prowling party of natives. Luckily no one was hit, but there were many narrow escapes. While stationed here Major Nelson, 40th Regiment, marched up one day with a detachment from Waitara, and called for volunteers from Bell Block to assist in attacking the Mimi Pa. The natives were seen there in the morning and a red flag was still flying. The Major was on horseback, and had, a minute before, been soundly rating Corporal Bush, 40th Regiment, for neglecting to take cover, when he suddenly galloped up to the pa (which had the usual crooked entrance), dismounted, and ran in. Messenger was close behind him, and when he got in Major Nelson was quietly rolling the flag up, and tucking it under his arm. The pa, fortunately for him, was deserted. Captain Messenger was soon afterwards attached to the Taranaki Bush Rangers, a corps whose special duty it was to patrol the country, under Captains Atkinson and F. Webster. He was at the battle of Mahoetahi. The troops marched from town before daylight, and firing began as they were crossing the river. They had orders to charge the hill—an old site of a village with banks and ditches, which were occupied by the enemy, chiefly Ngatihaua, under Wetini Taiporutu. The regular troops advanced at the same time, they taking one end of the rise, and the colonial forces the other. The natives stood their ground well for a time, but were driven out. The colonial forces had two men killed (Volunteers Brown and Edgecombe), the 65th losing the same number. The natives left 37 men dead on the field, including their chief, Wetini Taiporutu. They carried off their wounded, while, with the Bush Rangers, they surprised an ambuscade party of Ngatiruanui, who were lying in wait for an escort from Bell Block; the chief of the Ngatiruanui party being killed in the skirmish that ensued. At the battle of Allen's Hill, where there were about eight hundred natives engaged, Colonel Warre, C.B., being in command of the regular troops, the natives made a stubborn fight, and repulsed the troops more than once. The Bush Rangers were sent for, and went at the double nearly all the way from town, about four-and-a-half miles. As they got near they could hear that the firing was very heavy, and at Waiuku Hill they met an orderly sent to hurry them up. Directly afterwards, Captain F. Mace, who was in command of the mounted corps, galloped up on the same errand. They marched through the line of wounded men, extended and relieved the skirmishers; but were not allowed to charge the position held by the natives, who soon retired, and the colonial troops were ordered back to town. One of the regular officers received a Victoria Cross for bravery at this engagement.

Captain Messenger was next appointed to command a company of military settlers who had arrived from Melbourne and was sent with 150 of these men, before they were served out with arms, and only a few days after they landed, to build a redoubt at Sentry Hill, under the protection of the military. They finished the redoubt in a few days, and were complimented by Colonel Warre on their work. After a short time spent in drilling his company, Captain Messenger was sent to occupy a redoubt at Manutahi, and afterwards commanded at the Poutoko Redoubt. On the taking of Kaitake Pa by the Bush Rangers, he was sent to occupy that station.

An amusing incident occurred at Stoney River, to which place a reconnaissance under Major Butler went from Tataraimaka. They had just formed camp, and, as an attack was threatened, outlying pickets, etc., were posted. The men had piled arms, and were busy getting their supper, the bullocks, which had been dragging the guns, etc., all day, having been turned out to graze (in most cases with their yokes on). The only fodder was ground tutu, a stunted

growth of the ordinary tutu shrub (which drives cattle mad).
Suddenly thé brutes rushed the camp, staggering about apparently
quite blind, knocking down rifles, capsizing billies of tea, causing
tents to suddenly collapse, and playing havoc generally. It was a
curious sight. At one spot would be seen a pair of huge bullocks,
heels upwards, kicking furiously, with two or three drivers thrusting
sharp-pointed sticks violently up their nostrils, blood spurting in
all directions, this being supposed to be the only cure for a "tuted"
bullock; while at another place some maddened animal was
"running a muck" through the tents. A conspicuous figure in
this curious scene was a noted bullock-driver named Jack Phillips,
who, by-the-by, received a revolver with an inscription in silver on
the handle, as a reward for his bravery in remaining with his team
during a sudden attack from a native ambuscade. The commander,
Major Butler, was in a very anxious state of mind, fearing that the
force, in consequence of the misadventure described, would not
have sufficient bullocks to bring away the guns, etc. However, by
the morning most of the animals had sufficiently recovered (although
several were left dead) to do the work required.

In 1864 Captain Messenger was ordered to Pukearuhe, White
Cliffs. This post had just been occupied by the Bush Rangers and
70th Regiment, whom the colonial forces relieved, one company cf
the 70th, under Captain Ralston, remaining for a time. The men
had plenty of work clearing a site and building a redoubt. The only
means of supplying the post was by sea, and they were fortunately
not molested by natives until some time later. Skirmishing began
when the Imperial Government steamship *Alexandra* was wrecked
on the beach about a mile from the redoubt. She was engaged to
bring timber for a blockhouse and supplies for the post, and running
on a reef had a large hole knocked in her bottom. Being an iron
ship she would have sunk in deep water if Captain Williams had
not headed her for the beach at once. As it was, she filled and sank
just as her bows touched the sand. The natives came down from
Mokau to plunder the vessel and constant skirmishes took place.
Captain Messenger remained at White Cliffs until his company of
military settlers were placed on their land, and it was while living
on the land allotted to him that the massacre of the Rev. J. Whiteley,
Lieutenant Gascoigne and family, and two of his company of military
settlers named Milne and Richards, occurred. A short time before
this a communication had been sent to him by the Government
stating that from certain information received, there was reason to
believe that the Ngatimaniapoto natives intended to attack some
one of the outposts, either in Waikato or the White Cliffs, and that
the settlers, not being on pay, were to use their own judgment as
to remaining on their land; also requesting him to make the people
acquainted with this notice. The blockhouse at White Cliffs had
been for some time without any garrison, a half-caste from Urenui
Redoubt, ten miles distant, being sent up once a week to White
Cliffs, apparently to ascertain whether any of the out-settlers
were killed or not, but not a man was sent to garrison the post.

Things went on in this way for some weeks, when on the afternoon of Saturday, the 28th February, 1869, the Rev. J. Whiteley called at Captain Messenger's house, on his way to the Cliffs to hold service the next day. As it was raining he was pressed to stay the night, but did not do so. He rode away, and was shot dead immediately on his arrival at the redoubt by a party of natives belonging to the rebellious Ngatimaniapoto tribe, from Mokau, among whom the good old man had spent some years of his life as a missionary. This was the taua or war party that the Government had been warned about, and which had decided to make Pukearuhe their point of attack. They had arrived at Pukearuhe early in the day, and the main body had concealed themselves in the creek below the redoubt, while a few, armed with spears and tomahawks under their mats, induced one of the settlers, Milne, to accompany them to the beach to bargain for some pigs, when he was struck on the head, from behind, with a tomahawk, and fell dead. Richards was then led to his death in the same way. Lieutenant Gascoigne was in his garden, with his wife and children, some little distance from the redoubt. Hearing himself called, he came, carrying one of the children. Just as he reached his own door, he was struck from behind, and fell stunned. His head was immediately split open with an axe. The child was also killed, his wife and the remaining children being killed on their arrival at the house. It was some time after their massacre that Mr. Whiteley arrived. Meanwhile, the natives had ransacked the place for arms, ammunition, and valuables. When the Rev. Mr. Whiteley and his horse were killed, some of the war party became " pouri," and it was decided to return home, instead of, as at first intended, going as far as Urenui and killing all the settlers on the way. So, after setting fire to the blockhouse and other houses, and cutting down the flagstaff, they retired. The next day (Sunday) was very wet. On Monday, the two half-castes, McClutchy and Coffee, whose duty it was to make periodical visits to Pukearuhe, arrived from Urenui, saying they had been sent by Captain Good to ask Captain Messenger if anything was wrong at the Cliffs. The Captain advised them to go on and see, which they refused to do. So, after exacting a promise from them to stay until his return, and in case he did not come back, to see his wife and children safe to Urenui, he started on horseback. Before reaching the Cliffs, however, he met a man who had been told by one of the military settlers, named Skinner, that he had been on his way to the redoubt, and had seen a dead body on the road, and that the blockhouse was burnt. Captain Messenger, after assisting all the settlers over the river Mimi to Urenui, then tried, without success, to induce some of the native contingent to accompany him back to the Cliffs. He remained at Urenui until the arrival of an armed party, under Major Stapp, with whom he went to the Cliffs, and recovered the bodies. The Rev. J. Whiteley lay where he had fallen on his face, with seven bullet wounds in his body, his watch and coat being taken away. Mr. and Mrs. Gascoigne and family were put all together in a shallow pit, and slightly covered with earth. The two other men lay where they had fallen. Captain Messenger received the thanks of the Government for his conduct on this occasion.

After this melancholy tragedy, Captain Messenger was placed on duty under Captain Good, at Urenui, for a short time, when he was sent to Huirangi in command of a party of militia engaged in building a blockhouse at Te Arie. When that was completed, he was ordered to proceed, as second in command, with an expedition consisting of Armed Constabulary, Bush Rangers, and native contingent, to assist in the capture of Titokowaru, at Ngatimaru; but, on reaching Mataitawa, the expedition was recalled. Captain Messenger was now despatched to Wai-iti, two miles from Pukearuhe, to take charge of a company of Bush Rangers, where he built a redoubt, being joined by a body of Armed Constabulary, who erected a redoubt about half a mile distant. While on patrol duty, with a portion of his company, he came across Te Wetere and a scouting party in the hills, and nearly succeeded in securing him. As it was, they got such a scare that they never again ventured to return to the district for the purpose of fighting. They broke two or three guns in rushing headlong down a steep hill, then scattered in the bush, and were some days in reaching home. Captain Messenger was next employed in charge of a working party of Armed Constabulary, sawing timber for building bridges over the Urenui and Mimi Rivers, making the approaches, etc., for which work, when completed, he received the thanks of the Government. Lastly, he was placed in command of the post at White Cliffs, with rank of sub-inspector, and is still stationed there.

COLONEL LYON.

Colonel Lyon.

———

Service in the Imperial army—The campaign against Titokowaru.

COLONEL LYON, commanding officer of the Auckland district, was formerly an officer in the Coldstream Guards, one of Her Majesty's crack regiments ; he afterwards, to obtain active service, exchanged, as captain, into the 92nd Highlanders, serving ten months with them in the Crimea. On the regiment returning to England, after the peace, he met with an accident while sporting, which caused the loss of his right arm, and retiring from the service, he came out to this colony to settle down to agricultural pursuits. But the Maori war breaking out soon after his arrival, the Government called upon him to take the command of a company of volunteers, and he was appointed adjutant of a battalion, under the command of Colonel Balneavis. He gained his majority in 1863, and commanding a wing of the 3rd battalion of Auckland Militia, was sent on special service with 150 men, composed of imperial and colonial troops, to the Wairoa, in August of that year, where, after repulsing the Maoris in an attack on his redoubt, he drove them, with considerable loss, from their position, for which service he received the thanks of Lieut.-General Sir Duncan Cameron, K.C.B., and Major-General Galloway, commanding the colonial forces, and was favourably mentioned in despatches. He was appointed Lieut.-Colonel of the 3rd regiment of the Waikato Militia in October, 1863, and took the command of an expeditionary force at Opotiki, in 1865, returning after some months to resume the command of the Waikato district.

In 1869 he was appointed to the command of the colonial field force, collected at Wanganui during the absence of Lieut.-Colonel Sir George Whitmore at Poverty Bay. On Colonel Whitmore's return he continued to serve under him as second in command during the whole of the campaign against Titokowaru, being present at the fight at Otauto and capture of Te Ngahiere. After the campaign he remained for some time in command at Patea, until ordered back to the Waikato.

During the twelve months' leave of absence granted to Colonel Moule to visit the home country, Colonel Lyon performed all his duties as Under-Secretary for Defence and Commissioner of Armed Constabulary.

This brave and energetic officer has been on active service or outpost duty in New Zealand ever since the year 1860, and under fire so often that it would nearly lead one to suppose he had hitherto borne a charmed life.

The late differences existing between Russia and England which naturally, though unexpectedly, led to that spontaneous outburst of loyalty and offers of assistance from all Her Majesty's colonies throughout the globe, opened the eyes of hostile nations to the strength Great Britain could derive in case of need from her dependencies, and made them pause ere they forced a war upon us. Nevertheless, Her Majesty's colonial subjects at once saw their position, and taking the initiative, prepared to resist any invasion of their seaports, and Auckland—the principal port in New Zealand —a port of all others most liable to attack in case of war, was entrusted to Colonel Lyon to defend, one of the highest compliments the colony could bestow on so well tried a soldier.

CAPTAIN MERCER.

CAPTAIN MERCER.

———

Gallant conduct at the capture of Rangiriri—A soldier's death—Tributes by Sir George Grey and General Cameron to his memory.

CAPTAIN MERCER, of the Royal Artillery, was despatched to this colony to assist in putting down the rebellion, and had not landed many months when the capture of Rangiriri (one of the strongest of the native fortifications, manned by many hundreds of Maori warriors) was made which resulted in the death of this beloved and much lamented officer. General Cameron, well aware of the strength of the Maori fighting pa, and having the character of a shrewd general, it has surprised many that he should have ordered so small a force as 36 artillerymen, and, after their repulse, 90 seamen, to assault so formidable a palisading, surrounded as it was by rifle-pits in every direction. Neither would it appear desirable to take thirty-six artillerymen from their guns to attempt a duty foreign to their calling. The attack on the pa, though eventually successful, resulted in the loss of many of our best and bravest troops, no less than 130 having been either killed or wounded in the attack, as will appear in General Cameron's report of the engagement to Sir George Grey, and the latter's reply, copied from the *Gazette* of the 30th November, 1863 :—

[LIEUTENANT-GENERAL CAMERON TO THE GOVERNOR.]

"HEAD QUARTERS,
"CAMP, RANGIRIRI, *24th November, 1863.*

" SIR,—I have the honour to report to your Excellency that on the morning of the 20th instant I moved from Meremere with the force detailed in the margin (853 officers and men) up the right bank of the Waikato River, with the intention of attacking the enemy's entrenched position at Rangiriri, in which operation Commodore Sir William Wiseman, Bart., had arranged to co-operate with the *Pioneer* and *Avon*, steamers, and the four gunboats. The troops under my command and the steamers and gunboats arrived near Rangiriri at the same hour—3 p.m. The enemy's position consisted of a main line of entrenchment across the narrow isthmus which divides the Waikato River from Lake Waikare. This line had a double ditch and high parapet, and was strengthened at the centre (its highest point) by a square redoubt of very formidable construction. Behind the left centre of the main line and at right angles to it there was an entrenched line of rifle-pits parallel to the Waikato river, and obstructing the advance of troops from that direction. On a reconnaissance made on the 18th, I had determined on landing a force in rear of the position simultaneously with attacking it in front, with the view of turning and gaining possession of a ridge 500 yards behind the main entrenchment, and thus intercepting the retreat of the enemy. With this object 300 men of the 40th Regiment were embarked in the *Pioneer* and *Avon*, to land on a preconcerted signal, at a point which I had selected. Unfortunately the strength of the wind and current was such that the *Pioneer* and *Avon* were unable to reach this point, notwithstanding the persevering efforts of Sir William Wiseman and the officers and men under his command. The same cause deprived us of the assistance of two of the gunboats. After shelling the position of the enemy for a considerable time from Captain Mercer's two 12-pounder Armstrongs, and the Naval 6-pounder, under Lieutenant Alexander, R.N., in which the two gunboats joined, and it being now nearly five o'clock, I determined not to wait any longer for the landing of the 40th from the steamers, and gave the word for the assault. This was brilliantly executed by the troops, who had to pass over a distance of 600 yards in the face of a heavy fire, the 65th Regiment leading and escalading the enemy's entrenchment on the left. After passing the main line of entrenchment, the troops wheeled to the left towards the enemy's centre, and came under fire of the line of rifle-pits facing the Waikato River. This they at once stormed and carried, driving the enemy before them to the centre redoubt, which they now defended with desperate resolution. While the troops were forcing their way over the parapet of the main line, as already described, I was glad to perceive that the 40th were landing sufficiently near the point I had indicated to enable them to carry and occupy the ridge in rear, and to pour a heavy fire on a body of the enemy, who were driven by them from that part of the position, and fled by the Waikare Swamp. In this part of the attack they were joined by a portion of the 65th Regiment detached from the main body after the latter had passed the main line of entrenchment. The troops who carried the main line being still checked by the fire from the centre redoubt, two separate assaults were made on this work—the first by 36 of the Royal Artillery, armed with revolvers and led by Captain Mercer; and the second by 90 seamen of the Royal Navy, armed in a similar manner and led by Commander Mayne, under the personal direction of Sir William Wiseman. Both attacks were unsuccessful on account of the formidable nature of the work, and the overwhelming fire which was brought to bear on the assailants. An attempt was also made by a party of seamen under Commander Phillimore to dislodge the enemy with hand grenades thrown into the work. It being now nearly dark, I resolved to wait the return of daylight before undertaking further operations, the troops remaining in the several positions they had gained, in which they almost completely enveloped the enemy. Shortly after daylight on the 21st, the white flag was hoisted by the enemy, of whom 183 surrendered unconditionally, gave up their arms, and became prisoners of war. The exact strength and loss of the enemy I have been unable to ascertain, but he must have suffered severely. We buried 36 bodies, and there is no doubt a large number were shot or drowned in attempting to escape across the swamp at Waikare lake. Their wounded must have been removed during the night, as there were none among the prisoners. Our loss, necessarily severe in carrying so formidable a position, testifies to the gallantry of the troops I have the honour to command, and also, I am bound to say, to the bravery and determination of its defenders. I enclose a list of casualties. Your Excellency will observe that it includes a large proportion of officers, most of those who led in the different attacks being severely wounded.

PLAN OF GROUND
SURROUNDING
ORAKAU PA,
Showing the disposition of the troops under
Brigadier-General Carey,
2ND APRIL, 1864.

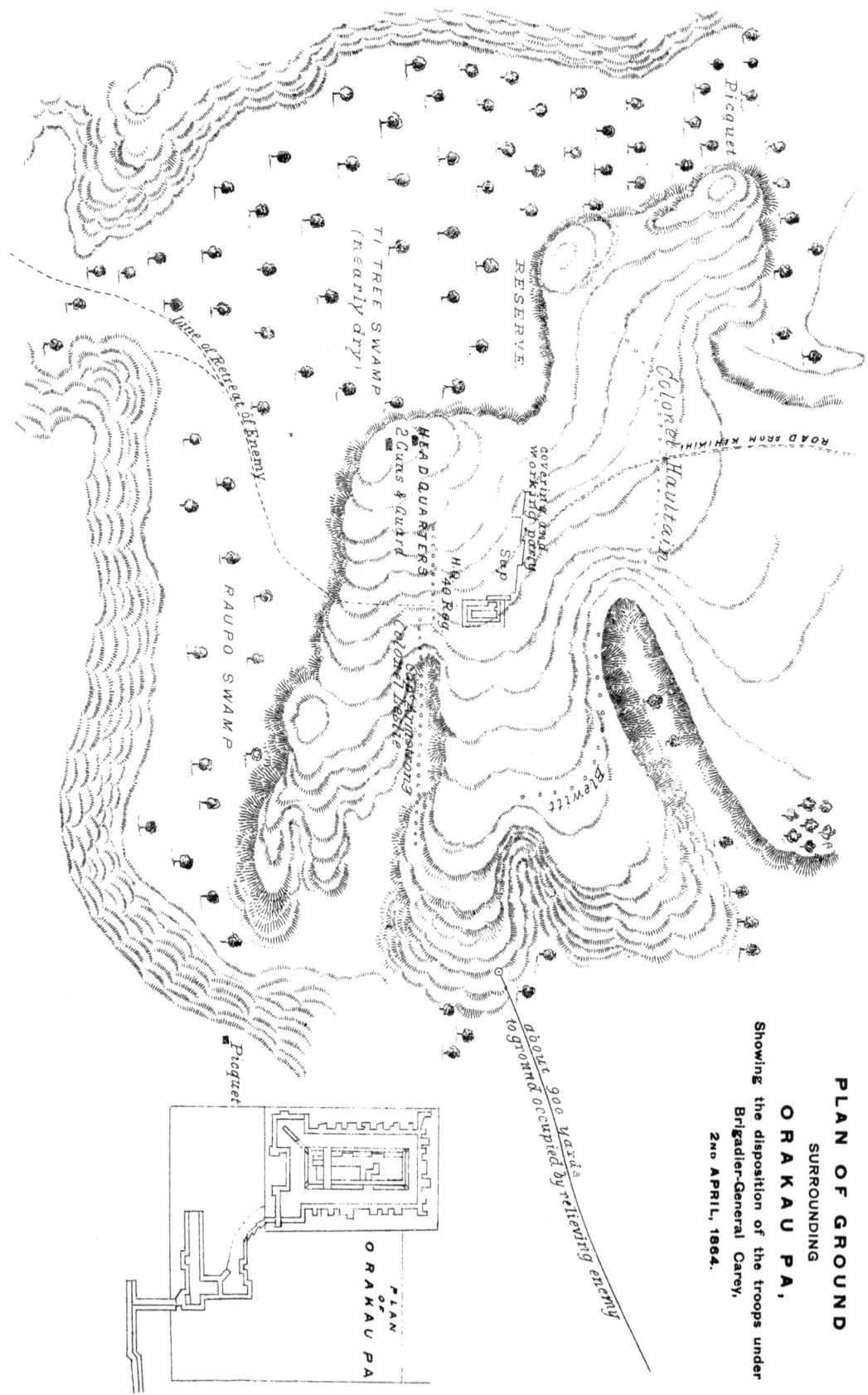

Picquet

RESERVE

TI TREE SWAMP
(nearly dry)

line of Retreat of Enemy

RAUPO SWAMP

Picquet

HEADQUARTERS
2 Guns & Guard

H.Q 40 Reg.

Step

covering and
working party

Colonel Haultain

ROAD FROM KIHIKIHI

Colonel Leslie

Colonel Havelock

Blewitt

about 900 yards
to ground occupied by relieving enemy

Picquet

PLAN
of
ORAKAU PA

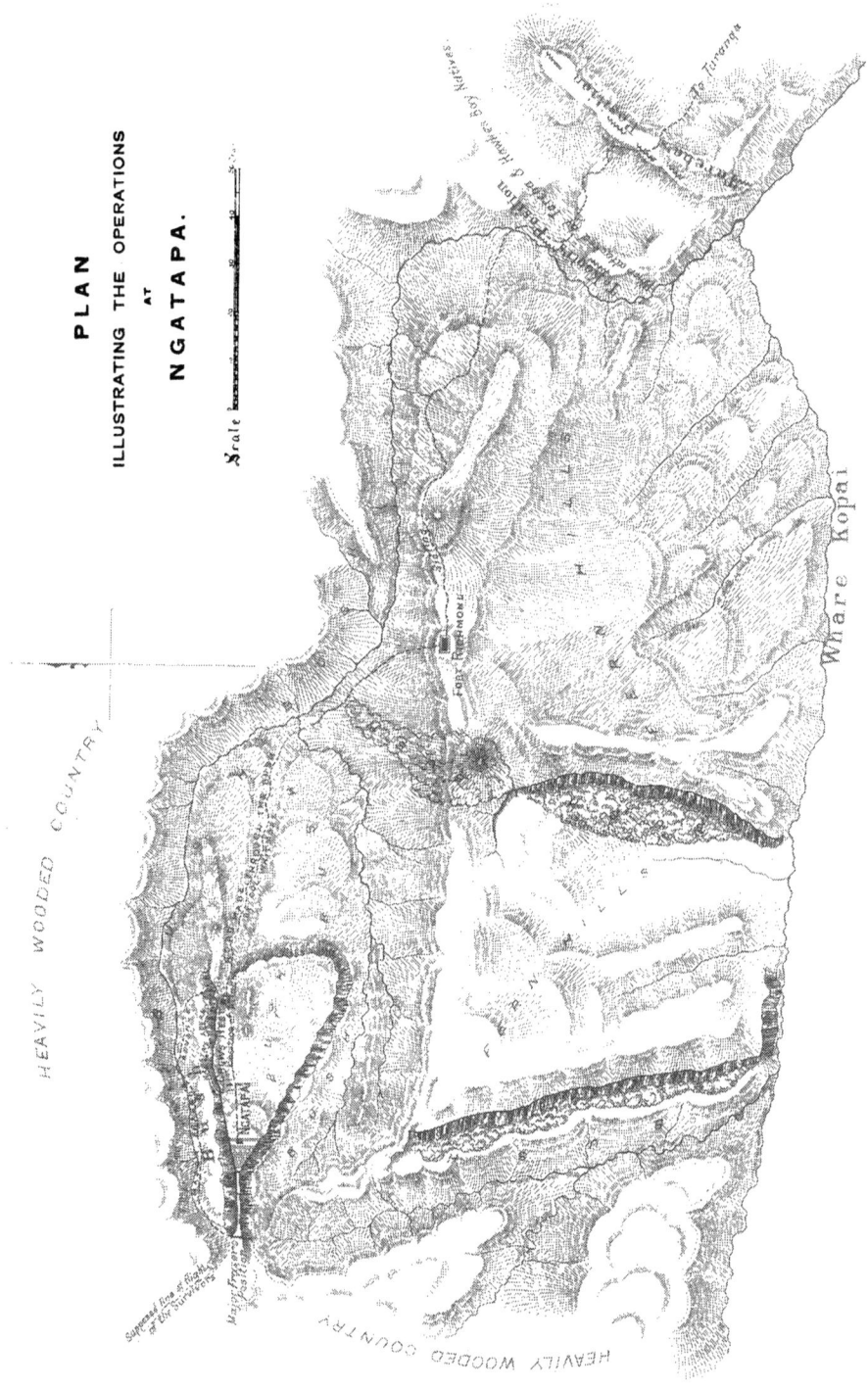

PLAN
ILLUSTRATING THE OPERATIONS
AT
NGATAPA.

Scale

HEAVILY WOODED COUNTRY

HEAVILY WOODED COUNTRY

Whare Kopai

Te Turaraqa

Station of Hawke Bay Natives

Fort Richmond

NGATAPA

Major Frazer's Position

Supposed line of flight of the Survivors

"It will afford me the highest gratification to report to the Right Honourable the Secretary of State for War, and to His Royal Highness the Field Marshal Commanding-in-Chief, the admirable conduct of the troops engaged on this occasion, and to bring to their special notice the names of those officers and men who more particularly distinguished themselves.—I have, etc.,

"D. A. CAMERON, Lieut.-General.

"His Excellency Sir GEORGE GREY, K.C.B."

[LIEUT.-GENERAL CAMERON TO THE GOVERNOR.]

"HEAD QUARTERS,

"CAMP, RANGIRIRI, *26th November, 1863.*

"Sir,—Since I closed my despatch of the 24th instant, I have received intelligence of the death of Captain Mercer, commanding Royal Artillery on this station, from the effect of wounds received in the action of the 20th instant, whilst gallantly leading his men to an assault on the enemy's strongest work. I regard the loss of this able, zealous, and energetic officer at the present moment as a serious misfortune. Your Excellency having been intimately acquainted with Captain Mercer, and appreciating his noble character and many sterling qualities, will, I am confident, participate in the grief felt by myself and by the whole force, for the death of this invaluable officer. I have also to deplore the loss of another brave and excellent officer, Captain Phelps, 2nd Battalion 14th Regiment, who died in consequence of a wound received in the action of 20th instant.—I have, etc.,

"D. A. CAMERON, Lieut.-General.

"His Excellency Sir G. GREY, K.C.B."

[HIS EXCELLENCY THE GOVERNOR TO LIEUT.-GENERAL CAMERON, C.B.]

"GOVERNMENT HOUSE,

AUCKLAND, *28th November, 1863.*

"Sir,—I have directed that your despatch of the 26th instant, which I received in the night, should be published for general information, at the same time as your despatch of the 24th instant.

"I entirely enter into your feelings of grief for the loss of the brave officers and men who have fallen in obtaining a victory from which may be anticipated such great advantages for this country. I can assure you that very deep sorrow for the heavy loss sustained and for the sufferings of the wounded is felt throughout the entire community, who will, I am aware, in a fitting manner, express their debt of gratitude to yourself and the forces under your command.

"You must permit me, whilst expressing my own sorrow for the loss of Captain Mercer, Captain Phelps, Lieutenant Murphy, Mr. Watkin, and so many gallant men, to add that my intimate acquaintance with Captain Mercer has caused me in his case to feel very keenly the loss of an officer whose many excellent qualities I regarded with admiration and esteem.—I have, etc.,

"G. GREY.

"The Hon. Lieut.-General CAMERON, C.B."

Mr. E. Hamlin.

Mr. Hamlin at Omarunui—The Uriweras routed at Waikare.

THE late Mr. E. Hamlin took so active a part in the late war that had I passed over his services, I should have placed myself in the position of an imperfect chronicler. In the early part of 1863, Mr. E. Hamlin, from his knowledge of the Maori language and character, was attached to Sir Donald McLean, who valued his services highly and brought him before the notice of the Government on several occasions. He was selected by Sir Donald to carry his ultimatum to the Hauhaus, then assembled at Omarunui, just before their extermination. A temporary staff had been erected, on which a white flag was hoisted when Hamlin started with the message "that if, within one hour, they did not lay down their arms and surrender, they would be attacked." This was an extremely bitter pill for them, and the only reply that Hamlin could obtain was "that the time allowed was short." For some time the Maoris took no notice of Hamlin, but sat glowering in their whares. They were puzzled how to act. They did not intend to surrender, nor did they wish to fight just then. We had evidently, by taking the initiative, upset all their plans; for had Te Rangihiroa been ready to operate from the western spit, there would have been no hesitation shown, and Mr. Hamlin's life would probably have been sacrificed as an offering to Tu, the Maori god of war. Again at Ngatapa, Mr. Hamlin particularly distinguished himself, being one of the first men in the pa. He was all through the Poverty Bay troubles, and took a party across the Waikare Lake, and utterly routed the Uriweras, after 800 men had abandoned the attempt.

MAJOR JACKSON.

MAJOR JACKSON.

Services at the beginning of the Waikato war—Gallant conduct with the Forest Rangers at Hunua—An account with some Maori murderers settled — The "Bathing Party" episode — The Forest Rangers at Orakau.

MAJOR JACKSON, at the commencement of hostilities in the Waikato, was farming his own land near Papakura, and as his was not the spirit to submit tamely to be driven from his homestead, with the loss of his flocks and herds, by rebel Maoris, he came forward and offered his services as a private in the volunteers, and in that capacity took an active part in driving the enemy out of his own neighbourhood. He first distinguished himself in repelling an attack made by the rebels upon a half-finished redoubt on the Wairoa road (known afterwards as Ring's Redoubt), being one of the most conspicuous in its defence, and was further credited with having by his unerring aim severely punished the attacking force.

After this Major Jackson came prominently to the front by engaging to raise a company of forest rangers, who would follow the Maoris from place to place and surprise them in their forest strongholds. The Government gladly accepted his offer, and he accordingly enrolled a body of men, composed of brave and experienced bushmen, whose general physique and equipments were superior to any other corps in the colony. With the utmost perseverance and daring Jackson and his men endeavoured to track the marauding and murdering bands of Maoris who for several months had infested the large tract of forest country lying between the Lower Waikato and our settlements, but their success in finding the enemy was not equal to their expectations or exertions.

On several occasions they had smart skirmishes, and did good service in showing the natives that we were both able and willing to follow them anywhere; but like the movable column, commanded by Imperial officers and employed at the same time on somewhat similar duty, they never had the good fortune to inflict any great loss upon the enemy. Major Jackson's original company of forest rangers were only engaged for a short period of service, and being a rather expensive corps, the Government, after six months' service, disbanded them, but authorised Major Jackson to raise a new company for special service like the first, but to be attached to and form part of, the 2nd Regiment of Waikato Militia. Although this act reduced their pay considerably, the men would not leave the Major, and most of them joined under the new conditions.

During the whole of 1864 Major Jackson and his company were actively engaged in the Waikato, and distinguished themselves on several occasions, more particularly at the siege and capture of Orakau. For this and other incidents of individual bravery Major Jackson received the thanks of the General commanding and was promoted to the rank of major.

At the conclusion of the campaign, the Major again settled down to farm life on land which the Government granted to him for his services at Rangiaohia; and although, from that time forward, there has been no actual fighting in the district, there was for years a deal of uneasiness and threatening among the Kingites; so much so that Major Jackson, seeing the state of affairs, was mainly instrumental in raising two troops of cavalry volunteers, of which he was appointed and still remains commandant. And it may be safely said that, apart from actual fighting, no body of volunteers ever did better service in New Zealand, their martial and determined bearing having reassured the settlers, and awed the rebels into submission against their will, thereby thoroughly protecting our exposed frontier and preserving peace and order in the district.

Major Jackson was elected by the settlers of the district to represent Waikato in the House of Representatives, and still continues to take an active and lively interest in all matters connected with the defence of the colony. It appears from documents before me, that a dispute arose with regard to land claimed as compensation for services performed by the members of the Forest Rangers while serving under the Major, and the following extract, in support of their services, I have taken from the evidence given, and papers laid before the Commissioner (Colonel Haultain) on the subject :—

THE FOREST RANGERS.

AT THE HUNUA RANGES.

During the month of December, 1863, Captain Jackson left camp at Papakura to scour the Hunua Ranges, it having been reported that natives had been seen in the neighbourhood. He had a force of about thirty, all ranks. These men were raised under instructions from the Defence Minister. When in the bush, they came upon tracks of the enemy, which they followed for two days. At about 8 o'clock on a Sunday morning, in the vicinity of the Papakura Valley, not near any post occupied either by Imperial or colonial forces, the whereabouts of the enemy was discovered through observing steam ascending from their ovens, when opened for the morning meal; and from the earliness of the hour, Captain Jackson concluded they were on the move. The party they had tracked so long, he was well aware, were travelling, and, from the appearance of the tracks, were evidently a small party; but there could be no doubt as to the strength of the camp whose whereabouts they had discovered, as each of the five puffs of steam they had noticed bore evidence of a separate oven, while others may not have been seen; and it must necessarily be a large party requiring such extensive cooking arrangements.

When the whereabouts and strength of the enemy became known, the Captain had great doubt on his mind as to whether he should attack the enemy's position or not, feeling that in doing so he incurred a great responsibility; for should he be unsuccessful in his attack, the probability, if not certainty, was that to a man they would be destroyed, being well aware that if once the natives succeeded in causing a retreat, so small a force would be considerably reduced ere that stage was reached, and probably so much embarrassed with the care of the wounded that few if any would be left to tell the tale; and, notwithstanding the anxious wish of his men to engage the enemy, should he unfortunately be defeated, the disaster would be credited to his rashness and want of judgment, more especially as he knew that the authorities looked upon his corps more as a scouting than an attacking force. He knew the ranges he had travelled through had been, since the commencement of the war, harbouring a murdering set of natives, who for nearly twelve months had caused great anxiety to the Government by murdering such settlers as they could surprise when visiting their abandoned homesteads, and thus causing a large extent of settled country to be deserted. Major Jackson knew that if he could succeed in dispersing this marauding band the result would be of incalculable benefit to the country; and consequently the mere probability of success warranted him in making the attempt, if, after consulting with his men and explaining to them the danger incurred, he found they would freely undertake the duty. He consequently called his men together and, as well as he could, showed them the position they were in, and the risk they would run by making an attack; that while in the bush, with proper precautions, they might be able to protect themselves from an attack of the enemy very much their superiors in number, yet it was necessary to well consider what would be the result of defeat ere they voluntarily made an attack upon a force that was evidently much stronger in numbers than their own; but, as these men were probably the murderers of our men, women, and children, he thought it was their duty, even at great risks, to endeavour to relieve the anxiety of the out-settlers, for should they happily succeed in dispersing the enemy, he felt certain they would not again return to the scenes of their former murders. The men were quite willing to leave the matter in the hands of their officers, and it was decided to make the attempt. Before they started, the men stripped themselves of everything but shirt, trousers, and boots, taking only their arms and ammunition with them.

Before leaving the Captain again addressed them. "Is there any man who feels that he is not equal to undertake this duty, either on account of illness or that his heart is not at present in the right place? If so, let he or they start at once for head-quarters, and they may perhaps do good service in bearing a despatch to Colonel Nixon, who would be soon on the move to assist us." Not a man stirred. The attack was successful, and from information obtained afterwards the natives were at least two hundred strong. Without going into details, the force completely surprised the enemy; the action was short, sharp, and decisive, with no casualties on our side, several of the enemy being killed and wounded—the actual murderers of the late Mr. Hamlin, Turt's children, Cooper, Calvert, Jackson, and Mr. and Mrs. Fabey being amongst the slain.

In this action an act of self-devotion on the part of a native deserves to be mentioned. About twenty minutes after the charge and capture of the enemy's camp a Maori was seen returning, and while the sentry was watching his movements saw him enter a whare and taking up a tin box; he was in the act of making off with it when the sentry challenged him, but as he took no notice he fired, wounding him in the arm, which caused him to drop the box before he disappeared in the bush. The Forest Rangers thinking they had a prize, rushed to the box, and forcing it open found it to contain only the king's flag, which had been entrusted to his care, but which in the suddenness of the surprise of the camp he had left behind him, and had risked his life to try and recover.

AT WAIARI, FEBRUARY, 1864.

Major Jackson happening to be with Major Heaphy in Colonel Havelock's tent before Paterangi when the news arrived of the attack of the enemy on a bathing party in the Mangapiko River, about a mile from the camp, hurried off to the scene with others. As the Major reached the river he found himself with three men of the 40th opposite to an old native pa (Waiari), the entrenchments of which, as well as the steep sides of the opposite bank of the river, were thickly covered with scrub and occupied by the enemy. The bank of the river on his side was low and flat, while the opposite side was steep and high, and about one-third down a wounded soldier was seen stretched on the ground. Several soldiers were on the top of the bank firing down into the scrub below, where the enemy were supposed to be. Jackson's attention was called to the wounded man by the men on the opposite bank (one being an officer) requesting him to come across the river and relieve the wounded man. Jackson replied, "It would be easier and better for you to get down the bank and take him up yourselves, and in the meantime if the enemy showed

I could keep them down without injury to the relief party." This the officer declined to do, and the men with Jackson cried out, "You are a lot of cowards;"and turning to Jackson said, "If you will lead us we will soon shift him." Jackson immediately agreed, and they proceeded to cross the river at great risk to their lives, the water in places being up to their chins. When nearly across Jackson saw the arm of a Maori above the scrub in the act of ramming down a cartridge, and while keeping his eye on him (waiting a favourable opportunity to get a shot at him), did not perceive at the moment another Maori had concealed himself in the scrub only a few paces from his landing-place, and had covered him with his double-barrelled gun. As the Captain placed his foot on the opposite bank the Maori pulled the trigger, but fortunately for Jackson it missed fire, and put him on his guard. Seeing his adversary now about to fire his second barrel, he let fly at him with his revolver, which did not seem to take any effect further than to distract the Maori's aim, as he fired and missed, and in his rage and disappointment hurled his gun at the Captain, and was in the act of bolting when Jackson's second shot killed him. After this they proceeded to the assistance of the wounded man, bringing him into a place of safety. General Cameron, who was apprised of this gallant action, ordered the gun taken to be given to Major Jackson, saying, "As it was so nearly the cause of your death, it will remind you in after years of your narrow escape." Although it was not until after the battle of Orakau that Jackson obtained his majority, it was dated back to this event, viz., 11th February, 1863, as an acknowledgment of his services on that occasion.

The enemy were by this time completely surrounded by the troops, yet they still lay concealed in the scrub, the soldiers not caring to enter it, when Major Jackson asked the General to send for his and Von Tempsky's Bush Rangers, who on arrival went in with bowie knives and revolvers and soon made short work of the natives, which pleased the General so much that he despatched Major Jackson into town next day to endeavour to procure more men of the same stamp.

AT ORAKAU, APRIL, 1864.

As a party of Forest Rangers were busy pushing forward the sap to the enemy's position, a militiaman was shot down about half way between the head of the sap and the pa—a distance of about twenty yards from the pa—and was left lying wounded and exposed to a heavy fire from the enemy. The Forest Rangers, twenty in number, under Lieutenant Whitfield, determined to recover the wounded man. To have sent two or more men to bring him in would, for a certainty, have resulted in more men being killed or wounded ; consequently, after an exchange of ideas, it was determined to effect his release by the majority of the men making a sudden rush across the open space between our works and the enemy's, thus causing a diversion by taking possession of the enemy's outworks, during which time the wounded man was brought in and handed over to the medical staff in attendance. In going across this open space, they laid themselves open to the fire of the whole native force in the pa, but owing to the suddenness of the movement, they were almost across ere their intention was suspected, and being so close under the enemy's works, were somewhat protected. It was not until some time after that Major Herford and others were shot down while trying to join the Forest Rangers. This movement had an important effect on the issue of events, for the Forest Rangers were not long in establishing themselves in comparative security and clearing the enemy's out-works of its occupants, thus enabling communication to be kept up with them and the covering party protecting those in the sap. A party with hand grenades were thus enabled to get into position immediately under the very walls of the pa, and by throwing grenades over the palisading amongst the occupants caused great consternation amongst them while endeavouring to escape.

MAJOR LUSK.

MAJOR LUSK.

Maning and Lusk's patriotic offer—Forest Rifle Volunteers raised—The battle of the Bald Hills—Exciting hand-to-hand conflict.

MAJOR LUSK, prior to the outbreak of the war, was employed by the Government in surveying a part of the North Island. When hostilities commenced he joined with the late Judge Maning (the author of " Old New Zealand ") in a scheme for marching 1,200 Ngapuhi warriors through the Waikato into the Taranaki district, and thereby crushing the rebellion at its outset by placing the Kingites between two fires. The Ngapuhi had given in their names to the Judge, who was to command the force, with Lusk as his lieutenant, which was duly reported to the Governor, Colonel Gore Browne, in the formal offer of their services; but as the Government were not then prepared for such vigorous measures, the offer was declined with thanks. Long after all concerned in this movement had given up the idea of their services being required, the Government intimated to Judge Maning their wish to accept the assistance of the Ngapuhi, and received for answer that the tribe had now changed their minds, the fact being that emissaries from the Kingites had been busy amongst them, and they decided for the future to remain neutral.

In the autumn of 1863 Mr Lusk was residing on his property, situated between the Maori settlement at Patumahoe and the Waikato river, and it becoming evident to him that the Maoris in his neighbourhood (who were a particularly bad lot) meant mischief, he called a meeting of the settlers of the district, and so forcibly pointed out to them the danger that existed to the out-settlers and the necessity for banding themselves together for their mutual support, that the Forest Rifle Volunteers was formed, Mr. Lusk being elected their Captain. The first act of the Captain was to advertise for a few men of the right stamp to make up his complement, which was readily responded to, and the corps was ready, when the crisis came, to take the field. For the first five months the Rangers had a lively time of it, as the Waikato natives and their allies made the forest country the principal scene of their operations, and for a time really believed they could not only drive in the settlers but take the town of Auckland.

The first fight that occurred was with a party of about two hundred rebels who were overtaken in the dense bush near Mauku,

on the 9th of September, 1863, when a sharp skirmish ensued in
real bush fashion, from tree to tree. It was the first time the
volunteers had met the Maoris in the Waikato, and the first time
the great majority of them had been under fire. But they behaved
so well that the Maoris, being out-manœuvred by a flank movement,
fled, and left their temporary camp to be ransacked by the volunteers. In this skirmish, thanks to the bad firing of the rebels, only
two of the company were wounded, whereas six Maoris were killed.
Several other slight skirmishes took place in the forest, and on the
15th September the Maoris, numbering over two hundred men,
suddenly attacked the small body of volunteers, who were posted
at the Pukekohe church, under Captain Lusk's command. The
volunteers were taken quite by surprise, and at the first rush the
enemy nearly carried the stockade, but our men, having rallied,
fought with such desperation as to drive the rebels back for a time
to seek shelter. The heavy firing which had been kept up on both
sides, brought up a number of regulars from the South Road,
also a company of militia from Drury. These reinforcements
joined the besieged force, and drove the enemy off at the point of
the bayonet.

On the 23rd of October, Captain Lusk and his men fought what
is known as the battle of Bald Hills. This was, in some respects,
the most desperate and remarkable action during the war. A
party of over three hundred Ngatimaniapotos, under two near
relations of the celebrated chief Rewi, together with 50 Ngatiporous,
who had just before brought a large quantity of ammunition from
the East Coast, had slipped quietly down the Waikato River, in
their canoes, passed our forces, who were confronting the rebels at
Meremere, and landing below Cameron Town, expressed their
intention of killing all the settlers between that place and Auckland. There were, at this time, at the Maukau stockade, under
Captain Lusk, 60 non-commissioned officers and men of his own
company, and 20 of the 1st Waikato Regiment, under Lieutenant
Percival, and at the church, further up the valley, which was
converted into a stockade, about thirty men also of the 1st
Waikato Regiment, under Lieutenant Norman, who was at that
moment absent from his post, having gone to Drury to draw the
pay for his men. Captain Lusk had that morning, as usual, taken
40 of his volunteers out on a reconnoitring expedition round the
district, and, on arriving at the church, found the small force there
in some alarm, their officer being absent, while a considerable
force of the enemy had suddenly appeared within a mile of the
post, seemingly intent on shooting cattle. Captain Lusk soon
took in the situation, and as there appeared to be upwards of
one hundred and fifty of the rebels in view, he considered it
prudent to get up reinforcements before attacking them. He
accordingly dispatched a mounted messenger to Drury, requesting
assistance, and suggesting "that the movable column stationed
at the Queen's Redoubt should be sent down the banks of the
river, so as to get between the Maoris and their canoes,"

Unfortunately, neither his request nor suggestion was attended to with sufficient promptitude to be of any service, as the reinforcement did not arrive until dusk in the evening —two hours after the battle—and the flying squadron only reached the Maori landing place (Rangipokia) early next morning, just in time to witness the last canoes, with a small rearguard of the enemy, disappearing round a bend of the river.

The consequence was that Captain Lusk and his men remained at the Church Redoubt for nearly six hours, fretting and fuming at seeing the rebels so near and no sign of assistance coming, which could easily have arrived within four hours of the time the despatches left. About three o'clock in the afternoon the engagement was brought on by Lieutenant Percival, who had been left in charge of the lower stockade, and who had received orders (when the enemy was perceived by Captain Lusk) to place the charge of the redoubt in the hands of the commissariat officer and to join him at the church with twelve men. Percival, being anxious to distinguish himself in having the first shot at the rebels, directed his guide to take him by a forest track past the church and within sight of the enemy, which was accordingly done, and the first notice Captain Lusk had of Percival's presence was witnessing from the Church Redoubt a small band of volunteers emerging from the bush to the west of the slope of the Ti Ti hill, lately occupied by the rebels. Fortunately for these twelve men the Maoris had just retired over the brow of the hill to a hollow beyond, probably to regale themselves on the cattle they had shot. Percival, who soon came within sight of them, opened fire at a long distance, and the Maoris seeing the handful of men firing at them did not condescend to return it, but despatched a strong party round the shoulder of the hill to cut them off.

Captain Lusk, seeing the state of affairs, at once advanced to their rescue, and Lieutenant Percival, perceiving at the same moment that it was time he beat a retreat, retired quickly on the support. It was a close shave, but the rebels seeing Captain Lusk's force hurrying to the rescue halted, and the junction was effected without loss. The Forest Rangers then advanced in skirmishing order, as the Maoris retired up the cleared slope of the hill, disappearing between two belts of bush land. Up to this time, as well as could be judged, not more than 130 Maoris could be counted, and as Captain Lusk had sixty-seven officers and men with him, including Lieutenant Norman, who had arrived in the meantime, he did not hesitate to advance upon the now retiring enemy.

When our line reached the brow of the hill, Captain Lusk observed that the enemy, instead of retiring straight on and down the slope on the other side, had turned off at right angles and taken up a position in the standing forest on the east of the clearing, and at once realised what the movement meant, viz., that the rebels had only shown a portion of their force, the main body being hidden in the bush, while the smaller body were the decoy-ducks, to try and draw the volunteers into the ambush laid for them. And so far they had succeeded, as at that moment there were 350 Maori warriors between the sixty-seven volunteers and their stockade. It was an anxious moment for all, and Captain Lusk had just time to change his front when the storm burst, as with terrific yells the whole body of rebels in a long line rushed from the shelter of the forest upon the volunteers, expecting an easy prey, while from behind each log and stump on the clearing leapt angry flashes of fire on this brave and devoted band. But they never flinched from their duty, and, shoulder to shoulder, kept their ranks, relying on their commanding officer to extricate them from the ambush they had fallen into. The men were too well used to the yelling of the savages for that to have any effect on their courage; but when the long line of rebels began to lap round them, Captain Lusk gave orders to retire slowly on to the belt of bush at their backs. Then it was that the flank fire of the enemy began to tell, and the first to bite the dust was the brave but rash Lieutenant Percival. He fell shot through the jugular vein. He had only time to say, "Fight on, men; never mind me," when the rush of blood choked him. A few moments later, Lieutenant Norman was shot in the chest by a Maori, who jumped from behind a stump within two yards of where he stood. The men now began to drop quickly, but the force by this time having gained the edge of the bush, a stand was made, and the advantage of shelter was all on the side of the volunteers. The Maoris soon learnt this to their cost, for when they rushed up thinking to finish the volunteers with their tomahawks, they were met with such a well-directed fire as considerably to check their ardour. Before this occurred, the volunteers had fixed their bayonets, in case of a charge occurring, and a few of the fanatics rushed madly upon the cold steel. Corporal Power had got his bayonet so fast in the body of a huge Maori that ere he could free it a long-handled tomahawk had split open his head; and while Private Worthington was striving to get a defective rifle to go off, his brains were dashed out with an axe. Such a hand-to-hand fight had it become that a chief rushing up close to our line was instantly shot through the heart, and while a dozen of his followers rashly came forward to drag away his body, six of them fell in one heap across him, while the rest, losing heart, bolted, and the whole line fell back and gave up the fight. Our men were too few and too encumbered to follow up their advantage, having eight killed and a large number of wounded to remove; whereas the enemy's loss was 32 killed and so many wounded that they fled across the Waikato River that same night and left the district.

The following was the despatch sent by Sir George Grey to the Duke of Newcastle, reporting the battle :—

"GOVERNMENT HOUSE, AUCKLAND, *2nd November, 1863.*

"MY LORD DUKE,—I have the honour to transmit for your Grace's information the copy of a letter I have received from Lieut.-General Cameron, C.B., enclosing a report from Captain Lusk, commanding the Mauku Volunteers, of a very smart engagement which the force under his command had with the natives on the 23rd ultimo.

" 2. The gallantry shown by Captain Lusk and all concerned in this engagement reflects the highest credit upon them. It was no enterprise which they undertook against the natives, but an attack upon one of those murdering and marauding bands, who had penetrated far into our settlements for the purpose of murder and plunder. I am satisfied that the spirit with which this party was assailed, the moment it was discovered by so small a body of men, and the punishment they received by an European force of only about one-eighth of their own, will do much to increase the respect of the natives for the courage and determination of the settlers, and to check the marauding parties who have murdered so many people.

" 3. I have every reason to believe that the loss of the natives was heavy, and although we have so much to regret the considerable loss which we ourselves sustained, it is impossible, at the same time, not to feel the greatest admiration for the resolute gallantry shown by the small body of men under Captain Lusk's command.—I have, etc.,

" G. GREY."

After the forces under General Cameron had advanced past Ngaruawahia, the transport service nearly broke down, partly through the shallowness of the river; and Captain Lusk was specially selected, from his knowledge of bush service, to open up communication between Raglan harbour and the Waipu valley, so as to transport the provisions across the forest ranges. After a short trial, and the crossing of a few convoys, the route was abandoned, the track being too steep. Captain L sk was then appointed to the command of the transport service at Te Awamutu, which place the force had just reached, and was present at the siege and capture of Orakau, after being the first to discover the whereabouts of the enemy. On this occasion he narrowly escaped being caught by the rebels. In 1868 Te Kooti escaped from the Chathams, and being in the neighbourhood of the Waikato, Major Lusk, in command of the Waiuku and Wairoa districts, assembled his men and made a forced march to Mercer, and within twenty-four hours' notice had marched his force of 300 men a distance of nearly thirty miles, showing the mettle the volunteers were then composed of. For this service, he and his force received the special thanks of the Government. The Major afterwards continued in command of the Waiuku and Wairoa districts until 1878, when the staff was reduced (the war being over), and his further services being dispensed with, he retired on his laurels.

Mr. Livingstone.

Gallant conduct at Ngatu-o-te-manu—The death of Sergeant Russell.

MR. LIVINGSTONE, one of the most energetic settlers at Waihi, on the West Coast, about half-way between Taranaki and Wanganui, accompanied the force on their second expedition to Te Ngatu-o-te manu as a volunteer. In the midst of the engagement, following the example of the rebels (who had posted themselves in the trees in the vicinity of the pa, and picked off many of our officers and men), he mounted a tree overlooking the pa, and, with Sergeant Davey, of No 2 division, did terrible execution amongst the rebels. So intent were they in their occupation that they were nearly left behind when the force retired. His mettle was severely tried in the retreat to Te Maru, being under fire the whole time. Coming up with Captain Roberts' party, who were separated from the main body, under Colonel McDonnell, he assisted in defending the rear, and behaved so gallantly that a few more of his stamp would have soon changed the fortunes of the day. About sunset Sergeant Russell had his thigh smashed, and as there was no means of carrying him off the field, his fate was sealed. This fact he recognised himself, and asked his comrades to shoot him. This they refused to do, but Livingstone put his revolver in his hand and bade him a sad adieu. Some months afterwards the facts of poor Russell's end were elicited from a Hauhau prisoner. He died game to the backbone. When the pursuing rebels came to where he lay, one of them, thinking he had an easy prey, rushed forward to administer the *coup de grace* with his tomahawk. Russell quickly drew his revolver and killed the Maori. After this reception, the Hauhaus stood off and shot him from a distance.

MAJOR SPEEDY, R.M.,
AND GROUP OF NATIVES.

MAJOR SPEEDY.

Friendly relations between the Mauku settlers and the natives. Plot to murder the Europeans—Organisation of the Mauku, Pukekohe, and Waiuku volunteers—Speedy's narrow escape—Maori gratitude.

MAJOR SPEEDY, a retired Imperial officer, who served in India as major of the 3rd Buffs, was one of our earliest settlers, purchasing his land at Mauku. This district was settled by a very intelligent and superior lot of settlers, who were on the best of terms with all the principal chiefs of the Waikato, taking an interest in the'r religious welfare, throwing open their houses to afford them English hospitality, and giving them entertainments, particularly at Christmas time. Major Speedy often welcomed a whole hapu, which the natives seemed highly to appreciate. Thus, up to the commencement of the war, the Lower Waikato natives and the Mauku settlers were seemingly the best of friends. But no sooner had the seeds of rebellion been sown by emissaries from King Potatau than all confidence ceased. The Maoris became "pouri" (dark) and morose, which bespoke the coming storm. They began to hold secret meetings, at one of which the massacre of the male Europeans, and the distribution by lottery of their wives and daughters, was not only proposed, but received such warm support that the East Coast natives were sent for to come up and take the leading part in the massacre, the instigators hoping thereby to remove the stigma of ingratitude off their own shoulders

A day was actually fixed for this atrocious deed, but the Princess Sopia, daughter of King Potatau, being at that time on a visit to her relatives at Mangare, it was feared she might be caught or shot by the soldiers, in revenge for the massacre. After her departure to the King Country, another night was fixed upon for the deed, but, by a strange coincidence, the settlers had chosen the same night to celebrate the Prince of Wales' marriage, and had lit bonfires on all the principal hills. The Maoris, mustering after dark, had actually started to commence their bloody work when the sudden glare of the fires startled them into the belief that their plot was discovered, and that the settlers had a counter-plot for their destruction, which caused them to slink back to their settlements, and remain on the watch all night. This was not made known, however, until some time afterwards, when Hakopa (Jacob), an old lay reader, called upon Major Speedy and informed him of the plot. It was a strange but significant fact that this man, and a few other Maoris who were regarded as friendly, gave Major Speedy, on several occasions, most important and correct information about the intentions and movements of the enemy, but in every case too late to be of any service.

Soon after this Major Speedy, being the Resident Magistrate and native agent of the district, was directed to read a proclamation of the Governor to the natives, the substance of which was that they were either to take the oath of allegiance to Her Majesty and deliver up their arms for safe keeping, or, by a certain day named, leave the neighbourhood of the settlement, and retire up the Waikato among the Kingites, so that the Government might discover their friends from their enemies. It being evident to Major Speedy, as to all who knew the natives, that they would never give up their arms and leave their land, he instructed Major Lusk to enrol and organise all the able-bodied settlers of Mauku, Waiuku, and Pukekohe into three volunteer companies, and for some time Maoris and settlers watched each other with the utmost suspicion, the former firmly believing that the pakehas would soon become so alarmed as to leave the country. But, as the day mentioned in the proclamation arrived, both parties began to entrench themselves, and, just before the volunteers were prepared to look up the Maori quarters, the natives suddenly deserted their settlements and defences, and fled up the Waikato.

Major Speedy, in discharge of his duties, had frequently to travel over dangerous ground with a very slight escort, and at times ran great risk of his life from ambuscades. On many of the journeys made by him to Waiuku and back he was accompanied by his daughter, a brave and intrepid girl, who would never leave her father while danger threatened. On one occasion his party had reached the Waitangi Bridge, Lieutenant Melsopp, who was accompanied by Miss Speedy, being the advanced guard. They had just crossed the bridge, within thirty yards of an ambush of ten natives of the Ngatiruanui tribe, who were concealed in the flax bushes half a chain from the bridge, when, luckily for the Major, a young Maori named Honi Ropea, one of the ambush, whom the Major had cured of a cutaneous disease, saw him amongst the party, and immediately exclaimed, "There is my friend; don't fire. Major Speedy is amongst them." And, although his party was most indignant at being baulked of their prey, Ropea, being a chief's son, prevailed, and the party passed on in ignorance of the ambuscade, unmolested. Some years after the war was over, Ropea met the Major and asked him if he remembered the day, while riding to Waiuku, his dropping his handkerchief and riding back to pick it up. The Major remembered the circumstance. Then Ropea told him of the ambuscade, and the difficulty he had in saving him and his party's lives.

MAJOR HEAPHY.

MAJOR HEAPHY.

MAJOR HEAPHY'S name is well known throughout New Zealand as the only colonist on whom the Victoria Cross was conferred. As a young man, he studied painting in the Royal Academy, and before the age of seventeen had gained both the bronze and silver medals and had entered as a competitor for the gold medal, from which he was obliged to withdraw on his appointment as draughtsman to the New Zealand Company. He left England for this colony in the ship *Tory*, in May, 1839. The sketches of many of the New Zealand views which adorn our early publications were by him. During the first ten or twelve years of his sojourn in the colony he employed his spare time in studying surveying, and in exploring the country, eventually settling in Auckland, where he married a daughter of the Rev. J. F. Churton, Colonial Chaplain. In 1852, he was located at the Coromandel goldfields, and in 1855 was appointed District Surveyor at Mahurangi. At the commencement of the volunteer movement, in 1859, he joined the city company, commanded by Captain Steward, Aide-de-Camp to Governor Gore Browne. He rose to be lieutenant of this company, and was afterwards elected captain of No. 3 (Parnell) company Auckland Rifle Volunteers.

When the first three detachments of volunteers were marched from Auckland to the front in July, 1863, Lieutenant Heaphy was with the detachment which erected St. John's Redoubt at Papatoitoi. In November, he was attached to the flying column, as guide, his intimate knowledge of the country rendering his services of great value. About the 20th December, 1863, some murders were committed near Kaipara, and it being feared that there was some political significance in them, a detachment of militia and volunteers was sent from Auckland. On their way they met Captain Heaphy, who had already, as a justice of the peace, held an inquest on the bodies, and committed the murderers for trial.

Being again attached to the flying column, Captain Heaphy was with Colonel Sir H. Havelock, V.C., on the 11th February, 1864, reconnoitring the country near Waiari, in the Waikato, when a party of the 40th Regiment, who were bathing, were fired upon. A number of soldiers from the adjoining camp appeared on the scene as quickly as possible, but in some disorder, and Colonel Havelock placed Captain Heaphy in charge of the detachment. A soldier was seen lying near the edge of the creek, wounded and bleeding to death, an artery having been severed. Captain Heaphy, having some knowledge of surgery, volunteered to go to his assistance, and, having reached him, was engaged in taking up the artery when he was fired at by a body of natives, who were concealed in the fern close by. He was struck and slightly wounded in three places, but nevertheless succeeded in completing his work of humanity and, with the assistance of some soldiers, in carrying off the man. For this brave action he received the New Zealand medal and the rank of major in the New Zealand Militia, and was recommended for the Victoria Cross. The warrant at that time, however, did not permit of its being awarded to any but regulars, and it was not until after considerable delay and special legislation in the Imperial Parliament that it was awarded to him in 1867.

On the termination of the war in the Waikato he held office as Chief Surveyor of Auckland. From 1869 to 1872 he represented Parnell in the House of Representatives, and in the latter year was appointed Commissioner of Native Reserves, and a trustee under the Native Lands Frauds Prevention Act. In 1877 he was further appointed Commissioner of Annuities, and shortly after received a judgeship in the Native Lands Court. At the end of 1880, finding his health failing, he applied for his pension, which was granted in 1881; and, in very feeble health, he left Wellington for Brisbane, to try the effect of a warmer climate. He gradually sank, however, and died in Brisbane on 3rd August, 1881. Thus ended the useful career of a man who, in private life and in every public position he occupied, won the esteem and respect of all with whom he came in contact.

MAJOR MAIR.

Major Mair.

Bravery at Orakau—Narrow escape from death—His interview with the Maori King—Services in command of the Arawas—Attack on Te Teko pa—Capture of the murderers of Fulloon and Volkner—Graphic account of the incident at Orakau—Assault on Te Ponga—Subsequent services.

MAJOR MAIR, the son of an old colonist and a proficient Maori scholar, was attached to General Cameron's staff as interpreter, at the commencement of the Maori war, and served through that campaign. At the famous siege of Orakau Sir Duncan Cameron selected the Major for the first post of honour when he opened communication with the brave defenders of the Orakau Pa to propose an honourable capitulation. The interpreter was ordered to advance to the extreme limits of the sap, and there to call upon the Maori warriors either to surrender or to send out their women and children. After delivering the ultimation, to which the reply from the pa was " We shall fight for ever and ever," Mair was suddenly fired upon by a native named Wereta, the bullet tearing open his tunic as it passed over his shoulder, yet leaving him unhurt.

At the end of the Waikato campaign the Major was appointed Native Resident Magistrate, and was located some time at Taupo. When the war broke out on the East Coast, Mair was gazetted a major in the New Zealand Militia, and entrusted with the command of the Arawas. After this he was constantly in action, and did good service to the State. Sir William Fox, in his " War in New Zealand," gives a graphic account of Major Mair's capture of Te Teko Pa in the Bay of Plenty, taking upwards of eighty prisoners, including the prophet Te Ua, and eight of James Fulloon's murderers. The Major on several occasions received the thanks of the Government for military services, and when the campaign on the East Coast was ended, he again settled down to the duties of Resident Magistrate in the Upper Waikato.

Years after he was mainly instrumental in bringing in the Maori King. The story is told by Rusden in his " History of New Zealand " in the following spirited manner:—" It was during the debates on the Native Lands Rating Bill that an event occurred which created surprise, both amongst the friends and opponents of the Government. Tawhaio had visited the European settlements in

I

Waikato, and in token of friendship had laid down before Major Mair, the resident officer of the district, about eighty guns. To Major Mair (whom the Native Minister, Mr. Sheehan, had so slighted) was due the token of reconciliation which Ministry after Ministry had laboured long and vainly to obtain."

Tawhiao met Major Mair at Alexandra, where the Waipa River divides the township from the mountains of Pirongia, and close to Matakitaki, where the firearms of Hongi, in years past, had laid low the flower of the Waikato, when the father of Tawhiao was young. Desiring Major Mair to stand back, Tawhiao laid his own gun on the ground, while at his gesture eighty of his people followed his example. "Do you know what this means?" he said to Mair. "It is the first of what I told you, that there should be no more trouble. It means peace." The telegraph flashed the information to all parts of New Zealand, and Major Mair, whom the Grey Government had not been sagacious enough to employ, had done more for the Ministry of the day than Donald McLean, or any of his successors.

The following is a sketch taken from the *Waikato Times* of 18th October, 1881 :—

MAJOR MAIR'S SERVICES.

"At a time when both races are reaping the benefit of the successful negotiations of Major Mair with Tawhiao and his people, and when the question of fitly recognising his efforts in this direction is before the Government, the following account of some of the services which that gallant officer rendered his country in the trying days of the Maori war will not be inappropriate. The e tracts are from a very interesting work by Lieutenant the Hon. Herbert Mead, R.N., entitled 'A Ride through the Disturbed Districts of New Zealand' :

CAPTURE OF TE TEKO PA, 1865.

"After the murder of Mr. Volkner (four months later) came the murder of Mr. Fulloon, Government Interpreter, and the crew of the *Kate*, by the Hau Haus, at Whakatane, both on the East Coast. By this time the whole country-side, from Taupo to the East Cape, was one seething hotbed of fanaticism, encouraged by the impunity which followed the murder of Volkner. The Government had avowed their inability to assist the plucky little band of loyal natives who yet remained at Taupo, and advised them to fall back on Rotorua, which they did. When Fulloon was killed, Mair was at Rotorua, organising an expedition against Kereopa, in the Uriwera country, and as soon as he heard of it he took measures to avenge his death. In about a week he collected and equipped a sufficient force, and at the end of that time he started from the lower end of Lake Tarawera with 200 Arawas, having sent about one hundred and fifty more to march down the coast from Maketu. On the 16th of August, the coast party attacked the Pai-Marire Pa, at the confluence of the Awa-o-te-Atua (river of the spirit) and the Rangitaiki, without success, having no boats or canoes. On the same day, Mair's party attacked Parawi, a very strong position on the same river, about seven miles from Mount Edgcumbe, but met with no better luck, and for the same reason. He then effected a junction with the coast party, which the enemy tried to prevent, but failed, losing a chief in the attempt. There were three pas near the sea, but all too strong to be taken without artillery and boats. Several days were spent in skirmishing, usually picking off one or two Hau Haus, and waiting in hopes of assistance from the Opotiki expedition (English troops which landed the 8th September); in this, however, they were disappointed. He then detached a party, who seized all the canoes at Whakatane (the scene of the murder), and got them by fresh water to the rear of the enemy, while the remainder dragged others overland into the lake behind the pas, and thus cut off their supplies. The Hau Haus evacuated all the pas during the night of the 10th October, and retreated up the intricate channels of the delta, leaving no traces of their route. But, on the 15th, Mair learnt that they had thrown themselves into the Te Teko Pa, and following them up, he captured all their canoes, with eleven barrels of powder, and lead for bullets. On the 17th, travelling by land and water, with 500 Arawas, he reached the pa. The place was very strong, having in its rear on one side the Rangitaiki—swift, broad, and deep—and on the other three sides three hundred yards smooth glacis, three lines of palisading, with flanking angles, and three rows of rifle-pits and breast-works. The pa itself was 90 yards long by 45 broad, and every hut within it was separately fortified. There was, moreover, a covered way communicating with the landing place of the river. Sapping was the only way to take such a place. Mair, who was present at Orakau when that place was sapped under the direction of Captain Hurst, R.E., seems to have made good use of his eyes. He started three saps under cover of a slight undulation of the ground, and, in spite of a heavy fire, made such good progress that, on the 19th, the Hau Haus craved a truce to arrange terms. Firing was suspended for twenty-four hours, but the saps were kept driving, and the only terms Mair would accept were unconditional surrender. By 2 a.m. on the 20th the Arawas had cut off the covered way and got close up to the southern angle. Mair then, for the last time, summoned Te Hura to surrender, assuring him that, if forced to carry the place by assault, no quarter would be given. They saw that the case was hopeless, and at sunrise the whole garrison marched out and laid down their arms. As they came out, each hapu of the Arawa sprang from their trenches with a yell, and immediately had as fine a war dance as ever was seen, old Pohipi and three or four other hoary old sinners giving the time. It must, indeed, have been a stirring sight—the long column of prisoners standing with drooping heads, while their captors danced the wild war dance with all the fury of excitement and success; the war cry of the Arawas echoing from hill top to hill top, while the earth trembled under the stamp of a thousand feet. Mair then placed the murderers under the special charge of the native police, and the remainder became prisoners of war to the tribe of Arawa. The murderers were first tried by court-martial and convicted, but the court being afterwards deemed informal, they were tried again by civil law in Auckland, and the sentences carried into effect. Thus ended one of the most completely successful campaigns that was ever organised and carried through during the New Zealand war, every one of the murderers having been brought to justice, besides the capture of a large quantity of ammunition and arms. Amongst them were some of the most rabid of fanatics, who carried with them the baked heads of Mr. Volkner and that of a soldier wherever they went, for the purpose of exciting other tribes."

Before the advance on Orakau, Major Mair obtained, through native sources, full information about the country, and had a map prepared showing tracks, swamps, etc. This enabled General Carey to send a force to the rear of the pa during the night, Major Mair acting as interpreter and intelligence officer.

The *Waikato Times* of 18th October, 1881, says (in reference to Major Mair's services at Orakau, already referred to):—"The troops moved up to Orakau from Te Awamutu about the 31st March, 1864, halted at Kihikihi, and arrived about five in the morning. The cavalry were ordered to advance under Lieutenant Rait, and were met by a few skirmishers from the pa. Shots were exchanged, but nothing serious occurred till the pa was attacked, when Captain Ring (18th Royal Irish) was mortally wounded, and Captain Fisher badly wounded, with eleven men killed and wounded; later on, two more officers (Captain Herford, 3rd Waikato Regiment, and Ensign Chaytor, 65th Regiment, the latter being buried at Te Awamutu). Sapping had been kept up steadily for three days, and had reached within five or six yards of the pa, when General Cameron sent Mair to communicate with the garrison of the pa, for which purpose he went to the end of the sap, which was then close to the native entrenchment, and, having called for a cessation of firing, stood up on a banquette within the sap and held a korero with the besieged. But he had scarcely finished the ultimatum which he had to deliver when one of the men within the pa fired at him. The Maoris concluded that Mair had been killed, and vehemently condemned the treachery of the man (Wereta) who had fired. However, he escaped, and received no further injury than having the shoulder of his tunic torn open. (From his coolness on this, as well as other occasions, some of the officers christened him Julius Placidus.) The message from General Cameron was to this effect: 'That he admired their pluck, but did not wish to see so many brave men die; that if they came out their lives would be spared;' but the reply from the Maoris was, 'We will fight you for ever and ever.' They were then appealed to to allow the women and children to come out, but they still said, '*No; if the men are to die, the women can die too.*' About 3 p.m. of the same day they bolted out of one end of the pa, surprising everybody, and commenced to fight their way desperately through a detachment of the 40th Regiment, but in this last struggle they lost about fifty in the pa, and about eighty lay thick about the fern and swamp. Te Karamoa, minister (or something of that kind) to Potatau, surrendered at the storming of Orakau, meeting the attacking party with a white flag in his hand, but was near being bayoneted, when Mair came to the rescue and saved him from the excited soldiery, who were jostling each other in their frantic efforts to get at him. Several months afterwards the part Mair had taken at Orakau, was very nearly bringing him to grief. Some Hauhaus at Taupo determined to take vengeance on him for having led the troops to Orakau, and laid an ambuscade for him on the road to the pa at Oruanui, where he was expected, but luckily he had gone off the road to examine a new steam jet; this brought him out on another track, and by this he escaped his assailants, little knowing the certain death he had accidentally avoided.''

Major Mair also tried to save a woman who was kneeling by the side of her dead husband. She was attacked by the soldiers, and threatened with their rifles. He had succeeded in knocking down one man when the poor woman was bayoneted in the *melee*. Her name was Hineiturama, mother of the well-known Tapsell family, of Maketu. Von Tempsky made a sketch of this incident, and gave it to the Governor, who, it was said, sent it to the then Secretary of State for the Colonies.

During the operations on the East Coast and raids into the Uriwera Mountains, the native scouts repeatedly refused to advance unless led by Mair. In one of the late Colonel St. John's expeditions, with European and native troops, up the Waimana Gorge, with his subalterns Pitt, Hunter, and Goring, Mair led the natives to the assault of Te Ponga, and carried it; but the Arawas were so impressed with the difficulties and risks attending a further advance with an ill-prepared force that they refused to go on, when the impetuous St. John said, "Then I will go on with my Europeans." The native troops retorted, "It is folly to attempt to advance on Moungapohatu; but if Mair persists in going with you, we will carry him off by force, and you will soon turn back then." Major Mair has been under fire upon more than thirty different occasions, and took an active part in the following engagements:—Paterangi, Rangiaohia, Haerini, and Orakau, in Waikato campaign; Ta Awa-a-te-Atua, Te Teko, and Whakatane, in East Coast campaign; Te Ake Ake and Whakamarama, in Tauranga campaign; Waimana, Omaruteangi, Hukanui, Ruatahuna, and Tatahuata, in the Uriwera campaign. Yet he never received any special reward

I*

for his military services.   In fact, it may be said that amongst
the leading spirits of the war, he and his brother, Captain Gilbert
Mair, are the only officers who did not get a portion of the
confiscated lands they had fought so hard to obtain for the colony.

Major Mair became a judge of Native Lands Court in 1882,
and still holds that office.   In 1886, he adjudicated upon the whole
of the lands comprised in the King Country, the parties concerned
having such confidence in him that they came forward to establish
their conflicting claims.

TE POKIHA TARANUI.

A remarkable incident—A run for life under a galling fire—How Pokiha
saved McDonnell and his men.

ON the 22nd of April, 1864, the Hauhaus, about eight hundred strong, were entrenched on the sand hills on the opposite side of the river Waihi, near Maketu, in the Bay of Plenty. The cliffs on this side, rising perpendicularly from eighty to ninety feet high above the flat on the river bank, were occupied by 200 men of Her Majesty's 43rd Regiment, under Major Colville, and about six hundred Arawas, under their old chief Pokiha. Considerable firing had taken place on both sides, when Major Colville ordered Colonel McDonnell, with nine men of the defence force, who had accompanied him from Waikato, to take possession of a rifle-pit immediately under the cliffs on the flat, on our side of the river, and opposite the enemy's rifle-pits on the other side, who were posted within 350 yards of the position. To reach this rifle-pit McDonnell and his men had to traverse about five hundred yards exposed to a raking fire, although the fire from the cliff poured down upon the enemy to cover the movement. Captain William McDonnell (the Colonel's brother) was the first in the pit, followed by the other eight, who all arrived safely. It was intended to make a general attack upon the enemy's rifle-pits at low water, when the river would be fordable. After the men were safely ensconced in their position the fire from the main body on the cliff ceased, the enemy only continuing a brisk rolling fire, principally directed on those in the pit, which was twenty feet long, six feet broad, and three feet deep, and had been dug by the men of the 43rd Regiment the day previous. McDonnell returned their fire with interest, as many were seen to fall. About noon the fire slackened, and for a few moments ceased, and as no support had as yet been given, the men in the rifle-pit, whose ammunition was getting low, began to consider their position. No good result had as yet been effected, and the Hauhaus had by that time got their range, which caused our men to crouch down and husband their own ammunition by only firing at intervals. In this dilemma, the bugle sounded the recall; but the sun was yet above the cliffs, affording a splendid light for the enemy's marksmen had McDonnell's party attempted to run the gauntlet over the 500 yards of space within rifle range of the enemy, so they turned a deaf ear to the bugle, more particularly as the main body had taken no precaution to cover their retreat. The bugle sounded again and again, but no one moved; and as the enemy fully understood what the bugle meant, they prepared, by a heavier fire than before, to cut them off from the main body, should they attempt to leave. On a sudden the whole fire of the enemy, from right to left, and from cliff to cliff, opened upon them, when, in the midst of the uproar, the old chief Pokiha suddenly leaped into the rifle-pit, saying, as he did so, "That fire was meant for me." Pokiha had seen their danger, and leaving his men on the cliff, had traversed the 500 yards, exposed to their fire to save the pakeha. This devotion and gallantry of the old chief was one of the bravest acts performed by either Maori or pakeha during that campaign. McDonnell asked him why he had run such a risk. "It was to save you," he answered; "do not obey the people on the cliff, but wait until the sun goes down. If you had left you would have lost half your men. Your brave fellows have been fighting all day the whole of the Bay of Plenty men. Let them bugle away; we will stay here, and I will take you out of it after dusk," which he did safely, for McDonnell and Pokiha were the last to leave, and as they flew over the five hundred yards the bullets snipped off the tops of the toi-toi all along the route, but the darkness saved them. Pokiha was afterwards recommended for the New Zealand Cross, but it was not bestowed on him. Soon after Major Jackson of the Waikato having to present a repeating rifle to the bravest man of the force, it was awarded to old Pokiha without a dissenting voice, a prize the old chief greatly preferred to the decoration.

PARIHAKA.
(TE WHITI'S SETTLEMENT.)

Ⱨon. J. Ⅽ. Ɍichmond.

<hr>

*Early Taranaki troubles—Destruction of his bush farm—Native Minister
in the Stafford Administration—The Poverty Bay massacre—Expeditions in pursuit.*

JOHN C. RICHMOND'S relations with the Maori wars
in New Zealand began with the formation of the
Taranaki Volunteer Rifle Company, commanded by
Captain C. Brown (now Major Brown), in 1858. He
was absent from the colony during the feuds which broke out
among the local tribes, and which led to the quartering at New
Plymouth of a detachment of the 65th Regiment, under Major
(afterwards Lieut.-Colonel) Murray, and his name does not appear
in the absurdly abused memorials sent to Governor Gore Browne
by the Taranaki settlers, previous to the arrival of that force.
He became a member of the volunteer corps as a private, and
studied rifle shooting with some success, ranking second after Mr.
Messenger as a marksman.

It was as Provincial Secretary that he first took any part
deserving of record in the troubles of the province. Mr. Cutfield
was Superintendent, and Mr. Thomas King and Mr. Richmond
were his executive officers, responsible to the Provincial Council.
Governor Gore Browne, having agreed to purchase the Teira
block at Waitara, subject to survey and detailed inquiry, wrote in
1860 a semi-official letter to the Superintendent, informing him of
his intention of going forward with the transaction, and asking him
to furnish surveyors for setting out the land offered, who, if
necessary, would have military support. This letter was placed in
the hands of Mr. King and Mr. Richmond, and they at once stated
their opinion that it would be right, in assenting to furnish the
professional help required, to state fully to his Excellency the
views of the local government as to the probable issue of the
attempt to survey. Mr. Cutfield did not agree with them, and
considered that the letter, being only half official, did not require or
justify any further answer than a simple assent to furnish the
assistance it asked. Mr. King and Mr. Richmond adhered to
their opinion, and Mr. Richmond drafted a letter, which appears
on the Parliamentary Blue Book of 1860, and in which the readiness
of the settlers to support the Governor's policy was affirmed.
It went on to state that the survey would certainly be opposed by

force, and that not only the non-selling party at Waitara, but their sympathisers among the local tribes, would join; and that it was to be expected there would be wide-spreading excitement and succour to the opponents of the Government from other distant tribes. It pointed out that the weakness of the Taranaki settlers was their scattered condition, their families, and their property; and suggested the erection of block-houses in the several districts. After a short "ministerial crisis," Mr. Cutfield accepted the draft, and it was despatched. This letter, which showed a clear foresight of the events that followed, was of special importance to the settlers of the day, and became a powerful support to their prayer to the Legislature to consider the ruin of their prospects and property. In particular, it gained the somewhat tardy assent of the late Mr. Sewell and Mr. J. E. Fitzgerald, C.M.G., to the provision honourably made by the New Zealand Parliament for compensating the local losses.

Mr. Richmond's share in the active operations which followed was small. He was at the Ratapihipihi *fiasco*, but not with the gallant combatants of Waireka, except in a night expedition after the fight to search for stragglers.

His bush farm having been destroyed, cattle driven off, and house burnt, he was obliged, with a growing family, to remove to Nelson; to which place he had been invited to take charge of the *Nelson Examiner* newspaper. He had been a frequent correspondent of the paper during the disturbances, and had made friends there in connection with the Taranaki refugees. It may not be out of place here to state that the large expenditure for the housing and maintenance of these refugees, as well as in housing and rationing the helpless non-combatants at New Plymouth, was incurred at the sole risk and responsibility of Messrs. T. King and Richmond; and that Mr. Richmond had, as a private member of the General Assembly, to ask for votes for these and other public local matters—the boating service for the troops among the rest—carried on and expended on their own risk and authority.

Living at Nelson Mr. Richmond continued to be honoured for ten years with the confidence of the constituencies of Grey, and Bell, and Omata; the latter place re-electing him in 1866, after four years' residence in Nelson. In 1865 he joined the Government of Mr. F. A. Weld, and held for a few months the portfolio of Native Minister. During this time he drafted the Order in Council confiscating the Ngatiawa Taranaki Ngatiruanui Block, under the "New Zealand Settlements Act, 1862."

In 1867-9 Mr. Richmond became a member of Mr. Stafford's Government, holding the portfolio of Native Affairs; Colonel Haultain being Minister for Defence. There was some difficulty in forming that Ministry, not merely owing to the peculiar position of the Prime Minister with relation to the former government of Mr. Weld and his colleagues, but chiefly owing to the jealousy of all expenditure on defence and native affairs which then animated the Assembly. Mr. Stafford had pledged himself to large reductions and Colonel Haultain declined to accept office on the proposed votes. In this Mr. Richmond seconded him, and was prepared to support him to the full. The negotiations were on the point of falling through, when a proposal by Sir George Grey, then Governor, satisfied Colonel Haultain, and avoided the deadlock. Sir George undertook to place the troops remaining in the colony in the towns of Napier, Wanganui, and New Plymouth; and thus to set free all the colonial militia and levies for any necessary active operations; the Imperial Government and the General Assembly alike objecting to any further active employment of the Queen's troops. This arrangement was deferred from time to time, and never fully carried into effect,—a failure which in no small degree aggravated the difficulty which fell on Colonel Haultain's shoulders in the troubles of the next three years.

Not very long after Mr. Richmond had charge of the Native Office a deputation from the Ngatiruanui tribe came to Wellington to ask if their submission was accepted, and where they would be allowed to live in peace, all their land having gone from them. Mr. Richmond explained that the Governor had full power to return part of their land, and appointed to visit the tribe at once. Summoning Mr. Parris, they proceeded to Patea, and after a tribal meeting, headed by Hone Pihama, the head of the Ngatiruanui tribe, five considerable reserves were made and promptly gazetted, upon which these hapus still live and from which they receive rents. Pihama, under all the difficulties of his position arising out of the pilgrimages to Te Whiti, at Parahaka, has remained orderly, and peacefully farms at Oeo in partnership with an experienced European, Mr Good.

With respect to the part of his public life in which alone he has any distinct claim to be remembered as one of the list of defenders of New Zealand, he was not personally responsible for the removal of Te Kooti and his party to the Chatham Islands. This took place during the government of Mr., now Sir F. A. Weld; but he was responsible for their continued detention. The Bay of Plenty was still disturbed; Kereopa, the murderer of Mr. Volkner at Opotiki, was yet at liberty and actively hostile. Mr. Rolleston, the Under-Secretary for Native Affairs, was sent to the Islands to visit the prisoners and report on their condition. On his report Mr. Richmond advised the prolongation of their exile, though not without promise of immediate release when the native affairs of New Zealand were quiet. Meanwhile Colonel Haultain was in personal command of the defence forces at and around Tauranga, until attacked by rheumatic fever, and incapacitated for service in the field and travelling for many months. Kereopa was taken, but the weakness of the guard at the Chathams let loose on the colony a more dangerous and able opponent, whom the bold and confident action of Major Biggs converted into our most active enemy.

During the Tauranga campaign Mr. Richmond had inspected the posts on the West Coast on behalf of Colonel Haultain. He found the military settlers had vanished, and that whilst the prospect of peace was yet remote the only real force under arms on the coast was the native contingent under Colonel McDonnell. The Defence Minister had asked him to send this force to his assistance at Tauranga, but he could not undertake that responsibility ; instead of which he dispatched its commander, Colonel McDonnell. On the resignation of Colonel McDonnell Colonel Haultain did Mr. Richmond the honour to ask his advice as to the selection of a successor for the retiring officer. He named to him two, either of them, in his opinion, competent to take active command of our forces, Major Atkinson and Major, now Sir G. S. Whitmore. By Colonel Haultain's request he spoke to both. The former gentleman had a most imperious call to visit England, but Colonel Whitmore was able to undertake the anxious work. It was towards the end of the session of 1868, shortly after the affair of Ngutu-o-te-manu, that news reached Wellington of the landing of Te Kooti a few miles to the south of Poverty Bay, and that the gallant Major Biggs had thrown himself between the returning party and the interior. Before the prorogation, Mr. Richmond set out in the Government steamer *Sturt*, at the request of Colonel Haultain, to see the East Coast in a state of defence. Mr., afterwards Sir Donald McLean, Agent of the Government at Napier, accompanied him.

After calling at Napier, they went to Waiapu to procure auxiliaries from the Ngatiporou. Along the coast they picked up Major Biggs, who had not thought the escape inland of Te Kooti a sufficiently serious danger to prevent him carrying on his ordinary visits as Resident Magistrate. A force of 170, or thereabouts, from the hapu of Mokena, Hotene, and Ropata, was obtained, and made for Poverty Bay. As they approached, they noticed considerable smoke up the Te Arai valley. No boat came off, and the tide did not serve for entering the river. A schooner at anchor was boarded, and from her people they learned that the idea had been entertained that the smoke was from the approaching party of Te Kooti. Mr. Richmond's mind hardly hesitated about it, and he desired Major Biggs to say what he required to put the settlers on the plain of Tauranga in safety. He asked for means to put a redoubt at the port in order, and a native force of 100 men to garrison it. On Mr. Richmond pointing out the scattered and scanty population on and round the plain he added to his demand money for a stockade near the few houses in the centre of the plain, amongst which was his own. All these things were agreed to and set about immediately, and the native force arrived in less than two days. Mr. Richmond's last words to Major Biggs were: "Do not let any loyal natives, Major Westrupp, or any outlying settlers sleep outside a stockade after this day." Biggs assented, but did not act on this caution, and ten days later was, with his whole family, among the victims of the massacre. Mr. Richmond then returned south to bring up the European forces, and returned with about 200 men, under Colonel Whitmore, but too late to prevent the disaster. At this time the total European force on foot did not exceed 500, probably not more than 400 men ; and this was divided between the west and the east coasts of the island. On arrival at Poverty Bay, they learned that Ropata's Ngatiporou, along with a party of Hawke's Bay natives, under Tareha te Moananui, were following Te Kooti. Colonel Whitmore and Mr. Richmond rode up the Arai Valley, and found that they had abandoned operations. Either the two tribes had disagreed, or they were tired, or did not like the look of the stronghold ; and both tribes were sent home, but the Ngatiporou were engaged to return after a rest. Colonel Whitmore arranged deliberately all his plans for the attack of the pa, which was undergoing improvements. In a few days Mr. Richmond brought back the Ngatiporou, and the siege proceeded. The place was most formidable to approach ; situated on a peak 1,000 to 1,200 feet high, bush covered, the top rendered more defencible by low, natural cliffs on one side. The approach on the easier side was by a narrow track, which a few resolute bushmen could hold against half a regiment. In the interval, Mr. Richmond had been to Maketu and Rotoiti and got from the Arawa a reinforcement of 120 young men, who arrived in time for the latter part of the operations, and had the honour of being first to enter the fortress. Ropata and his Ngatiporous also rendered magnificent service, for which the brave chief was awarded the New Zealand Cross, as narrated elsewhere in the biography of Major Ropata. The siege occupied about six days. The defenders were reduced to great straits The water, which curiously was found near the top of this isolated peak, was cut off by our lines of approach. Te Kooti and his body-guard escaped. Few prisoners capable of bearing arms were taken. The old men, the women and children were removed to Waiapu, where they have taken root among Mokena's people.

The geography of the East Coast and Hawke's Bay is favourable to a Maori general, and Te Kooti did his best to use it. After recovering from the affair of Ngatapa, he descended from his central position at Maungapohatu, on Mohaka in Hawke's Bay, and on Whakatane, Bay of Plenty. Our little European force had been meanwhile round to the Waitotata, and, in order to give Te Kooti a new lesson, we had to bring a body of men back by way of Waitara, Manukau, and Tauranga. The geography above referred to was not unknown to the Defence Minister. Colonel Whitmore had talked of a triple concentrating expedition by way cf Wairoa, Poverty Bay, and Whakatane ; and it was resolved to carry something of the kind out, omitting the Wairoa, and substituting Matata for Poverty Bay. Mr. Richmond assisted the commander in collecting his forces, which included a considerable number of Europeans, with Arawa and Whakatane (Ngatiawa) natives. These were divided into two parties, one, under Colonel Whitmore, starting from Matata by the Rangitaheke, the other, under Colonel St. John, striking at once into the bush by the ragnes. Mr. Richmond was with Colonel Whitmore at Matata, bar-bound on board the *Sturt*, up to the day before his setting cut

At the last moment he was asked to organise a third expedition, *viâ* Wairoa and Waikara Moana, and to lead it up himself. He agreed to assist but not to command such an expedition, but pointed out that it could not possibly form a junction with the others, as it must take ten days or a fortnight to get it on foot. He consequently handed it over to Major Herrick, of Hawke's Bay, telling him that the march of a colonial force by that route, if conducted with forethought and prudence, would be worth the expense in prestige and in exploring the fables about the difficulties of the country. A force was collected, a sledge track made up to the lake, boats built, and pontoon made; but the expedition did not start, the order having been countermanded the very day it was ready to march, and a Maori expedition was substituted.

This country is now explored in all directions. The mystery of Waikari Moana is now fully dissipated, and railways have penetrated, and are penetrating, the dark wildernesses behind Mount Egmont, and up to the foot of Ruapehu; but even now the peaceful tourist may look about him with a little surprise, and some respect for those earlier visitors, who, carrying their food, ammunition, and lives in their hands, threaded them in spite of an enemy, equal in bravery, superior in local knowledge and in the habits of life in the wilderness.

CAPTAIN NORTHCROFT.

CAPT. NORTHCROFT.

More than fifty times under fire—Services meriting the New Zealand Cross—Carrying a wounded comrade off under heavy fire—Dangerous exploit at Ketemarae—A wounded man shot in Northcroft's arms—Swimming a flooded river for provisions.

APTAIN NORTHCROFT, one of the bravest of our colonial defenders, joined in Taranaki at the very outset of the rebellion, taking a prominent part, although quite a boy, in the defence of that district. He was always to be found where danger threatened, and as the war extended itself to Wanganui, he was despatched there with the Taranaki Military Settlers, and took part in all the engagements and perils of a guerilla war. He was seldom out of the field, yet fortunately escaped even a wound. He gradually rose to a Sub-Inspectorship of Armed Constabulary, and received a commission as Captain of Militia. After the war he was made Resident Magistrate of the Waikato district, which position he holds to this day. During his sixteen years' of military life, he participated in no less than forty-nine engagements with the enemy, not to mention the daily skirmishes incidental to guerilla warfare, his services fully entitling him to the decoration of the New Zealand Cross, and which his modesty alone, one would be inclined to think, could have kept him from obtaining; as his bravery, while under fire, was mentioned in despatches so often as to occasion surprise that he could have been passed over, while so many possessing only a tithe of his colness in action, and his indomitable pluck and determination, were favoured with this distinction. The following (compiled by Mr. J. H. Wilkes) are a few only of the many acts of bravery this young officer was known to perform, any one of which would have entitled a soldier of the Imperial army to the decoration of the Victoria Cross :—

CAPTAIN NORTHCROFT'S RESCUE OF FARRIER-MAJOR DUFF.

On the 1st October, 1866, Colonel McDonnell made one of his favourite night attacks on the enemy. We had left the Waihi Redoubt about 10 p.m., and, crossing the Waingongoro near the mouth, came on to the Waimate Plains. From here we struck inland for the bush, and, following up a track for the best part of the night, we at last were rewarded with the sound of a cock crowing. This was just at day dawn. We continued in the direction of the sound, and, coming to the edge of a clearing, saw immediately before us a Maori village, which we rushed before the natives had time to escape from their whares. Ensign Northcroft, with two of his company—viz., Foley and Lufton—were, as usual, leading, and while in the act of getting over a fence into the clearing a Maori saw them, and attempted to run the gauntlet, but was immediately dropped by one of the three; I could not say which, as they all fired simultaneously. Ensign Northcroft on this day performed an act of bravery I had ample opportunity of witnessing. One of our best men on this expedition—Farrier-Major Duff —fell mortally wounded, and was carried and laid down under cover of a fence, so that Dr. Suther could attend to him. The natives of a neighbouring settlement, having heard the firing, came down in great force, and soon made it so hot for us that an order to retire was given. This was now somewhat difficult to obey, as the Hauhaus were pressing us very hard, and had already gained possession of the track by which we had entered the clearing. In the hurry of getting off the wounded, poor Duff was for the moment forgotten, the part of the clearing where he was lying being almost in the hands of the enemy; but to have left him to his fate would have disgraced the colonial forces for ever. Ensign Northcroft volunteered to bring him off. It was almost certain death to any one who should attempt it, as the natives held possession of the edge of the clearing within fifteen yards of where poor Duff lay, and to have endeavoured to dislodge them would have meant still greater loss of life, and almost certain failure, for the enemy by this time had considerably outnumbered us, and were under cover of the bush. Northcroft, at a glance, took in the situation, and said to me, as I stood beside him, " Take this rifle" (a rifle he had taken from another wounded man); and, without saying another word, he dashed off in the direction of where Duff was laid. We watched him eagerly as he ran, for no one expected to see him return. He had lost his cap in the early part of the fight, and had tied his white pocket handkerchief around his head, so that his men could distinguish him. I never shall forget the scene as long as I live—this brave, determined young officer, with the white band round his head, running, as it were, into the very jaws of death. The natives themselves did not seem to comprehend what it meant—what he was about to do—for on his first appearance they fired fifteen to twenty shots at him, and then for a time ceased altogether. But, nothing daunted, on ran Northcroft —the distance being from sixty to eighty yards—took up poor Duff in his arms, and ran as swiftly back again as he could with such a burden. Then, and then only, did the Maoris seem to realise what was happening, and two natives rushed out of the bush into the open, and deliberately took a pot-shot at Northcroft within a distance of twenty yards; but one of these fired for the last time, as Sergeant White (who fell some few months after) dropped him before he could re-load. The other native turned and fled into the bush. By this time Northcroft was safe, having escaped without a scratch; and as he laid his burden down, poor Duff, with his parting breath, paid him the highest compliment one brave man could pay another, as, while looking up into Northcroft's face, he in a whisper said, " I all along knew you would never leave me to be tomahawked."

CAPTAIN NORTHCROFT'S SPIRITED BEHAVIOUR AT THE DEATH OF ECONOMEDES.

Once again during the month of November, 1866, Colonel McDonnell left Waihi camp for another forage in the bush, hoping to catch or come across some of the broken parties of natives who had escaped from Te Umu, Popoia, and other places McDonnell had taken, and with the further object of getting to the rear of Tiritiri Moana, where the Hauhaus were supposed to be strongly posted. The force, consisting of Maoris and Europeans, started inland from the Ketemarae clearing, the Wanganui native scouts leading the way up to 2 p.m., when they came across two of the enemy, whom they foolishly fired at, the result being that they escaped and raised the alarm. Soon after we came to a deep and dangerous-looking ravine, with a creek running through, when our native scouts refused to lead further, and McDonnell called for volunteers, sixteen presenting themselves. Ensign Northcroft, Privates John Hall, Wilkes, Economedes, Lufton, and a very brave native named Tonihi were chosen as the advance guard, to be supported by Lieutenant Gudgeon with his Native Contingent, who would be followed by Captain Morrison and Lieutenant O'Callaghan, with their company of Taranaki Military Settlers. As the advanced party crossed the creek it was evident from the footprints that a strong party of Hauhaus had crossed it but a short time before, for though the stream was clear in the middle it was still muddy on each side, which fact was reported to McDonnell, and all felt assured that the advance under Northcote would soon be ambuscaded. Those who know anything of Maori warfare are aware that there is no greater trial of cool courage than leading in a bush track with the certain knowledge that before you have gone much further you will be fired into by an unseen enemy. Northcroft knew the danger he had before him well enough as he filed up the opposite side of the steep ravine at the head of his small party. When this party arrived at the top they found the track wound round to the right for some fifteen yards and then crossed a small karaka grove before entering some dense bush. At the edge of the grove Northcote held up his hand to indicate caution, ordering us to halt a few minutes while he and Economedes first crossed it. This they did with great caution, and were about to enter the thicket on the opposite side when Northcroft suddenly cried out, " Take cover," and sprang behind a karaka tree, none too soon, as

K*

a volley was fired from within a few yards in front of him, and poor Economedes, who was close behind him, was shot through the hips and mortally wounded. The rest of the party for the moment fell back, and so left Northcroft with his wounded comrade alone within a few yards of a lot of fanatical Hauhaus. We could hear them shouting "Kokiritia" (Charge), "Whakawaria" (Close in), and other cries used in Maori warfare. Gudgeon tried his utmost to get his Native Contingent to charge, but one of his fighting men having had a bad dream that foretold evil to come on that day, none would move. He consequently passed word to Lieutenant O'Callaghan to come up with his men, and as Gudgeon, O'Callaghan, the scouts, and No. 5 Taranaki Settlers dashed down the track we never thought to see either Northcroft or Economedes other than tomahawked corpses. But when we came to the karaka grove we found Northcroft kneeling down by the side of his brave Greek comrade behind a karaka tree, where he had drawn him for safety before the poor fellow died. By this act Ensign Northcroft saved Economedes from being tomahawked while he lay wounded, besides preventing his arms and ammunition from falling into the hands of the enemy, as well as a considerable sum of money he had on his person.

PRIVATE WATT SHOT WHILE IN NORTHCROFT'S ARMS.

On the 12th March, 1869, a column under Colonel Whitmore left the Patea township, crossed the river, and marched inland, between the Whenuakura and Patea rivers, in the direction of a place called Otauto, where the Hauhaus, under the redoubtable Titokowaru, were supposed to be strongly posted. On the following morning about dawn the Arawas, who were in the advance, stumbled across an outlying picket of the enemy. The morning being so misty we did not see them until we were fired into. Colonel Whitmore immediately ordered the advance division to extend and feel their way carefully, as the fog was very dense. We cautiously advanced through a small piece of bush, and entering an old cultivation continued on to the edge of a gentle slope, when we received another sharp volley, apparently only from a few yards' distance, which killed one man and wounded several others. The officers ordered us to take cover, as it was impossible to see what was in front. Colonel Whitmore then came up and tried to ascertain what was over the slope, but was received with a volley that convinced him that the enemy could see us, and to advance in that direction would be only useless waste of life. The Colonel very narrowly escaped death. He ordered Major Kemp to work round to the right flank of the enemy, and Sub-Inspector Scannell, with No. 2 division Armed Constabulary and the Arawa contingent under Sub-Inspector Gundry, to do the same on the left. I was with the party on the left, and it was soon apparent the Hauhaus intended to make it warm for us, as we soon had several men killed and wounded, while as yet we could not see further than the muzzles of our gun. Some of our men had at first taken cover under a row of flax bushes, which ran down the clearing in a direct line to where the enemy were posted. These poured in a raking fire on our fellows, killing and wounding many. A man of No. 2 division named Watt had, in his eagerness to find out the position of the enemy, crawled to within a few yards of them, when he suddenly called out that he was hit on the leg, the bone being broken. Although we were within a few yards of the Hauhaus, and could hear every word they said, we could not discover whether they were entrenched or under cover of their pa, the fog still continued so dense. It appeared almost certain death to advance to where poor Watt lay wounded, but Sub-Inspector Northcroft, sticking his sword into the ground, proceeded to pick Watt up. He had hardly got him fairly in his arms when the enemy fired a volley of five or six shots within a few yards' range, mortally wounding the man he had in his arms, while Northcroft himself escaped. Poor Watt exclaiming, " Oh, I am hit again," soon after expired. The whole of these circumstances I can vouch for, having been an eye-witness.

MAJOR SCANNELL'S ACCOUNT.

During the attack on Otauto a man named Watt, of No. 2 division Armed Constabulary, was severely wounded, and was lying amongst some flax bushes in a place much exposed to the enemy's fire. Sub-Inspector Northcroft, of that division, went forward, and taking the wounded man in his arms brought him from under fire, but while in the act of doing so Watt was again wounded whilst in Northcroft's arms, and died shortly after. The Victoria Cross has been granted in the Imperial army over and over again for such actions as this. The same officer marched with his division from Wairoa, Hawke's Bay, to Lake Waikaremoana. On the arrival of the division at the Waikare Taheke River, which it was necessary to cross, it was found impossible to do so owing to the heavy flood and rapid current. The division were out of provisions, and although every effort was made to attract the attention of the party in the Kewi Redoubt, about two miles' distant, it was found impossible to do so. The situation was becoming very critical, as the men were then two days without food. Under these circumstances Sub-Inspector Northcroft and one of the constables volunteered to endeavour to swim the river in company, and communicate with those stationed in the Redoubt. The river was swollen, the current strong, and the bed covered with huge boulders, against which the rapid current foamed and dashed in a most fearful manner, and to attempt swimming seemed certain death. At the last moment the constable declined the venture, and Sub-Inspector Northcroft, despite all opposition, jumped in alone. Before he rose to the surface he was carried fully twenty yards down the river, and after a desperate struggle with the current, succeeded in gaining the opposite bank, quite exhausted. After a short rest for recovery, he set off to the redoubt with only a shawl round his waist, and succeeded in procuring for his starved comrades all the provisions that could be spared, viz., a 50lb. bag of flour, which had to be dragged bodily through the river. Only those who witnessed the exploit could form an adequate idea of the danger he had passed through.

[LETTER OF RECOMMENDATION FROM COLONEL M'DONNELL.]

"WANGANUI, *March 30th, 1871.*

"Sir,—For the consideration of the Honourable the Defence Minister I have the honour to state, that at the attack on Tungarehu in October, 1866, Ensign Northcroft, of the Patea Rangers, and now a Sub-Inspector of the Armed Constabulary, did with great bravery and at the risk of his life, rescue Sergt.-Major Duff, who laid mortally wounded and helpless, from the enemy.

"Also, at the attack upon Tiritiri Moana, in November of the same year, Mr. Northcroft, being on that occasion in front in the bush, with Private Economedes, were met by the enemy, who fired and killed the latter. Mr. Northcroft held his ground until assistance came up, preventing mutilation of the body and the capture of his arms and ammunition, besides a considerable sum of money the man had on his person.

"This officer would have been recommended by me for the above to the Honourable Colonel Haultain as deserving of the Victoria Cross could it have been conferred on a colonial soldier.—I have, etc.,

"THOMAS McDONNELL, Lieut.-Colonel.

"To G. S. COOPER, ESQ.,
  "Under-Secretary, Defence Office."

WIREMU KATENE.

WIREMU KATENE, rebel, friendly, and friendly rebel, is now no more. At the begining of the war, he was one of our most powerful foes; but after a time, he brought in a portion of his hapu and, delivering them up, said he was tired of leading men who deserted him in the moment of danger, and for the future he would fight for the pakeha. He was given over to the custody of Major W. E. Gudgeon, who then had charge of the native contingent, with orders to keep a sharp look-out on his actions. The information he gave us, and his earnestness in the cause of the paheka, soon induced Colonel McDonnell to use him as his guide, and faithfully did he perform this duty. Katene was one of the bravest of Maoris, and the best of scouts, and would have remained true to us to the end had he not been imprisoned by the Resident Magistrate at Patea for some trifling peccadilloes.

One evening, while sitting round the camp fire, he suddenly placed his hand on Captain Gudgeon's knee, and, looking up in his face, asked him a question so full of meaning, and so illustrative of the Maori character, that the Captain never forgot it—" Do you believe in me now?" The Captain replied, "Yes, Katene, I do." "Well," said Katene, "you are right and you are wrong. You are right to trust me now, for I mean you well; but never trust a Maori, for some day I may remember that I have lost my land, and that the power and influence of my tribe has departed, and that you are the cause; at that moment I shall be your enemy. Do not forget what I say."

It was Katene who warned the force that in future they would have to meet the Hauhaus in the bush, as they did not intend to fight again in their pas, which they had come to regard as traps to be caught in, but that they would make the most of their knowledge of the country, surprising small parties, and only meeting the pakeha in the forest. He also warned us to be specially careful of the small redoubts, and see that they were well fortified, "For, mark me," he said, "their intention is to surprise and storm some of them immediately." The truth of these utterances was soon felt, both at Te Ngutu-o-te-manu and Turi-turi Mokai. Katene remained with us for some time after receiving repeated warnings from the rebels, and only left us in the quiet of one night to save his young daughter, whom the rebels had got possession of, and had sent him word they would destroy if he did not leave us immediately. He died only a few months ago, respected by both Maori and pakeha.

LIEUT.-COLONEL NIXON.

Lieut. -Col Nixon.

Early military services—Training the New Zealand Volunteers—Formation of Mounted Defence Corps—His great popularity and sad death.

LIEUT.-COLONEL NIXON retired from the Imperial service with the rank of major, having served in the 39th Regiment in India; was present at the Battles of Gwalior and Maharajapore; and was considered by the authorities to be one of the most promising soldiers of the day; receiving the Bronze Star for those actions. He settled in New Zealand, having reached this colony in June, 1852; and, on the first rumours of war, the settlers in his immediate neighbourhood looked to him as their leader in any defence they might be called upon to make; while he, on his part, as readily responded with all the energy and promptitude of his nature to their appeal. He quickly embodied and trained two troops of volunteer yeomanry cavalry, composed principally of the sons of country settlers, who were soon in a high state of efficiency; proud of their corps, and of their commanding officer. When hostilities in the Waikato district seemed inevitable Colonel Nixon, who was a Member of the House of Representatives, was entrusted by the Government to enrol a cavalry force of a somewhat different character, to be henceforth called the Mounted Defence Force of the Colony; and many of the officers and men of the volunteer yeomanry cavalry at once joined the new force, rather than be separated from their commanding officer, who at that moment was the most beloved, popular, and prominent man in the Auckland district. From the commencement of the Waikato campaign to the action at Rangiaohia, Colonel Nixon may be said to have lived in his saddle, and no affair of any importance occurred at which he was not present. He fell on the 23rd February, 1864, being shot by a Maori from a whare the natives had taken shelter in after the skirmish at Rangiaohia, while trying to induce them to surrender. His fate was more deeply felt, and more sincerely mourned, than that of any man who fell during the war. The whole country was in mourning, proving more real sympathy than even the stone monument raised by the colony to his memory, and showing how deeply the settlers valued his unblemished character, his high military talents, and his fearless bravery.

It is told of Major Nixon that, as a boy, he was so full of fun and devilment, that the authorities at Sandhurst told his widowed mother that she had better take him away, as he could never pass the examination. The lad, seeing the disappointment of his mother, begged hard for one more chance, which, in deference to his parent, was given him; and from that moment, long after the lights were supposed to be extinguished, he was seen with a candle under his table (which he had covered over with his blanket to hide the light), pursuing his studies half the night through; the consequence being, that he passed a brilliant examination, to the surprise of all who knew him.

He was adjudged a public funeral, and was buried in the Symonds-street cemetery. A monument has been erected to his memory at the junction of the Great South and Mangere Roads.

LIEUT.-COLONEL ROBERTS.

LIEUT-COL. ROBERTS.

Services with Forest Rangers—Gallant behaviour at Ngutu-o-te-Manu—
Cut off from the main force—Bravery at Moturoa—Command at Pari-
haka—The New Zealand Cross.

JOHN MACKINTOSH ROBERTS, in August, 1863, joined Major Jackson's company of Forest Rangers, and in the following November was appointed ensign in Von Tempsky's company, and finally promoted to lieutenant in March, 1864. From the first, he took a most active part in the war, was present at Rangiaohia and Haerini, and, on the day prior to the attack on Orakau, was ordered from Te Awamutu to Kihikihi, with 20 Forest Rangers, to join Captain Ring's Company (18th Regiment), which company, with the Forest Rangers, formed the advance guard to, and the storming party afterwards, on the Orakau Pa. In this attack the gallant Ring fell mortally wounded. In March, 1868, Captain Roberts was made sub-inspector of Armed Constabulary, and on the outbreak of hostilities in the Wanganui district, was transferred from the Waikato to Patea, with Von Tempsky's division of Armed Constabulary. He was present at the relief of Turi-turi Mokai, and was left in command of the redoubt. He took part in both attacks on Te Ngutu-o-te-Manu, and was the officer who, on the second attack, was cut off from the main body with 58 men and eleven wounded, and who, after so gallantly beating off the enemy, got benighted in the dense bush. Here he anxiously awaited the first streak of daylight to try and feel his way out to the open country, which was at last successfully accomplished, and Captain Roberts had the satisfaction of seeing his party in safety at Waihi Redoubt, about nine the following morning, thoroughly exhausted. (*Vide* his report attached, taken from the *Gazette.*) Captain Roberts with the 6th division of Armed Constabulary, was also present at the attack on Motorua, and again distinguished himself in covering the retreat of our forces, for which service he received his majority and rank of inspector. He, soon after, took an active part in the siege and capture of Ngatapa; was at the taking of Tauranga-a-hika Pa, and at the defeat of Titokowaru at Otauto and Te Whakamaru. He afterwards led the right column of the troops engaged in the pursuit of Te Kooti, in the Uriwera campaign, under Colonel

L

Whitmore, and was subsequently appointed to the command of the Taupo District. Here he remained until May, 1871, when he was transferred to the district of Tauranga, and made Resident Magistrate for the same. But, on the outbreak of active resistance and aggressive measures taken by the fanatics of the West Coast, Major Roberts' military services were again called into action, the Government conferring on him the rank of Lieut.-Colonel, and placing him in command of all the colonial forces gathered together at Parihaka on that memorable occasion. In 1886 he was removed to Auckland in command of the Armed Constabulary of that district.

The *Gazette*, conferring on Lieut.-Colonel Roberts the decoration of the New Zealand Cross, says :—" This gallant officer was awarded the New Zealand Cross, by His Excellency the Governor, Sir George Grey, for his resolute bearing on the 6th September, 1868, at Te Ngutu-o-te-manu, where, owing to a miscarriage of orders issued by Colonel McDonnell to retire, he and his men were left behind, and eventually had to fight their way back through the standing bush, closely pursued by the enemy. To Captain Roberts' coolness and determination on this occasion may be attributed the saving of the force under his command. And for the courage and judgment displayed by him at the battle of Moturoa, on the 7th November, 1868, when, having only arrived during the night, he with his young and newly raised division succeeded in covering the retreat of Colonel Whitmore's force, although greatly outnumbered, and at one time nearly surrounded. To his fortitude as a soldier, and the confidence he inspired, was mainly due the discipline of his men, who kept their ranks in a dense bush in spite of the repeated efforts of the enemy to close with them, and so enabled the force, encumbered with the wounded, to draw off in good order."

ENSIGN HUTCHINSON.

ENSIGN HUTCHINSON.

An incident at the White Cliffs—Delivering a proclamation to the rebels—
Humane behaviour of the chief Wetere.

IN September, 1865, the chief Wetere, in defiance of the Colonial force stationed at Pukearuhe, encamped his followers at the White Cliffs, the boundary line between Mokau and Taranaki, his main object being the plunder of the steamship *Alexandra*, as she then lay wrecked on the sands. His followers made continued raids during low water, carrying off everything they could lay hands upon This was the state of things at Taranaki at the time the Governor (Sir George Grey) offered the natives terms of peace under certain conditions, and had sent copies of his manifesto to each officer in command of a district, with instructions to have the same distributed amongst the rebels in their immediate neighbourhood with the least possible delay and risk to the party delivering it. As the only attempts to distribute it yet made—one by Mr. Broughton and the other by a half-caste—having proved fatal to the bearers, it was looked upon as a very hazardous undertaking. Major Baddeley, the officer in command at Pukearuhe, having received the proclamation, called for volunteers, whose duty it would be to go as far as prudence dictated towards Wetere's encampment, and after attracting the attention of the rebels to place the proclamation in a cleft stick, which they were to fix upright in the ground, so that the natives could see it. But Ensign Hutchinson, who had offered to conduct the party volunteering for the service, was anxious to do his errand effectually, and despite all previous warning he halted his men when within sight of the rebel camp, and, waving his white handkerchief as a flag of truce, bravely rode forward alone. As he approached the encampment Wetere himself came forward, accompanied by thirty or forty armed men, and ordered him back, wondering how he dared come on to his land without permission, and wanted to know what the soldiers were doing on his land at Pukearuhe. Hutchinson

L*

replied that, being only a junior officer, it was not for him to say, but he had brought a document from the Governor on the subject, and if after reading it he wished to reply and would display a white flag he would be sure of safety in approaching the camp and the officer in command would meet him. At this moment Wetere's men, who had all along been clamorous to kill the pakeha, asked Wetere and a chief, who were standing between them and Hutchinson, to move that they might shoot Hutchinson. Wetere, seeing the excited state of his men, cried out, "I am commander here; put up your guns; to kill him now would be murder, and I will only fight fairly." This speech somewhat pacified his followers, but it was as much as Wetere could do to control them, and taking the proclamation he hurried Hutchinson off, saying "Go back quickly, or I cannot answer for your life." This was the only instance of a proclamation being given into the hands of the rebels and the party delivering it escaping with his life; and although it led to a suspension of hostilities for a time, during which Mr. Parris, the Native Commissioner, was sent for, and obtained the interview desired by Sir George Grey of discussing the question at issue, Hutchinson (whose daring all must admire), instead of getting the New Zealand Cross for his pluck, received the warm congratulations of his friends, but his commanding officer gave him a good wigging for exceeding his instructions.

Wetere on another occasion saved the life of Mr. Wilkinson, the Government Native Agent, in defiance of his tribe, who had laid an ambush to destroy him. Wetere in this instance placed Wilkinson on his own horse behind him, and approaching the ambush called out, "If you want to kill Wilkinson you will have to shoot him through me, as I am much the stouter of the two." At the present day Wetere speaks of these occurrences with great glee, and shows the rings both Hutchinson and Wilkinson gave him in thanksgiving for his services, saying that having saved the lives of these pakehas he will always love them.

COLONEL ROOKES

COLONEL ROOKES.

Imperial services—His command on the West Coast—The story of the Wereroa Pa—Sir George Grey's bravery and narrow escape—Adventure of Colonels Rookes and McDonnell and Major Von Tempsky.

IN the year 1835, Colonel Rookes began his career as a midshipman in Her Majesty's Royal Navy on the China and West Indian stations, and from 1839 to 1841 was attached as a cadet, by special permission of the French Government, to the 6th Cuirassiers, at the Remount Military Riding School at St. Omer, eventually joining the 2nd West Indian Regiment, wherein he served for upwards of sixteen years, being ensign by purchase in March, 1842, lieutenant in the following December, and captain in 1846. He sold out to settle in New Zealand, in which colony he arrived in 1858. As an Imperial officer, he had received the thanks of the English, French, and Dutch Governments, of the Minister of War (Lord Panmure), the Commander-in-Chief (Lord Hardinge), and the Secretary of State (the Duke of Newcastle), for the able, judicious, and successful manner he had conducted the several military expeditions and operations entrusted to him, both in the field, on the Gold Coast, and in the Moriah country. On one of these expeditions he was placed in command of a combined naval and military, English and French, force, and captured the town of Malegeah, and severely defeated the rebels at Labadee. During this period of Imperial service, he was (*vide* Army List, 1846) selected as Aide-de-Camp and Private Secretary to the several Governors of the Bahamas and Trinidad, viz., Mr Mathew and the late Lord Harris, and for many years was a member of the Legislature of the former colony. He had also been repeatedly thanked by the Colonial Governments—by that of Gambia, in 1843, for opening up the navigation of the river from Fort George to the Barraconda Falls, and by that of the Bahamas, in 1846, for successfully negotiating with General O'Donnell, Governor of the Havannah, for the surrender of several British subjects held in slavery by the Spanish authorities.

Soon after his arrival in Auckland, the Maori rebellion of 1860 broke out, and Colonel Rookes was employed by the Colonial Government in organising the War Branch (now the Defence Office), and in recognition of the able manner in which this duty was performed, the Fox Ministry placed him by their recommendation in command of the Wanganui district as the deputy of the Governor. While holding this command, he raised, organised, and personally drilled seven separate troops of cavalry in the Rangitiki, Turakina, and Wangaehu districts so successfully that these forces were repeatedly thanked on the field and in general orders by Generals Cameron and Waddy. The latter officer, a veteran of considerable experience in India and the Crimea, remarked "that he considered these troopers, in physique and fearless riding, the beau ideal of what irregular cavalry should be." Colonel Rookes, in 1865, further received the thanks of the Colonial Government of New Zealand for the successful manner in which, under that distinguished Governor and statesman (Sir George Grey) he led the colonial forces at the capture of the Wereroa Pa, completely nullifying the assertion made in General Cameron's despatches, "that it would require a large addition of Imperial troops to reduce that stronghold of the natives."

The following account of the events leading up to the fall of the pa and Colonel Rookes' connection therewith will be of interest :— In the early part of 1863, when in command of the Wanganui district, natives brought in word that the heights above Perikama, at the embouchure of the Kiwi stream, were being fortified by three hapus or tribes—Ngatiruanui, Taranaki, and Waikato. Dr. Featherston, who was Superintendent of Wellington, asked Rookes to accompany him with his interpreter to the spot, situated about twenty-five miles from Wanganui. During this visit he obtained valuable information concerning this position. On this occasion, just before Dr. Hope's and Lieutenant Tragett's murder at Taranaki, the natives offered no obstacle to the crossing or re-crossing of the river, but would allow no one to enter their works, which were in course of construction. The position then might have been taken by a handful of men, the works destroyed, and a redoubt erected and garrisoned, which would undoubtedly have altered matters and obliged the natives to abandon a site which General Cameron estimated as something more than strong. (See correspondence with Sir George Grey, published in the ex-Governor's biography.)

The second time Rookes visited the place, 1865, was in command of a scratch force of volunteer cavalry from the Rangitiki, Turakina, and Wanganui districts. They preceded a force of 800 regular troops with three guns, and with a brilliant dash up to the pas by the cavalry (which they all wished to try) might have taken the three pas before their defenders could have climbed up from the Perikama flats, where they were planting potatoes. General Waddy, who was in general command, would not permit it, however, as General Cameron had given him strict orders not to attempt the capture. About a month after a messenger came in from one of the pas, saying if a force of natives and settlers were sent they would surrender to them, but that they declined to do so to the regular troops. Colonel Rookes went out with 250 natives and a few cavalry, and the natives again agreed to give up the pas. At this juncture Colonel Logan made his appearance on the ground and took command, and the natives declined further negotiating and ordered the force to retire. To ride into Wanganui, charter a steamer and send the friendly chiefs to Wellington, with instructions to see and explain matters to the Governor, Sir George Grey, did not take long; and Colonel Rookes, acting on the encouragement given to him by the Premier, Mr. Weld, who approved of his action, again, on the invitation of a well-affected portion of the Wereroa garrison, marched a mixed force of natives, Wanganui Cavalry, Von Tempsky's Rangers, and McDonnell's Contingent to the pa. On arrival he camped the force about eight hundred yards in front of the pa, at an opening in the forest that commanded the approaches from Wanganui. He was anxious that the natives should not surrender the pas except to Sir George Grey, who had through Mr. Weld loyally supported the Colonel's action, and he communicated with Sir George to that effect. In the meantime, leaving the force in front of the pas in command of Major Von Tempsky and Captain George, he accepted an invitation from the chiefs to come inside their works and arrange for a surrender; Captain McDonnell volunteered to accompany him and act as interpreter. They remained inside negotiating for three days, when suddenly, just after Captain McDonnell's return from Putahi, which he had most gallantly visited at the risk of his life, the natives broke off the negotiations, and Colonel Rookes and his companion returned to the camp disgusted. It was then that Sir G. Grey, who had arrived during the parley, rode up, accompanied by Mr. Parris, Hori King, and another chief, to within ten feet of the pa, the rifle-pits of which were lined with a lot of howling fanatics armed to the teeth, with their passions inflamed by the exhortations of their chiefs; and had it not been that one of the Hauhau chiefs came out and placed his mat before Sir George, the brave Europeans and native chiefs would all have blown into eternity. As it was, Sir George and the others rode back to the camp safely, when he planned the advance, which took place next morning, and led to the fall of the position. The legislature of the Colony (both Houses) voted thanks to Colonel Rookes and the men under him, which he got from the Upper House twenty-one years after they were voted. It was the fall of this position which first gave rise to the policy of self-reliance soon after inaugurated by the Weld Government, and which enabled General Chute so successfully to march (with his rear and flank free) through the forest at the back of Mount Egmont to New Plymouth, reducing on his route the various pas in the neighbourhood, and for which he received the honour of knighthood. On the day of Major Von Tempsky's arrival at Wanganui a large picnic party was being held at Alexander's farm, the boundary line at that moment of the contending parties, when Colonel Rookes persuaded the Major and Colonel Nixon to accompany him on a reconnoitring expedition to the enemy's country. They consequently rode away from the picnic in the direction of the Waitotara, and arriving at a gully some miles inland they dismounted to water their horses. While doing so a mounted native appeared on the opposite bank, and looking down upon them quickly disappeared. A short council of war was held, and they determined to make for the beach and return that way. When returning they had again to dismount to lead their horses over some rocks on the way, and Colonel Rookes, in dismounting, sprained his ankle, just as a volley was fired at them from an ambuscade amongst the high cliffs overlooking the beach, which caused Von Tempsky and Nixon to remount and ride away. Finding that Rookes did not follow them, being unable by his sprain to remount, they returned to his assistance, and, defending themselves with their revolvers, got him with some difficulty upon his horse and rode away under a heavy fire, but it was a narrow escape for all concerned.

Colonel Rookes, who was one of the bravest and most experienced officers, was superseded before the end of the war, the authorities regarding his outspoken advice on military matters as somewhat dictatorial.

CAPTAIN WILSON.

Captain Wilson.

The fight at Rangiaohia—How Colonel Nixon fell—Another of Rusden's statements refuted.

APTAIN WILSON, who came out to this colony in 1832, first served as a trooper in the Otahuhu Volunteer Cavalry, under Colonel Nixon, and in July, 1863, was made Sub-inspector of the Government Mounted Defence Force. He was one of our most active officers. He accompanied the Thames expedition, and was present at the actions of Paterangi, Rangiaohia, and Hiarini; was close to Colonel Nixon when he fell mortally wounded, and one of the first to render him any assistance. In 1865, the war having moved from the Waikato district and broken out at Wanganui, Captain Wilson resigned his commission, and was made captain of militia. The appended account of the fight at Rangiaohia, by an eye-witness, narrates very graphically the services rendered by Captain Wilson and the troops who participated in that engagement :—

THE FIGHT AT RANGIAOHIA.

(BY ONE WHO WAS THERE.)

"The picture of the fight at Rangiaohia, lately presented to the Auckland Free Library, is so vigorous and life-like that it carries me back to the Sunday morning (the 21st February 1864) when our colonel (Nixon) fell mortally wounded, and two of our corporals were killed—McHale, inside the whare, and Alexander, at the door. Corporal Dunn received a bullet, which I believe he carries to this day. Two of the 65th Regiment were wounded, one mortally, and one of the Forest Rangers. The night before, we paraded at 11 o'clock at Te Rore, and then moved off quietly. We knew that something was to be attempted, as we were ordered to get round the enemy and take him in rear, or something of that sort. The way was led by Von Tempsky's Forest Rangers, followed by the 65th and 70th Regiments, the Naval Brigade, the Mounted Artillery, and the Defence Force, while Jackson's company of Rangers brought up the rear. The night was dark, and we groped our way along a Maori track, passing pretty close to the enemy's position at Pikopiko. At cock-crow we entered Te Awamutu. The bridge had been destroyed, but the planks were there, and to relay them was but the work of a few minutes. This done, the order was given 'Forward, the cavalry,' and away we went, the Defence Force and Rait's mounted artillerymen following. It did not take long for the cavalry to clear the enemy out of Rangiaohia, our infantry being far in the rear. Having accomplished our work, we had turned about and were taking prisoners as we came along, when Captain Wilson's attention was drawn to a whare, near which a struggle was going on between Corporal Little, of ours, and a huge Maori. Little having secured his man, Captain Wilson ordered Corporal McHale to make prisoners of the other Maoris inside the whare, who we could hear talking. McHale entered the hut, but no sooner had he passed the door than two shots were fired, apparently from the Corporal's revolver, when Captain Wilson called out, "What the —— are you shooting the Maoris for?" and jumping from his horse was into the hut in a moment. The door was so low he had to stoop to get inside. The place was full of smoke, and as Captain Wilson entered he found under him McHale's body, his feet towards the door, and face down. The captain could not see anyone else for the darkness and smoke, consequently he soon backed out, calling out that McHale had been shot, which the men no sooner heard than with their carbines they commenced to riddle the house, which was built of slabs. The firing soon brought together the whole of the cavalry, and after a while some of the 65th and Forest Rangers, also the general and staff, came up. It was after General Cameron's arrival that Colonel Nixon was shot from the door of the whare. Then, as the Maoris did not surrender when challenged for the second time, the infantry fired the house. I saw one Maori walk out of the blazing hut, his blanket singed on his back. Poor fellow! he fell within ten paces of the door whence he and his compatriots had so wantonly shot our colonel and many other good men. There was nothing now to prevent us from recovering McHale's body, but its condition was such that we could hardly distinguish it from the Maoris around him. We succeeded in identifying it, however, and bore it away.

"The sun was overhead and baking hot as we moved slowly with our dead and wounded back to Te Awamutu. The wounded suffered much from fatigue and heat, and the enemy followed us up and fired at us along the way. I may mention that, in the pursuit before the whare was attacked, the Maoris, men and women, were jumbled together running away, and, being so much alike, the women were in danger of being killed. Captain Wilson, who had command of the advance guard, called to the women, telling them to sit down, 'E kotou, e nga wahine e noho ki raro, kei mate kotou.' They obeyed, and we passed them; they then got up and ran on. I heard some days afterwards that the big Maori, whom I mentioned before as having been taken prisoner, had said that his life was saved by a man who wore a silver band round his cap, meaning Captain Wilson. I write this simply to show that we did

McDONNELL   COL. NIXON   WILSON   ALEXANDER   DUNN
COLONIAL DEFENCE FORCE

THE FIGHT AT RANGIAOHIA FOR
FEBRUA

GEN. CAMERON AND STAFF

ST RANGERS   65TH REGIMENT

ECOVERY OF McHALE'S BODY.

try to save the natives. It was a sad day, of course, for all concerned; but, as they have asserted that we kohuru (murdered) them, I have endeavoured to show how they brought about their own destruction by wantonly killing our men at a time they were surrounded and had no chance of escape. At the great Maori meeting at Kopua, twelve months last May, Captain Wilson met two gentlemen—Wesleyan ministers—who informed him that there was but one thing the natives were sore about; namely, the kohuru at Rangiaohia. The captain replied, 'I can explain all about that affair, for I was present. It was I who sent the man whom the Maoris shot into the hut to make prisoners. Our man was dead inside the hut before the attack commenced.' After the action at Hairini, Captain Wilson made a rough sketch of the ground where Colonel Nixon had fallen, showing the position of the huts there; and the picture of the fight at Rangiaohia is based upon this sketch. Our old colonel's revolver is now the property of Captain Wilson, while he slumbers in the cemetery at Auckland, awaiting the great *reveille*, when those who fell in that hut will bear witness to the truth of this statement.

"21st February, 1864.—After the skirmish at Rangiaohia, the troops returned and camped at Otawhao, the Rev. John Morgan's missionary station (now known as Te Awamutu), bringing with them their dead, wounded, and prisoners. It was slow work carrying them under a broiling sun; no refreshment had been allowed since leaving Te Rore the night before. The wounded suffered much from heat and dust, and were glad to get the shelter of the mission station. Here the troops refreshed themselves with a bath in the stream, and the food given them. Then, as it was Sunday, they paraded and attended divine service at the mission church to hear Bishop Selwyn, who preached an appropriate sermon. The sermon and chanting of the service seemed rather a contrast to our morning's work. The slain were buried; the Maori wounded and prisoners kindly cared for, having tents pitched for their use."

MR. RUSDEN'S ACCOUNT OF THE RANGIAOHIA AFFAIR.

WITH THE MAORI CONTRADICTION.

The statements made in Rusden's "History of New Zealand," that women and children were wantonly shot and burned in their houses at Rangiaohia when that place was surprised by the troops, having been told to the Kingites, one of them, named Potatau, who is at present residing at Korokonui, has sent a statement of the facts as they came under his own observation. He was a little boy at the time of the Rangiaohia affair. The statement was written down in the presence of Potatau, and the translation was made by a half-caste who lives with the natives.

M

The translation is rough, but accurate, and it is given as it was received. First, I quote from the second volume of Rusden's history, page 199, his account of the Rangiaohia affair. He says :—

"At daybreak the general pushed on from Te Awamutu to Rangiaohia. 'The few natives who were found in the place were quickly dispersed, and the greater part escaped, but a few of them taking shelter in a whare made a desperate resistance until the Forest Rangers and a company of the 65th Regiment surrounded the whare, which was set on fire, and the defenders either killed or taken prisoners.' This was the official method of telling, or concealing, that women or children were burned to death. For the credit of General Cameron it may be hoped that when he thus wrote, four days after the occurrence, he did not know the truth, which was subsequently notorious. Of what avail was it to preach peace to the Maoris, and tell them to be merciful when a British force, commanded by a general and accompanied by a bishop, burned women and children in a Maori house? Was it to be wondered at that a grief came upon the bishop when he heard afterwards that a plot was laid by the enemy to take his life? The successful general returned to Te Awamutu with twenty-one women and children, who were not burned. . . . . The Maoris had not dreamed that heavy guns and a large body of troops would be turned aside against women and children. Their rage at being outwitted by the flank movement which left them idle, and destroyed their food and plantations, was exaggerated by the burning of their wives and children."

Potatau's statement:—"It took place on Sunday morning. Early in the morning I had reason to go outside the house. I then saw some troopers passing behind the house. I at once ran to my father's house. I had not been long there when my grandfather came to the same house. His name was Hoani. It was because he knew we were there that he came, so that he might die with us —Ihaia, Rawiri, and his son. At this time myself and my mother went outside the house, and sat at the door of the house. I heard my father say to my grandfather : 'Let us lay down our guns and give ourselves up as prisoners.' My grandfather said : 'Am I greater than your uncles who were taken at Rangiriri?' My father again said to my grandfather: 'Let us go in peace, and according to law.' My grandfather would not agree. At this time the soldiers came to us, and asked my mother in Maori : 'Are there any Maoris in the house?' She replied : 'No, there are no Maoris in the house.' My father at once said : 'Yes, there are Maoris here.' The European who spoke Maori came to the door of the house, and caught hold of my father, and handed him over to the soldiers. The European went inside of the house. My grand-father shot him and killed him. Some of the others dragged the body in the house. At this time my mother and self arose and went through the soldiers and between the troopers. They did not interfere with us, but allowed us to pass. We went to the house of

Thomas Power, who had a Maori woman to wife. After we left we heard the soldiers firing. Whilst we were at the house of Thomas Power, the Government interpreter came there. I may say that by this time a large number of women and children of our people had come to Thomas Power's house. What the interpreter said to us was that the general would have to deal with us. If he would allow us to take our departure it would be well; we could do so; if he sent us to Te Awamutu it would have to be so; but he told us to remain at this house. After this the interpreter left us. At this time the firing had ceased. We at once left the place and ran off to the bush, and made for Rangitoto."

The object of the march to Rangiaohia was to cut off the supplies which maintained the natives in the great pa at Paterangi. The above narrative (by one who was then a boy) shows that the Europeans desired to save all who were at Rangiaohia, and would have done so, but that one of the Maoris shot a man who was endangering himself to save life and opened fire on our forces. Not a shot was fired by the troops until this European was killed. The woman and children were protected, as far as possible, and some of them, like Potatau and his mother, got away and rejoined their friends.

Sir R. Douglas, Bart.

IR ROBERT DOUGLAS was born in July, 1837. He was educated at first in Jersey, completing his studies in Hampshire. He was gazetted into the 57th Regiment in 1854, and very quickly entered on active service in the Crimean war. He was present at the storming of Sebastopol, and the capture of Kinburn, receiving the Crimean medal and clasp, and the Turkish war medal. He next served against the Arabs at Aden, and was present at the capture of Sheikothman. From Arabia to India was but a short step, and the young officer took part in the suppression of the terrible Indian mutiny. The 57th were afterwards despatched to New Zealand, and Sir Robert served in the campaign on the West Coast, being present at various skirmishes, and at Nukumaru, receiving the honour of mention in general orders. For ten years he commanded a company of the old "Die Hards," finally retiring by sale of commission to settle in this colony. He was exceedingly popular in the regiment, the men looking upon him as a fearless leader and a considerate and liberal officer. From his residence in the North Island during a stirring period, he naturally made many warm friends.

Sir Robert Douglas was also a public man, well known in political circles. For many years he was a member of the Auckland Provincial Council, and at the general election of 1876, he was returned to the House of Representatives for the district of Marsden, which he represented until 1879. During this time he distinguished himself by great activity and energy, and perhaps did more than any other man in the House to keep the Opposition from falling to pieces during the ascendancy of Sir George Grey. He was never disheartened, and fought a losing battle perhaps better than any man in the House. He was a man of the most generous and kindly disposition, sparing no exertions to serve his party or his friends. The news of his death, which took place at Wanganui recently, was a source of deep regret to all, while the members of his old regiment, who had settled in New Zealand, testified their sincere sorrow at the early death of their late commander.

M*

LIEUT.-COL. McDONNELL.

LIEUT.-COL. McDONNELL.

Services in the Waikato and East and West Coast wars—Pursuit of Kereopa—Attack on Ngutu-o-te-Manu—Engagement with Te Kooti— Forty times under fire and four times wounded—Letter from General Cameron—Story of Ngutu-o-te-Manu by eye-witnesses.

LIEUT.-COLONEL THOMAS McDONNELL, eldest son of Captain McDonnell, of the Royal Navy, immigrated to this country about the year 1840. He received his first commission in August, 1863, as Sub-Inspector of the New Zealand Defence Force, under Colonel Nixon. Served in the flying column at Drury, Burt's Farm, Mauku, and Queen's Redoubt. Volunteered with Major Von Tempsky in the reconnaissance of Paparata, returning successful after a narrow and providential escape from the enemy, for which service he received letters of thanks in general orders, both from General Cameron (the Commander-in-Chief) and Colonel Nixon. Accompanied the Thames expedition, under Brigadier-General Carey. Was present at the taking of Rangiaohia on the 2nd February, 1864 (where Colonel Nixon fell mortally wounded), and in the action fought on the following day. Received his captaincy in 1864, and soon after was appointed Resident Magistrate for Upper Waikato. Was sent to the East Coast as second in command of the friendly Arawa tribes (being a good Maori linguist), where he encountered the enemy in several severe skirmishes, in one of which he was slightly wounded. Promoted to the rank of Brevet-major in July, 1865. Soon after received orders to take the command of a native contingent at Wanganui; became the moving spirit in the capture of the Wereroa Pa, under Major (now Colonel) Rookes; and accompanied the force in the relief of Peperiki on the following day. Was sent to Opotiki, under Major Brassey, where he defeated the Hauhaus, inflicting severe punishment on them by capturing their settlement and destroying their stronghold of Kiore Kino, with a loss to the enemy of thirty killed. Was in command of the force at Waimana, and in the pursuit of Kereopa, taking his village and killing seven of his men. Captured the Pua Pa, and defeated the enemy at the fight that took place at the gorge. Recalled to Wanganui with the Native Contingent, and served as advance guide to Brigadier-General Sir Trevor Chute, K.C.B., throughout his campaign; taking part in the actions at

Moturoa, Putahi, etc., where he was again wounded. Was made Colonel in April, 1867; and was at the taking of Ketemarae and Keteonetea, under Colonel Butler of the 57th Regiment. While protecting the surveying parties in the Patea district, he defeated the Hauhaus at Pokaikai, Pungarehu, Ketemarae, Waihi, Te Umu, Keteonetea, Tirotiro, Moana, Ahipaipa, and other places, at times against great odds, and always with many difficulties to contend against. He embarked again for the East Coast, and with the valuable assistance of Henry Tacey Clark, Esq., Civil Commissioner, succeeded in inflicting a heavy blow on the rebels at Hiria, above Lake Rotorua.

He was recalled to Patea, en route for Hokitika, on the West Coast of the Middle Island with 100 men to quell a political disturbance amongst the mining community. In July, 1868, he received his commission as Inspector of Armed Constabulary, and in the following August made his first successful attack on Te Ngutu-o-te-Manu. The second attack, made a few weeks later, was not so successful, he having been overpowered, with a loss of 50 killed and wounded, including five officers. This failure led to his resignation, which he was induced soon after to recall, and serve under Colonel Whitmore, who succeeded him. He fell into an ambush, and was again wounded. After taking part in the operations against Titokowaru, at Tauranga-ika and the Karaka Flats, he again resigned.

In July, 1869, he was requested by the Government to take command of the forces against Te Kooti, in the Taupo and Uriwera country, where, after enduring many privations from cold and hunger, through want of provisions in an unexplored and nearly impenetrable country, he was successful in defeating the rebel chief at Tokano, and at his favourite position at Porere, where he stormed the pa, and killed 40 of Te Kooti's best men. He afterwards continued the pursuit to Patetere and Te Papa, when, after again defeating Te Kooti, with a further loss of seven men, the Government recalled the European force from the pursuing column.

To sum up these important services, we find that Colonel McDonnell was under fire upwards of forty times; that he was wounded on four separate occasions; that he risked his life continually in reconnoitring, and in conferences with the enemy, sometimes in the very heart of the Pauhau country, being subject to treachery and ambuscades, from the orders he had to carry out, and from the peculiar position he was so often placed in; that, for these brilliant services, extending over a period of ten years, he repeatedly received the thanks of the Governor in Council, and of the Ministers of the day, of Sir Duncan Cameron, and Sir Trevor Chute (the generals commanding), and of the colonial officers he served under; that these thanks were indeed well deserved, as he never shrank from danger or failed in any duty, however disagreeable, but performed the work entrusted to him to the best of his ability The colonial forces under his command materially aided in the restoration of peace to New Zealand. For his personal bravery Lieut.-Colonel McDonnell has been awarded the New Zealand Cross, and received the following congratulatory letter from Sir Duncan Cameron on the occasion :—

CAMBRIDGE HOUSE, KIDBROOK, BLACKHEATH,
11th May, 1886.

DEAR COLONEL MCDONNELL,—I have to acknowledge receipt of your letter of 20th March last, and I assure you that it gave me sincere pleasure to hear that the Minister of Defence had taken up your case, so long and so unaccountably neglected by his predecessors in office, and that on his recommendation the Government had decided that the Silver Cross should be conferred upon you in recognition of the act of bravery which you performed more than twenty years ago, when under my command in the New Zealand War. You have had to wait a very long time for it, and yet among all those on whom that honourable decoration has been bestowed, I cannot conceive that anyone can have been more justly entitled to it than yourself in undertaking a reconnaissance which took you into the midst of the Maoris, from whom, if you had been taken by them, you could expect no mercy. You and that gallant officer, Captain Von Tempsky, gave proof of that cool, deliberate kind of courage which is so much more rare than the bravery displayed in the heat and excitement of an action, and for which such rewards as the Silver Cross are most frequently bestowed. I congratulate you most heartily on the occasion. —Believe me, very sincerely yours,

D. A. CAMERON.

As some difference of opinion existed at the moment of the Colonel's defeat as to his judgment in conducting the retreat from Te Ngutu-o-te-Manu I give *verbatim* the written statement of Adjutant Scannell, Lieutenant Hirtzel, and of the wounded he brought out :—

CAPTAIN AND ADJUTANT SCANNELL'S STATEMENT.

That, during the retreat from the second attack and repulse at Te Ngutu-o-te-Manu, on the 8th September, 1868, Lieut.-Colonel McDonnell, who commanded the expedition, used the most heroic efforts to have all the wounded safely brought out of the bush. That he remained in the rear of the force the whole time, encouraging his men, and fighting his way. That, if it had not been for his exertions and the assistance given him by Father Roland (a Catholic priest from New Plymouth, who accompanied the party for the purpose of administering spiritual comfort and consolation to the wounded and dying of all denominations), Captain Rowan, who was dangerously wounded in the lower jaw, would have been abandoned. That he saw Colonel McDonnell when the retreating force had reached the first clearing, on their way out of the bush. That the Colonel had then only a few of the constabulary and volunteers acting as a rear-guard, and very few fatigue men to carry off the wounded ; while the hostile tribes were keeping up a heavy fire from every part of the surrounding bush. That, when the fatigued bearers, who could get no relief, and the hard pressed rear-guard were for a moment inclined to waver, he again saw the Colonel (he was then on a high stump in the most conspicuous part of the clearing) calmly announcing to his men that, happen what would, he would not stir from that spot until every wounded man had passed on. That, how he escaped twenty deaths is more than the Adjutant could tell, for he was plainly visible to the enemy, being not more than fifty yards' distant, surrounded on every side as a clergyman in his pulpit is by his congregation. That his heroism and devotion were effectual, as the few brave fellows around him rallied, and checked the enemy, while the wounded were rapidly borne forward. That during the whole time occupied in the retreat along a bush track four miles in length, Colonel McDonnell remained altogether in the rear, killing several of the enemy with his own hand; the retreat lasting four hours. It is only fair, and no exaggeration to say, that it was mainly owing to Colonel McDonnell's exertions that so many of the wounded were brought off. That, near the edge of the bush, a few of the wounded were laid down, the carriers being fairly knocked up, and, to induce the men to persevere, Colonel McDonnell, the late Major Hunter, and many other officers placed themselves amongst the rank and file, to be told off as bearers in their turn. That the Colonel never left his post in the rear until long after the enemy had given up the pursuit; and that he was the last man to cross over to the Waihi side of the Waingongoro River.

TESTIMONY FROM THE WOUNDED.

The wounded in the hospital wrote as follows to Lieut.-Colonel McDonnell, commanding Expeditionary force :—

Sir,—We the undersigned officers and men, serving under your command at the front, but at present lying wounded in the Hospital at Wanganui, desire to express our sincere thanks for the kindness you have always endeavoured to show us, and to thank you for the support given us notwithstanding the difficulties and troubles by which you have been harassed. Having heard that a Court of Inquiry is to be held into the circumstances attending the fight at Ngutu-o-te-Manu, we wish to express our entire trust and confidence in you as a leader, and to state our firm conviction that but for the courage and presence of mind displayed by you and your brother officers, the casualties must have been much greater, inasmuch as the wounded would have been left on the field to the mercy of the enemy. We request you to forward this document to Colonel Haultain, and with respectful sympathy we beg to subscribe ourselves,

William G. Best, Assistant Surgeon, and eight others.

MAJOR NEWALL.

Major Newall.

———

AJOR STUART NEWALL enrolled for the Waikato militia, at Dunedin, in December, 1863, and joined Colonel Lyon's regiment, the 3rd Waikatos, on the 18th of the same month, at St. John's Redoubt, Papatoitoi. He did garrison duty at Drury, Papakura, and Queen's Redoubt with portions of the various Imperial regiments stationed there, and was appointed Colour-sergeant, in July of the following year, and in 1865 became Regimental Orderly-room Clerk, and so remained till the 9th March, 1868, when the regimental records were wound up. He afterwards joined the Armed Constabulary, No. 4 division, as a sergeant, and proceeded to Wanganui in February, 1869. He took part in Colonel Whitmore's West Coast campaign against Titokowaru; was present at the engagements at Otauto, Whakamaru, and Te Ngaire, thence through the bush from Ketemarae to Waitara, on to the East Coast, with Colonel Whitmore's expedition into the Uriwera country. He was present at the taking of Ahikeruru, and was on the following day with the column when Taranaki Jim, the half-cast, received his mortal wound from the ambuscade. He joined the force under Colonel St. John, at Tata-hoato, in the Ruatahuna valley, and took part in the various skirmishes of the next few days. He received his commission as Sub-Inspector in June, 1869, at Fort Galatea, after his return from the Uriwera country, and was ordered to Waikato in August, and, in January, 1870, accompanied Colonel Herrick's expedition to reinforce Colonel McDonnell, at Tapapa, where Te Kooti had shown himself with the intention of a descent upon Waikato. In 1871, he received a valuable gold watch from the Government in recognition of a military report and sketch map of the Waikato district. He was in charge of a party of Armed Constabulary at the opening of the Ohinemuri goldfields, where he remained for nearly a year, and with his party did good work in the formation of tracks and roads to Whaitekauri and Owharoa, as also towards

Kati Kati across the Waihi plains. He received a valedictory address of a highly flattering character on leaving from the miners, settlers, and others.

On recall to the Waikato, he was employed with a party of Armed Constabulary on the construction of bridges and the formation of roads towards Taupo, and continued at this work until June, 1880, when he took a party of men to Taranaki, Te Whiti having commenced his trouble at Parihaka. He, in command of the 4th company of Armed Constabulary, and Captain Gudgeon, of the A company, were the two officers selected to go in and take Te Whiti, Tohu, and Hiroki prisoners. After this he was constantly employed with his company road-making between Stoney River and Opunake until 1882, when he received the appointment of District Adjutant of Volunteers in Canterbury, which appointment he holds at the present time.

COLONEL KENNY.

COLONEL KENNY.

The old Fencibles—Threatened invasion of Auckland—Services in Taranaki and Waikato.

THE HON. COLONEL WILLIAM HENRY KENNY, M.L.C., came of a race of soldiers. He was the son of Major W. Crowe Kenny, of Her Majesty's 73rd Regiment, who carried one of the colours of that corps at the storming of Seringapatam, and grandson of Lieut.-Colonel Kenny, of the 11th Regiment, who was mortally wounded leading the storming party at the siege of Gawilghur under Sir Arthur Wellesley. The subject of this memoir entered the 2nd battalion of " The Black Watch " (then the 73rd Regiment) in 1828, at the age of sixteen, and, after doing duty in the Mediterranean for nine years, proceeded with his regiment to Canada, where he served during the rebellion in the Dominion, being part of the time on the staff of General Sir John Colborne, the commander of the forces, and being present at Colonel Wetherall's brilliant combat at St. Eustache and in some minor affairs at Napierville and elsewhere. Colonel Kenny returned to England with the 73rd at the conclusion of the rebellion, and served in the northern district and Wales during the Chartist disturbances in those localities. In 1844 he became Staff Officer of Pensioners at Sheffield and he brought the first detachment of New Zealand Fencibles to this country in 1847. In 1849 he succeeded to the command of that force, and, after the threatened invasion of Auckland by the Ngatipoua in 1851, he received the thanks of Governor Sir George Grey and of Colonel Wynyard, the officer commanding the forces, for the prompt manner in which he concentrated and led the Fencibles to Auckland for the protection of the town. The war of 1860-61 found him in command of the garrison of Auckland, which at first consisted, besides the militia and volunteers, of only a few sailors from the *Iris* and recruits from the 65th, together with small detachments of Artillery and Engineers ; but, in consequence of the threatening attitude of

N

Waikato after the battle of Mahoetahi at Taranaki, it was reinforced by two companies of the 40th and three companies of the 65th from New Plymouth. In 1863 Colonel Kenny again commanded the Auckland garrison until relieved by Colonel Carey, 18th Royal Irish. In August, 1863, Colonel Kenny sold out with the rank of Regimental Major and Brevet Lieut.-Colonel, and being then a Lieut.-Colonel in the New Zealand Militia, he was appointed Quartermaster-General to the colonial forces, in which capacity he served on the staff of Major-General Galloway until the conclusion of the war of 1863-64. In 1867 he was appointed Colonel of the New Zealand Militia and Inspector of Volunteers for the North Island. Colonel Kenny died suddenly at Ponsonby, Auckland, on the 17th August, 1880. At the time of his death he was the oldest member of the Legislative Council, his warrant of appointment bearing date 26th March, 1853. Colonel Kenny was a stern old soldier, of commanding appearance, a fine drill, and a strict disciplinarian.

MR. G. T. WILKINSON.

Mr. G. J. Wilkinson,

Surveying under arms—Baptism of fire at Orakau—Attack on settlers at Opotiki—Hunting the rebels down—Services in the Native Department.

MR. WILKINSON arrived in New Zealand in 1864, and, having joined Major Heaphy's staff, who had received orders to make a survey of the confiscated lands, started at once for the Waikato; and it was while marking out the boundaries of the township of Kihikihi, that the natives were discovered erecting their memorable pa at Orakau. Here it was Wilkinson received his "baptism of fire." Surveyors in those days, for their own defence, armed themselves with breech-loading carbines and revolvers; and, as Major Jackson's Bush Rangers, with Captain Ring's company of the 18th Royal Irish, marched to the assault of the pa, they having had conceded to them the post of honour, Mr. Wilkinson joined them as a volunteer, and during the *mêlée* which followed the rushing of the pa he had a lively time of it. Mr. Wilkinson continued with the surveying party on the frontier for some time, assisting in the surveys, and at times making raids into the enemy's country as far as Kopua, and even beyond, at great personal risk. He went from Waikato to Tauranga, and, with Mr. F. J. Utting, assisted in laying off the township of Te Papa; but soon after settled down on land at Waioeka, near Opotiki, with Messrs. Livingstone, Moore, and Biggs, where he had the most wonderful escape of his life possible from a sudden attack of Maoris, two of the party (viz., Moore and Biggs) falling victims to the attack. He returned to Tauranga. The surveyors being stopped in their work by hostile natives, formed themselves into an engineering company, with Skeet as their captain, and Gundry their lieutenant; and, smarting under the massacre of his two companions, Wilkinson joined forthwith, and was present at the engagements which took place at Te Akeake and Taumata, beyond Pye's Pa, some sixteen miles from Tauranga. It was all bush fighting, the natives having given up the foolish idea of meeting the pakeha on open ground. Being well and suitably armed, the engineer company generally led the van, and were left to discover and dislodge the enemy, who were always well planted, and who would allow our force to get pretty near to them before they discovered their presence by a volley.

N*

At Te Akeake Mr. Woolley was shot in the groin, and Mr Wilkinson had to defend him from being tomahawked until assistance arrived.   He was also present at the skirmishes at Te Irihanga and Te Whakamarama ; at the latter place they lost Mr. Jordan, who was shot in the groin, and died a few minutes after.   The firing was very heavy for the first half-hour.   The advance guard who sprang the ambush had a very narrow escape, more especially Mr. Goldsmith, of Tauranga ; their knowledge of how to spread and take cover alone saving them.

The Hauraki goldfields having been discovered, Mr. Wilkinson proceeded to that district, and his knowledge of the Maori language gained him the appointment of interpreter to the Resident Magistrate's Court, where he was called upon to translate the goldfields deed of lease to the Ohinemuri natives, and he was complimented by the late Sir Donald McLean for so doing.   The Government, wishing for correct information respecting the native feeling at Te Kuiti (the Maori king's headquarters), sent Mr. Wilkinson up soon after the outrage committed on Mr. Mackay, which service he performed very satisfactorily.   In 1878 he was appointed Assistant Land Purchase Officer to the late J. W. Preece (who then held the districts of the Thames, Ohinemuri, and Coromandel), and was subsequently appointed principal Native Officer for the Waikato district.

Three Military Chaplains.

Maori slaughter of the wounded—Resolution of the chaplains to inculcate humane principles among the rebel tribes—Dangerous missions for that purpose—Visiting hostile pas—Long and exciting koreros—The Maori forces reviewed—Incidents of the Taranaki engagements—Anecdotes of Commodore Seymour—Success of the perilous clerical efforts to secure respect for the dead and wounded.

THE battle of Puketakauere was fought on the 27th June, 1860, and was most disastrous to Her Majesty's forces, inasmuch as Lieutenant Brooks and twenty non-commissioned officers and men were killed, while Commodore Seymour and thirty-three non-commissioned officers and men were wounded. News of the success of this engagement on the part of the natives soon travelled the length and breadth of New Zealand, as part of the Grenadiers and light companies of the 40th Regiment under Major Nelson, and a small naval force under Commodore Seymour, were obliged to retire, leaving their dead and wounded on the field. The Rev. Mr. Wilson and Father Garaval, the Protestant and Catholic missionaries then in the Waikato, hearing the native account related by Epiha (the chief who led the natives), and from other tribes engaged in the repulse, their sympathies were so far excited that they resolved to interpose on behalf of Her Majesty's subjects; as, after the military had retreated, all the wounded were indiscriminately put to death. Some few spoke of the wounded who had survived a day or two before they were found, and even they were not spared. Epiha said that, on the morning after the fight, he sent natives to bury any of the dead unobserved the day before. That, when they came to the first body, the native who was about to dig the grave, sat down on the fern, and in doing so hurt a wounded man who was concealed beneath. The soldier instantly raised himself up, and drew his bayonet in defence, but was soon overpowered and killed by the native with the spade he had in his hand. The party soon after found a second body, and at his back sat another wounded man, who had crept out of the scrub and was eating the rations of his dead comrade. The poor fellow had just sufficient strength left to wrest the weapon from the native who found him, but, being crippled and unable to rise, was shot dead by another Maori. Mr. Wilson inquired of the chief why his men behaved with such cruelty and cowardice to men who could no longer resist them. He replied: "What else could we do; if we had spared them we should ourselves have been killed?" He spoke with great praise of Lieutenant Brooks, of the 40th Regiment, who defended himself for some time against three Maoris, until a fourth, coming up, shot him. Mr. Wilson had spent many days amongst the natives who had just returned from the seat of war, and as they were busy preparing to return to Taranaki, he used every argument to try and influence them for the future to spare and treat the wounded and prisoners kindly. To this, however, they would not listen. "What do you think we are going to Taranaki for?" they asked. "Do you suppose we are going to save men's lives? We ask no quarter, neither will we give any." However, frequent intercourse by degrees made some slight impression, and the night prior to their leaving Waikato for Taranaki, Wetene, Taiporutu, and the chief who was to lead them, said to Mr. Wilson: "To-night we hold a runanga to consider your words, and I shall try and induce the tribes, if possible, to comply. We leave at daylight to-morrow; return early and hear our decision." Early next morning the natives were under arms, and as they were leaving Mr. Wilson arrived. He found Wetene alone and pouri. His words were few, observing, "We held the runanga as I promised, but the tribe will not hear. Epiha, Tioriori, and myself were for mercy; all the rest against us. I now go to Taranaki, but should they persist and act as at Puketakauere, I shall return to Waikato. They agree to spare women and children, and" (after a pause) "perhaps they will." The result disappointed the Rev. Mr. Wilson so much that, as a last resource, he said, "Well, Wetene, I will follow you to Taranaki; perhaps when you are all assembled you may agree to act otherwise." The chief replied that the resolve was good. "Come and see us there, and hear our determination." Thus they parted: Wetene to fall only a few days after at Mahoetahi; Mr. Wilson to carry his point, at which he pressed so persistently at his own great peril. In pursuance of his resolution he returned to Auckland, and at an interview he had with the Governor, Sir Gore Browne strongly commended his humane mission, tendered him his good wishes, aud provided him a free passage to Taranaki. He arrived there on the 27th December, 1860. In the meantime, Father Garavel, with letters of introduction from the Governor to General Pratt, had left Auckland and landed in Taranaki the September previous, stating that the object of his visit was to try and lessen the ferocity of the rebels with respect to the wounded and prisoners, and to induce them to respect a flag of truce.

On the 10th of September a large expedition was organised under Major-General Pratt, having for its object an advance as far as possible into the interior of the North Island, towards Pukerangiora on the Waitara River. The force was told off in three divisions. No. 1 division consisted of 557 men, composed of a detachment of the 40th Regiment, under Major Nelson; Naval Brigade from

Her Majesty's ship *Iris,* under Commodore Loring, C.B.; and a Naval Brigade, under Commodore Seymour (now recovered from his wound). No. 2 division consisted of 464 men, being detachments of the 12th Regiment, under Major Hutchins; of the 65th Regiment, under Major Turner; the Royal Artillery, under Captain Strover; the Royal Engineers, under Captain Mould; and twenty men of the Mounted Escort, under Captain Desvoeux. No. 3 division of 333 men contained a detachment of the 40th Regiment, under Colonel Leslie; Royal Artillery, under Lieutenant McNaughton; and fifty Volunteer Rifles, under Captain Stapp. The whole force numbered upwards of 1,400 men, which with the guns and baggage waggons had a formidable appearance.

The day prior to this force starting for the scene of action, viz., Huirangi, Wi Kingi's stronghold, Father Garavel arrived, and being intimately acquainted with that portion of the Waikato Maori contingent, which had already preceded him, expressed a wish to General Pratt to be allowed to confer with them, which after some consideration the General allowed, saying, "You may go, but I will not be answerable for your life." He accordingly set out for their stronghold, alone and on foot, travelling through high fern up to their rifle-pits, and narrowly escaped being shot from the sentries posted in the trees before his sacred calling was observed. One had raised his rifle to shoot him, when a chief suddenly shouted out that he was a clergyman with white bands on his hat. Father Garavel had now a long interview with the natives with respect to the wounded and prisoners, the result of which was evident hereafter. The natives wished him a kind farewell and escorted him part of the way back to the camp. Shortly after, active hostilities again commenced.

On the Rev. Mr. Wilson's arrival, a day after an engagement, he rode into the enemy's country to ascertain the fate of a man of the 65th named MacKindry, whom the rebels had taken prisoner, and at the first rifle-pits the fighting captain of the Ngatiawas (Hapurona), a tall, rough, but honest-looking warrior, came out to meet him with a party of his people. They were not in a good temper, and said that MacKindry had died as they carried him off and that they had buried him near their flagstaff, the funeral service being read over his grave; Hapurona adding, "We are determined to fight to the last."

During the operations of the sap at Pukerangiora the Rev. Mr. Wilson observed the Maoris watching it, and warned our people to be on their guard. Luckily they took his advice, and were prepared for the attack made on the 23rd January, 1861, on No. 3 Redoubt, causing great loss to the natives. Mr. Wilson was originally in the navy, but for thirty years had laboured with great zeal and success as a Church missionary among the natives of New Zealand, highly esteemed by them, and greatly respected by his own countrymen.

When the Rev. Mr. Wilson first arrived at Taranaki, General Pratt was preparing to march into the interior of the country, with the three divisions before stated, and said to Mr. Wilson, "We start at daylight to-morrow morning. There is not time for you to go to see the natives; it would place you in an awkward position. You should have come sooner, as the Catholic clergyman did." But, obtaining an unwilling consent from the General, he left on his errand of mercy. Wetene and most of his men, whom he had conversed with at Waikato, had succumbed to their fate at Mahoetahi, and he had no supporters among the chiefs he was visiting. After three hours' ride through a beautiful country, deserted by settlers and wasted by the natives, he arrived at a native pa, situate on an elevation commanding the principal part of the Waitara, where the natives were waiting the advance of the troops. Seeing two men gathering thistles, he called to them, and was soon surrounded by a number of armed men, who were surprised to see a stranger amongst them, and refused to let him go further. When the chief men had assembled, Mr. Wilson told them his errand, and proposed the following terms:—1st. That all the wounded shall be treated with humanity. 2nd. That the prisoners shall be uninjured and exchanged. 3rd. That the dead be unmolested, and buried by their people. 4th. That persons approaching under a flag of truce be respected. Mr. Wilson here reminded them of the Scripture doctrine of mercy, of the uncertainty of success in war, and their personal interest in these conditions; but, being flushed with the events at Puketakauere, they were deaf to remonstrance, and refused to make any terms. Seeing Mr. Wilson smile, Hapurona said, "Do you deride my words?" Mr. Wilson said, "Why should I not laugh? You think you have only to speak and I must obey you. I bring you a message from above and you reject it. What I offer is for your own good as well as for the Europeans." Henere, whom Mr. Wilson had known in better days, checked his more furious comrades, and they, savage as they were, ceased further to menace, and, strange to say, requested Mr. Wilson to hold prayers with them before leaving, which Mr. Wilson refused to do, because, he said, "You knowingly disobey the will of God—a God of mercy— and yet you refuse to show pity."

On the following day, the natives were attacked at Matarikoriko, and Mr. Wilson again appeared amongst them on the second day of the encounter. It was Sunday, and the General consented to a truce, when Mr. Wilson walked over to their rifle-pits, little more than 130 yards from the troops. He was recognised by a Maori who had lived with him twenty years before at Matamata, and this native escorted him to the Maori encampment. Mr. Wilson again addressed them, saying it was the sacred day, and that if they would remain quiet the soldiers would do the same. They replied: "Tell your chief we never fight on the sacred day. It is they and not ourselves who desecrate it. There shall be no firing on our part." After placing refreshments before Mr. Wilson, and Rewi, the principal chief of Ngatimaniapoto, being present, he again spoke of the object of his visit, when Rewi replied: " It is well that you have come amongst us. Return to-morrow, and we will hear what you have to say." A chief then said: " We last night buried some of our men in the rifle-pits. Ask the chief of the soldiers to respect them; let them remain undisturbed. The funeral service was read over them in the night, during the battle. The ground is sacred." Thus, under no ord nary fire, and at a distance of from 100 to 150 yards from the enemy, these people thoughtfully, and without confusion, interred their dead, an act perhaps that has no parallel in the annals of war, the honours being literally paid by the guns of the artillery and the volleys of the 40th and 65th Regiments. Sir John Moore's burial (the theme of song) is tame contrasted with this.*

As the day advanced, Mr. Wilson moved into the woods, and found women weeping for the dead. With these were a few of Tarapipipi (William Thomson's) tribe. Mr. Wilson also visited them next day; they had been worsted at Matarikoriko, and were now falling back on the woods. The next day (December 31st) Mr. Wilson obtained the General's permission and proceeded to Huirangi, and was received by three or four hundred men all fully armed. They led him further into the wood under some karaka groves, and then the whole people collecting and seating themselves close together, desired him to speak. The arguments on this and on like occasions were drawn from Scripture,† and from the chivalrous usages of Christian nations in time of war. They approved, and even commended all this, but denied its application to themselves. One would observe, " We cannot reach so high." Another, " Our fathers taught us this mode of warfare, and we will adopt no other." A third, " Your customs are best for Europeans, ours for Maoris, " etc., etc. A pause now ensued, and Mr. Wilson thought all was gained, when a well-known leader from Kawhia, whose tribe had suffered at Matarikoriko, rose up, and boiling with rage declared that in this matter he would listen to no one. He was armed with a short-handled hatchet, to which the natives, when roused by passion, give a tremulous or vibrating motion. Coming at last up to Mr. Wilson, with that fierce stare which is natural to the Maori when the passions have attained supreme control, he approached so near, that his face nearly touched Mr. Wilson's, and in this menacing attitude declared, " he would never consent to such a contract; that, whatever other chiefs might do, he would never spare a European, he would never give quarter, " etc. This gave great offence to many who were present. " Take out your book now, and record our protest against all that he has said," they called out. " We cannot interfere with him, but he stands alone; do not be dark on account of what he says."

After the confusion occasioned by this outbreak was over, they again requested that the graves might be respected. Mr. Wilson

---

* The natives have a great dislike to remove the dead when once the burial service has been read over them.

† Micah vi. 8 ; 2 Kings vi. 21, 22 ; Proverbs xxv. 21, 22

asked, " Who will go with me and point them out?" The object
was to give them confidence in English honour, and the usages of
humanity practised by civilised nations, even in war. Two young
men shortly came forward to accompany him, but afterwards
thought it safe to decline. Much talking ensued, and Mr. Wilson
began to despair, till a man stood up and said, "I am the son of
Te Karu, who is buried there; I will go." The natives approved
of this. He then laid aside his arms, put on his girdle, and followed
Mr. Wilson. When they arrived, the Naval Brigade and 40th
Regiment were fast filling up the native pits, and Mr. Wilson
led his companion through the midst of these, to give him some
idea of the nature of "a safe conduct." As they passed to the
extreme right, which the natives had occupied during the action,
and where the troops were now at work, seeing the guide look
anxiously about, Mr. Wilson asked whether " he feared anything."
"No!" he replied; "not from the pakeha (white man), but from
the Maoris who may be among them." Mr. Wilson said, " You
have nothing to fear from them; your life here is as safe as mine."
They came at last to the spot where his father and some others were
buried. The bodies, through a mistake, had already been disturbed
by the Naval Brigade, but the graves were again covered before
they arrived. The native immediately detected it and said, " The
bodies have been disturbed," and seemed displeased. He added,
" There are others in the valley below."

At this spot Commodore Seymour and a few officers who were
amongst the men, inquired the object of the native's coming. It
was explained that the General had given permission, in order to
ascertain where the natives had been buried, that their graves
might remain unmolested. The following conversation then
occurred :—Commodore to Mr. Wilson : " What relation has he
lost?" Mr. Wilson : " His father." Commodore : " Does he lie
here?" Mr. Wilson : " Yes." Commodore : " Poor fellow! Has
he lost his father? Tell him I am sorry for him. Tell him we
bear no malice. It is war." Native : " I am not dark (unhappy)
on his account. He fell in open field—in battle. It was fairly
done. He was not murdered." This he said gravely and coldly.
Commodore : " Say that the graves shall not be injured; tell him
my carpenter shall fence them." In repeating this generous and
manly assurance, so characteristic of a seaman, Mr. Wilson said
to the Maori : " This person who speaks to you is the chief of the
English sailors." He looked satisfied, but made no reply.

A few days after this occurrence, the chief Te Wiona, who was
wounded and taken prisoner at Mahoetahi, was released from gaol
at New Plymouth, and Mr. Wilson had the pleasure of returning
him to the Waikato tribes. Arriving at Waitara, as Te Wiona
could with difficulty sit on horseback, the commissariat officers
(from whom Mr. Wilson and the Rev. Mr. Tresalet, Catholic
chaplain, had received many acts of kindness) immediately
furnished a bullock-cart for his conveyance. In this the wounded
chief, with his baggage, was placed, for, though taken all but

naked on the field, he returned to his people well clothed, and in the possession of several presents.

When Mr. Wilson arrived a mile from the woods he sent back the cart, put Wiona and some of the things on his horse and carried the rest himself. They were soon surrounded by natives, who crowded cut of their works and conducted them to the place where the prisoner's tribe was encamped. In a short time most of the principal chiefs were assembled. On solemn occasions the natives are very formal, and in this instance they placed the chief and Mr. Wilson (he still sitting on the horse and which Mr. Wilson was obliged to hold to prevent Te Wiona falling) in the centre of an open place in the wood, and commenced a wail for the dead who had fallen at Mahoetahi, addressing Te Wiona as their representative and fellow-sufferer, and which he by responsive moans fully appreciated. When this was concluded Te Wiona* retired among his own people, and Mr. Wilson saw him no more till the close of the day.

The chiefs now requested Mr. Wilson to remain till he heard the speeches and saw some of their tribes reviewed. The gathering was on elevated ground, where the flag was flying. On this occasion it was white. About a thousand men suddenly rushed down from the spot, throwing down several of their comrades as they advanced, and then with uncommon energy brandishing their arms and performing the war dance. Around stood the spectators, consisting of men, women, and children. Mr. Wilson sat near the front, where he was joined by the chief from Kawhia who a few days before had so fiercely opposed him. It turned out that the young man who accompanied Mr. Wilson to Matarikoriko was his nephew, and what passed on that occasion had sensibly impressed him. The native phalanx opened a line through their centre, along which the speakers ran to and fro, till either their eloquence or passions were exhausted. Some few spoke with quiet dignity, but the rest, carried away by their feelings, denounced war and vengeance against their enemies. By some the spirits of Wetene and his friends who had fallen with him were addressed in sympathising accents, and by others the tribes were rashly exhorted to abandon the rifle-pits and throw themselves headlong on the military—to act as their fathers would have done. But the great orator of the day was Hapurona, William King's fighting chief. When he arose he first passed slowly through the phalanx, his loins only covered with a small piece of sackcloth, his head thrown back, and his face frightfully distorted, turned upwards. His eyes were so contorted in their sockets that the whites only could be seen, appearing like small balls of chalk. Thus he twice passed through the square of warriors in perfect silence, giving at the same time a quick and tremulous motion to his arms, which were extended at right angles from his body, and which agitated a native weapon, carried in his right hand. Then suddenly starting into violent energy, he used

---

* This man never fought again, but nearly lost his life in an attempt to induce his own **people to return to Waikato.**

every possible argument to induce his countrymen to emulate the courage of their fathers and to annihilate their enemies.

The action which he gave to his weapon (the hani, or spear), always violent, yet often graceful, called forth acclamations from the people, and would have done credit to any theatrical performer. Mr. Wilson's new friend would not allow him to withdraw his eyes from him ; and he observed, " That man's action is wonderful. He has not his equal." Hapurona and others, while speaking, sometimes broke out into traditional songs ; these the men under arms would take up in chorus with admirable effect, their voices marking that nicety of time as though it had been the voice of one man, and the exact motion of their limbs and bodies giving additional excitement to the concourse. To such a pitch of frenzy did these harangues influence the tribes that Mr. Wilson thought they would immediately make an attempt upon the sap, and the thought glanced through his mind whether he should ever again pass from among them.

The principal chief of Mokau, Tekaka, after a long and furious declamation, sank to the ground from exhaustion ; and the energy and devotedness which this man displayed characterised the speeches of all the older men. But towards evening the more moderate addressed the assembly, and by degrees they cooled down to something like reason. When suffering under deep passions, the natives often regard the words of the dead more than those of the living. Therefore, when it at last came to Mr. Wilson's turn to speak, he reminded them of Wetene, and of what had previously taken place at Waikato in reference to the wounded, etc. He spoke of their late chief's (Wetene's) love of his countrymen, his humanity, and his desire that Mr. Wilson should meet them again at Taranaki to discuss again the question. He spoke of the praise the soldiers had expressed for his courage, and for those who fell with him, and the honourable interment his body had received at New Plymouth. He reminded them of the humanity of the General and troops to the native wounded and prisoners, and urged them by arguments to act as men who believed the words of God, and to follow in this respect the example the Europeans had set them.* Although only an hour before these men had wrought themselves into a delirium of passion, they answered all this with moderation and sense. " The works of the pakeha in this have been good ; for the future we will follow his example. The wounded and prisoners henceforth shall be treated with mercy. We will do as the European has done." Then Rewi, the leading chief of the Mgatimaniopoto, rose up and said, " Listen to me. These are the terms proposed ; say ' yes ' or ' no ' to them." He

---

* At Mahoetahi, before the struggle was over, a soldier of the 40th Regiment was observed to come up to a native who had been mortally wounded, and seeing his tongue out of his mouth (as he supposed from thirst), he placed his rifle on the ground, and ran with his canteen to the next swamp, and brought him water. This humane spirit characterised both officers and men. General Pratt, on the same occasion, shook hands with a native lying in the field in order to restore his confidence.

then with a loud voice repeated them twice; at the conclusion, at the second recital, the woods rang with the shout, " Ae! (yes) we consent!" Shortly after the people dispersed themselves, and all was quiet. Te Wiona now sent for Mr. Wilson to visit his wife and friends, who treated him with much kindness; but he reminded them that it was more to his countrymen than to himself that these friendly feelings were due.

Though the object which led Mr Wilson to Taranaki was now accomplished, and for which he felt sincerely grateful, he yet thought it right to remain some time longer on the spot, in order to see how far the natives would keep their promises. The contest was carried on nearly daily, and he was generally present on the field, with the object of being of use to the wounded; or, in the event of their falling into the hands of the natives, to demand them according to previous arrangement.

Mr. Wilson relates two original anecdotes of the Taranaki war, characteristic of the natives engaged; a fine race, enterprising and intelligent, in whom he took a particular interest. " Worthy of an ancient Roman was the conduct of the chief Mokau, at the close of the action of Mahoetahi in November, 1860. When the Maoris were driven from the old pa on the hill by the spirited charge of the 65th, the Taranaki militia and volunteers, they became 'whakawara,' or dispersed, and took to the swamp below. Mokau, retreating, saw at the edge of it a friend lying mortally wounded; he stopped, and though the avengers were close behind, he seized the hand of the dying man and stooped to say farewell, and to press noses in the native fashion. Raising himself up, he himself was shot through the heart, and fell across the body of his friend. His noble act of friendship had thus a fatal result. Of endurance and determination in a Maori, there was a remarkable instance at Huirangi in the summer of 1861. Natawa, a wild character, tired of firing away all day in his rifle-pit, got up into a tree, ten feet above the ground, to fire with better effect at the 12th, 14th, and 40th skirmishers, but he was dropped by a ball in the forehead. Having, perhaps, a thick skull, the Enfield ball stuck fast over one eye, without passing into the brain; and Natawa, recovering himself, went on fighting *for two days afterwards*. The second evening, some of his friends tried to get the ball out by moving it with their fingers, but perhaps a portion of bone was dislodged and touched the brain, and Natawa, after five days of raging madness, died."

Mr. Wilson shortly after re-visited his native land, and those of the united service who have, or may, read what he endeavoured to do for the combatants in the Taranaki War, who may have met him, doubtless paid him every honour. Judge Wilson, of Tauranga, and Captain C. J. Wilson, a gentleman residing at Howick, are sons of the Rev. Mr. Wilson, and served in the Defence Force in the Waikato.

Shortly after hostilities commenced at Taranaki, the Rev. J. M. Tresalet, then stationed at Wanganui, proceeded overland from there to the seat of war, for the purpose of ministering not only to the Catholic settlers at New Plymouth, but also to the Catholics in Her Majesty's Regiments there stationed. When he arrived, the Grenadier company of the 40th Regiment was encamped at the Henui, a mile outside of the township, and he was hospitably and kindly treated by the men of the 40th, until such time as he could conveniently be located at New Plymouth. The reverend gentleman, at that period, was entirely ignorant of the English language, having been located amongst the natives from his arrival in this colony; but in less than two weeks, thanks to the military, who took him in hand and taught him to read and write English, he was capable of conversing on various topics, and gave religious instruction. He was wholly dependent upon the liberality of the soldiers, and members of all denominations, to their honour, vied with each other who should present him with the largest sum, every man agreeing to give from one shilling per month upward, towards his support in his travels from camp to camp, at all seasons of the year, and subject to ambush continually, though, like Mr. Wilson, he luckily escaped. Previous to the troops embarking for Auckland, the men of the 12th, 14th, 40th, 57th, and 65th Regiments presented the reverend gentleman with an illuminated address, accompanied by a purse of sovereigns. Colonel Nelson and the officers of the 40th, whose wounded he had attended after the battle of Puketakaure, presented him with a cheque for twenty pounds, in token of the esteem in which he was held. The money was given on the understanding that it should be devoted entirely to his own private use, which he very reluctantly received, saying: "I want no money. You have done everything. Any man would feel a sacred pride in your benevolence since I came amongst you. I will never forget you." He afterwards erected a wooden church on which he expended the money they had given him. In it he had two stained windows in commemoration of the two special corps, the 40th and 65th.

MAJOR C. DEAN PITT.

MAJOR PITT.

———

MAJOR PITT was appointed to Pitt's Militia (400 strong) as lieutenant in July, 1863. This force was raised by Lieut.-Colonel Pitt (his father) for active service at the request of the New Zealand Government, their headquarters being at Otahuhu, and soon after joined Captains Stack and Moir's company at Drury. While at this station he took charge of the Maori prisoners, and escorted them to Otahuhu. He was then ordered to occupy the church at Mauku, relieving Lieutenant Norman, who was killed in an engagement with the natives soon after. He then moved up to Pukekohe with his company, No. 4 of the 1st Waikato Regiment, and was afterwards posted to Captain W. Fraser's company, No. 1, stationed at Shepherd's Bush, doing escort duty until removed to Tauranga, a few days after the Gate Pa disaster. He was present at the fight at Whakamarama, and shortly after received orders to join Major Mair at Tauranga. From thence he proceeded to Ohinemutu, to augment the force under Colonel McDonnell, who had command of the Native Contingent, and took part in the numerous skirmishes in that district. He raised a native force of Arawas, and was despatched to Opotiki, joining his forces with those of Colonel St. John. Returning to Tauranga early in 1868, he joined No. 4 company of Armed Constabulary, when orders were issued to unite his company with Colonel Whitmore's field force at Nukumaru, on the West Coast. He remained under Colonel Whitmore's orders to the end of the campaign, serving during this period also on the East Coast at Matata. The field force being now virtually broken up, Major Pitt was transferred, with his company, to the Waikato, and promoted to the rank of an Inspector of Armed Constabulary. From there he was ordered to Poverty Bay, as Commandant of the district, and of the Wairoa; where he resided up to 1874, when he sent in his resignation, and retired from the service.

Winiata.

WINIATA, one of the bravest of the brave, volunteered with the Wanganui tribe, under General Mete Kingi, to assist in putting down the rebellion, and all through the campaign on the West and East Coasts made himself conspicuous for his pluck and determination. He always headed his tribe, and was the last to retire from the field. His individual acts of bravery were legion, yet he was superstitious to a degree. On one occasion Winiata was seen in the rear of his company instead of leading it, and being asked the reason, said he had a dream on the previous night that as he was leading he was shot through the hip bone, and he felt all the pain in his dream as if it were true. This idea was soon forgotten on the march, until Economedes, who was leading, was shot down, when Winiata rushed forward, and examining the wound, said, " My dream has saved my life. See, he is hit just where I dreamed I was, and had he not taken my place I should have been a dead man." At the attack on the entrenched position of Te Kooti, at Porere, where our forces had been repulsed several times in their attempt to carry it by storm, Winiata on the last attempt climbed to the top of the parapet, some twelve feet high, and stood there loading and discharging his rifle, shouting out in Maori, " The pa is taken," when a shot penetrated his forehead, and he dropped dead, just at the moment of victory. McDonnell was near at the time and covered his face with his handkerchief, and his company buried him in the bed of a running stream, so that his remains should never be discovered or disturbed by the enemy.

ᠸ*

LIEUT. HIRTZEL.

LIEUTENANT HIRTZEL,

LIEUTENANT C. A. M. HIRTZEL joined the colonial forces in 1863, and served in the Defence Force Cavalry until 1866; during which time he took part in the principal engagements on the East Coast of the North Island. Being on active service he first distinguished himself when attached to the expedition under Major Brassey, who was sent to avenge the murder of the Rev. Mr. Volkner and settlers of the Bay of Plenty. In 1865 he rejoined his old corps in the Poverty Bay district, and was soon after engaged at the attack on the strongholds of the Hauhaus at Waerenga-a-hika; and while repulsing a sortie of the enemy, received a serious wound in the leg. On the disbandment of the Defence Force, Lieutenant Hirtzel received a commission in the Wanganui Yeomanry Cavalry, and at the attack on Pungarehu by the force under the command of Lieut.-Colonel McDonnell, he was in charge of a detachment of dismounted men. In the middle of the engagement, during the heaviest of the fire, he was in the act of climbing over the palisading erected around the pa, when he was struck down by a bullet, which entered his body near to his spine, and lodged in his shoulder; which wound nearly proved fatal. The ball was extracted with some difficulty by Dr. Spencer, at that time surgeon of the 18th Royal Irish, but now of Napier. Soon after recovery he again presented himself for active service, and was present at the disastrous repulse of our forces at the second attack on the village of Te Ngutu-o-te-Manu, where so many of our officers fell. Lieutenant Hirtzel was particularly commended for his conduct at Pungarehu during the action, and for saving the life of a Maori woman just before receiving his wound.

LIEUTENANT HIRTZEL'S ACCOUNT OF TE NGUTU-O-TE-MANU.

After Hunter and Palmer were shot McDonnell gave the order for the retreat. Whether Von Tempsky ever knew of the order I cannot say, but I remained behind with Captains Buck and Hastings, some of the Wellington Rifles and Palmer's men being with us. Captain Roberts at this time was with Von Tempsky further in the bush; and while Buck, Hastings, and myself were consulting as to what was to be done, Roberts came up and reported Von Tempsky's death, and asked Captain Buck to send some men to bring the body out. Buck immediately started off with Roberts, but the latter returned after a while bringing in poor Buck's body. We then commenced a retreat through the bush, having with us some of the Native Contingent (Von Tempsky's), Armed Constabulary, and the Wellington Rifles (I do not recollect how many of each), with Captains Roberts, Hastings, Livingstone, and myself. We marched through the bush for some distance, and could distinctly hear the firing and shouting of the rebels following up McDonnell's party, when, as well as I can recollect, the men composing the Native Contingent, with the exception of two, left us, and it was a little time after they had left us that our party was fired upon. It was at this time that Hastings fell and Russell and others were wounded. Poor Hastings happened to be close to me when hit, and telling me of it, begged me not to mention the circumstance to his men. Private Dore, who was shot through the arm, and another man, who was shot through the mouth, marched with us for some distance, but eventually fell out. Owing to his enfeebled condition at the time I do not think there is much dependence to be placed on Dore's statement "that he could hear the screams of the wounded being roasted alive." Darkness soon closed in, and we halted until the moon rose. I remember hearing several revolver shots fired by, I suppose, some of the poor fellows we had left behind; also that I had laid myself down by the side of Livingstone and had fallen asleep, but was awakened by Livingstone clutching me by the throat and telling me to shut up. I had been dreaming, and in my dream had yelled out. We started again as the moon rose, and reached camp the next morning. I have no recollection of the exact time, but met Major Hunter, with tears in his eyes, coming out to look for his brother. I also remember the squeeze McDonnell gave my hand while remarking, " Hirtzel, old fellow, I thought you were gone."

CAPTAIN H. HUTTON.

CAPTAIN HUTTON.

———

APTAIN HOWARD HUTTON joined the Otahuhu Volunteer Cavalry Troop in 1860, and served in all the events of the war up to 1865, when he left for the Cape, and took service in the Frontier Light Horse, under Lord Chelmsford, against the Zulus. He was mentioned in general orders, at Kambula, for his pluck in going to the front in the pursuit, where he acted as adjutant, and was highly complimented by Lord Chelmsford, Colonel J. North Crealock (Commander 95th Regiment), Brigadier-General Evelyn Wood, and Colonel Redvers Buller, who said in his despatches: "Captain Howard Hutton served under my command in the Frontier Light Horse from May, 1878, till August, 1879, during the latter part of the Kaffir war (1877-78), the operations against Sekukuni, in 1878, and throughout the Zulu war (1879). He was for the greater part adjutant of the Frontier Horse; but he latterly, at my request, undertook the duties of paymaster. In both positions, and throughout his service, he performed his duties thoroughly well." He is the possessor of the New Zealand and the South African medals and clasp.

The following testimonials from his commanding officers show the estimation in which Captain Hutton was held by them:—

[FROM LIEUTENANT-COLONEL BALNEAVIS.]

"AUCKLAND, *January 9th, 1866.*

"MY DEAR HUTTON,—As you are about to leave the colony, and have stated to me you might probably like to join some Volunteer force at home, I think it but right to testify to your having been appointed Lieutenant in April, 1860; Captain in July, 1863; and Acting Captain Commandant in January, 1864. We have had a good deal of official business to transact together, and I can state that I was always satisfied with the manner you conducted the duties.

" I have always considered you one of the best and most efficient officers in our Volunteer force.   In this opinion I am aware your late lamented Commandant, Colonel Nixon, coincided with me.—Believe me, etc.

"H. C. BALNEAVIS, Lieut.-Colonel,
"Late Deputy Adjutant General of Militia and Volunteers,
Auckland, New Zesland."

[FROM MAJOR-GENERAL T. GALLOWAY, C.B.]

"CANNAMORE, BALLINA, *February 23rd, 1868.*

"I had the pleasure of becoming acquainted with Captain Hutton in New Zealand in the early part of 1861, but when I was appointed to the command of the colonial forces in Auckland in July, 1863, I became more intimately acquainted with him.   He was then a captain of the Otahuhu squadron of the Royal Cavalry Volunteers, an admirable force, in beautiful order, and which did good service in the field.

"Captain Hutton was a good officer, well acquainted with his duties, and, very deservedly, was placed in command of the squadron previous to my leaving New Zealand in 1865.

"I feel a great interest in this gentleman, and can honestly recommend him for any appointment he may solicit and for which he may be eligible.

"J. T. GALLOWAY, Major-General,
"Late commanding the Colonial Forces in New Zealand."

CAPTAIN MAIR.

CAPTAIN G. MAIR.

Ambush in the East Coast campaign—The pursuit of Te Kooti—The rebel pas successfully stormed.

THIS distinguished young officer joined the first battalion 12th Regiment, under Colonel Haultain, as interpreter, at Tauranga, about November, 1866, and was present at several skirmishes with rebel natives. He had his horse shot under him at Whakamarama, on January 23, 1867. He took part in subsequent skirmishes at Irihanga, Whakamarama, Maeneene, Te Taumata, Oropi, Paengaroa, Pungarehu, and Te Kaki. At the last-named place he fell into an ambuscade laid by sixty Piriakaus. All the friendly natives on that occasion ran, with the exception of Pani, who assisted his leader in killing two of the enemy, while Mair and his brave companion also succeeded in rescuing their wounded comrade, Manparaoa. For these services, Colonel Haultain (then Defence Minister) promoted Mr. Mair on the field to the rank of lieutenant in the Auckland Militia, and praised him from personal observation, in his official despatch.

In 1868-69, he took part in various skirmishes against the rebel natives in the Bay of Plenty. On May 6, by direction of Colonel Whitmore, Lieutenant Mair led the attack on Harema Pa, Ahikereru. He was present in the fight at Tahoata, and in five or six other skirmishes in Ruatahuna ; and for these services was commended by Colonel Whitmore in his despatches, although erroneously described as " Major" Mair. On the 7th May, 1870, with a small force he attacked Te Kooti, at Rotorua, pursued him all day, killing twenty of his men—Henare Rongowhakaata, Timoti Te Kaka, and the notorious " Baker McLean " (Te Kooti's bugler) falling to his own rifle. For the last-mentioned services, he was promoted to the rank of captain, his commission dating from the engagement (7th February). On 19th August, 1871, Captain Mair led the Native Contingent into Te Kooti's

Te Kooti's pa, near Maungapohatu, inflicting great loss on the enemy, and with his own hand killing Patara and Wi Heretaunga, two notorious desperadoes. When the Hon. Mr. Bryce, as Defence Minister, made his famous march against Parihaka, in 1881, Captain Mair was appointed Aide-de-Camp to Colonel Roberts, who commanded the forces. Since that time he has continued to hold civil appointments in various districts as Native Resident Magistrate and Land Purchase Commissioner.

I have seen a letter from the Hon. Sir George Whitmore, in which this gallant officer expresses his opinion that Sir Donald McLean should have recommended Captain Mair for the New Zealand Cross. Captain Mair has since obtained this distinction which he so bravely earned.

SERGEANT CARKEEK.

SERGEANT CARKEEK obtained the New Zealand Cross for his conspicuous bravery at Ohinemutu on the 7th of February, 1870. While the force under Lieut.-Colonel McDonnell was serving in the Patetere country, Te Kooti with his force came out of the bush on the farther side of the ranges and attacked Ohinemutu, where Captain Mair and some Arawas were posted. It being of the utmost importance that immediate notice of the same should be despatched to Colonel McDonnell, Sergeant Carkeek used every exertion to get natives to convey a note to him at Tapapa through the bush, but as no one could be found to incur the risk, Sergeant Carkeek determined to carry the note himself, and finding a native who knew the road, started at daylight, and arrived safely at Tapapa about three o'clock p.m., having travelled upwards of thirty miles through dense bush known to be in the occupation of the enemy, with the danger of being surprised at any moment, when certain death would have been his fate.

P

CAPTAIN CORBETT.

CAPTAIN CORBETT.

JOHN GLASFURD CORBETT, eldest son of Major-General Sir Stuart Corbett, K.C.B., of the Bengal Army, came out to the Antipodes and settled down in Taranaki, the Garden of New Zealand, where he purchased of the Government a bush section, close to the confines of savage Maoridom. For nearly four years he worked on his farm, having the assistance of two English farm labourers he had brought out with him from the old country, when, seized with a desire for fresh fields and pastures new, he left this country for Australia, where, after going through all the phases of colonial life, viz., gold-digging, bullock-driving, timber-felling, stock-riding, etc., he offered his services to accompany Burke and Wills on their exploring expedition to the interior of Australia. His services were accepted, but want of camels so delayed their starting that in the meantime he went across to Dunedin with a cargo of horses, and there hearing of the outbreak in Taranaki started for the scene of action, determined to take part in it. Nine days after the first shot was fired he enrolled himself as a volunteer in Taranaki. In 1861 he obtained his commission as ensign, in 1862 as lieutenant, and in 1863 he had gained his company, and was present at Mahoetahi and at all the skirmishes in that district. He with eighty men made a night march and attacked the right flank of Kaitake, and held the key of the position while the troops attacked in front. For this service he received the thanks of General Cameron. Captain Corbett was then placed in charge of eighty-five military settlers and natives and ordered to take up a position at Tipoka, to turn the enemy's flank at Waikoukou. This could only be done by two nights' march through the forest, which he and his men accomplished, and for which he again was highly commended by General Sir Trevor Chute. Captain Corbett was educated for the East India Military Service, and while a member of the volunteer force of New Zealand, Colonel Gould, then commanding officer, offered to recommend him to the Horse Guards for a direct commission, which he declined. After the war terminated he met with an accident which deprived him of his right leg, and necessitated his retirement from military pursuits.

CAPTAIN ST. GEORGE.

CAPTAIN ST. GEORGE, a very promising young officer, lost his life at the battle of Porere, after doing good service, on the East Coast, under Major Biggs. His death was the cause of considerable grief in the camp, he being loved by both officers and men. It appears, from despatches received from Colonel McDonnell, that he met his death while gallantly leading on his men at the capture of the pa, having fallen mortally wounded on the plateau on which the pa was situated, in his attempt to reach it. He was buried in the pumice land, on the battle-field, wrapped in his blanket and waterproof sheet; and the story goes that some four years afterwards, his friends, wishing to have him buried in consecrated ground, sent up some natives to remove his bones, supplying them with a small coffin to pack them in. To the surprise of the party sent, on uncovering the body, they found it fresh as on the day it was buried.

The Maoris have a curious custom regarding their prisoners, which was carried out to the letter after the attack on Porere. In the engagement, several prisoners were taken, and all those belonging to tribes of any consequence were taken charge of by their nearest relations. But amongst the group was a very stout Maori woman, who had been severely wounded in the sole of her foot, and who could not lay claim to any tribe in particular; so to settle the question of ownership, she was put up to auction and knocked down to a native named Pokaika (Fox) for a horse valued at £10. When laughed at for his bargain and told that she would run away on the first chance given her, old Pokaika exclaimed, "Don't you see, she will never be able to run with that wounded foot. I wanted just such a one to cook my potatoes for me." And the old warrior was right in his conjectures, for she has remained a faithful servant to him up to the present time.

MAJOR VON TEMPSKY

Major Von Tempsky.

Formation of the Forest Rangers—Ambush at Mangapiko river—Distinguished service at Orakau—Badly treated by the Government—Subsequent services and death at Ngutu-o-te-Manu.

MAJOR VON TEMPSKY arrived in this colony from Central America (where he had passed through the eventful period consequent on civil warfare) just as the war had reached the Waikato district, and General Cameron, finding that the natives had established themselves in the wooded ranges between the Waikato and the settled districts south of Auckland, suggested to the Government the embodiment of a bush ranging force for Auckland similar to that so successfully employed at Taranaki, and the Government, in proceeding to raise this corps, accepted Major Von Tempsky's services as an ensign in August, 1863. The natives were then plundering the out-settlers' houses, and committing murders and every other atrocity unchecked. Hitherto it was thought by many that Europeans would be no match for natives in the bush; but these Maori advocates were soon silenced by the results, as the new force, the Forest Rangers, actually hunted the natives out of the unexplored and extensive forests. In this warfare Major Von Tempsky shone conspicuously. The Major's company of Forest Rangers was raised principally at his own expense, and from that day to the end of the war, his men, influenced by the determined spirit of their leader, rendered services of the most important chraacter to the colony. The first act in which Ensign Von Tempsky distinguished himself personally was in the reconnaissance of the rebels' quarters at Paparata, which place he stole up to, with Sub-Inspector (now Lieut.-Colonel) McDonnell, in the middle of the night, and remained concealed for nearly forty-eight hours in a flax swamp, without food or water, surrounded by the enemy. This was a voluntary act, but it resulted in giving General Cameron accurate information and greatly assisted his movements. This act won for him the respect of the commanding officer in New Zealand, and established him in public confidence.

He continued to serve with credit to himself in the Waikato campaign, principally in separate command, until the rebel

position of Paterangi was invested. Here he had an opportunity of distinguishing himself. He had taught his company
a drill suited to the warfare they were engaged in, and
which he had learnt during his career in Central America.
The natives had planted an ambush, and attacked a body of
soldiers, who had gone down to bathe in the Mangapiko River,
a tributary of the Waipa, the result leading to one of the sharpest
and best contested fights that had then taken place between the
Imperial troops and the rebels, and in which encounter the rebels
lost heavily. Reinforcements were sent up on both sides, and
what began as an ambush attack and skirmish ended in something
like a pitched battle and a complete rout to the natives. It was
here that Major Heaphy so greatly distinguished himself, and on
account of whose services the Premier urged his claims for the
Victoria Cross. Major Von Tempsky here added to his laurels.
Whilst the troops were posted on the left bank of the river, firing
at the natives, who lay under cover of the high fern on the opposite
bank, and kept up a constant and destructive fire upon our men,
Von Tempsky crossed the river with his men, in the teeth of the
enemy and exposed to their fire, armed only with revolvers and
bowie knives, charged through the fern, and for a time were completely lost to sight; but they soon dislodged the enemy and emerged
from the scrub carrying out a good many dead bodies of Maoris.

To Major Von Tempsky much of the success of that day
was due, and his services were heartily acknowledged by Sir
Henry Havelock and other Imperial officers. The next place we
find Von Tempsky is at Orakau, where the pa was defended with
such heroism by Rewi and his followers. During the action, it
was necessary for Major Von Tempsky to take up a position
commanding an angle of the works, to dislodge the natives. In
doing so, he was compelled to lead his men between a heavy cross
fire from the natives at almost point blank range. Exposed to a
shower of bullets, he worked his way, now lying flat till the leaden
shower passed over, now making a dash in advance, and again
falling to avoid the Maori bullets. The point gained, and fire
opened by the Rangers on the devoted garrison, the Maoris
soon found their works untenable, and forthwith effected that
brilliant retreat, glorious as sad in its consequences to the rebels.
For his services on this occasion Von Tempsky received his
majority. Major Von Tempsky was always sent on in advance of
the troops in the Waikato, skirmishing and clearing away all
obstacles; and this he did to the satisfaction of all Imperial
officers.

The services of Von Tempsky, at Wanganui, and daring and
successful expedition into the bush at Kakaramea, will not readily
be forgotten. At a dinner given to him by the Premier, all
there assembled endorsed the words of the head of Government:
"That Major Von Tempsky had done more to raise the character
of the colonial force than had been achieved by any officer during
the war; that he was the great bulwark of the self-reliant policy;

that he was the lion of the hour." But, like all the actions of Democratic Governments to their servants, civil or military, it lasted but the hour, as the next day he received written instructions to proceed to Waiapu and place himself and men under the command of Lieut.-Colonel Fraser. This he considered unjust to himself. That a junior officer, of but recent standing in the colonial force, should be promoted over his head, entirely overlooking his own individual services, was more than he could bear, and he immediately sent in his resignation, the effect of which action was that his men actually refused to proceed without him. The Government declined to accept his resignation, and as his men were fast drifting into open mutiny, sent Lieutenant Westrupp from the Defence Office with a request to the Major that he would proceed to the wharf and induce his men to go on board. This he declined to do, and Lieutenant Westrupp, whose conduct throughout was deserving of praise, obtained the command of the company, paraded the men, and called for volunteers, telling them that all those who remained behind would obtain their discharge. This appeal was not ineffectual, as about thirty-eight proceeded on board the *Lord Ashley*, which had been detained in harbour by order of the Government. In the meantime, Major Von Tempsky received a visit from one of the Ministry, to try and alter his determination, and being asked if he would proceed to Napier, without further delay, and report himself to his commanding officer, he further pressed his resignation on the Government, who immediately ordered him under close arrest, depriving him of his sword. This was his reward for nearly three years' service in the colony.

Lieut.-Colonel Fraser was at that time a very young man who had held an ensign's commission in the Imperial army, and came out to New Zealand in 1864, bringing with him letters of introduction from influential people at home. He was in consequence gazetted to a command in the New Zealand Militia, and ordered to Napier. He was sent up to Waiapu, to assist the chief Morgan, who was fighting against odds on behalf of Her Majesty; and at the head of a European detachment, aided by friendly natives, Fraser rushed a native pa in the most gallant style, and inflicted heavy loss on the enemy. This occurred about two months before, and was the chief service Fraser had then rendered, and for which he was made Lieut.-Colonel, while Major Von Tempsky, recollecting his own superior services, considered that he could not, with respect to himself and his brother officers of rank and long service, do otherwise than resign. Von Tempsky eventually withdrew his resignation, and served at Wanganui, although he had little chance of further distinguishing himself, being always under the orders of his superior officer, until he fell at Ruaruru, or Te Ngutu-o-te-Manu, lamented by all who knew him. The following was contributed by a friend of the late Major's :—

"The late officer was by birth a Prussian, and descended from a noble family. His brother is a colonel in the Prussian army, and was wounded in the campaign between Prussia and Denmark. Major Von Tempsky was a soldier born, and from his earliest youth was a wanderer over all nations. He was also a man of great literary attainments, and an expert linguist. His book of travels in South America is still read by the *literati* with intense interest. His youth, after service as an officer of Prussian Hussars, was spent chiefly in South America, and afterwards on the Californian and Melbourne goldfields; and his adventures in these places, as told by himself, have beguiled many a weary hour with his comrades over the picquet fires, during the campaign in the North Island.

"After the first advance of Her Majesty's troops beyond Drury, in 1863, the want of a body of bush-scourers was sadly felt, and Major Von Tempsky offered his services to raise a body of men, similar in equipment and tactics to those used by the South American Government against the Indians. His offer was accepted, and a reference to the files of the Auckland papers will show the immense service this corps, under his command, was to the Government. At Orakau, he was on the storming party, and the ready manner in which he brought his men into action to intercept the escape of the natives will never be forgotten by those engaged. After the suspension of hostilities in the Waikato district, Major Von Tempsky's services were again in requisition to accompany Major-General Chute in his famous overland campaign to Taranaki. In this he was under fire two or three times. When Colonel Hassard fell, Von Tempsky was there, and our beloved and respected general's order, '57th, advance! Forest Rangers, clear the bush!' will never be forgotten. He, after the campaign was over, returned to Auckland to recruit, and passed a short time with his family. Having resided some little time in Coromandel, he returned to Auckland, and devoted his time to literature and painting. His pictures of some of the most exciting scenes in the Maori war have elicited the highest commendation. When the Armed Constabulary was formed he accepted an inspectorship; how well he performed his duty, has been lately before us, and so fresh in our memory, that it is needless for me to comment on it. He is now gone and I will say no more. I see that the account of his death says, 'Von Tempsky is dead, but he nobly fell in battle.' I know all his old comrades will feel certain of this. His death is a national loss; although an alien, he zealously fought for the British flag, and, whether as a soldier or citizen, was universally beloved and respected. He has left a widow and three infant children as a legacy to his adopted country. As a husband and father, no man could have been more anxious and solicitous for the welfare of his wife and children, or more domestic in his habits; and to have seen him playing with his little ones at home, or attending to his flower garden, or painting, no one would have guessed him to be the terrible Von Tempsky, the terror of the Maori warriors of the Waikato, East Coast, and Taranaki."

COLONEL GORTON.

COLONEL GORTON.

———

OLONEL GORTON joined Her Majesty's 29th Regiment as ensign in July, 1855, obtained his lieutenancy in November of that year, and his company in 1860. During this period he served in Burmah and India. He exchanged as a captain in 1860 to Her Majesty's 57th Regiment, and joined it at Taranaki in June, 1861, and served till June, 1863. While in the 57th Regiment he was appointed extra Aide-de-Camp to Lieut.-General Sir Duncan Cameron, and was present with the General at the action of Katikare on 4th June, 1863; and his services were mentioned in despatches. In July, 1863, at twenty-five years of age, he was appointed a major in the New Zealand Militia, and to the command of the Wellington militia district, to which were subsequently added the Wairarapa and Castle Point districts; the strength of the militia and volunteers under his command being nearly 1600. He was specially thanked for his services when accompanying Dr. Featherston to the Wairarapa in August, 1863; the prompt arming and equipping of volunteers on that occasion having prevented the breaking out of hostilities in the district. In September, 1865, he was promoted to the rank of lieut.-colonel, and was sent to command the Wanganui district, to which was shortly added that of Rangitikei; and, on the departure of the Imperial forces from the West Coast, the supplying and equipping of the colonial troops came also under his control. For his services in connection with these duties he repeatedly received the thanks of the Government. In January, 1869, he took the field with Colonel Sir George Whitmore, as his acting quarter-master-general; and, to ensure the field force receiving rations while marching (*viâ* the back of Mount Egmont), he rode the whole coast from Keteonetea to New Plymouth, a journey of eighty to ninety miles, much of the distance being through the enemy's country, accompanied by only two native guides, thus completing the contract to supply the force from New Plymouth, and returned to camp in four days. In April, 1869, he took up his appointment as inspector of the Government stores of the colony, but resigned his public duties in January, 1878, for colonial pursuits of a much more profitable nature.

Cornet A. Smith.

———

ORNET SMITH obtained the decoration of the New Zealand Cross for his bravery and great endurance at Opepe. On the 7th June, 1871, when the party of the Bay of Plenty Cavalry in charge of Cornet Smith was surprised at Opepe, by Te Kooti's band, and nine men out of thirteen killed, Cornet Smith, though suffering agonies from a desperate wound in his foot, received during his escape, set out with the object of finding the tracks of his commanding officer, and apprising him and his party of their danger, when a less brave or thoughtful man would have proceeded straight to Fort Galatea, which post he could have reached in forty-eight hours with comparatively little risk, and with the certainty of getting immediate medical assistance.

On his road, Cornet Smith was captured by the rebels, stripped of all his clothing, firmly bound to a tree, and left to his fate. He was in this position for four days, without either food or water, when he managed to release himself and proceed to Fort Galatea, which he reached on the 17th, being ten days without food or clothing, being, on account of the wound in his foot, obliged to crawl for a considerable distance on his hands and knees, and further had to risk his life twice by swimming the rivers. He is an old Crimean veteran, and had his medals on when captured.

MAJOR BRASSEY.

MAJOR BRASSEY.

Defence of the post at Peperiki—Bottles asking reinforcements floated down the river—Ingenious fortification of the canvas camp with timber.

MAJOR BRASSEY as a young man entered the British navy, and served therein up to the year 1839. He then joined the East India Company's service, being present and taking part in all the operations in Scinde and Afghanistan, and subsequently in the Southern Mahratta campaign. He was acting Assistant Field Engineer at the siege of Panalla, Powenghur, Managhur, Mansingtosh, and Samunghur. He was five years adjutant of the regiment, and retired from the service on half pay, through ill health, with the rank of captain.

Being in New Zealand in the year 1865 the Government secured his services, and, with the rank of major, sent him in command of 400 Taranaki military settlers to take charge of the post of Peperiki, a native settlement sixty miles up the Wanganui river. Here the rebels tried to cut him off by taking possession in the night of the rising ground commanding his camp on the town side. He despatched a portion of his men under Lieutenant Cleary, and by a gallant dash they cleared the hill and rifle-pits, before the relief arrived from Wanganui, the garrison of that town having been apprised of Brassey's position by some bottles floating down the river from his camp, the writing inside asking for assistance. He was afterwards sent in command to the East Coast to avenge the murder of the Rev. Mr. Völkner, but being suddenly recalled to England on important private business, he on his return resigned his command. From the experience he had gained in India he was reckoned to be one of the best military officers.

RELIEF OF PEPERIKI.

[BY AN EYE-WITNESS.]

On the evening of the 17th July, 1865, when the Colonial troops under Sir George Grey were before the Wereroa Pa, a messenger arrived from Major Brassey, stationed at Peperiki, stating that the rebel natives had completely surrounded him, and that his post, being commanded on all sides, was in considerable danger. This circumstance hurried on the capture of the Wereroa, and on the return of the Colonial forces to Wanganui, they were ordered at once to proceed to raise the siege at Peperiki. The Commissariat officer had previously received instructions from Major Atkinson to keep the garrison rationed three months in advance, in case of extremities, which had been done. But as all the points of defence were now in the hands of the enemy, the relief was a work of some danger. Nevertheless, in spite of all difficulties, canoes alone being available for the expedition, the force started, and on the second day relieved the post, the corpses of several of the enemy half buried giving evidence of the gallantry of the attack and defence. When the enemy were first discovered firing down from the hills commanding the camp, which was in the valley, Major Brassey took measures for his defence, and ordered the church to be taken to pieces in sections. With this material he barricaded the tents, the tops only showing. The portions of canvas exposed were literally riddled with bullets. Having provided this temporary shelter, he ordered Lieutenant Cleary with a part of his force to clear the Cemetery Hill and rifle-pits, which they did in gallant style, losing only one man. Lieutenant Cleary was wounded. Had the natives held their ground the loss would have been very great, but they fortunately took fright and bolted before our men were half way up the hill.

GENERAL CHUTE.

GENERAL CHUTE.

The famous march from Wanganui to Taranaki—Narrow escape; a button shot off the General's coat.

GENERAL CHUTE, who assumed the command after the retirement of General Cameron, was a man eminently fitted for Maori warfare, owing to his great energy and decision of character. He never saw or made a difficulty, neither did he allow a few lives to stand between him and his object. His memorable march from Wanganui to Taranaki by the back of Mount Egmont through the dense bush, and his return by the coast line, carrying by assault every obstacle before him, was the greatest success of the war, and something so new in European tactics to the natives that, towards the finish of his campaign, the mere knowledge of his presence in the neighbourhood was the signal for a general stampede of Maoris from the district. The force he took with him was three companies of Her Majesty's 14th Regiment, two companies of Her Majesty's 57th Regiment, under Colonels Butler and Hassard, 200 friendly natives, under Colonel and Ensign McDonnell and Lieutenant W. E. Gudgeon, and a company of Bush Rangers, under Von Tempsky. The fortified pas of Okotuko, Te Putahi, Otapawa, Warea and Waikoko were carried by assault, his only word of command being "Go on, boys." He was afterwards knighted, and most deservedly so. At Okotuku Lieutenant Keogh and several of his men were wounded; at Putahi he had two killed and twelve wounded, amongst them Colonel McDonnell, a bullet having entered the muscles of his foot; a friendly native was shot through the chest, the bullet sticking in the muscles of his back, just under the skin (when it was removed by the doctor the native took no further notice of the wound); Lieutenant Gudgeon through the thigh, as he was in the act of picking off the wax from around the nipples of his revolver while preparing for the attack. At Otapawa were eleven killed and twenty wounded, amongst them Lieut.-Colonel Hassard mortally and Lieutenant Swanson slightly. Here it was that General Chute had a narrow escape of his life, a bullet cutting away the one breast-button of his coat. His only exclamation was, " The niggers seem to have found me out."

Q*

Paora Hape.

———

PAORA HAPE was a chief of Taupo, who had assisted us throughout the war, and in 1870, when Colonel McDonnell was in pursuit of Te Kooti, the tribes under Paora Hape rendered every assistance, and showed their loyalty to the last. Shortly after the engagement at Porere, Hape, with his tribe, crossed the Taupo lake for the purpose of making a raid on some of the rebel settlements in that quarter, and were so successful in killing and looting, that on their return they celebrated the event by a grand war dance. In the height of the dance, a brother-in-law of Paora Hape, who was in the front rank, by some mischance discharged his rifle, the ball lodging in the spine of Hape. Dr. Walker was immediately sent for from the camp, and on his arrival pronounced the wound fatal, the spine being nearly severed, although he lingered on for two or three days. This accident produced a great sensation amongst his followers, and there was an immediate gathering of all the tribes to hear the chief's last words. Paora Hape, as he laid on a stretcher under a flax awning, the tribes squatted all around him, began by saying "That his first words would be his last, which was to be strong, as he was strong in battle." (Here he mentioned the several events of his life, in which he had showed his strength, and continued :) "Be true to the pakeha. No good had ever come, or ever would come, by fighting against the pakeha. In the old days they were all strong, he was strong, but the strength only showed itself in the fighting Maoris. If any inferior pakehas come amongst you, you had better take no notice of them, but if they do wrong report them to the Government, who have good and righteous laws. The day of the Maori law had passed away —the pakehas and the Maoris could not live under two laws. The laws of the pakeha, being the best, must always be the law of the country," and repeating again his first words, "Be strong and be true to the pakeha," he turned over and died. He was afterwards buried with great ceremony on Moutiti Island, regretted as much by the pakeha as by his own tribe.

MAJOR-GENERAL SIR G. S. WHITMORE.

SIR G. S. WHITMORE.

Services at the Cape and in the Crimea—Arrival in New Zealand with General Cameron—Pursuit of Te Kooti—The disaster at Moturoa—Capture of Ngatipa—Successful campaign on the West Coast—Tito-kowaru's forces dispersed—Te Kooti defeated and pursued.

SIR GEORGE STODDART WHITMORE came to this colony as military secretary to Lieut.-General Sir Duncan Cameron, then in command of the Imperial troops in New Zealand. Prior to this he had served in the Cape Mounted Rifles, and held a position on the staff during the Kaffir wars of 1847 and 1851-1853, and also at the Boer insurrection of 1848. During these campaigns he had been repeatedly thanked in general orders and despatches, and was ultimately promoted when a junior lieutenant of his corps to a captaincy in the 62nd Regiment. He returned to England to join that regiment, in 1854, and finding himself attached to the depôt, with little prospect of getting out to the Crimea, he accepted the appointment of Aide-de-Camp to Sir H. Stork, at Scutari, and subsequently took command of a regiment of cavalry in the Turkish contingent, and served in the Crimea and at Kertch until sent on special service, to procure cavalry, artillery, and train horses and material, in Austria and the Principalities. At the termination of the war, he was one of the officers chosen to wind up the affairs of the army in the Crimea, and, as in these capacities, great financial and administrative responsibilities were thrown upon him, he was gratified by the Auditor-General, in a special report, certifying that although his accounts were the last rendered they were the first and easiest audited of any that had reached the department, being so thoroughly satisfactory that no objection was taken. He then assumed command of his depôt in Ireland, where he remained until his admission to the Staff College, where, during the Christmas of 1860, he passed first, after a brilliant examination.

In the following January, he left England for New Zealand with Sir Duncan Cameron, and served under him for two years, when Sir Duncan, feeling dissatisfied with the control placed over him, sent in his resignation, and Whitmore resigned with his chief. The Horse Guards declined to accept Cameron's resignation, but having no power to refuse the Colonel's, he, in December, 1862, became a settler in Hawke's Bay. In March, he was appointed Civil Commissioner for the East Coast, and on the murder of Hope and Traggett rejoined his old commander, as a volunteer, in the operations ending in the successful action of Katikare. Being appointed to the command of the militia and volunteers at Hawke's Bay, he returned to that district. He once more rejoined Cameron in the Waikato, and was with him at the taking of Orakau. In 1868, Colonel Whitmore was appointed to the Legislative Council, and has held a seat in that body ever since.

Being in England in 1865, he missed the operations on the East Coast, carried out by Colonel Fraser; but, in 1866, he commanded the force which completely defeated the rebels, under their prophet Panapa, at the Omaranui Pa, probably the most complete success obtained by our forces during the war, all the natives in the pa, to the number of 110, being either taken prisoners or killed. Our force, on that occasion, numbered 160, but many of them had little or no knowledge of the use of the rifle. His next military service was after Te Kooti's escape from the Chatham Islands, when the settlers of Poverty Bay applied to their fellow-settlers at Napier for help. Colonel Whitmore obtained the Government's permission to raise a small force of paid volunteers at Napier, altogether about thirty men, who with some friends were taken by Her Majesty's steamship *Rosario* to what is now Gisborne, but arrived too late to prevent the defeat at Paparata. Te Kooti, having on that occasion won a signal success, had pushed on to the Uriwera country with all the horses and camp equipage he had taken. Whitmore followed in pursuit, but could not induce the local settlers to join in the expedition until reinforced by No. 1 division of Armed Constabulary.

In the meantime, Te Kooti had achieved a second success over the Wairoa contingent, which attempted to bar his progress, and the rebels had six days' start. However, the Colonel pushed on, and after great difficulty, owing to the inclement weather, and the refusal of the Poverty Bay settlers to go further than the Whangaroa River, the boundary of their district, he overtook Te Kooti two days later, in the bush, and at once attacked him. The action began about three o'clock, in the bed of a stream, which had to be crossed seven or eight times, breast high, it being winter time and swollen with snow. Daylight was failing when the Colonel drew off his men, and at the same moment Te Kooti was being carried off into the bush, severely wounded. The colonial force had then been forty-eight hours without food, and to reach their enemy had been marching night and day, enduring hardship from hunger and cold unknown in any other incident of the war. Colonel Whitmore, being a man of iron constitution, could endure any amount of fatigue himself, and, unfortunately for his men, considered that they should all be made of the same metal. Consequently, in his anxiety to come up with the enemy, he often overtaxed their endurance, which at times led to a little grumbling, as Englishmen cannot keep their tempers on an empty stomach. The Colonel, much against his will, had now to retire, or rather retrace his steps, to save his men from actual famine, as supplies had not come up; and leaving his dead behind, but carrying his wounded, he did not meet the convoy until the following day.

The news of the disaster at Ngutu-o-te-Manu, on the East Coast, having now reached the ears of Colonel Whitmore, he hastened to the assistance of Colonel McDonnell, offering to serve under him as a volunteer. The force, by their defeat, was so diminished and demoralised that Colonel Haultain, the Minister of Defence, considered it necessary to order them back to Patea, and Colonel McDonnell tendering his resignation, the Government asked Colonel Whitmore to take the command. This he did at once, and proceeding to Patea, applied himself to reorganising the force, which was in a sad condition, both as to number and *morale*—one whole division of Armed Constabulary having mutinied had been disbanded, while the other two companies comprised few more men than were needed to tend the sick and wounded. The only division in number and discipline fit for service was the Hawke's Bay corps, which Colonel Whitmore brought from Napier with him, though at the cost of great unpopularity with the Hawke's Bay settlers for removing them. The Government now began to enlist recruits, both in New Zealand and the neighbouring colonies, while Titokowaru moved gradually forward, passing Patea in the bush on towards Wanganui.

Strictly speaking, Colonel Whitmore's command did not extend beyond the Patea district; but he threw himself with every available man between Titokowaru and Wanganui, and being joined that night by his first batch of recruits, namely, the No. 6 division of Armed Constabulary, he attacked the enemy at Moturoa. The natives were between six and seven hundred strong, entrenched in a formidable pa, so formidable that the Colonel was unable with his force to carry the works, which, being in the middle of a dense bush, and erected within the last few days, were not known to exist. The action was well sustained and very obstinate while it lasted; but, after three hours, the Colonel having personally examined the position, and finding no available point to force an entrance, drew off his men in excellent order, though with heavy loss. All the wounded were safely removed, though the dead had to be left on the ground. The retreat was conducted so as to leave no opening for attack, and the force fell back on Wairoa safely. Under the circumstances Colonel Whitmore resolved to fall back on Nukumaru, covering Wanganui, and strengthening Patea and Wairoa. This was soon accomplished, and a position taken up and fortified, where the expected recruits might be organised. But the massacre at Poverty Bay occurring in the meantime, the Government ordered him to fall back still closer to the township of Wanganui, namely, to the Kai-iwi River, and to proceed to Poverty Bay with the most reliable of his men.

This he accordingly did, and after some delay in waiting for native auxiliaries he invested Ngatipa, Te Kooti's stronghold, on the 1st January, 1869. This unusually inaccessible and almost impregnable work was taken on the 5th January, and the loss during the operations was so heavy on the rebels as to intimidate Te Kooti from ever again making a raid on Poverty Bay.

Ngatipa being taken, Colonel Whitmore hurried back to the West Coast, where meanwhile a considerable number of recruits had assembled, thanks to the energetic exertions of the Government, and although this force was thoroughly undisciplined and hardly trustworthy, Colonel Whitmore resolved on an immediate advance, trusting to train his men as he marched forward. Great caution was used to prevent any possibility of another reverse, which for the time would have resulted in retarding the prosperity of the West Coast. Although urged by the local Press to action of the most reckless nature, he moved slowly on for the first fortnight, discharging men unfit for the duty, and gradually teaching the rest the use of their arms in the field.

Taurangahika Pa was taken after a feeble resistance, and Titokowaru driven across the Waitotara; and Colonel Whitmore, satisfied that his force might now with safety be actively employed, threw a flying bridge across the Waitotara and marched to Patea, where, having rested two days, he moved off in the night, and at dawn next morning attacked Titokowaru's position at Otautu, which he surprised and took with some loss.

Having removed his wounded to Patea, he followed up his success, pressing the enemy by bush paths, while supplies followed by the coast road. He surprised the settlement of Whakamara, the enemy beating a precipitate retreat, closely followed by the bush column, which several times overtook the rearguard and inflicted some loss upon them.

Following on northward, Titokowaru's retreat became a flight, and when the column emerged from the bush at Taiporohenui, all traces of him were lost. Colonel Whitmore, relying on information received from Major Kemp, resolved to push on to Nga re, a post eight miles in the bush, surrounded by a swamp, almost impassable to strangers. Having arrived opposite the position, the force was set to work to construct hurdles of supple-jack, on which they crossed over the treacherous swamp, and succeeded in surprising the settlement the following morning. It was here that the Wanganui natives prevented the destruction of the enemy by running into the native camp declaring the occupants were friendly people. Meanwhile Titokowaru and the remnant of his force escaped before the ruse was discovered, but so panic-stricken and demoralised that they did not again pause in their retreat until they had found shelter far inland of Taranaki, at the Upper Waitara. This concluded the campaign. The troops, marching by the inland route round Mount Egmont, now reached the Waitara, where they were shipped to Auckland, *en route* to the Uriwera country.

NGATAPA FROM

THE EAST.

The operations on the West Coast were so successful that the war has never been resumed, nor a single shot fired since in the whole district, whereas settlements soon followed in the wake of the troops, and the coast was re-occupied by Europeans. So subdued were the natives at this time, that had the whole of the confiscated land been then offered by auction and occupied, no further trouble would have ensued.

The Uriwera expedition concluded the operations conducted by Colonel Whitmore. Finding Te Kooti established among the wooded mountains, from which apparent safe refuge he was making murderous forays on neighbouring districts, having just destroyed the Mohaka settlement, and murdered many settlers, the colonel resolved to follow him up. The country was then unknown. Provisions could only be carried on men's backs. It was dead winter, and the cold extreme. Nevertheless, he succeeded in reaching Ruatahuna with two columns from the north and east, jointly six hundred men, and in devastating the cultivations and stores of food collected.

Both columns engaged the enemy on several occasions, and caused, as well as suffered, considerable loss. But the expedition was otherwise eminently successful, by showing the natives that where they could go we could follow them, and the troops were withdrawn to Fort Galatea to await events. Colonel Whitmore confidently relied upon the retreat of Te Kooti to the open country of the interior through want of food; but unhappily the Colonel's iron constitution at last broke down, and he had to be carried to the sea, prostrated by dysentery. A few weeks later, having somewhat recovered, he returned to the field to hand over the command to Colonel St. John, and was directed by a medical board to seek rest and change of climate. On his recovery from dysentery, he found himself overtaken by rheumatism, and remained for several years in a crippled state.

A change of Government now occurred, and the policy of the former one reversed, their first step being to remove the Colonel from the command, he, notwithstanding his condition, being then about to proceed to Taupo to give Te Kooti the *coup de grace*, which in that open country could not have been doubtful, since, as the Colonel predicted, he had emerged from the mountains with a very reduced force. Unfortunately, the time was lost, and the policy of inertia and conciliation failed to restore peace, so nearly won by force of arms. This policy was adopted for eighteen months before operations ceased, and ended in Te Kooti taking refuge in the King Country. In six months Colonel Whitmore restored peace to the West Coast and Poverty Bay, never since broken, with a force hurriedly collected while the operations were proceeding. His services have been recognised by the Crown, the Queen having conferred on him the C.M.G. in 1869, and the K.C.M.G. in 1882. Of his further services in the Legislative Council it is unnecessary to speak. He was made Colonial Secretary and Defence Minister in 1877. On the resignation of the Grey Ministry in 1879, Colonel Whitmore resigned with his colleagues. On Mr. Stout's Government taking office in 1885, he was a Minister without portfolio for a few days only. On the accession to power of the Stout-Vogel Administration, he was appointed Commandant of the Colonial Forces and Commissioner of the Armed Constabulary, an office which he at present holds with the rank Major-General, conferred for the first time in New Zealand upon an officer of the colonial forces.

TE PUIA.

TE PUIA was Native Orderly, attached to the Native Contingent, then at Taupo, in 1869. Colonel McDonnell, having an important dispatch to send to Sir William Fox, who was then in Wanganui, organising an expedition of natives to co-operate with the forces under McDonnell at Taupo, was for the moment at a loss who to entrust it to, as no pakeha could be found who knew the road, the distance being upwards of one hundred miles, thirty of which would be through the enemy's country. Puia, seeing McDonnell's difficulty, volunteered to go. He knew it was important he should go by Hiruharema, on the Wanganui river, as being the shortest route, although the last thirty miles would take him through the country occupied by the enemy, where his life would be in peril every step he advanced. But, nothing daunted, the brave old man started on his journey, and got through unmolested. This is only one of the many brave acts Te Puia did while with us which equally deserve recording.

CAPTAIN W. McDONNELL.

CAPTAIN McDONNELL.

———

APTAIN WILLIAM McDONNELL, a younger brother of Colonel McDonnell, was appointed to the Native Contingent, and served throughout the war, both on the East and West Coasts. He was always the first to volunteer for any undertaking of danger; and acted as guide to Sir Trevor Chute all through his campaign. He was severely wounded in the groin while leading his men at a night atrack on Popoia, and probably never would have recovered from the injury, had not his native company carried him on a stretcher to the hot sulphur springs, a distance of at least one hundred miles, and immersing him therein for several hours each day brought him back perfectly healed. He was at both the attacks on Te Ngutu-o-:e-Manu, and was the officer sent round to the other side of the pa, during the action, with orders for Von Tempsky and his men to retire. He was under fire so often, and behaved so courageously, that his company would have followed him anywhere. He had a narrow escape of his life during the skirmishing that took place in the clearings around Putahi, after the pa had been taken. A rather grandly dressed Hauhau had shot a corporal of the 50th Regiment, who had been standing only a few paces in front of McDonnell, just as the captain had fired at a Hauhau a little to the right. As the corporal fell shot through the heart, it brought the captain and his adversary face to face, and it now became a simple question of life or death between them, as neither would retire, and he who could load first would be nearly certain to kill the other. Both commenced to load at the same moment, and a strange and exciting race it was, for both were men of strong nerve and determination. McDonnell first fitted the cap on his rifle. It was a happy thought, though contrary to all rules of musketry. The Hauhau commenced to load, keeping the capping for the last. Both ramrods worked freely, and, as the native was in the act of capping, McDonnell felt he had no time to lose; so, leaving his ramrod in his gun, he took a snap shot at his adversary from the hip, just as the Hauhau was in the act of raising his rifle to his shoulder, and fortunately succeeded in hitting him, as both ramrod and bullet passed through his chest, and he dropped where he stood. It was a race for life, and only won by half-a-second.

R

S. Black and B. Biddle.

THESE two men, privates in the Armed Constabulary of New Zealand, were rewarded with the New Zealand Cross for their brave and gallant conduct during the siege of Ngatipa, in June, 1869. During the attack on Ngatipa, under Colonel Whitmore, the rear of the enemy's position was assigned to the custody of Major Fraser, who commanded Nos. 1 and 3 companies of Armed Constabulary and Hotene's Ngatiporous. The extreme right—a scarped stony ridge—was commanded from the enemy's rifle-pits, and a lodgment could only be effected by cutting out steps in the cliff for the attacking party to ascend. Knowing this, the enemy made several determined sorties to try and dislodge our men, so much so that it became extremely difficult to hold the position so essential to the success of the operation. But a party of twelve determined men, having volunteered for the duty, continued the work in spite of all opposition; and, although suffering considerable loss during their operations, they continued to hold their ground (after repelling some most resolute attacks) to the end of the siege. The most conspicuous for their bravery were the two men above mentioned, and were rewarded accordingly.

Captain Scannell also reports that, on the morning succeeding the partial investment of the Taurangaika Pa, and while preparations were being made for the attack, Constable Solomon Black, of No. 1 division of the Armed Constabulary, noticing the unusual silence that prevailed about the pa, which was partially hidden from view by a small scattered bit of bush, declared it was his opinion the natives had bolted, and, in spite of all opposition, jumped over the ditch and bank fence, walked through the piece of bush, and straight up to the pa, where he had the satisfaction of verifying his statement. Had any natives been concealed in the pa—and there were no sufficient reasons to suppose the contrary at the moment—Black, as well as several others of Nos. 1 and 2 divisions who rushed after him, would certainly have lost their lives. This, although exhibiting Black's natural bravery, being regarded as somewhat foolhardy, was not considered when recommended for the New Zealand Cross.

MAJOR HUNTER.

MAJOR HUNTER.

The attack on Turi Turi—Major Hunter wrongfully charged and honourably acquitted—Gallant lead at Moturoa—His life sacrificed to disprove a false imputation—Colonel Whitmore's testimony to Hunter's bravery— Two courageous brothers who died in the war.

MAJOR HUNTER served through a portion of the war in command of a troop of the Defence Force Cavalry, and on the evening before the attack on Turi Turi Mokai (where Captain Frederick Ross and seventeen out of his force of twenty-five men were either killed or wounded), was stationed at Waihi, a post about two and a-half miles distant, where Major Von Tempsky was in command. Early in the morning of the 15th July the sentry on duty gave the alarm. He could not hear any report of firearms, but from the flashes around the Redoubt he could see that Turi Turi was attacked. Von Tempsky, being senior in command, immediately ordered his company (No 5 of Armed Constabulary) to stand to their arms, and marched them off to the rescue, leaving Major Hunter without orders. In the meantime Troop Sergeant-Major Anderson had got his men in their saddles and drawn up before Major Hunter's tent, expecting orders to follow. When the Major made his appearance he ordered them to dismount and feed their horses.

The circumstances which led to this order on the part of the Major have puzzled many to this day. Evidently, however, the Major thought his services were not required, and that had Von Tempsky wanted him he would have left orders to that effect, and under these circumstances he felt he could not risk the safety of his post by leaving it unprotected. The affair led to his being charged with having caused the destruction of fully half of the force at Turi Turi Mokai by not hurrying to their relief when he could have arrived in so short a time. The charge so irritated the force, that many officers and men who should have known better joined in his condemnation, instead of placing the blame on his superior officer, who had left him without orders. For it was no doubt the duty of Major Von Tempsky to relieve the beleaguered Redoubt; and as he did not take the troopers with him it argued that he considered his own company sufficient. Major Hunter was tried by court martial, and honourably acquitted. Those who knew the Major intimately knew him

R*

to be a brave man, although this affair had led many who did not know him so well to think otherwise. There is little doubt that those who blamed him so hastily must afterwards have felt they had a large share in the sacrifice he made of his life in giving the lie to an imputation under which he was unable to live, as his recklessness at the battle of Moturoa showed. This battle took place soon after the attack on Turi Turi Mokai. Major Hunter led the attack with fifty men of the Armed Constabulary and some of the local forces. Coming to a clearing in the standing bush, he charged gallantly across the open ground and made straight for the palisading around the pa. When within fifteen yards the whole face literally blazed—at least two hundred Maoris had opened fire on their assailants. Major Hunter's men falling fast, and finding the palisading too strong and well defended to be carried by assault, took cover and held their ground, although half the force were either killed or wounded, amongst the latter being Major Hunter himself, mortally. The survivors held on for half an hour, and so much were they encumbered by the dead and dying, that it was not thought possible to carry them off the field. But at this critical moment Colonel Whitmore brought up No. 6 Division of Armed Constabulary in skirmishing order, and by drawing the enemy's fire, saved the advanced party from annihilation, and enabled Major Hunter and the rest of the wounded to be brought off the field. Thus fell Major W. Hunter, who undoubtedly sacrificed his life to save his honour, his last words being, " I must show the world to-day I am no coward," the unjust accusations made against him still rankling in his mind.

In Colonel Whitmore's report to the Defence Minister (Colonel Haultain) he thus speaks of his death:—" I must now reluctantly allude, because it is with so much grief, to the death of the gallant Major Hunter. This brave officer, whose career has been so long before the country, who was so efficient in the every-day duties of his profession, and so prominent before the enemy, fell, as I believed, and he doubtless thought, in a moment of victory, when the loss of his brother, two months before, and of so many other gallant fellows, was about to be avenged. The Constabulary can boast of no better officer, the colonial service no braver, than Major Hunter, and the gallant manner in which he sprang forward before his division and led them to the assault, will never be forgotten by me, nor the whole force in presence of which it occurred. Happily, all saw how an officer should lead his men, and the other officers proved themselves worthy of the example. In falling as he has done, Major Hunter has left behind him an illustrious name in our colonial history, and will be followed to the grave by the regret of all colonial forces."

The evening previous to the attack on Moturoa Major Hunter informed a friend that he had obtained permission from Colonel Whitmore to lead the attacking party the next morning, and that he would let the world see he was no coward, and would avenge his brother Harry's death. *Requiescat in pace.*

CAPTAIN THOMAS.

CAPTAIN THOMAS.

WITH AN ACCOUNT OF THE CAREER OF TE KOOTI.

The Maori prisoners sent to Chathams—The guard numerically insufficient for their safe custody—Te Kooti practising on the credulity of his fellow-prisoners—Capture of the 'Rifleman'—Landing in Poverty Bay and subsequent events—The Poverty Bay massacre—A horrible tragedy—Hunting Te Kooti through the country—A series of successful engagements in which the colonial forces distinguished themselves.

CAPTAIN THOMAS was an Imperial officer, holding a commission in the 26th Regiment (Cameronians), and also as captain in the 2nd Cheshire, together with Sir H. B. Loch, the present Governor of Victoria. He settled in New Zealand, in 1857, and was appointed Resident Magistrate at the Chatham Islands. Happening to be in Wellington during the month of February, 1866, he was sent for by Cclonel Russell, the then Native Minister, who informed him of the contemplated idea of the Government deporting Maori prisoners to the Chathams under his charge. Captain Thomas distinctly stipulated that under such circumstances the guard should be increased in proportion to the number of prisoners sent; and on this understanding Captain Thomas left Wellington for Napier without delay to take over the first batch of forty-three prisoners, their wives and children, amounting to twenty-five more. The guard, half Maori, half European, under Lieutenant Tuke, twenty-six strong, accompanied them in the steamship *St. Kilda*. They arrived at the Chathams on the 14th March, and the first step Captain Thomas had to undertake was to proceed ashore and prepare for their reception with the natives of the Islands, informing them of the intention of the Government to locate them on suitable land for their habitation and cultivation. The prisoners were disembarked at Port Waitangi and marched up to the locality agreed upon as their place of residence; and being close at hand, by the evening of the following day they were all comfortably housed, having been hospitably received and fed by the island natives. After consulting Lieutenant Tuke, a redoubt of a suitable size and residence for the Resident Magistrate and commanding officer were being prepared, and the press of work was such that Captain Thomas did not consider it prudent to send half the guard back this trip, as Colonel Russell expected him to do.

On the 27th April a second batch of prisoners arrived, numbering in all eighty-eight, and the Government were reminded by Captain Thomas that if it was contemplated to send a large increase of prisoners the guard should be strengthened in proportion, as, according to agreement with Colonel Russell, when the number of prisoners reached 300 the guard should consist of two officers and fifty men. On the 10th June another batch arrived, making in all 272 persons on the Island. With this batch was Te Kooti.

It appears that a proposition had been made to the Government by one of the Chatham Island Maori chiefs (Toenga te Poki), when in Wellington, that the Island natives should be allowed to take charge of the prisoners, and it was greatly to the astonishment of Captain Thomas that he received, early in July, instructions to send back the whole of the military guard under his command with the exception of one corporal and three privates, without any further reference being made to him on the matter. Captain Thomas immediately ascertained the wishes of the majority of the Island natives, and they one and all were most emphatic in their desire not to undertake anything of the kind, neither did the prisoners themselves wish it. The European settlers also petitioned against being left under such inadequate protection, and all this was duly reported by Captain Thomas to the Government on the return of the *St. Kilda*, by which vessel the guard was sent back, with the exception of the four mentioned. On the 26th November fifty-six more prisoners arrived, making a grand total of 328, under a guard of two officers and twenty men, including ten natives, the officers being Captain Edmund Tuke and Lieutenant Hamlin.

The prisoners, up to this time, had behaved well, notwithstanding the inadequacy of the guard, and had hitherto been constantly employed in road making, and now had commenced planting seed potatoes for their own use. Again, at this time, Captain Thomas appears to have begged the Government, in the event of their sending any more prisoners, to strengthen the guard in proportion. No notice was however taken; but, in March, 1867, Major Edwards, of the New Zealand Militia, was sent down by the Government to inspect and report. On his return to Wellington, Major Edwards reported on the satisfactory behaviour of the prisoners, and recommended that the guard should consist entirely of Europeans, with two officers and thirty rank and file. He alluded in his report to having interviewed the prisoners, and to their expressing to him their desire that a few of them should be allowed periodically to return to New Zealand on their good behaviour, as the Government had promised. On the 24th June, 1867, Captain Thomas received instructions from the Defence Minister (Colonel Haultain) that the prisoners should not be kept under such strict surveillance as appeared to have been maintained; but Captain Thomas seems not to have adhered to this instructions, and everything proceeded favourably, the prisoners being chiefly employed in raising crops for their food.

In January, 1868, Mr. Under-Secretary Rolleston was sent down to the islands, and on his return reported most favourably of all that he saw, and stated that, with regard to the general control exercised by Captain Thomas in the Chatham Islands, so far as he could learn from personal observation, his kindness of manner and honesty of purpose had won for him considerable influence amongst the natives, and the way in which he discharged his duties to both races in a position made very difficult by the conflicting interests and animosities of a young and disorganised community appeared satisfactory ; also that the influence that Captain Thomas had obtained with the native prisoners had prevented any evil result, which probably might have been entailed by the unsatisfactory state of the military guard, and reported that he did not think that, as constituted, it would be of any material good had any serious difficulties arisen. One of the chief results of Mr. Rolleston's visit was that the guard, or rather a portion of the best behaved, were enrolled as a force of Armed Constabulary, numbering one senior sergeant, one corporal, and nine constables.

On the 30th March, Captain Thomas again wrote to the Defence Minister (Colonel Haultain), expressing his hope that, should it be the determination of the Government to leave the prisoners at the islands, he might be allowed some kind of assistance and support to enable him to exercise the present control he had over the prisoners, having regard also to any outbreak that might unexpectedly arise amongst them. This request, reasonable as it was, does not appear ever to have been attended to. At the same time, he also reported that the prisoners, without showing an open defiance, had not of late exhibited the same amount of willingness as they had previously shown. In the middle of April, 100 bushels of seed wheat arrived, with instructions from the Defence Minister that it should be sown by the prisoners for food. This step evidently showed the prisoners that their time of detention was not for the present to expire, as they had expected, and it was currently reported and believed amongst them that a latent promise had been made to some of them by Sir Donald McLean that two years was to be the period of their imprisonment.

Moreover, on the 19th May, Captain Thomas was instructed to warn the prisoners that the Government would not supply them with any more food whatever after the next harvest. In the latter end of June, one of the prisoners, who had had a quarrel with Te Kooti, reported to Captain Thomas Te Kooti's practise of rubbing his hands with matches, and imposing on the credulity of the prisoners on certain occasions, and of anointing some of them with oil, and from inquiries made he found the statement to be correct, and thereupon he at once separated Te Kooti from the rest of the prisoners.

On the 3rd July, 1868, the *Rifleman* schooner, chartered by the

Government, arrived with stores, etc., and on the following morning (it rained heavily at the time) the guard at the redoubt was suddenly seized and overpowered by the prisoners, one of them being tomahawked. Captain Thomas at the time was on the beach below attending to the customary duties at his office, and immediately on being informed of this unexpected event, proceeded to the redoubt without any arms whatever, knowing full well that he was entirely at the mercy of the prisoners, as he had been, in fact, all along, and not wishing to exasperate them. He found the prisoners in full possession, ransacking the magazine, etc. He called on them to lay down their arms and tell him what they wanted. He was upon this immediately seized, tied hand and foot, and carried into the guard's whare. One of the prisoners shortly afterwards came up to him and informed him that his life would be spared if he did not interfere to prevent their taking the *Rifleman* and proceeding to New Zealand. Shortly afterwards he was conveyed handcuffed to the gaol on the beach close at hand, and there he found the few European settlers incarcerated. After a delay of about half an hour they freed themselves, but by this time the prisoners were all on board the *Rifleman*, which finally, after two futile attempts to put to sea, got away the next morning, leaving the captain of the vessel ashore. Te Kooti held strict watch over the men at the wheel all the way to New Zealand, until he arrived at Whare-onga-onga, in Poverty Bay, the very spot he wished to land at. His plans were laid with so much secrecy, the attack was so sudden and unexpected, and the means of defence so limited, that resistance was out of the question. It is even very doubtful whether, had Captain Thomas received warning of what was intended, he could with so weak a guard have offered any effectual opposition to their proceedings. But there can be no doubt of this, that had Captain Thomas's repeated requests to the Defence Minister only been granted, of having the guard stengthened according to the number of prisoners sent, the prisoners might have been detained there to this day; but the escape of the prisoners, owing to the policy of the then Government, must altogether have involved the country in a loss of little less than a million of money and several hundreds of valuable lives.

Captain Tuke writes:—" In 1866, the native prisoners at the Chathams numbered in all about three hundred and sixteen, two hundred men, women, and children. Their first occupation was to build themselves houses of punga, five in all; the different hapus being divided and placed under a chief, who was responsible for their good behaviour and order. I found the system to work well, and the prisoners were exceedingly well behaved and orderly. They were visited every morning and evening by the doctor, and the roll called by the officer on duty in charge of the guard, which consisted of thirty men placed in a redoubt a short distance from the prisoners' houses. Rations were supplied daily to them, and they were found in clothing and tobacco. They were also allowed to fish three days a week, the Government supplying the whaleboats, etc; the principal steer oar in the first boat being Te Kooti Rikirangi, who was always well behaved. This man had not joined the Hauhaus at Poverty Bay, but was supposed to have supplied the enemy with ammunition (caps). He was a wild, rollicking fellow, about thirty-five years of age, a dealer in horses, and much given to drink; so it was thought advisable to ship him off with the rest of the prisoners, although it was never clearly proved that he did supply the enemy with ammunition. Te Kooti not being a chief, but only what the Maoris call a tangata tutua (common man), no objection was made by his hapu (Atuina Mahaki) to his being sent away. On visiting the prisoners one morning after the boats had returned from a fishing expedition, I found Te Kooti in a very bad state—spitting blood. The doctor (Watson) placed him on the sick list. The natives got permission to place him on the hill above the whares, in a small house by himself; an old woman attending him, according to native custom. He was well looked after, and supplied with medical comforts, port wine, etc. The natives, thinking he would shortly die, actually began preparing a coffin for him. I often used to visit him, at which he seemed much pleased and grateful. To the astonishment of the other prisoners he recovered, which they looked upon as almost a miracle. He then commenced the Hauhau practices and became a great prophet. At that time an order came from the late Sir Donald McLean, that all the chiefs who had behaved well were to be released. They were sent back to New Zealand by the *St. Kilda*, with the exception of Kingita, a troublesome fellow, who was afterwards killed at Poverty Bay. I wrote to Sir Donald McLean (by private instructions from him), that the prisoners, after Te Kooti's revival, had become altered in demeanour, and that I thought something evil was brewing amongst them. Some time before this Te Kooti had been married by Captain Thomas to a native woman named Martha. Major Edwards was sent down as commissioner, and recommended that the guard should be doubled, and a strong redoubt built, he fixing the position. This recommendation was not put into force, but another commissioner was sent (Mr. Rolleston) with instructions to take all surveillance off the prisoners; much to my astonishment, and also that of the Resident Magistrate, Captain Thomas. Our morning roll-call was done away with; the prisoners could roam about wherever they liked on the island. They were also told they were in future to grow their own wheat, which they looked upon as a great evil, having been promised, on good behaviour, their freedom in three years. If Major Edwards's advice had been carried out, the prisoners would probably have never got away, and thousands would have been saved to the country, the terrible murders in Poverty Bay would not have been committed, and the prisoners would have been quietly released after the three years. I do not wish, by this short account, to palliate Te Kooti's doings on his arrival in New Zealand, as I shall always look upon him as a murderer of the deepest dye, who never ought to have been pardoned; but he certainly had a grievance in being sent away without a trial, not being a prisoner of war. I was ordered from the Chathams in February, 1868, returning with the guard. The rest of the story is too well known; the prisoners escaping in the following July."

After the capture of the *Rifleman* and the imprisonment of the settlers, Te Kooti acted with great moderation. The women and children were kindly treated by Te Kooti's orders. So soon as the events recorded had taken place, the prisoners began to embark their wives and families. Not a moment's time was lost, and no precaution neglected, and in one hour from the time of the outbreak the prisoners were on board. The ketch *Florence*, lying at anchor near, was boarded, the crew sent ashore, and then the cable was cut and the ketch sent after them—a simple and expeditious method of preventing pursuit. Almost the last man on board was Te Kooti, and as soon as he came on board he ordered the crew on deck, and gave them the choice between instant death and working the schooner to Poverty Bay. They wisely chose the latter, and were subsequently informed that their lives would be spared and the craft surrendered to them on arrival. Sail was made that evening, but a strong westerly wind prevented them beating out, and the schooner returned to her anchorage; the sails were furled, the crew ordered below, and Te Kooti took charge of the deck. On the morning of the 8th another start was made, this time with success, and nothing of importance occurred until the 9th, when, the vessel having been delayed for two days by head winds, Te Kooti ordered all the greenstone ornaments on board to be collected and thrown overboard as a propitiatory offering to Tangaroa (Neptune). This sacrifice was evidently not sufficient, for the wind continued in the same quarter; so an aged man, a relative of Te Kooti's was dragged on deck, his hands tied, and despite his prayers and lamentations, over he went. For some time the victim could be seen struggling in the water, but no one pitied him; or if they did, were wise enough not to say so, for after all he might have been a Jonah, as the wind, hitherto adverse, suddenly veered round to the right quarter. The Hauhaus behaved quietly enough during the remainder of the voyage, though vigilant as ever. On the 10th July, the schooner arrived at Whareongaonga, about 15 miles south of Poverty Bay. During the whole night the prisoners were employed in landing the cargo, and by the 11th, seventeen tons of flour, 5000 lbs. of sugar, beer, biscuits, and many packages of merchandise were on shore, besides forty rifles, ten fowling pieces, revolvers, swords, etc. This done, Te Kooti released the crew and told them to be gone.

In due time the news of the landing reached Major Biggs, the Resident Magistrate of the district. At first he would not believe the warnings, it seemed so improbable that the prisoners had been able to escape; but to solve the doubt he raised a force of 100 Europeans and Maoris, and started at once for the scene of action, arriving there on the following morning. The prisoners, about

190 in number, were found holding a strong position near the landing-place. The first step taken by Major Biggs was to send a Poverty Bay chief of Te Kooti's tribe with a message, to the effect that he would try and smooth over matters with the Government provided they would all surrender and give up their arms. This arrangement was scornfully rejected, Te Kooti replying that " God had given him arms and liberty, and that he was but an instrument in the hands of Providence, whose instructions he carried out." Major Biggs gave orders to commence the attack, but the friendly natives refused to move. Under these circumstances fighting was impossible and impolitic, for in the event of defeat our men would have been followed into the settled districts and the whole bay ravaged before another force could have been organised to meet them. On the same day the Hauhaus avoided our force, and commenced their inland march, carrying with them, over one of the most rugged districts in New Zealand, the whole of the loot taken in the schooner.

When it was found they had escaped, Major Biggs ordered Mr. Shipworth to follow them up with some friendly natives until he had definitely ascertained the line of retreat, when he was to cut across country and join the main body, who by that time would have taken post at Parapatu. This was a strategical post of great importance, as by the nature of the country the enemy would have to cross the Arai creek, a point just below the position taken up, and would thus come into collision with our force, whether he liked it or not. After four days' waiting at Parapatu the camp was out of rations, so Major Biggs started for supplies. On the morning of the sixth day Te Kooti arrived, drove our men from their advantageous position, and compelled our force to take advantage of the night to retreat, leaving behind them their horses, swords, and baggage, amounting to about £1,200.

Another force attempted to intercept Te Kooti at a place called Waihau, but here again the Europeans and semi-friendly natives were compelled to retreat after an engagement.

After the Europeans had re-organised and had obtained the leadership of Colonel Whitmore, they pursued and came up with Te Kooti on the bed of the Ruakituri river. The men had been without food since the previous evening, were knocked up with long marches through rough country, and were certainly not in a condition to encounter a well-armed and determined enemy in a position of their own choosing. Here another misfortune befel the pursuers, as in reconnoitring the enemy's position Captain Carr, Mr. Canning, and three others were killed, and Captain Tuke and five of his men wounded. The result of the fight was fatal to the future peace of the settled districts, as it enabled Te Kooti, although severely wounded in the foot, and having lost eight of his men, to camp at Puketapu, just beyond the scene of the fight, from the 8th of August to October 28th, during which period he sent messengers all over the island, proclaiming himself the saviour of his people, and exaggerating his success.

Recruits, as might be expected, came up rapidly to him. The position held by Te Kooti at Puketapu was inland, and equidistant from the two settlements of Te Wairoa and Poverty Bay. Consequently it was in his power to attack either place by a march of two or three days. Moreover, it was well known that he had declared his intention of taking revenge upon the settlers for having attacked him at Parapatu, Te Koriaka and Ruakituri. There were two routes by which the Hauhaus might reach Poverty Bay, one by way of Te Reinga and the other by Ngatapa. The latter route was twice as long as the first, and was overgrown with fern and scrub. For this reason Major Biggs selected the Te Reinga track as the special point for observation.

For some time previous to the massacre at Poverty Bay a general feeling of insecurity was prevalent among the settlers, and it was felt that some steps ought to be taken to fortify a place of rendezvous in case of need. The friendly Maoris volunteered to erect a pallisade if the Europeans would do the earth works. This was readily agreed to, but Major Biggs vetoed the proposition as unnecessary, but appointed the Toanga Redoubt as the mustering place in case of alarm. Certain settlers, dissatisfied with this result, formed themselves into a vigilance committee to watch the Patutahi ford of the Waipaoa river. For nights this duty was carefully performed, and would probably have continued to the salvation of the Bay, but on the Thursday before the massacre a very old settler called on his vigilant neighbours and informed them that the Hauhaus were in the Patutahi Valley. Major Biggs was informed of this, and replied, " You are all in an unnecessary state of alarm, for I shall have twenty-four hours' notice before anything further can happen."

But about midnight on the 9th November, 1868, the Hauhaus crossed the Patutahi ford on their murderous errand. Mr. Wylie's house was the first on their line of march, and the owner was sitting at a table writing; but so sure was Te Kooti of this man that he told his men to go and finish the Matawhero settlers first, as they were certain to get Wylie on their return. From this point the Hauhaus appear to have broken up into small parties. Some went inland to Messrs. Dodd and Peppard's station, while the main body attacked the more densely settled districts of Matawhero. Messrs. Dodd and Peppard appear to have been the first persons killed. A Mr. Butters, who had been engaged to press wool for them, rode up to the woolshed wondering that no one appeared, and finally he walked up to the back door and found the two owners dead. Instead of seeking his own safety, Mr. Butters very gallantly rode to Waeranga-a-hiki and warned the inmates of the mission station and force. From there he went on to Matawhero to perform the same good office for the settlers there. How he escaped is a miracle, for he must have ridden through the midst of the enemy.

At Major Biggs's he found the Hauhaus in possession, and at Mann's house he saw the owner, his wife, and baby lying outside mutilated, and cne of them burnt. When the natives reached Major Biggs's, they found him writing, it is supposed, the orders for the out-settlers to muster at Turanga. They knocked at the door, and Biggs asked them what they wanted. The Hauhaus replied that they wished to see him. Biggs evidently saw that the long-dreaded raid had come, but before opening the door he called to his wife to escape by the back. She refused to leave him. As he stood in the doorway the Hauhaus shot him. He fell forward into the verandah, and the fiends then rushed in and tomahawked Mrs. Biggs, her baby, and the servant. A boy who was in the house escaped by the back door after the Major was shot, and, hidden in a flax-bush, witnessed part of the tragedy.

Another party went to Captain Wilson's. The Captain, like Major Biggs, was engaged in writing when the Hauhaus knocked at the door. They announced themselves as the bearer of a letter from the principal chief of the Bay. Wilson evidently suspected their errand, for he told them to put the letter under the door; at the same time he looked out of the window and saw a number of men moving about. This roused his suspicions, and he at once roused his man-servant, Moran. Meanwhile the Hauhaus were trying to batter down the door with a log of wood, but a shot from Wilson's revolver stopped them, and forced them to adopt the less dangerous plan of setting fire to the house at either end. Captain Wilson defended his wife and family until it was a choice between being burnt alive or taking the Hauhau offer of life for himself and family if he would surrender quietly. There was just a chance that they might keep their promise, and he surrendered. His captors led him in the direction of the river bank, when suddenly a Hauhau rushed at Moran and tomahawked him, and at the same moment Captain Wilson was shot through the back. Mrs. Wilson was savagely bayonetted, and only one little boy escaped; he was being carried by his father when he fell, and in the confusion managed to escape into the scrub unnoticed. Strange to say, the settlers in the vicinity did not hear the firing, for the Hauhaus found the Messrs. Walsh, Padbourne, McCulloch and others at their homes, unconscious of the tragedies that were being enacted in their immediate neighbourhood. McCulloch was shot while milking a cow; his wife, carrying a baby and attended by her young brother, tried to escape, but was overtaken and tomahawked, together with her child. The boy, more fortunate, escaped. Mr. Cadel's house was next visited. He had been away from home that night, and was returning in the early morning, when he walked right into one of these gang of murderers and was shot dead. His store was then looted. The Hauhaus got violently drunk, and galloped about the country, shooting all the friendly natives obnoxious to Te Kooti.

While the settlers about Matawhero were being murdered, the families living in the vicinity of the Patutahi Ford were reserved for the final *coup*, it being supposed they could not escape. Nor

S

could they have done so had not one of them—a Mr. Firmin—been awakened during the night by the sound of musketry. The sound was not unusual, but, in the then unsettled state of affairs, it was sufficient to keep him awake during the remainder of the night, and send him out at grey dawn to reconnoitre. At the ford he met a maori, and hailed him to know the meaning of the firing, which was still going on. The reply was, " The Hauhaus are killing the pakeha !" Mr. Firmin at once warned his neighbours—Wylie, Stevenson, and Benson—and these people, taking their children, fled towards Te Wairoa, across the Toanga Ford. Messrs. Hawthorne and Strong, who lived at some little distance from the others, had been forgotten in the hurry and confusion of their departure; but Mr. Wylie remembered them just before it was too late, and asked one of the men to return and warn them. This was a service of great danger, yet Mr. Benson never hesitated, but returned at once. About an hour after these fugitives had crossed the river, Te Kooti and twenty Hauhaus galloped up to the native village near the ford, and ordered the chief, Tautari, to point out the route taken by Wylie. The gallant old man refused to do so, and Te Kooti, finding his threats and promises disregarded, lost patience, and ordered his men to kill him and his two children. This was done before the wife's eyes, who was then questioned, and threatened with the same fate if obstinate; but she, equally faithful, and more prudent than her husband, misdirected the Hauhaus by declaring that the fugitives had taken the inland track. The murderers, completely deceived, galloped off on a wrong scent, Te Kooti boasting that he would cut pieces of flesh off Wylie until he died.

The young boy who escaped from Major Biggs's house succeeded in reaching Mr. Bloomfield's and roused the sleeping inmates. There were only ladies and children in the house, but they succeeded in escaping, though people were being murdered on both sides. While the enemy were attacking Mr. Goldsmith's house, a Mrs. James, mother of the boy just mentioned, was living in the barn with her eight children; she was roused by the shots, and saw sufficient to prove that the Hauhaus were in the Bay. She behaved with admirable coolness. Collecting her children she slipped over the steep bank of the river, and crawled for more than a mile under the shadow of the cliffs until she was able to enter the scrub, and reached Turanganui twenty-four hours after the first alarm.

The narrow escapes during this massacre would fill a volume. The most wonderful escape was, however, that of little James Wilson, who, as already mentioned, escaped into the scrub when his father fell. On the 16th November, seven days after the massacre, parties were sent out to bury the dead, and ascertain if any had escaped, and were in hiding. One of these parties, consisting of a Mr. Maynard and two comrades, saw a poodle dog run into a scrub of briars. Maynard recognised the dog as having belonged to Captain Wilson. They called and coaxed the animal in vain; it remained hidden, and this obstinacy led them to the natural conclusion that someone was hiding. A search was instituted, and, after nearly half-an-hour's work, their patience was rewarded by finding little James Wilson, with the dog held tightly in his arms. The boy had been too frightened to discriminate between friend and foe, but was greatly delighted when he recognised Maynard. He told him that he had lost his way while trying to reach Turanganui, to bring help for his mother, who was lying wounded in an outhouse at their place. After escaping from his father's murderers he had wandered about, sleeping in outhouses for several nights; often close to the enemy. At last he found his way back to what had been his home, and saw the bodies of his father, brothers, and sisters, but not his mother, until he happened to take shelter in the outhouse, where, to his great delight, he found her alive. When the boy had told his tale, Maynard galloped off to Wilson's. On arrival at the place they knocked at the door of the small building, but received no answer; they then called Mrs. Wilson by name, and instantly heard her say, "Thank God, help has arrived; bring me some water." After her husband fell, the poor lady was stabbed with bayonets, and beaten with the butt of a rifle, until the fiends thought her dead; but later in the day she recovered consciousness, and managed to crawl to what had been her home. Here she got some water, and then took shelter in the outhouse, which was less likely to be visited by the enemy than the house. Here she was found by her son in the manner already related, and fed with eggs or anything the lad could forage. Mrs. Wilson was carried that same day to Turanganui. For some time it was thought she would recover, but her injuries were too severe, and she died after her arrival at Napier. In the massacre thirty-three white people and thirty-seven friendly natives were killed.

Lieutenant Gascoigne, when warned by his scouts that the Hauhaus were in the Bay, rode as fast as he could to the Muriwai. On his arrival he found that he was senior officer in the Bay, and he determined to reach Turanganui at all risks, as there was no officer there to direct operations. To go by the beach was impossible, as it swarmed with the enemy, so he seized a boat and pulled across the bay. On arrival at Turanganui, Gascoigne found the old redoubt crowded with men, women, and children, and was told that a whaleboat had gone off to overtake the schooner *Tawera*, which was at some distance in the offing. She was fortunately brought back, and the women and children were shipped off in her to Napier. The friendly chief Henare Potae armed his men as best he could, and awaited with the settlers the expected attack of Te Kooti. The attack was never made, as Te Kooti was satisfied with what he had done, and contented himself with burning and looting the settlers' houses and coercing the friendly natives to join him. Within a week Major Westrupp and Captain Tuke arrived from Napier, and brought with them 300 natives, and the Hauhaus retired to Patutahi, where they collected their plunder.

The first duty performed was the burial of those murdered on the 9th. Most of them were found in a dreadfully mutilated condition. The bodies of Major Biggs and his wife were never found, but it is supposed that they were burnt in the house, as a lady's hand was found among the ashes. Mr. Cadel's body was found in a better condition than the others, for it had been guarded for seven days by his faithful retriever dog. By this time the friendly natives had arrived to the number of 600 men, but of a very indifferent class as regards fighting. They were placed under command of Lieutenant Gascoigne, and on November 21st that officer overtook the rear-guard of the enemy at Patutahi and shot two of them. Quantities of loot, which the Hauhaus had apparently been unable to carry away, were found at this place, and several dead bodies of friendly natives were seen, who had been shot by Te Kooti's orders. At Pukepuke another encampment was found, with more dead bodies, and the carts and sledges of the murdered settlers, which had brought the loot thus far. About dusk on the 23rd our men came up with the main body of the enemy, who were encamped on the Te Karetu creek with their women and children, and immediate attack was made, but our native allies were driven back. We lost five killed and twenty wounded, and the Hauhaus lost about twenty men. Our men rifle-pitted the ridge in front of the Hauhau encampments, and remained there a week without anything particular being done. Up to this time the force had been supplied with rations and ammunition from the depôt at Patutahi by means of a string of pack-horses, under the charge of Sergt.-Major Butters. But this did not last long, as the opportunity was too tempting for Te Kooti, who sent sixty men under Baker, the notorious half-caste, to take the depôt, cut off the convoy, and capture all the ammunition he could.

The party got in the rear of our men in the line of supply, and though the men escaped only by a timely warning, the Hauhaus captured sundry kegs of ammunition, and so large a stock of food that they were unable to carry it away. Ultimately, reinforcements having arrived, an assault was made on the Hauhau lines, and the enemy compelled to beat a retreat, losing over thirty-four of their men, including the celebrated fighting chiefs Nama, Kenu, and Henare Parata. Nama was wounded, but taken alive. Te Kooti himself had a narrow escape. He was still suffering from a wound he had received at Ruakiture, and was carried away up the bed of the creek on a woman's back. On the following morning the chiefs Ropata and Hotene went out to reconnoitre, and could see the Hauhau stronghold on the forest-clad peak of Ngatapa.

On the morning of the 5th, Ropata marched to attack Ngapata. The pa had tied lines of stony earthworks, extending across a small flat below the peak, either end resting on a cliff. A gun going off accidentally, the enemy answered with a volley, and instantly a general panic set in, our native allies retreating with the greatest celerity for nearly half a mile, and all efforts to bring them back were found unavailing. Ropata, with seventeen others, commenced the attack upon the pa, working up the sides of the cliffs, within twenty-five yards of the first line of parapet. Thirty-nine more men were induced to come to their support; but Ropata was compelled to retreat at dusk, and was so disgusted that he went right back to Turanga. Colonel Whitmore soon afterwards arrived at Ngatapa with 300 men, but hearing that the Hauhaus were burning their whares, preparatory to retreat, gave credence to the tale, and returned to Turanga. Te Kooti, on hearing that Colonel Whitmore had retired, raided down upon the Arai and Pipiwhakau bush, where his men murdered Mr. Fergusson, young Wylie, and a friendly Maori. Colonel Whitmore at once returned, and after some days compelled Te Kooti to retreat to the Uriwera tribe.

Colonel Whitmore, having driven Te Kooti from Poverty Bay, turned his attention to those troublesome people known as the Uriwera, to whom Te Kooti had gone. On the 19th of March, our force reached Matata. Whether Te Kooti had foreseen this combined attack or not it is impossible to say, but he certainly anticipated it by striking one of those rapid blows for which he is so famous. On the 18th, a kokiri of one hundred men, directed by Te Kooti, attacked the settlement of Whakatane. An old Frenchman, Jean Garraud, was tomahawked, but the Hauhaus were beaten off the large pa with heavy loss; although the pa, in a couple of days, surrendered to Te Kooti.

Major Mair coming up, Te Kooti fell back to a strong position in the hills, from which he retreated to Tauaroa, where Major Mair came up with him and surrounded him, but owing to the absence of proper support on the part of some native allies, Te Kooti effected his escape. Te Kooti, after his retreat from Tauaroa, retired to Ruatahuna, where he called a meeting of the Uriwera, and proposed to attack either Mohaka or Te Wairoa. The Uriwera chief proposed to join him, provided he would make a raid upon Mohaka, which was the more unprotected place of the two. With one hundred men, selected from the mixed tribes who accompanied him, Te Kooti pushed on to the Upper Mohaka, and arrived at a native village before daylight. The native inhabitants, thoroughly surprised, were taken prisoners and butchered without much noise, the tomahawk being the weapon used. He then crossed the river to attack the houses of the Europeans. Messrs. Lavin and Cooper were met on the road, and the latter was shot, but the former, who was not hit, attempted to escape with his wife. They were, however, overtaken and shot. Three little children of Lavin's, while playing on the river bank, were tomahawked, as also Mr. Wilkinson, making in all seven Europeans killed. Later on in the day, the Hauhaus marched down the river and attacked the Huke Pa, which had a garrison of six men and several women and children, the fighting men being away on an expedition against Te Wara. The defenders, though few in number, were under the influence of a courageous man named Heta, and they

s*

refused to surrender, and defended themselves all that day and night against Te Kooti, who, finding he was losing time, had recourse to stratagem. Heta was again summoned to surrender, but again refused; but another chief in the pa (Rutene) went out to meet Te Kooti, and was persuaded by him to go to the next pa and fetch the son of the head chief, Ropihana. Te Kooti rightly concluded that if he had this chief he could place him in front and march up to the pa with impunity, for none of the Mohaka tribe would dare to endanger the safety of their chief by firing. Rutene was successful in his mission. Te Kooti now felt safe, and put Ropihana in front of his men and marched on the Huke Pa, and demanded admittance. Heta was called upon to open the gate, but refused; but Rutene and the Hauhaus lifted the gate off its hinges, and the whole party entered. The defenders were disarmed. Heta refused, and, saying "We know we are being disarmed that we may be more easily killed; but if we have to die so must you," raised his rifle and fired at Te Kooti. A Hauhau, who was standing near, knocked up the muzzle, and Te Kooti again escaped. Heta was shot at once, and a general massacre ensued. Rutene was shot, and Ropihana wounded, but he succeeded in escaping to the big pa. All the women and children that could be found were soon dispatched, and then Te Kooti turned his attention tò the big pa.

News of Te Kooti's advance was sent to Te Wairoa, and a force was sent to the assistance of the beleaguered Maoris. A party of Mohaka Maoris, headed by Trooper Hill, broke through Te Kooti's lines and entered the pa, and after several days' siege Te Kooti moved off. Our loss by this raid was seven Europeans and fifty-seven friendly Maoris killed. Te Kooti advanced to meet Colonel Whitmore, but too late to meet him at Ruatatuna. The active rebel then at once marched for Heruiwi, an old native village on the edge of the main bush, overlooking the Taupo plains, where he could watch the movements of the pakeha. While at this place, two troopers of the Bay of Plenty Cavalry were waylaid, and one of them shot. On the 7th June, he came in sight of Opepe, and was astonished to see smoke rising from the deserted whares. Te Kooti ordered some of his men to saunter up and pretend they were friendly natives, while the main body crept up a ravine and cut the troopers off from the bush. The Hauhaus walked up to the unsuspecting men, who proved to be a party of the Bay of Plenty Cavalry. The party were somewhat startled by the sight of these armed natives, but became reassured, and entered into friendly conversation. During the conversation the Hauhaus gradually got between the troopers and their arms which had foolishly been left in the whares. Some of the men, seeing other Maoris coming out of the bush in skirmishing order, tried to get their weapons, but were stopped by the Hauhaus, who, having no further need of concealment, commenced the massacre. Nine troopers were killed immediately, but three succeeded in escaping. Te Kooti, after taking all the arms and ammunition of the party, continued his march to Waitahuna, where he camped, and Te Kooti's influence became supreme in the Taupo, and shortly after paid a visit to King Tawhaio. From this Te Kooti returned to defend himself from the systematic campaign that had been organised against him.

After one or two skirmishes, Te Kooti fell back, after capturing four scouts, while asleep in a whare, and having seen them chopped up and thrown into a swamp. At Tokanu, Te Kooti was attacked by a mixed force and sustained a signal defeat, which cost him his prestige among the inland tribes, and lost him the possible support of Rewi, with his 600 fighting men. At Kaikeriri, Colonel McDonnell's pursuing force again came up with the Hauhaus, who suffered severely in men, and were compelled to take to the bush. On our side we lost Captain St. George and Winiata, the most renowned fighting man of the Ngatihaus. Te Kooti himself was wounded in this engagement. A bullet wounded his thumb and forefinger, cut the third finger completely off, and passed through the fleshy part of his side. A smart search for the rebel was maintained, and our forces succeeded in finding him at the Tatapa Pa, but he and the garrison bolted, leaving 80 horses behind them. After his defeat, Te Kooti retired with his followers to Te Wera, a wild tract of bush country. In this *terra incognita* Te Kooti remained hidden from his pursuers, but at last was surrounded, and a party of eighteen Europeans got on a terrace not more than twenty yards from the huts, but divided from the Hauhaus by a deep creek. Te Kooti was seen and recognised by several of the Poverty Bay settlers, and could easily have been shot, as he was not more than thirty yards away, but our men withheld their fire, trusting the native allies would perform their share of the work. An alarm, unfortunately, was given and Te Kooti again succeeded in making his escape. Vigilant search was made for him by several search parties up to 1871, but without success, and in that year Te Kooti crossed into the King Country, where he has remained ever since.

From Te Kooti's first landing in Poverty Bay he seemed to bear a charmed life, as, although force after force was dispatched against him, something in his favour always happened to facilitate his escape, even when dangerously wounded, and three-parts of his followers killed. On one occasion an old woman took him on her back to a place of safety. Circumstances seemed to favour him in every way, for often when he was surrounded, seemingly without a hope left, he would escape as if by a miracle. There is perhaps nothing more astonishing in Te Kooti's career than the power he possessed over the minds of his fellow Maoris. Occasionally successful in his raids, yet invariably beaten in open fight, he could nevertheless persuade or frighten any tribe into joining him. After the hardships he endured and the losses sustained during the Poverty Bay campaign, where not less than 150 of his men were killed, the Uriweras joined him readily to attack Whakatane; and although they lost twenty men there, and were driven back to their own country, yet it did not prevent them from again coming to his assistance at Mohaka and following on to Taupo, where they were again beaten in three successive fights, losing upwards of fifty men, and being literally hunted out of the district. Yet no sooner had Te Kooti reached Patetere than a portion of the Ngaiterangi and Ngatiraukawa were ready and anxious to share his fortunes.

In 1882, the then Native Minister, Mr. Bryce, from motives of policy, condoned Te Kooti's offences by including him in the general amnesty extended to Te Wetere of Mokau and other natives implicated in tragedies during the dark period of our history. The reason offered for this clemency is the fact that Te Kooti professes that when he arrived from the Chatham Islands he had no other desire or intention but to return peacefully to his settlement, but being attacked by the colonial forces he was driven into retaliation, and that his mode of warfare was not different from that which Maoris considered perfectly fair. Since Te Kooti's pardon he has visited, with a large escort, many of the places rendered famous by his atrocities, and even contemplates a visit to Poverty Bay.

COLONEL BALNEAVIS.

COLONEL BALNEAVIS.

COLONEL BALNEAVIS, to whom the principal credit belongs for the efficiency of the Auckland militia, arrived in the colony in 1845 with his regiment the 58th). He took part in all the conflicts of Heke's war, and resigned his captaincy in the Imperial service in 1858, when the old "Black Cuffs," as the 58th were called, left for England. On the outbreak of hostilities in 1860, he took an active part in the organisation of the Waikato militia, and soon converted his raw levies into finely disciplined troops —steady under fire, and capable of enduring the hardships of a bush campaign. He had made a life-long study of field tactics and fortifications; and a model of a Maori pa, constructed by him, and sent home to one of the English military colleges, created great interest at the time amongst military scientists, in view of the astonishing resistance that these apparently flimsy strongholds had given to our troops, armed with all the appliances of modern warfare. The Colonel was also a most accomplished linguist, being able to converse freely in Maori, Arabic, French, Maltese, Italian, Greek, German, and Spanish. He came of good old military stock, his father being Lieut.-General Balneavis, who commanded the 65th Regiment through the Peninsula war, and was subsequently Governor and Commandant at Malta. Colonel Balneavis died at Auckland, in August, 1876, deeply regretted both by his old brother soldiers and by the general public. A public demonstration was made at his funeral, and the colours of his old regiment, which are now deposited in the Supreme Court buildings, Auckland, were sadly borne by his old comrades in the *cortege*.

CAPTAIN HANDLEY.

———

APTAIN HENRY E. HANDLEY entered the army as a very young man, and served with the Scots Greys during the Crimean War, commanding the right troop of the regiment at McKenzie's Heights, and in the charge at Balaklava, where he was wounded. He was also present at the battle of Inkerman and siege of Sebastopol. On leaving the Imperial service, and settling in this colony, he volunteered his services, and was appointed field adjutant to Colonel Herrick during the expedition to Waikare, Moana, and Taupo.

Extract from "Nolan's History of the Russian War":—"At the charge of Balaklava, Colonel Griffith, of the Scots Greys, got shot in the head; Brevet-Major Clarke, a sabre cut at the back of the neck; Cornet Prendergast, shot through the foot; and Cornet Handley, stabbed in the side and arm. This officer was at one time during the charge surrounded by four Cossacks, three of whom he shot with his revolver, and the fourth was cut down by his sergeant. I saw this gallant young fellow, a few hours after the battle, leaving the temporary hospital, saying his wounds were not of sufficient consequence to keep him from rejoining his regiment."

MAJOR TUKE.

MAJOR TUKE.

---

*Hand-to-hand fight at Kairomiromi—Pursuit of Volkner's murderers—
Wounded at Ruakitura—Command of the Taranaki district.*

MAJOR TUKE first joined the Volunteer Cavalry Corps, then just formed under Captain Gordon (late of the Enniskillen Dragoons), early in 1864, and was elected officer without opposition, and for some time both the training and the drilling of the corps were left in his hands. On the breaking-out of the war on the East Coast Major Tuke volunteered for active service, and obtained permission to accompany Major Fraser's company of militia to the scene of operations at Waiapu, where on arrival he was attached to the late Major Biggs's company of volunteers, then actively engaged against the rebels. He was present at the storming and capture of the pa Kairomiromi (where the fighting was of a most severe character, being a hand-to-hand struggle), and at the reconnaissance and capture of Pukemaire. He accompanied Major Biggs in his forced marches through the bush in pursuit of the rebels, and was present at the engagement at Kawakawa and capture of the Hunga-Hunga-Toroa pa, where he led his men up the cliff in the rear of the pa—a most perilous undertaking, but which soon decided the fate of the day; and on both of these occasions he was mentioned in despatches. In the meantime he was constantly engaged scouting the district, until he was ordered to Poverty Bay to take part in the attack on the Waerenga-a-hika pa. He was afterwards detailed for service at the Wairoa, and participated in many skirmishes involving loss of life. He received a commission in the Hawke's Bay Militia, and was shortly afterwards sent as officer in command of the prisoners at the Chatham Islands, where he remained for some months. Recalled to the Wairoa, he was again employed on active service against the enemy, and on the completion of his term of service was offered, and accepted, a command in No. 1 company of Armed Constabulary, and was sent to Opotiki after the murder of the Rev. Mr. Volkner, to avenge his death. He was actively engaged there and at Whakatane, and in the operations up the Waimana and the Waioeka Gorge, and other skirmishes more or less severe.

On the escape of the prisoners from the Chatham Islands he accompanied the division under Colonel Sir George Whitmore to

Poverty Bay, and took part in the pursuit of Te Kooti. At Ruakitura he was severely wounded, which caused him to be invalided for some time. After recovery, he was again detailed to the Wairoa district, in charge of Colonial forces during a very troublesome and anxious time, being daily threatened with an attack from a large body of insurgents. Here he received a most complimentary address from the settlers before leaving, which by the rules of the service he had to return. On the Poverty Bay massacre taking place he was immediately ordered to the scene of the disaster, and acted as second in command to Major Westrupp until the arrival of the reinforcements under Colonel Whitmore. He led the party who volunteered to go out and recover the bodies of the slain, when he was once more ordered to the Wairoa, and from thence to the West Coast on the murder of the Rev. Mr. Whiteley. He was then despatched with No. 7 company of Armed Constabulary to Pukearuhe, to guard the northern frontier of Taranaki, when he was promoted to the charge of the Taranaki district, and on the retirement of Major Turner, to the further command of the combined districts of Patea and Taranaki, where he remained until 1879, when the Parihaka natives began to be troublesome, and he had orders to organise the force assembled at Oakura under Colonel Roberts, preparatory to the demonstration made on that settlement. Serving as second in command on the day of the capture of Te Whiti, to him was given the post of honour, and, assisted by Captains Gudgeon and Newall, he arrested the prophets Te Whiti, Tohu, and Hiroki, and dispersed their followers, amounting to the number of 1,600. In September, 1883, in consequence of an expected disturbance at Kawhia, Major Tuke was despatched with a company of the Armed Constabulary to take the command of that district, where he still remains, and at the request of the natives was appointed Resident Magistrate.

This brave officer having served the Government of the colony for upwards of twenty years, being under fire often and seriously wounded once, one can only wonder how it is that the Government has managed to keep so valuable an officer a major ever since the year 1867, and without bestowing on him the decoration of the New Zealand Cross he so justly merited.

T

CAPTAIN CRAPP.

CAPTAIN CRAPP.

CAPTAIN CRAPP, who joined the colonial force about the year 1864, has the credit of performing one of the most daring acts during the war. On the 7th of May, 1869, the scouts led by Sergeant White were ambuscaded by the Uriweras, at a crossing of the Whakatane River, where the brave Sergeant White fell, and although quickly carried out by two of his comrades, under a heavy fire, to a place of safety, was found to be dead. At the time, the enemy held every piece of vantage ground, and had posted themselves very strongly on a fern and bush ridge that commanded the crossing of the river, up the bed of which the force had to march, it being impossible to cross while the enemy held the ridge. Colonel St. John, seeing the position, ordered Sub-Inspector McDonnell to support the scouts, with 40 men of No. 2 division Armed Constabulary, in dislodging them. White having fallen, it was necessary that an officer should take command of the scouts in his place, which Sub-Inspector Crapp volunteered to do. The track he and his men had to take wound up a spur of the Range, covered with high fern, scrub, and patches of bush, while at the top rifle-pits were so placed that the occupants could fire down the track for one hundred yards at least, which was too narrow for more than one man to advance at a time, and every man of the column felt certain that the leader of this small party would be shot ere he reached the top, for, if not ambuscaded at the turn in the track, certain death appeared to await him when within range of the rifle-pits. All these dangers did not deter or daunt Crapp, who advanced steadily up the spur, about twenty yards in front of his men, he having instructed them to keep that distance in rear, that he might draw the enemy's first volley on himself, and enable them to rush the pits before they could reload. Thrice the enemy fired from ambushes on this brave young officer, but luckily without effect; and at last, presumably fearing to come to close quarters with one so undaunted, backed by forty resolute men, they evacuated their rifle-pits and position, and disappeared in the dense bush before Crapp and his men could reach the summit of the range. This act of daring deserved the decoration of the New Zealand Cross.

MAJOR WESTRUPP.

MAJOR CHARLES WESTRUPP joined Von Tempsky's Forest Rangers towards the end of 1863, and soon after was commissioned an ensign in that corps. He was promoted to lieutenant early in 1864, and served under Major Von Tempsky, in the Waikato, until the middle of 1865, when he was promoted to a captaincy, and took a company of Forest Rangers round to Waiapu (East Cape), where he did good service, under the late Major Fraser and Captain R. Biggs, throughout the East Coast campaign. He was present at the attack on Pukemaire, the taking of Hunga-hunga-Toroa, Waerengahika, and the fighting in the Wairoa, in October, 1866-7. After the murder of Major Biggs, in November, 1868, he was placed in command of the Poverty Bay district, and gave orders for the pursuit of Te Kooti by the Napier natives, under Major Gascoigne, who overtook and defeated the rebels at Mangakaretu, killing 63 on the spot, Te Kooti himself being amongst the wounded, who retreated to Ngatipa.

Captain Westrupp now received his majority, and was left in command at Poverty Bay, while Colonel Whitmore directed the subsequent operations ending in the capture of Ngatipa. Major Westrupp shortly after retired from the service, settling down as a sheep farmer on a run in the Poverty Bay district. He was much liked by his officers and men, and was distinguished for his coolness and intrepidity in action.

T*

MAJOR GASCOIGNE.

MAJOR GASCOIGNE.

*Services in the East Cape expedition—Historical account of Poverty Bay
massacre—Guarding the wrong track—Burying the murdered settlers—
A gallant defence at Makaratu.*

MAJOR GASCOIGNE joined the Colonial Defence Force,
as lieutenant, in 1863, and served with the East Cape
expedition in 1865; was present at the attack on
Hatepe, and at the storming of Pakairomi-romi;
assisted in the assault of Pukemaire and several other minor
engagements. He served with the Ruakakuri expedition, and
was appointed officer-in-charge of the Poverty Bay Scouts, in
1868, and was also in command of the East Coast friendly natives
in pursuit of Te Kooti, after the massacre at Poverty Bay.
He took part in the attack at Patutahi, which, after eight days'
fighting, ended in the capture of the entrenchments. He was
present at Mangakaretu, as also at the operations and taking of
Ngatapa. He served against Titokowaru, 1869; was at the
capture of Tauranga-hika, Whereroa, Te Ngaiere, Waitotara,
Otauto, and Paingaroa. He rose to the rank of major in Militia,
and sub-inspector of Armed Constabulary, and is now stationed
with his company in Waikato.

This young and active officer was placed in charge of the scouts
chosen to watch the movements of Te Kooti and guard the district
from his threats to take utu on the Poverty Bay settlers for
transporting him to the Chatham Islands, and had his suggestions
been adopted, the massacre, in all probability, would have been
averted. His idea was that he was guarding the wrong track;
that Te Kooti would come in by an old track, now grown up, but
known to himself and Te Kooti, which he several times represented
to the commandant of the district, and had once or twice ridden
over to examine it, against orders, as Major Biggs was of a
different opinion. Consequently this track was left unguarded,
and the result was that Te Kooti, believing that he alone knew of
this old route, and that he would be safe from molestation in
coming that way, although many miles out of the direct road, took
it, and one night surprised the district, massacring Major Biggs,
Captain Wilson, their wives and children, and settlers to the
number of 33, besides 37 friendly natives, while Captain Gascoigne
and his men were carefully watching the more direct route. His

own account of the Poverty Bay massacre, never before published, is given *verbatim* below. It is concise and plainly written, no attempt to disguise or palliate the truth, but is a narrative of events as they occurred, and will one day be included in the future history of New Zealand. Captain Gascoigne was continually mentioned in general orders, yet shared the fate of so many of our bravest men, their services never having been recognised by the decoration of the Cross they well merited.

MAJOR GASCOIGNE'S ACCOUNT OF THE POVERTY BAY MASSACRE, 9TH NOVEMBER, 1868.

After Te Kooti had made good his escape from Colonel Whitmore's pursuit of him, up the Ruatakuri River, early in 1868, and obtained the alliance of the Uriwera tribe, he was said to have declared his intention of exacting utu from the Poverty Bay settlers for having tried to intercept him. Major Biggs represented the dangerous position of the settlers so strongly to the Government that at last he was authorised to place nine men and one officer to watch the country between the upper Wairoa River and Poverty Bay. This party was to act as an outlying picket. Previous to this the settlers had been paying three men to watch the valley of the Patutahi creek. Our orders from Major Biggs were as follows :—To camp at a bit of bush on the Te Reinga road from the Wairoa ; to watch that road constantly ; to have a sentry on the road at night and during the day on the top of the hill, which commanded a view of the road for several miles ; to scout daily to our right and left front, and to report constantly to him. Major Biggs felt sure that Te Kooti would advance by the Te Reinga road, and refused to spare men to watch the Ngatapa track, which was completely overgrown at the time, and supposed to be impassable.

On 7th November, three of us scouted in the direction of Ngatapa as far as Mangakaretu, but could not discover any signs of natives having been in that part of the country for years. The furthest part of the track was quite obliterated by the dense growth of scrub. We reported to Major Biggs, who ordered us not to scout any more in that direction, but to keep an extra sharp look-out on the main track, as he " expected Te Kooti would move down in a few days, and that he intended to order all the settlers to come into Turanganui." Our party consisted of five whites and five natives. Two of the latter were at the Big Bush, on leave, on the afternoon of the 8th, and at daylight on the morning of the 9th, these two men galloped into our camp with the news that Biggs and all the settlers had been killed during the night by the Hauhaus. We snatched up our arms and rode back to Poverty Bay as fast as we could, narrowly escaping from a large party of the enemy on the way.

We meant to get orders from Captain Westrupp, but on reaching his place at the Big Bush, we found that he had left for Wairoa, with a party of women and children, by the coast road

We determined to push on to Turanganui, and as the Hauhaus were in numbers before us, we seized a boat, sent our horses adrift, and pulled across the bay. Three of our men (natives) stopped at the pa on the big river, and, with all the natives there, joined Te Kooti next day. On reaching Turanganui, we found that a number of settlers, with women and children, had collected with the intention of escaping on board a couple of Captain Read's schooners, which were in the bay. We sent the women and children to Napier by the vessels, but detained all the men to defend Turanganui until assistance should reach us.

The Hauhaus reconnoitred our position, but did not attack us, and contented themselves with burning all the houses beyond the range of our rifles, and looting everything they could carry off. Te Kooti was employed in forcing or persuading all the Maoris about Makaraka and the Big Bush to join him, which they all did. We collected all the private property we could, and stored it in the redoubt, to save it from being stolen by the friendly natives, who began to join us.

In a few days Major Westrupp and Captain Tuke arrived from Napier with four hundred friendly natives, and the Hauhaus collected at Patutahi began to retreat with their plunder. The first thing we did was to find and bury the murdered settlers; this was sad and horrible work, and had to be done with strong covering parties of the friendly natives. The bodies of those killed had generally been dragged clear of the houses before the latter were burnt, and many of the bodies were dreadfully mutilated; some had been partly eaten by pigs, and some had numerous bayonet stabs. The men had been mostly shot, and the children tomahawked. We buried Major Biggs and his wife and child in one grave, and his two servants in another; also Captain Wilson and his children were buried together. Captain Wilson's son James, about six or seven years old, had escaped death in some way, and was found by one of our men in the fern next day; the little fellow pointed out where his mother was hidden, and both were brought into Turanganui; but Mrs. Wilson was so badly wounded that she only survived a short time. Besides these two families, Mr. and Mrs. Mann, Messrs. Peppard and Dodd, Sergt.-Major Walsh, and many others, whose names we did not know at that time, were slaughtered in cold blood during the dreadful night of the 8th of November.

On the 21st the Hawke's Bay natives, under the chiefs Renata Kawepo, Karauria, Henare Tomoana, and Tareha, and the scouts, marched in pursuit of the Hauhaus, and overtook a party of them laden with plunder at Patutahi; we shot two of them there. On the evening of the 23rd, we came up with their main body at Makaratu, strongly entrenched on the bank of the creek, and close to the edge of some heavy timber. The Hauhaus immediately attacked us on all sides, but we stubbornly held the ridge overlooking their main position, and contrived to entrench ourselves after a fashion by digging holes with sticks, bayonets, and knives.

For eight days the Napier natives defended themselves on this ridge, and on the third day we had nothing but fern root to eat, and had nearly expended the ammunition; for the enemy had seized the supplies sent up to us from Turanganui, and routed the escort that came with them. During this time we lost thirty-five men, killed and wounded; among the killed was the chief Karauria, one of the best leaders on our side. At last, by sending back a strong party as escort, we obtained a supply of biscuit and ammunition, which enabled us to hold out to the end of the month, when Captain Preece and the chief Ropata arrived with a reinforcement of the Ngatiporou tribe; and advancing by our right flank, they turned the nearest Hauhau rifle-pits, and then, with the scouts and part of the Napier natives, rushed down the slope, and carried the main position of the Hauhaus by storm, killing sixty-three of the enemy, including Nama and other noted Hauhau leaders. Two of the scouts were severely wounded here.

Te Kooti retreated to his almost impregnable stronghold, Ngatapa, which, however, was taken a few weeks afterwards by a force under the command of Colonel Whitmore, and where we again inflicted severe loss on him, killing many of the miscreants who, while living in Poverty Bay and professing loyalty to the Queen, not only assisted Te Kooti to surprise the district, but in many cases were the actual murderers of the settlers among whom they had been living on the most friendly and trusted terms up to the night of the massacre.

CAPTAIN HARDINGTON.

ſ·APT. Ĥ̨ARDINGTON,

APTAIN HARDINGTON, when Governor Gore Browne commenced the Taranaki campaign, was one of the first to volunteer for service in the Auckland Cavalry Corps, raised in Auckland for the defence of the settlers on the southern frontier of the province. The corps became popular, all the best men interested themselves in its progress, and it inspired a degree of confidence in the minds of the country settlers and their families. The muster at Otahuhu of about sixty stalwart troopers, mounted upon the best horse flesh in the community, in excellent drill, under the truly gallant Colonel Nixon, instituted a satisfactory surveillance over the outlying districts during a course of about two years; when, upon the arrival of Sir George Grey, they were disbanded from prudential considerations. In 1863, war, however, was declared in the Waikato, and Captain Hardington was asked again by his fellow-townsmen to take command, should a corps of cavalry be again raised. To this he assented. He was unanimously elected to the command, and commissions were issued by the Government accordingly. After being enrolled, and the usual drilling over, the corps was put into active service, and had harassing work at patrol and escort duties, also forwarding despatches. In November, the Auckland troop rejoined the Otahuhu troop, under Colonel Nixon, at Papatoitoi. The duties of patrolling were at the Karaka, Shepherd's Bush, and forwarding despatches between Otahuhu, Papakura, and Howick; and all of the three troops performed their respective duties throughout with the utmost zeal, and relieved the Defence Force situated at Papatoitoi and Papakura. Colonel Nixon went up with the regular troops, and was mortally wounded at Rangiaohia (returning to his farm at Mangere to die), when Captain Hutton became the senior officer in command of the cavalry. At the latter end of 1864, the cavalry were relieved from duty, after a course of over a year's active service, when Captain Hutton resigned, and Captain Hardington again became senior officer. Upon the unveiling of the Nixon monument by the Governor, in 1866, he was in command of the three troops. The late Captain Bassett, of the Otahuhu, and Captain McLean, of the Howick troop, resigned in 1868, and Lieutenant Marks was then appointed to the command. Their five years' service—viz., four years of parades and one of active service—were rewarded with thirty acres to each member of land scrip, hardly covering the expense of shoeing their horses.

Mr. Hardington, although now verging on the sere and yellow leaf, is still hearty and strong, with sufficient pluck left to go into harness again, should he ever be required so to do.

THE CHIEF TUKINO.

An incident of the war—How Tukino saved Colonel McDonnell's life.

TUKINO, a man of rank amongst the Maoris belonging to the Tangahoi tribe, and who had made himself known during the war by his shrewdness and skill in laying ambushes by which many an unfortunate fellow met his death, became, after the attack on Pokaikai (from whence he, with others, effected his escape), rather attached to Colonel McDonnell, as was shown from the following circumstance :—
It was just before the attack and capture of Pungarehu, a pa situate in the forest, that Toi, a chief of Ngatiruanui, came with a chosen band of fifty armed men to a ford of the Waingongoro River, a mile or so distant from the Waihi camp, and sent the Colonel a message saying that they wished to make peace, but were afraid to come any nearer lest they should be fired upon, and requesting him to come and see them, when they would sign for peace, being quite tired of war. The messenger further handed McDonnell a letter from the tribe in which the same sentiments were expressed. The Colonel, having so many times during the war visited hostile natives in their retreats and strongholds to try and induce them to surrender, it was nothing new or strange for him to receive such a message. Consequently, without a suspicion of treachery (although the tribe had been beaten in a sharp skirmish a short time previous), he replied, that as Toi wished to make peace, he was quite willing to meet him as a friend, but that he and his followers had better come into camp and tender their allegiance; and sitting down, wrote a letter to Toi to this effect, telling him to come in without fear, as no harm should happen to him. The messenger departed, but quickly returned, accompanied by Toi and two other chiefs. McDonnell received them in his tent, treated them most hospitably, and their protestations of friendship and wish for peace were apparently sincere. After some further conversation Toi intimated that he wished the Colonel to return with them to where his people were and repeat the good words he had spoken to them, which, he continued, would be gladly welcomed, after which they could all return to camp and make friends.

Just at this moment the Colonel heard the sentry outside the tent, who had been stationed there to keep prowlers off, order some one away. Again hearing the sentry threaten, he called to him to know what was the matter. He replied that it was a Maori bothering him to give the Colonel a letter. McDonnell, being pestered with native letters asking for everything they could think of, said, " Give me the letter, and send him off about his business." This was done and he resumed the conversation with Toi. McDonnell, while listening to Toi's wish to start soon, unconsciously opened the note, one glance of which showed him his position. It was an earnest warning from Tukino, who had just galloped in from Taiporohenui to inform McDonnell that a plot had been laid to capture and tomahawk him, under the pretence of making peace, and that Toi and Hauwhenui were the promoters of it. The Colonel's presence of mind did not forsake him, and carelessly throwing the note into a candle-box standing close by, went on with the korero. McDonnell asked Toi if they had not better ride to the river, that he would find the horses and take two or three of his officers with him to see his people. Toi, apparently much pleased, said that would be very good. To put him quite off his guard, the Colonel asked him what he thought his people would like to eat when they came into the camp, rice and sugar, or flour. Toi made answer, rice would be best. While answering this question the Colonel had taken down his revolver, and looking at it said, " Toi, do you believe in mata kiti ?" (a kind of second sight). " Yes," he replied. " So do I," McDonnell replied ; " I have just had a presentiment," and holding the revolver within a foot of his head, " One movement, Toi," said he, " and I fire. Confess that you came to trap me. Speak, or I pull—quick !" Toi turned yellow. " E tikaana" (It is true), he gasped, " you have divined our intentions. We are in your power, you will act as you wish," was the reply, as their eyes fell. McDonnell had called the guard in the meantime, and, as Captain Wirihana and Lieutenant McDonnell entered and took charge of the prisoners, the Colonel went out to look for Tukino. He found him smoking in the canteen and breathing anger against the sentry who had behaved so roughly to him. The Colonel told him he was going to shoot Toi and Hauwhenui at once. But Tukino entreated so earnestly for their liberty, that, taking into consideration that the pleader had saved, in all probability, the lives of himself and some of his officers, he reluctantly gave in, and as the Colonel returned to his tent, Toi looked up and said, " Do not keep us long, do the resolve quickly ; shoot, but do not hang us." " I have a little to say, Toi," he replied, " I give you your lives. It's lucky for you that the order to cook rice has not yet been given ; get you gone quickly ; you are safe this time for certain reasons of my own, but if ever I catch you hereafter you will be killed without mercy. Go quickly, or I may alter my mind. I see plainly I will never be killed by such as you." The Colonel saw them through the lines and they travelled at a rapid pace to the crossing.

Had it not been for Tukino's warning neither McDonnell nor any officer or orderly he might have taken with him would have ever seen the sun set. But as the Colonel promised Tukino not to let the natives know that he had given the warning, the fact has never been revealed until now, when Tukino is dead.

CAPTAIN BRYCE.

Captain Bryce.

*Defending the town of Wanganui—Mr. Rusden's attack on Mr. Bryce—
The affair at Handley's woolshed—Libel suit against Mr. Rusden—
£5000 damages awarded—The capture of Parihaka.*

CAPTAIN BRYCE, one of the oldest settlers in the district of Wanganui, had successfully farmed his land for many years prior to the rebellion of 1860; and, having a lively interest in all that concerned the future welfare of New Zealand, was always to be found taking part in the various discussions and public meetings of the province, where his straightforward and common-sense speeches soon attracted the notice of the settlers, inasmuch as they returned him as their member to the House of Representatives on the first occasion that offered. When the war reached Wanganui, he was one of the first to volunteer his services, by joining a troop of yeomanry cavalry, of which he was chosen one of its officers; and soon afterwards, when Titokowaru threatened the township of Wanganui, and Colonel Whitmore, the commanding officer, was suddenly ordered off, with all the available force at his command, to avenge the horrible massacre at Poverty Bay, Lieutenant Bryce's troop became the main safeguard of the district; and so well did they perform their trust—being always on duty, patrolling night and day the banks of the Kai-Iwi river (the then boundary-line of defence), that Titokowaru was awed from attempting his threatened attack on the township.

Years after, Captain Bryce joined the Atkinson Ministry as Native Minister, and by his firmness and determination to carry out his policy, staved off any further appeal to arms, which at times looked to imminent; for all must admit that, in warding off the danger so long threatened at Parihaka, he showed considerable skill and judgment, using the force at his command to such advantage that the fanatics lost all hope, and in the end quietly submitted themselves as prisoners. Yet the Hon. John Bryce was most unjustly attacked by Mr. Rusden, in his work on New Zealand, accusing him of indiscriminately shooting down men, women, and children, while in command of his troop at Handley's woolsheds; whereas the real facts were simply as follows :—

While the lieutenant with his troop were guarding the approaches to the township of Wanganui, by patrolling the boundary-line between the contending parties, Titokowaru's men, emboldened by their previous successes, were observed day by day pillaging the farm buildings and station of Mr. Handley, on the opposite side of the Kai-Iwi stream, near to Nukumaru, in broad daylight, which so exasperated our men, among whom were a number of young settlers in the immediate neighbourhood, that they determined to try and surprise the natives in their work of destruction, by riding round the back of the sandhills, and cut them off before they could get back to their pa. One day they were observed destroying the pigs and poultry on the station, and, while intent on their work, a portion of the troop did get round, and made a sortie upon them from between the sandhills, but were unfortunately soon brought to a momentary standstill by a high bank and ditch fence erected round the farm, which few of the horses could clear. Those who did get over—seven in number—made a charge at the retreating body of natives, and succeeded in overtaking and killing several in a swamp before they had time to reach the pa; amongst them two Maori lads fell in the general *mêlée*. It was clearly proved at the trial, and admitted by Mr. Rusden's counsel, that Mr. Bryce did not even take part in this charge; but if he had done, there was nothing to feel ashamed of. The skirmish was an ordinary brush with rebels under arms, who were in the very act of pillaging a settler's homestead. So insecure were the settlers of Wanganui at that moment, that it was absolutely necessary some demonstration should be made to check the further advance of Titokowaru; and this little event had all the desired effect, as, after the skirmish was over, little more was seen or heard of Titokowaru's threats. It is very easy indeed for members of the Aborigines' Protection Society, as they sit by their cosy firesides in merry England, to try and rake up cases of cruelty against the pioneers of a new colony. If a few of these gentlemen were transported to the Antipodes, and their lives now and then placed in jeopardy, as the colonists' continually were, by a bloodthirsty, fanatical crew of savages, I doubt if even Mr. Rusden himself would wait to ascertain the ages of the enemy at his door before he fired in self-defence. An idea of the issues tried in the action brought by Mr. Bryce against Mr. Rusden, may be gained from the judge's summing up.

"Mr. Baron Huddleston, in summing up the case to the jury, said: The defences which were set up were three—(1) It is said that the passages are true in substance and fact. If that be so, it is a complete answer to the action, for then there could be no injury to the plaintiff. By true in substance and fact he did not mean to say that it was necessary for the defendant to prove the truth of every fact in the passage. But the *onus probandi* was upon the defendant to satisfy them that what he had written was substantially true in fact. He must prove every material fact. To these facts he would presently refer in detail. The second ground of defence was one which had been fully recognised by all the legal authorities, and particularly those of recent date. It was that the passages complained of were fair and *bona fide* comment written about a public man's act in connection with a matter of public interest. His Lordship said he would shortly explain what was fair and *bona fide* comment. The third defence was, that it was written in the honest and *bona fide* belief that it was true in substance and fact and without malice. As regarded that defence, his Lordship had not the slightest hesitation in at once ruling that, in point of law, it was bad and no answer to the action. Take, for instance, the case of a gentleman engaged in commerce, about whom something wholly untrue and which affects his character has been written, and in consequence he is ruined and becomes bankrupt, both in character and capital—what answer is it for the person who has caused all that mischief to say that he honestly believed at the time he had written what he did that it was true, and that he had written it so believing and without malice? If such a defence were law, how could character and honour be maintained in this country? The law of England jealously protected the character of British subjects, and properly so. For if a man's character is attacked and ruined he is shunned by his fellow-men. Any man who chose to circulate slanderous accusations must be prepared to answer for so doing. Even were this subject new law he would have no hesitation in deciding it, but it was not, for it was laid down in the case of 'Campbell v. Spottiswoode' (3 'B and S,' 769) by Lord Chief Justice Cockburn in his judgment that 'in the interest of society the public conduct of public men should be criticised without any other limit than that the writer should have an honest belief that what he writes is true. But it seems to me that the public have an equal interest in the maintenance of the public character of public men, and public affairs could not be conducted by men of honour with a view to the welfare of the country if we were to sanction attacks destructive of their honour and character made without foundation. I think the fair position of the law is this—that where the public conduct of a public man is open to animadversion, and the writer who is commenting thereon makes imputations which arise fairly out of his conduct so that a jury shall say the criticism is not only honest but well founded, an action is not maintainable. But it is not because a public writer fancies that the conduct of a public man is open to the suspicion of dishonesty he is therefore justified in assailing his character as dishonest.' Again, in the same case, Mr. Justice Crompton had said, 'But it is always to be left to a jury to say whether the publication has gone beyond the limits of fair comment. A writer is not entitled to overstep those limits and impute base and sordid motives which are not warranted by the facts;' and 'I cannot for a moment think that because he has a *bona fide* belief that what he is publishing is true it is any answer to an action for libel.' Lord Justice Blackburn had also said in the same case, 'A question had been asked the jury whether the writer *bona fide* and honestly believed it to be true, and the jury have found that he did. We have to say whether that is an answer to the action. I think not; it is no defence.' His Lordship, continuing, said : You have, therefore, those authorities in addition to my own. The only remaining questions for us to consider, therefore, are whether it is true in substance and fact, and, if it is not, then whether it is a *bona fide* comment upon a public man on a matter of public interest. Sir John Gorst admitted in his admirable and candid speech that there were three things which he could not deny—viz. (1) That there were no women present at the Handley's wool-shed affair; (2) that Mr. Bryce did not take a personal part in the charge there made by the troopers; and (3) that if the passage ' Rangihiwhinui—(*i.e.*, Kemp)—declared that he would never have joined the colonial forces if he had thought them capable of such acts. He earned these by the hatred of Bryce, who long afterwards, when Native Minister, dismissed

U*

him (Kemp) from office,' bore the meaning that Bryce had dismissed Kemp for corrupt motives, it was a libel on Bryce. Those questions seemed to go to the whole matter. The learned Judge, having read the first libel, remarked that in considering the question of the meaning conveyed by the passage they must look at it not as Mr. Rusden might have thought of it, but as humble and ordinary individuals reading it for the first time. Could any such reader doubt that the words 'some women and young children emerged from a pa to hunt pigs. Lieutenant Bryce and Sergeant Maxwell, of the Kai-Iwi Cavalry, dashed upon them, cutting them down gleefully and with ease,' did not impute that Bryce took a personal part in the slaughter? Again, what did they think was the sense conveyed by the passage which discussed the cause of Kemp's dismissal by Bryce? Did it not mean to impute some sinister motive to Bryce? But the question was entirely for them to decide. That this statement about women being present is untrue is beyond all dispute, and now admitted. If, therefore, the other two passages convey the meaning which the plaintiff attributes to them, and they are also untrue, the defence that the libels are true in substance fails. This brings us to what I have seen from the outset would be the main issue in this case. It is this—Were these passages written by Mr. Rusden fair and *bona fide* comment upon Mr. Bryce in his public capacity about a matter of public interest? We may take it, I think, that the matters in question were of public interest. Was the comment fair? This is the question which you will have to decide in the light of the law as explained by me. The duty of the Judges, his Lordship continued, was, no doubt, to adapt the law to the times and circumstances of cases—so far as was possible. But, as Lord Cockburn had said, in a case to which he would refer presently, there must be some limit to public criticism of public men, and liberty must not be extended to licence. No doubt politicians gave and received hard blows, but it did not therefore follow that trespass into personal character was to be permitted. This doctrine was very aptly put in a judgment of Lord Cockburn's in the case of 'Seymour v. Butterworth' (3 'F. and F.,' 372). Again, Lord Bramwell said in 'Kelly v. Sherlock' ('L. R.' 1 Q. B., 689), 'A clergyman with his flock, an admiral with his fleet, a general with his army, and a judge with a jury are all subjects for public discussion and comment. All men who filled public positions rendered themselves open to comment.' Continuing, his Lordship said he had read those extracts in order to explain to them the effect of what he was about to say—viz., that if, in discussing a matter of public interest, a man chooses to condescend to personal attack, such comment is not fair, and is, therefore, actionable. For example, if when you are commenting upon and describing the acts or character of a public man in a general way, you add that in early life he had been a thief, such comment would not be fair. That being the law which would govern them, he would remind them before proceeding, once more, what were the questions upon which they must bring their minds to bear. They were— Were the passages true in substance and fact? And, if not, were they fair and *bona fide* comment, as explained by his Lordship? His Lordship then proceeded to detail the facts, first, as regarded the Handley's woolshed, and, lastly, as to the Parihaka incident. In a most careful and detailed manner, his Lordship took the jury through all the material parts of the evidence, commenting thereon. In dealing with the materials upon which Mr. Rusden had said he had written the first libellous passage, and which accused Mr. Bryce of cutting down women and children, the learned Judge commented very severely upon the discrepancy in the evidence of Bishop Hadfield on the point taken on oath and in the version of the affair which Sir Arthur Gordon had sent in a letter to Mr. Rusden in 1883 as reliable statements made to him (Sir Arthur

Gordon) by the Bishop relative to the same affair. In the latter Sir Arthur Gordon had stated that the Bishop had told him that 'he wished to be well within the mark, and that five women, and at least ten children, were killed on that occasion ;' while when examined on oath the Bishop had not said that any women at all had been killed. It was a remarkable difference, for which he failed to discover any satisfactory explanation. Speaking of the Parihaka incident, the learned Judge, having dealt with the circumstances under which it had taken place, remarked, with reference to the large force employed, that that seemed a very wise precaution if resistance was feared. It was the most likely manner of avoiding bloodshed. And there was, as a fact, no bloodshed. Mr. Bryce had no doubt destroyed the native medicine-house—doubtless of a somewhat sacred character—he said that it was necessary to have done so to check the growth of a dangerous fanaticism. No doubt in all such cases as these it was necessary for those in power to act with determination and firmly. Supposing Mr. Rusden considered this a cruel act, did he in his book discuss it in a fair spirit and without introducing personal attack? His Lordship then read the libel justification and particulars and remarked that it did seem a little as if Mr. Rusden was dragging in little unnecessary remarks in order to express such an opinion. There, however, was the article, and they must judge whether or not it was a personal attack or a fair and *bona fide* comment upon Mr. Bryce as a public man. No doubt these events were such as to challenge comment, yet that comment must be fair. If, then, they were of opinion that the defendant had not satisfied them that the libels were true in substance and fact, or that they were not fair and *bona fide* comment, then the plantiff must have their verdict. In that case it would be for them to say what damages Mr. Bryce should have. They must not give vindictive damages, but such a sum as, looking at Mr. Bryce's position and all the surrounding circumstances, might be considered a fair and reasonable compensation for the pain and annoyance occasioned him and for the damage to his reputation and character. In dealing with that question, his Lordship said he thought the jury would be fully justified in taking into consideration the fact that no apology had been made. In conclusion, his Lordship said that he considered Mr. Bryce was perfectly right in bringing the action in England and not in New Zealand. They had followed the case with such care and attention that he had no misgivings in now leaving it in their hands. They would have to say whether the passages in question were true in substance and effect. And, if not, then whether they were fair and *bona fide* comment written of a public man on a matter of public interest.

"One of the jury asked his Lordship whether the question as to the *bona fide* belief of the defendant in the truth of what he wrote might be taken into consideration when dealing with the damages.

"Mr. Baron Huddleston said that Mr. Justice Blackburn, in 'Campbell v. Spottiswoode' had said that 'it may mitigate the amount, but cannot disentitle the plantiff to damages,' and although he did not himself see how it could be so where it was a case of compensation to the plantiff they might on that authority consider it in that sense.

"The jury retired at 3.50 p.m., and returned at 4 p.m., finding a verdict for the plantiff, with damages £5,000.

"Mr. Tyrrell Paine asked for judgment.

"Mr. Baron Huddleston gave judgment accordingly.

"Sir John Gorst asked for a stay of execution on the ground that the damages were excessive, but Baron Huddleston said he could see no grounds for granting the request. He was quite clear upon the law of the case. He also certified for the special jury."

The following account of the skirmish at Nukumaru is furnished by an eye-witness (Trooper Francis J. Shortt):—"Towards the end of November, 1868, the colonial force, under Colonel Whitmore, were encamped at Woodall's Redoubt, some few miles out of Wanganui. The force consisted of a few hundred infantry and about thirty mounted troopers (exclusive of volunteers). I belonged to the troop under Captain Newland and Sub-Captain O'Halloran. On the afternoon of the 25th November, the troop received orders to be saddled up at midnight for a night expedition, the object of which was kept secret. At 12 o'clock we were all ready, but the rain descended so heavily we were ordered to unsaddle and turn in. On the following afternoon, we received a similar order, and at 12 o'clock at night we left Woodall's Redoubt, in charge of a guide, who led us down a precipitous path to the beach below, where we met the Kai-Iwi Cavalry. We proceeded together along the beach under the cliffs, forded the Kai-Iwi and Okehu streams, and turning inland, crossed the sand-hills on to the fertile land near Nukumaru, and then rode on to the Wairoa Redoubt. I was very tired and turned in. About two o'clock next day, we started back again. We did not return by the same road we came, but by the sand-hills along the sea coast. We had nearly arrived abreast of Nukumaru, when Sergeant Handley, of the Kai-Iwi troop, who was riding with Captain Newland, said, 'I should like to have a look at my brother's property.' I was riding behind Captain Newland at the time as he turned round and said, 'Shortt, you go with Handley.' We immediately galloped off, and soon arrived at the edge of the sand-hills, on the top of which was a post-and-rail fence surrounding some graves. While I held Handley's horse, he climbed the hill and disappeared through the rails. In about a minute, he came down and told me to go up and have a look, but not to expose myself. I did so, and from the top of the hill a grand view of the surrounding country was obtained. A placid lake lay to the right, a large woolshed close under the hill, clumps of flax extended everywhere. The whole immediate district seemed fenced in every direction. In front of the shed were three or four large fires burning, and I counted about twenty or thirty men and striplings busy about the shed. I took a good, steady five minutes' look at the place before I returned to Sergeant Handley, who was impatiently awaiting me. I said, 'Hauhaus, Handley.' He said, 'Yes,' and we galloped off at right-angles to the road we had come by, to intercept the troops, who had travelled on slowly a mile or two ahead. I fell into my place, and the troop immediately halted.

"Captain Newland, hearing what Handley said, ordered the return of the troopers as quietly as possible, telling the men not to allow their sword scabbards to hit the stirrup irons, or otherwise make a noise. We were soon halted again behind the same ridge of sand-hills, but fully half a mile to the right of the hill with the graveyard. Three or four of the officers, with Captain Newland, here started off for the scene of our first discovery. I went with them, to hold their horses while they reconnoitred the country. After a good half hour they returned, and ordering up the troops, gave them orders to dismount and proceed down the slope, leading their horses, so as to keep as much as possible under cover. The men dismounted and about six or seven of them had gone over the ridge, when one of the Kai-Iwi trooper's carbines went off acc'dentally. I was at the monent holding six horses, and hearing the report and an order given to mount and charge, I became so excited that I let the horses escape, and found myself galloping after the troop over the ridge, in company with the late Sergeant Maxwell and three or four others. But I unfortunately came to grief, being stuck in the swamp, and it was some time before I was able to get out and follow on. Eight Maoris were killed in the charge made. I saw three of them killed, and one I fired at, but missed, as he was running in front of my horse. This man I think was afterwards killed, as I saw him on the ground after the charge, and recognised him by his tattoo marks. The natives then swarmed out of their pa against us. Some of our men were eager to rush the pa, for which our force was, of course, totally inadequate, and they were only restrained by the peremptory orders that had been given to retire.''

It was during the Hon. Mr. Bryce's term of office as Minister for Native Affairs, in 1881, that the Parihaka troubles commenced. Ever since the suspension of hostilities, the natives of the West Coast had passively resisted the occupation of the lands confiscated as a punishment for their participation in the rebellion; but it was not until the year mentioned that any danger to the settlers was apprehended by the authorities. Te Whiti, a Maori tohunga possessing great influence, had collected a large assemblage of natives at his pa at Parihaka, near Mount Egmont, and did not hesitate to demand back the confiscated lands. Fully 1600 natives were collected at the pa, including many fanatics; and at last, after they had ploughed up the settlers' grass lands, and ordered them off their farms, there seemed every chance of a rupture. Mr. Bryce had been too great a sufferer himself during the war, to be further trifled with on this occasion, and determined on collecting a force, which would at once awe them into submission and save bloodshed. To effect this, he got together the Armed Constabulary of the colony, and calling upon the volunteer companies, Lieutenant Bennett, formerly of the Thames Navals, but then residing in Wellington, was the first to respond to to the call, by getting together one hundred men within twenty-four hours, and offering their services to the Government, which they gladly accepted; and, promoting Lieutenant Bennett to the rank ot captain, dispatched him with his men for the seat of action that same evening. This was followed by a general volunteering throughout the North Island, as in the meantime the lamented Miss Dobie was foully murdered near Opunake by a native named Tuhi, and the public mind was in fever heat over the occurrence; while the Government of the day were determined to carry out the Native Minister's scheme, of giving the Maoris a last salutary lesson, despite Sir Arthur Gordon's disapproval.

On the 30th of October, the roll, showing the strength of all arms, including the Armed Constabulary, collected at the various redoubts on the plains, were :—Pungarehu, 540; Rahotu, 250; Opunake, 119; Manaia Cavalry, 50; Armed Constabulary, 40. There were also on the march the Nelson volunteers (205), Wanganui volunteers (120), and Thames force (160), making a total of 1517 effective men, under the command of Colonel Roberts and a staff of officers, all of whom had seen good service.

The different contingents were now gradually moved forward to the level plains of Rahotu—the muster ground. It was some few days before the order was given to march onwards to Parihaka, owing to the inefficiency of camp equipage, want of tents, and even of ammunition. Luckily for the forces the weather continued fine, and on the evening the commanding officer's parade took place it was bright moonlight, showing Mount Egmont with its snow-capped tower, rising far above the few clouds discernible, with all its grandeur and beauty. The men were quickly brigaded together, told off in companies, served with ball cartridge, and in light marching order were minutely inspected. There were then on the ground 1300 colonial troops, well drilled, splendid shots, and eager to settle once and for ever the Maori question of supremacy. The men were cool and collected, and every word of command was distinctly heard. A finer body of colonial troops had never been got together. After the rations were served out for the morrow, the men were dismissed to their tents, with orders that no one was to pass the lines.

At 2 a.m. the following morning the camp was raised, and two hours after the 1300 men were in full march to Parihaka. Great care was taken to prevent surprise, as it was not by any means known at that moment whether the Maoris intended fighting or otherwise; nor was the fact ascertained until the stronghold was actually in our possession. Pungarehu Redoubt was safely passed, ere the separate divisions debouched off to surround the village. About 6 o'clock a.m. Parihaka was reached, and, the advance being sounded, the Armed Constabulary moved cautiously along at the double from stump to tree, in admirable skirmishing order, until the village was surrounded at pretty close quarters; every hill and dell round the pa being covered with armed men, waiting to hear the first shot fired,—the sign that the strife had begun. But it was not to be. Te Whiti, who had, no doubt, been informed of the effective force surrounding him, and the determined character of the men he had to deal with, decided on a non-belligerent policy. As I before observed, the village was surrounded with a precision and orderly advance creditable to any force, being as well handled, and with as little noise, as might be expected. But what might have turned out a disastrous movement, had fighting began, was the position of some of the contingents. These men, being marched through the entrance of the village to the rear, completed the cordon, but were in consequence exposed to the cross-fire of our own men. As they entered the village they were met by a body of young native girls, singing their songs of welcome, while the older women cursed them heartily.

The cordon being now complete, and no possibility of escape left, a body of the Armed Constabulary, under the command of Major Tuke and Captains Gudgeon and Newall, entered the mare (or sacred square), and in the name of the Queen called upon Te Whiti to surrender. The old prophet replied, " I am here if you want me; walk over my young men's bodies," he being surrounded by Maoris lying on the ground all round him. The gallant Major hesitated not, but picking his steps between the natives, arrested the prophet, and sent him out with an escort. The grand old chief Tohu then gave himself up, together with several others. Major Tuke's work was not as yet complete, for it had been mooted abroad that Hiroki, the murderer of a man named McLean, was amongst them. Major Tuke loudly called out the murderer's name, and on the fourth call a native jumped up. He seemed to rise mechanically, and, finding his mistake, was quietly settling down again, hoping he had not been noticed, when the escort pounced upon him, handcuffed him, and marched him off. This man's presence had been denied by the natives. The capture gave universal satisfaction, not only to the Europeans but to the better disposed Maoris, who would not tolerate murder. He was soon after tried for the murder, found guilty, and executed; showing to the Maoris that the Queen's warrant will eventually be served, if not at the moment. A large number of natives who refused to disperse were incarcerated.

Although the press cast some ridicule on the Defence Minister's presence while his plans were in operation, there can be but one mind as to his success, as it probably saved the colony many thousands, and the lives of many, both pakehas and Maoris; for, had it not been for the overwhelming force brought against them, the Maoris would most undoubtedly have fought, and probably might have been nearly exterminated. Consequently it was an anxious time for Mr. Bryce, for had only one rifle gone off by accident in the mare, it would have been followed by a general fusillade, which would soon have reduced the village to a shamble.

The Government of New Zealand have in many instances shown a niggardly spirit towards the volunteers. This was the case again at Parihaka. No sooner was the danger over than the Government treated the men with stinted justice (forgetful of the sacrifice many of them had made in leaving their employment to serve their country) by dismissing them then and there, causing many officers and men to retire in disgust—a " penny wise and pound foolish " policy, which will be remembered should they ever be again called upon.

The demonstration was brought to a close by a general return of all the volunteers to their respective districts, the Armed

Constabulary alone remaining for the purpose of preventing a return of the natives to Parihaka, who had been sent back to their own kiangas. Te Whiti, Tohu, and Titokowaru were tried, found guilty of assembling unlawfully, and confined as State prisoners during the Governor's pleasure. They were released shortly afterwards, and no further trouble worth speaking of was occasioned, showing the utility of Mr. Bryce's iron-handed policy.

CAPTAIN TURNER.

CAPT. A. B. TURNER.

The attack on Kennedy's farm—Fighting on the East Coast— Decisive victory at Te Rangi—Incidents of the fight—Various skirmishes— Pursuit of Te Kooti.

CAPTAIN TURNER, of Tauranga, the third son of Colonel C. B. Turner, K.H. (Knight of Hanover), one of the Duke of Wellington's old veterans, was educated in Canada as a civil engineer; and, when the Canadian Government arranged the active militia force, he was appointed an ensign in Brocknell's Rifles, which rank he held until 1861, when he resigned his commission, in consequence of his intention of proceeding to Auckland, where he arrived in August, 1862.

Upon the breaking out of the war in that district in 1863, he was appointed a sub-inspector in the Colonial Mounted Defence Force, under the command of Colonel Nixon, and was sent on detachment to St. John's Redoubt at Papatoitoi, for the purpose of patrolling in the vicinity of the forest. When at this post he was suddenly ordered to Kennedy's farm, where the Maoris had killed two children and wounded another; but he arrived too late, the natives having fled.

After the battle of Rangiriri, he was ordered to join head-quarters at Ngaruawahia, and captured a spy in the guise of a Maori postman. He was then sent on to Papakura, to take charge of the depôt, and remained in charge until headquarters returned.

On the 30th April he received orders to embark at Auckland for Tauranga; marched all night, and next morning was on board the transport steamer *Alexandra*, with a detachment of artillery under Colonel Barstow. The sudden movement was in consequence of the disaster at the Gate Pa. He arrived at Tauranga on the 1st May, just after the killed had been buried, and found there the 68th, 43rd, and part of the 3rd Waikato Regiments, the Flying Column, and Royal Artillery. Shortly after his arrival, he marched, under Sir Duncan Cameron, out to attack the Potorifi Pa, on the Wairoa river, but found it empty. A military post was established here, but abandoned on the arrival of Sir George Grey; when General Cameron left for Auckland, and Colonel Greer, of the 68th, took command.

On the 20th June, 1864, Captain Turner was ordered to reconnoitre the country beyond the Gate Pa, with three troopers only, so as not to attract the notice of the enemy. He returned late in the afternoon, reporting a large number of natives near the Waimapu river, transporting supplies. This resulted in an order being given after tattoo for a march out in the morning, consisting of Artillery, portions of the 68th, 43rd, and 1st Waikato Regiments, Flying Column, and Mounted Colonial Defence Force, the whole under Colonel Greer, who had not proceeded above a mile-and-a-half beyond the Gate Pa when the videttes were fired upon. But they soon drove in the enemy's picquets to the Te Rangi trenches, where the natives had made extensive earthworks. The Artillery, with one Armstrong gun, was placed on the rise in front of the trenches; two companies of the 43rd flanked the right (a very awkward position in heavy fern on the slope of a gully); the Mounted Force dismounted and flanked the left, until relieved by a company of the 68th; while the remaining portion of the 68th and 43rd, supported by the 1st Waikato Regiment, formed the attacking party. The Armstrong gun was shortly after removed to flank the trenches on the left, where it did good execution. In the middle of the fight a dog belonging to the Artillery was wounded while lying under the gun, and howled fearfully. The fight had lasted about three hours, when the advance was sounded, and a gallant charge was made, without a waver, against a most galling fire, and the affair was soon brought to a close, the enemy being completely routed. The natives suffered heavily, having 152 killed, besides those who fell in the swamps, and whose bodies were never recovered. Their loss in wounded was large. Our loss was ten killed and thirty-five wounded. In charging across the rifle-pits Captain Turner's horse fell with him into the earthworks, but he soon remounted. The natives here fought well, meeting the bayonet with their spears. Several acts of individual bravery were displayed in this engagement, and mentioned in Colonel Greer's despatches. One was omitted, where a Maori in close quarters was in the act of shooting an artillery sergeant, when Sergeant Charles, of the Mounted Defence Force, rode at him, and cut the back of his head clean off, thereby saving the life of the artilleryman. Here it was, also, that Rawiri, the native general, was killed, and a noble fellow he was; he was shot down by one of the mounted men. When I say Rawiri was a noble savage, I speak not so much in praise of his undoubted pluck as for his humane feelings; he having issued the order that, when Europeans were wounded or taken prisoners, they were to be well treated. This order was strictly carried out at the taking of the Gate Pa, when Colonel Booth, of the 43rd, and other wounded men were in the pa all night as prisoners, and were well treated by the natives.

Rawiri was buried with the others in their own trenches, and was the only one encased in a blanket. Some years later his body was exhumed by the Ngaiterangi tribe and buried in the cemetery, next the Europeans who fell at Te Rangi and the Gate Pa, the natives inviting Captain Turner to be one of the pall-bearers, as he was captain of the mounted men who had killed him. The captain accepted the compliment. After the fight at Te Rangi, Captain Turner was transferred to the 1st Waikato Regiment at Tauranga, and affairs remained in *statu quo* until the latter end of 1866, when the natives again began to be troublesome, first burning Captain Tovey's house down, next murdering a settler named Campbell, who had gone to cultivate his land; and as the natives had again collected in large numbers, it was thought advisable to disperse them. An outpost was accordingly established at Omanawa, about nine miles from Tauranga. Soon after a portion of the detachment under Captain Goldsmith (in reconnoitring) were suddenly attacked near Irihanga, and in the skirmish Sergeant-Major Emus was mortally wounded. It was then decided to attack their stronghold in force, and the 1st Waikatos and volunteer engineers were ordered to Captain Tovey's farm under Colonel Harrington. They crossed the Wairoa river at sundown on the evening of the 22nd January. Marching all night, they arrived at Irihanga at sunrise, and after a sharp defence the pa was captured; but the force being much annoyed at the enemy firing volleys from the edge of the forest, Captain Turner called for volunteers, who joined him quickly from the different companies and Volunteer Engineers, and having fixed bayonets, they, under a heavy fire, made a charge into the forest and took possession of the enemy's position. For this and other services Captain Turner was mentioned in dispatches and highly complimented in orders.

After this the force proceeded through the forest to the Whata-whata pa, and found it abandoned. Shortly after arriving there the 12th Regiment, who were acting as a moral support, were seen coming from the direction of Minden Peak. After burning down the settlement the force returned through the forest to attack Whakamarama, where the enemy had gathered in force, and quickly drove them out of their settlement some distance into the forest, returning to camp at 9 p.m., after a heavy day's work and the loss of two killed and several wounded. Captain Mair during the day had his horse shot under him.

It was supposed that after this the Maoris would remain quiet; but such not being the case, another expedition to the same place was made on the 15th February, and again the force lost two men and a number of wounded, remaining in possession for some days destroying crops, etc. The next action fought was at Akiaki, where, after a night march, the force attacked the pa and routed the enemy, having several men wounded but none killed. The natives in these skirmishes lost twenty-one killed, besides the wounded. Fighting then ceased in this district, the natives having retired into the interior, the blockhouse erected and garrisoned near the bush at Pye's pa having had a salutary effect upon them.

Nothing further of importance occurred until the end of 1869, when Te Kooti was at large on the warpath. Colonel McDonnell having followed him to Tapapa, a portion of the Armed Constabulary were instructed to go to Rotorua to try and intercept him, and Colonel Fraser, who commanded at Tauranga, applied for Captain Turner to join his staff, which he did, and two hours after was on his road to Rotorua, marching through the almost impenetrable forest for two days. It was hard work indeed, and proved to be Colonel Fraser's last march, as this gallant officer died shortly after of fever. Captain Turner was then appointed to the command of the East Coast Native Contingent, and returned to Akiaki. Here Te Kooti's advance guard laid an ambuscade, and, firing a volley, killed two of the Native Contingent and one Armed Constabulary man. After firing they retreated quickly to the bush, but the force succeeded in taking a prisoner. Captain Crapp here had a narrow escape, as the two natives shot were standing on either side of him.

On reconnoitring next day the force came upon Te Kooti's abandoned camp, some of his fires being still smouldering, which convinced them that he had taken the road to Rotorua. While on the march up the Waimana orders were sent for the force to return, and the Native Contingent being disbanded, Captain Turner sheathed his sword and returned to his civil duties.

THE HON. JOHN BALLANCE.

The Hon. J. Ballance.

THE HONOURABLE JOHN BALLANCE, in the early days of the settlement of Wanganui, started a paper in the district, which, I believe, was one of the first dailies of the North Island. It was called the *Wanganui Herald.* It was conducted so successfully that it soon became a paper of considerable circulation. Mr. Ballance had the gift of not only writing a good article himself, but of making his paper so interesting that his journal was sought for far and near. At the beginning of hostilities in 1868, on the West Coast, martial law was proclaimed, and every available man called upon to volunteer for service, or to join the militia. Mr. Ballance at once called a meeting, and the Wanganui Volunteer Cavalry Corps was formed, in which he enrolled himself a member; but before the services of the corps had been gazetted an order had gone forth from the commanding officer of the district, calling on all the inhabitants capable of bearing arms to enrol themselves in the militia. Mr· Ballance, among others, demurred to serving both as a volunteer and a militiaman, and sent a letter to the commander of the district, protesting against what he termed a tyrannical and senseless order. The result was that a picquet was sent to arrest him, and he was lodged in the guard-room, but was immediately released without conditions. Mr. Ballance was shortly after elected cornet of the corps, which rendered distinguished service throughout the war.

The most graphic accounts of the operations on the coast proceeded from his pen, and it was while doing duty as officer of cavalry and correspondent of his paper that he formed a lasting friendship with Colonel (now Sir George) Whitmore, both of whom were, ten years later, members of the same Cabinet. Towards the end of the war, Mr. Ballance fell foul of the Government, in consequence of an article violently attacking them for incapacity, which he was supposed to have written. His commission as cornet in the corps which he had raised, and

V*

which he had materially assisted to gain a colonial reputation, was cancelled without inquiry, and on no better evidence than mere suspicion that he was the author of the obnoxious article. In 1875, Mr. Ballance was elected a member of the House cf Representatives for Rangitikei, and in 1878, he joined the Grey Ministry, holding the portfolios of Colonial Treasurer and Minister of Education until, through a difference of opinion with the Premier, he resigned in 1879. At the general election of the same year he defeated Sir William Fox at Wanganui, but was himself defeated in 1881, regaining his seat, however, by an overwhelming majority, on the appeal to the country by the Atkinson Ministry in 1884. Upon the formation of the Stout Ministry, Mr. Ballance was asked to join, and at present holds the important portfolios of Native Affairs, Lands, Immigration, and Defence.

The Honourable John Ballance has, during his term of office, introduced and inaugurated the Village Farm Settlement Scheme of perpetual leases, thereby inducing the unemployed to turn their attention to the cultivation of the land, the true source of wealth in all new countries, and relieve the townships of their presence. These Village Settlements he has established in various parts of the North Island, and already upwards of a thousand persons have been located thereon, leaving it entirely to their industry to secure a happy and permanent homestead.

C. W. BROUGHTON.

Recovery of Captain Lloyd's head—The skirmish at Nukumaru—
Treacherously murdered in a Maori pa.

CHARLES WILLIAM BROUGHTON arrived in New Zealand in January, 1852, and during the early years of the colony carried on considerable business relations with the natives, his head-quarters during the grain season being at Marahowai, a settlement in the upper Wanganui, and the residence of the celebrated old chief Topine Te Mamaku. He was afterwards in the service of the Provincial Government of Wellington as interpreter, and was attached in that capacity to the staff of the late Dr. Featherston, who was acting as Land Purchase Commissioner for the province, and assisted in the completion of the purchase of the Waitotara block, the original negotiations having been initiated by the late Sir Donald McLean, who paid to the natives the first instalment of the purchase-money. At the outbreak of the Taranaki war, in 1860, he was employed in various capacities by the Government, and, at very great personal risk, succeeded in interviewing the rebel natives and getting them to deliver up the head of the late Captain Lloyd, of Her Majesty's 57th Regiment, who had fallen in an attack made on the escort outside New Plymouth, and which was being carried about the country in a manner horrifying to Europeans, being used as a trophy to excite the unsettled natives to throw in their future with the rebels. For this service Mr. Broughton received a written testimonial from all the officers of the 57th Regiment, accompanied with a valuable silver cup (26th June, 1864), as a token of their appreciation of his gallantry and zeal in putting an end to what was felt to be a most deplorable exhibition.

At the outbreak of the war in Wanganui, Mr. Broughton joined, in his official capacity as interpreter, the Imperial forces under General Cameron, and accompanied them from Wanganui to Alexander and Peat's station, at Kai-Iwi, on the 3rd January, 1865, was present at the skirmish (24th January, 1865) at Nukumaru, where Deputy Assistant Adjutant-General Johnston and two privates were killed, and seven men wounded. He was present also on the 25th January, 1865, when the rebels attacked the British camp, and succeeded, under cover of smoke, having first fired the fern, in breaking through the advanced pickets of the troops, and charged up to within thirty yards of the General's tent before being repulsed and driven back. The British loss on this occasion was ten killed and two officers and eighteen men wounded. The native loss was supposed to be heavy, nine killed and three wounded being brought into camp. He accompanied the forces to Patea, and was present at the action at Te Ngaio, when the natives, who met the troops in the open, suffered heavily, being thrown back in disorder, and their pa at Kakaramea taken and occupied by the Imperial troops. He was with the forces during their continued advance through Katemarae and Mana-wapo until reaching Wairongora, and remained in the field until the troops went into winter quarters. The campaign then languished, and the Government, wishing to circulate their terms of peace amongst the rebels, Broughton proceeded to the Wereroa, then held by a British detachment, and endeavoured through the medium of a friendly native named Kereti, to open communications with the hostile natives.

MURDER OF KERETI, OF MR. CHARLES BROUGHTON, AND OF TROOPER SMITH.

The Hauhaus on the West Coast having refused to receive the peace proclamation issued by His Excellency Sir George Grey, in 1865, it was found to be absolutely necessary, for the peace of the district, that they should be punished; for these tribes, taking advantage of the absence of colonial forces at Opotiki, had committed some very treacherous and barbarous murders. The first one was on a Wanganui Maori named Kereti, who had been attached to Brigadier Waddy's staff as native orderly. This man had been ordered to select some one among the Wereroa prisoners to carry the peace proclamation to the Ngarauru and Pahakohi tribes, a dangerous duty for anyone but a Hauhau to undertake. One of the prisoners, Tariu by name, was chosen, and he volunteered to do the work. Mr. C. Broughton, interpreter to the forces, approved of the choice, and warned Kereti not to proceed beyond the Wereroa, he being a Wanganui, and friendly to the Europeans. Kereti acknowledged that it would be unsafe to do so, and promised to remain at the Wereroa. On the 25th of September, he and Tariu started from Wanganui, and on the arrival at the redoubt Tariu was sent with the proclamation to the Putahi, while Kereti, forgetting Mr. Broughton's warning, proceeded on the same errand to the Ngarauru tribe. On reaching the village of Arei Ahi, he observed a strong party of Hauhaus, who were *en route* to waylay stragglers from the Wereroa. These men he avoided by hiding in the fern. After they had passed he went on to the Waitotara River, where he saw four women and a man named Rawiri on the opposite bank.

Kereti called to them and stated his errand, but was promptly informed that they would not consent to peace-making. He then asked them whether he was to return to the Wereroa. The women replied in the affirmative, but Rawiri said, " Return here to-morrow, and the tribes will then talk it over with you." Kereti very foolishly trusted to the good faith of a Hauhau, and on the following morning started to meet the tribe ; but he did not go far, for the Hauhaus, expecting him, had an ambuscade laid on the edge of the Karaka plateau, within sight of the Wereroa, and their first volley mortally wounded him. He fell, and was immediately stripped of his valuables, but, strange to say, was not tomahawked. The garrison of the redoubt saw the volley fired, and hastened to his assistance. They found him dying, and carried him to the camp, where he lived sufficiently long to make a statement to Mr. C. Broughton.

Even the ex-Hauhau Tariu was not well received, for the people of the Putahi refused to receive the proclamations, and kept him a prisoner for some days. Eventually he was allowed to depart; but his chief and relation, Hare Tipene, warned him to return by the sea coast, not by the track he had used previously, as ambuscades were lying in wait for him.

The treacherous disposition shown by these tribes ought hence-forth to have been a warning to those people inclined to trust them-selves to Maori honour. But such was not the case, as will be seen. On the 26th of September, a letter, signed by some Patea Hauhaus, was sent in to one of the redoubts. It contained a request that some person acquainted with the Maori language might be sent to confer with them on the proclamations which had reached them by the agency of Tariu. On receipt of this letter, Brigadier Waddy ordered Mr. C. Broughton to proceed to Kakaramea and communicate with the rebels. No time was lost, and, on the 30th, Broughton and a Maori assessor from Wanganui, escorted by ten soldiers, left the Kakaramea Redoubt, and proceeded in the direction of Otoia. Their flag of truce was seen, and a few Hauhaus went out to meet them, and invited them to enter the pa. This Mr. Broughton very properly refused to do, but proposed that the meeting should be held midway between their respective strongholds. The Maoris would not agree to this very reasonable request, and Mr. Broughton returned to the redoubt. On the following morning he went to the meeting-place of the previous day, and after hoisting the flag was met by three Hauhaus. One of them had been Mr. Broughton's servant some years previously, and now tried hard to persuade his former master to enter the pa, assuring him that he would be safe. Wi Pukapuka, the assessor, tried equally hard to prevent it, saying that treachery was intended, and absolutely refused to go a step further himself.

Mr. Broughton unfortunately trusted his old servant, and went on to the pa, while his companions returned to Kakaramea, feeling that they had seen the last of him. Of the tragedy that ensued there is no really authentic account, but the following statement made by an eye-witness, who belonged to another tribe, is probably true :—When Ruka and Broughton entered the pa, they found the tribe assembled; but instead of the loud welcome of "Haere mai! Haere mai!" usual in such cases, they were received in dead silence. As they entered the gate, Broughton saluted the Hauhaus, but received no reply, and saw, when too late, that his fate was sealed. He sat down for a few moments amidst the dead silence, and then, probably to hide his feelings, took out his pipe, walked towards the fire and began to light it. While thus engaged a native shot him through the back, and he fell partly upon the embers, where he writhed in agony until they dragged him off the fire and threw him over the cliff into the Patea River. Thus far the peace proclamations had caused two barbarous murders. The Ngarauru Pahakohi tribes having in this manner shown their desire for war, the people of Tangahoe and Ngatitupaea evinced the same spirit, for, on the 4th of October, five troopers of the military train fell into an ambush on the main road between Manawapou and Te Hawera. Two of their horses were shot. Trooper Smith, unable to move, his horse having fallen on him, was tomahawked; but his comrade escaped, after knocking down a Hauhau who tried to stop him.

RENATA KAWEPO.

RENATA KAWEPO.

A genuine friend of the pakeha—Gallant services on the East Coast—A tussle for life.

RENATA KAWEPO, a well-known chief of Hawke's Bay, took a prominent part on the side of law and order during the disturbances on the East Coast, and distinguished himself on several occasions by his personal prowess. In the same spirit in which he afterwards refused to offer himself for the House of Representatives and declined a seat in the Legislative Council, he took the field as a volunteer with his people. The proffered rank of major had no charms for him, as he was conscious that no mere creation of the kind could add to his influence or dignity as chief of his tribe. Renata's first service on our side was in the attack upon Omarunui (Hawke's Bay), where, under command of Whitmore, he led the Ngatiteupokoiri into the thick of the fight. The enemy was completely routed and defeated. For his services on this occasion Renata, who refused pay, received from Mr. Superintendent (afterwards Sir Donald) McLean a presentation sword. He afterwards went to Wairoa and took part in the fighting against the Hauhaus there, and subsequently at Turanganui. On the voyage to the latter place the people had suffered severely from sea-sickness. Hapuku counselled delay, to " give the young men time to recover." Renata insisted on immediate action, saying that was the best cure. They accordingly marched the same night, and Patutahi was attacked and captured at daybreak. He took part in the successful attack on Te Karetu, and was present at the subsequent operations against Ngatapa. When afterwards, at Tarawera, Colonel Whitmore called for a storming party against Te Waiparati, Renata Kawepo was the first man to volunteer. It was found, however, that the enemy had evacuated the place.

Renata's last performance was at Taupo, whither he had taken his people as "kupapas" (volunteers), under Colonel McDonnell, to fight against Te Kooti. After some skirmishing they attacked the Papakai pa simultaneously from three points, and then found that the enemy had retired on Porere. Without waiting to be attacked there, the Hauhaus came out, and a general fight ensued, the enemy suffering severe defeat. In the pursuit which followed there was much hand-to-hand fighting. Being well in front, and separated from his own people, Renata was attacked by a powerful Hauhau, and it became a trial of personal strength, each endeavouring to disarm the other. Whilst they thus struggled together on the ground the Hauhau's wife, like an enraged tigress, sprang upon Renata and gouged out his right eye with her sharp talons. She would have had the other eye also, but Renata, whose hands were engaged with the Hauhau under his knees, seized the woman's fingers between his teeth, and, biting them to the bone, held her firmly as in a vice. At this conjuncture Petera Rangiheuea, a Ngatiporou warrior, came up and "relieved all parties." By applying the muzzle of his rifle to the head of the unfortunate Hauhau, whom Renata held firmly down by the hair, with his face to the earth, he gave him his *coup de grace*. Renata was then taken to camp on a stretcher in an unconscious state, but recovered in time to prevent his people killing the woman who had come so gallantly to the rescue of her husband.

In consideration of the loss of his eye, and in recognition generally of his meritorious conduct, the Government bestowed on Renata a pension of one hundred a year. Being the owner of an extensive estate, and cultivating European tastes, the old chief now lives in comparative affluence at Omaha, about twelve miles from Napier.

OFFICERS OF THE ARMED CONSTABULARY.

(ENGAGED IN THE CAPTURE OF PARIHAKA.)

LIEUT. STANDISH.

LIEUTENANT FRANK STANDISH was one of the early settlers of Taranaki, and in the pursuit of colonial farming, was soon efficient as a good shot, a fearless rider, and had gained a thorough knowledge of bush life. At the outbreak of hostilities, he took up arms to defend himself and family; and, early in the year 1860, just after the burning of the Waitara Pa by the natives, Governor Gore Browne entrusted him with important dispatches to convey to Wellington, a distance of 270 miles through the enemy's country, which he accomplished in the short space of three days; the only places on the route where the natives showed any signs of stopping him being at Waihi and Patea. He spent his first night between Manawapow and Patea, amongst a large party of armed natives, camped in the open country, considering he was safer there, and less likely to be attacked alone amongst a number, than if pursued by a few. He reached Wanganui about 11 a.m. the following day, after which all went smoothly, and he eventually reached Wellington, and delivered his dispatches.

He was present and took part in the battle of Waireka, and accompanied Colonel Gold's expedition to Warea, and was afterwards with General Pratt at Mahoetahi, where he crossed the river with the friendly chief Mahau, to try and ascertain the probable number of natives located there. When within one hundred yards they were fired upon, and, upon reporting the same to Colonel Carey, he immediately advanced, and destroyed the pa. Standish was then ordered to Kihi with General Pratt, and discovering some rifle-pits close to the pa, was only just in time to save the lives of the force under Colonel Carey, who, after firing a few shots, marched into an empty pa.

The carrying of these dispatches through the enemy's country, at this period of the outbreak, was one of the most daring things of the war.

W

Sergt.-Major Maling.

ERGT.-MAJOR CHRISTOPHER MALING earned the New Zealand Cross for the valuable and efficient services he rendered as sergeant of the corps of guides on many occasions, and especially in going out to scout in advance with three men (two of whom were shot on the morning of the 26th February, 1869), by which an intended ambuscade was discovered, and many lives saved. And for a long reconnaissance with two men of the corps of guides (which lasted two nights and days) in advance, to ascertain the direction of Titokowaru's retreat after he had evacuated Tauranga-i-ka. This service was a most daring one, and of the utmost importance to the force, as intelligence was thus obtained which in no other way could have been procured.

From the moment of Maling volunteering for field service until he left—on conclusion of the war—he was conspicuous for his cool pluck and dash. He was much liked by his companions in arms, and never led them into any difficulty he did not share with them.

Many years ago Maling's parents, brothers, and sisters were murdered by the natives, the memory of which sad event appeared to be always present before him, urging him on to avenge their deaths. At the end of the war, Maling was engaged by the Government to construct telegraph lines through some of the roughest parts of New Zealand, at which work he was eminently successful. Mr. Maling is now in Japan, where he holds a post of some responsibility under the Government of that country.

MAJOR NOAKE.

MAJOR NOAKE.

Some incidents of the Crimean war—The relief of Pipiriki—Resident Magistrate at Upper Wanganui—Expedition up Waitotara river— Pacification of Patea.

MAJOR NOAKE, when only sixteen, left his boarding school for the ranks of a cavalry regiment then quartered in the South of Ireland, where he witnessed the painful scenes caused by the famine of 1847 and 1848, and was in Tipperary during Smith O'Brien's escapade, as also in Yorkshire during the Chartist riots. The war with Russia took his regiment to the East, where it formed a portion of the heavy brigade of cavalry. After serving some time in Bulgaria, where the regiment suffered severely from cholera, they were sent to the Crimea, took part in the siege of Sebastopol, and were present at the three Balaclava episodes—viz., (1) The unsuccessful defence of the advanced redoubt by the Turkish troops, when his regiment supported. In this affair there were many casualties; amongst them the Major's horse was wounded and his sword-scabbard broken by a bursting shell. (2) The charge of the Heavy Brigade and repulse of the Russian attack upon Balaclava, in which the Major took part, and assisted afterwards in taking prisoners. (3) The celebrated charge of the Light Brigade, whose attack was supported by Major Noake's regiment, the Scots Greys. While thus engaged the regiment suffered terribly from the heavy fire of the enemy. Major Noake had his sword knocked out of his hand, his revolver torn from his side, and his leg smashed. It was an unfortunate day for him, as, although he received the distinguished conduct in the field medal for his action therein, his wound caused him to be invalided home and discharged. Prior to this his promotion had been rapid, though so young, that his future would have been assured had he remained with his regiment in the Crimea. Some time after he was presented with a commission in his own country militia regiment, then embodied by the Lord-Lieutenant, and subsequently obtained his lieutenancy therein. He afterwards obtained permission and was attached to the garrison for qualification for a commission as riding master, and was appointed to the Military Train. A few months only elapsed when the mutiny in India broke out, which caused the King's Dragoon Guards to be suddenly ordered to India to assist in its suppression, and the riding master of the regiment obtaining his captaincy, Major Noake was appointed to the vacant post, and soon found himself with his new regiment in Calcutta, with every appearance of abundant active service, but was disappointed by being ordered to Madras, where they took no part in the stirring events beyond the disarming a mutinous native cavalry regiment. The climate soon caused his old wound to break out again, and undergoing an operation, he was for the second time invalided and transferred to a home regiment, until he ultimately left the service, and in 1863 came out to this colony. Finding the war in the Waikato was likely to continue, he applied for service and was appointed captain of militia and transferred to the Wellington Defence Force, which company as adjutant he materially assisted in organising. Major Noake afterwards commanded the force stationed in Rangitikei, which command he retained until it was disbanded, when the Major was appointed Resident Magistrate of Upper Wanganui district, succeeding Mr. White in that office. In his magisterial capacity he attached himself to the expedition sent to the relief of Pipiriki. He relieved Mr. Booth in the magistracy of Rangitikei, and was offered that of Raglan, which private affairs of his own in Rangitikei obliged him to decline. In 1868, the war having been brought to the doors of the Wanganui settlers, the commanding officer obtained his assistance as adjutant. On one occasion, having taken despatches to Colonel Whitmore, and finding him just about to attack Moturoa, he offered his services and that of his escort of Wanganui Cavalry, and consequently was by accident present at that disastrous affair. The command of the district being now given to Major Noake, he conducted an expedition up the Waitotara River after rebel natives. The force took three days' rations only, but were away eleven days, and received the thanks of the Government for the manner in which the expedition had been conducted, without tents, transport or commissariat, but that taken from the enemy. He afterwards searched the Whenua-kura and Patea Rivers, which resulted in the capture of the Pukekohe tribe, with their chief, Tauroa, and the despatch to Dunedin of 180 prisoners. For this service he was again complimented by the Government, and employed in the re-pacification of the Patea district, the object being to get the outsettlers back again on their land. Major Noake occupied Waihi with a garrison of Ngatiporou, built blockhouses, and was appointed Resident Magistrate, and entrusted with the construction of roads, etc. When these duties were successfully accomplished, and the district re-settled and prosperous, he was relegated to Wanganui. Te Whiti's action creating alarm by ploughing up the settlers' land his military abilities were again called into action, and he was dispatched to Patea to take measures for its defence in organising and arming the settlers, and retained the command until the termination of the disturbance, which ended in Te Whiti being taken prisoner.

SIR WALTER L. BULLER.

Sir W. L. Buller.

SIR WALTER L. BULLER, eldest son of one of out earliest missionaries, was born in New Zealand, consequently received his early education in this colony, and went Home to complete his studies. Before his return to the colony he obtained his degree as Doctor of Science, and was called to the Bar of the Inner Temple. He has since practised his profession as a barrister and solicitor, besides devoting himself to literature and science. He has been created a Knight of St. Michael and St. George, and elected a Fellow of the Royal Society. At the time of the West Coast campaign he was stationed at Wanganui as Resident Magistrate of that district, and had special charge of native affairs. At the taking of the Wereroa Pa in July, 1865, he as a volunteer accompanied Sir George Grey from Wanganui, and was present at the operations before that stronghold. He rode with His Excellency and others to within ten paces of the outer palisades, behind which the Maori rifle-pits were lined with barking fanatics, who covered the Governor's party with their guns, while the parley was proceeding, waiting only for the order to fire. On the night of the capture of the pa he undertook to carry from the camp to Wanganui some important despatches from the Commander-in-chief, relating to the complications that had arisen from the investment of Pipiriki, and the rising of the natives on the East Coast, which service he performed at considerable personal risk; as, without an escort, he rode alone at midnight many miles through the enemy's country. Sir George Grey, in referring to this act, spoke of it as " carrying despatches under circumstances of danger; " and Lieut.-Colonel Rooke, the officer in command of the district, in his despatch, described it as " an act of conspicuous personal courage, and a service which, in the Imperial army, would have been rewarded by some special mark of distinction." He afterwards, by order of the Governor, proceeded to Wellington with about one hundred Maori prisoners of war, whom he handed over to the authorities;

and when, in the following year, these prisoners made their escape from the hulk, he organised an armed party of Maori volunteers, and scoured the Ruahine Ranges in pursuit, receiving for this prompt and zealous service the official thanks of the Government. General Sir Trevor Chute has also placed on record his acknowledgment of Sir W. L. Buller's services in furnishing valuable native information before the commencement of his memorable campaign of 1866.

In one of the first engagements with the enemy Major (now Colonel) McDonnell, at the head of the Native Contingent, got severely wounded in the foot, and was reported disabled; whereupon Sir W. L. Buller, who is a first-class Maori linguist, promptly wrote to the Government, and volunteered for active service in his stead, believing that his knowledge of, and influence with, the natives would be of special use to the general. His offer was favourably received, but McDonnell, although suffering intense and personal inconvenience from his wound, gallantly refused to relinquish the command.

CAPTAIN H. A. LOMAX.

Captain H. A. Lomax.

———

APTAIN H. A. LOMAX was sent from the civil department, with which he was connected at Wellington, by Sir William Fox, to join Colonel McDonnell at Taupo, in his campaign against Te Kooti in November, 1869; the colonel having applied for trustworthy officers to accompany him. Soon after his arrival, on 24th January, 1870, he was present at the attack on the camp at Tapapa, at the head of the waters of the Thames River, where he distinguished himself by his coolness while under a heavy cross-fire, and subsequently in a skirmish at the foot of the ranges separating Waikato from the Lake Country; the force having been attacked on the march. The fire of the enemy was very sharp while it lasted, but the troops soon drove them off, with the loss of five killed and one prisoner. The force then moved on to Tauranga and Maketu, a most toilsome march through heavy bush up to Opotiki. On the force arriving at Tauranga a long discussion was held by the friendly natives as to the propriety of giving up the stern chase after a flying enemy, and one of the principal chiefs tried hard to persuade the Wanganuis to return; but old Governor Paipai, ever on the right side, sprang to his feet, and combatted his arguments by declaring that those men who feared a little hardship were cowards; and, pointing to Captain Morrison, Lieutenant Lomax, and the other thirty Europeans with McDonnell, said, " Even though you go back, these men will not." Nothing will so stimulate a Maori to action as the fear of resting under an imputation of cowardice, and the march was resumed. Presently a new earthwork was discerned, but whether occupied by our men or the rebels it was impossible to say. Shortly after the sound of musketry was heard, and bullets whistled through the air in all directions. This lasted for half-an-hour and suddenly ceased, to the great relief of the Wanganuis, who could not possibly understand it, no enemy being seen engaging the men holding the redoubt; and it was equally evident the fire was not intended for them. To ascertain who the strangers were was now a service of considerable danger, for, whether friendly or otherwise, they would be sure to fire on any scouts seen ; but the attempt had to be made, and forty Wanganuis, led by Lieutenant Lomax, were sent out to do it, Captain Morrison being at the time disabled, owing to having staked his leg. These men crawled up to within a short distance of the redoubt in true Maori fashion, unseen by the supposed enemy, and, to their astonishment, found the redoubt to be manned by a mixed force of Europeans and friendly Maoris, under Colonel Fraser, whom they could distinctly make out· How Fraser got there puzzled them, as they supposed him to be at Rotorua, guarding the passes to the Uriwera country. The only difficulty now was to make themselves known without being fired upon, when Lieutenant Lomax again undertook the duty, feeling assured he would not be taken for a Hauhau ; but he had forgotten his bush-ranging costume, and the sentry had actually covered him with his rifle, and would have fired, but for the intervention of Sub-Inspector Withers, to whom Lomax may be said to owe his life. For his services Lomax was promoted to the rank of captain, and received the New Zealand war medal at the close of the war.

MAJOR GUDGEON.

MAJOR GUDGEON,

Engagement near Wereroa Pa—Besieged at Peperiki—Command of the Native Contingent—Services under General Chute.

MAJOR GUDGEON entered the service, at Wanganui, as a very young man, just as the rebellion had reached that district, and from his knowledge of the Maori language and the drilling he had previously received at Taranaki, he was at once placed in the Native Contingent, as sergeant-major of that branch of the service. The first time he was under fire was while occupying the Karaka heights, the morning prior to the taking of the Wereroa Pa. Just before daybreak, Colonel McDonnell, taking with him Captain Wirihana, Sergt.-Major Gudgeon, and three or four of his men, started on a reconnoitring expedition, and had not proceeded far when they heard voices in the valley below, which they soon discovered was the village of Areiahi, containing several large whares, some of which were seemingly full of armed natives on their way to the defence of the Wereroa. It was still quite dark, and without waiting for the main body to come up, which the Colonel had hurriedly despatched a messenger for, he descended the hill and, approaching the large Rununga whare, called upon the natives inside to surrender, when a reply came in the shape of a bullet much too near McDonnell and his small party to be pleasant. This caused the Colonel to call out that any further action on their part was useless, as they were quite surrounded, that he would give them five minutes to lay down their arms, and that if another shot was fired he would blow the whare to pieces. This speech seemingly had the desired effect as no further demonstration was made, and the five minutes having expired, Captain Wirihana approached the door of the whare, and pushing it back, the sergeant-major crawled in on his hands and knees and demanded their arms. The natives denied having any, when on turning up the fern around the inside walls, 42 guns, mostly double-barrelled, were discovered, with the ammunition, which he handed out to Captain Wirihana, thereby disarming them. The force sent for was by this time coming down the hill, and the prisoners were handed over to them, and next day marched into town and shipped off to Wellington.

For this action he gained his commission. Two days after he

X

took part in the relief of Peperiki, a post sixty miles up the Wanganui River, which was besieged by Pehi Turoa, an Upper Wanganui chief, with several hundreds of his followers. He accompanied the native contingent, as second in command, to Opotiki, and was present in every engagement at Kiore Kino, the Hill Pas, and Waimana, where he surprised the notorious Kereopa (the eye swallower) with his twelve apostles, killing two of the party. He accompanied Sir Trevor Chute in his campaign of 1866, and was present at both attacks on Okotuku, and in the valley fight of Putahi, for which he was promoted to his lieutenancy, but unfortunately, while in the act of preparing for the next morning's fight, his revolver accidentally exploded, the charge passing through his thigh, which incapacitated him for the remainder of that campaign. On recovering from his wound, he was appointed to the command of the Native Contingent at Peperiki, where he remained until recalled to the Patea, where he took part in all the engagements fought in that district, with the exception of the disastrous one of Te Ngutu-o-te-Manu, being on that occasion left in charge of the camp. He served both under Colonels McDonnell and Whitmore during the West Coast campaign against Titokowaru, leading the Native Contingent throughout, their services ending in the severe action at Moturoa, where Colonel Whitmore encountered the full strength of the West Coast tribes under Titokowaru.

He followed Te Kooti into the fastnesses of the Uriwera country, and at the termination of the war was appointed Resident Magistrate at Gisborne. He was again recalled to take the command of his company during the disturbance at Parihaka, and was left in charge of the district of Manaia until April, 1885, when he gained his majority, and was placed in command of the land forces at Wellington (the seat of Government). A few months later, Colonel Reader, the Under-Secretary of Defence, finding his health giving way, applied for six months' leave of absence, and Major Gudgeon was appointed to take his place in the meantime.

Colonel Sir George Whitmore, in his despatch of the 7th November, 1868, thus speaks of this officer's conduct at Moturoa : "Captain Gudgeon and Mr. E. McDonnell, in charge of the Native Contingent, who, though unable to bring on their men, followed Kempt to the field, and shared the honour which he has won."

PLUCKY CONDUCT OF THE THREE GUIDES.

On the morning of the second attack on Okotuku, under General Chute, the three guides, namely, Lieutenant Gudgeon, Captain William McDonnell, and the brave Winiata, were some distance ahead of the attacking force, and not being aware that the main body had halted for a few minutes before ascending to the plateau on which the pa was situate, continued to advance until within twenty yards of the palisading, when they received a volley which caused them to adopt Major Von Tempsky's drill in bush warfare, namely, to throw themselves flat on the ground. The force had just arrived on the brow of the hill at the time, and witnessing the manœuvre thought at least they were either killed or severely wounded. But, in an instance, they were up again, and making for a potato-pit close by, had just time to throw themselves in before receiving the second volley. General Chute asked Colonel McDonnell what the devil they were about, when the Colonel answered he supposed they were going to take the pa. The General, enjoying the joke, ordered the advance at the double, and some of the natives, who had come out of the pa to intercept the guides' retreat, had to scamper back again quickly. As the force advanced the guides came out of their cover, and joining with the troops rushed the pa, which soon fell into our hands, but not without some heavy casualties.

Henare Kepa.

TE AHURURU OF THE NATIVE CONTINGENT.

———

CONSTABLE HENARE KEPA obtained the New Zealand Cross for his gallant conduct during the attack on the enemy's position at Moturoa. The storming party, failing to find an entrance, passed round to the rear of the pa, when Constable Kepa climbed to the top of the palisades erected around the fortifications to reconnoitre the position, and in doing so was shot through the lungs, yet he nevertheless walked out of action and brought his arms into camp.

x*

MAJOR GORING.

MAJOR GORING.

M AJOR GORING, at the age of sixteen, volunteered as a private in the third company of the 1st Waikato Regiment, and during the winter of 1863 was in active service under Lieut.-Colonel (then Major) Lyon at the Wairoa. In September, 1863, he received an ensign's commission in Pitt's Four Hundred, and remained with them about six months. He was then appointed an officer in Her Majesty's Transport Corps, in which he served two years, being present at most of the engagements that took place in the Waikato under General Cameron. He subsequently joined the Flying Column, under General Chute, which marched round the foot of Mount Egmont, and shortly after rejoined his regiment, then quartered in the Bay of Plenty district. He was present and took part in three engagements inland of Tauranga, under Colonel Harrington, and remained with his regiment until it was disbanded, receiving the compensation land allotted to him by the Government. In September, 1867, he was gazetted as Sub-Inspector of Armed Constabulary, but did not join for some months afterwards. He was then despatched to Opotiki, and saw service in the Uriwera country, under Colonels St. John and Fraser, being for a time attached to their divisions, until placed in charge of a native contingent. When Titokowaru's rebellion broke out in 1868 he was ordered to Waihi, and was present at the second attack on Te-Ngutu-o-te-Manu, in which engagement our forces were worsted. During the retreat, while showing a comrade the track Colonel McDonnell had taken, he got separated from his company, and finding himself cut off by the natives he had to follow on the same route. On coming up with the rear of Colonel McDonnell's party he found Captain Rowan seriously wounded and being carried out on a stretcher. He immediately volunteered his services as one of the bearers, the number around him being but few. While taking his share of this duty the natives twice got between them and the main body, but retired after a brisk skirmish and the loss of one of his men.

Colonel Whitmore soon after assuming the command, Major Goring (he had obtained his majority for his services at Te Ngutu) was present in the many skirmishes which took place at that time with the enemy, as also at the battle of Moturoa, where he had charge of No. 1 division of Armed Constabulary. Here our forces had again to retire, and the Major being in command of the rear-guard, he was one of the last to leave the bush, having to stand the brunt of a very heavy fire from the rebels the whole way out.   On reaching Wanganui news arrived of the massacre at Poverty Bay, and he and his company were ordered off to avenge the deaths of the many settlers, their wives and children, who fell on that sad occasion.· He was afterwards present at the taking of Ngatapa, and in the various skirmishes with Te Kooti in that district under Colonel Whitmore.   Returning to the West Coast, he was present at several engagements where loss of life ensued, including that of Otauto, where the natives suffered a terrible defeat.   He was afterwards placed in charge of the Waihi redoubt, when he obtained his majority in the New Zealand Militia.

GENERAL METE KINGI TE RANGI PAETAHI.

GENERAL METE KINGI.

TE RANGI PAETAHI.

———

ENERAL METE KINGI was ever a staunch friend of the Europeans. From first to last during the troubles that arose from the Maori war, his influence and help were freely given to the colonists, and right good and loyal were his services to the Crown during the governorship of Sir George Grey. At the time when the Wanganui European corps and the loyal natives were assembled before the Wereroa Pa, that stronghold of fanatics and murderers, the news was brought to camp late one evening, that the safety of the villages and settlements on the lower Wanganui was in danger. This was exciting news to our natives, who, almost to a man, were for striking camp and rushing to protect their wives and families. Much excitement prevailed in our quarters. Sir George Grey sent for Mete Kingi to his marquee, saying, " Mete, let us first take this Wereroa Pa, and afterwards we will go to the relief of Pipiriki. This is but a ruse of the enemy to cause you and me to abandon the taking of this noted place. The Europeans at Pipiriki are brave men, and will defeat their foes," etc. Nobly did Mete respond to this speech, and ordered the Wanganuis to remain. Information almost impossible to obtain now poured in, and Sir George Grey so matured his plan, that in twenty-four hours fifty-six Hauhaus were prisoners to the colonial forces, and the Wereroa Pa handed over by Sir George Grey to the Imperial troops, much to the disgust, by the way, of Mete Kingi and others, who wished it to be occupied by colonial men. For this assistance, Mete Kingi and the Wanganuis received the well deserved thanks of the Governor, and the title of general was conferred on Mete Kingi, which made him quite a lion in his tribe.

General Mete Kingi then, with the Wanganuis, joined the European force under Major Rookes, and all went up the river in canoes to the relief of the garrison at Pipiriki. After this expedition, the influence of Mete Kingi was necessary to induce the Wanganuis to go to Opotiki, and at length Mete and the Wanganuis accompanied the expeditionary force under the command of Major Brassey and Stapp in the steamer *Stormbird* to Opotiki, where they took part in every fight, and did good service. From Opotiki the Wanganuis, still commanded by their native general, returned to Wanganui to assist General Sir Trevor Chute in his West Coast campaign.

The Wanganuis gave valuable assistance to General Chute in penetrating the dense forest inland of Mount Egmont, where the railway now runs. A nice jungle it was then. Sir Trevor Chute speaks in high terms of the valuable aid he received at this time from Mete Kingi and others in his despatches. Then came Titokowaru's raid in 1868, when that notorious rebel neared the town of Wanganui and threatened to burn and sack it over the heads of its inhabitants, at the time when the majority of the European force was absent with Colonel Whitmore at Ngatapa, who again came forward with his influence, but Mete Kingi Paetahi? Europeans are apt to forget, in these piping times of peace, the services rendered in war. Others again are in ignorance of the services rendered by this old man, now no more. But those services deserve honourable mention in the history of New Zealand. Farewell, Mete Kingi! Peace to your ashes! You were kind and gentle to all. Aaere atu ra! Mete never affected to be a warrior. He was essentially a man of peace. He swayed his people with kindness, and preferred the *suaviter in modo* to the *fortiter in re*.

I do not suppose there ever lived a chief who was better or more favourably known throughout the country than the late Mete Kingi. For generosity and hospitality his name has become a proverb amongst the New Zealand tribes. He was close and careful in his own family, which earned him the name of being mean ; but he was not so really. He set his face against drunkenness, and blamed the pakeha law that allows people to drink and then punishes the drinker. "Why not," said he, "prohibit the sale of it?" Mete passed away full of years and honours at his pa at Putiki Uharanui.

DR. WALKER.

Dr. Walker.

DR. WALKER joined the Armed Constabulary, as surgeon, soon after the breaking out of hostilities, and was present at most of the actions fought both on the East and West Coasts of the North Island. He was very clever in his profession, although he had not allowed himself time to pass his degrees, so anxious was he to indulge in his love of travel and adventure in foreign countries. But at last, finding himself in New Zealand, just before the rebellion broke out, and few medical men anxious to take the field and administer to the wants of the sick and wounded, he volunteered his services for what they were worth, stating explicity what his experience had been and what he was equal to, all of which he greatly underestimated, as proved by the many clever operations he performed during his length of service—a period of eight years and upwards. Amongst others, he successfully extracted from the back of a Maori chief's eye a large tumour which other medical men had declined to operate upon, for fear of the results.

Dr Walker was a good officer, most assiduous in his duties, and extremely plucky in the field, and gained the New Zealand Cross for conspicuous gallantry in the performance of his duties as assistant-surgeon on many occasions during the campaign of 1868-69, and notably at the successful attack upon the position and encampment of Titokowaru, at Otauto, on the 13th March, 1869, where he was exposed to a very heavy fire, and bore himself with great courage. He has now passed away with the great majority, but his memory is still fresh in the hearts of many of his old comrades.

Thomas Adamson.

———

THOMAS ADAMSON, private in the Volunteers, gained the New Zealand Cross for good and gallant services as a scout and guide throughout the campaign of 1868-69, continually undertaking hazardous and laborious reconnoitring expeditions almost alone in advance of the force; and for personal gallantry when attacked, with other guides, in advance of the column beyond Ahikereu, on the 7th of May, 1869, where they unmasked an ambuscade, and Adamson, with others, was severely wounded, and the guide Hemi killed.

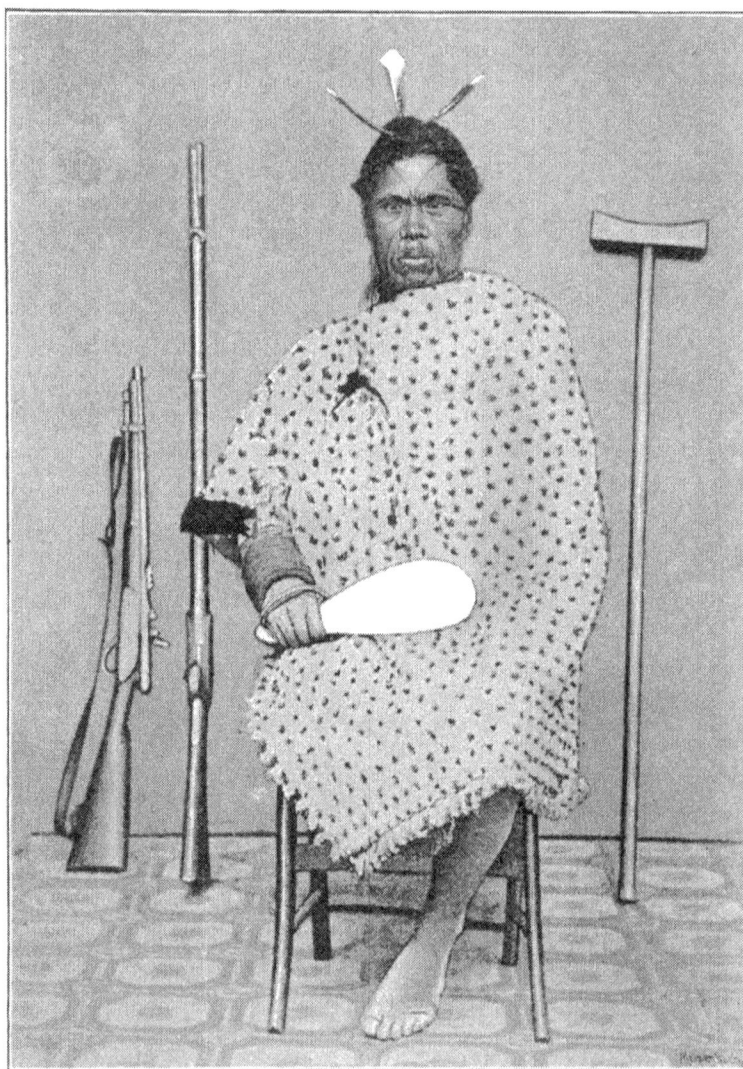

TAMEHANA.

TAMEHANA.

THE Hauhaus of the Upper Wanganui being determined to attack the town of Wanganui, sent messages to the Ngatihau tribe, at Hiruharama, a pa on the river, somewhat nearer the township, asking their assistance. These natives, instead of answering the request, despatched a swift canoe begging Wanganui and Ngatiapa to come to their assistance, well armed, to resist the attack, and holding a council of war, decided to abandon their pas of Hiruharama, Kanaeroa, and Tawhitinui, and fall back on Ranana, so as to fight the enemy on an old and classic ground, the island of Moutoa. These movements were made immediately after the meeting. Meanwhile the Hauhaus, ignorant of their intentions, advanced cautiously, and finding the three pas abandoned, took possession of Tawhitinui, about two miles distant from Ranana, on the opposite side of the river, from whence they could open up negotiations with the tribes of the lower district.

By this time the fighting men of Wanganui, Koriniti, Atene, and Parakino had arrived at Ranana, and were present when a message was received from the Hauhaus, demanding permission to pass down the river, and hinting they would resort to force should their request be refused. Haimona, chief of Ngatiapa Moana, a man of determined character, replied: "We will not let you pass; and if you attempt to force a passage, we will fight you at Moutoa." The Hauhaus accepted the challenge, and Haimona, with 100 picked men, occupied the island before dawn, awaiting the arrival of the Hauhaus, while Mete Kingi, with 350 men, took up a position on the left bank of the river. The advanced guard cn the island (fifty strong) was divided into three parties, each under a chief. Riwai Tawhitorangi led the centre, Kereti the left, and Hemi Hape the right—the whole under the general charge of Tamehana. A further support of fifty men, under Haimona, was posted at the other end of the island, at least 200 yards from the advanced guard, much too far to give effective assistance.

The 130 Hauhaus attacked vigorously. The main body of the friendlies, under Mete Kingi, being 300 yards away, and separated from the combatants by an arm of the river, were utterly unable to assist their friends. Why so small a party should have been detached to fight 130 Hauhaus, mad with fanaticism, and possessing a thorough belief in their own invulnerability, it is difficult to say, the more so as nearly, if not all, the friendly natives believed they were fighting against men who were assisted by the angels. Consequently we are bound to admire their courage rather than their discretion in putting themselves in a position comparatively unsupported, and from whence they could only retreat by swimming.

It must not be supposed that Wanganui fought only to save the town—far from it—for at that time they were strong supporters of the King, therefore in a measure inimical to the Europeans. They fought for the *mana* (influence) of the tribe. No hostile war party had ever forced the river, and they were determined none ever should do so. Our friends, whom we left at their posts on the island, had not long to wait, for the Hauhaus came down the river and grounded their canoes on a shingle spit of the appointed battle-ground. The warriors sprang on shore like men confident of success, Wanganui allowing them to land. A portion of the advance guard then fired a volley. The Hauhaus were not thirty yards distant, yet, strange to say, none of them fell, which increased the superstitious belief of their opponents regarding their invulnerability. At this moment a lay brother of the Catholic priest, Father Pezant, who had accompanied Wanganui, rushed forward and implored the opposing party to stop the fighting. No one listened to him, and the return volley laid him dead, together with many others, including the chiefs Riwai and Kereti. The centre and left, disheartened by the loss of their chief, began to give way, shouting that the enemy were protected by angels; but Hemi Hape held his ground, and soon proved to the contrary. Nevertheless, his warriors were driven slowly back by the overwhelming force of the Hauhaus. Two-thirds of the island had been gained, and the battle appeared to be lost, when suddenly Tamehana came to the rescue. He had vainly tried to bring back the fugitives, but, not succeeding, had returned to share the fate of those who still held out. Hemi called on his men to take cover from the Hauhaus' fire and hold their ground. He was obeyed by all but Tamehana, who fought like a demon, killing two men with his double-barrelled gun.

At this critical moment, Hemi Hape, the last of the three divisional leaders, was shot dead. His son Marino took the command. Nearly all his men were wounded, and as the Hauhaus rushed forward to finish the fight, Wanganui fired a volley into them at close quarters, killing several. But they still came on, and for a moment the fate of Wanganui trembled in the balance. Tamehana was equal to the occasion, for seizing the spear of a dead man, he drove it through the nearest Hauhau, whose arms he took, and drove a tomahawk so deeply into the skull of another as to break the handle in wrenching it out. Finding the gun unloaded, he dashed it in the faces of his foes, and capturing another gun was about fire it when a bullet struck him in the arm. He nevertheless killed his man. This was his last effort, as the next moment a bullet shattered his knee to pieces, and the tomahawk would soon have finished him ; but his gallant stand had given Haimona time to rally the fugitives and come up to his support. Ashamed of their conduct, they came determined to wipe it out. They fired one volley, killing a chief (brother to Pehi), and then charged pell-mell upon the Hauhaus.

There was no time to reload, so down went the guns, and all went in with the tomahawk. The enemy were driven in confusion back to the upper end of the island, where, followed by the tomahawks of their pursuers, and exposed to the cross-fire of Mete Kingi's people, they rushed in a body into the water, and attempted to swim the rapids to the right bank. Just then Haimona recognised the prophet amongst the swimmers, and calling to one of his best fighting men, Te Moro, said, "There is your fish," at the same time handing him his bone mere. Te Moro went for him, and caught him by the hair just as he reached the opposite bank. The prophet, seeing his fate, put up his hand and said, "Pai mariri ; mariri hau." The remainder of what might have been an eloquent speech was cut short by the mere, and Te Moro swam back towing his fish, and threw it at Haimona's feet. This day he shows two gaps in the mere with great pride. Over fifty Hauhaus were buried on the island, and twenty more were taken prisoners by Mete Kingi, who surrounded them in a gully. The loss of the friendlies was sixteen killed and nearly forty wounded—rather severe when it is remembered that not more than eighty men actually took part in the fight. It was only the gallant behaviour of Hemi and Tamehana with the men of Ranana that turned the scale and gave us the spectacle of a real old Maori fight in modern times. No other tribe can boast of an engagement like this for the last fifty years.

MICHAEL PIERCY,

AND HIS THREE COMRADES.

————

MICHAEL PIERCY and his three comrades belonging to No. 3 division of the Armed Constabulary, whose names with one exception I am unacquainted with, behaved most gallantly in rescuing Trooper Joseph Hogan who was severely wounded in the thigh early in the engagement at Te Ngutu. As soon as the order was given to retire they got the wounded man into a stretcher, took him on their shoulders, and through all the horrors of that retreat never left him until he was safe in the redoubt at Waihi, some twelve miles distant, and harassed most of the time by the enemy. They had no relief the whole time, although Hogan was a heavy, powerful man, over six feet high, and fully fourteen stone in weight. The only one of the four whose name I know was Michael Piercy, a son of one of our Wanganui settlers.

CAPTAIN ALFRED ROSS;

Captain Ross.

CAPTAIN ALFRED ROSS joined the Wanganui militia at the outbreak of the rebellion, and was chosen by Lieut.-Colonel Rookes, the commandant of the district, as his captain and adjutant. He carried out the duties of his office to the satisfaction of his superior officers during an eventful period of eight years, and deserves special notice for his pluck in volunteering and successfully carrying despatches from the commanding officer on the Karaka Heights through the enemy's lines to Sir George Grey at Maimene. This was a service requiring a considerable amount of tact, energy, and courage, all of which Captain Ross possessed; consequently he ably performed the service. Although many times under fire, and often placed in considerable danger in the discharge of his duties, and accompanying the commanding officer to and fro through the enemy's country, where the natives were lying in ambush to surprise and murder unwary settlers, he (unlike his brother, Captain Frederick Ross, who fell at Turi-turi Mokai, having some months previous been severely wounded at Ketemarae) escaped without a scratch. He was often favourably mentioned in general orders, and more particularly in Sir George Grey's despatches to the Secretary of State for the Colonies on the 20th July, 1865. After the war, in March, 1869, he was made a Justice of the Peace, and, turning his sword into a ploughshare, is now farming his estate in the Wanganui district.

Captain Percy.

C APTAIN PERCY volunteered for service in 1863, and soon rose to the command of his troop of yeomanry cavalry, and up to the end of 1865, did good service on the west coast of the North Island. In August, 1865, he was despatched with the force sent to Opotiki, to avenge the death of the Rev. Mr. Volkner, under Major Brassey, and during the attack on the Pua Pa, Captain Percy strolled out some distance to witness the attack, his troop not being engaged, and, while looking on, a spent ball lodged in his groin, which has not only disabled him for life, but nearly caused his death. This handsome and brave young officer is now in England, still under medical advice, the ball having never been extracted.

MAJOR KEMP.

MAJOR KEMP.

Awarded the New Zealand Cross for distinguished service—His quarrel with the Government—Gallantry at the capture of Moturoa—Pursuit of Te Kooti.

MAJOR KEEPA, or KEMP, son of the chief and chieftainess Rere-o-Maki and Tanguru, first distinguished himself as a young chief at the battle of Ohoutahi, near Hiruharama, on the Wanganui River, about the year 1847, but owing to a quarrel with his uncle, the late Hori Kingite-Anana, he entered the Maori police service for a time, and afterwards accepted the post of mailman between Wellington and Wanganui, an office in those days of considerable responsibility and danger. Soon after their reconciliation the war broke out in the Wanganui district, and Kemp with other chiefs succeeded in raising a Native Contingent amongst their own tribes, of which the Government made him captain, and he faithfully served his Queen and country during the war, distinguishing himself on so many occasions that he was recommended for and received the New Zealand Cross of Honour, for devoted and chivalrous conduct at Moturoa, on the 7th November, 1868, when at the head of a very small portion of his tribe, with which he covered the flank of the retreat, and assisted the removal of the wounded, although exposed to a very heavy fire at a close range; and for the gallantry and constancy shown by him in conducting the pursuit of Titokowaru's followers after their defeat at Otauto on the 13th March, 1869, hanging on their rear, and constantly harassing them during several days in dense bush. His force on this occasion was composed entirely of volunteers, several officers and many men of the Armed Constabulary having volunteered to follow this distinguished chief, besides the members of his own tribe. At the termination of hostilities he was made a Government Land Purchase Officer of the colony, and did good service, but an unfortunate quarrel with another land purchaser led to his dismissal from office, it is said, without any inquiry as to the cause of the dispute, although Kemp had demanded one. This circumstance afterwards resulted in a sort of civil warfare between Kemp and the Government, which completely shut up for a time the native trade on the Wanganui River, much to the disgust of the settlers.

After the battle of Moturoa Colonel Whitmore in his despatch to Colonel Haultain, the Defence Minister, thus speaks of Major Kemp:—"Captain Kemp, brave, modest, and generous in all his conduct; who never boasted before the fight, who has cast no reproaches after it, who has shown every officer that he is endued with great capacity for military operations, who has exhibited to every man of the force that a Maori chief can manifest a calm, deliberate courage in no way inferior to their own, who has laid up for himself in the hearts of many of the force the gratitude of men, who received a comrade's help in the moment of need, and who has tried hard to redeem the forfeited reputation of his tribe — this officer and chief merits a full recognition on my part of his deserts."

In the course of the ceremony of presenting New Zealand War Medals to certain loyal natives, the following interesting particulars, relative to the distinguished services of Major Kemp, were given in the speech of Dr. Buller, C.M.G., who said:—" Mr. Woon, you have asked me to take part in the proceedings to-day by presenting on behalf of the Government, to Major Kemp, the New Zealand War Medal. I have much pleasure in doing this; the more so because the events which this medal is intended to commemorate occurred during the period that I held office as Chief Magistrate of this town and district. I need not tell Major Kemp that the intrinsic value of this silver ornament and the piece of blue ribbon attached to it is little or nothing. The real value of the war medal is derived from the fact that it comes from the hand of the Queen, who is the fountain of honour, and is intended to show to all the world that the wearer has served Her Maje. ty in the field, and has exposed his life in the cause of his country. During the late operations in New Zealand, a large number of soldiers and friendly natives took part in the fighting, and, as a consequence, a large number of war medals have been distributed. But I think I may venture to say that, among all who have received this honourable badge, there has been no more worthy recipient than our staunch friend and ally, Major Kemp, the son of Tanguru, and therefore a high-born chief of the Wanganui River—related, on his mother's side, to the Ngatiapa, Rangitane, and Ngarauru tribe—own nephew to the late Hori Kingi, that good old chief who was the consistent friend of the pakeha, and the guardian of peace in this district—closely related also to another well-known chief, Te Mawae, who is in attendance here to-day to receive a medal—and, in addition to all this, endowed with natural gifts of a very high order—Major Kemp had better opportunities than most men of establishing a name for himself among the tribes, and making his mana felt in the district. Nor have these opportunities been neglected. In times of peace, always to be found on the side of law and order—in times of war, always in the foremost ranks of fighting—active as a Native Magistrate, and taking an intelligent part in the politics of the country—Major Kemp has succeeded in acquiring a larger measure of personal influence among the tribes than probably any other chief on the west coast of this island. But it is of Major Kemp's services in the field that I have now more especially to speak. I well remember that when I first came to the district, in 1864, Kemp had just received a commission as an ensign or lieutenant in the Native Contingent, under Captain (now Colonel) McDonnell. After performing good service at Pipiriki, Kemp was ordered, with the rest of the contingent, to Opotiki, for the purpose of breaking up a Hauhau combination there, and avenging the murder of the Rev. Mr. Volkner. On his return from that expedition, he served with McDonnell under General Cameron, and subsequently under Major-General Chute, throughout the campaigns on the West Coast. He assisted Sir George Grey at the taking of the Wereroa Pa; and he afterwards fought under Colonels McDonnell and Whitmore, distinguishing himself on all occasions by his daring courage. I believe I am right in stating that he was present at the taking of every pa, and that on more occasions than one he was instrumental in saving our native allies from defeat. To mention only a single instance, it will be in the recollection of the natives how, at the capture of Moturoa, when the friendlies had met with a temporary repulse, Kemp sprang to the front, and running along the parapet, shouted a challenge to the chiefs of the enemy to meet him in single combat, thus, by his daring example, stimulating the wavering courage of our native allies, and ensuring us the victory. In recognition of his services, he was first promoted to the rank of captain, and afterwards to that of major; and Colonel McDonnell has, on frequent public occasions, borne testimony to his intrepidity and valour. When the rebellion had been crushed on the West Coast, Kemp was instructed by the Government to organise an expedition into the interior for the pursuit of Te Kooti and his band of murderous fanatics. Of this force he took the chief command himself, and became known among the natives as 'General Kemp.' Starting from the head waters of the Wanganui, he pursued the enemy across the Murimotu plains to the East Coast, and thence back into the Ohiwa mountains, where, after much hard fighting, he succeeded in breaking up and dispersing Te Kooti's band, Hakaraia, one of the murderers of Volkner, and several other leading chiefs being killed, and Te Kooti himself barely escaping with his life. Major Kemp returned to Wanganui from this expedition covered with military honour, and received the thanks and congratulations of his pakeha and Maori friends in this district. He afterwards received in public, at Wellington, the handsome sword which now hangs at his side, the gift of Her Majesty the Queen, in recognition of his loyalty and bravery. Mrs. Fox, when handing over the sword, expressed on that occasion an earnest hope that it might always remain in its sheath. Up to the present time that hope has been realised; and I am sure all present will join with me in the same expression for the future. But if the occasion should ever arise, I think we may depend on its being promptly drawn in defence of our Queen and country." Dr. Buller then stepped forward, and affixing the decoration in its place, said, 'Major Kemp, I now hand you the New Zealand War Medal, and long may you live to wear it.'"

On the Stout-Vogel Ministry coming into office the Native Minister, the Hon. John Ballance, restored to him his position and pension, which he had been deprived of by the former Ministry. Major Kemp still resides at Putiki Pa, on the opposite side of the river Wanganui, his principal fighting men, Wirihana, Winiata, and others, the companions of all his late campaigns, having succumbed to the inevitable fate of all mankind.

MAJOR PITT'S COLUMN AT PARIHAKA.

THE VOLUNTEERS.

THE Volunteers of New Zealand, in order to uphold Her Majesty's supremacy in this colony, have enrolled themselves throughout the North and South Islands, ready for any emergency that may occur. They are mostly composed of old soldiers and the youth of the colony, vieing with each other both in drill and as steady marksmen. The only opportunity they have had hitherto of showing their pluck and determination as a body was at Parihaka, when they volunteered to a man to take the field in support of law and order, and were ready to lay down their lives at a call from the Government of the colony. They have gone to considerable expense in uniforms, etc., and put themselves to great inconvenience to attain efficiency in their calling, and if a foreign enemy should ever disturb the peace of the colony the citizen soldiery of New Zealand will not be found wanting. I have often witnessed the eagerness of the settlers to assist the Government in their trials during the ten years of native rebellion and the bravery they displayed on such occasions. Whenever the Government wanted volunteers there were double the number ready to serve, and at the present moment it would not be at all difficult to gather together five thousand men, well armed and equipped for any emergency, at a few hours' notice. Formerly it took time to make a man a soldier, but at the present day a slight knowledge of drill, joined to perfectness in the use of his rifle is sufficient to make him a steady, unerring, and cool marksman, with sufficient knowledge of military duty to be very serviceable in the field. The volunteers are all officered by men of their own choice, whom they have the greatest confidence in ; and to show their endurance, I may mention that I have known many badly wounded settlers more than once return again to their corps, forgetful of prior sufferings. The fear of further rebellion amongst the natives of New Zealand is now over, and the enemy who may next invade these islands will probably be one more worthy of our steel, being supplied with all the latest improvements in the art of warfare. But the colonists of New Zealand, to their credit be it recorded, are ready to double the numbers of the volunteer forces, leaving few to be compelled to join the militia. As an Englishman's home is his castle, he will defend it to the last extremity; and the New Zealand settler has brought with him from the land of his forefathers not only the pride of his nation, but his love of the old country, and his indomitable will to defend, and, if needs be, die under the British flag wherever threatened or assailed. It is upon this force the Government of New Zealand will have to depend, as the revenue of a new country is required in so many ways to open up its resources that the colony cannot afford a standing army even of small limits, consequently it would be suicidal to its own interests not to give every facility to foster and increase its army of volunteers. In years gone by a soldier was a mere machine, but at the present day he is an educated man, with a feeling of honour sufficient to carry him through great hardships and inspire him with indomitable courage. There is no doubt that the fall of all great nations has hitherto been due to over-population, and it is the over-population of the Continental nations that renders war so imminent at the present day. England's colonies have saved her from this calamity, by nursing her reserves, and increasing her help at hand, should she ever require it. For a long time even the Home Government seemed blind to this fact, by refusing to take possession of New Guinea and other islands of the South Pacific as a further outlet for her over-population; but her eyes are wide open now, while Continental nations are only just awakening to the fact that England possesses a source of strength in her colonies which will have to be reckoned with in case of any future disturbances of the peace of the mother country.

The experience of those who served during the late rebellion condemns the volunteers of New Zealand adopting the scarlet uniform of the Imperial army, not only as being unsuitable, but as leading to great confusion should the two forces ever be called upon to act together. Each colony should have a uniform of its own, as it has its flag, so that the forces may be distinguishable from one another, while fighting side by side. This would lead to a rivalry which would stimulate all to great and generous exertions. The fighting dress of a New Zealand volunteer should be a loose blue serge suit; their parade dress of blue cloth, with white facings. Even the Imperial forces, when in this colony, found their red regimentals so inconvenient that the Government had to supply them with blue serge suits, to enable them to take their part in the guerilla warfare of the country. Her Majesty, in visiting the hospitals after the Crimean war, is reported to have asked a severely-wounded man in what dress he preferred to fight in, and his answer was, " Your Majesty, in my shirt sleeves," and in his reply he spoke the feelings of the most experienced. All the money the Government can spare should be expended in the best of arms and ammunition, and for a fighting dress nothing can excel a loose blue serge shirt and trousers. Thus equipped, the issue of the day may be safely left to the pluck and determination of the men.

z*

LIEUTENANT W. HUNTER.

Lieut. W. Hunter.

LIEUTENANT WILLIAM HUNTER, the younger brother of Captain Hunter, who fell at Moturoa, had no fear in his composition. Arriving on the battle-field of Te Ngutu-o-te-Manu, he remarked to his men, "That, as the ball was about to commence, he should advise them to choose their partners." He had hardly delivered the speech, when, to the grief of all around him, he was shot down. On the side of the pa his company had advanced to attack was a small fringe of scrub, dividing it from a partial clearing, which had a break in it of about ten or twelve yards in length. This was only twenty-five yards' distant from the pa occupied by the enemy in force, and who had taken advantage of every cover, even to the standing trees around, which were all alive with armed natives. Captain Scannell, who was close to Lieutenant Hunter at the commencement, gives the following account of Hunter's contempt of danger. He says:—"I was passing the opening in the scrub, and saw Lieutenant Hunter walking up and down quite unconcernedly. He called me to him, and on my going he showed me the natives in the pa, quite visible through the opening behind their paling fortification, shouting and yelling in the most frantic manner. I remonstrated with him on the unnecessary manner in which he was exposing himself; but he merely laughed, and said it was capital fun to watch them. The brave fellow was soon after shot down on the same spot." Thus fell one of the bravest and most genial officers of the force.

An incident of this engagement may be mentioned here. On the 12th September, 1868, five days after the engagement, a half-naked man was seen coming from the bush towards the camp. A party was sent out to meet him, and found to their astonishment a man named Dore, one of the Wellington Rangers. He had been wounded on the 7th, having his arm shattered near the shoulder, and must have fainted from loss of blood, as the first thing he remembered after coming to his senses was finding himself stripped of everything but his shirt. He had probably been found by the enemy while unconscious, and they, believing him to be dead, neglected to tomahawk him, a most unusual piece of neglect on the part of the Hauhaus. The poor fellow hid in a rata tree until it was dark, and then attempted to find his way to Waihi, but for three days he had wandered in a circle, always returning to Te Ngutu, but on the evening of the 10th he managed to reach the open country, and made for the crossing of the Waingongora river. Here he felt his senses going, and feared he would never reach the camp. How he crossed the stream in his weak state is a mystery; and he himself is not aware, and from this time all was a blank to his mind, for all idea of time had left him, nor was he seen until the 12th. This was one of the most wonderful instances of endurance on record. A man with his arm shattered to pieces, without food, and nearly naked, struggling through five days and nights of frosty weather, and yet recovering of his wound more quickly than many whose injuries were of a slighter character.

LIEUT.-COLONEL FRASER.

LIEUT.-COL. FRASER.

LIEUT.-COLONEL FRASER was formerly an officer of Her Majesty's 73rd Regiment, and sold out in order to settle down in New Zealand, taking up the land allotted to retired officers of the Imperial army. Shortly after his arrival he was offered, and accepted, the command of the Hawke's Bay military settlers; and, when hostilities commenced on the East Coast in 1864, he was sent with a small force to the East Cape, to co-operate with the friendly natives in suppressing the Hauhau rebellion. He was rapidly promoted to the rank of major, and soon afterwards to lieut.-colonel, for his distinguished services during the campaign; as, with the force under his command—a mere handful of men—he was successful in compelling the rebels to surrender, after many well-contested engagements. At the assault on the pa, Karomiromi, Colonel Fraser, while leading the charge, had a narrow escape from being tomahawked; the axe was actually descending upon his head when a private soldier, named Welfitt, bayoneted the native in time to save his officer's life.

In 1865 Colonel Fraser took command of the force operating against the rebels at Poverty Bay, which campaign was brought to a close in November of that year, by the seven days' siege of Waerenga-a-hika. He was then transferred to the Bay of Plenty district, in command of the Forest Rangers; and active operations having recommenced in various parts of the island, Major Fraser, under Colonel Whitmore, took a prominent part both at the Wairoa and fall of Ngatapa, on the East Coast, in 1869, and during the operations on the West Coast in the same year. After the success of the campaign the field force again returned to the Bay of Plenty, where this gallant officer fell a victim to low fever, contracted at Tauranga, and died, deeply regretted by all who knew him.

COLONEL LOGAN.

AT early dawn on a peculiarly brilliant morning, in the beginning of the year 1865, the quiet settlement of Wanganui was startled from its slumbers by the booming of a gun, announcing the arrival of the first of seven regiments despatched to crush out the Maori rebellion in that district. The township of Wanganui is situated half-way between Wellington and Taranaki, and is surrounded by some of the finest agricultural land in New Zealand. It derives its name from the river which waters it and is navigable for steamers up to Pipiriki, a native settlement sixty miles from its mouth. As the troops landed all was bustle and commotion, and the quiet agricultural village suddenly became a centre of importance. I was soon on the wharf, and shall never forget the martial bearing of Colonel Logan as he marched up the beach in command of the 57th Regiment —as fine a body of men as ever had the honour of serving their country. Our Major Cooper, then senior officer in command, received and quartered them in the York Stockade taking precedence of Captain Blewett, in command of two companies of Her Majesty's 65th Regiment, who had been stationed there for some time. Soon after, Major Rookes, one of the most soldierly-looking men the colonial force ever had, with considerably military experience, gained in both cavalry and infantry regiments, and who had seen some service, was appointed commanding officer of militia and volunteers. I also had the honour to receive Her Majesty's commission as lieutenant and quartermaster, after having for months served as a full private, doing picket duty on alternate nights, subject to the orders of my son-in-law, who was captain and own adjutant, and of my son, who was a lieutenant. Such was then the fortune of war in New Zealand.

MAJOR R. BIGGS.

MAJOR R. BIGGS.

Suppression of the Hauhau rebellion at Waiapu—Killed in the Poverty Bay massacre.

MAJOR BIGGS, who resided for many years on his station in the Rangitikei district, was in 1860 one of the most active and energetic of our settlers, and the best shot and horseman in the whole island. He soon after left for the Poverty Bay district, and there joined the East Cape Expeditionary Force, and was one of the foremost in all the engagements that ensued, ending with the capture of Hunga-Hunga-Toroa, where he greatly distinguished himself—he and Ensign Tuke, with five or six men, having clambered along the face of the cliff below the pa, reaching a spot which so commanded the position that their fire soon compelled the surrender of over five hundred men, and a proportionate number of guns, fell into our hands, together with a large number of women and children, completely putting an end to the Hauhau rebellion at Waiapu. He was warmly thanked by the Government for this service, and promoted to the rank of captain; and his cool courage, which never deserted him, established him as a leader in all the subsequent severe fighting which took place at Turangahika and Waikare Moana during 1866. He was afterwards promoted to the command of the Poverty Bay district, with the rank of major, and on Te Kooti's escape from the Chatham Islands, and his landing at Poverty Bay, the Major collected the first party of volunteer settlers to oppose his progress, taking up a position at Paparata to prevent his escape into the interior; but being summoned at that moment to meet Colonel Whitmore at Turanganui, Te Kooti took advantage of his absence, surprised and defeated his force, and made good his retreat into the Uriwera country, followed by Colonel Whitmore, not only too late to stop him, but the pursuit resulted in the loss of Messrs. Canning and Carr (two of the principal Hawke's Bay settlers) and several other valuable lives. In 1868, owing to the threats of Te Kooti that he would attack Poverty Bay as "utu" for his imprisonment, Major Biggs placed nine men under Captain Gascoigne to watch the main track from the Uriwera country, but Te Kooti advancing by an old track at that moment grown over, succeeded in surprising the district on the night of the 8th and morning of the 9th November, 1868, and, dividing his men into small parties, attacked the outlying settlers simultaneously, murdering the settlers, with their wives and families. The Major was busy writing at the time (supposed to be the order for the out-settlers to come in) when he was shot, as he answered a knock at the door, and his wife, child, and two servants were tomahawked.

Major Biggs was acknowledged by all who knew him or served with him to be one of the most capable leaders we have ever had in the Colonial force, and his death was deeply regretted by both officers and men.

MAJOR ROPATA,

Major Ropata Wahawaha,

CHIEF OF NGATIPOROU.

———

MAJOR ROPATA was one of the bravest and most loyal of Her Majesty's subjects in New Zealand. He knew no fear, and was ready to lay down his life, as he in so many instances showed, in defence of law and order. At the commencement of the fight at Waiapu, he resisted one hundred rebels when he had but few men, and only seven guns. He seldom carried a weapon, except a pistol or walking stick. His strength was prodigious. At Tikitiki, the contending parties were ranged on each side of a ravine, when one of the enemy came forward, on the opposite bank, defying Ropata and his men. Ropata saw him, and went at him unarmed, and succeeded in dashing out his brains, whilst both parties stood looking on perfectly amazed. This was one of his earliest exploits. Afterwards, Ropata came down to Pukepapa, where some five hundred rebels were entrenched, and amongst whom were some of his own tribe. He had but two hundred followers with him at the time; but with this small force he soon overturned the pa. After this he followed down and took the rebel pa at Takitahupo.

Ropata was a man of iron nerve, who would never swerve from his purpose. At Ngatapa, he came with a small body of men, overturned the pa, and defeated the rebels. Most of his men deserted him; but, with only thirty men, he charged the last trench, carried it, and held it all night. For this he received the decoration of the New Zealand Cross and a pension of £100 per annum. Afterwards he joined the forces under Colonel Whitmore and gave valuable assistance in defeating the rebels.

On one occasion, when the Europeans and Ropata's men were engaged with the enemy, Ropata stood on a rock, at a distance, and guided the movements of his own men by waving to them which way to proceed, so well disciplined were they. At another time he and his men were advancing up the bed of a river exposed to a very harassing fire, so much so that they became panic-stricken and showed a tendency to retreat. But Ropata, bent on his purpose, resolutely advanced, come what would, and with his stick he thrashed all those who felt inclined to retire. Again, he actually took possession of the whole of the Uriwera country. When in the middle of the country, he was surrounded by rebels on all sides, who asked him to retire, promising not to molest him. The odds were fearfully against him, but nothing would make him turn from his purpose, and he merely replied that as he had got so far he would go right through. He did so, and the rebels for a day or so pursued him hotly, but eventually gave it up, and he got through safely. He afterwards said he knew that had he returned his force would have been massacred. This is only a tithe of his exploits.

Major Ropata has done an immense amount of good in the cause of order for the New Zealand Government, and so far from having his income reduced, it should have been doubled. He is as great a general in Maori warfare as ever lived in New Zealand—a wonderful man, for when fighting, he never took shelter, but remained in the open, yet was never hit. He never cringed to anyone, but went honestly forward, a creature of Providence. After the war, Her Majesty presented him with a handsome sword, in recognition of his services, and he gained the decoration of the New Zealand Cross, as the *Gazette* states, "for personal gallantry and loyal devotion on the occasion both of the first and last attacks on Ngatapa, and more especially for the courage he showed on the first occasion, at the head of only seventy men, when all the rest of the native contingent had retreated and left him without support. Major Ropata then pushed his way close to the entrenchments, and held a position at a pistol-shot distance all day, and until, under cover of night, he was compelled by want of ammunition to retire, having sustained heavy losses."

CAPTAIN ROSS.

CAPTAIN ROSS.

CAPTAIN FREDERICK ROSS, the second son of Hugh Ross, Esq., of Cokeley, on the breaking-out of the war, was chosen as one of the officers of the Rangitikei troop of Yeomanry Cavalry, and served in that capacity until appointed to a Sub-Inspectorship in the Armed Constabulary of the colony, from which time up to his death he was present in most of the engagements that took place. He was severely wounded while reconnoitring at Ketemarai, a bullet having entered his wrist and escaped at his elbow. Despite the painful nature of the wound, he was in a few weeks back again in command of his company. He soon after received orders to garrison with twenty-five men the old redoubt erected by Her Majesty's 14th Regiment at Turi Turi Mokai. It took some time to put in order, and when done, finding it too small for the necessary buildings, Captain Ross had his own tent pitched outside. All went well for two or three weeks, and the natives living in the immediate district came daily to offer their produce for sale, making friends with the officers and men, and lulling them into a false security, from which they were destined to be rudely awakened. The friendship of the natives was merely a ruse to inspect the redoubt and discover its weak points, as they subsequently made a night attack, killing or wounding nineteen out of the twenty-five defenders. Captain Ross was first awakened by the report of a rifle fired by one of the sentries, whose suspicions were aroused by the restless movements of some sheep feeding in the neighbourhood of the redoubt, and seeing a Maori raise his head above the fern he fired. In an instant a wild yell was raised by the natives lying in ambush around, followed by a general charge of the enemy. Captain Ross, having no time to dress, seized his sword and revolver and reached the entrance to the redoubt before the enemy, and there fell while gallantly defending the bridge across the ditch. The Maoris were led by their chief, Tautai, who in his charge missed his footing on the bridge and fell into the ditch. The next man fell by Captain Ross's revolver, and he had wounded another, when a native, crawling along under the planks of the bridge, shot and mortally wounded Ross through the openings, and driving a long-handled tomahawk into his body, dragged him into the ditch, where they cut his heart out. It is said that when Captain Ross was shot he called out to his men, "Take care of yourselves, boys, I am done for." And four of the bravest of his men, taking his words literally, actually jumped the parapet over the Maoris' heads, and, strange to say, three of them got clear away and gave the alarm. Thus ended the career of Captain Frederick Ross, one of the many colonial youths of New Zealand whose bravery, love of adventure, and open-heartedness wins the love and friendship of all they are thrown in contact with.

CAPTAIN NEWLAND.

CAPTAIN NEWLAND.

———

APTAIN WILLIAM NEWLAND was born in Taranaki, entered the Colonial service at the very beginning of the war, and took a most active part in it to its close, having been present at most of the skirmishes and engagements fought. He had the character of being a brave and determined man and a good officer, consequently his promotion was rapid. He served on both the East and West Coast campaigns of the North Island, being oftentimes in command of the cavalry or mounted force of the colony assisting in the operations against the rebel natives. He was essentially a cavalry officer, though well used to bush warfare. He also served under Sir George S. Whitmore at Taupo and in the Uriwera country when in pursuit of Te Kooti, and seemingly must have borne a charmed life, having escaped the numerous perils consequent on gueriila warfare. Captain Newland has now settled down to agricultural pursuits in the favoured district in which he was born. He was much respected by his men, who were a picked troop, many of whom fell at Okotuku and in other engagements. The names of Mick Noonan, Jim Lane, Kelly, and many others, will ever be remembered for their bravery and coolness in action, although some of them are numbered with the slain. Mr Shortt, of Queen-street, Auckland, also served in his troop, and afterwards acted as aide-de-camp to the late lamented Colonel St. John, and was for some time principal orderly to the Staff at head-quarters in Patea and Ngatipa on the East Coast. Captain Newland's distinguished services were frequently mentioned in despatches. He took a gallant part in defending the homes of settlers during the most critical period of the war. Colonel Sir George Whitmore, in his despatch after the Moturoa engagement, says :—" I beg to express my obligations to Sub-Inspector Newland, Armed Constabulary, who succeeded to the command of the force, and who behaved splendidly."

CAPTAIN LLOYD.

CAPTAIN LLOYD, while in command of detachments of the 57th Regiment and one hundred military settlers, was the first to come in collision with the Hauhaus while foraging and destroying Maori crops at Ahu Ahu, on the Kaitake ranges. The main body had finished work, and with piled arms awaited the return of Lieutenant Cox, 57th Regiment, who, with a small party, was destroying maize on the hill-side. Suddenly a large body of the enemy rushed out of the fern and scrub, with a terrific yell, firing as they advanced. The military settlers had been enrolled only a few weeks, many of them had never fired a shot, and their rifles were so clogged with oil that they would not go off; the few men who had seen service were new to Maori warfare, with its ambuscades, yells, etc.; the natural result was that both soldiers and settlers were thrown into confusion, and, after a little desultory firing, something very like a stampede ensued. Captain Lloyd stood his ground and was killed fighting bravely; Lieutenant Cox, with a handful of men, escaped by taking to the bush; and Captain Page, with ten or twelve men, who stood by him, got into high fern, and made his way through it to the Poutuku Redoubt. Our loss was seven men killed and twelve wounded; the enemy had four killed. Lieutenant Cox and his party, guided by a Maori scout, reached the town of Taranaki, and gave the alarm. The Bush Rangers, under Major Atkinson, always ready, were ordered to the scene of action, and reached the place in an incredibly short space of time. They found that the heads of those killed had been cut off and carried away. This act of barbarity was new in Maori warfare, and not understood at the time. Several men were missing, and as it was quite possible that they might be hiding in the thick fern, the officer commanding the Bush Rangers had the 57th regimental call sounded. The missing ones responded, and were brought out, all more or less severely wounded. They stated that the enemy rushed upon them barking like dogs, and seemed to have no fear of death.

CAPTAIN E. TUKE.

CAPTAIN E. TUKE.

APTAIN E. TUKE was ordered by the late Sir Donald McLean to Dunedin in 1863 to enlist the Hawke's Bay Military Settlers, and succeeded, with the assistance of Sergt.-Major Scully, in enrolling a fine body of 150 men, who did good service during the war. He was then sent to Poverty Bay, and was for a short time under the late Major Biggs' command, but was ordered back to Napier with forty men, to take up a position on the Ngaruroro river, and built a redoubt there. This was for the purpose of preventing a turbulent native, Paora Kopakau, from joining the Hauhaus from the Patea side. He was also present at the action at Petane, the late Major Fraser being in command, where nearly the whole of the Hauhaus were killed, including the most troublesome chief in Hawke's Bay, Rangehiroa. Captain Tuke was then ordered to the Chatham Islands in com mand of a guard of thirty men, and sailed for there in the *St. Kilda*, Captain Johnson, in October, 1865, with sixty prisoners taken in Omaranui and other places, relieving his brother, Major Tuke. The prisoners at the Chathams, then 317 in all, were well-behaved and orderly. They were supplied with rations, clothing, and tobacco, but had to work in planting their potatoes, fishing, etc. Te Kooti Rikirangi (his name tattooed on his breast), being a very quiet and well-behaved man, was placed in charge of the fishing boats. Te Kooti was suddenly taken ill, suffering from spitting of blood. He became so bad that his hapu asked permission to put him in a whare by himself to die, a native custom, with an old woman to attend him, but he had every attention paid to him by Dr. Watson, the surgeon, and was fed on port wine for some days. To the surprise of the prisoners Te Kooti recovered, which they considered a miracle, and the man became a great prophet and commenced preaching the Hauhau religion. Thinking that some evil was brewing, Captain Tuke wrote privately, by instructions from the late Sir Donald McLean, to that effect. A Commissioner (Major Edwards) was sent down. He recommended that the guard should be strengthened and another redoubt built in a stronger position overlooking the prisoners' whares. These recommendations were unfortunately not carried out; but another Commissioner (Mr. Rolleston) was sent, with instructions to take all surveillance off the prisoners—in fact, let them do as they liked, but give them their rations as before. The first step Captain Tuke had to take was to do away with the morning and evening roll-call, as the prisoners could go where they liked and could roam all over the island at their pleasure. This second Commission cost the country thousands of pounds, for if the first had been carried out the prisoners would not have escaped, but would have been released, according to Sir Donald McLean's promise, in three years. Another foolish act was pardoning the chiefs who had behaved well, who had been placed by Captain Thomas, Resident Magistrate, and Captain Tuke in charge of their different hapus. They were all released, sixteen in number, but one Kingita, a very bad fellow, who was killed afterwards at Poverty Bay. It was then that Te Kooti commenced his career as prophet. Te Kooti, when in Poverty Bay, was not a Hauhau, but was sent away for selling ammunition to the Hauhaus, a charge that was never proved. He therefore had a grievance, but always behaved well. Captain Tuke was present at his marriage by the Resident Magistrate, Captain Thomas, to a woman named Martha in the Court-house. How little anyone then present thought that he would afterwards revenge himself on men, women, children, and little infants. Captain Tuke was ordered back to Wellington in February, 1868, with the greater part of the guard and the released chiefs. He then retired from active service, but afterwards volunteered his services to Colonel McDonnell and joined the expedition to Potou Rotoaira, marching with a native force under Renata Kawepo by the inland route *viâ* Patea. On arriving at Potou he accompanied Colonel McDonnell in a reconnoitring party, who were fired at from the hills above Tokano. He was then sent back with despatches to Napier, making the journey in a day and a half, riding all night, accompanied by a half-caste, who picked up exchange horses on the road.

MAJOR PORTER,

MAJOR PORTER.

Carrying off a wounded soldier—Storming Ngatapa pa—Fighting Titokowaru—Pursuit of Te Kooti, and capture of two pas.

MAJOR PORTER'S first appearance amongst those who had so nobly volunteered to aid the Government in re-establishing law and order in the colony was in the Colonial Defence Force Cavalry. Colonel Whitmore, the then commandant, placed him in charge of the Block House at Mohaka, for the protection of that district, the native mind at that moment being much disturbed. From this time to the end of the war Major Porter's name was continually before the public as one of the most active and resolute officers in the force. At Waerenga-a-hika he greatly distinguished himself by bringing off the field (with the assistance of three others) one of his own men, who was severely wounded, under a heavy fire ; he sustained a wound on this occasion. In 1866, the false economy of the Government having disbanded the Colonial forces, Major Porter was entrusted by Sir Donald McLean and Major Biggs (who was afterwards killed in the Poverty Bay massacre) with some very important negotiations with the Ngatiporou, which he executed to the satisfaction of the Government.

In 1868, when Te Kooti and his band ot ruffians escaped from the Chatham Isles and landed at Poverty Bay, Major Porter again volunteered his services, taking part in nearly every action fought before and after the massacre.

At the siege of Ngatapa, he particularly distinguished himself. Being attached to the native contingent under Ropata, he formed one of the storming party who so gallantly scaled the outer works of the enemy, which action led to its capture. For this, Colonel Whitmore recommended him as sub-inspector of the Armed Constabulary, and gave him the command of No. 8 division of the Arawa tribe, who had orders to proceed to the West Coast to assist the field force raised against Titokowaru, who was then threatening the Patea and Wanganui districts.

During the Wanganui campaign Major Porter was continually on active service, and being a good Maori linguist, he was often detailed off, with Major Kemp and the Wanganuis, as a flying column of pursuit. In one of the ambuscades on the Waitotara, and also at Otauto, where so many of our scouts fell, Major Porter was again slightly wounded, and after the final scattering of Titokowaru's force at Te Ngaere, and the cessation of hostilities, he returned to the East Coast, with his company of Arawas, to take up the pursuit of Te Kooti, who had appeared in force and committed many massacres, both at Whakatane and Mohaka. Major Porter was afterwards placed in charge of the Transport Corps, and narrowly escaped being one of the party who were so treacherously murdered at Opepe. Te Kooti having retired to the fastnesses of the Uriwera country, Sir Donald McLean organised several expeditions to penetrate this stronghold of rebellion, which was quite a *terra incognita*, and Major Porter was ordered to accompany Major Ropata and an expeditionary force of Ngatiporou in marching through that hitherto supposed impenetrable country. At Maungapohatu, on the way, Major Porter, with a division of the force, successfully surprised a pa, and captured about 80 prisoners, the expedition culminating in the fight at Maraetahi, near Opotiki, where a number of Te Kooti's men were killed and 330 taken prisoners.

From that time to 1871 Major Porter was wholly engaged in bush travelling, in pursuit of Te Kooti, through the wild fastnesses of the country, enduring hardships and starvation, which so pulled him down that his nearest relations failed to recognise him.

The last engagement fought with Te Kooti was at Te Hapua, near Maungapohatu, from which place Te Kooti escaped with but few followers, and in one of these expeditions Ropata's force captured Kereopa, the murderer of the Rev. Mr. Volkner, and handed him over to justice. On the cessation of hostilities, to Major Porter was left the task of disarming our native allies, and by judicious diplomacy he succeeded in inducing them to return 2000 stand of arms, for which he was awarded just praise. Major Porter during these later years has held the post of Staff-Adjutant of East Coast Militia District, Native Office Land Purchase Commissioner, and many other appointments entailing great responsibility.

As Land Purchase Commissioner, he completed the Crown title to 547,381 acres in various parts of the East Coast of New Zealand. He has been elected Mayor of Gisborne four times, and has taken an active part in other local institutions.

RIGHT REV. BISHOP SELWYN.

Right Rev. Bishop Selwyn.

GEORGE AUGUSTUS SELWYN, D.D., was born at Hampstead in 1809, and consecrated Bishop of New Zealand in 1841. He was educated at Eton, and while manifesting his rare abilities as a scholar, he was very fond of all athletic sports, in which he excelled, and found to his advantage during the chequered life he spent while in New Zealand and the South Pacific Islands. The draft of his letters patent as Bishop of New Zealand, framed on those of the Bishop of Australia, shocked him greatly, more particularly the Erastian expression of the Queen giving him the power to ordain. But the Crown lawyers were inexorable, and the letters patent were issued with the offensive clauses in full. Against this the Bishop could only protest, which he did formally in a document delivered to the Colonial Office, saying "that he conceived that all spiritual functions were conveyed to him at his ordination." This feeling of High Church principles the Bishop carried out with him to the Antipodes, for on his arrival there he soon made his presence known, preaching the truths of the Church as by law established, and completely ignoring the doctrines of the Wesleyans and others who had for some years been instructing the natives in Christianity. This led to a series of letters between the Bishop and the Wesleyan minister of Taranaki, the Rev. H. Hanson Turton, all of which will be found in Brown's "New Zealand," published 1845, wherein the Rev. H. H. Turton asks the Bishop who invested him with the authority he denied to others, a question the writer says the Bishop very wisely refrained from answering. Like most of the missionaries, he took the part of the natives, right or wrong, advocated their cause, and at times placed himself in such a position during the war that had he been a person of less dignity he would in all probability have come to great grief. As it was it caused considerable annoyance to the military authorities. The Bishop was of opinion that the Governor was wrong in consenting to purchase Tiera's land at the Waitara (the cause of the war), which led to the action he took; otherwise His Lordship was highly approved of as the head of his own denomination, and generally admired and respected by all communions. He was a man of great earnestness, eloquence, and courage. He returned to England in 1867, and was soon after made Bishop of Lichfield, which position he retained up to the time of his death.

JOHN MCGREGOR.

———

Murder of the Gilfillan family—John McGregor's leap for life—Settlers
asking to be removed.

THE first outbreak in Wanganui occurred in the year 1848, when the up-river natives, led by their old chief Maketu, murdered the Gilfillan family, drove in the out-settlers, and actually occupied and held possession for a time of a portion of the town, although it was garrisoned by several companies of Her Majesty's 58th Regiment. During this siege a settler named John McGregor (late a wealthy settler there), seeing some of his cows on the opposite side of the river, crossed with the intention of bringing them in, and was ascending Shakespeare's Cliff, when an ambush of Maoris, from a ti-tree scrub, suddenly rose and pursued him. He turned and fled for his life, and as he looked round at his pursuers they fired. A ball entered his mouth and passed out of his cheek without displacing a tooth. Finding himself hard pressed, John McGregor leaped over the cliff on to the beach below—some say a height of fifty feet—and so escaped. This settler afterwards headed a deputation to Sir George Grey (who was always to be found where danger threatened), asking him to remove them to Wellington, and abandon the settlement. But Sir George Grey, with his knowledge of human nature, replied, " Before I assent to your request, I should like to see how many of you really wish it." He then directed all those who were anxious to run away from the natives to move to the other side of the room. Not a man stirred, Sir George having by this speech roused their courage and saved the settlement.

CAPTAIN PREECE.

Captain Preece.

———

APTAIN GEORGE A. PREECE entered the Government service as clerk and interpreter to the Resident Magistrate at Wairoa, Hawke's Bay, in December, 1864, and was attached to the colonial forces as extra interpreter, and served in the field through the East Coast campaign of 1865-66 under Colonel Fraser. After the cessation of hostilities he returned to duty in the Civil Service until July, 1868, when Te Kooti escaping from the Chatham Islands, he was again attached to the colonial forces with the rank of Ensign. He served under Captains Richardson and Tuke, Major Westrupp, and Colonel Lambert, and was in several expeditions against the rebel natives. After the Poverty Bay massacre he was made Lieutenant in command of the Wairoa Native Contingent. He accompanied Major Ropata and the Ngatiporou Contingent to Poverty Bay for the purpose of following up the rebels, and was present at the Mokeretu engagement, as also the first attack on Ngatapa, for which service he received the special thanks of the Government, and was subsequently rewarded with the decoration of the New Zealand Cross. He served through the East and West Coast campaigns of 1868-69 under Sir George Whitmore, and was several times favourably mentioned in despatches. He afterwards served under Colonels Herrick and McDonnell in Taupo and Tapapa, and was again mentioned in despatches on three occasions. He was promoted to the rank of Captain in February, 1870. The command of the Native Contingent was entrusted to him, and he was present in a number of expeditions, engaging with rebels on several occasions from 1870 to 1872, when Te Kooti with the remainder of his followers escaped into the King country. He experienced great hardships in the Uriwera country during these expeditions. He served in the Armed Constabulary as Sub-Inspector until May, 1876, when he was again transferred to the Civil Service as Resident Magistrate in the Opotiki district. On the occasion of the first attack upon Ngatapa his behaviour was so brilliant as to elicit the admiration of Major Ropata, who recommended him for special reward to the commanding officer with the very complimentary remark "that with two or three more like him he would have been able to break into the pa, at that time not fully completed."

MR. HEWITT.

Murder of Mr. Hewitt.—Head cut off and exhibited throughout the country.

EVERY day some fresh incident occurred to prove the hostile character of the natives around us, and an order was issued for the out-settlers to bring in their wives and children for protection. This order had not been in force many days when the murder of Mr. Hewitt took place. This gentleman, having settled on land in the neighbourhood of the Kai-iwi River, eight miles from town, had removed his family for safety, but continued, with his servant, to occupy the house, there being a military station within half a mile of his farm. He had ridden into town, and, having turned his horse into my paddock, he (on coming for it in the evening) requested my wife to go and comfort Mrs. Hewitt, who was in low spirits, and did not wish him to sleep at the farm, having a presentiment that something would happen. "But," he continued, "as I have left the man there, I cannot desert him." He accordingly rode out, and in the middle of the night was awakened by the furious barking of his dogs. He incautiously went outside with his man to ascertain the cause, and, hearing Maoris talking in the bush around his house, was in the act of returning when he was shot down. His man fled from the place, and, leaping a bank and ditch fence, caught his sock on a stake, which held him head downwards in the ditch. This saved his life. It was very dark, the Maoris gave chase, thinking he was far ahead, and he escaped to the station. On returning with assistance, he found poor Hewitt's lifeless trunk. The head was gone, and the heart had been cut out. The head was afterwards placed on a pole and carried by the natives through the country as a trophy, together with that of Captain Lloyd, who had been shot at Taranaki a short time before.

LIEUTENANT O'CALLAGHAN.

LIEUT. O'CALLAGHAN.

LIEUTENANT WILLIAM G. O'CALLAGHAN, the son of Admiral O'Callaghan, entered the Royal Navy in April, 1855, as a cadet, having passed his examination at the Royal Naval College, Portsmouth, and was duly entered on the books of Nelson's immortal flagship, the *Victory*. From thence he was sent to the Baltic to take his part in the campaign against Russia in Her Majesty's ship *Hawke*, an old block ship of sixty guns. Soon after he was drafted to the *Exmouth*, of ninety guns, the flagship of Sir Michael Seymour, and was present at the bombardment of Sveaborg, the reduction of Narva, and the blockade of Revel and Cronstdadt. Returning home in October, he received the medal awarded for the Baltic campaign before he was thirteen years old. He was afterwards, appointed to Her Majesty's ship *Calcutta*, of eighty-four guns a sailing line of battle ship, to which vessel Sir Michael Seymour had shifted his flag, as commander-in-chief in the China seas; and from the *Calcutta* he changed about to various ships, taking part in the war with China, which broke out in 1856. He was on board the *Encounter*, of fourteen guns, when she fired the first shot against the city of Canton; was present at the first storming of that city, when the British force, being engaged by overwhelming numbers, had to retire; took part in the bombardment and capture of the Bogue Forts, the French Folly, and Stameen Forts, besides several boat actions. He was sent to England, and changed to the frigate *Actæon*, of twenty-six guns, and, again proceeding to China, was present at the final bombardment and storming of Canton, in 1857, in which action his captain, W. T. Bates, was shot through the heart. He served afterwards in the *Retribution*, when Lord Elgin, the British plenipotentiary, proceeded with a squadron consisting of the *Retribution*, *Furious*, and *Cruiser*, with gunboats *Dove* and *Lee*, to open up our trade on the River Yangtse-Kiang, and in the engagement had two officers and three seaman wounded, and a marine killed. He was then invalided home in July, 1859, but proceeded to New Zealand in 1861, and, liking the country, he left the Imperial service, and was sent by the New Zealand Government to Sydney, to aid Captain Bilton in bringing over a gunboat (the *Pioneer*), returning in her as first lieutenant. On arriving in the Manukau, the *Pioneer* was handed over to Commodore Wiseman, who put his own officers and men in her. He then offered his services as a volunteer and was appointed lieutenant in the Taranaki Military Settlers, and took part with them in the capture of Kaitaki, Manutahi, Mataitawa, and other rebel posts round and about New Plymouth, and subsequently joined the Wanganui Rangers, under the late Captain Frederick Ross. While in that company, he saw a lot of service, both at Opotiki, on the East Coast, and in the Patea on the West Coast of the North Island, being present at the engagements that took place at the Kiori-kino and the Hill pas, Katemarae, Kateonetea, Turi-turi, and Pungarehu.

After acting as adjutant to the field force at Waihi, his position as senior subaltern in the expeditionary force, he thought, required consideration, and he naturally looked for promotion, the tardiness of which caused him to retire from the service. For his services in the navy, he received the Baltic Medal and the China Medal and clasps, besides £30 prize money. For his services in New Zealand, he received the New Zealand Medal and 200 acres of land in the Patea district; but, as he could not then settle on it, he accepted the office of clerk of the Magistrate's Court at Invercargill, where he is doing duty at the present moment.

TROOPER LINGARD.

TROOPER LINGARD.

———

TROOPER LINGARD, who had joined the Wanganui Cavalry, was awarded the New Zealand Cross for his gallant and determined courage in rescuing Trooper Wright, whose horse being shot dead, had fallen in front of the palisading surrounding the pa on Trooper Wright's leg, thereby holding him a prisoner. Trooper Lingard, seeing his position, immediately went to his assistance, and having with some difficulty extricated him, rode deliberately back to the palisading, and cutting away a Maori horse tethered there, put Trooper Wright thereon and brought him off the field, being all the time under heavy fire, thereby saving his comrade from being tomahawked. Trooper Lingard at the time was a very young man, and quite a stranger in the neighbourhood, consequently had neither interest nor friends to push his case, which made the honour of the decoration, awarded entirely on his merits, all the greater.

Captain Waddel.

APTAIN WADDEL, of the Auckland City Guards, on the 9th of July, 1863 (then Lieutenant Waddel), had the honour of commanding the first escort of the Auckland volunteer forces that marched out to the front. After morning drill it was the custom to detail on parade guards as pickets for the night. Mr. Waddel, being in charge of the picket, was inspecting the men, when the late Colonel Balneavis, the then commanding officer of the volunteers, being still on the ground, received a telegram from the front instructing him to at once furnish an escort to act as convoy to several dray-loads of ammunition which was required at Otahuhu, whereupon the Colonel informed Mr. Waddel that his picket would have to perform that duty. The Colonel further said that rations would be drawn and everything be in readiness on their arrival in camp at Otahuhu. But on their arrival there the late Major Hunter, an old member of the volunteer force, merely inspected the ammunition and then dismissed the men to their quarters for the night. They were not provided with either blankets or overcoats, and at evening parade it was decided, rather than risk the chances of taking cold, to return to town. Many of the men still living will remember that night march homewards. After Major Hunter had done the honours in camp to Mr Waddel, his men were anxious to interview him. They were hungry, footsore, and angry at the fact that the rations served out were in a raw condition, and the inquiry was made, " Is this what Colonel Balneavis meant by saying that everything was in readiness ?" Mr Waddel replied, " Let us see what the others are doing." They then proceeded to the camp fires at the rear of the huts, where not only frying pans, but pot-lids had been brought into requisition, the men being hard at work making the best of the circumstances. Mr Waddel's men were new to military duty, and not inured to the rough experiences of camp life. The volunteers and militia of Auckland, however, were not long in becoming initiated, and rendered good service as the war proceeded. Lieutenant Waddel, who has since held many public offices, must, like many other Auckland citizens, remember with satisfaction this episode in his life when he was called upon to assist in defending the city from an enemy who were literally at its gates.

cc*

PRIVATE J. SHANAGHAN.

James Shanaghan.

RIVATE JAMES SHANAGHAN joined No. 5 Company of Armed Constabulary, under Major Von Tempsky, on the 11th of March, 1868, not having then attained his nineteenth year, and soon after was at the relief of Turi Turi Mokai, and took part in the many skirmishes in that neighbourhood. He was present at both attacks on Te Ngutu-o-te-Manu, and at the latter engagement was near to Lieutenant Hunter when Major Von Tempsky fell mortally wounded, and on the cry arising that the Major was shot, he and Lieutenant Hunter both ran towards the position the Major held when he fell to try and recover his body. Before they had got half way across the clearing, Lieutenant Hunter also met his death, which caused Shanaghan to pause, and while attempting to carry Hunter off the field, several who had seen the occurrence hastened to his assistance and bore the body to the rear. By this time the men were in a very disorganised state, and on Shanaghan asking a comrade to assist him in a second attempt to bring in the Major's body, Captain Buck was the only one who responded, saying, "I will go with you, young fellow. Do you know the spot where the Major fell?" Shanaghan answering in the affirmative, the two proceeded to cross the clearing and reach Von Tempsky's body. The firing being still kept up briskly on the part of the Maoris, Shanaghan and Buck decided on getting away as quickly as possible, but as Shanaghan was in the act of picking up the body his left hand thumb was shot away, and while changing his rifle to his other hand, a second shot pierced his right hand, entering at the back, and lodging in the palm, at the same time striking his rifle with such force as nearly to knock him down. Captain Buck asked him where he was hit, when Shanaghan, turning round to show the Captain his hands, a third volley was fired, and Captain Buck fell dead at Von Tempsky's feet. Shanaghan then retired. Colonel McDonnell soon after this began to retire, finding it impossible to stop the fugitives. He began by collecting the wounded, and sent them on ahead, staying himself with the rear, fighting his way through ambushes nearly all the way out, and only reached the outskirts of the forest some hours after dark, when Shanaghan was borne on the shoulders of Colonel McDonnell and Sergeant Blake across the Waingongoro river, which was greatly swollen by the incessant rain. Shanaghan feeling nearly exhausted, started with a comrade for the camp at Waihi, two miles off, and on arriving was taken into hospital. On their way they met Captain Gudgeon and Captain George McDonnell, who had been left in charge of the camp, and who were inquiring into the truth of a report in circulation that Colonel McDonnell was also killed. Shanaghan says he owes his life to Colonel McDonnell, as it was entirely due to his untiring exertions and care that the wounded succeeded in getting out of the bush that night. It will naturally be a wonder to most of my readers why Shanaghan was not recommended for the New Zealand Cross, but this is only one case of many where justice was overlooked.

DR. I. E. FEATHERSTON.

Dr. Featherston.

D R. FEATHERSTON, one of the recipients of the New Zealand Cross, was formerly Superintendent of the Province of Wellington. During the war, finding that the General, Sir Trevor Chute, had some difficulty in managing the Native Contingent, he volunteered his services, and accompanied the General on his memorable march round Mount Egmont as a non-combatant, taking part in all the hardships of that campaign. The following despatch from Sir Trevor Chute to the Governor fully explains the grounds upon which this much-coveted decoration was in this instance conferred, and never having hitherto been published, may be of some interest to his many friends and admirers.

"Army and Navy Club, Pall Mall,

"London, *February 1st, 1873.*

"To His Excellency the Governor of New Zealand, etc.

"Sir,—I deem it my duty to bring under the notice of your Excellency and Government the distinguished and valuable services rendered to the colony during the campaign on the west coast of New Zealand in the early part of the year 1866 by Dr. I. E. Featherston, late Superintendent of Wellington, and now Agent-General for the colony in Great Britain.

"I have the honour to state for your information that this officer, who volunteered to accompany me on the expedition and to take charge of the native allies, rendered me valuable and important assistance in every respect, and was on all occasions most conspicuous for his bravery and gallantry. He was present at the capture and destruction of the following pas, viz., Okotuku, Putahi, Otapawa, Ketemarae, and Waikoko, and accompanied me in the march round Mount Egmont. I venture to bring more particularly under the notice of your Excellency and Government the intrepid devotion of this officer to the public service on the occasion of the assault and capture of that almost impregnable stronghold, the Otapawa Pa, the occupants of which were under the delusion that it could not be taken. The conspicuous gallantry displayed by this officer at the storming of that pa, in leading the Native Contingent into action, almost at the sacrifice of his own life, not only elicited my warmest approbation, but the admiration of the whole force present on that memorable occasion. As I have already acknowledged in my despatches the eminent services rendered to me by Dr. Featherston throughout the campaign, I now consider it my imperative duty to recommend this officer in the strongest terms for the distinctive decoration of the New Zealand Cross, in recognition of his meritorious and intrepid services during the period referred to, and more particularly at the storming and capture of that formidable pa, Otapawa, where I must in truth say Dr. Featherston so exposed himself in the service of his Queen and country as to become, as it were, a target for the enemy's fire, thus by his noble example stimulating the courage of the native allies.   I deem it my duty to make this recommendation under Clause 5 of the Regulations ordained in that behalf by Order-in-Council dated the 10th day of March, 1869, and published in the *New Zealand Gazette* of March 11th, 1869 (No. 14).

"I have the honour to be, etc.,

"TREVOR CHUTE."

INSPECTOR SCANNELL.

JNSPECTOR SCANNELL.

INSPECTOR SCANNELL, as a young man preferring a military career, enlisted in the 57th Regiment, then *en route* for the Crimea, but was detained at Malta, to serve as orderly-room clerk until the peace and the removal of the army from that country. In May, 1858, his regiment was ordered to proceed overland, viâ Egypt, to India, to assist in quelling the Mutiny; but he was again employed in the orderly-room at Aden for two years before he rejoined headquarters. On arrival at Bombay, he was appointed to the non-commissioned staff of the Indian establishment as quarter-master-sergeant of the Queen's Depôt, and acted in that capacity up to November, 1860, when he embarked with his regiment for New Zealand, arriving in Auckland harbour early in January, 1861, proceeding thence to Taranaki, then almost in a state of siege. He remained there, doing picket and reconnoitring duty, until the temporary cessation of hostilities, when his company was despatched to Wanganui to relieve one of the companies of the 65th Regiment, under orders for England.

While in Wanganui, he accompanied the expeditionary force under General Cameron to Alexander's farm, arriving at Nuku-maru in time to assist in repulsing the second attack made on the camp at that station. He was present at the action at Ketemarae, and in all the skirmishes that took place between Patea and Waingongoro River, the most advanced post occupied by the Imperial forces. Early in 1866, he served under General Chute, then commanding in New Zealand, who took the field intending to attack and reduce all hostile settlements between Patea and Taranaki. He was present at the attack at Otapawa, when Colonel Hassard and ten of his men were killed. Took part in all the skirmishing at and capture of Ketemarae, until the following July, when, having completed his twelve years' service, he claimed his discharge, to settle in the colony. He immediately after joined the Wanganui Bush Rangers, under Captain Frederick Ross, and was present at the skirmish when Captain Ross was so severely wounded, and for the next few months participated in all the skirmishes and raids made on the enemy's strongholds, until the force, having acquired complete possession of the whole of the open country from Patea to the Waimate Plains, the natives appeared so completely subdued that many gave in their allegiance.

This was the state of things in the early part of 1867, when the Government, from a false idea of retrenchment, disbanded all their well drilled fighting men, substituting in their place a sort of volunteer militia for garrison duty, although it was believed by many that the natives were only biding their time to fight again. And as the eyes of the General Assembly began to open, they passed an Act embodying an Armed Constabulary force for field service, and Sergeant Scannell was the first enrolled, as senior sergeant of No. 2 company. In 1868, No. 2 company was despatched to Hokitika, to quell a disturbance amongst the digging community, and Sergeant Scannell remained in charge of part of the force until after the trial of the ringleaders. In June the natives began to show their intentions in the murders of Cahill, Clark, and Squires, and reinforcements of untrained men were sent up by the Government from Wellington.

In August, 1868, the first attack on Te Ngutu-o-te-Manu was made, No. 2 division of Armed Constabulary with Sergeant Scannell leading. At this attack they lost four men and several wounded. He was also present at the second attack on the pa, which the natives had in the meantime strongly fortified, and our newly trained force were repulsed with great loss—upwards of fifty men and five officers being killed, besides the wounded. For his services on this occasion, he received his commission as sub-inspector of No. 2 company in the Armed Constabulary, and took part in all the operations that followed. On Colonel Whitmore's departure to avenge the massacre of the Poverty Bay settlers, he was made adjutant of the force left to defend the town of Wanganui under Colonel Herrick, and consequently held a command in the skirmishes at Taurangaika and the Karaka Flats; and on the return of Colonel Whitmore, took part in the battle of Otauto. He was then despatched to Whakatane to penetrate the Uriwera country, in search of Te Kooti, under Colonel St. John, and took a prominent part in all the operations, capturing two strongly fortified pas and several native villages, traversing the country to Waikaremoana, from thence to Taupo and Tokanu, on to Lake Rotaira and Papakai, where Te Kooti's force was seen occupying a strong position under his generals, Te Heuheu and Tahau. He led the attack, killing fifty natives, and taking many prisoners; but Te Kooti, although severely wounded, escaped in the dense bush surrounding his fortification. The European force being recalled from further pursuit, Scannell was appointed to the command of the Taupo district, made Resident Magistrate, and first-class inspector, and was gazetted to an equivalent rank in the New Zealand Militia.

DD

MAJOR RICHARDSON.

Major Richardson.

MAJOR RICHARDSON, a descendant of an old Cumberland family, arrived in the colony in the year 1864, and proffering his services to the Government, was appointed ensign in the Hawke's Bay Military Settlers, and in the latter part of 1865 was first engaged with the enemy at the storming of the Waerengahika Pa, under Major Fraser, which engagement lasted from the 16th to the 21st of November, where we had six men killed and ten wounded. He was then despatched to the Wairoa, and took part in the capture of Te Maru Maru Pa, again losing six men, amongst them the brave Captain Hussey. Ensign Richardson by this time had not only made himself a general favourite, but he was further highly esteemed by his commanding officer (Major Fraser) for his intrepidity and coolness in action. Seven or eight days of desultory fighting followed this attack, during which time we lost at Te Kopani, by ambush, thirteen friendly natives killed and twenty wounded. In October, 1866, Ensign Richardson fought at Petane, near Napier, on the occasion of the natives threatening the township by taking up a position on two sides. Colonel Whitmore attacked the enemy at Omarunui, while Major Fraser held them in check at Petane. It was here that Fraser and Richardson, by manœuvring, got to the rear of the enemy, and charging in amongst them, cut down twenty of their number, wounding five. For this, and the expedition used by Major Richardson in bringing reinforcements up from Wairoa to meet the emergency, he received the personal thanks of Sir Donald McLean, and was soon after gazetted Sub-Inspector of No. 1 Division of Armed Constabulary. In March, 1868, Major Richardson took part in the engagement at Whakatane and Opotiki, reinforcing Major St. John's force, and assisted in reducing the Otara and Te Ponga Pas. In the following June the Major was again under marching orders, his instructions being to intercept Te Kooti and engage the rebel and his followers at Te Konaki, on the Waihou Lake, but owing to the defection of his friendly allies, he had to retire under a heavy fire, which lasted from 8 a.m. to 5 p.m.

In the month of September, 1868, Major Richardson was engaged, under Colonel Whitmore, hunting up the chief Titokowaru, on the West Coast, and in November following, fought at Otoia, up the Patea River, not to mention the various other skirmishes that took place in this district. In April, 1869, the Major was appointed to the mounted division, under orders for Napier, and reached that township a day or two after the Mohaka massacre, and received orders to join Colonel Lambert's division, already on the march to Mohaka ; but as Te Kooti was found to have retired upon Waikare Moana, the mounted division was ordered to Wairoa to join Colonel Herrick's command, who was organising a force to cross the Lake in pursuit of Te Kooti. But after the punts had been built and other difficulties surmounted, the expedition was countermanded, and the force recalled to Napier. Major Richardson, with his mounted division, was then despatched to Taupo, and joined the force under Colonel McDonnell, and soon came across Te Kooti's track, both at Tokano and Porere. At the latter place Te Kooti lost two of his fingers and thirty-five of his best men, while we lost the brave Captain St. George and Lieutenant Winiata. Following on, the force again surprised Te Kooti on his return from Taupo, at Tapapa, capturing nineteen stand of Enfield rifles and all his camp equipage, horses, etc., but Te Kooti himself again escaped to the bush country, where he was for a time constantly harassed by Pitt's, Westrupp's, and Richardson's command, until he finally escaped into the Waikato or King's country. In 1874 Richardson gained his majority, and in 1879 retired to settle down on his estate at Petane, near Napier, after nearly ten years of active service, taking part in some of the smartest engagements both on the East and West Coast. One matter worthy of note is, that the first five men on whom the New Zealand Cross was conferred, were members of No. 1, the company to which Major Richardson was attached.

FATHER ROLLAND.

FATHER ROLLAND.

AMONGST those attached to the colonial forces, and who never flinched from his duty, more particularly if danger was apprehended, was Father Rolland. Although of a delicate constitution, no weather or other difficulty ever prevented him from accompanying the force, so as to be near the men in the hour of trial. He was present at both attacks on Te Ngutu-o-te-Manu, and on the occasion of the disastrous retreat consequent on the second attack, he not only volunteered his services to assist the wounded, but bravely took his turn in carrying the stretchers, so that none should be left behind. It was on the 21st of August, 1868, that orders were issued for all available men to hold themselves in readiness to start on an expedition before daybreak to attack the stronghold of Te Ngutu-o-te-Manu. The morning broke with torrents of rain, which delayed their departure, but about 10 a.m. the rain ceased, and a thick mist shrouded the whole country side. This being even better for our purpose than darkness, the order was given to start. The column consisted of detachments of Nos. 2, 3, and 5 divisions of Armed Constabulary, the Wellington Rangers, and Wellington Rifles, in all about 300 men, accompanied by Father Rolland. It was this march that called forth from Major Von Tempsky the following eulogy on Father Rolland, which appeared in the papers of the day. He said : " On a grey and rainy morning, when the snoring waters of the Waingongoro were muttering of flood and fury to come, when our 300 mustered silently in column on the parade ground, one man made his appearance who at once drew all eyes upon him with silent wonder. His garb was most peculiar ; scanty but long skirts shrouded his nether garments ; an old waterproof shirt hung loosely on his shoulders ; weapons he had none, but there was a warlike cock in the position of his broad-brimmed old felt, and a self-confidence in the attitude in which he leaned on his walking-stick that said — Here stands a man without fear. Who is it ? Look underneath the flap of that clerical hat, and the frank good-humoured countenance of Father Rolland will meet you. There he was lightly arrayed for a march of which no one could say what the ending would be. With a good-humoured smile he answered my question as to what on earth brought him there. On holding evening service he had told his flock he should accompany them on the morrow's expedition, and there he was. Truly there stood a good shepherd. Through the rapid river, waist deep, along the weary forest track, across ominous looking clearings where at any moment a volley from an ambush would have swept our ranks, Father Rolland marched cheerfully and manfully, ever ready with a kind word or playful sentence to any man who passed him. And when at last in the clearing of Te Ngutu-o-te-Manu the storm of bullets burst upon us, he did not wait in the rear for men to be brought to him, but ran with the rest of us forward against the enemy's position. So soon as any man dropped he was by his side. He did not ask, 'Are you Catholic or Protestant?' but kindly kneeling prayed for his last words. Thrice noble conduct in a century of utilitarian tendencies. What Catholic on that expedition could have felt fear when he saw Father Rolland at his side smiling at death—a living personification, a fulfilment of many a text preached? What Catholic on that day could have felt otherwise than proud to be a Catholic on Father Rolland's account?—Waihi, August 24th, 1868."

GENERAL SIR DUNCAN CAMERON.

GENERAL CAMERON.

ENERAL CAMERON served throughout the Eastern campaign of 1854-55. Commanded the 42nd Regiment at the battle of Alma and the Highland Brigade at Balaklava; on the expedition to Kertch; at the siege and fall of Sebastopol; and the assault on the outworks on the 18th June, for which he received a medal and three clasps, was made a C.B. and officer of the Legion of Honour. He also received the Sardinian and Turkish Medal third class of the Medjidi, and was afterwards despatched to New Zealand in command of the twelve regiments in that colony, from 1863 to 1865, being finally recalled at his own request, in consequence of the Governor (Sir George Grey) and himself having disagreed on some important points touching their individual responsibilities. This far is certain, that a deal of mischief was done during the uncertainty that prevailed as to their separate duties and responsibilities in connection with the conduct of the war. The General, up to the time of his taking command in New Zealand, had been mainly employed in operations against civilised forces in the field, whereas in New Zealand he had to contend against a brave, determined, fanatical savage race, in the fastnesses of the New Zealand bush, who took every opportunity to waylay and murder all opposed to them; whose fighting pas were a network of skilled underground engineering, difficult to approach, and still harder to take. When General Cameron first marched out to the front at Wanganui he passed the Wereroa pa without attacking it, which caused Sir George Grey to write to the General asking him how he could leave a strongly-fortified pa in his rear. The General replied, " That it would cost too many valuable lives to attack it at that time." And further, that he should require a much larger force before he attempted it. In this the General was right and he was wrong; for had any Imperial force attacked it they would have done so from the front, and the sacrifice of life would have been great indeed. The British soldier was brave enough, but he had no knowledge either in bush warfare or Maori tactics; even his uniform was a check to his entering the bush and taking advantage of his wily enemy. But when Sir George set his mind to take it he gathered together the friendly natives and European bushmen, who by following a known track during the night through the dense bush arrived in a roundabout way just before

daylight on the Karaka heights, a spur of the range just behind
the pa, and which from some points so commanded it that the enemy
were easily driven out without loss to themselves; consequently
by a little stratagem he accomplished what was easy enough with
bush rangers, but nearly an impossibility with newly-landed red-
coated Imperial forces. Again, Sir Duncan, after fighting with a
foe worthy of his steel, was disgusted with the foe before him.
There was neither honour nor glory to be gained fighting with
savages; and yet, strange to say, more officers in proportion to the
number engaged fell in New Zealand than in the Crimea. It was
the settlers only, smarting under the loss of their homesteads and
the lives of their friends and relations, that were fitted to cope with
the difficulty. They had something to avenge; and when the
colony clamoured for responsible government, they, on the withdrawal of the Imperial forces, rose as one man to defend their
rights, and did so effectually—peace and harmony having reigned
ever since the natives learned who were to be their future masters.
To General Cameron, however, is due the conquest of Waikato.
He advanced with military precision, sweeping the rebels completely out of the country he occupied and thoroughly conquering
it, and winning it for the Crown. As narrated in other pages, he
on many occasions displayed great personal bravery, and well
earned the gratitude of the colonists of New Zealand for his
services.

LIEUT.-COLONEL ST. JOHN.

LIEUT.-COL. ST. JOHN.

COLONEL ST. JOHN retired with the rank of captain from Her Majesty's 20th Regiment of the line, and joined the Colonial forces of New Zealand in 1863. He had served with the 20th Regiment at the Crimea with considerable distinction, his services being commended in the army reports of that period. When the Waikato Regiment, known as Pitt's 400, was first raised in 1863, Colonel St. John joined as senior captain, and on the formation of the regiment, he received his majority. During the subsequent operations throughout the Waikato, at Tauranga and Opotiki, he took an active part in the principal engagements.

In 1868 Lieutenant-Colonel St. John joined the Field Force of Armed Constabulary as inspector, and during the campaign against the Uriweras in 1869 he led the left column of assault by the Whakatane Gorge, his division being ambuscaded several times throughout the advance, but owing to Colonel St. John's indomitable pluck and dash, he succeeded in reaching the Ruatahuna with but little loss.

When the Field Force were in quarters at Taupo, Colonel St. John, with a party of officers, being in advance of a reconnoitring party, narrowly escaped being cut off by several hundred rebels, at a place called Opepe, the small escort with him being all cut off but two, who escaped severely wounded.

After the cessation of active military operations, Lieutenant-Colonel St. John held the position of private secretary to Sir Donald McLean, who was then Defence and Native Minister, and whom he survived but a short time, his death no doubt hastened by the fatigues and privations undergone in pursuit of the enemy. There was no pluckier fellow in the service, and as a marcher, he was unequalled.

DR. J. M. GIBBS.

Dr. Gibbs.

R. J. MURRAY GIBBS, who was in private practice at Waipukurau at the time of the Poverty Bay massacre, having been ordered into Napier with the rest of the outsettlers, finding there was no medical man to attend to the wounded at Poverty Bay, placed his services at the disposal of the Government, and left Napier with the first relief party on the 13th of November, 1868. Finding Mrs. Wilson, although desperately wounded, yet alive, he had her conveyed to town and attended to her, until called away by Captain Gascoigne, who with some friendly natives was following up Te Kooti, and his first baptism of fire was at the attack made on this arch-rebel's rifle-pits at Mangakaritu. It was here that one of our scouts (Thomas Lake) was dangerously wounded, a bullet entering below his left eye, coming out under the right ear, and he was carried off the field and placed in a gully at the back of the camp. While the doctor was attending him the native force moved off the field, and had proceeded a considerable way before the doctor was missed. Captain Gascoigne, in his report of the 6th December, 1868, says:—" The natives, having been encamped at Mangakaritu for some time, suddenly determined to return to Turanganui, carrying their wounded with them. That he remained some short time to destroy stores, etc., and on coming up with the force he inquired for Dr. Gibbs, and was informed that he was still in camp attending to a wounded man; that he returned and found the doctor sitting by Thomas Lake; that he asked the doctor to make a rough stretcher whilst he tried to overtake the natives, but meeting with McDowall, a mounted man, he brought him back to assist in carrying the wounded man out, as it was of the greatest consequence to get round the hill before they were observed by the enemy; that they carried him at their utmost speed for more than a mile, until, getting exhausted, the captain took McDowall's horse, determined to overtake the friendly natives and force some of them to return and assist; that on overtaking them they refused to return until he threatened to stop their pay. Some men then returned with him, until they met Dr. Gibbs, with McDowall and the wounded man, they having contrived to carry him another mile down the valley. That from November Dr. Gibbs had been in constant attendance on the wounded, half of that time actually living on biscuit and tea, and for three days on fern-root, the enemy having cut off their supplies; that during this period the doctor had a sunstroke from exposure, aggravated by severe work and bad living; that he considered that Dr. Gibbs's action in remaining with this wounded man after the whole force had left, more especially as he knew no one in the force would be likely to think of him but himself, is deserving of the notice of the Government. In fact, he knew of nothing better than his behaviour from first to last during the whole native war." Dr. Gibbs next served under Lieut.-Colonel Herrick at Waikaremoana, and afterwards with Lieut.-Colonel McDonnell throughout the Taupo campaign, as principal medical officer, and was recommended by the latter officer for the New Zealand Cross, " for gallant conduct under fire at the attack and capture of those two well defended positions at the Iwa-tua Range, Te Porere, and Te Heu-heu, on the 4th October, 1869. That his gallant conduct and his constant anxiety to relieve the wounded during the five hours' hard fighting, until the position was stormed, was the admiration not only of the force engaged, but also of the enemy, for the attention he paid their wounded also at the close of the engagement." After the Taupo campaign he was appointed principal medical officer of the Taupo district, which position he resigned in 1873 to again attend to his private practice.

MAJOR TURNER.

Beginning of the war—First tears of doubt shed—Major Turner wounded.

DURING the summer of 1860, while travelling down the coast to the Wellington races, accompanied by Captain Blewett and Dr. Gibson, we were overtaken by a messenger who had been despatched to bring up two companies of the 65th Regiment then stationed there, the Taranaki natives having shown fight by the erection of a strong pa on land which Governor Gore Browne had notified his intention to take possession of. We arrived in Wellington on the day of the embarkation, which a great crowd had assembled to witness. The wives and children of the soldiers had received orders to take leave of the men at the barracks; but one young mother, more anxious than the rest, had, despite all orders, taken up her station under the wharf, and as the troops commanded by Major Turner passed over, she held up her baby so that its father by going on his knees could kiss it. The sensation this circumstance caused was indescribable, and the first tears of doubt and anxiety for the fate of those about to engage in the struggle were shed by that young wife. In vain did the clergyman assure her that the troops had only to show themselves and all would be over. Those who knew the Maoris best thought otherwise, and the clergyman himself was but too soon convinced of his mistake, as the returning steamer brought back the commanding officer (Major Turner) seriously wounded, a ball having entered his mouth and lodged in his neck. Thus began a war which speedily assumed such proportions that the Governor considered it necessary to send to England for assistance, which was readily and liberally granted by the British Government, as ten regiments, with their commissariat staff and transport corps, were soon located in the Taranaki and Auckland provinces, the outbreak having been confined principally to those districts up to the summer of 1865, when the disaffected natives, finding the Imperial troops more than a match for them in the open country of the Waikato, left that district and joined the Wanganui natives in their bush fastnesses, determined to fight to the bitter end.

SUB.-INSPECTOR ROWAN.

SUB.-INSPECTOR ROWAN.

SUB-INSPECTOR F. C. ROWAN volunteered his services against the West Coast natives under Titokowaru in 1868, and commanded, as lieutenant, the Taranaki volunteers, perhaps the best body of volunteers in the colony. In August, 1868, he was present at the first attack upon Te Ngutu-o-te-Manu, and led one of the attacking parties with distinction. On the 7th September he took part at the second attack, and fell dangerously wounded, being shot through the jaw whilst foremost in the attack. He rejoined the force in 1871, and was appointed a sub-inspector in the Armed Constabulary, in which force he served at Te Wairoa and White Cliffs until the year 1877, when he resigned the commission as senior sub-inspector, and left the colony.

CAPTAIN MACE;

Capt. F. J. Mace.

APTAIN MACE, who had been a resident in Taranaki for some years, distinguished himself so conspicuously on the outbreak of the war in that province by his intrepid conduct, as to merit from the Government of the colony the highest military distinction they could bestow on a colonial officer, viz., the New Zealand Cross, which honour was conferred upon him for conspicuous bravery in the performance of his duty throughout the war ; for most valuable and efficient services in conveying despatches through the enemy's country, and in acting as guide upon many important expeditions. Notably his conduct at the Kaitikara river, on the 4th June, 1863 ; at Kaitake, on the 11th March, 1864 ; and at Warea, on the 20th October, 1865. Captain Mace served from the commencement of the war in 1860 under Captain Burton, watching for two days the enemy's approach to Waireka, thereby saving the lives of many of the outsettlers, who were collecting their cattle for safety. He acted as one of the guides to Captain Cracroft's party, who so gallantly carried the Waireka pa on the 28th March, and for this service the Government of the day presented Mace and his brother guides, Charles and Edward Messenger, with a revolver each. He then joined the Mounted Troop, and served through the Waitara campaigns under Generals Pratt and Cameron, he and his company's services being publicly noticed by both Generals on several occasions. He was further sent for and thanked personally by Governor Browne for his action at the capture at the Peach Grove. Captain Mace subsequently served under Colonel Warre, and was employed carrying despatches between New Plymouth and Opunake, twenty-five miles of which was through the enemy's country, where no troops were stationed. This service he performed several times, accompanied by twenty-five of his troopers as an escort. His troop was in every engagement and most of the skirmishes that took place, and was mentioned in most of the military despatches, and twice brought before the special notice of the Government by

Colonel Warre, and in a letter from the Defence Minister (Colonel Haultain) to Colonel Lepper he acknowledged that the past services of Captain Mace's troop were second to none in the colony. He had one horse killed under him at the taking of the Ahu Ahu pa and two others wounded under heavy fire on other occasions. In July, 1863, he was sent by the Government to Dunedin to raise men as Military Settlers, and returned with 215, these being the first landed in Taranaki.

EXTRACTS FROM DESPATCHES IN THE NEW ZEALAND GOVERNMENT GAZETTE.

[COLONEL WARRE TO MILITARY SECRETARY.]

(No. 23, 1863.)

"As I consider Mr. Mace's conduct deserves special notice, I beg to state that he has lately been in charge of the mounted orderlies as ensign in the Taranaki Militia and has frequently been of great service to me since I have been in command of the outposts. His courage is proverbial, and I myself saw him gallop after three or four Maoris and shoot one of them."

[COLONEL WARRE TO ASSISTANT MILITARY SECRETARY.]

(No. 53, 1863.)

"I must also beg to be allowed to mention the excellent conduct of Captain Mace, who with his troops were unceasing in their efforts to assist the wounded and distribute ammunition."

[COLONEL WARRE TO ASSISTANT MILITARY SECRETARY.]

(No. 4, 1864.)

"The mounted men under Captain Mace did the skirmishing through the thick scrub and fern for the troops."

[COLONEL WARRE TO QUARTERMASTER-GENERAL.]

(No. 11, 1864.)

"And especially to bring to the notice of the Governor the gallantry of Captain Mace, who on this occasion, with trooper Antonio Rodriguez, so nobly assisted the wounded men."

[MAJOR BUTLER TO COLONEL WARRE.]

"The Mounted Volunteers who accompanied me behaved throughout with their usual conspicuous courage and coolness. Of these I beg to name Captain Mace and Antonio Rodriguez, the latter of whom again distinguished himself by carrying the wounded men to the rear under heavy fire."

Dr. Grace.

DR. GRACE arrived in the colony in the month of July, 1861, with a detachment of engineers and infantry, who were landed at Taranaki. The following day he was placed in charge of the town hospital to attend the wounded consequent to Major Nelson's attack on Puke-te-Kauere. On General Pratt's arrival from Australia the doctor was attached to the Flying Column under Major Hutchinson, which had its head-quarters at Waireka camp, from which point these flying columns swept the whole country round about, being daily engaged with the natives in preventing a concentration of their forces against their contemplated attack on the township of New Plymouth. Dr. Grace was also present at the attack made on the pa erected on Dr. Rawson's land, and from his kindness of disposition and readiness to give his services to all, he became a great favourite with the whole colonial force. Being now on the General's staff he was more or less present in every affair that took place at this period, and was soon after placed by Dr. Mouatt in charge of the field hospital at Waitara, where the first ambulance corps was organised. On the 28th of December he marched with the advanced guard of the 40th Regiment to Matarikoriko. The skirmishers had taken up their position at dawn of day so well supported both in rear and flank, as to give them that feeling of security that for a moment they piled their arms, but they had hardly done so when the natives fell upon them, rising suddenly out of the scrub immediately around them with fearful yells. Taken completely by surprise, the 40th began to waver, and would probably have fled, but were saved by the doctor, who, not daring to leave his wounded, cried out, "Tipperary boys to the rescue. Give them the bayonet. Ireland for ever!" This brought the men to their senses, and like magic the tide was turned and the credit of the British army saved. For this act of cool courage he was thanked by General Pratt in orders.

Dr. Henry, of Wellington, and Drs. Gibbs and Carroll, of New Plymouth, also saw a deal of hard service and were many times in imminent peril.

CAPTAIN BOWER.

CAPTAIN BOWER.

CAPTAIN M. N. BOWER, who had seen long service in the Crimea, on arrival in this colony, was (in June, 1863) made sub-inspector of the Colonial Defence Force, and inspector in the following year, captain in the New Zealand Militia on the 6th June, 1864, and of the Auckland Militia, on the 3rd February, 1865. He served as adjutant of the Colonial Defence Force, under Colonel Nixon, until the force was disbanded; was adjutant of the flying column under General Carey, accompanied the column, under General Cameron, from Te Rori to Te Awamutu; was present at the attack and capture of the village of Rangiaohia, and was with Colonel Nixon when wounded. He served with the 1st Waikato Regiment at Tauranga; was district adjutant at Opotiki; took over Fort Colville, Maketu, from the Imperial forces, on their withdrawal from New Zealand; served with the force under Colonel Harrington at Pye's Pa, and attack and capture of the village of Ake Ake and others. He also served with Lieut.-Colonels McDonnell and St. John, as district adjutant and quartermaster of the field force expedition to Ohinemutu, Rotorua, and to the field force at Wairoa, Hawke's Bay. He was ordered to Poverty Bay after the massacre, and served until the fall of Ngatapa under Colonel Whitmore. He was afterwards made adjutant of the Waikaremoana field force under Colonel Herrick; and, lastly, served as adjutant and quartermaster of Taupo field force, under Lieut.-Colonel Roberts, until the force was disbanded.

Sergeant Hill.

ERGEANT HILL, of No. 1 division of the Armed Constabulary, obtained the New Zealand Cross for his intrepid conduct at the relief of the Jerusalem Pa, at Mohaka, on the 10th of April, 1869. Constable (now sergeant) Hill accompanied the Wairoa natives, who, under their chief, Ihaka Whanga, proceeded to relieve Mohaka, then under attack by Te Kooti. Constable Hill volunteered with a party to run the gauntlet of the enemy's fire, and dash into the pa, then so sorely pressed. This was a desperate and dangerous service, and it was in a great measure due to the example set by Constable Hill (who led the party) that it was successfully carried cut. During the subsequent portion of the siege, Hill so animated the defenders by his exertions, that the repulse of Te Kooti may be attributed to him; his conduct being spoken of with admiration by the natives.

ASSIST.-SURGEON WEBBER.

ASSIST.-SURGEON WEBBER.

EVERYONE acquainted with the late Dr. Webber, of the Taranaki Military Settlers, knew him to be one of the bravest of the brave, and to such, the following anecdote will not be needed to convince them of the fact, that though an excellent surgeon, he was by no means at heart a non-combatant officer.

In 1865, while quartered at the White Cliffs, Taranaki, a subaltern and twenty men (whom he accompanied as medical officer,) were sent down to the wrecked steamer *Alexandra* to save her from pillage by the natives in the district, and while dispersing some Maoris on the beach, were suddenly fired upon by a party in ambush from the cliffs above. Finding themselves between two fires, and at a disadvantage owing to their exposed position with a hidden enemy in their rear, the officer in charge took prompt steps to get his men under cover. To do so a projecting cliff had to be repassed, as it stood between them and the camp, in rounding which they would again be exposed to the close fire of the ambush party in addition to the fire from the natives in front, who were now fast returning. Consequently our men had to run the gauntlet. The doctor being appointed to the command of the first party of five to make the trial rounded the point safely, when the supposed non-combatant was seen returning alone, and taking up a position on the point of the cliff, defied the rebels to hit him, while he coolly emptied his revolver in return. Luckily for him, at this moment he was seized by the second party on return, and quickly dragged into safety, with a brief but terse reminder, that it was not a part of his duty to be shot at. This brave and generous doctor, gallant and genial soul, beloved alike by officers and men, has finished his earthly campaigning, but his memory lives in the affections of every member of his company who survives him.

LIEUTENANT GUDGEON.

LIEUT. GUDGEON.

LIEUTENANT GUDGEON, the author, arrived in New Zealand on the 10th of January, 1850, having resigned a Government appointment, after seven years' service in the Income and Property Tax Office, Somerset House, London. He took his passage in the good ship *Berkshire*, which vessel being laid on for Taranaki direct, he made that district his home for the first ten years of his pilgrimage, settling down as a bush farmer on one of the furthest back sections in the district, six miles at least from the township. Finding his family increasing, with no chance of educating them, he, in 1859, removed to Wanganui. He had not been there many months when the war in Taranaki broke out, and he had just cause to congratulate himself on his removal, as the two little boys, Pote and Parker, who were the first to fall under the tomahawk of the natives, were the daily companions of his children, going to the same infant school together, their parents occupying the adjoining sections.

The war after a time left the district of Taranaki and travelled northward to the Waikato, and in 1864 broke out in Wanganui, when all capable of bearing arms were called upon to enrol, and he soon found himself in the enviable position of a full private in the Wanganui Militia, doing alternate night picket duty until he was appointed quartermaster and commissariat officer to the colonial forces with rank of lieutenant. Being on the commanding officer's staff, he was one of the first to hear of the movements and disposition of the colonial forces, and every circumstance as it occurred, having oftentimes the painful duty of conveying very sad news from the front to the wives and children who remained in the township. The Maori war was very distasteful to the Imperial forces, and no wonder either, as most of the regiments had come flushed with victory, direct either from the Crimea or the Indian Mutiny, and were disgusted with the guerilla bush fighting of New Zealand. As they had not suffered by the rebellion they had nothing to avenge. No hard earned property destroyed; no homes broken up; no wives and children slaughtered; no honour to gain. Consequently they looked upon the Maori as a foe unworthy of their steel. This feeling it was that led eventually to the withdrawal of the Imperial forces. Then it was that the Government fought the natives with our colonial lads, who were as much at home in the recesses of the New Zealand forests as on the open plain. They soon terminated the war, which but for the attempt to capture Te Kooti would have come to a close long before. In September, 1869, the war being virtually over, Lieutenant Gudgeon applied for and obtaining leave left Wanganui for the Thames goldfields, residing there till the end of 1879, when he settled down in the city of Auckland, and collecting together his manuscripts, published his reminiscences of the war, the doings of the Maoris from 1820 to the signing of the Treaty of Waitangi in 1840, and this present volume; and if, in so doing, he has passed by anyone whose deeds deserve recording, or has been guilty of errors, either of commission or omission, in the descriptions he has given of the services he has chronicled, let it be attributed principally to the innate modesty of the colonial forces, who, in most instances, referred the author to their comrades for the information he sought rather than give it themselves. The author trusts, therefore, that whatever mistakes may be found in these biographies they will be looked upon as unintentional, and not arising from any want of inclination to do justice to all the men who so gallantly defended New Zealand.

A

MAORI HISTORY

BEING

A NATIVE ACCOUNT

OF THE

Pakeha-Maori Wars in New Zealand

BY

LIEUTENANT-COLONEL McDONNELL

OF THE NEW ZEALAND MILITIA

Auckland
H. Brett, Printer and Publisher, Shortland Street

DEDICATION.

———

THIS BOOK, CONTAINING OUR HISTORY, IS MOST RESPECTFULLY DEDICATED

BY

KOWHIA NGUTU KAKA

TO THE

OLD RANGATIRA PAKEHA TRIBE

AND TO THE

VOLUNTEERS AND MILITIA

WHO ARE NOW RESIDING IN OUR COUNTRY, CALLED BY THEM

NEW ZEALAND

BUT BY US

TE IKA O MAUI.

INTRODUCTION.

IN the following pages, I have endeavoured to give a brief Maori account of the early colonization of New Zealand, as also a history of the native wars that have taken place in this colony, which I gathered from a Maori chief, who was an eye-witness of many of the events recorded, and had learned from others on good authority. In every instance I have strictly adhered to the facts related, and have allowed my Maori historian to draw his own inferences from them. Of course, many of these inferences will be found absurd, as, for instance, the missionary who denounced Kahu and his people for fishing on the Sabbath, and assured them that they would "all go to hell and be burnt with fire for ever and ever, just like their wicked forefathers, who knew not Jehovah," did not mean to insult them. He merely did what he conceived to be his duty; while Kowhai Ngutu Kaka's inference was that as these fits of cursing, so dangerous to the tribe, might come upon these missionary wizards at any time, it was necessary for their own safety to destroy them. As a rule, the early missionaries were well-meaning men, and some were high-minded and self-sacrificing; but some were what we might expect men to be who, taken from inferior positions in society, suddenly found themselves at its head. Power is always a dangerous temptation, and a narrow theological education does not lessen its force. Religious enthusiasm was largely mixed with spiritual pride, and as time lessened the former it increased the latter in too many cases. Despite the idiosyncrasies of those early soldiers of the Church, they were, with few exceptions, faithful servants of their Master, and we cannot but admire the heroic self-sacrifice and devotion to duty of the pioneer missionaries, who were the bearers of the banner of the Cross in primeval New Zealand. Unfortunately, the Christian graces of the missionaries did not at first make so much impression on the natives as the rough-and-ready methods of the runaway sailors, who were amongst the earliest colonists, and were the progenitors of the class of Europeans still known as pakeha-Maoris. The Maori thought the Maori pakeha a good sort of fellow, and the missionary a mere visionary. His judgment was wrong in both cases; but it was his own, and I have studiously avoided giving my own impressions. What I have written are merely Maori ideas, and what I *know* to be such.

In the same way, I must not be considered responsible for what Kowhai Ngutu Kaka says about the folly of distinguished Imperial officers, or of Colonial Governments. I am no more responsible for his opinion of these persons and institutions than I am for his opinion that Te Ua caused the wreck of the steamship *Lord Worsley* by his incantations. In like manner, I leave him to say what he really thinks about confiscation and other matters. In short, I only wish to be regarded as the translator of the thoughts of a people in regard to ourselves whom I know thoroughly. I understand their language and traditions. I have fought with them and against them. I have dealt with them as a settler, bought land of them as a Government officer, and sold it for them as their agent. I have lived amongst them as one of themselves, helped them, and have been helped by them in peace and in war. I know their good qualities and their bad, their knowledge and their ignorance, their wisdom and their folly. I have often taken an active part, and often a leading part, in public matters, where European and native interests came into collision. I am no Philo-Maori, nor am I blind to the faults of my own countrymen. I think if we had acted more on the motto " Be just, and fear not" in our dealings with the Maori it would have been better for both races. I believe our intentions have been excellent, but most of them have gone to pave a well-known road. All I can hope is that the road will never reach its terminus. Purgatory is fair enough for both pakeha and Maori. We have, I fancy, just reached that stage, and I think I have done no harm in showing how the natives of New Zealand think we have got there.

THOMAS McDONNELL.

CHAPTER I.

My Tanewha ancestry, and how I manage to prove my claims to land.

AM descended from a long line of ancestors. The first mortal or man ancestor of mine was the offspring of a great Tanewha, who lived in the whirlpools and dark caves about Tongariro. From such a source is my origin, and as such it has been acknowledged by the Native Land Courts, one of your legal institutions; so I hope that no one will doubt this account of my original and immortal descent. I have, too, with my tribe, based our rights—well, I will say our claims, as it is a better word than rights—to many a block of fair land. I always took money when it was offered to me on account of my claim from commissioners. As the fact of having sold and accepted money was certain to secure, if not the entire block, an interest therein, I always took as much as I could get. When in Court, to support that claim, I always swore to the truth on your Bible. I rubbed my nose well on it (our form of kissing, or substitute for it), and then I traced my descent from that old and ancient Tanewha. In the main my accounts did not differ much, and I always claimed my Tanewha for my ancestor. I always won my case, as I always sold to the Government. I invariably did thus, thanks to a teaching I had had from my Tanewha ancestor, who appeared to me in a dream, and said, " All this country was mine when I dwelt in Tongariro. You are my descendant, so grasp all you can. If you don't others will. Stick to your Tanewha; quote him well; chant songs of no meaning. People don't like to expose their ignorance, and they will agree with you as to what you say is the meaning, for the less they know the more stubborn they will be to agree to it. Go to! Arise, my son! The Courts wait for you! Go, and the white Christian race will protect you! Obey their behests, and love yourself, even as they love each man themselves. *E noho !"* (Farewell !). And he vanished. But I often see him in my dreams, and his teachings are ever the same. My ancestry, eighty-nine generations back, each generation marked on this notched stick; the top and biggest notch is my Tanewha's mark, made with a stone axe by himself. My mother was a Waikato; my father, the one who begat me, for I have many fathers, originally came from Ngatiruanui. The tipuna (grandfather) of my mother's sister was a Uriwera chief, who again was the grandson of a Ngapuhi, who had killed an Arawa chief under the great Hongi-Hika. Fortunately for me this Ngapuhi grandfather of mine ate a portion of that

Arawa chief, so by our law he became entitled to his estates, to which I have a large right, and to Taupo and the Lake district (as your Courts acknowledge). So, as I explain to the Court, I am entitled to receive advances on the land occupied by the Ngapuhi, Arawa, Uriwera, Ngatiruanui, Rauru, and Waikatos. I could give you my own mother's ancestry, but it is totally different to that of her sister's. My father's ancestry was again different. Through him I claim at the Thames and Maketu, and Whakatane, and on a yet undiscovered goldfield. I cannot say I know where it is situated; but no doubt my Tanewha does, and will tell me in time to send in my claim, so I am in no hurry. My father's father died, his mother threatened to marry again, so my father married his own mother to keep the estate in the family. Then she died, when in her right he became possessed of the manor which has by right descended to me. So you see I am a large land owner, and always am willing to sell to anyone, but prefer the Government to buy. Further, I am related to all the Hauhaus and Kingites, and until the last few years have fought against you. That is over now for me, and now I will tell you why I have addressed you. It has long been my wish to seek out a good European, if I can find one, who understands our ways, and get him to put into your language what I tell him in mine, but who at the same time can be trusted to keep my real name a secret. Well, I have found this European translator, seen and talked him to attention, and told him that he must put down what I say word for word. I will give our history of the past war, and the fights, and the causes that led us to fight against you. Governors have written, premiers have written, generals have written histories of the war. Missionaries have written. Some of them have told the whole truth, others have when it suited them. Rusden has written, ugh! such a book; but, alas! the majority of the writers have lied and cheated. Before I commence my history of the fighting, as witnessed by me, for *our history*, will you consent to publish it when it is sent to you? I shall only speak the truth. What I have witnessed I will speak of as that I have seen, and what I have been told as that I have 'heard. My book will be better than the books of those pakehas who have written solely from what they have been told or read of.

CHAPTER II.

Our history—Captain Cook—The arrival of the missionaries.

I WILL commence with, I will say, one hundred years ago. Many years ago (it may be one hundred years or more, for Maoris do not remember dates or time,) a people who called themselves missionaries came to our shores and distributed themselves all over our country. Until the arrival of these persons we had, on the whole, lived a happy life. In the spring we cultivated our yam and kumera fields; we searched and obtained the substantial fern root that was to us, when pinched by failure of our crops, a never-failing source of food. There it grew, and at all seasons of the year, but especially in the spring and summer months, it was eaten by us. The fern root of these days is not what it once was, as the pigs brought here by the pakehas have almost entirely destroyed the good kinds by their eternal rooting. With bundles of this dried root our people who resided far inland used to come in the season to their recognised fishing places on the coast, and there live on fresh fish, dried fish, and the fern root they had packed down with them, until it was time to return and weed their kumera beds, and snare the rats, who at this time began to burrow in the kumera hillocks in search of the young and sweet roots. It was a necessity with us to snare these little animals, as otherwise they would have destroyed our plantations.

It is generally believed, though it is an error of the pakehas, that we principally lived on fern root; but we only used it in conjunction with other food, except when we were hard pressed. We ate these rats; they were game to us in their season. They were totally unlike the large pakeha rats who live on offal and sewerage. Our rat was fat, tender, and sweet, living only on nutritious roots. He was to us an article of food—a delicacy—what the pheasant and hare is to the pakeha; only we ate ours when it was pure and sweet; they eat theirs when it is decomposed by long keeping and stinks like a dead hawk. But yet they express disgust at us because we steep maize and potatoes in fresh running water to make them soft. What a blind and self-conceited race the pakehas are! I have known many Europeans, the late Sir Donald McLean, Parris, and other pakehas, eat our steeped maize; ay! and enjoy it greedily; but I have never known a Maori attempt to eat a putrid pheasant or a decayed hare. Well, as I was saying, we lived merrily. We had our moaris—long slender spars we used to swing from by ropes attached to the top of it. It was firmly fixed in the ground on the grassy and

EE*

mossy banks of our rivers and streams.   Many ropes were fastened
to the head of it, and our men, women, and little ones used to swing
off the ground and, when over the cool river, let go the rope and
be plunged into the water.   It was great fun.   This way of taking
our bath lasted all the summer months.   Then we had kiwi and
weka hunting, pigeon and kaka (parrot) snaring and spearing, eel
spearing, and fish spearing by torchlight on the sandy and muddy
flats of our rivers.   There was no dearth of sport for ourselves and
our young ones.

At the fall of the leaf, and in the winter, we lived on the harvest
we had gathered in the summer and autumn.   We had our games,
too.   The kaihotaka (humming top) was a great amusement to all,
and the different tones sounded by these tops as they flew off the
ground and bounded in the air from the lash of the muka (dressed
flax) whips, sounded like the string of a harp when one of them is
struck singly.   We had the haka, too, and the dance.   We loved
music—not the discordant scraping sound of the fiddle I have
heard played in a public house, danced to by intoxicated pakehas,
who at one time, it was thought by us, were so maddened by its
horrible noise that they tried to drown its scrapings by shouting
and gesticulating.   We know better now what it all meant.   Not the
crashing sound of drums and brass bands, or the bugle.   No, such
was not our music.   Our music was what even our oldest warriors
and priests used to listen to with pleasure   The flocks of little birds
who welcomed the rising and sang the setting sun to rest, mingling
their liquid notes with the distant hum of the waterfall and the
rippling of the water of our mountain stream, as it raced rapidly
on to the sea over the pebbles   Such was our music; but our bird
bands have now gone for ever.   Nothing softens the crashing sound
made by the water as it is hurled over the precipice, and the
murmuring of the brooks creates a desolate feeling in our hearts.
When I think and muse over these shadows of the past my soul
grows dark; then my heart begins to throb and my right arm to
tingle, and I exclaim, "Oh! had not my sinews been cut by the
pakeha? Oh! why did he ever come to disturb us in our happy
country? Why did not our ancestors foresee our ruin, and slay
all who first touched our shores?   Why did not our sacred Tanewha
warn us?   Too late! alas, too late!   We cannot kill them now."
Although, when we found them out, we had a try for it, as in
the course of our history I will tell.

Let us return to our missionary.   When those people came here
first we were very much surprised at their appearance and bearing.
We had seen Captain Cook and his sailors.   They were a cheerful
and merry tribe—good-natured, very affectionate (especially to our
women), and gave us a quantity of useful things without asking for
payment, such as hooks, axes, iron hoops, etc.   We liked this tribe
very much.   But this new tribe, the missionary, puzzled and vexed
us.   The majority of them were very solemn, and had a gloominess
about them as if all their relations had been eaten and they were
powerless to get their revenge.   We asked our priests, "Are they

spirits?" Some replied they were good spirits, others that they were bad spirits, others again that they were a mixture of good and bad. "Say you so?" said a chief named Poata. "Well, then, let them be killed. We are quite good enough, and want no more evil." A "hui" (gathering) took place to discuss this view of the question, but I believe the meeting broke up without doing anything definite in council. That meeting years ago did then what the pakeha meetings of Parliament do now. They met, they talked, they ate, and drank—though they did not get tipsy—and did nothing; but after it was over the women of the people had to work extra hard to replace the quantity of food that had been wasted. A great many meetings took place in different parts of our country, and it was generally settled that the missionary tribe should be allowed—though tolerated would be a better word—to try and persuade those who were willing to listen to their incantations or prayers. Our country was a free country, and everyone did as he liked, so long as nothing was done injurious to the welfare, prestige, or mana of the tribe. Mark that. But a few missionaries were killed, and that some of them were eaten is true. You will say that this was wrong, but I say it was right and only just in many instances. Listen! Some of our chiefs, bold, brave men, were somewhat of short temper, and though good-natured enough and keen for a joke, would on no account stand undue familiarity. They had a high-spirited, though very affectionate, race to lead—not control, mind—or guide, and to have put up with insult without avenging it according to its nature would have been fatal to a chief occupying a leading position; and not only so, but injurious to the tribe, as it would render it contemptible to its neighbours. Taking this into consideration, will any reasonable person be astonished at the following action taken by my great-grandfather Kahu, as fine an old warrior as ever led men to battle. One day, as he was returning from a whapuku fishing excursion, in which some visitors, Ngapuhi chiefs and their favourite wives had accompanied him by invitation, he was met by a missionary on the beautiful surf-beaten beach of Tatahi, and as the men of the tribe dragged the large red canoe, fish and all, ashore, this person thus addressed my great-grandfather: "You are a wicked, bad man. You have not listened to my teachings; you have broken the Sabbath commandment by going over to fish. My God is angry. You and your people will all go to hell, and be burnt with fire for ever and ever, just like your wicked forefathers, who knew not Jehovah. Repent, or be lost!" All eyes were turned from this man's face, and became fixed on my great-grandfather, who had been threatened by this missionary that he would be burnt with the fire that was now burning up his ancestors, male and female; that he was to be cooked with fire, and *never* to be done. Not a doubt existed—could have existed—in the hearts of the tribe as to what the result would be. No harm had been done to this stranger of a stranger tribe. He had asked for, and obtained, a piece of land in our tribal district to build upon; houses had been built for him and his gods; yams, kumeras, fish, crayfish, shellfish, eels, pigeons, kakas, and rats, each in its season, had been largely heaped up for him, as he said it was good to give to him and his god; and then, without any provocation at all, he had cursed my great grandfather! True, this man would be killed, and his flesh would be cooked with fire and sent to the neighbouring tribe, who would, of course, hear of this awful cursing. Each tribe would have its tana muru (robbing party), who would come and ravage the settlement, dig up and trample our kumera and yam plantations; blood would flow from wounds received and given, and perhaps it might be necessary to have someone killed to wipe away the disgrace of this cursing. My great-grandfather's mats and kiwi mats would all go, as they would be brought from their places of safe keeping and exposed to view. These robbing parties it would never do to allow to return empty-handed, for my great-grandfather was a powerful chief, and the tribe would feel insulted if they and their chief were not well robbed, as otherwise it would appear as if their mana (prestige) was so small that it was not worth taking notice of.

So far so right; but otherwise it would be a great loss to the whole tribe, and the man who was the cause of all this coming trouble was one we had befriended. Yes, it evidently was about as nasty a piece of kohuru (unprovoked maliciousness) as ever we have been told of or dreamt of. "Lay hold of him," cried my great-grandfather; "take him out of his kotiroa (long coat) and other clothes." This was done more quickly than a boiled kumera is taken out of its skin. "Remove his head and place it on to the short pole in front of our big house; stick it upright, and cook the rest of his body in a priest's sacred oven." This order was quickly obeyed, and in less time than it takes to remove the feathers from a fat pigeon the man of incantations was in an oven, and prevented from creating further mischief. He had done quite enough as it was. Some of him we ate, but the most part of him was cut up into many portions and sent away to the tribes far and near, to show and to prove that my great-grandfather was not a chief to be insulted with impunity, or a man to allow his ancestors to be cursed for nought. Every day for a whole moon after this tauas came upon us, robbing us first and then condoling with my great-grandfather, and showing their respect for him to such a degree that when the tauas left off coming we had not a kumera left, nor had my great-grandfather a flax or kiwi mat in his house.

A few other missionaries were, by distant tribes, killed at once by the tribes they had taken up their abode with, as they said, "Who could tell when a fit of cursing might seize them and cause the same trouble to fall on them as has fallen on us?" Some of these missionaries were afterwards eaten out of curiosity to see what they tasted like, but they were not approved of, as I have heard tell. The rest of the missionaries met when things had cooled down a bit, and told us through some of our slaves, who had been baptised and made catechists of, that a letter was being written to King George (George the Fourth), who would send war parties in big ships, and batter us. We believed this, as it was natural and right that the English king chief would want payment for the death of one of his wizards, and we felt uneasy, though why he should have sent that style of men to our shores to curse us we could not tell. On the receipt of this news, two lines of action were recommended to us by our chief men. The first was to kill all the missionaries, and cook the lot ; then they could not make personal complaints against us when the ship of King George came. We decided, however, not to molest them further, and to await the current of events.

Then King George's ships never came to get utu (payment) for the missionaries who had been killed ; and we afterwards found out, from other Europeans, that King George had never heard anything about us. By this time many of our inferior men had joined their churches and ways of praying ; and other ships brought fresh tribes to our shores. You must know that the missionaries had names for our people. Those who were baptised, and said they believed all they were told, were called missionaries. Those who would not be baptised were called by them Teweras (devils)—a nice name for us, don't you think ? But, when these other people came, these wizards of priests said they were devils too, just as we were called devils ; and we were glad to hear it. Anyway, we would be even with them now, and give a welcome to the new tribe called the Pakeha Devil Tribe.

CHAPTER III.

Devil Pakehas.

BEFORE I go into the matter of the new tribe of pakeha rewera (devil pakehas), I must relate to you a new code of laws laid down for us to follow by this wizard tribe of missionaries lest, by neglecting them, we incurred the anger of the new gods, whose powers were being made known to our people. The Ten Commandments we had already been made acquainted with, and, on the whole, we thought them good. But we were much puzzled about the new laws made for our tribe and people. We were not to spin humming-tops on Sunday, or peel kumeras or potatoes. They were to be peeled on Saturday evening, or we must boil them in their skins. We were not to gather firewood on a Sunday, or fish, or bathe, or go into the woods to get tawharas (fruit), or catch eels; and if any traveller came to our village on Saturday evening, he was to be asked if he meant to continue his journey on the morrow, and, if so, he or they would not be permitted to rest there, but would have to move on, as it would be desecrating the Sabbath.

I remember hearing that, one season, a native of our village, who had been created a teacher of the new religion, broke our law with a betrothed maiden, and then took shelter with his chief wizard missionary. The tribe resolved at length to ask for him, fully expecting that, as he had broken their own commandments about taking other people's goods, to say nothing about his having broken our laws, too, that no difficulty would present itself. But this wizard missionary would not give the transgressor up to be punished and spoke to us of a woman who had sinned, and who was going to be stoned to death for the offence, but who was pardoned *without payment*. That settled the question, and they dragged the Maori who had committed the wrong to the clear place in the middle of the village, where he was speared through and through by the chief to whom the young woman had been betrothed. But had this Maori teacher of new incantations been a chief, or a brave man, he would have known how to meet his antagonists, and have warded off the blows aimed at him; then the tribe very likely would have interfered to save him. As it was, all the kaiaka tanga (science) was on one side, and he fell ignominiously, as a woman falls, without defence worth calling such. As the man who now lay dead from the spear wounds was of our tribe, we prepared to place him in the fork of the puriri tree in our waihi tapu (sacred place), but the missionary begged us to let him have the body, saying he would bury it in a hole he would dig for it, that at last our chief consented. "It will be something new to gaze upon," said he ; so a hole was dug in the ground, then the dead man was put in a long box, which was nailed down to prevent him getting out, as we thought ; then the missionary put the box in the hole, first of all writing a direction, as we supposed, on it, and then covered him up, after performing an incantation, and told us all he had gone to heaven.

Well, we welcomed the first devil tribe, and each chief and head of a hapu (family) exerted himself to obtain a pakeha ; wives were given to them to induce them to settle down and live with us, and be " our pakehas." It is true that some of them, as we look back now, were rough, and we found that some of them had, from motives of policy, left their own tribe without saying " hekona " (good-bye) ; but it was no use writing other people's names on bits of paper in our country, as nothing could be got by it, and there was nothing worth stealing they could carry away. We think they were good men, the most of them ; they worked hard, and their wives bare them lots of children for our tribe, and they treated their wives well, as a rule. Only one man, a whaler, beat his wife on one occasion for nothing. But when her relations heard of this they belaboured him so soundly with the butts of their spears that he was ill for some time. His wife afterwards told us that he had been drinking some waipiro (stinking water). We afterwards found out what this waipiro was, but did not drink it for many years. It has since proved to be our greatest curse, but we drink it whenever we can get it. These pakehas of ours laughed at the missionary wizards and would not attend their incantations. Nevertheless, on the whole, we preferred our devil pakehas to the missionaries. Thus we lived on until other pakehas came, who were an improvement on the former ones, as we thought, and who brought their pakeha wives and children with them.

CHAPTER IV.

*A terrible crime—Arrival of a Governor—Treaty of Waitangi—War in the
North—How we were taught repudiation—Causes that led us to war—
Land purchase and spoliation.*

NOTHING stands still, and guns were brought to us as
an article of trade. Iron hoops had been discarded for
tomahawks. A flint musket was a valuable article, but
a double-barrel flint gun was a weapon to be turned
over and over again to be admired; and pistols with a large bore
were precious, indeed, and showed to us that the pakeha knew how
to get rid of his foes by a sudden surprise, when it became
necessary.

To prove the value that we placed in muskets about the year
1830, I will relate the following story, and will tell it as it was
told to me, but I can vouch for its truth. There lived on the
Hokianga River two men who were sawyers. Both were pakehas
belonging to chiefs. They had several muskets and some pistols,
and each had a native wife. A slave man had been given them
by the chief, who had great authority. He had, with his people,
consented to be baptised, and his name went home to the Wesleyan
Mission Society. The chief was a good man, though his temper
was somewhat gusty and uncertain. He seized a double-barrelled
gun and shot a man one day at the Bay of Islands, because he
got the better of him in some argument. Well, one day, as these
sawyers were heaving a log on to the saw-pit, something gave
way, and the log fell on one of the men, hurting his leg badly.
The other, with his wife, went down the river to get assistance,
leaving his mate and the slave. The injured man during the
absence of his mate, had proof that his domestic arrangements
were all going wrong, and that the slave had been making a fool
of him. On his companion's return, he told him; but his wife had
eloped with the slave. Recovering from his hurt, the sawyer and
his mate went to the chief to see about getting back his wife and
to have revenge on the slave. The result of the conference
was that the chief promised to punish the slave, provided that
his pakehas gave him one musket afterwards, and one pistol as
payment in advance. This bargain was agreed to. The slave
and the woman had gone to the Ahu Ahu, a settlement not far
from Ohaeawai, to seek protection. The chief, accompanied by
his friend Hehi, went in search of them, and found them in
the above-named village. With fair and oily words the chief
induced the slave to return with them to Hokianga, telling

him never to mind the pakehas, as no notice would be taken of their complaint. Nearing the entrance of the bush that divides the country in this locality, they halted to roast some potatoes in the ashes of a fire they made. After partaking of these, the chief said to the slave, "Go on," and the slave said, "Lead on." The chief rose to go, the slave following him, carrying the bundles, Hehi bringing up the rear. Suddenly Hehi brought down his weapon on the man's head. The blow was not sufficient to stun him, and he sprang upon the chief, who had turned round to face him, and as they clutched each other both rolled on the ground. Hehi now despatched the slave, the chief holding him tight. They cut his head off, and pitched his body into the fork of a tree, and came on to where the sawyers lived. It was night when they got to the house (a wooden one). The pakehas arose and began to get them some food. "I have come for my musket, and I want one too for Hehi," said the chief. "Not till you have revenged us for the wrong the slave did us," replied one of the men. The chief, who had been sitting on the floor of the house, now arose and, letting the head roll off his lap, said in a stern voice, "There is your head; give me muskets." And they were given. I don't know if this account was sent home to the society of the wizards, but if it wasn't it ought to have been.

Nearly all the new arrivals bought land from us. Some of these pakehas paid fair prices; others obtained a right to thousands and thousands of acres for very little. Missionary Williams, Davis, and a score of others, bought land—Captain McDonnell, R.N., Judge Maning, Russell, St. Aubin, Busby, and others. But, be what they gave little or much, we were quite satisfied with it at the time, and knew what we were doing. Then the New Zealand Company bought land, and settlers continued to arrive.

At last a Governor arrived. This was in the year 1840. The Governor's name was Hobson. A paper called the Treaty of of Waitangi was signed by a few chiefs, who had only a right to sign for themselves, and not for the New Zealand Maoris as a whole. But it is doubtful, in spite of what has been said and written, if these old Maori chiefs really understood the true meaning of what they did sign. I don't believe they did. It was all great rubbish and nonsense.

After a time new laws were made. Ngapuhi, objecting to these laws, and seeing, with a troubled spirit, our independence slipping from us, cut down the flagstaff—the emblem of the Queen's authority over these islands at the Bay—and had a fight, which ended in the defeat of the Queen's troops, and the sacking of Kororareka town. The red-coat tribe were driven away; but the sailor tribe of Her Majesty's ship *Hazard*, commanded by Captain Robinson (or Robertson), fought like braves and Robinson slew several of our men in a hand-to-hand fight at the corner of the church, on Kororareka beach, and the marks of his cutlass are to be seen on the posts of the church-yard there to this day. After this victory of ours we erected a pa at Okaihau. The soldier tribe came to attack it, and boasted that they would eat their breakfast inside it. Tamati Waka Nene, Wiremu Repa, and Te Taonui, of the Popoto tribe, attempted to dissuade the English commander from attacking the pa in front, and said, " Let us go to the rear, where there are no rifle-pits, and only a slight fence." But he would not listen to them, such was his self-conceit. And then the bugle sounded, and this red-coated tribe came on like a pack of fowls when grain is thrown to them. Oh, what a brave but foolish tribe !

Hone Heke was in the pa with 250 men. Kawiti lay in ambush outside, in some scrub, with twice seventy warriors, all clothed in the pillage of the Bay of Islands town. " Wait till you see the eye of the enemy !" cried the chiefs. " Wait, be brave ! Wait, be ready ! Now, give them their breakfasts ! Haere mai ! Haere mai ! Bang ! Fire ! Ha ! ha ! ha !" And fifty men lay dead and wounded before the pa, not twenty feet from the palisading. Then they fell back. At this time, Kawiti charged with gun and tomahawk. Alas ! this was a fatal mistake. A bugle sounded, when the enemy, now reinforced by a number of men who had not joined in the assault on our pa, faced about, and came at our people with a rush, grinding their teeth, with their bayonets fixed on their muskets. And then it was all over. Down went Kawiti's choicest warriors. The ground was strewn with them. Kawiti lost half his men in that charge. We never tried that move again. Once was quite enough. On the return of the troops to camp, we afterwards heard that Tamati Waka Nene was so enraged at the useless sacrifice of men that he tore from a Maori whare a long stick, and hit the commander of the Queen's forces a blow on the head with it.

We left the pa that night, and built another at Ohaeawai. The soldier and sailor tribes drew up big guns from the Bay of Islands to batter it down. But all the posts of our pa were of puriri ; they fired plenty of balls at us, but they did not knock down our pa. Then they rushed it, but we drove them back with a killing fire, and they retreated, leaving their dead and dying, whom we tomahawked. We left that night, after Pene Tawi had lit a kauri gum fire on the breast of a wounded soldier—the only instance of torture resorted to in that war.

Then we went to Ruapekapeka (Bat's hole) Pa. Here we intended to take a stand, and give the Queen's troops a good thrashing and drive them into the sea. We had constant intercourse with the missionaries at this time, and no settler pakeha was touched by us. Not one hoof did we deprive them of. As our allies passed through pakeha settlements they bade them "Good day," and came on. The reason for this was threefold, as I will explain. First of all we had invited these pakehas to come and dwell amongst us, and we thought they all belonged to different tribes, like ourselves. We understood there was English Church, Wesleyan, and Catholic (the wizard missionary tribe of three hapus=families). Jews had not then arrived. They are a clever people. We are of this race. These families hated each other, it is true; but then it is natural for families to disagree, though of one tribe. Then came the tribe of inferior pakehas, called " rerewas " (devil pakehas), because they would not attend to what the wizard tribes taught. Then came the superior pakeha—"rangitira," gentleman tribe—and the children of these old pakehas are respected to this day. Then the red-coat tribe, and then the sailor (Captain Cook) tribe. Ah! these last were a fine lot of men—worth ever so much more than the red-coat tribe. Afterwards we found out, but not so very long ago, that all these people and tribes really comprise one tribe. It was very puzzling to us, and is now. The third reason was, we feared to do any wrong to our friends lest payment be demanded of us, and taken, if we did not give it. This was a very good reason.

How we came to lose the Ruapekapeka Pa will seem to you very absurd now. But it was the innocent fault of the missionaries. I feel sure if they had known of our doings they would have warned us. We never did them the injustice to think that they behaved treacherously to us in this war.

We generally understood (for we had been taught by the pakeha) that the seventh day being Sunday was set aside as a day of rest, as was stated in the Ten Commandments; and in the enemy's camp the missionaries had, they informed us, performed divine service, and prayed with and for the army of the Queen. Well, one Sunday we all went out of the pa to have prayers too—to pray for ourselves—and only a few of the devil ones remained inside. No thought had crossed our minds of misfortune, when all of a sudden the army of the pakeha were inside and outside our pa. We fought, but it was of no use. We were beaten, and lost heavily, and our stronghold was captured by the soldiers.

This was the last fight worth recording, and shortly afterwards peace was made and all were friends again, only that the Queen's flagstaff was not attempted to be re-erected until many years afterwards. We would not have that. No heartburnings were felt, because no land was confiscated.

It was after this war with Hone Heke that the pakeha passed a law to prevent Europeans selling us guns and ammunition. Perhaps this was a wise act on their part. But I could tell you of pakeha traders and whalers who paid little or no attention to it. They used to get out double-barrelled guns in cases, hidden in bales of blankets, and plenty of powder and shot. A score of guns and a hundredweight of powder was as much as one could get secretly from our friends the traders at one time; but we often got a ton or so of powder from the American whalers when on the eve of starting home to their own country. The ships used to lay off and on the coasts from Coromandel up to the Bay of Plenty and Poverty Bay. Plenty of tobacco, too, we got in that way.

The Northern natives were not so well off as the East Coast tribes. I remember some of those Ngapuhi chiefs, anxious to be allowed to purchase openly, sailed from Hokianga to Auckland to see the Government. For a chief to make that voyage in the days I speak of (thirty and more years ago) was a great event. Well, they at last got to Auckland, after great expense and trouble, and had an interview with the Government, related their errand, spoke of their past and present loyalty to the Queen of England, and hoped that permission would be given to them to buy powder and shot. After some talk they were informed that this permission was allowed them, and they returned highly elated with the success of their mission. Fancy their disgust, and how they were laughed at when, on going to the traders to purchase ammunition, they were informed that though permission was accorded them to buy the prohibition had not been taken off against selling! They had been put off with this in Auckland, and sold in a rascally manner. Nice treatment for men who helped the pakeha in his time of need with men and guns.

Letters were now received by us, and communications were sent to the chiefs in the different districts to the effect that a commission would be appointed to inquire into the various land transactions between the pakeha and the Maori. So that if we liked (for so we read it, and our race can quickly take a hint) to repudiate our bargains, we could do so. This commission sat. We claimed back all our land we had formerly sold to the pakehas, and got most of it. We felt ashamed after this to visit our pakehas for some time, but a great many of them went away and never came back any more. But the Government said we might do this unjust thing, and rob them. So it was not us who really were to blame. When the Maori people declared war against the Government years afterwards (a war that has cost millions of money to prevent us regaining the lands they had for the most part robbed us of), we had a vivid remembrance of who taught us repudiation in the first instance. Nothing, as I have before said, stands still, and some things travel in circles. If anyone starts a wrong, it will come back to him again, and we all get punished in turn for our robberies. The Government bought, with a strong hand, our fair tracts of land for from one penny up to fivepence an acre; but they had far better have purchased it in an honourable way—ay, and given us twenty pounds an acre—than have fought with us for it.

I will try as well as I can to explain the later reason we had for going to war. First of all, we thought it would be easy to vanquish and kill the pakehas. We looked upon them as merely a large number of thistles, easily cut down and rooted up; and, after we had endured much wrong, the thought of an easy victory was very fascinating to our nature. But the chief, the very chief reason of our commencing to fight—the reason that had attracted so many tribes, and attached them to the King movement—was the unjust manner in which our land was being torn from us. There were no Native Land Courts in those days to even make a semblance of doing justice ; but one man was appointed the land purchase officer for the Government. I am only a native, and am not able to go into all the pakeha policy of those dark, black days, which ought to have been bright days for us.

At last these land purchases brought trouble at the Waitara ; but if Cooper, who was subordinate to the chief officer of the Government, had been left to manage native affairs in Taranaki, no war would have arisen there ; and if Searancke had been left alone in his district, no trouble would have arisen in the Waikato. But these subordinate gentlemen were shifted about, and their decisions altered and amended by their chief, who made the Government believe that the future welfare of the country rested solely upon him —as if the welfare of a country depended upon one man! What fools the pakehas are! Well, as I said, the land purchase policy caused a disturbance at the Waitara. The rightful owners refused to sell, but the tribes which had no claim sold, and the land was taken possession of in the name of the Queen. This time the rightful owners took up arms to defend their rights. The tribe rallied up. And this is how the war commenced ; but it had been smouldering a long time before it burst into the flame that has scorched our country and has taken so much blood to extinguish.

CHAPTER V.

OUR one great motive in organising this political movement was to unite the Maori race and bring them together as one people. Many of our wisest chiefs foretold failure in this. They urged that the tribal independence was too strong. There were tribal jealousies and ancient feuds to overcome. To entirely do away with these latter was impossible. And then, who would be chosen to rule over us all as the King Chief?

There were two great tribes in this country before whom all other tribes must give way. The first was Ngapuhi, who as a whole comprise, roughly speaking, all the tribes north of Auckland —very powerful tribes, several thousands strong in their day. The hapus were usually about two hundred to five hundred strong. The Rarawa tribal boundary extended to the North Cape and to the mouth of the Hokianga River; the warlike tribe of Ngatiwhatua, at Kaipara, Riverhead, and Hauraki. Then, who could withstand the Ngapuhi from Hokianga, where even the great Hongi Hika met his death trying to conquer the river, and Ngapuhi of the Tokirau, Bay of Islands? Did not Hongi Hika, on his return from England, dressed in the armour King George had given him, lead all these warriors to battle, and slay from the Auckland hills —those rich volcanic kumera grounds—right away to the barren lands of Ngaiterangi, at Tauranga, proceeding on to the Arawa country, swooping on to Ahuriri, Hawke's Bay, where they slew the Ngatikatiungunu, and made them fly like dust before a gale? Then putting to one side a slight repulse, fearfully avenged on the confines of Waikato, returned to their own districts along the coast from Auckland, in their huge sea-going kauri war canoes. Such a fleet was never seen before, nor ever will be again, laden with spoil—the captive women of many a hapu, and the flesh of their enemies.

Waikato knew too well, for the bones of many of their warriors whitened the soil of Ngapuhi, the geographical strength of their country. To get there nothing could be easier; but to get back again across the narrow strip of land was another question altogether. Then the Ngapuhi were better armed, and had learned much that the Waikatos and other tribes had not had the chance to learn. Under these circumstances there was small chance that Ngapuhi would consent to recognise a Waikato King. However, a deputation of diplomatic chiefs, wizards, tohungas (no missionaries), and

warriors, known and trusted for their wisdom, and whose words
and speech could be made as enticing as the fat pigeons fed on the
" miro " berry are to a hungry man, was sent to sound and to tempt
the Ngapuhi. Ngapuhi met the Waikato heralds on the Hokianga
river, at Opara, and with haughty patience listened to all that the
Waikato deputation had to say. It is related that all the fat of
the tuis and the pigeons in the " miro " season was as naught to
compare with the oiliness of the Waikato speeches. If only the
Ngapuhi would consent to be the backbone, the sinew and mana of
the Waikato King.

" Your speech," replied Ngapuhi, " is as a sperm whale for fat-
ness ; but you can return, and take back our reply. If we ever
elect to join our tribes under one head, we have the race of Hongi
Hika to fall back upon, and Matiria shall be our queen ; but we
choose to live as we are, and under the Queen of England, and at
peace with our friends the pakehas. All the pakehas are ours."
We knew what this meant, and that Ngapuhi perceived that we
intended to go to war, and wished to intimate to us that old battle-
fields could be fought on again. It was enough ; and we turned our
attention south, and Waikato drew all the southern tribes into the
meshes of her net, excepting the Arawa ; but even some of the
hapus of the Arawa were induced to join when it came to fighting
in their locality, and at Tauranga, when half of Ngatipikiao came
over to assist us at the Gate Pa, at Tauranga. But our wish was
to confine the war to the neighbourhood of Waikato. At length
the Taranaki, Mokau, and the brave Ngatiruanui tribes joined, and
so did Ngatiraukawa ; but the Lower Wanganuis and Ngatiapa
were undecided for a time, and swayed to and fro like a tall tree in
the wind, but the friendship for the pakeha prevailed. The confidence these tribes had in Sir George Grey in the old war of 1845
remained firm, and though he was absent from the colony his
words and advice remained with them. Then there was Dr. Featherston, Sir William Fitzherbert, and other old pakeha friends,
who had proved themselves to be "rangitiras" (gentlemen). And
no doubt all this, combined with tribal dislike to old enemies,
turned the scale, and they elected to abide by the Queen of England,
whom they had never seen. We looked upon these people as
" lick plates " of the pakehas and cookies. But what cared Hori
Kingi, Mawae, Kawana Paipai, and Mete Kingi. They laughed
at us, and said " taihoa " (wait).

Strange as it may seem, no one at this time appears to have
warned the Government that the King movement meant war ; that
it was a plot to kill all the pakehas and drive them into the sea,
and recover our land that they had stolen from us through their
agents. During this time we were allowed to purchase arms and
ammunition, the prohibition having been taken off, and we laid in
a heavy stock of powder and guns.

We cast our eyes back, and saw nothing but cheating and taking
advantage of us. Even in small things it was the same. The large
P-weight belonging to the steelyard that would weigh up to 500lbs.,

was used by dishonest traders to weigh our wheat with the small steelyards that weighed up to 250lbs., but when anything was sold to us by weight the p's were reversed. It was the same system, and our innocence in the dark ways of the pakeha, and our credulity and ready forgiveness of injuries were utilised to our disadvantage. We had noticed also that the Government were not brave enough, nor had not confidence in themselves to carry out the laws that they made. The cry was, "We are afraid to send policemen here, lest," as they urged, "they be cooked and eaten."

I have said that the Government were afraid to carry out their own laws. I could give many instances of this, but I will content myself by relating one. It was about the year 1857 or 1858 that an old man fell sick at a village on the Wairoa river, in Hawke's Bay. It happened to be planting season; and though the sick man was a chief the tribe could not delay their planting, so they left one of their number to look after him until he died. His death was daily expected, but he lingered on. The native deputed to look after him was angry because this old man would not die, and he thought he would be too late to put in his own corn and potatoes. "You ought to die, as you are keeping me here doing nothing," said the man to the sick person, who would reply, "Perhaps I may die to-morrow." But the morrow came, and still he was there. At last the man got a spade, an old blanket, and a prayer-book. He put these into a canoe, and then carried the old man and placed him in it, jumped in himself, and pulled down the river for a short distance to a sandy point, got out and dug a hole, placed the old man in it, read the burial service over him, and covered him up alive! He then returned to the village, and from there went up to the plantation, where his tribe were. He told them that he had buried the sick man. "When did he die? Why did you not tell us, so that we could have a 'tangi' (cry) over him?" he was asked; but all they could get was that he had read the burial service over him. At last they got at the truth of this dreadful murder. The head men of the tribe, Paora Rerepu and others, sent to the Magistrate at Napier to send up policemen and take the native who had committed this crime, but no notice was taken of the information or request. The natives, therefore, held a meeting, but were puzzled to know what to do. At last a young chief got up and said he would end the difficulty. The murderer was placed with his back against a cabbage tree. The young chief then loaded his double-barrelled gun, and took his position about one hundred yards distant. "I am," he called out, "going to fire two shots at the murderer. If I hit him, there is an end of the matter; if I don't hit him, he shall go free." And he fired at him, and the bullet went clean through his brain, and he fell dead, and was there and then buried. It was apparent to all that it was the Government who were afraid to act.

The big fighting began in Taranaki about land some time in the year 1860. We commenced by killing some men and children. All the Kingites were involved. To seek payment for this, a force, composed of soldiers and settler-soldiers, marched up from Taranaki to attack us at Waireka. Soon after the fighting commenced the soldiers went away, leaving the settler-soldiers to stem the attack. We now hurried on, and the fight grew hotter and hotter. I must tell the truth in our history. Well, these men beat us; but still we might have had better fortune had it not been for the unexpected arrival of some man-of-war sailors, who attacked us from another quarter. They rushed at our pa and climbed over the palisading, regardless of the storm of bullets we sent at them. We lost heavily in this remarkable fight, but we killed many of the enemy.

The war grew, and all the settlers were driven into town. We tomahawked many a pakeha. The soldiers now sent away, by force, the settlers' wives and children to Nelson. When we heard of this we said, "The town will be abandoned soon," as we had no doubt all the men were going to march away in a body, when they had sent away their women and children. But one never can calculate what pakehas will do, except that if we laid an ambuscade they would be certain to walk into the midst of it. Sentries were now placed round the town, and settlers were forbidden by the troops to go and save their houses from being burnt, and their stock from being killed and driven away. It was very considerate of the troops for us. To prove that the alarm caused by us was very great, I will give you one or two of the proclamations issued at this time.

PROCLAMATION.

Dated 20th April, 1860, signed by Colonel C. E. Gold, commanding the forces, New Zealand.

"The inhabitants will in future be required to have a candle or lamp at their front windows, ready to light in case of alarm, and are desired to secure their doors and lower windows. The police to see to this."

PROCLAMATION.

"The Major-General hereby gives notice that it is imperatively necessary that all persons should come within the lines of entrenchment at nightfall; and that, in the event of alarm, all women and children repair at once to Marsland Hill. It is also requested that lights are then put in windows of all houses.

"By command.   R. CAREY,
                              "Lieut. Colonel, Deputy Adjutant-General,
Headquarters, New Plymouth,
   "October 16, 1860."

"Many complaints having been made to the Major-General that Europeans are in the habit of intriguing with the wives and daughters of the friendly

Maoris in the pa in the neighbourhood of the town, which not only creates ill-feeling, but is not unlikely to lead to the murder of the person so offending and to the withdrawal of these Maoris and their families from their allegiance all Europeans are cautioned against the continuance of such practices, which, if persevered in, will oblige the Major-General to issue orders that no European, excepting the medical attendants and others specially sanctioned, shall enter into any of the pas. And, on the other hand, that no Maori, male or female, shall pass the barrier into town without a pass from Mr. Parris, Assistant Native Commissioner.

" By command.   R. CAREY,

" Lieut.-Colonel, Deputy Adjutant-General.

Headquarters, New Plymouth,
  " November 23, 1860."

Brown, Atkinson, Stapp, and others fought us bravely at Waireka, and had it not been for Atkinson and his toas (braves), who prevented us from killing more of the 57th Regiment when we killed Lloyd and his men and cut off their heads, we would not have been beaten back. At Puketekauri, too, when the 40th Regiment were defeated, their loss in killed and wounded would have been much heavier than it was had it not been that the settlers saved them. We got a fine lot of rifles and ammunition that day. We understand that the Queen of England instituted an Order for any act of " conspicuous bravery." The Order is called the " Victoria Cross." There is no order for " conspicuous caution " yet instituted. However, in a fight a soldier was hit by us badly, and could not get away with the other wounded. He would have been tomahawked by us, but a man—an ordinary pakeha—named Antonio, at a fearful risk of his life, rushed to the rescue, and getting the wounded soldier upon his back, carried him away to a place of safety. This, we all said, was a brave act. Listen to the result. Antonio, after he had got the man out of danger, gave him up to an officer of the Imperials, who was recommended by his Colonel, and afterwards received the Victoria Cross. Antonio got no reward until the New Zealand Cross was instituted, when he received one for his brave act in 1864.

Seeing the state of things that existed, we sacked and burned homestead after homestead, for we knew, or thought we knew, that Atkinson and Stapp with their men had been sent away to Nelson lest they should sally forth and molest us in our work of destruction. After some weeks had passed (but not until we had destroyed the whole of the settled district) General Pratt, the English General, arrived with his tribe of soldiers. " Now," we said, " we will have some fighting." For so we thought.

Soon after this we erected a pa, as we were tired of burning houses and waylaying and tomahawking people. We determined to await the attack of the troops. Day after day passed on, but all remained perfectly quiet, and our European clothing began to get shabby and rotten. At last the General commenced a sap. A big roller was made, and the friendly natives under Parris, the Civil Commissioner——Now, I am pledged to tell the facts. Well, then, these friendly natives under the Civil Commissioner were our good friends. When the Civil Commissioner told them what was going to be done they let us know all about it, though the Civil Commissioner did not know that all he told them was conveyed to us. Then we assisted the troops to make their sap and bridge over the bad places approaching to our pa. Yes, I believe that without our valuable assistance they could not have done even what they did. I daresay you who read this will think that I am joking; but listen. Fascines were required of green manuka brushwood in large quantities. Now, this manuka grew upon our land, for we had driven the pakeha from it, and by right of conquest it had become ours; but, as the troops did not like to fetch it themselves, they asked the friendly natives to get it for them. These natives did not wish to take our brushwood without our permission; but it was no use to us, so we had an understanding in the following manner. We cut the brushwood, and tied it up into the different sized bundles that General Pratt and his army required, and we really did try hard to please them, lest they should take their custom elsewhere, and send to Auckland or Nelson for what they required, as they did for their fuel. After we had stacked the fascines, the friendly natives came and fetched them away, first paying us the cash they had obtained from the commissariat. We were well paid for our labour. We returned a portion of this money to them to purchase clothing for ourselves and our wives and children, and the next time they came to get more fascines, they brought us blankets, shirts, and trousers for us, and underclothing for our wives, and little clothes for our children; so the sap progressed steadily, and did nobody any harm; and when, after a time, it came too near, we left that pa and built another one.

I think it was soon after this that the fighting commenced near Auckland, and war parties, from Rangiriri and other strong places of ours, sallied forth to kill anyone and everyone they came upon. The first people we killed were at a place called Burt's Farm. It was occupied by a farmer, his wife, and children. Our war party came upon the little children, whom they found playing in the woods near the house, and tomahawked them. We then killed the others. One of the men, however, I fancy, got away. We were very successful, and killed a good many children and people by surprising them. We thought the pakehas were very foolish in not sending their families to safe places.

We now assembled in force at Koheroa, and made strong rifle-pits. A new general (General Cameron), who had fought with the Russians at the Crimea, came to fight us with his tribe of soldiers. This general was a different man to General Pratt. He did not sap up to our position here at the Koheroa line of rifle-pits, but with his tribe of soldiers, charged up and into our earthworks, so that it was doubtful at one time who would win, our enemies fought so well. But now this general came up in person and encouraged his men—just as our chiefs encouraged our men—and

so they charged us, with strange yells, and alas! we were beaten,
and lost heavily. We retired in disorder, leaving our dead and
wounded. Some of them were bayonetted; but this is right in
war, for what is the use of fighting unless you kill your man when
you have got him down? To do otherwise would be to waste all
your efforts to get him into a position so as to be able to kill him
properly, and the pakehas who blame us and their own people for
this are very foolish, and write nonsense merely because they don't
know what fighting is. We knew that there were some settlers
living at the Mauku, so we sent a large party from Rangiriri
to tomahawk them. As we were on our way there, we came
across a Magistrate (Armitage), who had been appointed by Fox
(now made a big rangatira) to spy upon us. So we killed him, as
a warning to others, and then continued on our way. On our
arrival at the houses of the settlers, we found they had left; but
the garrison stationed at the Mauku Church Redoubt came out
to attack us, and a battle took place on some cleared land, which
resulted in their defeat. We killed a good many of them, and
chased the remainder back to the redoubt. We laid those of their
dead we could find in a row, after well tomahawking the bodies,
stuck up a stick and placed the courier-bag we found on one of the
officers on the top of it, and went back with our dead and wounded
to Rangiriri. Our chiefs were very angry at the loss of men we
had sustained, as they termed it a useless fight, though we had
come off victorious.

After the fight at Koheroa, we entrenched ourselves strongly at
Rangiriri and Meremere, having had to retreat from Whangamarino. The main body of the enemy were at Queen's Redoubt,
and now we harassed their convoys as they used to pass between
Queen's Redoubt and other parts, and cut off stragglers, whom
we tomahawked. One day we caught two soldiers going up from
Queen's Redoubt to Pokeno. We caught them, and chopped them
up. After this the enemy were more careful how they strolled
about looking at our country.

To keep the enemy from getting to the rear of our people at the
Thames, and at the rear of Meremere and Rangiriri, we commenced
to build a strong pa at Paparata, and to dig a line of rifle-pits near
a bush. This position was about twelve miles from Queen's
Redoubt and about five from Pickard's Redoubt, where they had
an Armstrong gun that overlooked Meremere on the Waikato.
This gun was a great nuisance to us, and we laid an ambuscade
for Pickard, but it was unsuccessful. General Cameron sent two
officers to spy us out at Paparata. These men came in the night
and hid themselves, and returned the next night. Had it not been
a very wet day we would certainly have found them. As it was,
we discovered where they had been the morning after they left, and
found a compass and a box of preserved fish and some empty tins.
This made us feel uneasy, as we did not know what information
they might carry to the General or the Governor, and it was partly
in consequence of this that we decided to abandon this place. One

of these officers was Von Tempsky, the other was McDonnell. You will hear more about these two men anon.

Rangiriri and Meremere were now attacked. This was a dreadful battle, and the loss on both sides was very severe. The flower of Waikato fell here. Our rifle-pits were carried by a series of charges, but were not taken until the red blood flowed like water. Then the soldiers tried to storm our redoubt, but were repeatedly repulsed, and each time with great loss. Many of us escaped by swimming the Waikato river, and going by the lake in rear; but those inside the redoubt could not get away so easily; so they at last, after having done all that brave men could do, hung out a flag of truce and surrendered. "Shall we be all killed in payment for the loss sustained by the enemy?" we asked one another; but we were well treated, and our wounded were well looked after by their doctors. And then some of us thought that perhaps that if this class of men had been the first to arrive in this country we might all have lived in peace. But, alas! that could never have been, for our doom was pronounced on the distant day when Captain Cook first came to New Zealand. From that day our fate was sealed, and we know now that in a few short years we will have to follow the moa and our ancestors to oblivion. To oblivion? No; to a better and happier world, where there are no bad pakehas to trouble and perplex us, and when the natural ignorance of the Maori and the unnatural ignorance of the pakeha will be enlightened.

After Rangiriri fell overtures were sent to us for peace. But while these negotiations were being talked over, and before anything was settled, a large body of troops was slipped past us and took possession of Ngaruawhia, at the junction of the Waikato and Waipa rivers. This movement was carried out so suddenly that we only saw the advantage that had been taken of us after it was too late to try and prevent it. It was a smart trick. This we attributed to the Governor. Others said it was the General's doing. But whoever was to blame for this, there were the troops in possession, and when we sent to tell them that it was not fair, and that they were to return, they refused to budge. So we determined to fight it out—as, by the way, we all along had made up our minds to do—but we wanted to gain more time after our defeat, and engage the enemy in talk. Large parties of soldiers were sent up the Waipa river to different parts, and up the Waikato, and the troops spread over the country like a stream that had overflowed its banks in a flood. Many skirmishes took place, in most of which we were beaten, but we made up our loss for this by laying ambushes and by firing on the steamers from the banks of the river as they passed up and down. This kind of warfare suited us. Soldiers always walked right into our traps, they are so stupid. We shot and tomahawked scores of men in this way during the war, but we could not, as a rule, contend successfully against them in the open ground; but then they were always better armed and provided than we were.

We now erected two strong pas at Paterangi and Pikopiko, to

bar the advance of the Queen's troops on Te Awamutu, Rangi- aowhia, and Kihikihi, the heart and lungs of Waikato. General Cameron now began to concentrate his men at Te Rore, and big guns were brought up, and huge mortars, and we saw that a tremendous battle would soon take place, for we had more than one thousand men in these pas, all of them warriors and eager for a fight—the greatest number ever concentrated together at one time against the enemy in the Waikato or at any other place in our country. Our pas were double palisaded and rifle-pitted. The pits were deep and roofed over with logs eighteen inches through. These again were covered with bundles of tightly-bound fern, and a thick layer of earth was shovelled over the whole and tramped smooth. Only small holes were left for the men to fire through. Each of our pas was flanked, and the strength of one part was made equal to the other. Our rear was protected by a swamp, and the only approach was up a gentle slope from the position taken up by the enemy. A good dray road extended from the rear of one of the pas to our farms at Rangiaowhia, Te Awamutu, and Kihikihi, from where we were kept supplied with provisions. Having made our fortifications complete, our young men amused themselves by firing at the steamers, and this at last became so serious to our foes that they had to get iron sheets to protect their men with. But still we made our bullets whistle about their heads. We kept a good watch for an attack to be made, for we felt certain of beating them off with ease. About this period the Governor arrived at Te Rore, and told the General to attack us, but the General would not obey the Governor. How it would have been I cannot tell, but we felt certain of defeating him if an attack had been made. However, nothing of this kind was attempted. One or two men used to take pot shots at us with their rifles, but nothing more.

Traitors, however, were at work. A half-caste, for a few shillings, betrayed us, and offered to show the general a way round our pas, so that he could get to the back country and cut off our supplies, rendering our positions useless. We knew nothing of this until one day a mounted man rode into our camp covered with dust and foam, and astounded us all with the information that Te Awamutu, Rangiaowhia, and Kihikihi were in the hands of the enemy, and that severe loss had been inflicted upon us at the village of Rangiaowhia, and that a number of people had been burnt in a house there; also that a number of prisoners had been captured. On receipt of this news we put on our belts and at once evacuated our pas, and fell back inland of Te Awamutu, where we found the troops had encamped. We wept bitterly over our dead in the burnt and once beautiful village of Rangiaowhia, and prepared to dislodge the enemy from the position they had taken up at Te Awamutu mission station. It was on a Sunday morning the troops attacked Rangiaowhia, and on the following day we advanced from there to give them battle. We attacked them in three columns, and drove in their pickets. Then the troops poured out ot their camps and came at us. A short conflict took place. They drove us at the point of the bayonet to some distance, to a swamp. Here we rallied and had another fight; but two bodies of cavalry, one on each side of the troops on foot, charged us, and one party of cavalry came upon us in a corn field. Then we had a bad time of it, and our men were cut down with the sword right and left. Our other wing and centre had been defeated. We were utterly routed with heavy loss. Our killed numbered twenty-five men, and we lost many in wounded and prisoners. Soon after this Tamihana Tarapipipi sent in messengers to the General. A correspondence ensued, but nothing came of it.

On the same evening of this battle, as a party of our scouts were in ambush at a bush on one side of the cornfield where our dead warriors lay about, we noticed two mounted men, one without arms and the other apparently a cavalry officer, ride up, quietly dismount and fasten up their horses, and proceed to investigate the bodies of our dead. We could not understand their conduct, for they were far away from the troops. They then separated, and went looking all over the field, meeting again. At last the one not in uniform called out in a loud ringing voice, " E hoa ma ko au tenei ko Pihopa haere no mai, ko au tenei Ko Pihopa Herewini." (Friends, this is I, the Bishop. Come to me in safety. This is I, the Bishop Selwyn.) " Ha," we said, " it is Bishop Selwyn with a soldier officer come to gaze on our dead. Let us call them to us, and then tomahawk them." Some of us were afraid to kill the Bishop, others were for letting a volley fly at him. He and his companion were not more than two hundred yards distant, but while we were making up our minds as to what we should do they proceeded to untie their horses. The Bishop called out once more, and then the two got into their saddles; and now we sent a volley of fifty guns at them, but they rode rapidly away, apparently uninjured.*

We now made other pas, and the fighting went on. Kihikihi was occupied, and troops were located in redoubts all over the country.

The last big fight we had in the Waikato was at Orakau. Here again we lost heavily, but if the most wonderful blunders had not been made not one man of us had escaped, and this fight would have annihilated us. As it was we put our women and children and wounded in the centre, and surrounded them with our band of warriors. Watching our time, all of a sudden we marched out of the pa in a dense column right over the heads of a small portion of the Regiment (I think it was the 40th) guarding this outlet. This movement, as we had calculated, took everyone by surprise, and we got clean away from the whole of the troops in array against us. Still our loss was heavy, but we had taken our mana (prestige) safe with us. The General had

---

* Bishop Selwyn rode out in the evening after the fight accompanied and guided only by Sub Inspector McDonnell, of the Mounted Defence Force, to afford relief to a wounded Maori who had been cut down that day.

offered terms if we would surrender, but Rewi, the chief in command, replied "Never! We will fight for ever and for ever." This was because of our lands. We thought after the defeat at Orakau, and seeing our fine country and pastures in the occupation of our foes, that indeed our affairs seemed hopeless. We could not afford to lose any more of our men. There were none to fill up the gaps made in our ranks. This was not the case with the pakeha. If he blundered, as he nearly always did, and lost men, ten replaced every one he had lost. Nevertheless we fought on, lest we should become worse than slaves. Far better, we thought, to die in battle than lose the heritage that had descended to us from our ancestors.

CHAPTER VI.

Hauhau religion—War on the West Coast, Wanganui district.

IT was about the year 1863 or 1864 that a revelation was made of what we thought to be the real God. We had been told of so many different religions, and at different times, that each one was right and the other was wrong, that we were puzzled. So at last a man called Te Ua determined to search the foundation stone of all these creeds, and extract a religion for himself and the race. He did so, and the result was this new religion, which was named " Hau," and his disciples were called Hauhaus. We worshipped before a pole placed firmly in the ground, and rigged as a top-mast of a ship.

It had been manifested to us that we were the ten lost tribes of Israel. We chanted our prayers in an unknown tongue, as we marched and danced round, trusting, with all faith, that, sooner or later, we would be able to comprehend the meaning of the apparent gibberish we gave utterance to. A spike nail was driven into the pole or Niu, about three feet from the ground, upon which we used to hang the head of one of our enemies we had killed. " Paimariri " was our watchword, and " Riki " was our god of war, and the spirit of Joshua was our guiding general. It was a very nice, cheerful sort of religion. Te Ua, our prophet, caused the *Lord Worsley* steamer to come on shore near the White Cliffs, by his prayers of Hau; but the spirit of the angel Gabriel forbade him to kill any of the passengers or crew.

Our form of prayer was a chant after the following : " God the Father, Hau ; God, the Son, Hau, Hau ; God the Holy Ghost, Hau, Hau, Hau. Attention, save us ; Attention, instruct us ; Attention, Jehovah, avenge us, Hau ; Jehovah, stand at ease, Hau ; fall out, Hau, Hau ; Paimariri Hau, big rivers, long rivers, big mountains and seas, attention, Hau, Hau, Hau."

We were then sanctified by the Three in One. Each person now touched the head hanging on the spike nail in the Niu, as they revolved round the pole, and the prayers were over for that time. Then, if about to start on an expedition to seek the enemy, Joshua's spirit led us forth, and he who had told the moon and sun to stand still led us forth with power to smite the Gentile and our spirits assisted him.

The first Hauhau fight was near Mount Egmont, and was fought bravely by us. Here we killed Captain Lloyd and several men, and cut off their heads for our Nius. Some of our people that were faint-hearted got hit, and we lost two killed, who at once became orderlies for Joshua to help us. We now fought the battle of Mutoa, about which such a fuss has been made. It was more a tribal faction fight than anything to do with the pakehas. The friendly natives were very clever indeed to twist that fight into the form they did.

The war in the Wanganui district commenced by our throwing down the challenge by killing several pakehas and slaying Mr. Hewitt at Kai Iwi. We called Mr. Hewitt out of his house one night when all was still. He came out with his man-servant to see who it was calling to him, and then we seized him and cut off his head for our Niu, but the servant escaped. This was our signal for fighting, and we now awaited the attack of the troops at our pa, the "Wereroa," which we had made exceedingly strong with double palisading, covered in rifle-pits and strong earthworks. There were three pas—one big centre one and two smaller ones flanking the centre one.

One morning our scouts brought in the news that the pakeha taua (European force) was advancing to attack us in thousands. Our men at once assembled, and we planted an ambuscade in a karaka grove near to Nukumaru. Soon after the taua came in sight, kicking up the dust with their feet. But in place of coming to attack us, as we had made up our minds they would, they pitched camp near to some tall flax and toitoi, not far from where our ambush was concealed. The chief in charge, Hone Pihama, sent at once to the pa to inform the garrison. A conference was held on the spot, and it was decided to attack forthwith, which we did. We shot down the outlying picket and tomahawked several men. Then a general charge was made, and a small party rushed on the General's marquee, thinking to catch and kill him; but owing to some of our people (so it was said at the time) having disregarded the commands of our high priest, the attempt was not so successful as it ought to have been. The real victory, however, remained with us, as the General moved his army to the sea coast after this and never again attempted to fight us near the bush.

The next fight we had with this commander was between Papawhero, Patea, and Kakaramea. The army of the pakeha was on the line of march to somewhere, but just as they filed through the sand hills and drew near to a small swamp, they were attacked by the Pakakohe tribe, who, by the way, had sneered at the attack that the Ngarauru had made on the army of the pakeha before at Nukumaru. The Pakakohe, however, were defeated, and nearly annihilated. It was a brave but very foolish thing for their chiefs to lead these men (about one hundred) to attack in broad daylight about one thousand, who were wide awake and on the line of march, especially when they had over one hundred cavalry with them. The result ought to have been foreseen. The Pakakohe were horribly beaten, and lost sixty of their best men— cut down by the troopers—for nothing. It was like the charge we read of made at Balaclava—a brave but foolish affair.

A few more fights took place between Patea and Taranaki, but as General Cameron would not permit his troops to attack us near the bush, where our pas were, no battles of any importance were fought. But we sent out parties to lay ambuscades daily, and succeeded in killing a few carters and military trainmen now and then. It kept our young fellows out of mischief, and in good humour and training to be ready to seize any chance that might present itself to inflict a severe blow on our enemies. Thus we instilled a fear of us, by constantly tomahawking and shooting down from ambushes.

About this time our friends, the Upper Wanganuis, sent us word that a European force, and some traitors of our race belonging to the Lower Wanganuis, had taken possession of Pipiriki. They were under the command of an officer (Major Brassey), who had made a name for himself in India. Queen's troops were also sent to Tauranga and Maketu, and the Arawas (the traitors!) were enrolled for service under Hay and McDonnell. Colonial troops were also sent to Poverty Bay, under Fraser, Biggs, and George.

CHAPTER VII,

*Defeat of the English troops at Gate Pa (Tauranga)—Fight at Makelu—
Battle of Motata—A spirit's warning unheeded—The result, defeat and
heavy loss—Fighting at Tauranga—Te Kooti—Escape of prisoners
from Kawau and the hulks—Capture of Wereroa Pa by His Excellency
Sir George Grey, K.C.B., Governor of New Zealand, with a scratch corps
of Colonials and Maoris.*

THE Ngaitirangi, our allies, now induced half of
Ngatipiako, a hapu of the Arawa tribe, to join them
in an attempt to drive back the invaders of their
district, now at Tauranga. Only a few paltry skirmishes had taken place as yet, and the Ngaitirangi had not yet
tried their strength with the troops. That was to come, as will
be seen. When the hapu of Ngatipiako and Ngaitirangi
assembled we advanced to within a short distance of the camp
and town at Tauranga, and dug a straight line of shallow rifle
pits across a narrow strip of level land and stuck some tokorari
(flax sticks) in the earth we had shovelled out of this ditch. Behind
this we built a small square redoubt of sods, but made no loop-
holes or palisading, and well in rear of this we erected a flagstaff
on the level and open ground. We had about five hundred men,
and here we awaited the attack. We were about three miles from
Tauranga Camp. There was no bush near, and we had to go to
the river beach for firewood. After waiting a few days more then
half our men left—owing to a difference of opinion amongst our
leaders—and fell back to Te Ranga. Those that left urged that
our position was not tenable, but weak and dangerous, and that
when we were attacked the enemy would drive us into the mud
flats that were on each side of our position, which the pakehas
afterwards named the "Gate Pa." There had been an old
stockyard here at one time, but all that was left of it was one
of the gates, hence, I suppose, they called it the "Gate Pa," but it
was no pa at all.

One morning we discovered that one regiment—a thousand
strong it must have been—had got to our rear. We were
on a narrow strip of land, with water on both sides of us, an
enemy in our rear and an enemy in front. Our chiefs now took
in our position, which was very similar to that of a snared
rat or parrot, but we determined to make the best of it. The
attack was about to commence from the front. We could see them
dragging up their big guns to fire at our flax-sticks. It put us in
mind of a man trying to tomahawk a mosquito or namu (sandfly).
Our chiefs told us to keep low in the ditch, and not poke our heads

above the level, and let the enemy fire away at the redoubt and flagstaff. Perhaps they might continue firing till evening, when we might get an opportunity to slip away. This was good advice, so we followed it, and waited for results.

The uproar soon commenced, and we had a lively time of it; but we sat and smoked our pipes. The cannon roared, the big mortars banged away, and so did the little ones; the rifles cracked, and the shower of lead and iron and bursting shells rattled over our heads. Every now and then a report like thunder was heard loud above the din. This was the hundred-and-ten pounder Armstrong gun, making a big noise, and the shrieking of the shot as it flew along, here and there skimming up a long piece of grassy sod that covered us with dust, made us think it would be well to be out of reach. We picked up several of these projectiles some miles in rear of our position next day nearly two feet long. Well, they kept up this furious fire, but it did us no harm. Not one of us had as yet been touched, and the day was getting on, and our courage began to improve.

We cannot make out, even to this day, how our enemy in rear escaped the fire of the tribes in front (the 43rd Regiment and Naval Brigade). Towards the evening the enemy in front came on with a rush and a cheer, and charged up to our ditch. We saw them coming, and passed the word along. When they were close upon us, we ran into the little redoubt behind us. We could get no further, for the enemy in our rear (the 68th Regiment) now advanced, firing volley after volley, intending them for us, but they passed on to their friends in front, who returned them with interest, thinking it came from us; but we had not fired at all. Then both sides retreated from each other, and then, and not till then, we rose and gave them the contents of our guns, and they fled in haste, leaving their dead and dying with us, some of them having been shot down by their own men.

We treated their wounded well, by the order of a Ngaitirangi chief, and gave Colonel Booth, of the 43rd, a resting place for his head, and placed a calabash of water near him to slake his thirst. We considered that the slaughter of these men was a judgment from heaven. We only lost three men, and one or two were slightly wounded; but the enemy lost about thirty killed, and their hospitals must have been filled with their wounded. We left the battlefield early the next morning. This victory for us was, I regret to say, the only set-off against other fights that ended in sad defeats for our race.

At this time the Bay of Plenty tribes, the Ngatiawa, Whaka-tohea, Ngatipukeko, and Ngatiporou—in all 800 strong—marched up the coast from Opotiki, Whakatane, Ohiwa, Matata, and other places to do battle with the Arawa and Europeans stationed at Maketu and Fort Colville. On we came, and nearly caught two officers, who were stupidly enough out shooting ducks at Waihi, but they escaped from our fire. Shortly afterwards we were engaged in a smart skirmish, in which we lost four men, but we

GG

must have killed many of the 43rd Regiment. The next day
a rifle-pit was taken possession of by a few men—twelve in
all—and they kept up a sharp fire upon us all the day. These men
were officered by McDonnell and his brother William. Only one
man came to support them, and we tried to shoot him down as he
advanced to the pit, but we could not hit him, although we concentrated the whole line of fire upon him as he came forward at a
sling trot with his gun at the trail. He was a brave man, though
a traitor to us. We afterwards learnt that he was Pohika Taranui,
the fighting chief of Ngatipikiao, of the Arawa. There were
hundreds of men on the cliff above the pit, but after a little firing
in the early part of the morning they did not trouble us much. We
could not make it out, but so it was. When the sun fell the men
in the pit got up and ran away one by one, and our whole line of
pits in the sandhills opened fire upon them, but they all got away
alive. That night we crossed over, and took possession of the
ground occupied by the enemy the day before. All this day and
for a week afterwards there was daily fighting and skirmishing
between us and the Arawa and the few men under Hay and
McDonnell. The troops in Fort Colville did not trouble us much,
but fired a few shots at our rifle-pits with a big gun. At last a
man-of-war ship steamed up and shelled us from the sea ; but none
of us were hit, but albeit the shells and firing prevented the Arawa
from following us up, and in that way served to cover our retreat,
for which we were very thankful.

When we got as far as Otamarakau, on the beach, a little
steamer (colonial gunboat *Sandfly*) that had been in chase of us
fired a shell as we were rounding a cliff, which hit and killed four of
us, making our losses in killed twenty-two men ; but we had—
must have — killed a great many of the Arawa—so our leaders
said. Night fell, and we camped at the Matata, not thinking the
Arawa were after us.

Strange to say, on the same day our people had defeated the
troops with such slaughter at Gate Pa, we received a worse defeat
at the hands of the Arawa and their pakeha leaders, for the next
morning early they fell like a tremendous landslip upon us. We
made a short stand, and then turned and fled. The ebb tide was
at its swiftest in the Matata River, and those who escaped the
bullets from the carbines of Hay's men, and the long-handled
tomahawks of the cursed Arawa, tried to swim across the river,
but many were swept out to sea over the bar, and were strewn
along the coast afterwards—food for the seagulls and sharks. We
lost about eighty men ; only one prisoner was taken- -a chief named
Aporotanga. He was shot dead the next day by the wife of the
head chief of the Arawa, old Winiata, who fought his last fight at
the battle of Matata. This was only right, and proved her affection
for her husband was sincere. Shortly after this battle, we all turned
Hauhaus, and were called Kingites no more for a long time.

Soon after the defeat of the united tribes at the Matata, the
Ngaitirangi and Pikiao, who had won the victory at the Gate Pa,

commenced to strengthen their position at Te Ranga. Rifle-pits were dug, and earthworks had commenced to be thrown up, when, one morning before daylight, one of our women, who had lost her husband at the Gate Pa fight, said that she had heard voices in the distance. We turned out and listened, but could hear nothing, and so rebuked her, telling her it was the distant noise of the surf on the beach. But she replied that the noise she had heard was the voices of a war party on the march to attack. We derided her, so that she got angry and left, taking her two sons with her But we knew afterwards that it was the spirit of her husband which had made her hear the music as a warning to move off with his sons, for the enemy were soon upon us with a vengeance, and we had barely time to man our first line of rifle-pits when they charged up with fixed bayonets. We lost very heavily, and fled, leaving more than one hundred of our warriors to be buried in the pits they had made. This victory completely did for us on this coast, as the best men of Ngaitirangi and Pikiao were nearly all killed, and we paid dearly for our strange victory at Gate Pa.

A great deal of fighting was going on at Turanga, Poverty Bay. The European commanders were Biggs, Fraser, and George. Many pas were taken, and scores of our people were made prisoners. In fact, all the news that we got from that quarter was most disheartening. Of the prisoners made there some were sent to the hulk in Wellington, while Te Kooti was, with many others, sent to the Chatham Islands. Te Kooti was a nobody at this time, only rather notorious as a horse thief. He eventually became a great man, as I will relate in due course. The prisoners taken in the Waikato, Turanga, Rangiriri, and other places were sent to Auckland and placed on board a hulk there.

And now a curious thing happened. All the prisoners were removed from on board the hulk and sent to the Kawau, and these ridiculous pakehas thought that they would remain there quietly, while the mainland and liberty, a few miles off, were beckoning them to come over. So one calm evening they quietly rowed over in boats. They then borrowed a few spades and old guns, and quietly entrenched themselves on some ranges, much to the terror of the neighbouring settlers and of the Aucklanders.

I will now relate how the Wereroa Pa passed away from our hands, and how our famous chief Tataraimaka was taken prisoner. General Cameron's army, or part of his tribe, was stationed at Nukumaru, in a large redoubt, and we watched their proceedings from our stronghold—the Wereroa Pa. We watched the roads too, and laid ambuscades for carters, orderlies, and in fact anyone and anything we could safely kill and capture. On the whole we were very successful. At one time we nearly caught Major Rookes, who commanded the Militia of Wanganui, Major Nixon, and Von Tempsky, who were out reconnoitring on the Okehu stream. We drove a volley into them, and had it not been for Major Nixon and Von Tempsky, who kept us back, we would have tomahawked them and got their horses. These two officers did not get the

Victoria Cross, because they did not belong to the Imperial troops, but a similar act was performed by a brave man, Colonel McNeil, a staff officer in the Waikato, who saved Vosper, a trooper in the Defence Force, when they were fired upon by an ambuscade. For this act he earned and obtained the Victoria Cross. Our bullets, it was considered by the Queen, I suppose, could only kill and wound Imperial and not colonial men. What superstitious people the pakehas are!

We now heard that the Wanganuis, who had been stationed at Pipiriki, were coming to attack us, having been excited thereto by McDonnell, who commanded them. Soon after the receipt of this news, a woman brought us a letter from Hori Kingi, Mawae, and Kawana Paipai, telling us to surrender the pa to them at once. A few of our people seemed inclined to listen to these chiefs, especially the Nga Rauru, who were related to them. After this we received a number of messages from McDonnell, who, with a mixed force, was now camped at Okehu. At length the Waitotara tribe, urged by their chief Pehimana and others, agreed to surrender this pa to the Wanganuis, and a day was fixed for the occasion. But one of McDonnell's officers rode to the Nukumaru camp, where he had some men, and told the officer there in command (Colonel Logan) what was going to happen. Colonel Logan at once thought he would get the pa surrendered to himself. So he collected his staff and, with the officer who had brought him the information, rode off to the Wereroa, and asked the natives to go out of the pa, and let him take it. But this did not please us, so we told him to return at once to his camp, or we would fire upon him, and we manned the works. So they rode back. They had not long been gone when the Wanganuis came in sight. But we refused to give up the pa now, as we thought they had been playing us a trick to get us to give it up to Colonel Logan. That night McDonnell came by himself right up to our pa, but as he arrived, a large party of our men went out of the principal gate, with torches, and were astonished at seeing this officer. We did not know what to think, but he at once told us who he was and what he had come for, and asked us to keep our word to the Wanganui chief and to him. The strange coolness of this proceeding staggered us exceedingly, and some of our older men said it would be the wisest thing to kill him at once; but we suspected an ambush. Our priests had told us to take food to our relations, the Wanganuis, and now desired us not to hurt McDonnell, but to escort him back, and take the food with us as a present, and Pehimana promised to visit the united camp in the morning. So we escorted McDonnell back to his camp, and left our presents of food there. But when the morning came we observed that Colonel Logan had moved up a lot of his troops from Nukumaru, between our pa and the camps of the Wanganuis, and intercepted Pehimana on his way there and again demanded that the pa should be surrendered to him and not to the Wanganui chiefs. He turned round to McDonnell, before our envoys, and asked him, saying, "Why am I not in the Wereroa Pa?" to which he got the reply from McDonnell, "I cannot tell you. There stands the pa, you can go and take it." Colonel Logan then ordered Rookes, who commanded the Wanganui force, to return to Wanganui and not take the pa. At last this mixed force returned, but came back again after Colonel Logan had gone to Nukumaru. Rookes, McDonnell, Kawana Paipai, Tamati Puna, and Kemp were invited by us to the Perekamu village, below the Wereroa, in the valley behind it, and we again entertained the question of the surrender. But we feared what the Pakakohi would say, who lived at the Putahi, some distance off. If the consent of this tribe could have been gained, we would not have cared for what all the tribes of the Ngatiruanui might say or do, as we felt our hearts warm towards our relatives, the Wanganuis. So we proposed to McDonnell that, as he had risked coming to see us, he might as well go and talk it over with the Pakakohi tribe at the Putahi stronghold, and he at once said he would. We found horses for him, Tamati Puna, and Kemp, and off they started, Kawana Paipai and Rookes remaining in the Perekamu village. On McDonnell and the two chiefs who accompanied him reaching the flat below the Putahi Pa, they were met, as had been previously arranged, by a scout, who desired them to dismount, and leave their horses and saddles on the flat below, as they could not ride up the steep bush hill. They were told also that they must discharge their revolvers, and leave them with their saddles. They fired off their revolvers, but returned them to their waist belts, and then ascended the hill.

On their arrival at the pa they were met by the priests and taken round the niu, and they joined in our prayers, etc. After this they were left alone in a small house, while the tribe assembled to discuss matters. The result of the deliberations was that Tamati Puna and Kemp should be sent back to Perekamu in the morning, but that McDonnell should be killed for having come to ask for the pa, and who, as they were informed, had been the chief cause of getting this expedition up. In the evening we re-assembled in our big runanga house, and then sent for McDonnell and the two Wanganui chiefs. Our chief priest, Te One Kura, now stood up and told McDonnell he must at once unbuckle his sword and give it up. McDonnell said in reply that he would do no such thing, but asked for the Wereroa Pa, or he would take it, and spoke to us all as we had never been spoken to before. Much talking now took place, and Kimball Bent, a deserter from the 57th Regiment, pressed us hard to kill McDonnell at once, but our talk had not yet finished. Tamati Puna rose to speak in favour of his pakeha, saying, "You must kill Kemp and me first, if you have to kill McDonnell." Kemp afterwards said the same. This we thought was the speech of warriors and brave men. McDonnell drew his sword out of its sheath, loaded the revolvers, and then handed them to his companions. We did not interrupt Kemp or Tamati. At last daylight began to dawn upon us. We had been talking the whole night long. Presently there was a loud cry, and then a volley of musketry. None of us knew what it could mean, and we all rushed outside with our arms, and met a body of the Tangahoe tribe, who lived at Manutahi, who had come to bring a prisoner (a 57th soldier) they had taken as a companion for Kimball Bent. On our return to the pa McDonnell, Kemp and Tamati had gone. We sent after them, but they had got their horses and galloped away.

After this the Governor, Sir George Grey, came up, and again the negotiations were re-opened for the surrender of the pa, but we refused. Aperahama te Maiparea, who is now alive and knows this, now invited Sir George Grey to come up to the pa, and he would give it to him. Sir George Grey rode up with several officers, General Waddy (we saw that he had one eye like our chief Titokowaru), Colonels Logan, Rookes, McDonnell, Dr. Buller, and other Europeans. This aggravated us, as we did not wish to see Waddy and Logan. We manned the pits of our pa, and would have ended the matter there and then had we not feared for the Maiparea, who was between the pits and the Governor of New Zealand. We saw him looking down our barrels, or we would have shot them all. After this the Governor sent McDonnell twice in one day to tell us to surrender; the second time, as he returned, he just missed a party who would have tomahawked him as he ascended the Wereroa hill from Perekamu village. He took another track that he had not taken before, and so escaped. We all thought this very strange luck, that boded bad for us.

CHAPTER VIII.

Taking the Wereroa pa—Capture of Opotiki—Murder of Völkner—Murder of the crew of the Kate—General Chute's campaign against us in 1866, aided and abetted by Dr. Featherston.

OUR Pipiriki allies now attacked Major Brassey, so as to cause our pa to be relieved, but this morning, after the news had reached us, Sir George Grey and a large force appeared in front of the Wereroa, while a detachment was marched secretly round our position, taking the bush for it. These last captured a large number of our warriors at Areiahi— fifty-five men and all their guns and ammunition. Rookes and McDonnell did this. We know now that these two officers had found out this road during their stay at Perekamu village. It was a great mistake not to have killed them when we had the chance, and Sir George Grey too, when we could have done so without any difficulty. The defenders of the Wereroa now abandoned their strongholds, and the Queen's troops—though nothing had been done by them to capture it—were now placed in possession, and the prisoners were sent to Wellington and placed on board of a hulk in the harbour. Our great Taranaki chief, Tataraimaka, was one of them. The prisoners soon got tired of living there, so they picked out the bow port-hole and swam ashore one rough and stormy night. A few got drowned, but the majority got away. We all laughed at this, and gave Tataraimaka—a sly old warrior—great credit for the way he had planned and effected their escape.

This is the true history of how the Wereroa Pa was captured by Sir George Grey Rookes, McDonnell, and Mete Kingi were the officers. Mete Kingi was made a General, but none of us could make out why, as Rookes and McDonnell did the fighting and captured the prisoners, while Mete remained in camp.

Just before this time we discovered, or thought we had (it was all the same to us after we had made up our minds), that the Rev. Mr. Grace, who used to live at Taupo, and Rev. Mr. Völkner, of Opotiki, had been acting treacherously to us. So their death was resolved upon by Kereopa, who was then our high priest of Hauhauism, and the tribes of the Bay of Plenty met at Opotiki to decide how the sentence should be carried out. We had at this time boiled quantities of peaches, and, letting the juice ferment, we drank it, and it made us brave to act, and filled us with energy. Many of us held the opinion that Völkner was a good man. He was gentle and very kind to all. Many of those who were his own natives knew that he would not do anything underhand, or to our hurt. He had always recommended us not to join in the fighting, and he had kept aloof from interfering in land questions. If all the other missionaries had followed his example, and had minded their own business, Völkner might not have been sacrificed. I always thought we made a great mistake in taking his life away from him, as he was not our enemy, being a German. But alas! so it was. Judgment was pronounced by Kereopa, and Völkner was hanged. When nearly dead Kereopa cut his head off, swallowed his eyes, and filled the communion cup of the church, which we had found, with his blood. The chief men and women of our people were then drawn up in two files inside the church, and the silver cup was passed round. Each person drank or wetted their lips with the contents, returning the cup to Kereopa, who drank what remained. The Rev. Mr. Grace had pleaded hard for Völkner's life, with many tears and to his own peril, but without avail. We intended to hang him too, but somehow we let him escape. Kereopa said it was a great mistake. We would have killed him, and in all probability cut his body to pieces.

After this we captured and shot a half-caste, Fulloon, a Government agent, in a vessel, the *Kate*. We killed all the crew, by direction of Horomona, a Hauhau prophet. Most of the leaders in Hauhauism distinguished themselves in this way, but when the pakehas caught them they always hanged them. But it was only one of our many methods of fighting our enemies. When a man goes to fight, he goes to kill, and it does not signify how he kills his enemy, so long as he does kill him. If he won't kill his enemy when he catches him, what is the use of going to fight? A man goes to fish for whapuku. Well, he catches a fish. What does he do with it? Does he let it go again? That would be a foolish thing! No, for if he did, he would be laughed at, and people would say he was mad. So he eats it. What else did he catch it for? And so with fighting. When you go to kill men, kill them, and don't make fools of yourselves.

The Government now prepared to take "utu" (payment) for the death (murder they called it) of Völkner; the Wanganuis were commanded by McDonnell. Major Atkinson was War Minister, and gave instructions to Brassey and Stapp, who commanded the expedition, to give us a bad time of it, and to hang and kill those who had taken part in Völkner's death. As I wish to tell the truth, I must confess that this was sensible of Major Atkinson. He meant fighting to be fighting; there was not to be any catching and letting go again, and that kind of nonsense. I wonder how long the war would have lasted if each side had acted in this way! We heard of all this from our friends, who were friends of civil commissioners, and prepared for the reception of the expedition. This punishing force sent to fight us arrived in the Bay of Plenty in their ships off the entrance to our river of Opotiki. We had a success against them at first, for our Hauhau priest, Kereopa, caused the little steamer to drift on shore near the bar, by his incantations to Joshua. All the pakehas on board the steamer got on shore, and some of them made a small pa on the top of a hill for their protection, and another party of them took possession of one of our burying places. We intended to attack them in force, as all the other steamers had gone away, the wind was so great, but it came on to rain and it grew quite dark before we had settled our plan. The next morning we attacked them, but after firing a few shots in return they embarked in their vessel again. The heavy flood from the rain the night before drifted their vessel, though they had full steam up, right out towards the bar. They got aground broadside on, and we took possession of the sand-hills and rained bullets upon them, Kereopa encouraging us to the attack. Night again fell, but it rained and thundered, and the lightning was all round the vessel. The storm was raised by the incantations of Kereopa, who wanted us now to rush the vessel; but it was postponed till the following day. The next morning one of our people, who was suddenly inspired with the idea that he was gifted with supernatural powers, went up to where the vessel lay high and dry to sing the paimariri hymn to complete the destruction, when a rifle bullet laid him dead on the sands, and the enemy got possession of his body. This rather surprised us, as he had told everybody he was ball-proof. Next morning the steamers returned, and the whole of the enemy landed. We met them on the beach, but we could not stand before them. We fled, then rallied, and then broke again, their attack was so impetuous. Our villages and settlements were attacked, taken, and destroyed, and we lost a number of men. Our cattle were eaten, our kumeras were dug up by the Wanganui (who, I am sure, never ate such fine kumeras before). Our pigs—such fat ones!—and poultry went the same way. Then our horses were caught, appropriated, and used by the enemy to ride us down with and kill us. At the Kiorikino Pa we recognised our best horses in a charge that some of them, with men on their backs, made upon a number of us who had made a sally from three large pas on the hills to relieve the besieged in the Kiorikino Pa that Stapp and McDonnell had surrounded. They cut down a number of us, and then the pa was taken and many more of us were shot. We were now followed up to Ohiwa, where Raku Raku gave McDonnell and his men information as to the whereabouts of Kereopa and his disciples. From the intelligence thus obtained, the force was divided, and a simultaneous attack was made on two of our positions. Kereopa was not, however, caught, but some of our best men were killed. Only one man was wounded, and he was shot dead by the Wanganuis, by order of McDonnell. But the only thing this man had done was to assist in hanging Völkner. Then Smith, a civil commissioner too (most wonderful!), and Mair, of Orakau Pa celebrity, with the Arawa, had captured, after hard fighting at the Teko Pa, the men who had killed Fulloon. This was also called a murder, and the prisoners were brought to Opotiki to be hanged by Major Stapp; but they were, for some reason or other, with our great chief Mokomoko, sent to Auckland and put to death there.

War now commenced on the West Coast. General Cameron had gone home. He was tired of fighting, for we would not give in, because there were too many Pakeha-Maoris working for us, and because the land that had remained to us from the Government sharks had all been confiscated. "We will never give in now," we said. General Chute and Dr. Featherston sent to Opotiki for McDonnell, the Native Contingent, the Patea Rangers under Newland (all tried Taranaki warriors), and the fierce Wanganui Yeomanry Cavalry. These men arrived at Wanganui, and the following is the pakeha version of the arrival of the Native Contingent, which I would pass over as of no account, but for a circumstance that occurred afterwards, which proved how very selfish the pakehas are when Maori interests are concerned :—
"Immediately the steamer cast anchor His Honour the Superintendent of Wellington, Walter Buller, Esq., R.M., Major Von Tempsky (Forest Rangers), and others went on board to welcome our native allies. Foremost to meet them was the undaunted British chief, Major McDonnell, the able leader of the contingent; next came Ensigns Gudgeon and Walker, the old veteran (general) Mete Kingi, Captains Kemp and Aperaniko, Adjutant Wirihana, and others. They were agreeably surprised to find their old friends, Dr. Featherston and Mr. Buller, ready to give them a right hearty welcome, and, after many congratulations, disembarked to meet their more intimate relations and friends. The Putiki natives have won the admiration of the European community for their unflinching loyalty, and will, I hear, after the withdrawal of the Imperial troops, form an important branch of the colonial force."

Such was the reception by the Government of the Warganuis under McDonnell. The following account by this officer will tell you how the Government treated these men for "their unflinching loyalty," and the encouragement they received at their hands. McDonnell's memo. to Dr. Featherston at the request of the latter :—
"On the 29th December, 1866, the Native Contingent crossed from Putiki, the native settlement on the other side of the river Wanganui, where they camped ready for marching. The following day they fell in, but on the word 'quick march' they to a man grounded arms and remained standing. Kemp, their native captain, stepped forward and said, 'The men of the Native Contingent, not having received any pay for three months, refuse to march until paid. Many, perhaps, will get killed, as we are always placed in the front. This is as it should be, but we want our pay for the past before we enter on the future.' This I felt to be just, and could not blame them. I made a short speech, in which I acknowledged the unfairness of not having been paid, but I said that to speak of such matters on parade, and at the moment of marching, was hardly fair to me, or to General Chute, who was waiting for them at the Wereroa to advance on the enemy. I had, I told them, no Government money in my hands—I only wished I had—but that I had one hundred pounds I had saved up of my

own money in the possession of a friend who was going to invest it for me. That under the circumstances I would forego the investment and distribute the sum amongst them; it would purchase pipes and tobacco for the campaign, if no more, and that on their return to Wanganui they would receive their pay in a lump, and could enjoy themselves at their ease. 'But do not,' I added, 'disgrace yourselves now.' I fetched the money (one hundred pounds) and placed it on the ground. 'There is all I have; you are welcome to it; pick it up, and in one hour's time parade again. But if any of you get drunk that man shall remain behind, and of course will not have the chance of capturing any horses.' There was a general rush forward and a scramble, but the money was equally divided, every man, I believe, got an equal proportion, and to the hour they were again on parade. If any of them were shaking on their legs, or had to lean against their comrades to shoulder their rifles I did not notice it—but they had brought very little tobacco. I afterwards got my money back in driblets, excepting about ten pounds. As a whole it was a dead loss to me." McDonnell sent in this account to the Government, and was told by an authority that some mark would be given to him for his services; but he informs me that he has not even got the ten pounds back, let alone the " mark!" Comment is superfluous. The contingent refused to march until they were paid. McDonnell went at five o'clock in the morning to His Honour Dr. Featherston, who was in bed in the Wanganui Hotel, and asked him for the pay due, or even £100 of it. Dr. Featherston begged him to get them to march without it as he had no money, and could not get any, and was at his wits' end what to do, as he had promised to join General Chute that day in company with the contingent. McDonnell said he could raise £100 of his own money, but if he happened to be shot in the coming campaign who would see it paid to his family? Dr. Featherston promised he would see to this, and McDonnell obtained the cash and gave it to them.

Well, in January, 1866, the whole army of this general took the field, and he and Dr. Featherston pitched their camp on the site of the famous Wereroa Pa. On the 3rd of January they all marched for Okotuku Pa, where the Ngarauru awaited them, eager for the fray. While the enemy were pitching their tents, we came out of the bush to do a little tomahawking; but McDonnell and Featherston, with the Native Contingent, attacked us, and drove us back into the bush, and before we could rally they had possessed themselves of our pa at the top of the hill. We afterwards heard that Dr. Featherston took the sacred dove at the top of our niu. By the time we had collected ourselves together in the bush, to endeavour to retake our position, the enemy had retired to their camp below on the level ground. We now set to work to fortify our position. We gathered all the firewood that lay in heaps about our plantations (our winter reserve), and stacked it up closely against the palisading of our pa, and then remained perfectly quiet, so that our enemy might think we had gone right away.

The next morning the army marched up the wooded hill, and
presently stood in front of our pa, which was at the narrow end of
the plateau. We kept quiet, as we wished the enemy to come
quite close, when we would pour one volley into them and slip
away. But two Europeans and one Maori, whom we had noticed
the previous day, attempted to take the pa by themselves. We
thought they were out of their mind. We let them come within
twenty yards, and then fired a whole volley at them; but just at
that instant they tumbled into an empty potato pit, and so saved
their lives. [The three men here spoken of were Ensign Gudgeon,
William McDonnell, and Winiata.] The troops now charged our
pa, but we could only send them a straggling volley, as we had no
time to reload properly; and then our palisades were scaled by
the soldiers. We now slipped out of our pa at the rear, after
losing a number of our men. Only one man of ours was taken
prisoner, and we have heard he was afterwards shot.

Why need I relate the whole of the campaign of this victorious
general and his army? The storming of Putahi Pa, the plan and
approaches to which we found afterwards had been remembered
by one of the pakehas who visited this stronghold at the time of
the Wereroa Pa negotiations, and which information he now gave
to General Chute and Dr. Featherston. We expect he got well
rewarded for this intelligence, as he went nigh to lose his life in
obtaining it; but we understand McDonnell was wounded in this
engagement, and lamed for life. Then Otapawa was taken, the 57th
Regiment being led by the brave Major Hazzard, whom we shot as he
entered our works sword in hand, leading his warriors like a chief.
The march round the mountain of Taranaki and the fight at
Waikoukou followed. It is not a pleasant task to have to record
how in less than five weeks we were all scattered to the winds, and
all our pas and settlements utterly destroyed and burnt. This
dreadful General and his men never slept, and did not fight
in accordance with the laws of warfare laid down by civil commissioners for pakehas to follow. So we complained to one of the
civil commissioners, who then went to have an interview with the
General, who was then camped near Taiporohenui, after defeating
us at Otapawa, and tried to reason with him. But we heard that
the General spoke to this commissioner in such a way that he
left in a hurry. When we were afterwards informed of this by
Wiremu Hukarunui, a neutral, but our friend and intelligencer, we
feared that a new state of things had succeeded to the old, and that
commanding officers of armies were no longer to be under the
control of civil commissioners and pakeha-Maoris. " If this is the
case," said we, " our game is up." We could not stand that kind
of thing.

We, to speak truly, looked upon Chute and his army as the best
fighting force we ever had to oppose, or that had ever been in
array against us. Bush or open it was all the same to them, and
the 57th Regiment and 14th and 18th Royal Irish fought with the
colonial troops, amongst whom were many old warriors of the

Hikitipiti (65th) like proper devil-pakehas. Many months elapsed after this campaign, but as no one came to take possession of the country, and as we were informed by our pakeha-Maori friends that the commissioners and the bishops had said that it was wrong to confiscate our lands, we took heart and returned to the district, and rebuilt and reinhabited our pas and settlements, forgot our past troubles and prepared to resist any attempts the pakeha might make to settle upon the country that General Chute and his men had conquered. But the remains of General Cameron's army tribe still occupied positions near the coast at Patea, Kakara-mea, Manawapou, Tangahoe, Waingongoro, and in Taranaki. But these, we thought, would follow General Cameron when the ships came back that had sailed with him to England, for we are but a simple people in some things.

CHAPTER IX.

Campaign under McDonnell—Pokaikai—Survey of district—Fight at Hairini—At Rotorua—Waikato defeated.

NOW I will give you an account of the fighting under McDonnell and his Bush Rangers and Wanganui Cavalry, and the means he took to steal our country by surveying it. It will be but a short account, as it is very painful to have to relate how we were duped and beaten by this man and his force.

First of all, McDonnell met some of us at the Kauwae, Wiremu Hukanui's place, and asked us to give in. This is an act of his that we thought weak and unworthy of a warrior. But, alas! how we were deceived in him. Colonel Haultain was the War Minister at the time, and the instructions he had given to McDonnell were, we heard, that he should get the district surveyed, and kill as many of us as he could if we objected, as, of course, Colonel Haultain, being an old warrior of vast experience, made sure that we would. Having heard all this and more from our pakeha-Maori friends, what business had this cunning man, McDonnell, to try and get us to make peace, so that he and his men might rob us with impunity? This is what we thought then, though we hoped at the same time that the civil commissioners would take care of our interests. Well, we pretended to McDonnell that we would think over what he had proposed, and that one of our principal chiefs, Ngahina by name, a Hauhau priest, should go to Wellington. But we arranged, in the meantime, to shoot McDonnell down, by a well planted ambuscade, the following morning, as he returned to Patea from the Waingongoro camp. This settled, we at once sent off a messenger to consult with the civil commissioner as to the future. Now, this commissioner, Parris, was a hundred miles away, at Taranaki. McDonnell left the next day for Patea. Our ambuscade, seventy strong, of Ahitana's people, divided into two parties, and planted themselves so that McDonnell should get between them on the banks of the Waihi stream. The trap was beautifully arranged for his death; nothing could have been better planned, and when McDonnell and his few friends, six altogether, including Carrington, the chief surveyor, rode up, we let them get just past the first ambush, and then poured a volley into them at thirty paces, calling out aloud to our Hauhau god " E Riki Kawea, E Riki Kawea!" to make the bullets go straight to their mark. Then the second ambush fired at them, crying out "O Joshua O Joshua!" but, though we sent volley after volley after them as they wheeled and galloped back to Waingongoro, we missed them all. In revenge for this very natural attempt of ours to kill him, McDonnell sent a woman to spy out our pa, Pokaikai. We tore the woman's clothes, and sent her back. McDonnell then sent us a very curious letter of hidden meaning, like to our own Hauhau letters and sayings, which we write to this day when we wish to nonplus and puzzle the pakeha, and confuse them; like that saying of Te Whiti's, "the potato is cooked." McDonnell's letter told us he was coming to visit us. We received this note in the morning, and the following is a copy of the letter :—

"Camp, Manawapou, Tangahoe.

"To the Enemy,—

"Salutations.—In a short time I will truly visit you. You will then see me. Why do you plot to kill me and my women? The kao (preserved kumara) is dried. Sleep, that the taha (calabash) be filled; that the journey be successful. There is a whale on the sea; spear him for the tribe. From your friend,

"McDonnell."

We said, "This man McDonnell is a fool to come and visit us; we will show this note of his to the commissioner, and ask him to tell us what it means." But it is true that it was ourselves who were bewildered by McDonnell, for in the grey dawn of the very next morning he kept his word and did visit us. Our pa, Pokaikai, was entered into pell mell, and after a short but fierce struggle and a few shots we had to fly out of it. The ground was hard with white frost, for it was in the cold weather of August. Many of us were shot down and killed, and all our women and children were taken prisoners, we had to fly naked. We lost our clothes, our weapons and ammunition; our pa and houses were burnt, except one house which they left to shelter a woman who had been wounded. We also lost McDonnell's letter, which he found in a meeting house, so that we could not show it to Parris, the commissioner, to whom we carried our sad, sad tale of complaints. Village after village and pa after pa were taken at all times of the day and night. When our scouts would tell us McDonnell was at Waitotara, fifty miles away, that hour he would drop upon us with his bands of trained men, Wanganui Troopers, and Ross's and Newland's Wanganui and Patea Rangers, who were all as bad as himself. They laid ambuscades for us, and thus we lost more men. It was not fighting according to pakeha rule, and again we complained to the civil commissioners. But we tomahawked away whenever we got the chance, and occasionally we killed some of his men.

Now we were told by the Commissioner, Parris, that a Royal Commission was coming to try McDonnell for not fighting by Commissioner rule, and in attacking us at Pokaikai and elsewhere. We all said "Kapai" (good), and prepared to assemble and give evidence against this commander and destroyer of our people. We pretended, too, that we wished to make peace, and a truce was proclaimed for the purpose. The Royal Commission sat, but all the Civil Commissioner proved was that a woman had been accidentally hurt with the point of a bayonet at the attack on Pokaikai, by a man named Bezar, who did not belong to the force; that she had been well attended to afterwards, and that Bezar, who had accidentally hurt her, had taken her to himself with her consent and the consent of her tribe, for a wife; that she was now Mrs. Bezar, and that shortly she expected to present him with a son and heir. Now the Civil Commissioner had reported that this woman had been brutally murdered, by command of McDonnell. It is true we had told Parris all this, but we told him a good many things, and to our credit be it said, he believed them all. The Commission could not hang McDonnell, we regretted to find; so they acquitted him, and said he had done quite right. So they then departed to their homes, and the woman, Mrs. Bezar, went home with Mr. Bezar and bare him a son, and the Commissioner Parris got on his horse and went home too; and the Government wrote to McDonnell that the Commissioner, Parris, now said that he could not make peace with us, and that he could go on with the fighting. That very night McDonnell and his devil pakehas laid an ambuscade for us, but we laid one for them too, and, strange to say, we both picked on the same spot. The ambuscades met and fought, but we were beaten, and lost some men; but we wounded Captain Ross, the officer we afterwards killed at Turi-turi Mokai. We all attributed this, at the time, to anger on the part of McDonnell and his men for having been tried by us—the very men that he and his bands were paid to fight and destroy. Verily, O pakeha, you are a puzzle to us!

Our large fortified village of Pungarehu, a mile in the forest, was now attacked at daylight. We lost over thirty-five men, and many were wounded and taken prisoners, one of whom was put to death. Many other places were attacked, and we severely wounded McDonnell's brother William. McDonnell now erected a platform at Waihi forty feet high, and when the surveyors were sent to survey the banks of the Waingongoro river, where the scrub was high and good for our ambuscades, the prisoners were told off to do sentry-go on the top of this platform, and told to keep a good look-out for us and report if they saw any danger, but that if the survey party got fired into that they would be at once hanged. We knew McDonnell's men would obey him gladly, so we did not interfere any more with the surveyors, lest our relations should be hanged by McDonnell's men. Well, we were getting tired, and had all but given in, as our country was opened up and conquered again right away to Warea, and drivers used to trade in safety right away over our land to Taranaki, and no one molested them. The roads, too, were safe. We had discovered that McDonnell was a man of his word, and he had promised to leave us alone so long as we behaved ourselves. Our prisoners he released, and they returned to us by consent of Colonel Haultain, the War Minister.

CHAPTER X.

Civil interference—Successful attack on Te Ngutu-o-te-Manu with old force—Defeat at same place—Death of Von Tempsky and others—More civil interference.

BOUT this time Waikato sent an armed force of two hundred and fifty picked warriors to fight and get revenge on the Arawa tribes living at the Rotorua lakes. Waikato got the better of the Arawa on three occasions, and drove them to their pas at Rotorua; and began to plunder the country, and threaten to attack Tauranga, and had got the better of some troops who attacked them there. So McDonnell was taken away from the West Coast and sent to command his old Arawa tribes. He soon organised a band of that brave and loyal tribe to the Queen, but disloyal to their own country, and attacked us on the mountains above Lake Rotorua, at Hirini. Here a desperate fight took place. We stood firm for some time, but the Arawa scooped the brains out of one of us whom they had shot, and smeared their faces over with them, and then, urged by their native and pakeha chiefs, charged us. We could not stand this sight; we broke and fled, and were hotly pursued by the Arawas. We lost heavily, and did not pull up till we reached the head waters of the Thames.

Now, during McDonnell's absence from the Ngatiruanui country, the people of our race had been made uneasy from the action of a Government officer, who began to preach to us; and by this time McDonnell had returned from Rotorua. Things were ripe for disturbance. The name of this man was Booth, and he had once been a catechist. Some of our men stole horses. An attempt was made to capture the young chief who took them. One was caught by Booth, but he afterwards escaped; when, in return and revenge for the insult, we killed three men who were working in the bush. This led to revenge again, and to get payment McDonnell attacked us at the Ngutu-o-te-Manu, defeated us, and burnt our fortified village. We lost nine men in the attack. Our pa was burnt, including our large new place of worship.

After we had killed three pakehas in the bush, whom we knew afterwards were called Cahill, Squires, and Clark, we thought of trying to surprise the Turi-turi Mokai Redoubt, near Te Matangarara. The commander of this pa lived outside the earthwork in a small whare, near where the canteen was. We sent some of our people the evening before, under the pretence of selling some onions, to have a look at the defences, and to ascertain, if possible, if Ross, the captain, was going to sleep in the whare outside the

redoubt. Our spies returned, and reported that the ditch was in a
bad state, and that Ross and the canteen man were each in the
habit of sleeping in their own whares outside and that the planks
over the ditches of the redoubt, serving as a bridge, had not been
moved for some time. Early in the grey dawn we approached,
crawling stealthily up, and had all but got into the ditch when a
sentry challenged, and we heard the click of the lock of his rifle,
and then he blazed away at us. The door of Ross's house now
flew open, and Ross appeared with his sword and revolver. We
fired at him, but he flew to the entrance of the redoubt, shooting
one of us dead ho had just crawled inside; and where a bloody
fight took place, Ross cheering his men, some of whom leaped,
half asleep, over the parapet of the redoubt into our hands. These
we at once killed. Ross now fell in the entrance, and we dragged
him into the ditch and cut out his heart, but the man who did this
fell dead. We tried hard to get at the rest, but several men in one
corner of the earthwork swept it clear, and we lost some of our
warriors ; but help was now on its way to the redoubt from Waihi
camp, and we had barely time to collect our wounded and dead,
leaving three in the ditch at the entrance of the redoubt that had
been shot by Ross in the hand-to-hand conflict. Ah ! he was a
brave man. I think we killed six men, besides Ross and the
canteen man. Our loss in killed was five we carried away, three
we left in the ditch, and eight wounded. Had the captain been
inside this redoubt our loss would have been heavier. The people
living at Matangarara only knew of our intention to attack this
position the evening before we attempted it, and detained an officer
at their village (Northcroft, one of the bravest of the pakehas) who
seemed desirous of going to Turi-turi Mokai to sleep there, as he
was on his way to the Waihi camp. Tuwhakaruru was accused of
bringing this about, but he did not know of our intention until
after we had attempted it and failed.

During the absence of McDonnell at Rotorua, the Wanganuis
came to visit us at our settlement at the Ngutu-o-te-Manu, and
there we all made a compact of peace with each other—a tribal
peace that had nothing to do with the Europeans or their
Government. Few pakehas know of this ; but there are some who
do right well. After the successful attack on the Ngutu-o-te-
Manu, McDonnell made another attack, and we defeated him with
great loss at the same place, but the Wanganuis, as a whole, and
many of his new men left him in the forest, and did not help the
pakeha, but ran away to the stream of Waingongoro, and then
remained in perfect safety till the column came out of the bush.
The Europeans separated in the forest, and retreated with their
wounded. We soon found, as the column commanded by
McDonnell retreated, that he had not many men. Most of them
had gone, all but Roberts and Livingstone and their band of
warriors, who fought bravely, but who were cut off from
McDonnell, who was encumbered with wounded; so we left
Roberts and his men, after we had fought them, and followed

McDonnell's force, and pressed them in rear and on both flanks; but his brave band fought hard, and shouted to us to come nearer; and McDonnell called to us in Maori all the way, and taunted us; and thus we fought from noon till night, until they got out of the bush. Then they turned on us, and gave us a parting volley as we were in the act of dancing a war dance, that wounded some of us. We returned to our dead—a few—and to theirs—a great many —twenty. It was a good victory for us.

It is not true, however, that we tortured the wounded, but we tomahawked them. The bodies we collected together, and heaped them up upon two altars, Von Tempsky's body being placed on the top of one of them, and then we burnt them, and the smoke went up in a cloud to the sky. Then we crossed the Waingongoro River, and had a skirmish at Tangahoe, where we dug up the dead bodies of the men who had been buried, and cut off their limbs, and cooked them in a fire, and ate them, and made soup of them; and we burnt many houses.

McDonnell now wished to make prisoners of all the men from Tai Porohenui to Waitotara, as he thought the Pakakohe tribe would join Titokowaru; but the Resident Magistrate prevented this, and went to see the tribe at Hukatere. The Pakakohe, of course, were going to join, but wished for time, so they talked with their tongues, and the Resident Magistrate foolishly believed them; and on his return to Patea published the following notice, which amused us considerably:—

NOTICE.

" The undersigned chiefs of the Pakakohe tribe pledge themselves that they will give protection to all Europeans, men, and women, and children in their district, namely, from Waitotara to Mokoia Taurua, Warematangi, Te One Kura, Paraone, and Rangihaeata. JAMES BOOTH, R.M.

" Patea, 10th 6—68."

Heiaha i Korero tia ae; which means " comment is needless."

CHAPTER XI.

The fight at Moturoa—Gallant defence of Wereroa redoubt—Defence of Wanganui—Poverty Bay massacre — Moturoa pa—The comparative value of heads.

TITOKOWARU advanced and built a pa at Moturoa, at the edge of that bush. Here we were attacked by another man, Colonel Whitmore. This caused us to think we had perhaps killed McDonnell, as he was not present. Colonel Whitmore proved himself to be a good warrior and cautious. The officers and men under him made a gallant attack on our pa at Moturoa, but we defeated them with heavy loss. Whitmore and Roberts encouraged their men, but the defeat was complete, and we chased them away, right away in the open, nearly as far as the Wairoa, Roberts and Newland, with their hapu division, keeping us back. These men were those who had fought so well at the Ngutu-o-te-Manu. Our victory cost us only one man, who had left the pa to go and tomahawk a wounded pakeha, but he was shot dead in the act. This man was he who had killed Broughton, the interpreter to the troops, because he came to propose terms of peace to us inland at Kakaramea, about the year 1865. We did not torture the wounded, but we tomahawked them all and burnt their remains on the altar, as we had done before at Ngutu, and the sweet savour ascended to the heavens. The burnt bones were afterwards collected and buried at the Wairoa church by their own people. We laid twenty bodies on our altars, and got thirty-five stand of arms. Colonel Whitmore had fought at Poverty Bay, Wairoa, Hawke's Bay, and other places, but he had to learn that the tribes living south and east of us, of Ngatiruanui, were as puwha (sow thistle) when compared with our savage warriors.

Titokowaru, before the above victory, had determined to advance on Wanganui. This was resolved upon, and the expedition started; but, though the plan of attack was cut and ready, and three columns of two hundred each had got their orders, certain events had happened, and fresh councils prevailed. Te Oti Takarahgi, of Kaiwhaike, sent us word that all the Wanganuis and the whole of the tribes from the Wanganui Heads to Otaki, had been roused at the intelligence of our advance that had been conveyed to the Putiki chiefs by McDonnell at midnight. He had been communicated with by Colonel Fraser, from Patea, and the tribes were now assembling to take the field under Colonel

McDonnell, Kemp, Kawana Paipai, and Te Hakeke; but he (Te Oti Takarangi) said that he would have to smother his feelings if his relative Mete Kingi and Wanganui were attacked, as he would have to stick by them. The next day, so very rapid had been this collecting together of men, our scouts brought us the information, as we were on the line of march to Waitotara, that McDonnell, with the contingent, and 500 warriors under Kemp, Paipai, and Haimoana Hiroti, was erecting a redoubt on the site of the old Wereroa Pa, and that they had been fired upon. After this we gave up the idea for some time, and this is the cause why we did not attack Wanganui that time; but we heard that the news of our approach had caused great alarm and consternation in the town.

Shortly after this the Wanganuis were removed from this redoubt to Patea by Colonel Whitmore, and it was garrisoned by a European force from Wanganui, officered by Powell, Broughton, Witchell, and others. We now made up our minds to attack them, take the redoubt, and tomahawk them all. We made sure of an easy success, when we would then march on and sack Wanganui, and have a fine time of it. We attacked, but though we fought for many hours, we were repulsed so often that we got sick of it, and Broughton enraged us by his taunts, asking us in Maori, after each repulse, to " try it again." At length we withdrew, for we were beaten, strange to say.

Soon after this the redoubt was abandoned, and many stores were destroyed in a hurry, and the canteen keeper was well nigh ruined. We were much surprised at this, but suspected a design ; but, when we found that the place had really been left, and that the way had been left clear for us, we again made preparations for attacking the town of Wanganui, and crossed the Waitotara, being now reinforced by the Ngarauru tribe, led by Uru te Angina and other braves, and came on to Kai-Iwi stream, which we crossed ; we plundered and burnt as we went. Nevertheless, flushed as we were by our successes, some of our warriors did not approve of pushing the pakehas to desperation. We thought they would defend their wives and children, and there were some good men in Wanganui; those, for instance, who had so well defended the Wereroa Redoubt when we attacked it, and, though we were six hundred strong, had beaten us off. We heard also that a body of the 18th Royal Irish, under Captains Dawson and Butts, had come from Wellington, and held the stockade at Pukenamu. We pondered over this, though why everything had been left clear for us to advance, as it were, with impunity, our leaders and priests could not make out. The cavalry, too, were in Wanganui, and our experience of these men, before whom the brave Pakakohe tribe went down, the time they attacked General Cameron on his line of march at Patea, had not been forgotten by us. We knew also that if we were successful of the rich spoil we would get, and that what had occurred at Taupo in the time of Te Wherowhero, who slew 250 persons after they had

HH*

been prisoners with his own hand, every now and then refreshing himself with a draught of blood, would have been surpassed by many who longed to make a great name for themselves, the slaughter would have been great. But if we proved to be unsuccessful—what then? How could we have retreated? And we met the scouts of the Wanganui army under Colonel McDonnell, his brother William, Wirihana Puna, Pini, and Haimona Hiroti at Kai Iwi, and exchanged shots with them from the bush; so that it was plain we could not surprise the town at night as we intended. Besides, to tell the truth, we were much divided in opinion, and our priests had dreams and some of them saw bad omens, and one bad omen in war time is very demoralising. I recount these things because some have doubted the intention of Titokowaru, Toi, Tito, Hauwhenua, Ihaka, Wharematangi, and others to sack and burn the town of Wanganui. But twice it was resolved to do this at our councils of war, and no mercy was to be shown to anyone. But the action taken each time saved that settlement; and of this there is no doubt at all, as the panic there was very great.

Colonel Whitmore was absent at this time. He had had to go to Poverty Bay to see after Te Kooti, who with his band of warriors, had escaped from the Chathams. This we heard of by a special messenger from Kaiwhaike. Te Kooti, we were told, had seized a big ship, an English man-of-war, though we doubted this seizing of a sailor's floating pa, and had landed at Poverty Bay. Te Kooti and Whitmore had previously had much fighting together, and Te Kooti, taking advantage of the absence of his experienced antagonist and brave warrior, made a sudden and well-directed attack on Poverty Bay, and in one night slew, without mercy, over forty Europeans—men, women, and children; and Te Kooti, to encourage his men to commit excesses on the women and girls, which they had no wish to do, himself set the example. Over fifty Maoris were slain, too, the same night by Te Kooti and his band. And this is what Whitmore left Wanganui to avenge. We considered this a great victory for Te Kooti, and it proved the stamp of man he was. He did perfectly right, in our opinion, in killing all these people, but we considered he was both wrong and foolish in treating the women as he did; and, although Bryce has pardoned him, there are some who will kill him yet, if a good chance occurs, for the acts he has committed, pardoned though he may be. This I hear from many pakehas, and they are right.

To sum up, Te Kooti, after this victory (termed by the pakeha as usual when we had a success, a massacre), entrenched himself at Ngatapa. This strong ancestral pa was stormed by the brave Whitmore and his men, assisted by the chief Major Ropata, of Nga te Porou, a terrible warrior. Over one hundred tattooed warriors bit the ground. Colonel Whitmore has earned, in our opinion, a decoration for bravery as a warrior for his personal conduct at Ngatapa. He then returned to Wanganui to renew the fighting with us, and after a few skirmishes and ambuscades we made a stand at Taurangika, where we built a strong palisaded pa. One day a body of Kai-Iwi troopers attacked a party who were out looting, so we turned out to the rescue from our stockade and engaged them, keeping in the scrub and swampy ground. We drove them away and followed them up some distance. Another time a party of troopers rode up to our double-palisaded pa to try, as we thought, to ride it down. The majority of us were in the bush, but the guard of the Taurangaika Pa made a great noise, and shot one trooper—Maxwell—but his comrades bravely rescued his body. We laid ambuscades, and a party of Ngatiruanui laid an ambush for Wirihana Puna at Okehu stream one evening, but were just too late, as he rode by the beach to Wanganui. They nearly, however, succeeded in shooting McDonnell, whom they wounded in the leg. He fired at us, and then galloped back to the beach, and we retreated up the creek, as we had done before at the same place when we ambuscaded Rookes, Nixon and Von Tempsky. We had, the day before this, sent a large party to take messages to Kaiwhaiki, asking Te Oti Takarangi and his brave people to join us and help us to fight Whitmore, but he sent back word that it was too late to ask him now. Whitmore now attacked our pa with mortars, and shelled and blazed away, but they did us no harm. Seeing now that no good could result by remaining here any longer, we left one night, after first tying up a female dog and three puppies to keep up a noise. Whitmore entered the pa next day, and the puppies were taken and made pets of by his army. Whitmore, after finding we were gone, lost no time but followed us up, but we shot some of his men at the Karaka. We had several skirmishes after this, and ambuscaded and killed seven men who were stealing our peaches. But Whitmore pursued us and we retreated to the country of the Ngatimaru.

Had we been followed up here we would have turned again on the force with renewed vigour, as we took our mana with us. As it was they left us alone; we were tired, and wished for rest. I am pledged to tell the truth. Well, had the Waimate Plains been occupied then, all trouble would have ended; but, instead of settling the land that had been conquered, first by General Chute, secondly by McDonnell, and now again by Whitmore, the late Sir Donald McLean promised to give these lands back to us, after we knew they had been taken; and he paid one of us £60 a-year to keep guard at the crossings of the Waingongoro River, to keep pakeha cattle from straying on to OUR LAND! We got blamed for destroying the settlers' sheep and cattle on the Waitotara, as if we were going to let them graze quietly before our eyes, when our insides were yearning for the meat on their bones. We would have been fools, indeed. But thousands of our cattle had been killed by McDonnell and his men in the Patea district, and by the army of Colonel Whitmore.

Whitmore was made a great rangatira by England's Queen for his valour; but his officers made a mistake when they informed him that we lost heavily in these fights and skirmishes. Neither was it a right thing for the Governor to do, by the rule of the

Christians, to offer a reward for heads. We thought that the trade in our heads, formerly carried on between the Christian pakeha and the savage Maori at the Bay of Islands, called the "Preserved Head Trade," had come to an end in or about the year 1830, but it was recommenced by a Governor of New Zealand. If our heads are buried at one place and the bodies elsewhere, at the last day these bodies won't know where to find their heads, and the heads won't know where their bodies are, and the confusion will be great; and probably some bodies will have to suffer for the conceived wrong of heads that did not belong to them; but this is by no means an unusual thing to happen. We should not in any way have blamed Whitmore if these things had been done by his order; we should have served him the same if we had caught him, out of respect, as this is the custom of our race, and it is natural to wish for trophies; and even now we had much rather he had taken our heads to ornament the door of his pa with than bury them. But it was Sir George Bowen who offered £1000 for Titokowaru's head, not that Titokowaru felt annoyed at this, as it was only natural that having failed to remove his head from his shoulders by fair means that unfair means should be tried to obtain it; it was all fair in war. So Titokowaru offered in return half-a-crown—two shillings and sixpence—that being the amount of cash voted for his military expenditure, and which was kept tied up for security in an old shirt, for Sir George Bowen's head. No doubt each of these great rangatira warriors knew the value of each other's head. But it is strange that pakehas will call themselves Christians and preach Christ to us, and then offer rewards for our heads; but pakehas are strange beings! Sir George Bowen put us in mind of Herodias, who wished for the head of John the Baptist. Only that Herodias was successful in obtaining what she wanted, because she knew how to set about it, and Sir George Bowen was not, because he didn't.

Now the remnant of the Pakakohe tribe surrendered to Major Noake. They felt no disgrace in doing this, for they gave in to a man who had proved himself a warrior at Balaclava, and were not deceived, but were sent to Otago. Another force, commanded too by this officer, went up the Waitotara river in canoes, and got past Piraunui village and near to Oruanga village, when they met a canoe pelting down with three young men in it. Uruti Angina, our chief, had, with his people, retired four miles past Oruanga. The pakehas fired on this canoe, but the men escaped, and returned quickly to their people. Uruti Angina, hearing that the pakehas had come so far up the river, took canoes with his men, and went to meet them, intending to cut them off overland at the bends of this tortuous river; but, fortunately for them, as not one would have returned to tell the tale, they had pulled back. We followed them up until we past Te Iringa village, but they had gone. So we returned. A few days after this we accepted terms sent to us through the Wanganui natives living at Hiruharama, and gave in for good. This was the Ngarauru tribe, who have never fought against the pakehas since.

CHAPTER XII.

Taupo campaign under Colonel McDonnell—Defeat of Te Kooti at Tokano and at Porere—Escape of Te Kooti into the King Country—The end of the war.

TE KOOTI, the great warrior, who had so often defeated the Europeans, and the trading tribe of Ngati Kahu-ngunu at the Wairoa, Mohaka, Wai Kari, and other places, had retired into the bush after his defeat at Ngatapa by Whitmore. He now went to Taupo with his followers, and there came upon a party of troopers at Opepe. These men did not recognise them, but mistook them for a party of friendly Arawas. Te Kooti seeing this, told his people to get between them and their arms. The troopers, fifteen in number, were thoroughly off their guard. Te Kooti now gave the signal, and they were all shot down but two or three, who managed to escape, and tomahawked. It was a great success for Te Kooti. Then he wrote a letter cleverly accusing the Arawa of the " massacre," and moved on to Tokano. This affair of Te Kooti was only second to his clever "massacre" of people at the Mohaka and Wairoa, where he killed over forty people. But neither of these affairs, in our opinion as Maoris, came up to the attack on Poverty Bay. That was a great success and victory. Te Kooti now surprised Te Heu Heu's settlement at Tokano, when he gave them the option of joining him against the Arawas and Europeans or being killed. There was no second course with Te Kooti, and the end of it was they all agreed to make common cause against the enemy.

About this time I joined Te Kooti with a few of the Whaka-momonis. We all went to Waikato now and tried to induce the Waikato tribes to join, and thus pave the way to a rising in that district, and there repeat what had been so successful in Poverty Bay. But the Waikatos wished to find out first whether Te Kooti's atua (god) was as invincible as he had declared it was. Te Kooti replied, "Come with me, and see for yourselves," and Rewi, of the Ngatimaniapoto tribe, agreed to return to Tokano with him, when, if Te Kooti proved by his valour that his god was really as powerful as he had represented, he would assist him with all his power, and let him plan out a campaign for Waikato. So Rewi and a small following of tried men accompanied Te Kooti back to Taupo. On our arrival at Poutu, at the lake of Roto Aira, we caught and killed four scouts belonging to the Ngatituwaharitoa tribe, of whom Hare Tauteke was the chief. We shot them down the morning after we captured them. Te Kooti asked one of these men (who had fought well in the Waikato, at Rangiriri, and

Koheroa against the pakeha) if he would join him, and thus save his life. We all thought the reply a noble one, though it cost him his life: "If you had asked me to join you before you slew my comrades, I might have thought about it; but with those lying dead before me, I say that I will not join a tutua (common fellow) like you." Te Kooti had him immediately killed, to Rewi's disgust, and chopped up, and thrown, with the others, in a swamp, where McDonnell's force afterwards found them.

We were now informed that the Ngati Kahungunu, under Henare Tomoana, had arrived on the banks of the Taupo lake, at a village named Tauranga Taupo, distant from where we were at Tokano some fifteen miles. "Oh," said Te Kooti, "Henare Tomoana is it? Ugh! a fat Leicester wether. Ngati Kahungunu are the dust under my feet. Let us go and kill them." He was a great warrior was Te Kooti. Off we went, and Rewi with us to look on. As we got near the Ngati Kahungunu tribe rapidly began to throw up earthworks. They turned their horses loose, and those we had captured, so they could not gallop off, and had to fight, for Te Kooti never gave any quarter, and he hated Ngati Kahungunu.

By the next morning those fat people (I expect they had never worked so hard in their lives before) had erected a palisading, and we commenced to attack them. We sapped up to their defences from the sides and from the lake. In a few hours we would have them, and Rewi looked on approvingly, but they called out to us from the inside that McDonnell and Renata Kawepo, an old warrior, were close on our rear, and that Herrick with the cavalry and George with the Arawa tribe were coming up to their assistance in front from Runanga and from Tapuwaeharuru; and while we were turning this over in our minds we suddenly saw two mounted men on the rise of a hill in front. Thinking these to be the advanced guard of Herrick and the Arawa under George we at once raised the siege and retired on Tokano, taking all the Ngati Kahungunus' horses with us. These two mounted men afterwards turned out to be two orderlies from Runanga, and we would have had plenty of time to have killed all those fellows had we remained. As it was we got all their horses. The next day McDonnell arrived at Poutu, Lake Rotoaira. He rode up to Tokano with a few men, and we nearly caught him before he discovered who we were. He then rode away rapidly to Tauranga Taupo.

The next day Herrick and George arrived with the Arawa. They took possession of Tokano, and we fell back over the ranges to Papakai, intending to return and fight directly the weather moderated. We commenced the next fight by laying an ambush, commanded by Te Heu Heu, for McDonnell, as we found he was in the habit of riding from Poutu to Tokano, a distance of about twelve miles, sometimes with only one orderly; but on the day we had determined to attack Tokano we commenced firing, so that McDonnell could hear and ride in that direction. He soon made his appearance with twelve troopers after him. We waited till they came up hot with haste, and then fired a volley into them from some timber and broken ground, but they dashed past none the worse, fired a few pistol shots at us, and joined the Arawa, who were now coming to the attack under George, who was cheering them on. Up the hill they came, Ngati Kahungunus' main body well in the rear as usual, as Te Kooti remarked. As our people fell the Arawa cut their heads off, and held them up for us to see. We broke and fled over the ranges back to Papakai, leaving our dead and wounded that McDonnell had killed as payment for the Poverty Bay massacre and the Opepe troopers.

The next fight was at the Porere on the Iwituaroa Range, near Tongariro; but Rewi told Te Kooti that he and his gods were imposters, and that he had no skill in battle, and returned to Waikato in a rage, having lost one man, who would go and fight at Tokano. The fight at the Porere was on the 4th of October, 1869. This was the last stand-up fight that occurred between the Europeans and our race. The battle lasted several hours, and we lost very heavily—more than forty killed and left on the field and in the pa, and many of us died from exposure and from wounds afterwards. The last charge—and many were made, for we fought hard—took the position. George, the commander of the Arawas, fell dead, shot by Te Kooti; and Winiata fell too, whose name had reached us for bravery. The Wanganui native contingent, under Major Kemp, now poured over the parapet of our earthwork in front; at the same time our pa was stormed from the rear by the Europeans and the traitor Arawas, under Major Scannell, commanding No. 2 division of the Armed Constabulary. A terrible revenge was now taken by the native contingent for the death of Winiata, and by the Europeans and the Arawa tribe for the loss they had sustained in the death of Captain George. No quarter was given by McDonnell and his officers; all went down before the bayonets and clubbed rifles. Nearly all our women were captured, and were shared between the Arawas and Wanganuis. These men fought well under Captain George and Major Kemp, who recaptured most of the horses we had taken from Henare's men. Te Kooti barely escaped with his life, but he got wounded in the hand, supposed to be by McDonnell. Lieutenant Northcroft was instrumental in saving Renata Kawepo's life, as one of our women had got him down and gouged out one of his eyes and tore his ears. But we were beaten, and the pakehas showed us no mercy. We were terribly hard put for want of provisions, but we got some potatoes from Tuhua. If our enemies had had provisions they could have annihilated us; but one time, as they were quite out of food and expecting the convoy to bring them kai (rations) from Napier, the convoy came, they rushed to meet it, but it only brought candles and soap. Candles and soap! Nice food for warriors to fight on. No wonder they all cursed and swore at the way they were treated. But we were delighted to hear about this and the rotten meat biscuits they had to eat or starve to death. They ate horses, ha! ha! ha! How we laughed in Waikato at the idea of sending a convoy all the way from Napier to Tokano with candles and soap, to feed five hundred warriors fighting for the peace of the island! Funny pakehas!

After this there was another fight at Tapapa, when Te Kooti lost many men and all his pack-horses and pack-saddles in trying to surprise McDonnell early one morning at daybreak; but the force were standing to their arms and we were terribly sold. The Ngaraurus from Waitotara had joined McDonnell to help him against us. This fact so disgusted me that I slipped back to Waikato. Te Kooti now tried to effect his escape to the Uriwera country, and on his way to massacre the Arawa women and children who had congregated together for safety at Rotorua. McDonnell divined his intention, and dispatched Tawa, Captain Mair, with the Arawa warriors to prevent this being carried out. Tawa arrived just in time, neatly intercepted him, and slew many of his followers, shooting with his own rifle Te Kooti's best man, a half-caste. Te Kooti's force hardly could have escaped from the Arawa this time, but night fell, and so they got away. Te Kooti now wandered about, seeking rest but finding none, for Captain Mair was ever on his track. He was attacked several times, but at length effected his retreat to Waikato, where he humbly sought refuge with Rewi and the King.

We have had some great generals and captains, Te Wherowhero, of Taupo, who with his own hand tomahawked at one time over two hundred prisoners taken in war. I can't say whether this was before or after he had embraced Christianity. Then there was Hongi Hika, Kai Karu, and the other celebrated brave warriors; but the last war with the pakeha proved that the same spirit which had actuated our forefathers was still in existence, and brought to our help the splendid warrior leaders Kereopa, Titokowaru, Te Kooti, and others, of whom it can truly, to their praise, be said, that they were true descendants of Arohakore, who was "a man without fear." Poor Kereopa was betrayed in cold blood, and hanged at Napier. What a shame! But the brave warrior Te Kooti has not met with this treatment; thanks to his Tanewha, he has reached a haven of rest. This ends the fighting. Soon after this I became converted, and my present belief is in Te Whiti and Tohu, who are striving to redeem their people from destruction. We have been greatly injured by the pakehas, and thousands assembled to crush us at Parihaka, led by Mr. Bryce; but, to save their people, who were not allowed to fight with carnal weapons, Te Whiti and Tohu gave themselves up. No injury was done to these two good men, and shortly afterwards they were returned to us by Mr. Bryce; and we now await patiently the day when it shall please the god of Te Whiti and Tohu to cause the removal of all the pakehas, and the lands we have been plundered of will be returned to us, but without a renewal of bloodshed. How this is to be done none of us know, but we feel that it is sure and certain to come at last, for have not Te Whiti and Tohu said so?

CHAPTER XIII.

Kowhai Ngutu Kaka's opinions on certain slanders—He vindicates his own race, and offers advice for the future.

SOME time since a pakeha who wishes us well, and whose warnings have ever been for our good, wrote a parable— a history of a pretended outbreak. The plot was that we were made to kill numbers of people, but the result told heavily upon us, and in a fight on the slopes of Mount Egmont we were all slain; only one man, the last of our race, was left to tell the tale, and then he died too. But even a better organised and real plan had been talked about amongst Titokowaru's people. It was nipped in the bud, however, by Te Whiti and Tohu. Afterwards, when this story was explained to us by those of our race who could read, with its melancholy ending, we appreciated the wisdom of our leaders in abstaining from any more war. We heard that this pakeha was much abused for this parable, as it was said that he was trying to teach us how to fight, as if, for one moment, we required any pakeha to teach us how to go to work. But we knew the tale had been written as a warning to us, and we knew who wrote it.

Another work, I believe the last published, relating the doings in this country, has been read and explained to me. I am not sufficiently acquainted with the disreputable portion of pakeha politics to judge the truth of the political part of it; but it seems to me to contain, in the spirit of its writings, a great deal of petty slander, and that ignorant kind of Christianity peculiar to the pakeha kuias (old women) of Exeter Hall. Therefore I can only form my estimate of the whole work by comparing those portions of it that relate to things and incidents I am personally acquainted with, and then judging how far the writer has confined himself to fact and truth. In the same way, when the writer of this book makes mention of officers and other gentlemen, whom I have first known as brave enemies and afterwards as sincere friends, I will not wrap up my speech in raurekau leaves, but say that this man Rusden is telling lies!—lies that possibly were told to him (unless he dreamt them); but he, not possessing the courage of justice, has not paused to investigate the truth before he wrote about the conduct of men in every way his superiors. I judge, therefore, of the value of his book, as to its being a truthful, reliable history of the past, from that portion of it which I am able to understand, and which I know to be false. But then I am only a New Zealand savage, and therefore am not well versed in the doctrine of that kind of Christianity practised among the Christian race away from Christ and His glorious charity.

Now, if that scribbler thought to please us by slandering the pakeha chiefs who were leaders against us he has made a great mistake in our character. Rusden would, if we had happened to tomahawk one of his kith or kin (if he has any), have rubbed noses with us, told us we had acted quite right, and have pointed out where the others lived so that we might serve them the same. As a race we respect those who fought against us, hand-to-hand, but who always saved life where circumstances (in a European point of view) warranted their doing so. Customs differ; and we kill prisoners, such being our rule, as I have before explained in this our history.

After our defeat at Rangiriri, overtures of peace were proposed to us; but though we had lost our pa and many men we never sued to the pakeha for peace. To sue for peace is a confession of weakness—an acknowledgment that one is beaten. We invariably treated all these offers with contempt. Numbers of times the pakeha sent heralds of peace to us, proclaimed it (almost without our knowledge) in the *Gazette,* sent flags of truce to us to treat for peace, just as if they had experienced all the reverses and losses themselves that we had. Why could they not have waited until we made signals to that effect? This persistence irritated us more than our defeats had. We tore up their *Gazettes,* fired upon their flags of truce, and shot and tomahawked their messengers, both pakeha and Maori, yet they still persisted. We sustained defeats from the Queen's troops and from the colonial troops often; but we had our victories—" massacres " they mostly called them—and yet the soldiers gave us no credit for our cleverness! When they hastened to occupy any pa that we had evacuated, after they had failed with their appliances to take it from us, such as Wereroa, Rangiriri, Paterangi, Pikipiko, Gate Pa, and other places, they exclaimed, "Maoris never could have designed these works; some deserter of a sapper or engineer has shown them how to flank this angle, make this rifle-pit bomb proof," and so on. And this mythical deserter of a sapper, whose name was never heard, got the credit of designing our fortifications! The strange part of it was, that they could never make anything half so good for themselves. They built a redoubt on the other side of the Wanganui River on the hill, for the settlers to send their families to during Titokowaru's raid in 1868. It was never occupied; but the first wet day after it was finished all the sides tumbled in. It was the same in the Waikato and everywhere else, and then they laid the fault on the soil of the country. That they did not know how to conquer or manage any of our kuias (old women) would have known better. Then only look at the foolish sap carried on by them at Taranaki. Truly the empty vanity of the pakeha is great.

The pakeha can beat us in masses, but if the average single pakeha meets the average single Maori, each with his own weapons, our man would, in ninety-nine cases out of a hundred, come off victorious, killing his antagonist each time, and I am ready to prove my words against any man of my age any time before competent judges. I don't speak of the billiard-playing, degraded Maori; I speak of warriors. How can ignorant men know how to pona, rapa, marangae, or piki a spear? And as for warding off a rallying whakaoho or a wero, it would be ridiculous to see them try it, because they have not been taught how. But nothing seems to come to them naturally. They have even to be taught how to row in one of their own boats and to speak their own language correctly. Then to see some of them attempt to paddle a canoe is simply ridiculous to contemplate. They are a strange people! We have been beaten because the pakeha outnumbered us in men. But we are not conquered or rubbed out, and not one of these pakehas can name the day when we, as a race, sued for peace. The most that can be said is that on such and such a date we left off fighting. Haka! wah! ha! ha! ha! We can still dance our war-dance! In what have the pakehas proved better than we, or intellectually our superior?

So, I say, let the pakeha cease to plunge about in his pride, praising himself alone. God will judge all men, Te Whiti and Tohu say, in due course of time, and each man will receive the due reward of his deeds, be they good or evil; but as for sanctimonious cant and hypocrisy, we don't want that rubbish to interpose between the races. Leave us alone, I say, to such meannesses, and in time we may learn to respect, if we cannot love, each other. Try, O pakeha gentlemen! those of you whose thoughts and "whose talk is not all of bullocks," and whose learning we acknowledge, to give us credit for a little common sense. We contribute largely towards paying the taxes, and we are, we know, much plundered. We wish, in our very natural struggle for existence, to have a real and not a sham voice in the way we are to be governed; and though we, as a race, are disappearing—such being the will of God—yet we still number over 46,000 people Do you know the power of passive resistance? We do. You had better take a lesson how to overcome that, as you have hitherto failed to understand many things connected with New Zealand. Who broke the Treaty of Waitangi? Let the Europeans know the facts of the past, though that cannot be recalled, but let it be remembered in time to come, lest more trouble unhappily arise. Note the words of Wiremu Kingi, in his letter to the Governor, written in 1859, and quoted by Sir George Grey, in 1863. "It was settled so in consequence of your bad system of purchasing land. For we had lost numbers of our own people through this same land purchasing. Whenever the Government shall have laid down some equitable system of land purchase, and when calm is once more restored, then the tribes who are for selling will sell their lands under a properly registered system, etc." The Treaty of Waitangi, as far as any of us can be said to have understood it, was not broken by us, but by the pakeha. By it our rights to all our lands, forests, fisheries, etc., etc., were guaranteed in every way, so long as it was our wish to retain the same in our possession; and, in 1859, Wirimu Kingi gave notice to the Governor that he would allow no land to be sold within forty miles north of the European boundary at Taranaki. Contrast these things with the system of land purchasing adopted, and then say truly, who broke the Treaty. But might is right, and right is right only when it suits might.

Now, you pakeha who may read this simple but truthful history, do not be surprised at the sentiments contained in it. I am aware that in many things you, the pakehas, will condemn us, and no loyal pakeha will or can say we were right in many things we have done. You will say to us, "You murdered innocent women and children purposely, though it is true some were killed by us unintentionally, and some of your women fought against us in the field with gun and tomahawk." This is true, I acknowledge, but it was our custom so to do, and I know that in relating the past we must each tell our history from this point of view, but at all events the results were the same to those killed. You, the English nation, have given your account of the battle of Waterloo and how you won it; the French nation have given their account of how they lost it. But in this point only do the two accounts agree. In all the rest they differ. And so it is here. You have written your side of the question many times, I have now written ours once. Kaati! Enough, till I write again, or until the god of Te Whiti or Tohu return to us all the lands you have robbed us of, and quietly but effectually remove you from amongst us.

KOWHAI NGUTU KAKA.

Incidents of the War

TALES

OF

Maori Character and Customs

ETC., ETC., ETC.

BY

LIEUTENANT-COLONEL McDONNELL

OF THE NEW ZEALAND MILITIA.

Auckland

H. BRETT, PRINTER AND PUBLISHER, SHORTLAND STREET

INCIDENTS OF THE WAR.

I WAS residing in Hawke's Bay in 1862, when hearing that a mounted corps was about to be raised in Auckland, to be used as a defence force for the colony, I proceeded to that town, which was then the seat of Government, to offer my services as a colonist in assisting to quell the native disturbance, that had from small beginnings now assumed the proportions of a war of some magnitude, and promised to become still greater. Week after week brought news of fresh disasters, and of such and such a tribe having joined the King natives, who thought that the lands of their ancestors were being wrested from them and slipping from their hold, which was sufficient of itself to rouse every savage feeling in the breast of the New Zealander. Many, no doubt, had private reasons for hating the Europeans, but the one absorbing feeling in their hearts was : " Our lands are going from us against our wills! Let us kill every pakeha we can. They are but thistles! Let us cut them down and save our country." No one pakeha knew this feeling existed, and had existed, among the natives better than I. My knowledge of their character was not as poets love to pourtray it, but as it really is—nothing worse and nothing better. I had hunted, fished, and travelled with them (with all tribes), and had been much thrown with them in their districts, kaingas, and pas. I had not become acquainted with their character by second-hand means or translations through Government or other interpreters, few of whom, alas! were then fitted for the very important position they filled, and many of whom were only Pakeha-Maoris—*sans culottes*—who had private ends to work, which the twisting of a sentence would materially aid. A great portion of the misery and desolation this country has suffered has been caused by men of this description. I repeat, I had not gained my knowledge of the natives by these means. I had the advantage of knowing the Maori language from childhood thoroughly, and by mixing with them had become acquainted with their habits and customs and the practical use of their native weapons, which has often proved of good service to me. My father, a captain in the Royal Navy, had on certain occasions only one argument. If a native grossly insulted either himself or his family he knocked him down. The natives understood this argument, which had rarely to be repeated.

Otherwise he was their friend. No settler was more respected or more beloved by the Northern tribes, and the name of " Kapitane" (the native name for captain) is, though he is no more, well known and remembered in the North.

On my arrival in Auckland, I called upon the Premier (the Hon. A. Domett), from whom I had received much kindness and consideration during his residence in Hawke's Bay, where he had filled the office of Resident Magistrate. I told him why I had come to Auckland, and asked for a commission in the Colonial forces, which I understood were about to be raised. Mr. Domett told me that the time had not arrived for raising this corps, but that, when raised, I should receive a commission in it. In the meanwhile he gave me an appointment as interpreter to Mr. Lawlor, Resident Magistrate at Coromandel. I thanked Mr. Domett, and went to assume my new duties, feeling certain in my own mind that this corps, or some corps, must soon be raised, and that Mr. Domett would never have promised had he not intended to perform. So I left Auckland for Coromandel in high spirits. There was little or nothing to do in Coromandel, as everyone was too busy to engage much in litigation I managed to arrange many matters between Europeans and natives out of Court. It answered the purpose quite as well, saved me much trouble, and the Resident Magistrate much annoyance. I used to occupy much of my spare time in digging in a creek for gold, in company with some friends. It put me in mind of my digging days in Australia, and served to kill time. We used to work hard to keep the claim dry; but at last we bottomed the creek. My share of the expenses came to thirty pounds; there were five of us. The result of our labour we looked upon with no small pride, for, under a strong magnifying glass, it looked very rich, the point of the penknife which held it looking like a broad bar of steel covered with huge nuggets of gold. One of my mates, a careless sort of fellow, opened the door of the room we were in, and a puff of wind flew away with our riches. Our party broke up, we dug no more, though I am certain there is plenty of gold in that creek. If any one disputes this he can go there and try for himself.

Several months flew by, when the whole of Coromandel was placed in a state of ferment by the receipt of the news of the diabolical murder of Traggett and Hope, who were killed by an ambuscade on the West Coast, near New Plymouth, with several others. This happened in May, 1863. Soon afterwards the Defence Force was raised, a splendid fellow appointed to command, and I received my commission, giving me the rank of sub-inspector in the same corps. My friend Von Tempsky received an ensign's commission, and raised a corps of Forest Rangers. Lieutenant Jackson raised a similar body, and these two corps, and the names of their two skilful leaders, Jackson and Von Tempsky, are entwined with the history of New Zealand. Jackson and Von Tempsky will ever be remembered. I joined our headquarters at Otahuhu, some eight miles from Auckland,

and was there introduced to my brother officers, and our major, and commanding officer. The corps consisted of two troops of fifty each ; each troop was under an experienced officer—Captain Walmsley and Captain Pye, V.C.—and there were two sub-inspectors to each troop. A gentleman named Mr. Mair was attached to us as interpreter. We all soon became fast friends, and I look back with feelings of pleasure and pride to the many pleasant hours we all spent together. Alas! how many of those gallant settlers have fallen in seeking to restore peace to their adopted country.

RECONNOITRING THE REBEL CAMP AT PAPARATA.

Camp life during our stay at Selby's farm was very monotonous. A parade in the morning, a walk round our horses at stables, and now and then a light puff of blue smoke, accompanied by the faint sound of a shot from the high wooded range about Queen's Redoubt, fired by some of the enemy's scouts, showing that every movement in our camp was watched with the eye of a hawk, were almost the only break in our camp life. It was a weary time. We were forbidden to stray from camp, as the enemy were always on the look-out to cut off stragglers, and many an unfortunate man met his fate quite unexpectedly and unprepared in this way; but in spite of such sad warnings these orders were not too strictly obeyed. I believe I felt the inaction more than the majority of us. I was unaccustomed to confinement, and loved to roam in the woods, and being an expert bushman I had little fear of being surprised. In a rather melancholy humour one afternoon I started for a prowl by myself, and ascended the hill at the rear of our camp that over-looked the broad river Waikato, and where I could obtain a bird's-eye view of the valley below and the country to the right, where the river sailed on to the sea. Gaining the summit of the hill, I sat down, and taking out a glass I had borrowed from our Colonel, commenced to take a survey of the country. The enemy's strong-hold, Paparata, I could see remarkably well from my position, and on closely examining the earthworks, distant about twelve miles, I formed a resolve to scout up to the position and obtain intelligence that was much wished for, and report to the General for his infor-mation. I took another long look, and, full of ideas, retraced my steps to our camp, not knowing how best to frame my request to our Colonel. I sought advice from my old friend Von Tempsky, who promised to do all in his power to obtain permission if I would promise him one thing in return, his request being that he should accompany me. This being agreed upon, we started together in search of Colonel Nixon and laid the matter before him. For a long time he would hear nothing of it, and withheld his consent to speak to the General, pleasantly remarking that we were too valuable officers to lose. He said that Sir Duncan never would give his consent, that he had reconnoitred the position before with a large body of troops, and had thought it best to let it alone for the present. After much persuasion, the fine old fellow promised to see about it the next morning, but gave it as his opinion that the General would not allow us to risk our lives. I thought differently, and that any information about Paparata would be very acceptable, as he wanted information. Next day Von Tempsky and I were requested to attend at headquarters at 1 p.m., when, introduced by our Colonel, we met the chief, who told us the heads of the information he wished for, and gave his permission for us to go, and wished us a safe return. We received a letter to the officer who commanded at the next post to allow us to pass, and early the following morning we started. Our reception here was very ungracious, and we were forced to quit the camp before dark, and march to Koheroa, a post some seven miles off, and out of our way. The road between the two posts was only used by strong escorts, and a corporal of the 18th had been waylaid a week before, having ventured alone to start to walk the distance, and was tomahawked by the natives. However, we reached Koheroa safely about 3 p.m., and met with a hearty welcome from the garrison, who proved old acquaintances of mine. We had scarcely got rid of the dust of our march when His Excellency Sir George Grey and Sir Duncan and staff arrived in camp. Sir Duncan was surprised to see us here out of our road; but I informed him of the cause. The following day we took notes of the country, and made ourselves as familiar as we could with the position of the hills and general features of the neighbourhood, so as to be prepared for any emergency that might happen to us. We then returned to camp, and after partaking well of our friends' hospitality, we started at dusk on our enterprise. We had to retrace the steps we had come some six miles along a razor-backed ridge, with gullies and swamp on either side—the very places for ambuscades; and supposing scouts to have been out that evening, they must have seen our figures against the sky. This idea gave us much anxiety afterwards. In a short time we came to the branch track leading in the direction of Paparata, now about seven miles distant. The country was quite level up to it, with the exception of a few small gullies. A very large swamp was to our left hand, backed by a high wooded range, intersected with deep ravines running into the swamp. To our right was the road we had just come along, the Waikato River, and the enemy's position at Meremere. Before us lay Paparata. The path we were now on was scarcely discernible, it being very dark, and at times, we could scarcely tell if we were off or on the track, but by keeping the night air on our left cheek, and stooping down now and again to feel for the road, we moved slowly along. Any tree and dark object was carefully approached, lest it should prove an enemy. Our object was to avoid a meeting, if possible, for many reasons, and we did not know but that we might fall in with scouts sent to shoot stragglers and pick up information. Presently we heard the buglers at Queen's Redoubt sound the last post, the echoes replying and dying away in the ranges. All again was still, and nothing broke the silence but the boom of the bitterns from the swamp—a rather melancholy sound at any time. Perhaps it was not till now I fully realised the risk of what we had volunteered to perform. Onward we went, gradually nearing our destination. We had gone over six miles, when we came to a little swamp, over which we had to pass. Pungas were growing in the middle of it, and in the dark we mistook these for a picket of the enemy. We crept up on hands and knees, and to our no small satisfaction found our mistake. We had made up our minds for a small fight if there proved occasion for it, but, of course, anything in this way would have spoilt the object in view. We crossed over and entered a broad track, fenced in on both sides with toitoi and flax. On our right was a long narrow clump of forest. We passed a small village on our right, and could detect the odour of the cooking ovens of the inmates. We continued on for about 500 yards, now and then getting into clear patches of grass and clover.

Presently we heard voices approaching, so we began to retrace our steps till we could get to one side and allow the natives to pass us; but we had not gone far when we heard other voices approaching in what had been our rear. " We are in for it now," I whispered to Von Tempsky, and it struck us both that we had been seen by scouts as we had passed over the razor-backed ridge before mentioned, and that we were in rather a mess, and were being hunted. One chance seemed open—to leave the path and strike for the narrow belt of forest. This we did, and went a short distance and sat down to rest for awhile. The two parties of natives met nearly opposite to where we were seated, muttered a few words too indistinct for us to understand, and then they moved off in the direction we had been going. We remained quiet for a short time, but, as we commenced to move off again, the day began to break, and cocks to crow all round us. We did not know where we had got to. About this time I was lying on my back, when I imagined I saw a man standing over me. I fancied I recognised the features of a high-caste named George Clarke, a noted character in Hokianga. I had presented my pistol, and in another moment would have pulled the trigger, when the figure faded away, the object taking its real form, a koromiko bush. For the time I could have sworn it was a man. I suppose the strain on the nerves caused this strange hallucination.

We now heard a horseman approaching, and presently a native galloped past on a grey horse. A brute of a dog yelped at his heels. The dog stopped close to where we lay. He evidently scented mischief, and was trying to attract attention to it; but at last he obeyed a shout from his master and made after him, a great relief to us. It was now light enough to distinguish objects more plainly. The flax we found ourselves hidden in was about four feet high. This was all the shelter we had, and to our disgust we found it would be impossible to gain the forest without being seen by the natives, some of whom were on the alert. Our position was such that we required to use the greatest caution lest we should be discovered. We were in a small piece of flax swamp that stood in the centre of a level bit of country, showing a very different aspect to what it had borne as we had marched on it by night. I stood upright to get a good view of the position, when Von Tempsky gave me a tug. I turned, and he pointed silently to a native standing about twenty paces from us, holding a bright double-barrelled gun in his hands. I at once threw myself down on the ground. Fortunately he had not seen us. After the sun had risen we took another view. Good heavens! we were almost in the centre of the natives, and on two sides of us, and about 500 or 600 yards off, were newly-dug rifle pits, and some earthworks, and new roughly-made whares.

"After the natives have had their breakfast," whispered Von Tempsky, "they will find us out, old fellow."

"Very likely," I replied; "some horrid hag will be coming to cut flax and discover us hidden here. Of course she will yell out her discovery, other natives will come up, and we will be tomahawked."

We resolved, should we be discovered, to fire right and left and make a dash for it as well as we could. Von Tempsky, I could see, was thinking of his wife and little ones. I blamed myself for bringing him. It did not at that time so much matter for myself. I had no one to care for me. Having arrived at the conclusion that we were in what the Yankees term a "considerable fix," we determined to make the best of it, and commenced our breakfast off biscuit, two cakes of chocolate, and a tin of kippered herrings, and prepared for what might happen. The natives were all now on the stir, and after their morning meal a certain proportion commenced work at the pits (the pa was on the hill above us), others making speeches ; and we gathered that a large body of natives had arrived the previous day from Meremere to talk affairs over with the men at Paparata. Some natives now began catching pigs, and sometimes a porker would dash close by us, pursued by all the curs in the place. We dared not stir, and at times our very breath seemed suspended, our nerves were strung to the uttermost, and several times I was on the point of rushing out and having the suspense over. Anything was better, so it seemed, to silent endurance. The wind, now proving our best friend, continued to rise, and soon increased to a gale, and rain fell in torrents, continuing without intermission all day, and to this change in the weather, thank God, we owe our lives. The little hollow where we lay commenced to fill with water, which soon rose five or six inches. The high wind beat down the flax, so we could not sit upright, but had to lie on our sides in the water, keeping ourselves dry as we best could. It was trying work. For twelve long hours we were forced to keep this position, every moment expecting to be found out. At last the day passed away into night and the rain ceased. We tried to resume our sitting posture, but we were so cramped we could hardly effect this. After chafing our limbs as well as we could we prepared for our return. We had run the risk, but had gained a considerable part of our object, and had a tolerably correct estimate of the enemy's strength, and from speeches we had heard we collected a certain amount of information needless to repeat.

We now commenced our return, and after re-crossing the swamp with the punga roots we waited a short time, thinking the man who had ridden away in the morning might return. Luckily for him, or maybe for ourselves, he did not make his appearance. We resumed our journey, and reached Koheroa about one a.m. Captains Phelps, R. Langtree, Green, and Picard, of the Artillery, were anxiously waiting up for us, and had almost given us up for lost. Captain Phelps was afterwards killed at Rangiriri, and I lost a dear friend. Langtree, too, has also gone to his long home. Wherever Green and Picard may be, I trust they are as happy as I wish them to be. The next day we returned to Queen's Redoubt and headquarters, reporting ourselves and the result of our trip to the General, who was pleased to thank us for the service by letter and in general orders. Our dear old Colonel was delighted to see us safe back, and threw up his cap and cheered; indeed our welcome back to camp was very flattering to us. So began and ended our trip to Paparata. The enemy shortly afterwards evacuated the position, in reality not a very strong one. Colonel Nixon, beloved by all those who knew him, met his death-wound some months afterwards at the fight and taking of Rangiaoahia, and this country sustained in him the loss of one of its bravest and best leaders. My friend and comrade Von Tempsky has also met his fate at the hands of the Hauhaus, shot dead in action at Te Ngutu-o-te-Manu. I have gone through much, yet I am still here; and I often, when musing with myself, think with softened feelings of those dead and gallant friends of mine who have gone, but whom I some day hope to meet again.

THE BATTLE OF RANGIRIRI.—GENERAL CAMERON'S BRAVERY.

Soon after our return from Paparata, No. 1 troop, under Captain Walmsley, was ordered to accompany a force of regulars to the Thames, who were to march across the country from there and get to the rear of the Paparata. We marched to Auckland and shipped our horses on board the steamer *Cairo*. The Forest Rangers accompanied the expedition, which sailed from Auckland to the Firth of the Thames in five steamers, two of which were men-of-war—the *Esk*, commanded by Captain Hamilton, and the *Miranda*, commanded by Captain Jenkins. A heavy gale brought us to anchor near Mareitai. During the time we were anchored here, we heard of the storming of Rangiriri, the fortifications of which pa were constructed with much skill and care. Our troops suffered severely. General Cameron exerted himself to the utmost, regardless of his person. "Let us kill the General," said the natives; "he is too much for us;" and many a gun was levelled at him; but the natives then were indifferent marksmen, and happily the General escaped. I notice a singular error in a work on New Zealand ("New Zealand—Past, Present, and Future," by Missionary Taylor), in which, referring to Sir Duncan Cameron in this very fight, it states that "the General exposed himself, and the natives might have killed him, but, in admiration of his boldness, said, 'Don't shoot him; he is a brave man.'" But the natives of New Zealand, although capable of admiring a brave man, will nevertheless, if he is opposed to them in fight, shoot him if they can, like sensible fellows. Captain Mercer, R.A., Lieutenants Davis and Alexander of the *Miranda*, lost their lives at the storming of this place. Many a brave fellow bit the dust that day. The natives lost one hundred and ninety men, and about one hundred and eighty surrendered, and were placed on board a hulk in the Auckland harbour. The expense of keeping them there must have been something considerable. Bread and meat of the best description, port, sherry, brandy, and beer were provided, besides sago, sugar, jams, sardines, potted meats, and butter. The butter being found fault with (I have been glad to eat worse), pots of the best Scotch marmalade were substituted. They lived well. By Jove they did!—that is if they got all these good things. Many visited the hulk to see the prisoners and learn Maori!

LIFE AT SURREY REDOUBT.—LOOTING HORSES.

The weather having cleared up, we weighed anchor, and steamed for the Thames. The force disembarked, and we marched to Wainongo, over the hills, taking it in rear, Major Drummond Hay acting as our guide. This settlement was deserted, but the rebels had made preparations for our reception, if we had tried to effect a landnig in the boats in front, rifle-pits having been dug in the scrub that fringed high-water mark, and newly-cut boughs of trees had been artfully stuck in the ground, in front of the pits, so as to hide them, and to appear as if they were simply bushes that had grown there. We erected a redoubt at this settlement, and christened it the Miranda. Herds of cattle roamed the neighbourhood, and many a capital hunt we had, spearing and shooting the bulls. This was at last attempted to be stopped, but the temptation was too strong for some of us. Our horses would stray over the ground occupied by the cattle, men were sent to look for them, and this nearly always ended in a cattle hunt. The force now moved on. Not a rebel was seen, but there were plenty of tracks, and we wondered where the Maoris had vanished to. We camped on some rising ground that commanded a good view. Here another redoubt was erected named the Esk. We moved onward again, and finally camped on a hill above Paparata, from where we could see Queen's Redoubt and the broad, clear river Waikato. Paparata had been left by the natives, who had got intimation of the force in rear of them. The rebels were very daring in their attempts to gain information. I know for a fact that natives used to leave Paparata and go through the forest, keeping on the ranges, coming out at a flat bush near Otahuhu. They would remain in this bush till nightfall, and then find a way over the fields into Auckland, purchase tobacco and newspapers, see their friends, and return the same way they came.

A redoubt was erected at Paparata named the Surrey. A series of operations now commenced of hunting up the enemy; but most of them had cleared out and gone up the Waikato. I here amused myself by looting several horses, which I managed to pass on to Auckland. Many a hand-gallop I had on my trusty horse Retribution. One evening I had secured a fine chestnut mare, five years old, and a perfect picture, worth forty guineas to anyone. A certain officer—a colonel—sent his groom to me to ask if I would sell this horse and name the price. I mentioned £30, and I would give a week's trial, or a four-mile gallop with any horse. After dark I was in my tent when the Colonel came to me. I invited him in, and he produced a bottle of brandy—a very scarce article with us subalterns. The Colonel placed the brandy, corked, on the ground, and spoke pleasantly. "I wish for the mare you have looted; I want her for my wife, and will give you £5 for her." I laughed. "She is worth £40, Colonel. You shall have her for £30." "No, no," he replied. "If General Carey knew you had been looting horses he would be very savage. You had better let me have the mare. I will give you £7 for her.' My friend was now desired to draw the cork of the brandy. "Now, about the mare; you had wiser, by far, let me have her." "You can have the mare, Colonel, for £30, and not a penny less." "Very well," said he, "all loot horses will have to be given up to the transport corps, to-morrow," and he flung himself out of the tent. We kept the brandy. If he had asked me for the mare politely, I would have made her a present to him, but I was not to be frightened into selling her. Feeling that the Colonel would make good his threat on the morrow, I resolved to lose no time. I saddled my horse quickly, and, taking a trusty man with me, led the horses round and galloped to Queen's Redoubt, passed the sentries at a gallop, with "Officers' horses, to be shod," and placed them in a fair way of being forwarded to Auckland, returning myself to the Surrey Redoubt in the morning. I was at the stables when a groom came up to me. "Compliments, sir, from Colonel ——, and he will give you £10 for the mare." "My compliments back to your master, but the mare and all the loot horses galloped last night in the direction of the Queen's Redoubt. Your master had better send you after them." The mare brought me £30 by auction. I looted a fine black horse a day or two after this, and presented him to Brigadier-General Carey, who commanded the expedition, and I believed it carried him well afterwards.

A strong garrison was placed in charge of the Surrey Redoubt, and I was sent to Armitage's farm, on the bank of the Waikato river, with twenty-five men, where a detachment of the 14th Regiment was stationed. The remainder of the Defence Force, under Major Nixon, moved to Whatawhata, on the Waipa, a branch of the river Waikato. I had little or nothing to do at Armitage's farm. I detested the place. We had to provide orderlies to carry despatches, a work the men hated. The commissariat for the troops and officers' messing went up by boats, principally manned by sailors of Her Majesty's ships of war ; and fine pickings these fellows got. There was a low wooded island in the middle of the river. Here the sailors used to land and overhaul the stores. Many a case of brandy, wine, and now and then champagne, were confiscated by them ; and the rum—the fellows used to drink it as only British sailors know how. " Hang the old Commodore ; tap another cask, Jack," said they. They had what is called " plants " on the river bank, and well Jack remembered them. They worked hard though, and were often wet through to the skin.

One morning some of the enemy's horse were reported on the other side of the river. We made a party up of two officers of the 14th, myself, and a couple of men, and went across the river. The horses gave us the slip and galloped away. One fine horse, however, continued galloping along the bank until he reached the margin of the Mission Station at Kaitotehe, and jumped into a large orchard there. " Now we have him," I cried, and we paddled the canoe up the river, then landed and went after him. Now it so happened that a certain naval officer was at this time stationed at Kaitotehe, and had made it a practice, when any unfortunate devil of a sailor or marine looted a horse or found a piece of greenstone, to take both horse and greenstone from him. We had heard of this, and here they all were, supposed to be guarded by a sailor whom we found up a tree eating cherries. " Are they all the loot horses ?" I inquired. " They are," replied the man, swallowing a mouthful of cherries, stones and all ; " I have to do guard over them and the fruit." I determined to take all the horses, and we sent them galloping down the river bank. My friends jumped into the canoe, and I with two men ran after the horses, and with some trouble got them safely across to Armitage's. We had fifteen. They had all belonged to the enemy, excepting a grey mare, the property of the missionaries. We had ten good horses, five yearlings and foals. We gave six horses to the men and kept the other four. The yearlings and foals were a nuisance ; what to do with them we did not know.

The next morning an orderly rode up and handed me a note demanding the horses. " What horses ?" " The loot," replied the man, grinning. " Then you will not have them," I said. He rode back, and I received a letter threatening to report me to General Cameron. In the meanwhile we sent our horses to Auckland and sold them. I now received a letter from head-quarters, telling me to deliver up the property of Mr. ——, the missionary. I sent back the grey mare, which we had no intention of keeping, and I sent word the yearlings and foals would follow the next day. Two mounted men came up to fetch the yearlings and foals, but they, as soon as they got out of the yard, plunged into the Waikato and swam across the river. No more correspondence on the subject took place that I know of. I believe it created much amusement at headquarters, and gladdened the hearts of the sailors who had been done. I gave them a fair proportion of what the horses had fetched as their share.

THE FIGHT AT RANGIAOHIA.—DEATH OF COLONEL NIXON.

At length I received instructions to join our headquarters with my detachment. Never was an order more cheerfully obeyed, and soon we joined the troops under General Cameron at Te Rore, where the pas of Te Rangi and Pikopiko were, two of the most formidable pas I had ever seen. After the loss of life at Rangiriri the General was reluctant to storm these pas in front, and having procured guides, determined to march to the rear of them by Te Awamutu at night. Preparations were made; a large force told off of foot and horse; a troop of mounted artillery were under Lieutenant Bate, R.A.; Von Tempsky's and Jackson's Rangers, and our Defence Force—the whole comprising 1,200 men. On Saturday evening after dark the forces fell in. The strictest silence was enforced as we moved off parade, the General commanding in person. Our guides led us over hills and through valleys. I was so fatigued that I slept half the night in the saddle as we moved slowly on. As we neared Te Awamutu the sun rose on a glorious morning, fresh and fair; but there was little time given for thought. Our corps was ordered to the front, and as we passed the mission station at Te Awamutu, every house of which was familiar to me, the order was given to advance and capture the village of Rangiaohia, two miles ahead. "Forward! trot!" A few more minutes—I knew the ground well—and we would be there. The native village rapidly came in sight. I was close to our major. He gave the word "Charge!" and we galloped up. A few natives rushed out of their whares, firing their guns at us, and then ran to the right and left over the kumera and corn plantations; our men pursuing them. One fellow I singled out was running slowly towards a large peach grove; he reached it about six horses' lengths before me, slowly turned round, dropped on one knee, shouted "Kia mate" (for death), and fired. The ball passed by me, and before he could rise I fired at him with my revolver. I now found myself rather detached from my comrades, but a hundred yards or so to my left I saw half-a-dozen of our fellows cutting at something with their swords I galloped up, and the following scene was taking place:—The men had surrounded a small peach tree, rather tall, and the branches of which spread out some distance from the stem. A single native held the stem of the young and pliant tree with both hands, and was jumping from side to side, using the tree to keep off the horses, and twisting to avoid the cuts which were being made at him. His activity was extraordinary. As I got close up I determined to save him; this, from my eye, he must have divined, for he made a feint, a dive under a horse's belly, avoiding two cuts made at him, and, with a leap like a kangaroo, lit on my saddle bow, clasping me round the shoulders. The violence of the shock, for which my horse and myself were not prepared, threw the animal right back on his haunches. "I will save you," I cried; "but jump off, quick!" He did so, but held my leg tightly with one hand, beseeching with the other. I sent the men away to look for more natives. After a pause I looked round, but could see no one in sight, though firing was going on. I now asked the Maori where his gun was, as he had a couple of cartridge boxes on. He pointed out some docks, and said it was there. I told him to fetch it, but promised to shoot him if he played any tricks. He brought me his arms, and I then desired him to fetch my horse round to where my own people were. So we went on for about six hundred yards, until we came to a group of our men who had dismounted. I gave them the prisoner, and inquired where our colonel was. They pointed to the other side of an enclosure containing some huts, and I saw Colonel Nixon, Walmsley, Pye, Bowen, Wilson, and Mair standing with a few men on the other side. Leaving my horse here I sprang over the fence, and advanced through the huts towards them. They waved me back and shouted, but I could not hear what they said, and kept on. As I passed one of the whares, in the low doorway I noticed a trooper—as I thought—kneeling and looking in; but as I passed before the door several shots were fired at me. One glance now showed me that the trooper was dead, and the hut occupied by Maoris. I quickly ran forward. The colonel had only just come up with the others as I had appeared, and now requested Captain Walmsley and myself to come with him and charge the hut—a low, slabbed whare, about five feet high, with sloping roof. The doorway we were going to charge could only have been entered in a stooping position. It was almost certain death, but I could not argue the point. I advised our Colonel (Nixon) to take off his scabbard, which he did, and we advanced, revolver in hand, round the corner of the hut, Nixon leading. A flash, a report, and our gallant and beloved commander fell back in our arms. We carried him out of the line of fire, and laid him on the grass. I cannot describe the great sorrow felt. At last he rallied a little, and I went for some water, and was returning when two natives made after me. I, however, gave them the slip. Our Colonel had been hit in the left side, the bullet passing through his body, and breaking two of his ribs. Our men, now in a fury at seeing the Colonel fall, rushed the house, but were driven back from the low doorway. A sharp fire from the house kept the place. The Rangers now came up, and at it we went again. Bang! bang! two more fellows dead; another charge, two more fallen. The floor of the house was two feet below the level; it was a covered in rifle-pit. The Imperial troops now came up; they ordered us to stand back. They charged the house, but it was of no use; they were beaten back. One man made a rush forward, and put his head in at the door, but staggered back with a ball through his head. Strange to say, this man (65th Regiment) lived a week. Someone now set the thatch on fire. Volley after volley was poured into the hut, and we concluded that all had been killed inside, when a naked little child, about four years old, darted out of the burning whare, and rushed first to one side and then to the other, its large brown eyes dilated with terror as it dashed about, trying to escape, like a wild bird. Several shots were fired, but the men, in their excitement, did not know what they were firing at. At last, seeing that escape was impossible, and being exhausted, the child sank down on its knees by a young bush, as if appealing for its protection, and, covering its eyes with its baby hands, sat panting. Mr. Mair wrapped it in a great-coat, and the men put biscuits before it. The child gazed from one to the other, trying every now and then to repress a deep sob. At last it looked shyly at the food, and presently commenced to eat heartily. Another rush from the burning house, and a man came out. Many shots were fired, and I and Von Tempsky could hear the thud of the balls as they struck him. He staggered and reeled, and the firing ceased. The Maori lifted his head and gave one earnest look around, as if bidding us a mournful farewell, then taking up the corner of the half-burned blanket he had on, he covered his face and lay down and died.

The troops now fell in, and marched back to Te Awamutu. Mr. Mair, Major D. Hay, a half-caste lad, who had acted as guide, and myself, rode towards a house I had remarked, built in European style, and near a grove of trees. We had noticed a little white flag flying from the roof. We dismounted, fastened up our horses, and I knocked at the door, which was locked. I heard whispering inside, and called out in Maori to open the door. The bolt was withdrawn, and we entered. There were about thirty young women and girls inside, some of whom I knew. Most of them were crying. I requested Hay to ride after the troops, and inquire what the General wished done with these women. He left, but did not return. I told the women that they had no cause to be frightened, gave them what tobacco I had in my pouch, and shook hands with them. They begged me not to make them prisoners. The half-caste guide now spoke to them. "You dog," said the women, "you slave; you led the pakeha to kill your mother, your sister, and," holding up a pretty little girl, "your cousin, too. Stand off! stand away! It suddenly struck me we had better clear off. All the troops had gone, and some natives would be sure to return. We wished the women good-bye, mounted our horses, and rode up to the smouldering whares; but we were glad to turn away. Mr. Hale's body, that had been drawn inside the hut, was burnt into a cinder; only his feet were left in his boots. We now heard natives entering the house we had just left; so we galloped after the troops. Our corps camped in the graveyard of Te Awamutu, and I slept wrapped in my plaid, the grave of some infant serving me for a pillow. I was tired out, and slept as soundly as the ashes that reposed beneath me.

We rose early next morning to bury our dead. There were two brothers in our corps, one a sergeant, the other a private, named Alexander, and they were much attached to each other. One of them, the private, had been shot before the hut and was buried with the other dead. The sergeant swore to be avenged. He had not long to wait. The news of our attack on Rangiaohia had been rapidly conveyed to the pas of Te Rangi and Pikopiko. The natives, furious at being outwitted, and goaded to desperation at their beautiful and pet district round Te Awamutu and Rangiaohia being in our hands, turned to drive us back. The King's force now evacuated their pa, and marched at night by the broad dray track to Rangiaohia, where, if they had been doubting whether to attack us or not, the charred remains of the village destroyed the day before caused them to hesitate no longer. We had taken possession of the district on Sunday. On the Monday morning following they made a desperate effort to regain what had passed away from them for ever. Our camp at Te Awamutu was protected by strong pickets. One of these pickets, about ten a.m. on Monday, was attacked. The sentries on duty held their ground, and the enemy drew off to return in greater numbers. The trumpet sounded "Boot and saddle," and in a few moments we were all mounted on parade, and moved off under the command of Captain Walmsley. The General rode with us to where two roads met. The enemy had taken possession of a double ditch and bank that ran along the top of a rise. We were ordered to gallop past this bank and take up some ground to the right. This order was carried out under a heavy fire from the embankment as we thundered past. Where we were going to and what we were about to do I knew no more than a child. The thick yellow dust that rose in clouds prevented me from seeing anything, and nearly choked me. We pulled up in some ti-tree, where we dismounted. The 50th and 65th now came up, and as they prepared to charge the ditch and bank from which the natives (several hundred) were firing rapidly, we remounted and waited for the order to charge. One of Bates' men, a few paces from me, suddenly tumbled from his horse, shot through the head. The Imperial troops fixed bayonets and, cheering loudly, rushed up the rise, our force following them slowly. A few hot moments passed, several men and officers went down, and the Maoris left their position, running down the other side of the rise into a raupo swamp, nearly dry, and a number of them took to the right and left   Had the soldiers, after driving the rebels from the ditch, continued in pursuit, instead of halting to form up, they might have killed a great many of the rebels. The cavalry divided, No. 1 taking one direction, and No. 2, thirty strong, taking another. Sergeant Alexander cut down two of the enemy, and so avenged his brother's death. One native fired off his musket at me about a yard off. I just got singed. I shot him with my revolver, and got one good clip at another fellow, just as he was about to shoot a man named Wyatt, since drowned at Manawapo, Patea district, while carrying despatches. These thirty had knocked over eleven, wounding many more, who, however, managed to gain a rough piece of bush close by. We ought now to have pushed on, but were ordered to halt. I dismounted to secure a flint musket, when hearing a native groan near me, I turned to look at him. He was lying on his back, with a severe sabre wound on his head, and a thrust through the chest, from which the blood was oozing. I poured some spirits down his throat, which seemed to revive him a little, and placing some leaves under his head for a pillow, I left him.

The General and staff now rode up, and I was directed to come with them. I rode with the staff for about an hour, when I managed to secure another horse for myself. The enemy had lost considerably, and we had a few killed, and many more wounded. A strong force was posted on the side by the ditch and bank, and we returned to Te Awamutu just before sunset. I was going down to the river to bathe, when I happened to remember the wounded man I had seen. Bishop Selwyn, who had, I suppose, marched from Te Rore with us, asked whereabouts the native was lying. I volunteered to accompany His Lordship and point out the spot. We rode out to the scene of the late fight, and hunted about. everywhere, but I could not find the man. He must have crawled towards the bush on our left. The Bishop called out in Maori, " It is I—the Bishop! Any wounded man come out—be not afraid!" I shouted, too, with all my might. We proceeded to the edge of the bush and looked in. I strongly recommended His Lordship not to remain any longer. On our return to where the bodies were lying, we called out again, when, from a bush on our front, shots were fired at us. We then rode slowly away. As we neared the troops that were posted at the bank and ditch, we remarked that one of the sentries had been placed in such a position that, to anyone in the bush or raupo swamp, the figure of the sentry would stand out in bold relief against the sky, and afford an easy aim to the enemy. "Stupid fellow," said Bishop Selwyn ; " that sentry will certainly be shot. I will give the officer the hint." He did so as we passed the post. The man was not removed, and the natives shot him the same night from the swamp.

The dead Maoris had been sent for at the request of the Bishop, and His Lordship read the burial service over them next day. The native we had gone to look for had been found in some scrub, where, no doubt, he had crawled to die.

SWORD VERSUS SPEAR.

One evening Wilson and I paid Von Tempsky a visit to where he was camped, and while we were amusing ourselves with a song and a smoke, a European, who had accompanied the force, joined

KK

us at our camp fire, and commenced to relate what he would do if he had command. We were awfully bored, but when he drew Von Tempsky's sword out of its sheath, and only wished he had half a dozen Maoris before him, with their spears, such as those (pointing to some the men had captured), I thought it time to put an end to his nonsense. "You might find it rather difficult," I said, "to ward off one of those spears, if properly handled." He rudely told me I knew nothing about them. "Well," I said, "I do not know, perhaps, as much as you do." Here I laid hold of a six-foot spear, a stout one made out of manuka wood, called a matia. Von Tempsky chuckled, and so did Wilson. They both knew what I was going to do. Our visitor said, "I might hurt you with the sword." "I will chance that," I replied. "I am now—look out!—going to give you a choice. I will either hit you right on the crown of the head, or give you the point in the stomach." He placed himself in an attitude. "Come on." I gave a spring and war whoop, danced round him for a moment, and, after a feint or two, brought the butt end of the spear heavily on his head. Down he went. I rushed at him, and in a quick way asked Von Tempsky to make haste with the tomahawk. I let him get up at last, and he walked off a wiser man as regarded his knowledge of native weapons. Von Tempsky was the only man whom I had tried that I could not touch ; but he was an excellent swordsman.

PAT'S STRATAGEM.

During the war with the Maoris many of the soldiers deserted from the regiment they belonged to and scattered themselves over the country. Scores of them went North, where they were employed by timber merchants and others. Little effort was made, as a rule, to recapture these men, but after the troops had gone home a *Gazette* was issued proclaiming a free pardon to all deserters from Her Majesty's service. Attempts had been made previous to this to capture a few, and a reward of ten pounds per head offered for their capture.

One strapping young fellow, a son of Erin, had taken "French-leave" of his regiment. Pat, as he was called, ran away, and after roughing it some time in the wilds, engaged himself as cook to a large party of sawyers. Now Pat had been an officer's servant, and was a first-rate groom ; so really his loss was more than his master could bear with equanimity of temper, wherefore many inquiries were made as to where he had taken refuge, with a view to his arrest.

At last, a mean-spirited, sanctimonious devil-dodger betrayed the hiding place of poor Paddy, but the distance was too great to send a corporal's guard to arrest him ; and, in fact, to have done so would have been useless, as he would have had timely warning of his danger. Two natives, however, for a reward of twenty pounds, offered to capture Pat, handcuff him, and deliver him bound, like Samson, into the power of his enemies.

The plan of these brawny savages was to entice Pat to their village, which was not far distant from where the sawyers were working, where he was to be overpowered by numbers and tied up. But, though many plans were laid to accomplish this, they all proved failures. Brown, dusky-eyed girls were sent to lure Pat from home; but, though more than willing to make love to these charming children of nature, Pat kept his beat round and about the hut and sawpits. It is not at all unlikely that he received a quiet hint or so to be on his guard from one of his brown adorers. But the stealthy Maoris, ever on the alert, contrived to ascertain that on a certain day all the sawyers were going some distance back in the bush, and would not return till the evening. The Maoris thought that Pat, with two against him, would have no chance of escape if they happened to light on him unprotected. They had obtained full leave to knock him down in case of resistance, so they started on their expedition. They crept up to the hut about dinner time, armed with a gun, a hard-wood spear, and a pair of handcuffs. On looking through the window, they saw Pat sitting by the fire, alone, smoking his pipe, and half asleep.

"He is ours," they thought as they opened the door and went in.

Their entrance aroused Pat, who looked up. He took in the situation at once. It has been said that Irishmen are wanting in ballast; but when was ever a true Irishman placed in a dangerous predicament that he did not act with perfect *sang froid* and all his mother wit come to his rescue? Pat rose and welcomed his visitors.

"Come in, Johnny, my boy; shure all the sawyers chaps 'ave gone to the bush, and won't be back till to-morrow; sit ye down. Where are the illigant wahines (girls) and how are yez all; begorra we'll 'ave somethin' to ate—pork chops and plum-duff, and bile some praties, and put on the billy, for a cup of tay is the right thing in the cowld weather, Johnny me boys," said Pat, looking at his visitors with the "tail of his eye."

The Maoris understood quite enough English or Irish to comprehend that they were going to have a delicious feed of fried pork chops and potatoes and tea. They no doubt felt that their man was safe and their prisoner, and it was but fit and right that he should prepare a good dinner for them.

After the chops were eaten, they could, of course, handcuff him and take him off; so they loosened their flax belts in anticipation —pork chops was not an every-day meal with them. Pat bustled about, cut up the chops, pitched more wood on to the fire, filled the kettle, though he remarked that, "Divil a cow them sawyers had, so there was no milk and the two goats is dead, rest be to their sowles." So chattering merrily on he took down the huge old and worn frying-pan, and placed it on the tripod. In went the pork chops and plenty of lard; on went the potatoes and kettle. Pat set the table in order, tin plates, pannikins, knives, and forks.

"We can eat by the fire," said the Maoris.

" Divil a fear," said Pat, " two grate jintlemen rangatiris like yer two selves to ate on the floor ; you will just sit down at the table wid me.   Take yer seats boys, till I bring the praties."

Each native having piled up his plate with potatoes, Pat fetched the hissing frying-pan full of chops swimming in fat.

The time had come !

In the twinkling of an eye—an Irish eye—the whole of the contents of the pan, chops, scalding fat, and all were capsized over the head of the most powerful of the two Maoris, and before he could give utterance to his howl of terror and pain, Pat brought the frying-pan with his two hands and all his might on the head of the other, and with such force and good will, the fellow's head came through the bottom of the old pan, which rested like a collar on his shoulders.   The two Maoris rolled on the earthern floor of the hut.   Pat went out at the door, snatching up the gun as he went after wishing them good-bye, and telling them to make themselves perfectly at home, he slipped away into the forest.

" Batheshin," said he, " the dirty varmints to make me waste the mate and praties and spoil me frying-pan "

No one attempted to molest Pat after this, and he became a first rate bushman, and is now, I believe, doing well as a small farmer.

THE TRIAL OF KEREOPA.—HORRIBLE DISCLOSURES.

The preliminary trial of Kereopa commenced at Napier, on 11th December, 1871, before B. Sealy, Esq., R.M., and J. A. Campbell, Esq., R.M   The magisterial inquiry was commenced on the 12th, when the prisoner was committed to take his trial at the Supreme Court, on 21st December, on a charge of murdering the Rev. Mr. Volkner   We give below the leading points of evidence taken by the Magistrates.   Penetito deposed : " I saw the prisoner in 1865, at Te Tuku   He urged the people of that place to become Hauhaus.   It was in the spring of 1865.   He went from Te Teka to Whakatane   He asked the people of that place to give up the Roman Catholic priests that he might kill them.   They had not agreed to it.   Kereopa then went to Opotiki.   He asked the chiefs there to let him have Mr. Volkner, that he might kill him.   I myself heard him do so.   Mokomoko, one of the chiefs, agreed to do it   Mokomoko was hanged by the Europeans at the Wairoa. The day after I heard Kereopa make the demand, I started for a place called Te Puio.   I returned the same day.   When I got back, I saw the people assembling in a church.   Then I saw Kereopa with Mr Volkner's head.   He was standing in the pulpit. It was wrapped in calico.   Then I saw him gouge out Mr. Volkner's eyes   The right eye was in his right hand, and the left eye in his left hand.   Then I saw him put the right eye into his mouth and swallow it.   I then saw him put the left eye into his mouth.   It stuck in his throat.   He drank something that I thought was water, till I saw the blood running down his chin. After I saw Kereopa with the head, I saw the body lying outside

VIEW OF REV. VOLKNER'S CHURCH, OPOTIKI.

the church. My brother wrapped it up in a blanket." Pihana
Tiwhai deposed : "I saw him and Petara at Opotiki. The prisoner
had a basket with him with a European's head in it. The first
words that I heard him say were, 'Friends, this is a word from
God to you. If any minister, or other European, comes to this
place, do not protect him ; he must die! die! die!' Petara said
next, 'I am come to bring the new God to you. This is the true
God. If a minister or European come within these boundaries, he
shall not be spared.' I knew Mr. Volkner. He arrived after
Kereopa and Petara had come to Opotiki about five days. He
came by vessel. The vessel came up the river, and lay close
against the bank. As soon as the vessel came alongside the
Taranaki natives tied up the Europeans, including Mr. Volkner
and Mr. Grace, and led them away to the gaol. I saw the whole
transaction—I mean by the Taranaki natives—Kereopa and
Petara, and those that came with them. Next thing I saw was
Mr. Volkner being led away. I could not see who the native was
who was leading him. I was too far off. It was one of the
Taranaki natives. My wife said to me, 'Don't follow them ; they
are putting Volkner to death.' I went away to a mill near. In
the evening I returned. I was told that Mr. Volkner was killed,
and was shown where his body was. The body had on black
trousers, boots, and white shirt. There was no head on it. I
asked Kereopa to let me have the body to bury it. (The witness
here gave some very disgusting details of the treatment the corpse
subsequently received.) I saw Mr. Volkner's head, and that of
another European, afterwards, at Opotiki, in a tent." Wiremu
Pahi, sworn, deposed : "I remember when Kereopa came to
Opotiki in March, 1865. Mr. Volkner was then absent in
Auckland. The first the Taranaki natives did was to rob
Mr. Volkner's house. Kereopa said Mr. Volkner was to be
killed. At the time of Mr. Volkner's arrival Kereopa was
inland. The vessel when it arrived was robbed, and the
Europeans put in gaol. Kereopa returned on the arrival of
Mr. Volkner. Kereopa then sent some people to bring Mr.
Volkner from the gaol, that was my house (the names of some
of the party were given). Kereopa was also with them. Mr.
Volkner was brought to the church. After the talk was done there,
he was led off to be hung. Kereopa gave orders to take him to a
tree and hang him. The last I saw of Mr. Volkner was when he
was being led to the tree. I went to my plantation ; when I
returned Mr. Volkner was hanging on the tree. I went straight to
my own house. After a short time I returned to the church, and
saw Mr. Volkner's body lying outside it, without the head.
Thauraira Kari cut the head off. Kereopa told him to do it. The
head was put in the church through the window. Kereopa placed
the head on the table before him, and took out the two eyes with
his two hands. He said : 'Listen, O tribe, this is the parliament
of England.' Then he swallowed the eyes. After this the head
was carried round to all the people in the house. I went out. I
KK*

saw the body." Renata deposed : " Two Jews, besides Mr. Volkner and Mr. Grace, arrived in the same vessel. After the vessel arrived he went inland and saw Kereopa there. He was telling the people that he had received a message from his god that he was to kill Mr. Volkner. I went back to Opotiki. After I arrived I saw Mr. Volkner led from a whare to the church. Kereopa was alongside of Mr. Volkner. I did not go to the church. The next thing I saw was Mr. Volkner being led from the church to a tree. Kereopa was a few yards behind Mr. Volkner. Kereopa had Mr. Volkner's watch and waistcoat on, and Mr. Volkner had on a shirt and trousers. I saw them lead Mr. Volkner up to a bush. After that I went to my own place on the opposite side of the river. I stopped at my place some time. When I got back I saw Mr. Volkner's head in the church. I looked in at the window. I saw the head on the table, and the two eyes in Kereopa's hand. Kereopa first offered them to his god, and then ate them himself. Kereopa had seagull feathers stuck in his hair." Hori Wetere Te Motutere deposed : " Kereopa asked the people of Te Teko to let him have a European named Aubrey, a miller there; they did not give him up. He went next to Whakatane. There they asked the people to give them up the Catholic priest, Father Grange, to kill him. They did not agree to do so. They next went to Opotiki. I went into the church. I saw there the head lying on the table, and Kereopa with one of Mr. Volkner's eyes in each hand. He said : ' These are the eyes that have looked on the destruction of this Island, I will eat them. He has eaten me, and I will now eat him. He crucified me, and I will crucify him.' Then he swallowed the eyes. He drank something out of a pannikin. I don't know what it was. He then said : ' All men, women, and children, must eat of this sacrifice.' I jumped out of the window and ran away." Hautakura being sworn, deposed : " I live at Waiotahi. I remember the arrival of Kereopa and the Taranakis at Opotiki in 1865. Kereopa explained the Hauhau religion and laid off boundaries. ' Whatever European comes within these boundaries,' he said, ' whether minister or otherwise, they shall be killed.' After this Mr. Volkner arrived, and was taken to gaol by Kereopa's orders. I heard him give them. They then assembled at the Catholic Church Kereopa said, ' Listen! Mr. Volkner must die this day.' I went home. I came back some time afterwards, and found the people all assembled near the church. I was at the doorway. I heard Kereopa say then again, ' Mr. Volkner must die this day.' He then sent a party to fetch Mr. Volkner. Keramita, Kahupaia, Hakaria, and Kereopa himself were of the party. I remained in the doorway, and saw them leading up Mr. Volkner. Kereopa had Mr. Volkner's clothes. When they got to the doorway of the church Kereopa ordered some men to lead him to execution. The words he used were : ' Come some people, and lead Mr. Volkner to kill him.' The same persons that went to fetch him on the former day led him away together with Kereopa and the whole population. They were Taranakis. Kereopa was close behind

Mr. Volkner when he was being led away within a yard of him." The prisoner was then asked if he wished to say anything for himself. He declined to do so. The prisoner was then committed for trial before the Supreme Court on the 21st December, 1871, and afterwards he was hanged.

ON THE EMPLOYMENT OF NATIVE FORCES.

During the war at the north with Hone Heke and Kawiti, which, on our side, was conducted principally by Col. Despard, many natives from Hokianga under their chiefs—Tamati Waka Nene, Te Tao Nui, Wi Kipa, Wi Hopihana, and others—rendered us great assistance, partly from a good feeling they entertained for the whites, and partly from hatred to their old enemies, and a natural love of fighting which is inherent in the New Zealander. Tamati Waka Nene held a prominent part throughout the war, and his word carried great weight with the majority of the friendly natives. The first Maori stockade, or pa, attacked by our troops was Okaihau. This pa, much to the astonishment, and against the advice of the chiefs, was rushed by the soldiers, and resulted in about thirty of our men being shot down within a few feet of the palisading, and we had to retreat. Kawiti's men, who were in the front, charged our troops; but they never again tried this, many of them being killed by a charge of bayonets.

After this, Colonel Despard depended greatly on the advice of our native allies, as he wisely saw he did not understand the enemy's mode of warfare, and that our natives had ways and means of knowing what the others were about, and manœuvred accordingly. But however Tamati Waka obtained his knowledge of passing events he never, as a native general or chief, thought of ordering the natives to do what he considered best but when he had arrived at certain conclusions. As, for instance, at Ohaiowai he wished to take possession of a certain eminence, which commanded a portion of the enemy's work. Perhaps this had been the result of a secret conference with two or more old chiefs. Early in the night Tamati Waka would have a dream and a huhi (a convulsive starting of his right or left arm). The dream might have been a successful weka hunt, or that a taniwha (a fabulous sea monster) had invited him to a feast, as the case might be, which would denote to the tribe's success. The order would be given in the following manner: "The enemy have (the oracle informs) determined to attack our camp, and in doing so will succeed in killing some of us; to prevent this a strong party will take possession of the hill over the pa to-night;" when, before morning, it was occupied by 250 men, and then Colonel Despard was informed of the movement, and desired to do certain things, but almost always when the arrangements had been nearly completed by our natives for destroying the enemy after their own way of advancing and fighting, an abortive attempt at storming would be made, never once successful, and always ended with the enemy escaping, and us losing many valuable lives, to the anger and disgust of the friendlies. Towards the close of the campaign the officer in command admitted that, owing to the peculiar mode of warfare, to be successful against the enemy, it was necessary for his troops to act as a contingent to the friendly natives, and not the natives as a contingent to the troops; and he was right, as there were then several hundred friendly natives in the field, by nature independent, impetuous, trickish, and impatient of control, who could only be managed by their chiefs through their superstitions, and not by ordering them about, and they were not fighting so much for love of the pakeha as from the memory of old grievances. The love so often prated about for the Queen weighed not a feather in the balance. Letters and speeches, commencing—"O Governor! great is my love for you," "O Queen! we are your children, and our love for you is great," means no more than, "I remain, yours truly," or "I have the honour to be," etc. At this time they were receiving no pay for their services, but this was nearly forty years ago, and the conduct of Hone Heke and Kawiti was condemned by most of the northern tribes. We will now turn to the present and the last few years.

When the Arawas assisted the Government in 1864 they received no pay, but were only supplied with arms and ammunition during this time; though I had considerable command over them, I was careful not to let such appear. I gained the confidence of their chief, and certain successes were obtained, as they fought to revenge themselves on their enemies and not on ours. It gave them no little confidence, too, the fact that they were fighting under our law, and were considered to be helping the Government and the Queen's general.

Shortly after this they were placed on pay, when they soon found out, if the fighting lasted one week and the enemy were beaten, the pay only lasted one week, and then abruptly ceased. The result of this discovery was, they used all their cunning to prolong hostilities. This was only to be expected would occur when under their own chiefs, who if they had ever urged them to action, would have less influence with their tribes. But a European placed in command had no reason to fear the loss of any influence he might have obtained if he considered himself as a gentleman ought to, and if properly supported by the Government; for the natives who know when a man does his duty respect him accordingly, but they will, to attain their own ends, write letters to the Government requesting that so-and-so be removed, mentioning some childish reason, in the hope that another pakeha may be sent to replace the one in command, in the further hope that the new-comer may fall more easily into their ways, and they have an easier time of it while the pay goes on. As one instance out of scores I could mention, I will relate what happened to my friend the late Captain St. George. He at the time was stationed at Taupo in command of a body of Arawas, who had to do their duty. Returning one day with his native orderly from a long wet ride, he retired to change his clothes. The two principal chiefs of the settlement or pa came to

him, and begged for one of the bottles of rum he had by him. This
request he refused. Had he given it to them they would both have
become tipsy. Shortly after this, Captain St. George sent for his
orderly and gave him a glass of grog. The two chiefs heard of it,
and wrote a letter to the Commissioner (a gentleman), and begged
he would cause the officer in command to be removed, as he was
giving the men rum, and making them drunk, causing neglect of
duty. The Commissioner, Mr. Clarke, enclosed this production to
Captain St. George, asking an explanation. The chiefs acknowledged to the letter, said they had written it in a moment of anger,
and wrote to Mr. Clarke explaining the truth, and confessing they
had told a falsehood to spite the officer for not giving them the
bottle of rum.

I have obtained many successes with the Arawas serving under
me when in receipt of pay; but I have made allowance for their
customs and superstitions. Up to a certain point I have often given
in to their wishes, when I had my way in return. I have my secrets
worth knowing, the advice of an old and noted Tohunga chief, and
if we have to fight again, which, perhaps, we may, a few of the
secrets of my Tohunga Karakai (praying wizard) may be found
useful, even though times are altered from what they were, and the
officer who may then be placed in command of our forces (if he is not
too proud to inquire) shall be made acquainted with at least a few.
My sword belt has got so stiff, and the lock of my rifle so rusty that
it would require more soft soap to soften the one, and more sweet
oil to lubricate the other, than the Government stores can perhaps
provide. No chief, however he may wish to perform his duty to the
country, has sufficient power among the hapus a tribe consists of
to get the men to make short, quick work of a campaign against
their wishes, and retain his influence; for that, amongst the Maoris,
is subject to their changeable opinion. The tribe led against our
enemy have little or no feeling of hostility to those they are
expected to fight. They have had their day of utu (payment) for
the past, and think now that five shillings a day under their own
chiefs, who are bound, as their chiefs, to look after the interests of
the tribe, is a good thing. And let any chief beware lest he strain
this point too much, as there are those who would quickly thwart
any apparent intention from one of themselves to *use* the tribe for
the pakeha.

The power of a chief is well hinted at by "Old New Zealand" in
the scene of the wrestling match with "Melons." The head chief
appears, and is very angry. "'Look at that; the pakeha does not
bear you any malice. I would kill you if he asked me. You are a
bad people—killers of pakehas. Be off with you—the whole of you
—away!' This command was instantly obeyed by all the women,
boys, and slaves; but I observed that *the whole of you* did not seem
to be understood as including the stout, able-bodied, tattooed part
of the population—the strength of the tribe—the warriors, in fact,
many of whom counted themselves to be very much about as good
as the chief." The sympathy of the natives is for themselves, and

not for the pakeha; and this is very natural. Why should it be otherwise?

Tribes sent out under their own chiefs are expensive and sometimes mischievous, and little is done for the reasons I have mentioned, though much may be reported, etc.; but the same natives, in concert with Europeans, under a European officer who has some knowledge of the Maoris, will not fail of success, always provided the natives are honestly told the European is in command, whose word must be obeyed, and from whom there is no appeal, then good will result. The Europeans otherwise had far better go by themselves, when, if not worried and harassed with the telegraph from all quarters all at once, will in the end have their opportunity, and succeed.

The old Wanganui contingent, when acting with the European forces, was a happy and successful way of employing natives, and would be so again, but the European portion of the force ought to number two or three to one, and a European to command the whole is indispensable, if certain success is looked for.

Such is my practical experience during eight years' compaigning in New Zealand, and of more than forty years' residence among the natives.

One time I particularly wished to march in a certain direction, and had concluded, as I thought, all arrangements with the fighting chief; but he, feeling his way with the tribe, preparatory to giving the order, found that for some reason or another they were not willing to go, and looked to him to frustrate the march and my plans. He returned and told me of the feeling existing. It was absolutely necessary for the success of certain designs that we should march, and he knew this. "Exert your influence," I said, "and make them go." "That would never do," he replied, "they would soon cease to listen to me; but as we are all on pay—you appear to be angry with me—I will then speak to the tribe, and get them to march." I did as requested, and had the satisfaction of hearing my friend complain loudly to the tribe that I was a pakeha, a hard pakeha, one who would not listen to reason ; that this march was not requited, it being only a whim of mine, etc. ; but they must remember they were only on pay, and some weeks in arrears. Perhaps after all they had better march; he would write to the Government to remove me; so they would all march now he had decided it. In a short time they paraded, declared their chief was a "Tangata whai whakaaro" (man of understanding), and knew how to manage affairs. The chief returned to me with laughter in his eye, and said, "Come, be quick, while they are in the humour; I had to abuse you, but I hope you are not angry; they are my tribe, and I must not lose my influence." I replied I was much pleased, and that he might abuse me to his heart's content as long as good results were obtained. Two or three days afterwards, when the tribe saw the good our march had helped to, they took great credit to themselves for what had been achieved.

ILLUSTRATIVE OF NATIVE ALLIES.—THE MARCH ROUND MOUNT
EGMONT.

After the capture of Otapawa, and the total defeat of the natives
at Katemarae, Ahipaipa, Pa Poaka, Mawhitiwhiti, and other places
by General Chute, arrangements were made by the General for one
of the most hazardous enterprises ever undertaken in New Zealand.
This was to march through Mataitawa, by the old track round
Mount Egmont. As far as the contingent and Wanganui kupapas
were concerned, Maori ingenuity was fairly exhausted in trying to
persuade the General from such an arduous task, but he was not to
be put off. Men were told off for the expedition from each
regiment in camp, and the Forest Rangers, under the personal
superintendence of their gallant leader, Von Tempsky, cleaned up
their trusty breech-loaders, and made preparations. As I was *hors
de combat* from my wound, which my late exertions had made very
painful, the General came to my tent, where every information that
could be procured from the Maoris was obtained, and laid before
him in the presence of Commissariat-General Strickland and His
Honour Dr. Featherston.

I was instructed to tell off as many natives as I thought would
be sufficient, procure special guides, and report progress with the
least possible delay. The General then left us. I then asked the
doctor to collect all the chiefs into our tent. This was done, and
a long korero (talk) ensued. At first the chiefs declared that it was
impossible to go round the mountain by the proposed route ; that
the force would never get out of the bush, and that it would be
better to go round by the coast. We combatted every argument
that they brought forward, and finally wrung an unwilling consent
from them that the natives should go with the expedition. I may
here remark that it was absolutely necessary that the natives
should go, as no one knew the direction to be taken in the pathless
forest about to be entered. Doctor Featherston communicated
the result of our consultation to the General, who, naturally
concluding that all obstacles were removed from his undertaking,
ordered a certain number of rations to be issued to the men of all
corps about to march, and to be cooked at once.

Somehow or other a kind of instinct which I seem to have,
whenever Maoris are concerned, caused me to feel certain misgivings when they consented to go. I could not feel sure in my
own mind that any of them would really start. True they had said,
"Yes, we will go, you can tell the General that so many shall
accompany the force," and that they had also drawn fresh
ammunition and rations ; but yet, knowing them as I did, I was by
no means easy on that point. This worried me. I felt that any
blame would naturally fall on myself, and as I lay in my tent
thinking the matter over, the uncertainty gradually established
itself as a fact. The natives did not intend to go, but I had no
proof to lay before the General.

I knew Mete Kingi and others had from the commencement of

the campaign endeavoured to raise obstacles in the way, and the reserved look Mete had on his face during the korero in my tent helped to confirm my suspicions. I felt miserable and helpless. It was now about 9 p.m. The echoes of the bugle, sounding "lights out," had scarcely died away among the hills when the curtain of my tent was slowly raised, and a native crawled in. I recognised him as one of the most faithful of my followers. Many were the plots which he had given me timely warning of. "What is up now?" I said, in a subdued voice. "But a word," whispered the man; "when the General parades to-morrow morning, one native alone will be present, and that is myself. Mete Kingi and the rest have been deceiving you. None of the natives will go round the mountain. The tribes have their orders. I must go now," he continued. "I could not come near you before." "Kapai (good)" I replied; "it is enough. Go away quietly, as you came." Soon after he had gone, Dr. Featherston returned (we occupied the same tent) from the General's quarters, when I mentioned the visit I had had. We sent for the native chiefs, my brother William (who now commanded the contingent) taking the message. They soon collected. On putting the question plainly, and demanding an immediate reply, they said (like the hypocrites they were), "It is true the men will not go, in spite of all our endeavours to induce them." Mete added that his heart was broken utterly; he might get over it, but he thought not; his heart would remain dark for ever. I frankly told him and the others that they lied, and that he had, through his superstition, tampered with the men; that my familiar spirit had told me so, and it was therefore no use denying it; and I ordered the whole of them—contingent officers, and all— out of the tent.

The doctor lit his cigar, I filled my pipe, and we gazed at each other for a few seconds in silence. "It's that beggar, Mete Kingi," I said, breaking silence. The doctor ground his teeth, and smoked away vigorously, uttering short but pithy sentences between each puff of smoke. "The General will be in a towering rage. I have only just left him, and he was delighted at having overcome all difficulties. It is now half-past twelve, and he ought to know this. What's to be done?"

Only one chance occurred to me to try—being unable to move about—and with Dr. Featherston's consent, I prepared to put it to the test. Hori Kingi te Anana, at this time the principal chief of Wanganui, had with his tribe received much kindness from Dr. Featherston. They looked up to him for advice, not only from the high position he held, but privately. Hori Kingi respected him as one who had never deceived him, whose word, once passed, was good for the performance of what had been promised, but who, at the same time, was not easily imposed upon by threats in whatever shape they were made. I awoke my brother, Capt. McDonnell, and asked him to find Hori Kingi, and bring him by himself to our tent. I then advised Dr. Featherston to recount to Hori, when he came in, the events that had taken place between them during the past few years. The friendship that had during that time existed between them—his own fixed determination that the expedition should march as already agreed upon, at 3.30 p.m., and then telling Hori that the other natives might remain if they chose, to then ask him, as his old and trusty friend, to accompany him. Dr. Featherston caught at the idea, and I prepared to translate word for word what the doctor might say.

Presently the old chief entered, and squatted on the floor of the tent. "So the natives won't go to-morrow, Hori," I said. "They will not," he replied. "They are not required to now," I rejoined, "but the doctor has something to say to you before he leaves in the morning, and he will now speak." Dr. Featherston then made a short, straightforward speech, and to the point, that understanding the natives at the eleventh hour had resolved not to go, he had sent for his old friend Hori to request that he would accompany him in the morning with the troops.

Old Hori was much excited, and moved about uneasily. "I would, oh Featherston, go with you," he said, "but I am lame. Behold my foot."

"I sprained my ankle severely some days since," replied the doctor, "yet I accompanied your natives wherever they went. My ankle is much swollen and very painful now, but I will go to-morrow, and you, Hori, shall accompany me. It shall never be said that the whole of the Wanganuis were frightened. You and I must prevent this evil thing."

The blood of his ancestors rose to the old chief's brow, and his face underwent a change. "Patatone, but for you, were would the tribe be? If Europeans had acted like you, like chiefs, we would not now be fighting. You have been—you are—our father. Hori Te Anana speaks now. Hori Kingi will go with his father—go by himself with you, but will not return again to his tribe. I will, in future, go where you go, and stay where you stay. You will hear me tell my tribe this. I go to bid my people farewell. Listen, both of you!" As Hori uttered these words, he rose and stood upright at the door of the tent.

It was a clear night, and the contingent and kupapa tents showed out white and distinct, and not a rustle was heard as the old warrior spoke. "O Whanganui! Whanganui! farewell. The tribe, farewell! The past, farewell! Farewell for ever! Listen to me now. Hearken to me. I cast off my tribe, and they are no longer mine. The spirit of the tribe has fled, bewitched by Ngati-manui. They have become strange. They are now what they were not. I cast them on the dark side of the path. I, Hori te Anana, leave with my father, Dr. Featherston, and the Queen, to-morrow. Farewell to you, O tribe farewell! I have spoken; it is enough."

A low hum, like the working song of the bees, like the murmuring of a stream, arose in the camp of the Maoris as the old chief spoke. I could feel that everyone was drinking in his words, and now and then a low moan was heard, which proceeded from the women of the tribe. Hori re-entered the tent, and grasping each of us by the hand, said, in a subdued voice, "They *are* my children, I think. Some of them will come with their father."

A shrill voice was now heard addressing the tribe, and, my ears being quick, I told Hori, word for word, what was going forward. Chief after chief of the plotters succeeded the man now speaking; but a muffled roar from the contingent presently echoed through the camp. The young warriors, the best and the bravest, had been worked up to a pitch of frenzy. Mete's name was coupled with English oaths, and he was most unromantically told to "shut up." "He is a coward," said one. "He is always meddling," added another. "We thought you did not want us to go, Hori," said they; and, although it wanted an hour of the time to parade, tents were struck, baggage packed, and over seventy of the flower of the contingent (with cries of "To Taranaki! to Taranaki!") formed up on parade, with arms and accoutrements, ready to march.

The reaction was complete, but the excitement had cost old Hori a struggle, and he asked for a glass of spirits, which, by the way, he had scarcely ever tasted before. The General now looked in to wish me good-bye. He little knew then of the previous night's work we had had. One of the plotters (Paora) now came to the tent, and began to tell me and the doctor how very glad he was that the natives had consented to go, and how superhuman his endeavours had been to accomplish the result. "I feel cold," he continued, and stretched out his hand to a flask of commissariat. I jumped up, regardless and oblivious of my situation, and kicked the rascally hypocrite out of the tent; but I hurt myself worse than I hurt him. The force fell in, and my friends bade me adieu, and marched away on their uncertain journey.

A CURIOUS MISTAKE.

During one of our long and hungry marches through the Tuhua forests in search of the notorious Te Kooti, Major Kemp, who was leading at the head of a column of 400 men, committed a curious mistake. We had from the plain seen fires that were supposed to be those of Te Kooti's bands, and the smoke rose in a high pillar to the sky. I took the bearings with a small compass I had, as there was no known road, intending to guide the force myself in search of the enemy. Kemp, however, earnestly begged me to let him lead the column, so, as I knew him to be a splendid bushman, and that his instincts were of the right kind, I resigned the first post of honour, and took the second, that is the rear of the whole. The duty of a leader of a column in a trackless forest is, first, not to march too quickly; secondly, to notice every log and creek the men have to cross over, and regulate the pace accordingly, halting occasionally to allow the men in the rear to close up. I of course thought that when Kemp made the request he did he was going to trust to his native instinct But I was mistaken; a brilliant idea had occurred to him! He noticed that a compass Mr. Maling, one of a corps of guides, had pointed in one direction, no matter which way the case containing it was placed. Now, the direction the fires were in from us was about due south. One end of the compass was as good as another to Kemp, and he came to the conclusion that the compass pointed for Te Kooti himself, and that if he held the compass, it would soon take him to where Te Kooti was, and in this way he would cheat the other sections of tribes now on the march, out of the honour and glory of killing this miscreant. Full of these ideas, and chuckling to himself, he entered the bush at the head of the column. On we went over hill, creek, and dale, clambering up steep ascents, and carefully descending all but precipices, halting ever so often. Such a scramble I never had before or since, and I have gone over some rough country. To make matters worse, it poured as if a second deluge had been let loose. At last darkness set in, and we camped without fires, as Kemp assured me from signs he had seen, we were not far off from Te Kooti now. But the other chiefs declared we had passed the place where the smoke had been seen hours ago, and that we would soon reach Waikato or Auckland. For my part, although I had no suspicion of the truth, I felt sure we were all at sea, and were off the scent. The next morning this proved to be the case, and the column had to return to camp the best way it could, as our meagre stock of biscuits had given out. Several days after this Kemp came to my quarters, and looking curiously at my compass, said, "I cannot quite make out this instrument." I explained it to him as well as I could, and how vessels were guided by it on the trackless ocean. "I know they are," said Kemp, "but it is because the needle points out the direction the ships must take. Is this not so?" "Eureka, I have it now," I thought, as the truth flashed upon me. "Did you have a compass the other day when we were out after Te Kooti?" "Yes," replied Kemp: "I halted too, every now and then, to see if we were going in the right direction, but somehow or another we did not go right." I could not help laughing; but it had caused one of the roughest and most wearisome marches we had at Taupo. I satisfied Kemp of his mistake, and I think he will trust to his native instincts in preference to any compass in future.

TALES OF THE MAORI.

TOENGA POU.

N the left bank of the Hokianga River, about twenty miles from the Heads, was once a famous native settlement. The rich kumara grounds belonging to it were celebrated far and near, and right in front, half way across the river, was an island, fringed with mangrove trees, on the extensive flats of which, at low water, an unfailing supply of shell-fish, eels, and patiki were to be procured. Stingrays were also very abundant here, and I have seen them caught measuring five feet across. At the back of this settlement a high hill, the summit of which had, after great labour and skill, been fashioned by many hundreds of pair of hands into a formidable pa, hewn, as it were, out of the solid earth. It was the principal stronghold of the settlement; and even to the present day, though most of the outer lines have been filled up with dry leaves and rubbish, and the outer and deep ditch is now less than half its original depth, enough remains to form a good idea of what this fighting pa once was. It would probably have taken five hundred navvies, working with pick, shovel, and barrow, twelve months' hard work to cut down and form this work; but when one knows that all the tools with which this was undertaken and accomplished were only bits of hard wood, pointed and burnt hard in a fire, and the only means of carrying away the thousands of tons of earth, stones and gravel, were small buckets made of flax, one is forced to admire the courage and perseverance of the New Zealander in those days.

This pa was called Karewa Ki Runga (the Lofty Reared on High). Hence the Maori canoe song—

> Puke tiki tiki te puke ne Karewa,
> Iri noa aki taku aroha to maunawa.

> O lofty hill, the hill Karewa ;
> Yet my love is loftier within my soul.

"Karewa Ki Runga" was the fighting pa of the Popoto tribe at the time I speak of, and they numbered over one thousand warriors, the most powerful tribe of the Ngapuhi, and Muriwae Te Tuku Take was its head chief, and at the period I tell of was in the prime of his life, a just man according to tradition, but a stern and terrible warrior in battle. He was the grandfather of Te Taonui, who proved himself such a staunch friend to the Europeans at the time of the war with Hone Heke. Taonui (Big Spear) was then about sixty years of age. His father, Te Ahuriri, died about 1849, and was supposed to be at least 110 years old at the time of his death. He remembered Captain Cook well, and at that time he had, so he said, wives and children, so Muriwae Te Tuku Take (his father) must have been about forty or fifty years of age when what I am about to relate occurred, and several years before the arrival of the great navigator Cook to these shores.

The Maori villages under Karewa Ki Runga were Otaehau, Te Horeke, Parepare, Mangatete, Mangaraupo, and Waikahanganui, and the slopes of Karewa, part of which were cultivated as calabash grounds. Karewa Ki Runga frowned aloft some 700 or 800 feet above the villages, and commanded the whole; but about a mile from this hill were two other pas, which had also been cut out of a solid hill top, but they were inferior to Karewa in height.

At the back of the Waikahanganui settlement, the village furthest off from the centre, was one of the most beautiful wooded valleys I can remember. A narrow brook of clear, ever-cold water ran through the middle of it; here and there were gigantic kauri trees, but the graceful miro were crowded on both banks of the little stream, and lined the valley stretching away to the ranges on each side of it. This stream, in the pigeon season, when the berries on the miro trees were red ripe, used to be covered from sight by thickly-leaved branches, which were placed over it. It was but a moss-lined little brook, about eighteen inches wide, but deep, and ran the same winter and summer. This covering over was a work of care, but places were left at intervals here and there for the birds to come to bathe and drink. Each of these drinking places was provided with innumerable perches for the birds to light and plume themselves upon, but rows of snares were placed in every direction, and meshes out of number. These were made out of the cabbage tree leaves, being much stronger than flax, and kept their shape like very thin steel. When this valley was used for bird meshing, about three miles of it was laid under snares, and during the season it was under strict tapu, and only visited each evening before sundown, to remove the captive and drowned birds and replace any of the snares which had chanced to get broken or displaced; but under no pretence whatever were strangers permitted to go there, either in or out of season; in fact, it was never thought that anyone could have dreamt it possible to go to places of this kind, not being one of the tribe, and death would have followed to a certainty anyone who so transgressed tribal rights. The usual take, or harvest, of birds in one month, during the full fruiting of the miro in its season, was from 4500 to 5000 birds, such as pigeons, parrots, and tuis; but even in my time, when I was a youngster, I used to accompany old Toenga Pou, when he went out bird snaring to this valley, and have helped to lift between 300 and 400 birds from the few hundred

LL

yards of the stream he had prepared in the way I have described. There were other valleys and places, bird snaring grounds, in plenty on the estate of the Popotos; but the Puna Valley was far away the best and most valued, as it was so complete and near to the settlements. Each of three pas, even when no war party was expected, was held by an efficient garrison, and the tribe took turn and turn about, naturally and by instinct, to guard them. Hundreds of short darts, so pointed at the ends that on striking an object the point would remain in the wound and, being barbed, prove difficult to get out, were kept in covered pits. Heaps of round iron stones, weighing from one to five pounds each, were collected from the beach and piled up for the use of the slingers (kotaha); and heavy logs and boulders were kept in place on the outer ditch to use in case of an assault, and ready to launch over the precipitous sides of the pas, in case such a defence was required. Before early dawn, which the tui and bell bird heralded each morn, the war note of the watchers in the pas proclaimed all was well, and a good watch kept. The slumbering tribe in the villages beneath now bestirred themselves, and soon hundreds of columns of white steam, shooting upwards to the sky, showed that the morning meal of the Popoto tribe was being prepared in the ovens. After this was eaten, the tribe betook itself to its different occupations, which varied according to the seasons. Behind the hills on which these pas stood were forests, extending for many miles, and where the young men and maidens used to go bird-hunting, and snaring and spearing tuis and parrots, and to gather the wild fruits of the forest, and collect scented moss for their hair.

I will now as well as I can remember, for it is many years since old Toenga Pou recounted his strange story to me, and which had been handed down to him by his forefathers, relate what he told me one night when we two were camped out in a miro bush on the Mataki Hills, where we had gone to get birds.

TOENGA POU'S TALE.

The once great Popoto tribe, of whom I am one, gave a feast in the pigeon season to the whole of Ngatiwhatua who lived on the Kaipara and Wairoa runs; the scaffolding alone which was to support the piles of food was six kumis long (a kumi means sixty feet, so the total length would have been 360 feet). Each scaffolding was one kumi in length, and tapered up from its base, which was twice the stretch of a man's arms (12 feet) to 40, 50, 60, and 75 feet in height, according to the strength or amount of food the hapu of the tribe it belonged to had, and tapered off at the top to about 18 inches broad. On the bottom tier would be about 600 baskets of kumeras; a strong platform was lashed over this to support the next tier of, say, 500 baskets; then another platform, and so on, until a single row of baskets graced the top of the pile. In all, to each piece of scaffolding there would be between 3,000 and 3,500 baskets of kumeras; nere and there would be calabashes of preserved birds-- pigeons, tuis, kakas, weka, kiwi, curlew, ducks, and widgeons ; fish of all kinds, tons of them taken in immense tidal bag nets 70 feet long by 25 feet square at the mouth, narrowing off to 18 inches, an immense basket capable of holding two hogsheads fastened on the other end. These nets used to be set near the mouth of a creek in the tide way, and held in position by two stout spars firmly driven into the river-bed, and were filled to tightness each tide—bundles of dried dog-fish, sharks and eels, and baked dogs, preserved rats, etc., but at these tribal feasts, unless under peculiar circumstances, such as returning from war, or an impromptu feast on the death of an old chief, when, if a lazy slave taken in war could be spared, he would be eaten; no human flesh would form part of a feast such as described. Even when human flesh was eaten it was cooked in a separate oven, and not tossed about as a common article of food, except on the battle field, whatever may be said to the contrary.

The Ngatiwhatua accepted the invitation of the Popotos and came to Hokianga by the coast from Kaipara, first assembling at Mangawhare, on the Wairoa River, making that their starting point. The party consisted of two thousand men and women ; the young children were left behind, and all those who were old and infirm. They all, of course, went fully armed and prepared for war, for one could never tell what might happen. Besides, it was not wise or prudent to go unarmed and place undue temptations in the eyes of their hosts, the Popotos, or not to be able to take advantage of any good chance that might occur to themselves ; but the head men of each family hapu of the tribe received a hint, in a speech addressed to the whole by the head tohunga, Puni, to keep the young men within bounds during the intended visit. (A large party of natives travel slowly; and though I walked once for a wager from Mangawhare to the sea beach, and on then to Hokianga to the settlement of Waimamaku in one day, and without anything to eat by the way, but which was not included in our wager, for I lost my provisions in the surf of a stream I crossed, Ngatiwhatua took one month to go this route.) At the head of the Hokianga River the party were met by a fleet of war, fishing, and other canoes, sent to convey them up the river. Each pa had its usual garrison doubled, and an extra row of manuka stakes was shown to have been placed round the already double palisaded pas. The green boughs and leaves were left on each stout stake, as a hint that any attempt to surprise the garrison would be vain and without hope i f success.

The fleet of canoes drew near after the morning's meal had been consumed, and the noses of the canoes touched the landing-place pointed out for them at the settlement, and 1,500 warriors, not including the women, formed up in array. They were met by the Popotos and their allies, and a terrific war-dance took place on both sides, until (as Toenga Pou said) Karewa Ki Runga reeled again. Then the distant garrisons had each their war-dance, which contained, said Toenga, a very strong hint of power. The guests were then shown to their quarters, and after an abundant meal night closed over the whole

The next day the feast was karangaed (called) that is each piece of scaffolding was formally handed over to a hapu of Ngatiwhatua by a corresponding hapu of the Popotos, and this was subdivided again and again until all the food and delicacies were distributed, and a week's feasting and unbridled license of all kinds was indulged in   But any vestige of morality that may have existed before amongst these children of nature was, as such, according to Toenga's strict account, considered out of place, and carefully put by where nobody could find it ; but as it was not required, it was not sought for   The pigeon portion of the feast was extolled to the skies—the freshness, the flavour of the aromatic, miro-berry fed birds, the lumps of yellow fat !   Alas ! such have never been seen since   The backbone and thighs melted away in their mouths, and fairly bowled over the conceit of the Ngatiwhatua, who asked, " Where did you get these delicious birds ?"   This question was a breach of Maori etiquette ; but a young chief without any brains replied, " These birds came from the Puna Valley.   We had ten takings in one month, but only a few birds are here of what we took, and there are many large calabashes of preserved birds in the storehouses in the valley now," but this was a bit of bounce.   Now, gluttony pure and simple, and before which passion all has to go down to gratify it, is unfortunately a leading trait in the Maori character (said Toenga Pou).   Once let gluttony get possession of a chief and his tribe, and they will not rest till it has been appeased.

" Ugh !" said Ngatiwhatua, amongst themselves, " more of these fat pigeons in calabashes at Puna Valley, are there ?   Why should these Popotos have retained these ?   If we could surprise and slay these people we could have all their nice settlement and the rich bird valley," and the water ran out of their jaws at the bare idea of continual feasts of pigeons and other birds.

Now, Te Koukou, a famous warrior of Ngatiwhatua, and his giant brother Ngahe, had been overtaken by this spirit of kaihoro (gluttony) and an opportunity was sought for ; but our garrison never relaxed their vigilance, and it was hopeless to attempt anything unless these were overpowered first.   But the time drew near for the guests to disperse and return to their homes, so the canoes were accordingly prepared to take them to the heads, so far on their way back, but all Te Koukou's and Ngahe's men declared they would return overland by way of Mangakahia, that being so much shorter than going by the round of the sea beach.   At this a large proportion of the warriors said they would go that way too.   So about 800 men left one morning for Mangakahia, and the rest left for the heads, accompanied by a number of Popotos in the canoes, little dreaming of what was about to take place.

Te Koukou had, according to custom, asked a small party of Popotos to see them as far as the forest, through which they would have to pass to get to their own country.   This forest was about fifteen miles distant, and about twenty of them accepted and went, and one girl named Ponaiti (small joints). On reaching the forest, Te Koukou slew every man and ate them, but saved the girl, whom he told he intended to make his wife, a proposal and alliance which she cheerfully assented to then and there. The other division of Ngatiwhatua, on reaching their former camping place at the heads of the river, contrived to quarrel with their late hosts about a woman. This led to blows, and some of the Popotos were slain, and the rest fled back in dismay with their canoes to the settlement, vowing vengeance. They had barely ended their tale to the assembled tribe when Ponaiti, the girl, stood in their midst, nearly dead from fatigue and running; but she managed to tell her people of the slaughter of her father and other relatives, and what her destined fate had been, ending her horrible tale of blood by saying that Te Koukou was on his way to surprise the pas and kill everyone.

"Get ready for them," was the only sentence that fell from Muriwai to Tuke Take. The tribe was like a flock of birds all at once. Men with tapued back and still more tapued heads and arms seized huge baskets of kumeras, bundles of dried fish, calabashes of water, and streamed up the hill sides to their pas. In less than the roasting of a small kumera in the ashes, the villages were deserted, and all was quiet in the fighting pas and ready. Ponaiti said that she had so deceived Te Koukou as to lead him to think she had remained at Mangakahia till he returned; but she had made tracks through the forest after they had left, to get home before they could attempt their surprise. "They won't go to the villages," said the leading warriors, "but will attack us at dawn to-morrow; and they think they are sure to surprise us, when the destruction of the settlements would follow." Scouts were sent out down the hills to give notice of their approach. They returned soon, and reported the advanced guard of the enemy creeping up the hills, followed by the main body. "Let them come close, and be ready with the logs and boulders, and slings and spears. I will give the charge," said Muriwai te Tuke Take, and several trusty messengers were despatched, by the rear of the pa adjoining the bush, to warn the river natives at Opara, and at Taheki and Wairua, close to the Mangakahia forests, to warn them to look after and close up all the roads, so as to let not one of Ngatiwhatua escape after they were defeated—for that result was looked upon as a certainty, as the Tohungas had foretold. Silence now reigned supreme in the three pas, as the occupants waited the coming storm; but as the objects began to form out of the darkness, the enemy were seen within a few fathoms of the pa, preparing for the final rush up the steep rise in overwhelming numbers.

The chief Tohunga's son had been killed and eaten by the enemy before him, and the fighting chief passed the word, and then one horrible yell burst from Karewa ki Runga, quickly followed by two more frantic war cries from the two other pas. These were returned by the enemy, who had to win now or be eaten. It was in reality your head or mine, and the enemy sprang up the rise to the assault, but the varied collection of rocks and logs, and a shower of slung iron stones, accompanied by well-aimed darts, whistled about their ears and heads, and bore them down. But the enemy fought with determination, knowing the terrible result of defeat, especially in a case like theirs. Each pa was attacked simultaneously, but heavy logs rolling down the steep sides of the pas bore down tens of warriors, and many jaws were broken and skulls cracked by the slingers. At last, seeing their attempt was hopeless, the enemy broke and fled in every direction. " Now then," sung out the chief, " let them smell the pigeon's fat in the valley of Puna. The empty calabashes of our tribe will be filled before night. Show no quarter. Kill everyone, and we will have enough Mokai Mokai's preserved tattooed heads to adorn every post in the pa and village, and our women will sing to them from the flutes we will make out of their thigh bones," and the pas poured out their forces on the retreating enemy, while the old and infirm priests, who viewed the battle from the pas, cursed them in their flight. One special curse was so curious I have not forgotten it. " Haere ! haere ! Katahuna-e-au-ngahinu, o-to-tua- roa, he Turamahaeriwi i to wairua ki te reinga, haere ! ha-e-re ! Tenei au te haere nei." " Run ! ay run ! but I will render down the grease out of your backbones to light your soul to the reinga with. Run ! ay run ! Here I am now, in full chase."

Run they did. Many brave deeds were done ; but what was the use of defeated men fighting ? So many of them never warded off the blows given in anger, lest they should be made prisoners and tortured. Te Koukou and his big brother were both killed after a tough struggle. The majority of those who escaped fell into the hands of those who had been warned by the scouts to be on the alert, and their varied tortures afterwards amused the people for several days, until finally they were eaten. A very few ever reached their homes. The whole hillside, from summit to base, smelt of blood and the flesh and fat of men, for the slaughter had been great, and the Popotos rejoiced exceedingly at their splendid victory over Ngatiwhatua, who, in numbers, were once able to cope with them ; but now their principal warriors were slain, and their heads would be preserved and stuck up on the edge of their pas, and on every carved post in the settlements beneath.

Many years afterwards, the Ngatiwhatua tried to retrieve their loss and get payment, but were met on the sea beach between the heads of the Kaipara and Hokianga rivers, and on this occasion the Popotos were accompanied by one European ; this was the notorious Jacky Marmon. Here a fierce fight took place, which ended in the total rout of Ngatiwhatua, of whom many scores were killed and eaten.

Jacky Marmon himself related the history of this fight to me personally, and his description at the time made my blood run cold in my veins.

The top of Karewa Ki Runga was oblong in shape, about 80 feet long by about 50 feet broad, about 35 feet above the rest of the hill from whence it had been formed, and the sides were steeper than an angle of 45 degrees. A deep ditch surrounded this fortified mound, which was 6 feet deep and 12 feet wide, and the earth taken out of it and from the cutting away to form the pa itself was used to make outer lines of breastworks, and make the rest of the hill steeper and smoother in doubtful places. A double palisade had stood on the outer edge of the ditch, and I remember several of the old puriri posts that had formed part of it as sound in their positions as if freshly placed there, but I believe puriri will last as long as iron.

During the war with Hone Heke in 1845-46, my father, Captain McDonnell, R.N., fortified Te Horek, then our homestead, and had two 32-pounders dragged up to the top of Karewa Ki Runga and placed in position there, and at one time we had a garrison of 300 river natives, whom he partly armed with flint-lock Tower rifles and no end of ball-cartridges ; and there is no doubt the news of our garrison, and one upper and lower battery of two 32-pounders, seventeen pieces of cannon lower down, consisting of 18-pound carronades and long sixes, had a grand moral effect on those natives who were hesitating which side to join, and also on Heke and Kawiti's men ; but we had lively times of it for several months, and many Europeans were scared and left the district, never more to return to it. We saw it out ; but few know, or would credit it at this distance of time, the hardships, troubles and dangers some of the pioneer settlers went through, or of the miserable returns made to them for their dogged perseverance and courage.

THE TRIBAL PAKEHA —STORY OF A FEAST AND A DOUBLE SUICIDE.

A favourite pastime of the Maori in the "good old times" was the "moari," or swing, formed by placing a long tapering ricker or spar firmly on some rising ground, and sometimes, for a love of peril, on the brink of a precipice. A number of ropes, according to the size of the spar, were fastened to the top of it, one below the other at intervals of a foot, from which the people would swing, grasping the ropes in their hands and then running swiftly round and swinging off into the air over the sloping ground, river or cliff, as the case might be. Then as each person alighed, the spar being relieved from the weight springs more erect, causing the individuals yet revolving in the air to be lifted higher with a jerk, and experiencing a feeling as if the ropes were being dragged out of their hands.

Serious accidents often used to occur. I have a very vivid recollection of losing my hold one day as I was swinging round a thirty-foot moari and of revolving through mid-air. I was flung into a swamp, where I was picked up much bruised and shaken. I once saw a Maori named Tamati Tutonu sent spinning through the air from a sixty-feet moari and disappear through the tops of some puriri trees. Fortunately for him he was not killed, but he could not bear us to touch him, as many of his bones were broken. A Job's comforter improved the occasion, and told him it had happened as a punishment to him for swinging on a Sunday; but the poor, ignorant, unsophisticated Maori said that if the rope had been new, in place of being old and rotten, it would not have occurred.

A rather romantic, though sadly tragical, affair occurred in connection with one of these swings. It chanced to be one of the tallest ever known, had ten ropes attached to it, and was situated near to a precipice that overlooked a mountain torrent, that hissed and dashed wildly over huge black-looking boulders and rocks. No accident had hitherto occurred from using this celebrated moari; perhaps the reason of this was that few dared stand the jerks of the outer ropes as the inner swingers landed. A great feast was given by the tribe at their chief settlement, where this moari stood, and which on this occasion was handsomely decorated with feathers and painted with red ochre. Thousands of dried sharks, eels, pigeons, whale-birds, tuis, wekas, potatoes, kumaras, and the large kai pakeha and taro were provided. Steamed dog, too, but the latter delicacy was for the chiefs and the men of high rank who were expected. There were several hundred pigs, dead and alive, which had been killed in the most approved way. Their legs had been tied, and then they were cast into the deep water. Piggie was soon drowned, when he would be dragged on shore and cut up. The reason the natives killed pigs in this way was to avoid losing the blood, as the meat ate shorter, and pleasantly reminded the converted cannibals of old repasts eaten in the blood. There were numerous bundles of the sugar ti plant. There never had been, said some, such a prodigious feast; but, as with the pakehas, so with the Maoris, there always will be croakers and wet blankets, and a few old and toothless men were heard to grumble. Certainly they had not been permitted to partake of the steamed dog that their mouth watered for. It was too bad! They spoke slightingly of the feast. "As a feast it was well enough; but to compare it with those given in their day by Kaikaru and Te Ngaungau, of the Patu Powhaitere tribe (eat eyes and the gnawer of the paraqueet-killing tribes, who used to serve up crushed and steamed infants in raurekau leaves) would be too ridiculous; but men were men in those days—gone, alas! never to return. We then lived upon our enemies; but now—ugh!" etc., etc.

Well, the feast was attended by many hundreds of men, women, and children, who had assembled from far and near. The flax belts were discarded now, and shark oil and pigeons' fat were used copiously, being well rubbed into the skins of the gluttons of the various hapus about to be pitted against each other, to enable them to eat the greater quantity. No Government officer or painstaking missionary were there, so no bursts of loyalty were recorded or frantic expressions of love and attachment to Queens and Governors,

which sound so loud, and mean so little. No, this was a time for
relaxation and real enjoyment. Everybody was allowed full
swing, and to do just as they liked. This was true happiness!
Only one pakeha was present—the tribal pakeha, " Our pakeha,"
who was owned by the chief of the tribe, though they all had a
share in him, as will be seen by and by. He had been solemnly
invited, and here he was, proud of the honour. Other pakehas,
who were jealous, hinted, in a shabby sort of way, that it was
because he had lately received an instalment of goods from
Auckland, which instalment now dangled and streamed out from
the scaffolding that supported the huge piles of food. These
jealous pakehas used to relate afterwards that for the goods
displayed that day " Our pakeha " merchant did not get paid.
Paid? All I know is, that two years afterwards, at a return feast
for the one mentioned in this account, he got for his share a nice
little kit of dried tapued eels, of which none could, or dare, partake
of, except himself; and he was, with great ceremony, presented
with an ancient spear that had once belonged to the famous
Horopuku (swallower of stomachs), and earnestly desired to take
the greatest care of it. Not paid, indeed! He ate all the eels,
and his emotion was visible when the ceremony of presenting him
with the spear was over, and whenever he walked abroad through
the village afterwards with the spear, as he often used to. After
filing his schedule, and being allowed to wander out of prison
a free man, he was, although destitute of cash or credit, ever
certain of being saluted and welcomed by " Advance, the man
who ate the sacred eels! Welcome, the pakeha ngawari (a
complimentary term, meaning soft pakeha) who guards the spear
of Horopuku!" This tribal pakeha died shortly after he was
released from prison. The honour of the spear was either too
much, or the sacred eels had disagreed with him, perhaps. He
was buried by the tribe that owned him. The women composed
a sweet, poetic lament over him, in which he was spoken of as
" Tino pakeha ngawari, he pakeha pai (a real, good, soft pakeha,
whose like they would never, never see again)."

I have forgotten the swing. On the afternoon of the day of the
feast the guests began to gather about the maori, and inquiries
were made aloud, " Will anyone show us how the swing works?
Will anyone swing?" when presently six young men and four
young women, one a handsome girl named Takiri, who was
betrothed to a young chief named Te Whetu, came forward, and
an old chief, a kind of Master of Ceremonies, sang out, " Clear
away from the maori, so that the view be not intercepted." The
six young men were stripped to the waist, and wore shawls firmly
girded round their loins, reaching down to their knees. The
girls were dressed in short bodices, reaching below the waist, over
which they had bright-coloured shawls, fastened around the middle
by gay scarfs. Te Whetu did not wish his betrothed to swing,
but she would not be deterred. At a given signal they gave one
strong pull all together to see if everything was safe, and the tall

kauri ricker trembled and quivered from top to butt. Takiri sang
the usual chant in her clear voice, and then away they whirled
around, and off the brink of the precipice. Then came the cries
of applause. "Well done! well done! Look! look at the
muscle! Hold firmly! Well done! well done!" When suddenly
there was a pause in the cheering. Takiri's shawl had given way
at the waist, and, floating over the precipice, was wafted away by
a current of air. "Takiri, Takiri," cried some of the women,
"you had better send Te Whetu for your shawl." Te Whetu rose
and walked away to one side. As soon as the young girl had
alighted, she went, upright as an arrow, to the pa, dressed herself
in her best mats, and returned. "Oh, Te Whetu, farewell! Do
you not comprehend? I am going now to swing on the outer rope
of the moari. Te Whetu, I am going." Then, turning to the
crowd, she said, "Man the inner ropes—all of them. I am going
to show I am brave, though I am but a girl. I don't care for the
accident, or for your sneers, you women that have driven away my
betrothed husband. Man the ropes!" The young men came
forward and, in compliance with her request, seized the ropes.
Then, with a loud cry as they stamped round, away they went, all
alighting except Takiri. The moari, relieved from the weight,
straightened with a spring, when, at that instant of time and trial,
the poor girl cried, in a rapid, clear voice, "Farewell, tribe!
farewell, Te Whetu! Here is for the reinga haere ake! Follow!"
and relaxing her hold, she, as from a catapult, was hurled away
and dashed out of all form on the rocks beneath. One loud wail
of terror broke from the assembled natives. Te Whetu went
straight to his hut and closed the door. Immediately after a dull
sound was heard, the hut was entered, but Te Whetu had joined
Takiri in the reinga. He had placed his double-barrelled gun to
his chest, and pulled the trigger with his foot. After this the
moari was cut down, and the settlement was deserted for many
years.

HOHAIA-TE-RARAU'S VISIT TO ENGLAND AND THE RESULTS.

A young Ngapuhi chief went on a visit to England in the
good ship *William Hyde*, sailed by Captain Gordon. The
captain had taken a fancy to the chief, and offered him a free
passage home. Hohaia te Rarua was the name of this New
Zealander. He had a desire to visit England, and was much
influenced by many things he had heard, and wished to see for
himself as to the truth of the wonders he had heard of. He was
a modest, well-behaved young fellow, and of the bluest Ngapuhi
blood. It was in 1843 that he went home. His old father, the
Taonui, was very much against his going, and after the ship had
sailed away, used often to express himself somewhat as follows:—
"He will never, never return, either to his tribe or to his country;
he will see the Queen, and she will make him an offer which he will
be forced to accept; he will become her husband, and I shall not
see him any more with my eyes. The Queen is only a woman

after all, and will have no thought for me, his father, but only for herself, women are so wanting in thought." Te Taonui got some young fellows (Europeans) to write to the Queen for him, and to Hohaia. He begged Her Majesty on no account to have anything to do with Hohaia, and cautioned the latter on no account to marry anyone, whatever else he did.

When Hohaia returned to New Zealand after two or three years' absence, he was an English-speaking Maori, and as finished a rogue as ever Exeter Hall raved over. The Taonui fondly imagined that his letters had prevented him from making any misalliance, and when Hohaia assured him they had, the old man gathered himself unto his fathers in peace. Hohaia became so outrageous in his ways that had he lived in Australia he would speedily have come to grief, but his career was brought somewhat suddenly to a close.

EXHUMING OF NATIVE DEAD.

It is (or used to be) a native custom after the death and burial of a chief, to state at the time of interment when the remains were to be disinterred to allow the bones to be scraped and conveyed to their final resting place in the sacred caves belonging to the tribe. In the "good old days" the New Zealanders used to place their dead either in the fork of a puriri tree, or on a platform until the flesh had wasted away; but this ceased to be practised a short time after the introduction of the honey bee, as the bees used to visit the decaying bodies of the dead, and the natives had a prejudice to honey made, as they termed it, out of the fat of their deceased relatives. I used to tell them the bees were the best judges, and wished, no doubt, to flavour their honey and convert the fat into wax, but the Maoris could not see it in that light!

Great feasting used to take place at these gatherings to exhume the dead, and the office of bone scraping and polishing was always performed by tohungas (priests). A truly correct account of one of these hahungas (exhumings) would be too ghastly and sickening to give here. The priests would convey the remains to the nearest stream or creek, and literally scrape the cheesey flesh that adhered to the bones into baskets with their skinny fingers, and then empty the disgusting mass into the stream, and compliment the departed in a chant as the water swept it away. The skeleton would then be pulled to pieces, joint by joint, until the body was dismembered. The skull would be most carefully gone over, and all the flesh and hair that remained would be carefully picked off with their long nails. Then the bones would be scraped and polished, and then smeared over with a preparation of shark oil and pigeons' fat and red ochre, and carefully wrapped in newly-dressed flax. The stench that came into the camp, where the tribe had assembled to feast in honour of these ghoul-like proceedings, was high in the extreme.

TE ERIA: OR, CALIBAN THE ROBBER, AND HOW HE WAS LEGALLY
ROBBED IN TURN.

The natives at the North were, as a rule, an honest and well-behaved people, and if proper respect were paid to their time-honoured customs and sacred places, were always hospitable and civil. But of course there were exceptions to this rule.

There was one noted thief on the Hokianga river named Te Eria. Theft was inbred in him; he would steal anything. He excelled in all his performances. In snaring pigeons, ducks, or snipe, none could equal him, and as he used to rob from the snares of others, he used always to bag more birds, though he often got into trouble in consequence. Being a fearfully ugly fellow, with double-jointed fingers, and a body somewhat inclined to deformity, his repulsive aspect had earned for him the name of Caliban; but robber though he was, he was never at a loss for employment in other ways, being so handy with either oar, axe, or spade, while on a wild cattle-hunting expedition, to have him as one of the party was to ensure success, as he was such a good tracker and bushman.

One evening it had been arranged that Caliban should accompany a hunting party I had organised, and I took him into the house I occupied to consult as to the best route to take. I showed him a bright brass cartouche-box full of ball cartridge, also my powder flask and shot belt, and about twenty figs of tobacco, the latter intended for the use of the natives going with me. Our talk over, I showed him out of the house, and shut the door. (We never used to lock the doors until after the natives had become civilised or demoralised—as far as the natives are concerned, it is a distinction without a difference.)

I rose at daylight to assemble our party, but Caliban could not be found; neither could my brass cartouche-box, flask, shot belt, tobacco, or my spare rugs. "Caliban again!" I exclaimed. Instinct led me to the beach by the river—to the shed, where I used to keep a pet racing canoe. That had gone too. I sought one Ipu, Toenga's son, and we held a council, and both of us solemnly declared war to the knife on Caliban.

The result of our deliberations suggested that the thief had crossed the river, and would make off with his spoil to the Rarawa tribe, from whom he came. Another canoe was quickly procured, and away we started, first arming ourselves with a couple of Tao's spears. I also took with me a heavy dog whip, perfectly new (for I never flogged my dogs), and an ugly weapon it was. We soon reached the other side of the river, where we found my canoe comfortably stowed away amongst the young mangroves, and presently we struck Caliban's trail, as we were familiar with his footsteps; they bore a marked resemblance to the Roman letter V, rounded off at the lower end. We hastened on, and about an hour's run on his track brought us to a native fishing village. I asked the first man I met, "Is Te Eria here?"

"Yes," was the reply.

"He has robbed me," I said, "and we are going to have a *taua* on him."

"Not with the whip?" I was asked.

"Well," I said, "no—that is, if he will fight like a man."

The native pointed to a house, saying, "He is in there; call him out."

"Puta mai ki waho" (come outside), I cried, "and defend yourself. Here I am ready to be killed. What is the good of life to me, now I have lost my brass cartouche-box, flask, and belt? Come out, I say, and finish the work you have commenced."

Ipu and I were ready to pounce upon him with our spears and give him a sound drubbing, and kept running up and down, not at all like persons waiting to be killed—that being merely a form of speech and a sort of apology to the inhabitants of the village in conformity with Maori politeness. As Caliban would not come out, we went in, and discovered him sitting on the earthern floor of the hut with one of my rugs on his shoulders. I tore it off, leaving him naked. "This is my rug."

"It was given to me," he replied.

Ipu by this time had found his bundle, and on unfastening it the desire for life returned, for here was the brass cartouche-box, flask, and all. Caliban grinned, but declared that for those articles to be found in his bundle was the most remarkable and curious thing he had ever known to happen.

"You will," I answered, "O Caliban, ever remember this remarkable occurrence by one just as curious and more unexpected," and out came the dog whip, and as he would not take his reward standing I gave him while sitting a sound lacing over the back and shoulders. He made some horrible faces, but never uttered a cry or stirred hand or foot.

After I had finished he said, "If you haven't finished you had better go on."

"I have ended," I said.

It was the first time he had been caught red-handed by us, and he richly deserved what he got.

Caliban now rose slowly, and declared he would go straight to the Rarawa tribe and return with a party of his friends, and thus he proceeded to tell what he would do, but his threats were too horrible to mention. Ipu at length cut him short with, "No Rarawa who can fight would ever follow a man who has showed himself to be no more than a dog. You had a chance offered you to defend yourself, but refused to do so; now, like a coward, you boast of what you are going to do with women and children." Then, addressing himself to me, he said, "It is too late now to go cattle-hunting to-day, and Te Eria must be punished for the threats he has made. Let us return and row up to his place with our party and *muru* (legally rob) him of his kumaras and hogs."

On our return home we launched the boats and pulled up the river to Caliban's farm and sacked it, and returned with two boatloads of kumaras and several fat hogs bearing Caliban's ear-mark. We were well fed, too, by the other inhabitants of the village. The natives, when they heard of our taua, said that we had, under the circumstances, acted strictly within the law of muru (robbery), and that Caliban had been in the wrong all through, *because no one would help him!*

Caliban avoided our settlement for some time after this, as he was of opinion that he might be shot or speared for having tried to get a party to help revenge him, though he had failed. But one evening I chanced to see him paddling past our place in a great hurry. I was just starting for a pull in my canoe, so I gave chase, and in spite of his exertions I overtook him, and peace was made. A cattle-hunting expedition was got up, and my robber friend was to the fore as usual. Caliban continued to keep his name up as a robber until he died, but I believe we were exempted from his pilfering.

A MAORI SALUTE AND ITS CONSEQUENCES

A tribe of natives, who lived near the head of the Hokianga River, having by some means recovered two cannons from the wreck of a vessel that had been cast away, were in high glee at their prize. What, indeed, were tuparas (double-barrel guns) and ngutu-pareras (duckbills, the name they had given to flint-lock pieces) to these puripos (guns of thunder).

This tribe determined to force an opportunity for displaying their treasures to their less fortunate neighbours, and trusted to make them play second fiddle in the matter of salutation. They would, in future, be known as the tribe who owned the thunder guns. To accomplish this much-to-be-desired notoriety, it was requisite to give a feast and invite the neighbouring tribes. They had plenty of powder, and set to work to put these guns in position on the sand, using a log of wood to elevate the muzzles. But, at the trial discharge, it was found that the guns would jump up in spite of various contrivances to keep them down. So, as carriages were unknown to the natives, a couple of ponongas (slaves) were told off to sit straddle-legs across the guns while they were discharged, and the ears of the multitude were ravished by the loud reports that woke the sleeping echoes in the opposite ranges of hills. The fame of these two guns got spread abroad, and the tribe became the envy of the river in consequence.

The eventful day of the feast arrived, and the visitors came from far and near in their canoes. The two cannons were placed in position about twenty feet from the palisading of the pa, and were loaded to the muzzle with powder and stones to discharge into the river. The two men told off for the duty now mounted on one of the cannons. "Fire," cried the chief in the pride of his heart. Flash! bang! and a tremendous report, followed by a shower of stones on the water, astounded the natives, and doubtless the visitors all felt small But the gun had bounded up after the discharge, and the two natives were sent sprawling, one one way, and the other the other; but this was taken to be part of the performance by the lookers-on. They now prepared to fire off the other gun, a long nine-pounder, cast goodness knows when. Several pounds of powder had been well rammed into it, and some scores of round iron stones were packed on top of the powder. One native sat in triumph upon it with his face towards the touchhole, holding a lighted fire-stick in his hand. The word to fire was again given, and the light was applied, and a mighty explosion took place. As might have been expected, the old honey-combed gun had burst into fragments. None of the bystanders were hurt, but where was he who had fired the gun? Portions of him were found and gathered into baskets; a woman picked up a piece of the front part of the skull.

But as it was only a slave who had been killed, the sorrow was for the poor dear gun, the departed glory of the tribe. "Where are the eyes?" cried out the native lads, when the women exclaimed, pointing at the same time to the palisading of the pa, on which was seen plastered one temple, cheek and eyebrow of the unfortunate wretch who had been blown up, "Aue! a-na na! chara i te hanga! e kamu mai ana ki au katahi ano." (Alas! well, well! was ever the like seen! he is winking at me, upon my word.) The quivering of the muscles of the eyelid had been mistaken by the woman for a piece of facetiousness on the part of the dead man's spirit as represented by his eye, and "he is winking at me," was passed about for several days afterwards by the native wits of the settlement.

THE MAORI ATUA (GOD).

Respecting the Maori Atua, the conception of the New Zealander with regard to the future state after death would seem to be very vague. They supposed there were many gods, but there were only two or three of them of any recognised importance, such as Maru, Tu, and Tauwhaki. After the death of anyone his spirit proceeded rapidly to a cliff near the North Cape and sprang off, disappearing into the sea and re-appearing again in the reinga, the abode of dis-embodied spirits; here they all assembled, the good, bad, and the indifferent. They carried on their contentions here as they used when they formerly inhabited the human form when on earth. They fought, they loved, and died again, but after this second death no one seems to be able to tell what became of them; even their tohungas do not pretend to say, except they became ngaro-noiho, viz., disappeared. Maru, Tu, and Tauwhaki ruled the destinies of man on earth, but it does not appear that they had anything to do with the reinga, and flitted about from place to place, appearing only to the seers and tohungas (priests). These deities were, on the whole, antagonistic to mankind, but if pro pitiated through their priests would permit the tribe to be successful in war or in any tribal undertakings. Then they would assist individuals in their pursuits. If a tribe was going to war they would make presents to propitiate the gods through the priests, who would place a number of reeds in the ground, and then retiring a short distance, pronounce an incantation, and then send short clubs whirling amongst the reeds, and judge by the way they fell whether the gods would crown the expedition with victory. If a man caught an unusually large or fat eel it was expected he would give, if not the whole, at least a portion, of it to the priest as a present for Maru or Tauwhaki, and thus secure a continuance of good fortune. Woe betide the unhappy person who should steal Maru's presents; certain death would follow such a transaction. There was no hope of reward hereafter or punishment for good or bad conduct during the life upon earth. Opinions differ as to the food eaten by the spirits in the reinga. Some say they live on large kumaras; other priests say they catch flies and insects and subsist on these, over which they quarrel and fight. On my return once to Wanganui from the North I happened to mention that I had been to the Rerenga Wairau (Spirit's Flight)—the cliff. An old man drew near me, and asked me if I had noticed any spirits leap off into the sea. I told him that they came so rapidly one after the other that the noise made as they jumped into the water made quite a disturbance. "Ah," he replied, "then it is true. I thought it was so, and what the missionaries have told us is wrong."

MAORI COURTSHIP.

In the good old days young Maori girls were seldom if ever consulted as to their inclinations as regards marriage, though occasionally a damsel would show such determination and power of will as to get her own way, accepting or refusing a partner for life, or may be until she got tired of him, in spite of any previous decision of the tribe; but sad scenes used to occur too frequently, and often a young girl fell a victim to the manners and customs of her race. Desperate struggles used to take place between tribes somewhat related to each other, one party forcibly resisting another who came prepared to seize a girl as a wife for one of their young chiefs; the recognised law being that if the tribe who came to take the girl, by force if necessary, succeeded in dragging her away from her relations and the tribe she belonged to, their right to have and retain her became established and recognised, and no future tribal attempt would be made to recover possession of her, though single attempts at revenge were not altogether unknown to happen, when it would depend upon circumstances—supposing the person who made such an attempt got injured or killed—whether his people would make it a tribal affair. To sum up, it depended very much upon circumstances whether justice reigned triumphant, or was strangled for the sake of a tribal reason, but in this way they were no worse than their white brothers. At times the policy was to take the part of the revenger, when the tomahawk would be dug up, and bitter feuds take place.

To illustrate this state of things, I will relate the following occurrence that happened on the Hokianga River. I became slightly concerned in these events, but I had been fully cognisant of all that had previously transpired at the Taua tango wahine.*

With her tribe at Pakanae, a settlement nigh to the heads of Hokianga, lived a young and handsome girl named Pupu,† who was deeply attached to a young man of her own tribe called Te Ngaru o te Moana,‡ and a very fine young fellow he was. At a feast given to Pupu's tribe by another tribe who lived near the source of the Hokianga River, up the Waihou, the beauty of Pupu attracted the eye of an influential young chief named Toetoe, who began, after the custom of the Maori—and really the customs in this way are pretty nearly the same all over the world—to make love to Pupu. But she would have nothing to say to him— would not give him " encouragement," as it is usually termed. All her heart was in the possession of The Wave. But Toetoe declared he would have her, and that, as no other way was open to him, he would take her by force; and Pupu knew too well what this meant.

The feast over, the guests returned to Pakanae, and soon after assembled in committee to decide whether they should permit Pupu to be taken away quietly when the abduction party appeared in their canoes, or whether they should seriously oppose them. It was just a matter of policy, as the other tribe were distant allies of theirs. But up to this moment the fact that Te Ngaru and Pupu had arranged their future was unknown to the tribe—or at least no official notice had been given by the young parties. It would have saved a lot of trouble if they had done so.

The argument in committee was rapidly going in favour of letting Pupu be carried away with or against her will, when Te Ngaru bounded up and made his speech. Te Ngaru's speech, of course, was opposed to anything of that kind. He declared that, cost what it might, his betrothed should never leave or be taken away as a wife for Toetoe, and he at once claimed Pupu for his wife, and called to the tribe to stand by him and the girl whom they had brought up.

After many hours of consultation and argument, it was definitely settled by Te Anga, the head chief of the tribe, saying, " The girl can remain and be your wife, O Te Ngaru, if you can get the willing hands of the tribe to help you to retain possession of her when Toetoe comes to take her away. But first of all, perhaps Pupu wishes to go. I dare say she gave Toetoe encouragement at the haka,§ and spoke soft words to him, and would prefer living between the mountains up the river to remaining at Pakanae, where she can see the sea beach and hear the rumbling of the breakers over the home of Tamure and Araite Uru."‖

---

* The forcible abduction of a woman.   † A shell.   ‡ The waves of the sea.   § A dance. ‖ Two celebrated tanewhas, whose house is on the Hokianga bar. The first-named was a chief, and the second his slave, who gave constant employment to his master by always disobeying his orders.

Pupu demurely replied that she was content to remain where she was—and with Te Ngaru.

"Enough, then, has been said!" exclaimed Te Anga, "the meeting is ended."

About three weeks after these events four canoes, containing about a hundred men and women—for the latter play an important part in affairs of this kind—and a few elderly chiefs to see fair play, approached Pakanae; and about an equal number on shore at the village were ready to resist them in the coming struggle. Football is nothing to what used to take place, the girl being the ball, as it were. Poor Pupu had seated herself at a little distance from her party in a clear space, and was surrounded by a few old hags, who coquettishly related in a vain way what troubles they had gone through on account of their good looks in their time, and contemplating with the greatest possible satisfaction and delight the coming events of the day.

The visitors were now welcomed with loud cries and the waving of shawls and mats by the Pakanae natives, who formed up to meet them. The strangers were shown to a place of honour, and every luxury in the way of kumaras, shark, and mutton-fish, etc., was placed before them. Loud were the grunts of satisfaction as the baskets were rapidly emptied, one after the other, until all was consumed. Half an hour's rest, and then up rose Toetoe.

"I have come to fetch Pupu for my wife; we have a long way to return. Let Shell listen to this: we must go."

Then a few women, probably his sisters and aunts, and four or five strong-limbed young men, rose and went to where Pupu was sitting. A similar number of Pupu's people rose and sat down again by the side of Pupu.

"I have nothing more to say," cried Toetoe, who then went up to Pupu. Stooping for an instant, Toetoe caught Pupu by the waist, and placed her, in spite of her struggles, on his shoulders. Pupu now gave a loud wailing cry, in which horror, hate, and despair were strongly mingled. This acted as a signal, and at once poor Pupu became the centre of a surging, yelling, frantic mob of men and women, one party trying to carry off the girl to the canoes and the other trying to detain her.

In affairs of this kind, should the girl really wish to go, the struggle is but a sham—a make-believe. The girl is unhurt, and gets away with a little damage to her dress, and a few single wrestling bouts end the affair. But in Pupu's case the girl did not wish to go, and the blood of the young men was roused. No weapons were permitted to be used, though rough tumbles, tugs, and blows were exchanged to such an extent that the unfortunate girl was nearly pulled to pieces, and in less time than it takes to relate this Pupu was almost denuded of clothing. Now she was lifted high in the air, then pitched forward, dragged over the sand and back again by her limbs and hair, torn and mauled by the men as well as by the women—each side equally rough. But as yet no advantage had been gained by either side. At length the poor victim was left gasping, senseless, and bleeding on the rugged sandy beach, while each party mutually rested to get their breath. A short time elapsed, when at it they went again, and again the vile work was gone through.

Alas! poor Pupu. She was in the end borne off triumphantly by Toetoe's party, placed in one of the canoes, forcibly held down, and rowed away. "Cease the struggle," cried Te Ngaru; "let them take her." But Te Ngaru, though fate this time had forced him to relinquish his bride, had no intention of giving her up altogether; he knew that a certain time would be allowed to pass before Pupu would be forced to take Toetoe for her husband, and weeks probably would go by before she recovered from the terrible pulling about she had undergone.

About a month after the struggle, Te Ngaru, with his two brothers, came to the Horeke in a canoe. I knew them well; they often had worked for us on the station. Te Ngaru told me that he was going to steal back his betrothed, and wanted me to lend him our four-oared gig. One tide would, he said, take them to the place where Pupu was kept, one tide to wait in ambush, and the next ebb return. I had felt very sorry for both parties, and I thought it would be a splendid thing to help restore Pupu to Te Ngaru, so I made up my mind to run the risk from a certain quarter, and take the boat and go with them. I got my friend Ipu to go with us. We started away after all but ourselves had retired to rest, and a few hours' pull took us to a creek near to Toetoe's village. Ipu was sent to reconnoitre. To explain his presence there, he was to say he had come to visit an old relative who lived in that neighbourhood. This was carried out in the morning. We waited impatiently for his return, or for some sign, the place being about half a mile away. The day passed by, yet no sign. The tide began to ebb, and Te Ngaru now became more restive. He wanted to go to the village, and it was with difficulty I restrained him. Whether I would have been able to do so for long I cannot say; but we now heard footsteps rapidly approaching, and a great noise in the village.

"Cast off the ropes—out with the boat-hook—make ready to shove down the creek!"

This order had scarcely been whispered by me, when Ipu and Pupu, bright, but out of breath, sprang into the boat. In less than a minute we were in the main stream, and had the satisfaction of seeing several dusky figures on the edge of the river. They were calling out for Pupu, and wondering where she could be hidden, for we were in the deep shadows of the river.

We let the boat drift a bit, and then shipped the oars, and in a few hours we were safe at home. Pupu and the others at once got on board of their canoe and reached their home at Pakanae at day dawn.

Toetoe made an attempt to get back his wished-for wife, but he could only raise a few followers, as he had been dreadfully laughed at for not being able to keep what had been won for him. He got no sympathy, but in an encounter he had with Te Ngaru, he received from him a severe spear bayonet thrust through his thigh, which laid him up for some time, and as public Maori opinion went this time happily in the right direction, Toetoe had to become reconciled to his bad fortune. An old warrior tried to console him for his loss by telling him that it could not matter much; he could get another wife, who probably would attend to his requirements, and cook for him far better than the girl he had been deprived of.

MAORI CRUELTY.

Kai Hau (Eat the Wind), a Ngapuhi chief, once related to me an account of an expedition he had taken part in when a young man, that went from Hokianga and the Bay of Islands to the Auckland district and commenced a war on the natives there. He went on to say—I will give the account as nearly as I can remember him to have told it:—

"Ah, that was a taua! The number we killed was very great; and oh! the quantity of kumaras and human flesh that was eaten! I was a young man then, and one day I had, with a few others, returned to where Auckland is now, from Onehunga, which was then a fine kainga, with large kumara plantations. But all the land there is spoilt now, as stones have been placed upon it for carts to run upon. But that is just like pakehas' work. Well, I had captured a young girl (by his description about sixteen or seventeen years of age). I was young, and had intended to make her one of my wives when we returned to Hokianga, as she was a kohio pai (nice girl); but on descending the hill near the watu (Shortland Crescent) we were met by another party of our own fellows who had returned unsuccessful after their day's work. They asked me when I had captured the girl. (They noticed her, as she was momona—fat).

"Never mind where I got her," I replied; "I am going to take her back with us to Hokianga."

They asked me to let them have her to eat, as they were hungry, and seeing she was tetere (plump).

"I won't," I replied.

"We must have her," they cried, and before my companions could come to my assistance they seized her.

I held on by one leg, when presently one of them tomahawked her. I was very, very angry at this. If they wished for food they ought to have hunted for themselves. But I cut off the leg I held, and that was all I got of her for my trouble.

"What did you do with the leg?" I inquired.

"Do with it?" he asked. "Ate it, to be sure. What else should I do with it? But I *was* vexed, as I wanted to be kind to the girl, and the other natives had no right to act as they did. It was not fair. However, I had utu (payment) for it. I picked a quarrel with the man who tomahawked her, and speared him through the thigh, and several days afterwards the men who were carrying him were set upon by the enemy, and had to leave him; so he was cooked and eaten.

"I think, now," he continued, after a pause, "that I am old, perhaps it was foolish for us to have eaten one another; and if the pakehas were to go away, I would not again eat human flesh. But we have pork and cows now."

"It is because the missionaries have told you how wrong it is to eat such food that you are now a Christian, I suppose? You have been baptized, have you not?"

"You are wrong," he answered, stoutly; "I have nothing to do with that tribe. They are nothing at all to me, and I won't be baptized. They told me that Tu, my ancestor, and Wharewera, my father, are in a big fire, being burned, and that I am a rewera (a devil), and, unless I am baptized, I will be burnt, too; but I don't believe it. Tu was killed and eaten, and he cannot be burnt now. I don't want anything to do with the tribe of missionaries. Tu and my father were toas (braves), and I prefer going to where they are. No, I will follow my ancestors to the reinga (spirit world) and to the kumara grounds; but if I *am* to be burnt, I am to be burnt, and don't provoke me to be talking about it."

Some of the tortures inflicted at times on prisoners of war may be interesting, to show the strange spirit that existed, especially in those who were acknowledged by the tribe to be *first-class warriors*. The prisoner to be tortured was brought forward amidst screams and yells from the women. One method was to lash the arms and legs to two strong stakes driven firmly into the ground and the width of the victim's body apart. The head was secured from rolling about by being lashed to a cross piece of wood placed behind the neck, and fastened at each end to the stakes to which the prisoner was tied, who was, of course, naked. An incision was now made with a sharp shell or piece of volcanic glass or tattooing chisel across the shoulders on each side of the spine. The operator would then cut slowly down by the side of the spine (but not to touch the bone) to the small of the back. The blood would then be licked from the wound by the women and children. Another cut would then be made, and the slice of flesh would be torn down the whole length of the back. This strip of flesh would be slightly roasted before the victim's eyes and swallowed, and he would be asked to look at a piece of his own back. Slices would be cut off in this way, and the children would be encouraged to throw hot ashes on the prisoner and pierce between his ribs through and through with long reeds, etc., until the unhappy wretch expired. Another way was to fasten the man down to the ground with cross stakes, and heated round stones would be placed on his body and allowed to burn out the flesh; and to finish off, the eyes would be burnt out of their sockets, and red-hot gravel put in the mouth to stop the screams. Heated rods would be placed in children's hands, and they would be desired to burn holes in the legs and arms for the amusement of the lookers-on.

The man who could stand by and see all this without showing by speech or action that he pitied the sufferer was considered a

MM*

warrior of the first degree, as his heart was hard and all pity had left his breast.

DEATH OF THE CHIEF WILLIAM RIPA.

William Ripa, a northern chief of high rank, and the head of the Matapungarehu tribe, was one of the handsomest Maoris of his day The tattooing on his face and his brow was beautifully done, every line had its graceful curve. He was a powerful chief, and as brave as a lion. His two brothers—younger than himself—were named Hetaraka te Ngo and Hone te Ware. Some dispute had arisen between the Matapungarehu tribe and the Whanau Pane. Turau, a chief of the latter, had insulted a near relation to Wi Ripa, who had avenged the insult according to Maori law, and had seized a horse belonging to Turau as payment. Here the affair was supposed by Ripa to have ended, but Turau had determined otherwise, and only waited a favourable opportunity to have his revenge.

The Matapungarehu had dispersed to their villages, as it was planting season. Wi Ripa, with his two brothers and a slave, had retired to their home on the banks of the Waihou River, and engaged in their usual occupations.

Turau heard of this and formed a plan to kill the chief. During the war at the North with Honi Heke, the Matapungarehu, under Wi Ripa and his brothers, rendered great service to the country, assisting to put down the enemy, many of whom, though now friendly to the whites, bore Wi Ripa and his tribe a deep grudge for what they had made them suffer. One of these, a chief of Te Taheke (I forget his name, but will call him Taheke) never forgot the treachery. This man was of high courage, but bore a bad character, and was noted for his animosity to Wi Ripa To this chief Turau went and unfolded his designs, and Taheke promised to aid him all he could. They collected about thirty followers, all of whom hated Wi Ripa for his daring and pluck. Kepa, one of these men, said that nothing would please him better than to kill Wi Ripa, but that he would fight him fairly and face to face. Against the wish of the others he sent a messenger to the three brothers, that on a certain day a war party would attack them.

Wi Ripa demanded of the messenger the names of the chiefs who were to attack him. The man mentioned all excepting Taheke. "You can return now," haughtily replied Ripa; "four men will meet them. I will not disturb the tribe to drive those dogs away." Te Ngo wished his brother to let him fetch five men who lived close by, but could not win his consent. "No," said Wi Ripa; "they would summon the tribe from their cultivations." The day before the attack, a lad brought the news to Wi Ripa that Taheke was one of the thirty. Ripa regretted now he had not allowed his brothers to collect a few men. Te Ngo then proposed they should leave the village. "What!" cried Ripa, "and let Taheke say I fled before him? I killed his relations and will now kill him, though now, I foresee, I will fall also. I know my time draws nigh; but it is well."

The same evening, Wi Ripa, taking his gun and spear with him, walked to the bank of the river, and desired his favourite wife to bring him his son, and seated himself by the water's edge. When the lad was brought to him, he addressed his wife thus:— "Listen to my words and be brave. Take the child away from here to-night, at once. See well to his food, let him have plenty to eat; be careful of him; the actions of his fathers, my ancestors, will teach him what a chief ought to be. Go, enter the canoe, and pull up the river to the tribe." The wretched but obedient wife acted as she had been bidden. Who can tell what they both suffered, for each knew they would see one another no more.

Wi Ripa now returned to his brothers and requested them to leave him. "I am to die to-morrow; before this time I will have gone—get you to the tribe." They both refused to leave. "It is well," said Ripa. "Listen to me; the spirits call me. I am a dead man, they sound through the forests. Yes, I come; the tall fern trees will bow their curled heads in sorrow as I pass. I'll bid them farewell as I hurry on—farewell. On land, farewell! O rivers, my home, all parts, farewell! The mullet leap as the flood tide runs. I leap on the ebb. Remain here, O river Hokianga. I'll retire with the morrow's evening sun. Farewell, O tribe; all echoes repeat my words; be brave, be strong. It is enough my brothers, I have spoken. Apopo! apopo! i te ata!" (To-morrow, to-morrow in the morning we will be brave, to meet our enemies—the enemies of our tribe.)

Early the following morning the canoe containing the war party landed about 300 yards below the village, and where there was a huge block of stone, behind which Turau placed himself, sending the party on. As they advanced, Wi Ripa and his brothers stood up and cried, "Haere mai, haere mai" (Welcome, advance; welcome the strangers).

The party came up rapidly, Taheke leading.

"Stand!" cried Wi Ripa; "what seek you?"

Taheke advanced nearer. "I seek a horse; I seek blood. Give me your wife for Turau."

Te Ware levelled his gun. "Friend," he cried, "retrace your steps or I'll fire."

Taheke came nearer. Te Ware pulled the trigger, but the cap missed fire. "Advance, charge!" cried Taheke. "They have no powder in their guns."

There was a rush forward. Wi Ripa shouted his war cry; four double reports awoke the echoes, and two chiefs fell dead. Three bullets in Taheke's heart finished him.

"Re-load my gun, Te Ware," cried Wi Ripa, putting down his gun, and he dashed forward with his spear among the enemy.

Katahi, karua, katoru (one, two, three), and at each count a man fell, pierced through with the spear. Some badly-aimed shots were fired at Wi Ripa, who ran back to his brothers, and they gave Turau's party another volley, who now commenced to retreat. Te Ware rushed after them, but was shot through the chest. He sank on the ground, but managed to re-load and fire, bringing down one of the enemy.

Wi Ripa jumped forward, and kneeling, embraced his brother. Te Ngo and the slave tried to part them. " I remain here," said Wi Ripa, " Te Ware is dead; take our guns and my mere (greenstone weapon) to our tribe. Go quickly."

Turau's party seeing Te Ware lying still on the ground, and his brother with his head on his breast, concluded both were dead, and returned. But Ripa jumped up, struck one down with his spear, and then seated himself on the ground. A man came up from behind and struck him down with a heavy spade; one more blow killed him.

Turau's party now placed the two bodies in a hut, collected their dead and wounded, five killed and seven badly hit, and made for the canoe. The tribe came down and took the bodies of their chiefs away, and hundreds of natives came to show their respect. A small Maori war ensued. Other chiefs and Mr Maning, an old settler, arranged terms of peace.

William Ripa's son, the lad his wife had conveyed up the river the night before the death of his father, was serving with the Ngapuhi Contingent on the West Coast (Patea) during the disturbances of 1868, and I had many conversations with him. He was apparently a fine young fellow, and was much moved when I told him I recollected his father's and uncle's death.

JEALOUSY.

A well-known settler in Hokianga was one day seated in his house, the doorway of which fronted the river. A white pipi shell walk ran in a curve to the gate, which was fastened to the gate-post by a curved piece of iron hoop and a latch. The distance to the gate from the house was about one hundred yards. A chief, who had already killed three or four fellows in sudden fits of passion, had visited the settler this day, and brought his youngest and most favoured wife with him. The chief, whose name, by the way, was Kaitoke (eater of worms), was sitting just inside the threshold of the doorway, keeping his wife in view, who was seated on the grass a little to one side of the house, but out of sight of the settler, and had a huia (white-tipped feather of the New Zealand crow) stuck in her hair as an ornament.

It was about dinner time, and the settler's native servant had laid the cloth and knives, and had brought in the dish of potatoes. In fetching the things in he had to pass and repass the girl where she was sitting. On his return to the kitchen he halted, plucked the feather from her hair, and made as if he would place it in his own hair, and then replaced it and passed on. Kaitoke had seen this while conversing with the European (about spars, I think), when he quietly asked if there was such a thing as an axe or an adze in the house. " Yes, you will find an adze in that room, if you want one," replied the settler. Kaitoke rose, got the adze, and resumed the former subject of conversation.

When the native man returned with the dish of meat, his eye caught Kaitoke's, who then rose to his feet. The man now dropped this dish, and ran for his life towards the gate. Kaitoke jumped up in hot pursuit. The settler saw the two running, but did not know the reason, not having seen the by-play. He rose and looked beyond them to see what they were running for. The man gained the gate, but, whether paralysed with fear, or otherwise stupefied, I cannot say, he fumbled at the fastening, and could not at the precious moment open the gate. Kaitoke came on him, and, with a hideous yell, buried the adze in the back of his head, leaped the gate, and was away round a stoney point. The settler, a powerful, wiry man, took down his loaded rifle, and started away in hot pursuit, but only got one snap shot at him as he wound in and out of the huge boulders; and Mr. ———, I believe, never met him again, as he kept close. The murdered man was buried. He had been killed in a fit of mad jealousy by this chief. This occurred about 1845.

WITCHCRAFT.

The influenza was very prevalent in Hokianga about the year 1846, and many of the natives fell victims to it through their mode of treatment, rushing when the fever was on them to the river and bathing themselves in the cold water. One tribe had suffered in particular, and many of them had died. The chief Tio (The Oyster) had successively lost three of his children, and the fourth, a fine lad of six years, was at the last stage of that sickness, when Tio summoned the whole tribe to assemble, and addressed them somewhat as follows :—

"Listen to me, O tribe! I have had a dream and a hui (a starting of the limbs in sleep), and I have discovered the cause of the many deaths that have taken place amongst us, including the death of my three children and of that which will soon follow—the death of my son now lying here. We and they have been all bewitched by the old man and woman, his wife, both of whom are now sitting yonder, and unless they die for the evil they have caused and brought upon us they two alone will soon represent this our tribe gathered together here. Therefore it is, O tribe, I have called you here to see justice done. I will kill them this day with my own hands as utu for those who have died through them, and in order that we may live and be saved alive. Lead them forth to the end of the beach to yon sandy point."

The old man and his wife said nothing. Probably they knew it would be of no use. They were led about a hundred yards away and seated by the edge of the river. Tio now stripped, and, taking his long-handled tomahawk, advanced towards them. The old grey-haired woman rose as Tio approached, and, avoiding the thrust he made at her, clasped the chief round his knees, and cried, "Kill me not. Alas! do not kill me. I am innocent, I am innocent. But he said she was guilty. It was of no avail; she was quickly dispatched. The old man now rose. The tide had, as if in mockery, drifted a branch of a tapakehi shrub to where he had been sitting. This he laid hold of, and—vain thought—attempted to do battle for life with his armed and powerfully-made chief. Alas, poor old man! bend your head to your fate, it will save you a few moments of pain. He warded off two blows, poor wretch! when the rotten stick broke in his hand, and he fell and joined his old wife in the spirit world.

TOENGA'S VISION.

One night I was returning home with a party of six natives from a fish spearing expedition we had undertaken the same evening. The fish we speared at night by torch-light during the run in of the young flood tide.

My old friend Toenga Pou, who, among his many accomplishments, prided himself on being a tohunga (priest), was sitting next in front of me in the nose of the canoe, humming a weird sort of chant to himself in a low dreamy tone, and keeping time with his paddle.

It was a beautiful clear starlight night, and midway up the sides of the two ranges of wooded hills that formed the background to each bank of the river, lightly floated a thin soft line of white mist, the tops of the ranges showing out distinctly against the starlit sky, the surface of the water might have been likened to a mirror in which the stars, mountains, and trees were clearly reflected.

It was a warm night, not a breath of air could be felt. All was serenely still. Our canoe cut her way rapidly through the water, urged forward by our paddles, leaving a long trail of phosphoric light in our wake. We were steering across the river to avoid the effects of the strong running tide, and were nearing a low line of mangrove trees, whose overhanging boughs, dipping and trailing in the tide, caused a ripple as the current swept past, and now and then was heard the gurgling sound made by the water, as it washed up and receded again from the hollow stems of the mangroves.

Suddenly, without warning, Toenga threw up his paddle and stopped in his chant. The action was so marked and unexpected that we all stopped paddling, and the canoe drifted with the tide.

"Heaha?" (what is it?) I asked.

"Taihoa" (wait) replied Toenga; "resume your paddles till we land."

Not a word more was spoken until the canoe touched the shore.

By the time we reached home it was nigh morning, and I went to my house, Toenga following me until I reached the door.

"My son," he said, "I must away to my home. Listen to me; the spirit of Nga Ripene (a young girl I knew well, and a niece of Toenga's) has passed up the river; it crossed the nose of the canoe just when I threw up my paddle on its way to my settlement and huts to carry her love and leave it with her relatives and with me. Alas! alas! Nga Ripene is dead; but I fear her spirit will try and get my daughter Haupu to go with her to the reinga (the next world). I must go now, as her people will be sure to bring her body up to-morrow to our settlement."

Old Toenga had been very merry over our fishing, and had been more successful than of any one of us. As his aim was so true and his sight so quick, he often succeeded in spearing fish that had been missed by others of our party. But now his mood had changed, and he walked towards his home with his head down, looking careworn and sorrowful. I doubted the truth of old Toenga's vision, as I had seen the girl a few days before, she having been one of a party of Maoris who had called at our settlement on their way down the river, when she had seemed in good health and spirits, and had looked remarkably handsome ; and now Toenga had said she was dead ! I could not believe it.

Toenga described the sensation he had felt by saying that his hair and flesh had moved of their own accord, doing a kind of obeisance to the spirit as it passed on its way.

About noon on the following day, a native named Puakawau came up the river on his way to Waikahanganui, where Toenga lived. He told me Nga Ripene was dead. She had died suddenly the previous day towards sundown. I told Puakawau the occurrence of the previous night, and what Toenga had said ; but he expressed no surprise, only saying he was glad of it, as he would be prepared for the message he was taking to him.

The last request Nga Ripene had made was, that she might not be buried in the kari tupapaku (corpse garden) of the missionaries. She had been christened Matilda, but Toenga was to place her remains with those of her ancestors. Of course Toenga carried out to the letter this last request.

Nga Ripene's death was attributed to her having eaten some peaches that had been grown on a piece of tapued (sacred) ground by mistake. This occurred about 1850.

MAORI CANNIBALISM.

About the last act of cannibalism that occurred in this colony happened in 1845, at Kaiwhaiki, on the Wanganui River. A war party, led by the old Heu Heu and his tribe Ngatitunharetoa, of Taupo, swept down to Wanganui. On reaching Kaiwhaiki settlement, they found it had been abandoned. They dug up a corpse that had been buried for some days, took it to the river side, washed it free from the earth and clay, cut it up in pieces, cooked it and ate it. Several natives are now alive in Wanganui who witnessed this act of cannibalism. But, now I think of it, I am wrong in saying that the above was about the last piece of cannibalism that occurred in New Zealand, as Titokowaru's people ate and converted into soup portions of our men who were killed in action. In 1868 a man who had been shot dead in action, and who had been buried at the Manawapou Redoubt, was taken up, cooked, and eaten.

The following is an account of a strange crime committed at

Murimotu some years ago. I believe it to be a true account of what then took place. A woman of Wanganui married a man from Tongariro, Taupo, and afterwards went with him to live on his lands at Murimotu. The result of this marriage, after a number of years, was six children—all boys. In the course of time, the woman was seized with a desire to go and see her relations at Wanganui. So, bidding her husband take care of the youngsters, she started away on her journey. Shortly after her departure a severe storm came on, which, for violence and duration of time, was without precedence. Snow fell heavily for ten days, covering the face of the country lying near the base of Ruapehu and Tongariro mountains, and the Patea and Murimotu plains. Day after day passed, but still the snow fell, and buried one after the other of the plantations, kumara, and taro pits. The very houses even were buried, and the snow lay thick in the forests and on the trees. In a few days' time the stock of food in the house where this man lived with his six sons was consumed, and hunger stared them in the face. They dug their way out of the hut and gazed around, but nothing but snow and the line of forest met their view. No food was apparently procurable, and the fall of snow showed no signs of abating. Two more days passed over. At length the father, roused to action by the cries of his starving children, said to the youngest, " Son, let you and I go to the forest to try and get some birds and firewood, lest we all starve to death." The young lad assented, and following his father's footsteps, they struck for the nearest point of the forest. On reaching their destination, the man said to his son " See, there lies a bird." The boy turned to look, and was at once killed by a blow from his father. The flesh was stripped from the bones, and made up into small parcels, and taken back to the house and there cooked and eaten. The other children were made to believe it was preserved birds' flesh. Time rolled on, and the man again requested one of his sons, the fifth, to accompany him to get food, and to assist him in searching for his brother, whom he declared had lost himself in the forest. On reaching the bush, this lad met the fate of his brother : the flesh was removed from the bones, and done up in leaves to represent hua hua, but one limb was left in the fork of a tree. Back trudged the man with his terrible burden, which he cooked for food on his return. The following day the snow began to melt away before a warm northerly wind. Pina, the mother of these lads, had been frightened at the bad weather in Wanganui, and on the first signs of clearing, she started on her journey homeward. On arriving at the settlement she asked her husband how he had managed to procure food. He told her he had picked up some frozen birds in the bush, adding, '' We have still some of the flesh left ; you are hungry, and had better eat of it." Pina said, " I cannot eat until I see all my children ; only four are here, where are the two youngest ?" " They were here just now," replied the man. But at last he said, " They have lost themselves in the forest during the snow storm while searching for birds." Pina's suspicions were now awakened, and catching up a mat she said, " I will return presently." She made straight for the bush, and in a short time she found the remains of her two sons, and their heads. On her return home she sent her husband away on an errand to the bush, and in his absence she left for Taupo with her family to seek protection and revenge on her husband. The presiding chief, on hearing her story, sent an armed party to capture or kill the man, but on reaching the settlement he was not to be found, nor was he, they say, ever after heard of. All his land was confiscated as payment by order of the head chief of that district.

The above facts were related before the Native Land Court to prove how a certain block of land came into the possession of a particular family, who had not based their claims to it upon ancestral titles.

THE LAW OF UTU.—A TOURNAMENT.

When I was a lad of eighteen, the following occurred, which may not be without interest :—My father had gone on a trip to Auckland on some business or other, and I was left in charge till his return. But to understand what is to follow, a description of our house is necessary. The "Cottage," as we called the house my father and mother and younger members of the family lived in, was situated on the banks of the beautiful river Hokianga. A large fenced garden and vineyard enclosed these premises, and separated them from the business part of the establishment. The outer fence on one side formed one end of a large yard one hundred yards long, and was bounded by the river on one side, and the base of a hill on the other. A row of small cottages, including a large building used as a storehouse, lined the base of the hill. At the further end of this yard stood another cottage, having a passage through the centre of it leading into another large garden, orchard, and vineyard. This cottage I occupied with my brother George. Another row of houses had been built at right angles to those that fronted the river, running up behind them. One of these was used for an office. My brothers, George and William, in company with one of our native lads (a tall, ill-grown fellow), intended to go tui shooting, and while George went to our father's office to get the guns, we—that is, Moko, the native lad, my brother William and myself—were standing at some little distance from the office, and nearly opposite my house, looking at some cattle that were now walking between us and the office door. My brother George now appeared in the door way with a double-barrelled gun, which he levelled at the cows as they walked past, and he snapped the piece several times, thinking the gun was not loaded.

I called out, "Don't do that ! The gun may be loaded ; some of them are ; and you might shoot the cows."

"It's not loaded," he replied, and pointed it at my head.

"Don't," I said ; "it might go off."

"No, it won't," said he, and shifted his aim on to Moko, who was standing by my side, and just before William, who was a head shorter than Moko. He pulled the trigger, and bang went the gun. Moko gave a howl, fell backwards, and remained motionless on the ground. The gun dropped from George's hand.

"There—I told you so!" I said. "You've done for Moko now, at anyrate. A precious mess you have got us into!"

George was so troubled at the thought of what would happen that he made a clean run for the bush, to some caves we knew of. William and I turned Moko over and shook him, but, to all appearances, he was stone dead. However, when we commenced to lift him he groaned.

"Ain't you dead, Moko?" we asked.

"Kna mate rawa ahau" (I am quite dead), replied the corpse.

At last, with some trouble, we got him on his legs. The gun had been loaded with ball, which had struck him a little above the left temple, and running along his sloping forehead had ploughed a line over his head, leaving the skull bare, but untouched otherwise. We got him into the house, and seated him on my bed, and with my pocket knife I cut the strip of scalp away with the hair attached to it. I bound up his head as well as I knew how, and gave him a glass of wine we fetched for him. We were very vexed for Moko's accident, but I was in a terrible state of mind for the results. According to the Maori law of utu (payment) we would be robbed, and if our whole place was not burned down, we might consider ourselves lucky. I blamed myself much for permitting George to enter the office. I desired William to stay with Moko and help him into the house, while I went to look for the other lad we had named Ipu, a fine brave young fellow, and about my own age. I soon found him, and told him of what had occurred. He came to see Moko; and I afterwards sent him to tell his father, old Toenga, a great friend of mine, and a tohunga (priest) of the accident, asking him to return as quickly as he could. I knew that Toenga would collect a few men and come to me at once, after he had sent messengers to Wi Hopihana, a chief of the Popoto tribe, to convey the news to him; for it was a most serious affair. During Ipu's absence I noticed a canoe putting towards the settlement. I went to the beach to meet it, and as it touched shore, I saw it contained Whakarei, a chief of some rank, and his daughter, who were related to Moko. I knew Whakarei very well, and the Maori custom also, which would, when I told him of our trouble, bind him to remain and assist us out of the ill-effects of the morning's work. So I told him what had occurred.

"Lucky for you," said Whakarei, "I happened to come down the river this morning. You have sent for Toenga?"

"Yes," I said.

"That was wise," he replied: "he will know and do what is required. Toenga will, of course, have a taua (war party) on you, a mere matter of form, but it will strengthen your cause against other tauas." (A family "taua" might consist of knocking you down, or sticking a spear through your leg or arm, seizing your cattle or any other property you happened to possess. It depended very much on the estimation your friends held you in; it was a toss up, in fact, what they would do. I knew old Toenga very well though, and he had partly adopted me as his white son.) "You must have plenty of food for those who comprise the tauas to-day, as they will remain to defend you against the Ihutai's tribe (it was only this tribe of blackguards I dreaded) who will hear of this by to-morrow. You had better give me the gun with which Moko was hit. I am his relation, and you can then say you have made restitution, and have given me the gun."

We now went to see Moko, and Whakarei unbound his head.

"You are badly hit," said he, "but you won't die, and I have got the gun."

*　　*　　*　　*　　*　　*　　*　　*

Toenga's party soon arrived, and were met by Whakarei, myself, my brother William, and Ipu, who had returned.

The next day another friendly taua came headed by the Chief Wi Hopihana. This over, news came that two war canoes containing a taua from the Ihutai were fast coming up. On they came with loud yells and brandishing their guns and spears, but I had armed our side with some fowling-pieces and old Tower rifles. The canoes landed their party, who formed up and then charged up the beach towards us, who were kneeling to receive them. They stopped short when within about fifty yards, and a dead silence reigned. At last, with a hideous yell, they sprang as one man erect, and had their war dance. We now shook our guns up and gave them a more awful dance than theirs had been. Again all was silent. At last old Toenga passed from left to right with his bayonet spear and challenged the enemy, calling out to their best man named Kaka.

"You challenge me, Toenga, do you?" said he.

"Yes," said the other, "come and be killed."

"Here I am," said Toenga, and as his opponent advanced to the right, Toenga advanced to the left. Then each of them tacked about, and so on, till they met at striking distance in the centre of the space between the tribes. (They set at each other just as I have seen game cocks do before they fly at one another.) Toenga now made a spring, the other man made a rapid feint, followed by a quick thrust at Toenga's thigh, but to touch my old tutor was not such an easy thing to accomplish, and the old fellow's blood was up. He did not attempt to parry the dangerous thrust, but uttering a frightful yell, he bounded off the ground, avoiding the bayonet, which he had jumped over. Round went his spear with a whiz, and down came the butt end on his antagonist's neck, knocking him off his legs, and laying him on the ground; then bringing the spear's point to the front, he buried it in the ground within an inch of the prostrate warrior's stomach. "Ha! ha! i tohungia ano koe!" (Ah, there, I've allowed you to live). Howls of applause came from our side. Two more now challenged. At last my turn came. Old Toenga gave me his spear, and bade me recall one particular feint and underthrust he had taught me. (Many a rap I got in learning it from him, to say nothing of what always awaited me at home whenever it was found out that I had been taking lessons from him.) "You do it," continued Toenga, "just as I taught you. Attract his attention before you allow him to close. When making the feint, dart your eye into his with a glare, yell, and at the same time sink the butt of the spear and push forward instantly; the spear will do the rest, and if it does not run through his stomach it will stick into one of his legs, which will answer the purpose just as well He can't ward off your thrust, as he will be deceived by your eye. Now, my son, move forward; keep your body limp, allow every muscle to have play, and as you close stiffen yourself into your spear." I advanced first to one side, then to the other, to meet my foe. On he came, a beetle-browed fellow, armed with a heavy hard-wood spear. I obeyed my instructions to the letter, and a howl informed me that the spear had done the rest. It had entered above his knee cap, and had gone home to the bone. As he stooped with the pain I brought the butt round with a swing, and down on his head. "Me he toke!" I cried. Ipu now sprang forward, and was met by another lad, and a pitched battle took place, which ended in the victory for Ipu. The Ihutai now asked for payment for the injury done to Moko. "I have given Whakarei the gun. I will give no more, and if I did, Kapetana would kill me when he returns from Auckland," was my reply. "Three of your men have been beaten; do you want any more?" They now moved towards the store which held goods to a large amount, and threatened to break in the door if I would not unlock it. "We cannot prevent them breaking the door open," said one native, "as they want payment, but we will fight them afterwards."

"Yes, I thought, and who will get the goods then?"

"No man breaks open that door," I cried, as three natives advanced with axes towards it.

I resolved to shoot them. I longed to do so now; a change had come over me.

"William," I said, "go to the cottage."

I levelled my short rifle. "Now, break down that door," I said in English, "and I'll shoot you!"

"Come back," cried Wharepapa, the chief of the tribe; "he means what he says, he'll fire. Hokimai come back," and they drew back. For a few seconds I felt sorry they had, but intensely glad for it a moment afterwards. This ended the affair, and a general shake hands all round soon took place. I gave Moko's avengers a feast of pork, potatoes, rice, and sugar on my own responsibility. The Wharepapa took his wounded grandson and the gun which Whakarei handed to him, and the tribe departed in peace to their own place. Wi Hopihana collected all the arms we had issued to our people, but the ammunition was not offered to be returned, and I did not ask for it. The next day they all returned to their different villages in great good humour. This happened about thirty-two years ago.

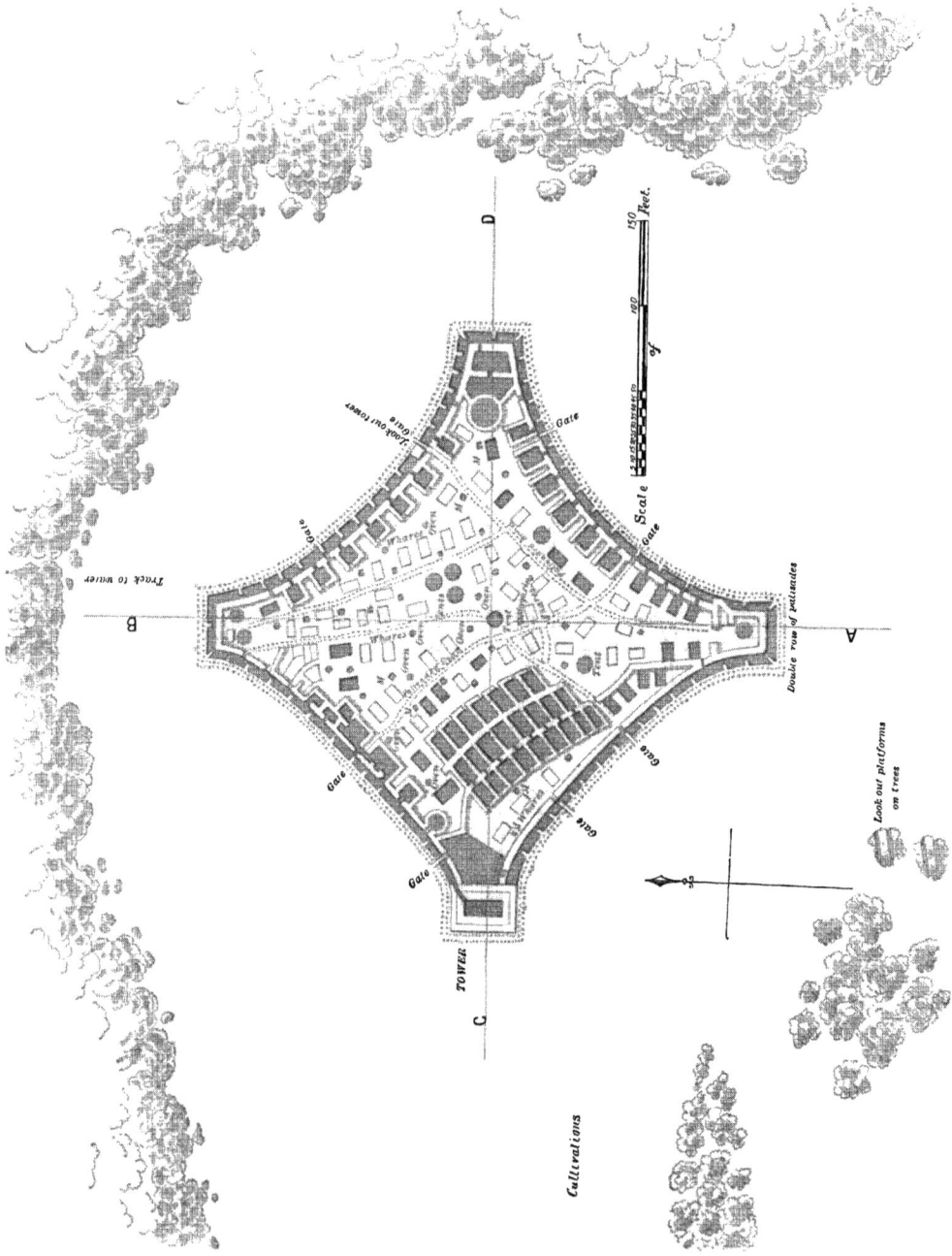

PLAN OF TAURANGAIKA PA.

WEST COAST.

Abandoned by Titokowaru when attacked by the Colonial Force under Col. Whitmore, Feb. 3, 1869.

Scale of Feet.

150 Feet.

Track to water

Double row of palisades

Look out tower

Gate

Cultivations

Look out platforms on trees

TOWER

Gate

ADDENDA.

AN ALPHABETICAL LIST

Of Volunteers and Militia men who received the New Zealand Medal, *having been either under fire, or attached to Her Majesty's Imperial Forces, during the War of 1860—1870.*

Col. D. Force	.. ..	.. Colonial Defence Force
Com. Dept.	Transpt. Corps	.. Imperial Commissariat and Transport Corps
Auck. Vol.	Auck. Rifles	.. ⎫ Auckland Volunteers, Rifles, Volunteer En-
Auck. Vol. Eng.	Auck. Mil.	.. ⎭ gineers, and Militia
H. B. Mil.	H. B. Cav.	.. Hawke's Bay Militia, and Cavalry
Nap. Mil. ..	.. ..	.. Napier Militia
Forest Ran.	.. ..	.. Forest Rangers
Patea Mil. ..	Patea F. Force	.. Patea Militia and Patea Field Force
A. C. ..	.. ..	.. Armed Constabulary
1st W. Regt.	2nd W. Regt.	.. ⎫ 1st, 2nd, 3rd, and 4th Waikato Regiments
3rd W. Regt.	4th W. Regt.	.. ⎭
Well. Mil. ..	.. ..	.. Wellington Militia or Rifles
Tar. Vol. ..	Tar. Mil.	.. ⎫ Taranaki Volunteers, Militia, Military Settlers,
Tar. Mil. Settlers	Tar. B. Ran.	.. ⎬ Bush Rangers, and Cavalry Volunteers
Tar. Cav. Vol.	.. ..	.. ⎭
Wan. Y. Cav.	Wan. V. Cav.	.. ⎫ Wanganui Yeomanry Cavalry, Volunteer Ca-
Wan. Vol.	Wan. N. Con.	.. ⎭ valry, Volunteer, and Native Contingent
Kai Iwi Cav.	.. ..	.. Kai Iwi Cavalry or Rifles
M. V. ..	M. Mil. ..	.. Mauku Volunteers or Militia
O. V. Ran. ..	.. ..	.. Opotiki Volunteer Rangers
N. Z. Mil. ..	.. ..	.. New Zealand Militia

———

Aagaard, Michael, trooper, Patea Y. Cav.
Acker, John, private, 3rd W. Regt.
Adams, Thomas, private, 3rd W. Regt.
Adams, W., private, 3rd W. Regt.
Adams, R. A., private, 2nd W. Regt.
Adam, Alex., sergeant, Well. Mil.
Adam, Samuel, private, A. C.
Adams, jun., Francis, corporal, Tar. Vol.
Adams, R. R., bugler, 3rd W. Regt.
Addiss, Daniel, private, 1st W. Regt.
Adamson, Thomas, private, Wan. Rifles
Addis, Thomas, bugler, 1st W. Regt.
Adamson, Stephen, trooper, Wan. Y. Cav.
Adamson, William, trooper, Wan. Y. Cav.
Aitken, John, private, 2nd W. Regt.
Airth, Stephen, sergeant, Well. Rifles
Allan, John, sergeant, Tar. Mil.
Allan, W. A., corporal, 1st W. Regt.
Allan, Walter, corporal. 2nd W. Regt.
Allan, John, private, 2nd W. Regt.
Allan, A. J. private, Tar. Mil. Settlers
Allan, Thomas, sergeant, Wai. R. Vol.
Allen, W. S., private, Tar. Vol.
Allen, David, private, 2nd W. Regt.
Allen, Henry, private 2nd W. Regt.
Allen, David. private, 3rd W. Regt.
Allen, Henry, boatman, Com. T. Corps

Allen, Samuel, private, Thames Vol.
Allen, Thomas W., private, Forest Ran.
Allen, Thomas, private, Tar. Bush Ran.
Allen, John, private, Tar. Mil.
Alexander, F. M., lieutenant, Wai. Vol.
Alexander, Horatio, corporal, Col. D. Force
Allison, Thomas, private, Tar. Mil.
Allison, Robert, private, 2nd W. Regt.
Aldridge, William, private, 2nd W. Regt.
Aldridge, George, private, 2nd W. Regt.
Alwell, Edward, private, 2nd W. Regt.
Alcock, John, corporal, 3rd W. Regt.
Alley, George, private, 3rd W. Regt.
Allnutt, J., Clerk, Impl. Com.
Allender, John, private, Auck. Vol.
Alfrey, William, constable, A. C.
Aines, Joseph, trooper, Col. D. Force.
Amois, William, private, Tar. Mil. Settlers
Anderson, James, captain, Nap. Mil.
Anderson, J. E., private, 1st W. Regt.
Anderson, James, private, 1st W. Regt.
Anderson, George, artificer, Com. T. Corps
Anderson, James, private, 3rd W. Regt.
Anderson, Alexander, private, 3rd W. Regt.
Anderson, J., bullock-driver, Com. T. Corps
Anderson, S., clerk, Com. T. Corps
Anderson, J., corporal, 2nd W. Regt.

I

Anderson, J. C., issuer, Com. T. Corps
Anderson, Samuel, private, 2nd W. Regt.
Anderson, John, private, Wan. Mil.
Anderson, Andrew, constable, A. C.
Anderson, David, segt.-maj., Col. D. Force
Anderson, G. B., private, Tar. Mil.
Anderson, James, trooper, Wan. Y. Cav.
Andrews, John, private, Tar. Vol.
Andrews, H. F., ensign, Auck. Vol.
Andrews, W. A., private, 3rd W. Regt.
Andrews, William, private, Tar. R. Vol.
Ansell, Thomas, private, 3rd W. Regt.
Anson, James, private, 3rd W. Regt.
Anes, John, private, 3rd W. Regt.
Andrehan, Edward, constable, A. C.
Appleton, William, private, 1st W. Regt.
Apjohn, Michael, sergeant, 2nd W. Regt.
Appleyard, William, private, 2nd W. Regt.
Armstrong, John H., private, Com. T. Corps
Armstrong, Patrick, private, 1st W. Regt.
Armstrong, J. H., captain, Tar. Mil.
Arbuckle, James, private, 2nd W. Regt.
Arnold, John, butcher, Com. Dept.
Arthur, J., private, Auck. Mil.
Armitage, Erasmus, private, Tar. Vol.
Arden, Hansen, private, Tar. Vol.
Arthurs, John, trooper, Col. D. Force
Arden, Francis, private, Tar. Mil. Settlers
Archer, Edmund, private, Auck. Mil.
Arden, F. H., private, Tar. R. Vol.
Arden, Henry, trooper, Tar. Cav. Vol.
Armstrong, J. Wilson, corporal, Wan. V. Cav.
Armstrong, Thomas, trooper, Wan. V. Cav.
Ash, John, private, 1st W. Regt.
Askin, R., bullock-driver. Com. T. Corps
Ashcoft, W. T., private, Tar. Mil. Settlers
Ashton, Edward, private, Nap. Mil.
Austin, Samuel, qr.-mstr. sergt., Wan. N. Con.
Austray, George, private, 1st W. Regt.
Autridge, H., bullock-driver, Com. T. Corps
Autridge, James, trooper, Tar. Mil. Vol.
Autridge, Humphrey, private, Wel. Rifles
Avery, George, baker, Com. T. Corps
Avery, George, private, Wel. Mil.
Aveling, Henry, sergeant, A. C.
Avent, John, sergeant, 1st W. Regt.

BABINGTON, W. H., private, Forest Ran.
Baker, sen., Robert, private, Tar. Vol.
Baker, jun., Robert, private, Tar. Vol.
Baker, Thos. F., ass. surg., Nap. Mil. Serv.
Baker, J. W., cornet, Kai-Iwi. Vol. Cav.
Baker, Richard, private, 1st W. Regt.
Baker, Henry, issuer, Impl. Com. Dept.
Baker, John bullock-driver, Com. T. Corps
Baker, Thos., constable, A.C.
Baker, Charles, constable, A.C.
Ball, George, private, 2nd W. Regt.
Barrett, Richard, private, 2nd W. Regt.
Barriball William, private, Tar. Vol.
Barton, Samuel, private, Auck. Mil.
Ballance, John, Cornet, Wan. Vol. Cal.
Bauer, Chas., private, 1st W. Regt.
Bannister, William, corporal, Auck. Mil.

Barrett, William, artificer, Com. T. Corps
Bassett, Richard, private, Auck. Mil.
Bates, David, private, Auck. Mil.
Baldry, John, private, Auck. Mil.
Barnett, Thos., private, Auck. Mil.
Barnes, Zechariah, private, Auck. Mil.
Bartlett, Chas., artificer, Com. T. Corps.
Bartlett, Joseph, private, 1st W. Regt.
Ball on, John, private, 1st W. Regt.
Baskerville, John, private, 1st W. Regt.
Ball, William, private, 1st W. Regt.
Bamford, T. J., sergeant, 2nd W. Regt.
Barry, Michael, private, 2nd W. Regt.
Bray, Bernard, private, 2nd W. Regt.
Baird, Walter, private, 2nd W. Regt.
Badderly, John F., trooper, Tar. Cav. Vol.
Barry, John, private, Wan. Rifles
Bacon, Thos., private, Auck. Mil.
Barrett, James, private, 3rd W. Regt.
Barker, John, private, 3rd W. Regt.
Bath, Michael, private, 3rd W. Regt.
Bates, Samuel, private, 3rd W. Regt.
Ballantine, Alexander, private, 3rd W. Regt.
Baggs, Thos., private, 3rd W. Regt.
Barrie, Robert, corporal, 3rd W. Regt.
Ball, Richard, private, 3rd W. Regt.
Bartlett, Daniel, private, 3rd W. Regt.
Bartlett, Thos., private, 3rd W. Regt.
Bainbridge, Henry, trooper, Col. D. Force
Banks, Alfred, private, H. Bay Mil. Settlers
Banks, George, private, H. Bay Mil. Settlers
Barriball, Henry, private, Tar. Mil.
Batten, James, private, Tar. Mil.
Barry, David, constable, A.C.
Ballard, Wm., corporal, Tar. Mil. Settlers
Baskerville, Wm., private, Tar. Mil. Settlers
Barker, John, bullock-driver, Com. T. Corps
Bartley, J., corporal, Auck. Mil.
Bacon, A., issuer, C. T. Corps
Barry, Daniel, private, Napier Mil.
Bassett, W. H., sergeant, A.C.
Bamford, George, private, Tar. Mil. Settlers
Banbury, jun., Francis, corporal, Tar. Vol.
Bassett, W.M., private, Tar. Mil.
Batchelor, J. O., corporal, Wel. Mil.
Bayley, R., private, Tar. Vol.
Bayley, Percy F. W., private, Tar. Vol.
Bailey, Alfred, private, Tar. Vol.
Bayley, James, private, Tar. Vol.
Bayley, Walter, bullock-driver, Com. T. Corps
Bayley, James, bullock-driver, Com. T. Corps
Bayley, Arthur, private, Tar. R. Vol.
Bayley, Daniel, private, Tar. R. Vol.
Bayley, Geo. J., private, Tar. R. Vol.
Bayly, Isaac, private, Tar. R. Vol.
Beagley, W., private, Wan. Vol.
Bear, Jonathan, sergt.-maj., Tar. Mil. Settlers
Beetham, Wellesley, trooper, Col. D. Force
Bentley, George, col.-sergt., Tar. Vol.
Berridge, William, sergeant, Tar. Vel.
Beamish, J. G., constable, A. C.
Beaven, Frederick, trooper, Wan. V. Cav.
Beere, E. H., private, Auck. Vol. Eng.
Beates, Charles, private, Auck. Mil.

Bennet, John, private, Auck. Mil.
Bell, James, private, Auck. Mil.
Bell, T. R., private, Auck. Mil.
Begg, John, private, 1st W. Regt.
Behems, Hendrick, private, 1st W. Regt.
Bell, William, private, 2nd W. Regt.
Bell, James, private, 2nd W. Regt.
Beny, Robert, private, 2nd W. Regt.
Begg, Andrew, private, 2nd W. Regt.
Bell, George, private, 2nd W. Regt.
Bergin, William, private, Wel. Rifles
Bertie, John, private, Wel. Rifles
Bertram, A. J., sergeant-major, F. Rangers
Benny, James, private, Tar. Mil. Settlers
Bee, George, private, Nap. Mil.
Belling, Thomas J., private, Tar. Vol.
Bezar, Zechariah private, Tar. Vol.
Bentley, J. D., sergeant, 1st W. Regt.
Beggs, James, private, 3rd W. Regt.
Beetham, F. W., private, 2nd W. Regt.
Beet, William, private, 2nd W. Regt.
Bell, Fraser, private, 3rd W. Regt.
Berger, Charles, private, 3rd W. Regt.
Bear, Thomas, sergeant, Tar. Mil. Settlers
Bear, William, sergeant, Tar. Mil. Settlers
Beckefield, Richard, constable, A. C.
Bertrand, George, private, Tar. Vol.
Beavan, J., bullock driver, Com. T. Corps
Bedford, J., bullock driver, Com. T. Corps
Bee, Thomas, butcher, Com. T. Corps
Beamish, George, private, Tar. Mil. Settlers
Bennett, John, private, Nap. Mil.
Beatty, James, constable, A. C.
Beauchamp, George, constable, A. C.
Bennett, C. D., sergeant-major, A. C.
Beetham, Wellesley, trooper, Col. D. Force
Bell, William, private, F. Rangers
Bell, J. N., private, Nap. Mil.
Berkley, John, sergeant, A. C.
Bell, George, ensign, 3rd W. Regt.
Bell, C. M., private, 1st W. Regt.
Biddle, Edward, private, Tar. Mil. Settlers
Billiard, Thomas, private, Tar. Vol.
Binnie, Alexander, private, Tar. Vol.
Birmingham, Robert, private, 2nd W. Regt.
Birr, Isaac, private, 1st W. Regt.
Bill, David, private, 1st W. Regt.
Bird, Joseph, private, 1st W. Regt.
Bilton, Francis, private. Tar. Mil. Settlers
Bird, William, private, 2nd W. Regt.
Bishop, Walter, private, Tar. Mil.
Biddle, Benjamin, constable, A.C.
Bidgood, John, private, F. Rangers
Bishop, John, private, Tar. Mil.
Bigley, Charles, sergeant, A.C.
Bissett, William, private, 3rd W. Regt.
Bird, John, private, 3rd W. Regt.
Bishop, W., bullock driver, Com. T. Corps
Bishop, J., bullock driver, Com. T. Corps
Bishop, A. E., bugler, Napier Mil.
Bishop, Daniel, private, Tar. B. Rangers
Biddulph, Charles, private, 2nd W. Regt.
Birchfield, William, sergeant, 3rd W. Regt.
Birch, John, private, 3rd W. Regt.

Birch, James, private, 3rd W. Regt.
Biggs, James, private, 3rd W. Regt.
Birch, Azim S., captain, N. Z. Mil.
Billing, William, private, Tar. Mil. Settlers
Biggs, Samuel, private, 1st W. Regt.
Billing, Thomas J., private, Tar. Regt.
Blackstock, George, private, Nap. Vol.
Bland, John, constable, A. C.
Blakie, Thomas, private, Auck. Mil.
Blygh, Dunbrick, private, 2nd W. Regt.
Blyth, W. T., private, Tar. Mil. Settlers
Blakeney, James, private, 3rd W. Regt.
Blackburn, William, private, 3rd W. Regt.
Blythe, Frederick, private, 2nd W. Regt.
Bluett, H. P., sergeant, A. C.
Blane, John, bullock driver, Com. T. Corps
Blackburn, R., bullock driver, Com. T. Corps
Blazil, John, bullock driver, Com. T. Corps
Blazil, James, bullock driver, Com. T. Corps
Blyth, Donald, constable, A. C.
Blackmore, E. G., private, Tar. R. Vol.
Backmoor, H. G., ensign, 4th W. Regt.
Black, Charles, private, 3rd W. Regt.
Black, William, lieutenant, Tar. Vol.
Black, John, sergeant, Tar. Vol.
Black, Walter, private, Tar. Vol.
Black, Alfred, corporal, Tar. Mil. Settlers
Black, Solomon, constable, A. C.
Black, Hugh, sergeant, Col. D. Force
Black, Hugh, private, 2nd W. Regt.
Blake, A. H., private, Nap. Vol.
Blake, Richard, captain, Patea Mil.
Blake, J. G., corporal, A. C.
Blake, George, farrier surgeon, A. C.
Blake, James, constable, A. C.
Blake, E. J., sergeant, Patea F. Force
Blake, R. T., captain, Patea Mil.
Blake, Michael, private, 2nd W. Regt.
Bond, William, sergeant, Forest Ran.
Bond, Philip, private, Forest Ran.
Bowler, Harry, trooper, Patea Y. Cav.
Booth, Joseph, private, Auck. Mil.
Bourke, John, private, Auck. Mil.
Bodde, James, private, 1st W. Regt.
Boyd, Robert, private, 1st W. Regt.
Boyle, John, sergeant, 2nd W. Regt.
Bongardo, James, private, 2nd W. Regt.
Bowden, Alexander, private, 2nd W. Regt.
Boland, Michael, sergeant, H. B. Vol.
Boyd, J. McN., assistant surgeon, H B. Vol.
Borne, John, private, 3rd W. Regt.
Bond, John, private, 3rd W. Regt.
Bowen, Samuel, private, 3rd W. Regt.
Bondfield, Patrick, private, 3rd W. Regt.
Box, William, private, 3rd W. Regt.
Boye, Christopher, private, 3rd W. Regt.
Bond, William, private, 3rd W. Regt.
Boyle, Thomas, private, 3rd W. Regt.
Boce, Helier, private, 3rd W. Regt.
Booker, William, private, 3rd W. Regt.
Bowen, Henry, private, 3rd W. Regt.
Bourke, Peter, constable, A. C.
Bolton, C. E., trooper, Col. D. Force
Bolton, H. H., sergeant, 3rd W. Regt.

Boggs, George, private, 1st W. Regt.
Bould, Robert, bullock driver, Com. T. Corps
Bond, James, bullock driver, Com. T. Corps
Booth, James, boatman, Com. T. Corps
Bond, Chas. J., issuer, Com. Dept.
Borrell, W., boatman, Com. Dept.
Bowler, Alexander, sergeant, Patea F. Force
Bowden, John, private, 1st W. Regt.
Boylan, Michael, sergeant, Nap. Mil.
Bousfield, O. L. W., private, Nap. Mil.
Bolton, W. H., trooper, Wan. Y. Cav.
Bower, M. N., captain, 1st W. Regt.
Bowen, J. R., private, Tar. Mil. Settlers
Brassey, Willoughby, major, Tar. Mil. Set.
Brewer, John, private, Nap. Vol.
Brighouse, John, trooper, Col. D. Force
Brighouse, Thomas, private, Nap. Mil.
Brook, R. A., private, 1st W. Regt.
Bradley, J. T., colour sergeant, 1st W. Regt.
Brett, sergeant, A. C.
Brewer, H. M., ensign, N. Z. Mil.
Bryce, John, captain, Kai Iwi Vol.
Breton, G. R., captain, 3rd W. Regt.
Brien, William, corporal, Auck. Mil.
Broadbent, John, private, Auck. Mil.
Brady, John, corporal, 1st W. Regt.
Brashill, John, artificer, Com. T. Corps
Bryce, William, private, 1st W. Regt.
Brennan, Thomas, private, 1st W. Regt.
Breden, George, sergeant, 2nd W. Regt.
Brady, Patrick, corporal, 2nd W. Regt.
Bright, James, private, 2nd W. Regt.
Broadhead, George, private, 2nd W. Regt.
Bree, Helier, private, 2nd W. Regt.
Bray, Bernard, private, 2nd W. Regt.
Bravne, Robert, private, 2nd W. Regt.
Brennan, Thomas, private, 2nd W. Regt.
Bruce, Robert, private, Auck. Vol.
Brodie, Charles W., Well. R.
Broadmore, F. A., private, Tar. Mil. Settlers
Brooking, William, corporal, Tar. Vol.
Brewer, Henry William, private, Tar. Vol.
Broughton, Edward, captain, Wan. Rifles
Bridle, R. C., private, Tar. Mil. Settlers
Brooks, J. H., private, Tar. Mil. Settlers
Brearly, Michael, Butcher, Com. T. Corps
Bridgeman, W. R., sergeant, Auck. Mil.
Brock, Adam, private, Auck. Mil.
Brownlie, John, private, 1st W. Regt.
Bryce, Thomas, private, H. M.
Bryson, Alex., constable, A. C.
Brodkort, Werner, constable, A. C.
Brathwaite, Robert, private, Nap. Mil.
Brooking, John, trooper, H. B. Cav.
Bryne, John, private, 3rd W. Regt.
Bresnahan, S., private, 3rd W. Regt.
Brook, Robert, private, 3rd W. Regt.
Broad, F., clerk, Com. Dept.
Bruce, C., storekeeper, Com. Dept.
Brand, J., clerk, Com. Dept.
Brownlow, Henry, constable, A. C.
Brunt, W. M., constable, A. C.
Brannan, Thomas, private, 1st W. Regt.
Brennan, Kyran, private, 4th W. Regt.

Brooking, R., private, Nap. Mil.
Brooking, W. F., private, Tar. Mil.
Brosnan, Patrick, private, Auck. Mil.
Bradley, George, constable, A. C.
Brett, Frederick, corporal, 3rd W. Regt.
Brien, Frederick, artificer, Com. Dept.
Bruce, Robert, artificer, Com. Dept.
Brien, James, private, 3rd W. Regt.
Bryant, George, private, 3rd W. Regt.
Broadbent, Anthony, private, 3rd W. Regt.
Bray, John, private, 3rd W. Regt.
Bryant, John, private, 3rd W. Regt.
Bryne, Martin, private, 3rd W. Regt.
Brisland, James, private
Bruce, Donald, private, 3rd W. Regt.
Briggs, William, private, 3rd W. Regt.
Brindle, Coosdale, private, 3rd W. Regt.
Bryan, John, private, 3rd W. Regt.
Brilly, Henry, private, 3rd W. Regt.
Brennan, Patrick, private, 3rd W. Regt.
Brigg, Thomas, sergeant, Auck. Mil.
Brooking, H. L. S., constable, A. C.
Brennan, John, constable, A. C.
Brooks, Robert, private, Tar. Mil.
Brennan, W., constable, A. C.
Brown, Henry, private, Tar. Mil.
Brown, W., assistant-surgeon, A. C.
Brown, Cartwright, lieutenant, Nap. Mil.
Brown, William, sergeant, Tar. Mil.
Brown, Charles, major, Tar. Mil.
Brown, Harry, constable, A. C.
Brown, Patrick, sergeant, A. C.
Brown, David, private, Auck. Mil.
Brown, Thomas, private, 1st W. Regt.
Brown, John, private, 1st W. Regt.
Brown, James, private, 1st W. Regt.
Brown, William, private, 2nd W. Regt.
Brown, John, private, 2nd W. Regt.
Brown, Robert, private, 2nd W. Regt.
Brown, J. H., sergeant, H. B. Mil.
Brown, John, private, 3rd W. Regt.
Brown, Patrick, sergeant, 3rd W. Regt.
Brown, Robert, private, 3rd W. Regt.
Brown, William, private, 3rd W. Regt.
Brown, Charles, private, Well. Rifles
Brown, W. W., clerk, Com. Dept
Brown, Charles, sergeant, A. C.
Brown, Daniel, constable, A. C.
Brown, C. S., private, 2nd W. Regt.
Brown, Thomas, trooper, Col. D. Force
Brown, William, private, Tar. Mil. Settlers
Brown, John, constable, A. C.
Browne, Hugh, private, 1st W. Regt.
Buchanan, John, captain, Nap. Vol.
Bullot, Charles A., sergeant, Tar. Mil.
Bullot, Frederick, constable, A. C.
Burgess, Alexander, private, Tar. Mil.
Burrett, Thomas, trooper, Well. D. Force
Burrow, John, constable, A. C.
Burlton, John, sergeant, Nap. Mil.
Butter, Alexander, sergeant, Forest Ran.
Burke, John, sergeant, Auck. Mil.
Bulman, Robert, private, Auck. Mil.
Burns, William, private, Auck. Mil.

Bull, Alfred, private, Auck. Mil.
Bullock, Cornelius, private, Auck. Mil.
Burns, A. T., private, Auck. Mil.
Burke, John, private, 1st W. Regt.
Burr, Jesse, private, 1st W. Regt.
Burroughs, John, private, 1st W. Regt.
Busse, Charles, private, 1st W. Regt.
Bull, John, private, 1st W. Regt.
Burleigh, William, private, 1st W. Regt.
Burke, Michael, private, 1st W. Regt.
Burner, William, private, 1st W. Regt.
Burns, John, sergeant, 2nd W. Regt.
Buck, William, private, 2nd W. Regt.
Burnett, James, private, 2nd W. Regt.
Bullen, Samuel, private, 2nd W. Regt.
Busst, T., issuer, Com. Corps
Burslam, G. I., private, 1st W. Regt.
Burrows, A. W., private, Tar. Mil.
Burter, John, private, 1st W. Regt.
Burdett, Charles W., sergeant, Auck. Eng.
Burns, Andrew, private, Auck. Rifles
Burns, Henry, constable, A. C.
Burgess, Alex., private, Tar. Mil.
Burgis, J. C., trooper, Col. D. Force
Burtt, Thomas, private, N. M.
Burton, W. Y., private, H. B. Mil.
Burton, Benjamin, private, 3rd W. Regt.
Burnes, William, private, 3rd W. Regt.
Bulmon, Robert, private, 3rd W. Regt.
Burke, Thomas, private, 3rd W. Regt.
Butterworth, John, private, 3rd W. Regt.
Burgess, W. R., storekeeper, Com. T. Corps
Buchanan, James, constable, A. C.
Bullen, John, sergeant, 1st W. Regt.
Burbridge, Henry, corporal, 3rd W. Regt.
Burgess, Alex., private, 3rd W. Regt.
Bullen Samuel, private, 3rd W. Regt.
Buchanan, William, private, 3rd W. Regt.
Butters, Alex., private, 3rd W. Regt.
Burton, Patrick, private, 3rd W. Regt.
Burke, Francis, private, 3rd W. Regt.
Buttell, Raynor, private, 3rd W. Regt.
Busby, Abraham, private, 3rd W. Regt.
Bullot, Henry, private, Tar. Cav. Vol.
Butt, N. A., sergeant, 3rd W. Regt.
Burns, Robert, constable, A.C.
Bullott, E. A. N., private, Tar. Mil. Settlers
Busst, J. A., private, 1st W. Regt.
Buller, W. C., volunteer, Staff
Bygum, Hans, private, Forest Ran.
Byrne, Charles, private, 1st W. Regt.
Byrne, H. Le Foler, sergeant, 1st W. Regt.

CADELL, THOS., superintendent, Riv. Trans.
Callaghan, Daniel, private, 3rd W. Regt.
Cann, J. G. W., sergeant, 1st W. Regt.
Capper, Samuel, corporal, 1st W. Regt.
Carey, John, assistant-surgeon, Auck. Mil.
Carey, Matthew, private, Tar. Mil. Settlers
Carnie, David, private, 3rd W. Regt.
Carr, H. H., constable, A.C.
Carrington, Wellington, cap'ain, Tar. Mil.
Carthew, Edward, captain, Tar. Mil.
Carven, Edward, private, Wan. Rifles

Casey, P., private, 2nd W. Regt.
Caulton, S. C., Nap. Col. Def. Force
Carver, R. P., ensign, Auck. Mil.
Calvert, C. A., vet. surgeon, Auck. Mil.
Calvert, John, private, 1st W. Regt.
Carter, John, private, 1st W. Regt.
Callaghan, Thomas, private, 1st W. Regt.
Campion, George, private, 1st W. Regt.
Caldicott, William, private, 1st W. Regt.
Carty, James, corporal, 1st W. Regt.
Cameron, William, private, 1st W. Regt.
Carroll, Michael, private, 1st W. Regt.
Campion, John, private, 1st W. Regt.
Carty, James, private, 1st W. Regt.
Carr, Robert, private, 1st W. Regt.
Carstairs, David, private, 1st W. Regt.
Cameron, Dugald, private, 1st W. Regt.
Carleton, Henry, private, 1st W. Regt.
Cave, W. J., corporal, 2nd W. Regt.
Cairns, Thomas, private, 2nd W. Regt.
Carter, Edward, private, 2nd W. Regt.
Camell, Henry, private, 2nd W. Regt.
Catgill, Robert, private, 2nd W. Regt.
Cain, Thomas, private, 2nd W. Regt.
Casey, John, private, 2nd W. Regt.
Carnell, Henry, private, 2nd W. Regt.
Campion, George, corporal, 3rd W. Regt.
Carson, James, private, 3rd W. Regt.
Cane, John, private, 3rd W. Regt.
Caddigan, John, private, 3rd W. Regt.
Carr, Thomas, private, 3rd W. Regt.
Cane, William, private, 3rd W. Regt.
Cahill, Edward, private, 3rd W. Regt.
Callaghan, Daniel, private, 3rd W. Regt.
Cahill, Patrick, private, 3rd W. Regt.
Carey, Edward, private, 3rd W. Regt.
Cayle, Peter, private, 3rd W. Regt.
Calder, Andrew, private, 3rd W. Regt.
Casey, William, private, 3rd W. Regt.
Cahill, Philip, private, 3rd W. Regt.
Carey, Langer, bullock driver, I T. Corps
Cairns, Robert, bullock driver, I.T. Corps
Cram, James, bullock driver, I.T. Corps
Caddy, E. B., bullock driver, I.T. Corps
Cavanagh, Patrick, bullock driver, I.T. Corps
Cameron, Angus, bullock driver, I.T. Corps
Castray, F. W., clerk, Com. Dept.
Capes, Joseph, boatman, Com. Dept.
Casey, Patrick, baker, Com. Dept.
Cargill, J., labourer, Com. Dept.
Carey, William, private, Auck. Def. Force
Campion, John, private, 1st W. Regt.
Calvert, Sylvester D., private, Wairoa Rifles
Carey, John P., private, Tar. Mil. Settlers
Carroll, James, private, Nap. Cav.
Catherall, James, private, Nelson Mil.
Carrington, Nelson, private, Tar. B. Ran.
Carver, Robt. W. J., private, H. B. Mil.
Carnell, Charles, private, Tar. B. Ran.
Callaghan, Joseph, private, 1st W. Regt.
Cambie, D. S., sergeant, 1st W. Regt.
Cameron, Colin, private, Tar. Mil.
Carson, Gilbert, private, Auck. Vol.
Capel, Sidney A. B., sub-inspector, A.C.

1*

Carlyon, P. F., lance-corporal, A.C.
Carroll, James, trooper, Kai Iwi Vol. Cav.
Carson, Robert, private, Well. Rifles
Carey, Henry, private, Patea Rifle Vol.
Carter, Harcourt, constable, A.C.
Cameron, Richard, private, Bay of I. Vol.
Carter, William, bugler, O. Cav. Vol.
Calvert, G. A., vet. surgeon, Col. D. Force
Cameron, John, private, Mauku R. Vol.
Cammell, George, petty officer, Auck. N. Vol.
Cain, Thomas, constable, A.C.
Carroll, I. N., private, Wan. Mil.
Carren, Henry, sergeant, Forest Ran.
Catanach, John, private, Nap. Mil.
Cameron, John, captain, Wan. Y. Cav.
Cass, Thomas, mate, Col. Steamer
Callender, Adam, private, Tar. Mil. Settlers
Cameron, George D., constable, A. C.
Cahill, Patrick B , sergeant, A. C.
Capper, Alfred E., trooper, Kai Iwi Vol. Cav.
Carkeek, Arthur Wakefield, sergeant, A. C.
Cannon, Charles, private, 3rd W. Regt.
Campbell, Alexander, constable, A. C.
Campbell, Charles S., constable, A. C.
Campbell, Peter, private, Wan. Rifles
Campbell, James, private, Tar. B. Ran.
Campbell, Duncan, constable, A. C.
Campbell, Archibald, sergeant, Auck. Mil.
Campbell, Dugald, private, 3rd W. Regt.
Campbell, George, private, 3rd W. Regt.
Campbell, John, private, 3rd W. Regt.
Campbell, Lawrence, private, 3rd W. Regt.
Campbell, David, private, 3rd W. Regt.
Campbell, John, labourer, Com. D pt.
Campbell, H., boatman, Com. Dept.
Campbell, Jos., bullock driver, Com. Dept.
Campbell, James, clerk, Com. Dept.
Campbell, W. W., private, 1st W. Regt.
Campbell, Archibald, private, 2nd W. Regt.
Campbell, Joseph, sergeant, 1st W. Regt.
Campbell, John, private, 1st W. Regt.
Campbell, James, private, 1st W. Regt.
Campbell, Allen Z., cornet, Kai Iwi V. Cav.
Campbell, George W., trooper, K. I. V. Cav.
Chapman, N. E., lieutenant, Tar. Mil. Settlers
Cherry, George T., private, Tar. Vol.
Chicken, John, private, Tar. Vol.
Chitty, Charles, sergeant, Col. T. Corps
Churton, A. H., sergeant, Auck. Vol.
Churton, J. F., sergeant, Auck. Vol.
Chadwick, J., quarter-master, Wan. V. Cav.
Chapman, Chas. S., private, Well. R.
Chawner, Edward, sergeant, A.C.
Cheve, G. S., ensign, 3rd W. Regt.
Chapman, Thomas, private, 1st W. Regt.
Chaplin, Samuel, private, 1st W. Regt.
Charlton, John, private, 2nd W. Regt.
Chandler, William, private, 2nd W. Regt.
Chitty, Charles, corporal, 3rd W. Regt.
Churchouse, W. R., issuer, Com. T. Corps
Chalong, Michael, baker, Com. T. Corps
Charles, Samuel, labourer, Com. T. Corps
Christy, Walter, trooper, Wan. Yeo. Cav.
Chapman, Daniel Y., corporal, Well. R.

Chilman, John, corporal, Well. R.
Churchouse, W. R., major, Tar. Mil. Settlers
Chase, John, constable, A.C.
Chalmers, Robert, private, Auck. R.
Chalklin, W. W., private, 1st W. Regt.
Charters, Luden, priva e, 3rd W. Regt.
Churchall, Thos., private, 3rd W. Regt.
Chapman, James, private, 3rd W. Regt.
Cheshill, Jacob, private, 3rd W. Regt.
Chapman, Francis, private, 3rd W Regt.
Chapman, Isaac, private, 3rd W. Regt.
Christie, John, private, 3rd W. Regt.
Clare, William, major, Auck. Mil.
Clery, H. A., ensign, Tar. Mil.
Clifton, Theodore, sergeant, 2nd W. Regt.
Clifton, W. S., private, Auck. Vol.
Clinton, P. J., private, F. Rangers
Clode, George, sergeant, 2nd W. Regt.
Clotworthy, George, private, F. Rangers
Clifford, Dennis, private, 1st W. Regt.
Clutterbuck, John, private, 1st W. Regt.
Clough, August, private, 1st W. Regt.
Cleming, Thomas, sergeant, 2nd W. Regt.
Clancy, Michael, private, 2nd W. Regt.
Clement, Archibald, corporal, 3rd W. Regt.
Clifford, Michael, corporal, 3rd W. Regt.
Cleath, George, artificer, 3rd W. Regt.
Clapworthy, William, private, 3rd W. Regt.
Clinton, Charles, private, 3rd W. Regt.
Clelland, Archibald, private, 3rd W. Regt.
Clementson, Robert, private, Tar. Mil. Settlers
Clare, Thomas, private, Tar. Vol.
Clarkson, D. K., private, Auck. Rifles.
Clayton, Henry, private, Nap. Mil.
Cleary, Joseph, private, 1st W. Reg.
Clime, James, private, Tar. Mil.
Clarkson, John, private, M.R.
Clansey, Samuel, constable, A.C.
Clifford, Henry G., corporal, Forest Ran.
Clark, H. T., staff interpreter
Clark, H.M., private, 1st W. Regt.
Clark, Milton, corporal, Auck. Mil.
Clark, W. H. S., lieutenant, Auck. Mil.
Clark, William, private, 1st W. Regt.
Clark, Samuel, private, 1st W. Regt.
Clark, Archibald, corporal, 2nd W. Regt.
Clark, John, private, 2nd W. Regt.
Clark, William, sergeant, 3rd W. Regt.
Clark, H. M., sergeant, Auck. Mil.
Clark, George, sergeant, 1st W. Regt.
Clark, J., storekeeper, Com. Dept.
Clark, James M. C., captain, Auck. Vol.
Clark, W. C., lance corporal, Tar. Mil.
Clark, J. H., captain, Tar. Mil. Settlers
Clark, Owen, private, 3rd W. Regt.
Clark, John, private, 3rd W. Regt.
Clark, Michael, private, 3rd W. Regt.
Claypole, A., butcher, Com. Dept.
Cloran, Patrick, baker, Com. Dept.
Clansing, Henry, constable, A.C.
Codd, George, private, 2nd W. Regt.
Coffee, Martin Y., sergeant, Tar. Mil. Settlers
Colson, Thomas, private, Tar. Mil.
Colthart, John, corporal, Well. Rifles

Comrie, James, private, Patea Vol.
Corbett, George, private, Tar. Vol.
Corbett, James, private, Tar. Vol.
Corbett, J. G., captain, Tar. Mil. Settlers
Corry, John, private, Nap. Mil.
Cosgrove, Patrick, private, Nap. Mil.
Cossey, J. T., private, Auck. Mil.
Collins, James, constable, A.C.
Collins, Robert, captain, N.Z. Mil.
Connely, J. F., trooper, B. of P. Vol. Cav.
Connoll, Thomas, trooper, Wan. Vol. Cav.
Cotton, Edward, private, Auck. Mil.
Coates, W. N., ensign, 1st W. Regt.
Connell, D. W., ensign, 4th W. Regt.
Courtney, Nicholas, private, 1st W. Regt.
Cox, John, private, 1st W. Regt.
Corbett, Edward, private, 1st W. Regt.
Coleman, Michael, private, 1st W. Regt.
Coulan, Bernard, private, 1st W. Regt.
Connor, Hugh, private, 1st W. Regt.
Cookson, Joseph, private, 1st W. Regt.
Cootie, George, private, 1st W. Regt.
Cosgrave, William, private, 1st W. Regt.
Connelly, Jeremiah, private, 1st W. Regt.
Cookson, Edmund, private, 1st W. Regt.
Connor, George, private, 1st W. Regt.
Coates, William, private, 1st W. Regt.
Cook, J. G., private, 1st W. Regt.
Cobine, Joseph, private, 1st W. Regt.
Coventry, Robert, private, 1st W. Regt.
Coleman, Peter, private, 2nd W. Regt.
Cowley, Richard, private, 2nd W. Regt.
Comerie, George, private, 2nd W. Regt.
Conroy, Arthur, private, 2nd W. Regt.
Connor, Patrick, private, 2nd W. Regt.
Cox, Richard, private, 2nd W. Regt.
Colthurst, William, private, 2nd W. Regt.
Coombs, George, bullock driver, Com. Dept.
Corbett, Wm., bullock driver, Com. Dept.
Cox, Hewing, bullock driver, Com. Dept.
Cook, William, clerk, Com. Dept.
Cowie, Andrew, issuer, Com. Dept.
Cowie, Edward, issuer, Com. Dept.
Corby, —, issuer, Com. Dept.
Cook, E. R., issuer, Com. Dept.
Cook, J. G., issuer, Com. Dept.
Corbett, Michael, baker, Com. Dept.
Coombs, W., baker, Com. Dept.
Connelly, John, labourer, Com. Dept.
Collingwood, A., boatman, Com. Dept.
Cook, George, private, Tar. Vol.
Courtney, Frank, private, Tar. Vol.
Cox, Alfred W., private, H. B. Mil.
Collingwood, H. A., corporal, A. C.
Conolly, Charles, trooper, B. I. Vol. Cav.
Corri, Albert T., sergeant, 1st W. Regt.
Coffey, Dennis, constable, A. C.
Collart, Robert, constable, A. C.
Compton, Alfred, private, Patea Rifles
Cooke, Philip, sergeant, 1st W. Regt.
Collins, Michael, constable, A. C.
Cock, Henry, private, Tar. Mil.
Cockerton, Levi, sergeant, 1st W. Regt.
Coombs, Frederick, petty officer, Nav. Vol.

Condie, David, private, Patea Mil.
Copeland, John, private, Auck. Nav. Vol.
Collinson, Joshua, B., private, Well. Rifles
Cocking, William, private, Hutt Mil.
Codling, Elijah, private, Forest Rangers
Cook, George, private, Auck. Mil.
Cole, George L., private, Forest Rangers
Coulton, Robert J., lieutenant, 2nd W. Regt.
Corney, Joseph, private, Tar. Vol.
Coston, Dennis, trooper, Col. D. Force
Cox, Henry, bugler, Tar. Mil.
Cowan, David H., sergeant, 1st W. Regt.
Crossman, George, constable, A. C.
Cornice, John, artificer, Com. Dept.
Costello, William, artificer, Com. Dept.
Cox, George, artificer, Com. Dept.
Collins, William, private, 3rd W. Regt.
Covey, William, private, 3rd W. Regt.
Cobham, William, private, 3rd W. Regt.
Cowley, Richard, private, 3rd W. Regt.
Coyle, Thomas, private, 3rd W. Regt.
Cox, William, private, 3rd W. Regt.
Courtenay, John, private, 3rd W. Regt.
Cook, F. W., private, 3rd W. Regt.
Collins, J. J., private, 3rd W. Regt.
Collins, Joseph, private, 3rd W. Regt.
Coope, Thomas, private, 3rd W. Regt.
Conn, Edward, private, 3rd W. Regt.
Cox, George, private, 3rd W. Regt.
Coxhead, John, private, 3rd W. Regt.
Collins, Joseph, private, 3rd W. Regt.
Cox, James, private, 3rd W. Regt.
Collins, James, private, 3rd W. Regt.
Cobley, William, private, 3rd W. Regt.
Cowie, George, private, 3rd W. Regt.
Cotter, Peter, private, 3rd W. Regt.
Coleman, James, private, 3rd W. Regt.
Conway, Bartholomew, private, 3rd W. Regt.
Cook, John, private, 3rd W. Regt.
Coventry, Robert, private, 3rd W. Regt.
Collingwood, E., blck. driver, Transpt. Corps
Cooms, Wm., bullock driver, Transpt. Corps
Cook, Henry, trooper, B. I. Cav. Vol.
Collins, John, private, Tar. Mil.
Cox, Geo. W., trooper, Waiuku Cav.
Cox, John, private, Tar. Mil.
Collins, John, private, Well. Rifles
Cody, William, private, Col. D. Force
Combes, Robert, sergeant, Auck. Rifles
Connelly, James, petty officer, Auck. Nav.
Cook, Samuel, private, Col. D. Force
Cornes, Alfred R., private, Col. D. Force
Connell, Maurice, trooper, Wan. Y. Cav.
Constable, Wm. S., sergeant, Patea Rifles
Coombs, James, private, 1st W. Regt.
Cooper, George, constable, A.C.
Cooper, Henry S., private, 2nd W. Regt.
Cooper, George E., sergeant, 2nd W. Regt.
Cooper, George, private, 1st W. Regt.
Cooper, A. R., ensign, 2nd W. Regt.
Cooper, George, private,
Crispe, Heywood, sergeant, Forest Ran.
Crosby, Henry, private, Tar. Mil. Settlers
Crapp, Arthur A., sub-inspector, A.C.

Davis, James T., private, Tar. Mil.
Davis, J. C., cornet, Tar. Cav. Vol.
Davis, John, private, 1st W. Regt.
Davis, James T., private, Tar. Mil. Settlers.
Deane, H. E., s-rgeant, Well. Rifles
Dempster, Alexander, private, 2nd W. Regt.
Denholme, William, private, Nap. Mil.
Dent, William, private, Auck. Vol.
Dette, Charles, private, 1st W. Regt.
Devoy, Henry, bugler, 3rd W. Regt.
Denholme, William, sergeant, Auck. Eng.
Dennis, F. B., trooper, P. B. Cav.
Deacon, Thomas, private, 1st W. Regt.
DeCarbert, Samuel, private, 1st W. Regt.
Dempsey, William, private, 1st W. Regt.
Dennis, John, private, 1st W. Regt.
Deckan, John, private, 1st W. Regt.
Dette, Charles, private, 1st W. Regt.
DeBlackguerie, G., corporal, 2nd W. Regt.
Dempster, Alexander, private, 2nd W. Regt.
Devett, Edward, private, 2nd W. Regt.
Dee, William, private, 2nd W. Regt.
Desmond, Michael, private, 2nd W. Regt.
Desmond, John, private, 2nd W. Regt.
Denburgh, William, private, 2nd W. Regt.
Deans, James, private, 2nd W. Regt.
Dean, Mark, private, 3rd W. Regt.
Dennis, T., private, 4th W. Regt.
Dempsey, William, driver, Transpt Corps.
Delaney, James, driver, Transpt. Corps.
Denk, William, driver, Transpt. Corps.
Dempsey, William, clerk, Com. Dept.
Delaney, John, boatman, Com. Dept.
DeLeon, Henry, issuer, Com. Dept.
DeNorvill, Alfred, sergeant, M. S.
Dent, Mark, sergeant, V. A. Com.
De Thierry, George, B. of I. Vol.
De Thierry, Richard, private, Auck. Mil.
Dempsey, James, private, Well. Mil.
DeFangerand, Pierre, constable, A.C.
Deerness, William, trooper, Col. D. Force
Deery, David, private, Auck. Rifles
Delaney, John, private, 1st W. Regt.
Dean, Edward, corporal, A.C.
Dillon, Michael, private, 2nd W. Regt.
Dingeldy, H. J., private, Tar. Mil. Set.
Dinwiddie, Peter, private, Nap. Vol.
Dickson, Mauley, private, Tar. Vol.
Dickey, Alexander, private, Wairoa Rifles
Dickey, senr., John, private, Wairoa Rifles
Dickey, junr., John, private, Wairoa Rifles
Dillon, Henry, private, 1st W. Regt.
Dillon, James, private, 1st W. Regt.
Dillon, Robert, private, 1st W. Regt.
Diggles, John, private, 1st W. Regt.
Dicken, Thomas, private, 1st W. Regt.
Diggles, John, private, 1st W. Regt.
Diebricht, Godley, private, 1st W. Regt.
Divine, William, private, 2nd W. Regt.
Dickson, Samuel, private, 3rd W. Regt.
Dillon, Joseph, private, 3rd W. Regt.
Digham, Henry, private, 3rd W. Regt.
Dickie, James, labourer, Com. Dept.
Dillon, P., labourer, Com. Dept.

Dick, James, private, Tar. Mil. Settlers
Divine, James, constable, A.C.
Dickman, Thomas, private, Well. Mil.
Dickson, Joseph, private, Tar. Mil. Settlers
Dick, William, private, 1st W. Regt.
Dismore, Nathaniel, sergeant, A.C.
Dickson, Fetcher, private, Tar. Mil. Settlers
Dinwiddie, John, private, Nap. Rifles
Dillon, Daniel, private, 3rd W. Regt.
Dingall, James, driver, Transpt. Corps.
Donelly, James, trooper, Well. Cav.
Dolan, Patrick, constable, A.C.
Donelly, Thomas, private, 1st W. Regt.
Doody, Michael, private, 1st W. Regt.
Doull, William, private, 1st W. Regt.
Douse, Arthur, sergeant, 1st W. Regt.
Donelly, John, corporal, 1st W. Regt.
Donnall, James, corporal, 1st W. Regt.
Donelly, John, private, 1st W. Regt.
Douglas, Robert, private, 1st W. Regt.
Downey, James, private, 1st W. Regt.
Donovan, Wm., private, 1st W. Regt.
Donovan, John, corporal, 2nd W. Regt.
Doherty, Patrick, private, 2nd W. Regt.
Double, Richard, private, 2nd W. Regt.
Donelly, Patrick, private, 2nd W. Regt.
Dowe, Anderson, sergeant, 3rd W. Regt.
Donelly, Thomas, private, 3rd W. Regt.
Downs, Joseph, private, 3rd W. Regt.
Douglas, H., private, 3rd W. Regt.
Dobbins, Thomas, private, 3rd W. Regt.
Donovan, Denis, private, 3rd W. Regt.
Doyle, Thomas, private, 3rd W. Regt.
Dorgan, William, driver, Transpt. Corps
Doyle, James, butcher, Transpt. Corps
Dobbyn, Stephen, private, 1st W. Regt.
Donnelly, John, private, 1st W. Regt.
Dolbie, Charles, private, Nap. Mil.
Dowle, Albert, private, 2nd W. Regt.
Downer, Benjamin, bugler, Auck. Cav.
Doyle, John, private, 1st W. Regt.
Dougherty, Patrick, private, Wan. Rifles
Downs, Benjamin, bugler, Auck. Cav.
Dore, Geo. Hy., private, Well. Rifles
Dorsay, Victor, private, 3rd W. Regt.
Drummond, Jno. Ed., constable, A.C.
Drew, Robert, artificer, Auck. Mil.
Drew, John, private, 3rd W. Regt.
Dryburgh, John, private, 3rd W. Regt.
Drew, James, private, 3rd W. Regt.
Drake, John, sergeant butcher, Com. Dept.
Drew, James, butcher, Com. Dept.
Drew, James, constable, A.C.
Drory, Henry, private, Tar. Mil.
Dribery, W. T., private, Nap. Mil.
Dromgool, Charles, private, M.R.V.
Drury, H. K., captain, 2nd W. Regt.
Dromgold, James, private, M.R.V.
Drake, Wm., trooper, Col. D. Force
Dunfry, Charles, private, Nap. Vol.
Durie, D. S., inspector, A.C.
DuMoulin, J. P., captain, 3rd W. Regt.
Dumford, G. W., private, 1st W. Regt.
Dunn, W., private, 1st W. Regt.

Duncan, John, private, 1st W. Regt.
Durden, James, private, 2nd W. Regt.
Ducksberry, James, private. 2nd W. Regt.
Duckworth, John, private, 3rd W. Regt.
Dudgeon, George, driver, Transpt. Corps
Duffin, John, private, Tar. Mil.
Dunckley, W., private, Forest Ran.
Dunn, Arthur J. N., corporal, Col. D. Force
Dunn, John, constable, A.C.
Durbridge, Henry, trooper, Col. D. Force
Duncan, Jos. R., private, Tar. Mil.
Duffy, Thomas, constable, A.C.
Duncan, G. E., private, Tar. Mil. Sett.
Dundass, Henry W., sergeant, A.C.
Dybell, Alfred, private. Tar. Mil. Sett.
Dyer, Henry, private, 3rd W. Regt.

Earl, R. A. N., sergeant, Tar. Mil.
Easton, George, corporal, Patea Vol.
Easton, James, private, Patea Vol.
Earles, Stephen, private, 1st W. Regt.
Eady, James, driver, Transpt. Corps
Earl, William, private, 1st W. Regt.
East, Charles, constable, A.C.
Early, Hugh, sergeant, Tar. Mil.
Easton, Robert, private. 1st W. Regt.
Ebberley, Peter, constable, A.C.
Ebbett, William, constable, A.C.
Edwards, Edward, sergeant, Transpt. Corps
Edwards, F. R., corporal, Auck. Mil.
Edwards, Frederick, private, 1st W. Regt.
Edwards, John, private, 1st W. Regt.
Edwards, Henry, corporal, 1st W. Regt.
Edwards, John, corporal, 2nd W. Regt.
Edwards, John, private, 2nd W. Regt.
Edwards, Robert, driver, Transpt. Corps
Edwards, B. F. J., col.-sergeant, 1st W. Regt.
Edwards, Jas. Thos., private, Auck. Rifles
Edwards, Chas., private, Tar. Mil. Settlers
Edhouse, Henry, corporal, 1st W. Regt.
Edmunds, Thomas, private, 2nd W. Regt.
Edmunds, William, private, 2nd W. Regt.
Edmonds, J. J., boatman, Transpt. Corps
Edmonds, Thomas, private, 1st W. Regt.
Edinburgh, C., sergeant, issuer, Com. Dept.
Edgeworth, Robert, corporal, A.C.
Eden, Thomas, private, Nap. Mil.
Egan, John, private, 2nd W. Regt.
Egan, James, trooper, Well. D. Force
Ellaby, C. H., trooper, Wan. Y. Cav.
Elliot, John, private, Tar. Vol.
Elliotte, R. H., trooper, Col. D. Force
Ellenburgh, C. A., sergeant, 1st W. Regt.
Ellew, Walter, corporal, 1st W. Regt.
Ellis, Robert, private, 1st W. Regt.
Elton, William, corporal, 2nd W. Regt.
Ellis, George, corporal, 3rd W. Regt.
Elliott, Alexander, corporal, 3rd W. Regt.
Elmslie, Peter, corporal, Wairoa Rifles
Elberry, John, private, 3rd W. Regt.
Elliott, Peter, driver, Transpt. Corps
Elliott, John, driver, Transpt. Corps
Elliott, William, driver, Transpt. Corps
Elliott, Thomas, driver, Transpt. Corps

Elder, William, private, 3rd W. Regt.
Elliott, Frederick, constable, A.C.
Elley, Reuben, constable, A.C.
Elliott, John, private, Nap. Mil.
Elliot, George, private, Tar. Mil.
Ellis, William, private, Wan. Mil.
Emerson, C., boatman, Transpt. Corps
England, Thomas, private, 1st W. Regt.
England, Charles, private, 1st W. Regt.
Enright, Timothy, private, 1st W. Regt.
English, William, private. 2nd W. Regt.
English, Joseph, private, 3rd W. Regt.
Ensor, Thomas, trooper, Col. D. Force.
Erskine, James H., private, Wairoa R.
Erskine, Robert, constable, A.C.
Esther, Patrick, private, Tar. Vol.
Etheridge, Thos., artificer, Com. Dept.
Etherington, George, private, Patea R.
Everett, Chas., sergeant, Tar. Mil.
Everett, Thos., private, 3rd W. Regt.
Eva, Stephen, driver, T. Corps
Eva, William, private, Tar. Mil. Settlers
Evans, Chas., corporal, P. Bay Mil.
Evans, Frank W., trooper, Wan. Cav.
Evans, John, constable, A.C.
Evans, John, private, 3rd W. Regt.
Evans, James, private, 3rd W. Regt.
Evans, R., clerk, Com. Dept.
Evans, Herbert L., trooper, Wan. Cav.
Evans, Robert, Vol. officer
Evans, Henry, constable, A.C.
Ewarth, James, driver, T. Corps
Ewing, Geo. B., private, 1st W. Regt.
Egton, Thos., sergeant, A.C.

Fallon, Joseph, corporal, Forest Ran.
Fawcus, George, private, 1st W. Regt.
Farrell, Benjamin, private, 1st W. Regt.
Farrer, Frederick, private, 1st W. Regt.
Farrar, Simeon, private, 2nd W. Regt.
Farrell, Charles, driver, Transpt. Corps
Farrell, Robert, private, 1st W. Regt
Farrelly, Thomas, constable, A C.
Farmer, George, private, H. B. Mil.
Fahey, David, constable, A. C.
Faulkner, Elijah J., private, 1st W. Regt.
Fairchild, John, captain, Gov. Steamer
Fairburn, Thos., lieut-corporal, Tar. Mil. Set
Fairbairn, Robert, private, 3rd W. Regt.
Featherstone, J. E., superintendent, Well.
Featon, E. H., private, O. N. Vol.
Featon. John. private. O. N. Vol.
Feehan, Thomas, private, 4th W. Regt.
Ferris, C. W., trooper, Nap. Com.
Fenton, William, sergeant, 3rd W. Regt.
Fergusson, Robert, private, 1st W. Regt.
Fergusson, Michael, private, 2nd W. Regt.
Ferdinando, Antonio, private, 3rd W. Regt
Ferrand, Edward, private, 3rd W. Regt.
Fennell, Patrick, private, 3rd W. Regt.
Fencoe, William, driver, Transpt. Corps
Fleming, Andrew, sergt-issuer, Com. Dept.
Ferrell, Henry, issuer, Com. Dept.
Fee, James, butcher, Com. Dept.

Fernandez, Joseph, labourer, Com. Dept.
Fellow, C., boatman, Transpt. Corps
Ferraby, John, constable, A. C.
Felgate, John C., private, Tar. Mil.
Feltus, Richard J., issuer, Com. Dept.
Fielder, J. B., private, Nap. Vol.
Finney, John, private, 1st W. Regt
Fitzgibbon, G. C., private, Auck. Mil.
Finnimore, William, major, Wan. Y. Cav.
Finlay, William, constable, A.C.
Finch, Thomas, sergeant, 2nd W. Regt.
Finch, George, private, 3rd W. Regt.
Fisher, J., boatman, Transpt. Corps
Finnigan, A., labourer, Transpt. Corps.
Finlay, James, private, Forest Ran.
Fielding, John, private, 1st W. Regt.
Fisher, John, private, Col. D. Force
Firman, Thomas, sergeant, Hawke's B. Vol.
Fitzmaurice, Gerald, trooper, Col. D. Force
Figg, Henry, lieutenant, Auck. Vol.
Fisher, Albert, private, 1st **W.** Regt.
Fitzgerald, Michael, captain, Nap. Mil.
Fitzgerald, L. C., captain, S. O. C. F.
Fitzgerald, John, private, Wan. Mil.
Fitzpatrick, Patrick, private, 1st W. Regt.
Fitzpatrick, Thomas, sergeant, 1st W. Regt.
Fitzpatrick, Thomas, private, 1st W. Regt.
Fitzpatrick, Armstrong, private, 3rd W. Regt.
Fitzgerald, William, private, 3rd W. Regt.
Fitzgerald, Henry, issuer, Com. Dept.
Fitzgerald, Thomas, private, 1st **W.** Regt.
Flanagan, Edward, private, 3rd W. Regt.
Flavell, William, sergeant, Wan. Vol.
Flint, G. B. constable, A.C.
Flanaghan, John, private, 1st W. Regt.
Flack, Peter, sergeant, 2nd W. Regt,
Fleming, Robert, private, 2nd W. Regt.
Fleming, George, private, 3rd W. Regt.
Flynn, James, clerk, Com. Dept.
Flanagan, Charles, boatman, Transpt. Corps
Fletcher, —, labourer, Transpt. Corps
Flower, C., boatman, Transpt. Corps
Flatt, Joseph H., private, Auck. Rifles
Flyger, William Henry, private, Wan. Mil.
Flynn, Thomas, sergeant, Patea R. Vol.
Fletcher, James, sergeant, H. B. Vol.
Fletcher, Henry, private, Nap. Mil.
Flanagan, John, private, Nap. Mil.
Flanigan, Michael, private, Tar. Mil. Settlers
Flynn, John, private, Tar. Mil. Settlers
Flockton, Hamilton, private, 1st W. Regt.
Fookes, A. C., lieutenant, Tar. Mil. Settlers
Foot, C. J., trooper, Wan. Y. Cav.
Ford, W. A., sergeant, 2nd W. Regt.
Forster, A. L. B., sub-inspector, A. C.
Forster, H., sergeant-major, A. C.
Ford, Arthur S., private, 1st W. Regt.
Forbes, Robert, sergeant, Auck. Mil.
Fowler, Frederick, sergeant, 3rd W. Regt.
Foster, Michael, private, 1st W. Regt.
Folkhard, Thomas, private, 1st W. Regt.
Forceman, Marshall, private, 1st W. Regt.
Fort, Andrew, private, 1st W. Regt.

Fosbury, Richard, private, 1st W. Regt.
Forrest, James, private, 1st W. Regt.
Folkhard, R. W., private, 1st W. Regt.
Fox, Godfrey, private, 1st W. Regt.
Fort, W. H., artificer, Com. Dept.
Fory, James, private, 2nd W. Regt.
Fortune, John, private, 2nd W. Regt.
Fowlaston, Matthew, private, 3rd W. Regt.
Foster, William, private, 3rd W. Regt.
Fogherty, Thos., private, 3rd W. Regt.
Ford, Francis, driver, T. Corps
Fort, Adam, driver, T. Corps
Foreman, John, driver, T. Corps
Forsyth, Robt., clerk, Com. Dept.
Foreman, Sergt. Henry, baker, Com. Dept.
Fooks, Fred. P., private, Tar. Mil. Settlers
Fortescue, P.T., ensign, Tar. Mil. Settlers
Foster, Fred. W., private, F. Ran.
Foreman, Richard W., private, Patea R.
Ford, Harris, sergeant, Tar. Mil.
Foreman, Thos. private, Tar. Mil.
Forster, Richard, private, 2nd W. Regt.
Fraser, Samuel L., private, H. Bay Vol.
Fraser, William, captain, 1st W. Regt.
Fraser, James, lieut. col., N.Z. Mil.
Frazer, John, sergeant, A.C.
Frazer, J. T., ensign, 1st W. Regt.
Fraser, John, private, 1st W. Regt.
Fraser, Henry, private, 1st W. Regt.
Frazer, John, private, 1st W. Regt.
Fraser, William, sergeant, Auck. D. Force
Fraser, William, private, Col. D. Force
Fraser, Thomas, private, 1st W. Regt.
Francis, W. D., bugler, Tar. Mil.
Frank, Chas., private, 1st W. Regt.
Frewin, Thos., corporal, 1st W. Regt.
Freeman, Henry, private, 1st W. Regt.
Frost, Edward, private, 2nd W. Regt.
Fry, Lewis, private, 3rd W. Regt.
Frost, William, private, 3rd W. Regt.
Fry, Henry, private, 3rd W. Regt.
Frank, Charles, private, 3rd W. Regt.
Fritze, Geo., driver, T. Corps
Franshaw T., issuer, Com. Dept.
Free, William Henry, lieutenant, Tar. Vol.
French, William, sergeant, A.C.
Froggart, Henry, constable, A.C.
Freeman, Isaiah, bugler, Tar. Mil. Settlers
Freeman, Edward, private, 3rd W. Regt.
Furlong, Thomas, trooper, Tar. Cav. Vol.
Furnival, G., private, Tar. Mil.
Furlong, Andrew, corporal, 3rd W. Regt.
Furze, W., driver, Transpt. Corps
Fulton, W., private, Tar. Mil, Settlers
Fuller, W. E., trooper, Wan. Cav.
Furley, Samuel, private, Tar. Mil. Settlers
Fussell, James C., trooper, Col. D. Force
Fyfe, John, artificer, Com. Dept.
Fyfe, David, private, 3rd W. Regt.

GALLAGHER, JOHN, trooper, Col. D. Force
Gallagher, Thos., private, 1st W. Regt.
Gallagher, John, private, 1st W. Regt.
Gallagher, Peter, private, 3rd W. Regt.

Gallagher, Edward, trooper, Col. D. Force
Gallagher, John, private, Tar. Mil. Settlers
Gallagher, Bernard, lance-corporal, Well. Mil.
Garner, Frank W., private, Well. Mil.
Gascoigne, F. W., sub-inspector, A.C.
Gay, M. J., constable, A.C.
Garrett, Roland, lieutenant Kai Iwi Cav.
Gage, William, artificer, Com. Dept.
Gazeley, William, private, 1st W. Regt.
Galt, William, private, 1st W. Regt.
Gaffney, Thos., private, 1st W. Regt.
Garner, Chas., private, 1st W. Regt.
Galbraith, Albert, private, 1st W. Regt.
Gaffney, James, private, 1st W. Regt.
Gates, Henry, private, 2nd W. Regt.
Gay, Archer, private, 3rd W. Regt.
Gammond, Edward, private, 3rd W. Regt.
Garrett, William, private, 3rd W. Regt.
Galloway, William, private, 3rd W. Regt.
Galloway, Peter, private, 3rd W. Regt.
Gale, Augustus, driver, Transpt. Corps
Garlly, William, driver, Transpt. Corps
Gardner, James, driver, Transp. Corps
Gates, Edward, boatman, Transpt. Corps
Gale, W., boatman, Transpt. Corps
Gabert, Sergt. B., issuer, Com. Dept.
Gay, J., issuer, Com. Dept.
Gayne, Chas., private, 3rd W. Regt.
Gatland, Jas. B., private, Auck. Vol.
Garsed, Edwd., private, Tar. Bush Rangers
Garrad, Thos., private, Hawke's B. Vol.
Gannon, M. J., constable, A.C.
Gamble, Robt., trooper, Col. D. Force
Galway, Theophilus, private, 3rd W. Regt.
Garrod, William, sergeant, Tar. Mil. Settlers
Garbes, Peter, private, Well. Rifles
Gage, John, guide, Napier Vol.
George, F., Nelson, major, 3rd W. Regt.
George, John, private, 1st W. Regt.
Gee, James, private, 3rd W. Regt.
George, William, driver, Transpt. Corps
Geraty, —, baker, Com. Dept.
Geshagan, William, baker, Com. Dept.
George, Robert, private, 1st W. Regt.
George, Henry R., private, Auck. Vol.
George, Thomas J., private, Tar. Rifles
George, James C., private, Tar. Rifles
Geary, Hamilton, private, Well. Rifles
Gibbons, C. R., private, Tar. Mil. Settlers
Gibbons, M. C., trooper, ———
Gibbons, Patrick, private, 2nd W. Regt.
Gibbons, James, constable, A. C.
Gibson, Thomas, sergeant, Col. D. Force
Gibson, Harrison, trooper, Wan. Y. Cav.
Gibson, William, trooper, Wan. Y Cav.
Gibson, James, private, 3rd W. Regt.
Giddy, W., private, Tar. Vol.
Gilander, John, private, F. Rangers
Gilmore, William, sergeant, Auck. Mil.
Gill, Charles, private, 1st W. Regt.
Gibbs, James, private, 1st W. Regt.
Gibb, T. R., corporal, 3rd W. Regt.
Gilliland, Samuel, private, 3rd W. Regt.
Gilbert, John, private, 3rd W. Regt.

Ginger, T. E., private, Tar. Vol.
Ginger, Diston, private, Tar Vol.
Ginger, Stanley, private, Tar. Vol.
Gilbert, John J., private, 3rd W. Regt.
Gibbes, J. M., assist. surgeon, Napier Mil.
Gidall, Jacob, private, Tar. Mil. Settlers
Gillmer, E. B., corporal, Col. D. Force
Gibbs, Charles, trooper, Kai-Iwi Cav.
Glennan, Michael, private, 1st W. Regt.
Glennis, Wm., constable, A.C.
Glassock, H., ensign, 2nd W. Regt.
Gleeson, Michael, private, 2nd W. Regt.
Gledhill, John, private, 3rd W. Regt.
Glenn, J. A., private, Tar. Mil. Settlers
Glover, John, private, Tar. Mil. Settlers
Glover, Robert, private, 3rd W. Regt.
Goldsmith, Henry, captain, 1st W. Regt.
Goldsmith, E. C., sergeant, Auck. Eng.
Goldsmith, William, private, 1st W. Regt.
Goldsmith, John, corporal, 3rd W. Regt.
Goldsmith, Chas. Geo., trooper, P. Bay Cav.
Goldsmith, J. W. P., sergeant, A.C.
Gold, Robert, corporal, Auck. Mil.
Gold, Wm., private, 1st W. Regt.
Gold, Chas. Y., corporal, Tar. Mil. Settlers
Good, Thos., captain, Native Con.
Goring, Foster Y., sub-inspector, A.C.
Gordon, Thos., trooper, Wan. Y. Cavalry
Goldthorpe, Wm., private, 1st W. Regt.
Goss, Daniel, private, 1st W. Regt.
Golding, Edward, artificer, Com. Dept.
Goodman, Henry, sergeant, 2nd W. Regt.
Gordon, James, private, 2nd W. Regt.
Gower, Joseph, private, 2nd W. Regt.
Golding, John, private, 3rd W. Regt.
Goymier, Edward, private, 3rd W. Regt.
Goodhall, John, private, 3rd W. Regt.
Goring, John, private, 3rd W. Regt.
Gollen, Alexander, private, 3rd W. Regt.
Goodwin, John, private, 3rd W. Regt.
Gorton, G. J., driver, Transpt. Corps
Goodman, Joseph, driver, Transpt. Corps
Goscombe, G., boatman, Transpt. Corps
Gossling, G. J., lieutenant, Tar. Mil. Settlers
Gordon, Thomas E., captain, H. B. Cav.
Gorman, William, private, Patea Rifles
Goff, John, private, 2nd W. Regt.
Grant, William, sergeant, Transpt. Corps
Grant, A., constable, A.C.
Grant, Thomas, private, 1st W. Regt.
Grant, Thomas, sergeant, 2nd W. Regt.
Grant, Francis, private, 2nd W. Regt.
Grant, Iram, bullock driver, Transpt. Corps
Grant, William, clerk, Com. Dept.
Grant, David, private, 2nd W. Regt.
Grayling, Irwin, W., private, Tar. Vol.
Gray, C. M., private, Wan. Mil.
Graham, Charles, private, 1st W. Regt.
Grace, Thomas, private, 1st W. Regt.
Graham, Alexander, private, 1st W. Regt.
Gray, Peter, sergeant, 3rd W. Regt.
Gray, R., bullock driver, Transpt. Corps
Gray, C., bullock driver, Transpt. Corps
Gray, B., bullock driver, Transpt. Corps

Gray, John, coxswain, Transpt. Corps
Gray, John, baker, Com. Dept.
Gray, William, labourer, Com. Dept.
Gray, Charles, private, Tar. Mil.
Gray, Charles, private, Wan. Mil.
Grace, William H., trooper, Tar. Y. Cav.
Gratton, T. A., private, 1st W. Regt.
Graham, Samuel, private, Nap. Mil.
Grantham, Henry J., private, 1st W. Regt.
Gravatt, Edward, private, 1st W. Regt.
Graham, Andrew, private, Nap. Mil.
Green, J. H., corporal, 2nd W. Regt.
Greene, Thomas, sergeant, 2nd W. Regt.
Greene, Joseph, issuer, Com. Dept.
Green, Charles Henry, trooper, Col. D. Force
Grey, Charles, private, Wan. B. Ran.
Grey, W. G., private, Tar. Vol.
Greenwell, G. S., private, Nap. Vol.
Greenwell, S. T., private, Nap. Vol.
Greenwood, Robert, cornet, Tar. Cav.
Greenwood, R. W., private, Tar. Mil.
Gregory, Walter, private, 1st W. Regt.
Gregan, L. W., private, 2nd W. Regt.
Grestock, George, private, 3rd W. Regt.
Gregory, John, bullock driver, Transpt. Corps
Greenway, J. W., clerk, Com. Dept.
Greenway, C., private, Tar. Vol.
Gregory, Edward, sergeant, Tar. Mil. Settlers
Greenfield, Robert, sergeant, 2nd W. Regt.
Gregory, R., sergeant, Tar. Mil. Settlers
Griffith, J. J., private, Tar. Mil. Settlers
Grindell, James, private, Nap. Vol.
Griffith, William, private, 3rd W. Regt.
Gridall, T., labourer, Com. Dept.
Griffith, William J., sergeant, A.C.
Griffith, Chas. E., col.-sergeant, 1st W. Regt.
Grounds, William, corporal, 1st W. Regt.
Grogan, Charles, private, 1st W. Regt.
Grooves, Jas., bullock driver, Transpt. Corps
Groves, George, private, Tar. Mil.
Grubb, —, labourer, Com. Dept.
Gudgeon, Walter Ed., sub-inspector, A.C.
Gundry, W. J., sub-inspector, A.C.
Gunter, Frederick, private, 1st W. Regt.
Gubbins, William, private, 2nd W. Regt.
Guthies, Wm. J., constable, A.C.
Guthie, William, private, Patea Rifles
Gurney, E. W., private, Auck. Mil.
Guirk, Patrick, corporal, Tar. B. Ran.
Gwinneth, Wm. H., private, 2nd W. Regt.
Gwynneth, John, captain, B. of P. Vol.
Gwinney, Michael, private, 1st W. Regt.
Gwan, Robert, private, 2nd W. Regt.

HAGUE, JOHN, private, Nap. Mil.
Halbert, C. J., private, Nap. Mil.
Haldane, Richard, private, 4th W. Regt.
Hannay, John, private, Forest Ran.
Hardy, Adolphus F., private, Forest Ran.
Harper, George, private, 2nd W. Regt.
Haultain, T. M., colonel, 2nd W. Regt.
Hawes, Robt. N., corporal, Tar. Mil. Settlers
Hair, Robert, cornet, Wan. Y. Cav.
Hallett, Charles, constable, A. C.

Handley, John, sergeant, Kai Iwi Cav.
Handley, Thomas, trooper, Wan. Y. Cav.
Handley, William, sergeant, Wan. Mil.
Hare, George, constable, A. C.
Haselden, F. H., lance-corporal, 1st W. Regt.
Hawbel, John, private, 1st W. Regt.
Hanson, Andrew, private, 1st W. Regt.
Hare, Henry, private, 1st W. Regt.
Hardwick, George, private, 1st W. Regt.
Hawarth, Edward, corporal, 1st W. Regt.
Hannan, Isaac, corporal, 1st W. Regt.
Hadden, John, private, Com. Trans. Corps.
Hawthorn, Thomas, private, 1st W. Regt.
Hayes, Thomas, private, 1st W. Regt.
Hannon, William, private, 1st W. Regt.
Haldane, Thomas, private, 1st W. Regt.
Harkins, James, private, 2nd W. Regt.
Harfield, John, corporal, Forest Ran.
Hayden, John, constable, A.C.
Hayes, Thomas, constable, A.C.
Hargrave, James, private, Wan. Mil.
Harrod, W. D., private, Tar. Mil. Settlers
Hayan, Patrick, private, Wel. Rifles
Haggard, W. R., private, 1st W. Regt.
Halse, William, private, Tar. Vol.
Hawes, R. S., private, Nap. Mil.
Halloran, Richard, constable, A.C.
Hanson, Carl, constable, A.C.
Hawkins, David, private, Tar. Vol.
Hamblyn, James, private, Tar. Vol.
Haigh, G. B., private, Tar. Vol.
Harper, Robert, trooper, Col. D. Force.
Hallett, Henry, corporal, 2nd W. Regt.
Hawthorne, James, private, P. B. Mil.
Hart, Patrick, constable, A. C.
Haslett, William, private, 1st W. Regt.
Hartwell, Michael, private, Transpt. Corps
Hastings, Henry C. H., lieutenant, Well. Rifles
Hawke, Joseph, trooper, Tar. Cav. Vol.
Hamblyn, Charles, private, Tar. Rifles
Hamlin, F. E., interpreter, Col. Forces
Harkness, Thomas, private, O. Rifles
Hart, George, private, Auck. Mil.
Hawke, Joseph, private, Tar. Mil.
Hanham, James, private, 1st W. Rifles
Hany, Thomas, sergeant, 3rd W. Regt.
Halifax, Francis, sergeant, 3rd W. Regt.
Hart, Thomas, corporal, 3rd W. Regt.
Haskill, Herbert, corporal, 3rd W. Regt.
Hain, John, private, 3rd W. Regt.
Hames, George, private, 3rd W. Regt.
Hampton, Samuel, private, 3rd W. Regt.
Hamley, Patrick, private, 3rd W. Regt.
Hayes, Robert, private, 3rd W. Regt.
Hanson, Gordon, private, 3rd W. Regt.
Harding, Charles, private, 3rd W. Regt.
Hayes, William, private, 3rd W. Regt.
Halliday, David, private, 3rd W. Regt.
Halifax, Thomas, private, 3rd W. Regt.
Hannon, Joseph, private, 3rd W. Regt.
Harvey, John, private, 3rd W. Regt.
Harvey, Nathan, private, 3rd W. Regt.
Haslem, John, private, 3rd W. Regt.
Hampton, Jn., bullock driver, Transpt. Corps

Hancock, Jn., bullock driver, Transpt. Corps
Hansom, C., bullock driver, Transpt. Corps
Hayes, John, bullock driver, Transpt. Corps
Haddock, T., bullock driver, Transpt. Corps
Hagerty, M., bullock driver, Transpt. Corps
Hayes, Henry, bullock driver, Transpt. Corps
Harvey, Jas., bullock driver, Transpt . Corps
Harvey, John, bullock driver, Transpt. Corps
Hamblyn, C., bullock driver, Transpt. Corps
Hacket, J., clerk, Com. Dept.
Hayward, Henry, clerk, Com. Dept.
Hayward, John, issuer, Com. Dept.
Hawkes, George, baker, Com. Dept.
Hawcroft, George, labourer, Com. Dept.
Hart, William, boatman, Com. Dept.
Hazelgrove, J., boatman, Com. Dept.
Hassell, George, private, 2nd W. Regt.
Halpert, John, private, Tar. Mil. Settlers
Hart, Theodore, private, Tar. Mil. Settlers
Hardinge, H. D. C., private, Wan. Rifles
Hayward, George, private, Patea Mil.
Harding, Chas , constable, A. C.
Harington, Philip, lieut.-col. 1st W. Regt.
Hamlin, H. M., interpreter, Col. Forces
Hamon, jun., Joseph, private, Napier Mil.
Harvey, John, private, Napier Mil.
Hardy, John T., private, Patea Rifles
Harper, Ralph, private, Tar. Vol.
Hamlin, Ebenezer, col.-sergt., 3rd W. Regt.
Hall, A. C., sergt.-major, Wan. Y. Cav.
Hall, J. C., corporal, Tar. Vol.
Hall, Charles, artificer, Com. Dept.
Hall, John, constable, A.C.
Hall, H. T., private, Tar. Vol.
Hammond, Edwin, private, Tar. Vol.
Hammond, J. E., private, 1st W. Regt.
Hammond, John, private, Pov. B. Vol.
Hammond, James, private, 3rd W. Regt.
Hammond, Thos. C., Tar. Mil. Settlers
Hay, William, trooper, Tar. Cav. Vol.
Hay, W. M., ensign, Forest Ran.
Hay, J. B., lieutenant, 3rd W. Regt.
Hay, Charles, private, 1st W. Regt.
Hay, Henry, private, 3rd W. Regt
Harris, Benjamin, lieutenant, O. Cav. Vol.
Harris, J. D., colour-sergeant, 3rd W. Regt.
Harris, Thomas, constable, A.C.
Harris, sen., Robert, private, 1st W. Regt.
Harris, jun., Robert, private, 1st W. Regt.
Harris, Wm. Henry, corporal, Patea Rifles
Harris, D. M., private, Wel. Rifles
Harris, Corbyn, private, Tar. Rifles
Harris, William, private, 3rd W. Regt.
Harris, John, private, 3rd W. Regt.
Harris, R., bullock driver, Transpt. Corps
Harris, George, labourer, Transpt. Corps
Harrison, H. S., captain, Auck. Vol.
Harrison, H. F., constable, A.C.
Harrison, H. B. R., lieutenant, 2nd W. Regt.
Harrison, George, private, 1st W. Regt.
Harrison, William H., private, 2nd W. Regt.
Harrison, John, private 1st W. Regt.
Harrison, Job, sergeant, Tar. Mil.
Harrison, W., bullock driver, Transpt. Corps

Harrison, A., bullock driver, Transpt. Corps
Harrison, Alfred V., private, Nap. Mil.
Hamilton, J. B., private, 2nd W. Regt.
Hamilton, J. D., trooper, Nap. Cav.
Hamilton, J. A., corporal, 1st W. Regt.
Hamilton, James, private, 1st W. Regt.
Hamilton, Samuel H., sergeant, Auck. Mil.
Hamilton, James S., private, Auck. Mil.
Hamilton, Dupre A., trooper, Col. D. Force
Hamilton, W., boatman, Transpt. Corps
Hammerton, R. E., lieutenant, Tar. Vol.
Hammerton, T. E., bugler, Tar. Cav. Vol.
Hammerton, G. D., bugler, Tar. Vol.
Heaphy, Chas., lieutenant, Auck. Vol.
Hempton, Thos., private, Tar. Mil.
Hendry, James R., private, Mil. Vol.
Hendry, C. F. H., private, Forest Ran.
Hewitt, William, corporal, Auck. Mil.
Henwood, Samuel, artificer, Com. Dept.
Herford, W. V., brevet major, 3rd W. Regt.
Healey, Peter, private, 1st W. Regt.
Hefferman, Cornelius, private, 1st W . Regt.
Hennessey, William, private, 1st W. Regt.
Heisfield, W. G., private, 1st W. Regt.
Hewitt, William, private, 1st W. Regt.
Hendry, James Thos., private, Auck. Vol.
Heslop, George, private, Napier Mil.
Heslop, John, coporal, Wan. Vol.
Heslop, William, private, Napier Mil.
Henry, Robert, private, Wairoa Vol.
Hennessay, Patrick, private, 1st W. Regt.
Hector, Geo. N., volunteer, Field Force
Herbert, Patrick, corporal, 1st W. Regt.
Herbert, George, corporal, 1st W. Regt.
Hemsworth, Wm. Henry, Constable, A.C.
Heaton, James, sergeant, 3rd W. Regt.
Heaton, James, corporal, 3rd W. Regt.
Herbert, Harry, private, 3rd W. Regt.
Henry, Thomas, private, 3rd W. Regt.
Henley, John, private, 3rd W. Regt.
Hewitt, Vincent, bullock driver, Tran. Corps
Hellier, John, bullock driver, Tran Corps.
Henshaw, J., clerk, Com. Dept.
Hertford, C., boatman, Com. Tran. Corps
Hearfield, W. G., butcher, Com. Tran. Corps
Hedderwick, John, private, Tar. Mil. Settlers
Hegarty, James, private, 1st W. Regt.
Herbert, Michael, private, 1st W. Regt.
Healey, Thos., trooper, Col. D. Force
Hecker, Henry Chas., sergeant, Napier Mil.
Hennessey, James, private, Hawke's Bay Vol.
Henry, Joseph, assist. surgeon, 1st W. Regt.
Henry, Patrick, sergeant, Tar. Mil.
Hearle, Edward, constable, A.C.
Herrick, Jasper L., lieut.-col., N.Z. Mil.
Hesketh, James, constable, A,C.
Heard, William, sergeant, 1st W. Regt.
Hewlett, W. H., private, Col. D. Force
Heaney, Alex., sergt.-major, A.C.
Henderson, James, private, 1st W. Regt.
Henderson, Joseph, constable, A.C.
Henderson, James, private, 1st W. Regt.
Henderson, William, private, Wairoa Vol.
Higham, George, private, 3rd W. Regt.

Hickey, John, private, 3rd W. Regt.
Hindon. Wm., bullock driver, Transpt. Corps
Hickey, Lawrence, bullock driver, Trans. Corps
Higgins, David, private, Tar. Mil. Settlers
Higginson, William, private, 2nd W. Regt.
Hickman, Jeremiah, private, Well. Rifles
Hillier, William, private, Tar. Mil.
Hinds, J. W., corporal, Napier Vol.
Hirst, James, sergeant, Tar. Vol.
Hiscox, Andrew, sergeant, Tar. Mil. Settlers
Hickey, Patrick, constable, A.C.
Hicks, Richard, trooper, Kai Iwi Cav.
Hindley, James, trooper, Wan. Cav.
Hind, G. R., sergeant, Auck. Mil.
Hindel, Chas., private, 1st W. Regt.
Hislett, William, private, Col. D. Force
Hinde, T. G., private, 1st W. Regt.
Hinds, John, private, 1st W. Regt.
Hinckman, George, private, 2nd W. Regt.
Hilbert, James, private, 2nd W. Regt.
Hinton, John, constable, A. C.
Hinde, Thos., private, Tar. Vol.
Higgins, James, bugler, Patea Rifles
Hirst, Israel, sergeant, Auck. Mil.
Hirtzel, C. A. M., lieutenant, N. Z. Mil.
Hickman, Thos., constable, A.C.
Hine, Chas. E., private, 2nd W. Regt.
Hill, E. Arnold, trooper, Col. D. Force
Hill, Matthew, private, Tar. B. Rangers
Hill, Rowland, private, Nap. Mil.
Hill, Matthew, trooper, Nap. Cav.
Hill, Roger, ensign, Auck. Mil.
Hill, H. W., lieutenant, F. Rangers
Hill, W. J., private, Auck. Vol.
Hill, George, private, F. Rangers
Hills, F. J., major, 2nd W. Regt.
Hills, Charles, private, 1st W. Regt.
Hill, John, private, Tar. Mil. Settlers
Hodge, William, corporal, Patea Vol.
Hogden, John, private, M. Vol.
Hogarth, Hugh, private, Auck. Vol.
Holland, J L., private, Auck. Vol.
Holmes, Alfred, private, 1st W. Regt.
Hope, E. L., private, 2nd W. Regt.
Hoskin, Richard, private, Tar. Vol.
Howard, William, private, Nap. Vol.
Howell, Simson, private, Tar. Vol.
Howe, John, trooper, Wan. Cav.
Horne, Copley, private, Nap. Cont.
Hobin, W., ensign, Auck. Mil.
Horne, George, lieutenant, 2nd W. Regt.
Howe, W. H. D., lieutenant, 2nd W. Regt.
Hodge, Robert, artificer, Com. Dept.
Hodge, Andrew, artificer, Com. Dept.
Horton, Isaac, private, Transpt. Corps
Hobbs, John, private, 1st W. Regt.
Hoff, John, private, 1st W. Regt.
Howard, Edward, private, 1st W. Regt.
Holmes, Anthony, private, 2nd W. Regt.
Holmes, C. W., private, 2nd W. Regt.
Holland, George, private, 2nd W. Regt.
Hodges, Henry, private, 2nd W. Regt.
Howe, Robert, private, 2nd W. Regt.

Holdsworthy, William, private, 2nd W. Regt.
Hope, Edwin, private, 2nd W. Regt.
Holt, James, captain, 2nd W. Regt.
Hooker, Nathaniel, corporal, Tar. Vol.
Hoskin, A. J., private, Tar. Vol.
Hoskins, Josiah, private, Tar. Vol.
Holmes, Henry A., private, Well. Rifles
Holden, Thomas, sergeant, Forest Rangers
Hoby, George, private, Tar. Vol.
Hoby, jun., George, private, Tar. Vol.
Holt, Francis, private, 1st W. Regt.
Howell, Henry, private, 1st W. Regt.
Hollister, Robert, trooper, Col. D. Force
Hodges, F. O. D., sergeant, H. B. Vol.
Hodson, James, sergeant, 3rd W. Regt.
Hoolaghon, John, private, 3rd W. Regt.
Howes, James, private, 3rd W. Regt.
Howes, Robert, private, 3rd W. Regt.
Holland, John, private, 3rd W. Regt.
Hogan, John, private, 3rd W. Regt.
Hodgson, Henry, private, 3rd W. Regt.
Hodgson, James, private, 3rd W. Regt.
Howell, Henry, private, 3rd W. Regt.
Howard, Charles, private, 3rd W. Regt.
Howiss, Henry, private, 3rd W. Regt.
House, Robert, private, 3rd W. Regt.
Hogan, Charles, private, 3rd W. Regt.
Holland, George, private, 3rd W. Regt.
Howlder, John, bullock driver, Trans. Corps
Houghton, T., issuer, Com. Dept.
Horne, T., butcher, Com. Dept.
Hodgin, James, butcher, Com. Dept.
Horne, T., labourer, Com. Dept.
Hoby, Oliver C., private, Tar. Vol.
Holloway, Henry, sergeant, Tar. Mil. Settlers
Honeyfield, J. C., private, Tar. Mil. Settlers
Hooper, Clarence, surgeon, N.Z. Mil.
Hopcroft, James, ensign, 1st W. Regt.
Hollis, Edwin, sergeant, Tar. Vol.
Horsford, Samuel, sergeant-major, A.C.
Huntley, R. H., private, Auck. Mil.
Hussey, J. E. W., sergt.-major, Wan. Y. Cav.
Hursthouse, C. Wilson, lieutenant, Tar. Mil.
Hutton, Howard, Captain, Auck. Cav. Vol.
Hunter, Andrew, trooper, Kai Iwi Cav.
Hunter, Moore, trooper, Kai Iwi Cav.
Hurley, Daniel, corporal, Wan. Cav.
Hurley, William, trooper, Wan. Cav.
Huddy, W. C., trooper, Auck. Mil.
Hunter, H., lieut., 1st W. Regt.
Hutton, John, corporal, 1st W. Regt.
Hudd, James, private, 1st W. Regt.
Hutton, John, private, 1st W. Regt.
Hudson, Owen, private, 2nd W. Regt.
Huntley, Walter, private, 1st W. Regt.
Hunt, Philip, private, 2nd W. Regt.
Hull, Thomas, private, 2nd W. Regt.
Hulme, Andrew, private, 2nd W. Regt.
Hudson, George, private, 3rd W. Regt.
Hutton, John, private, 3rd W. Regt.
Huston, Thos., bullock driver, Transpt. Corps
Hunt, Ed., bullock driver, Transpt. Corps
Hunt, W. T., supintendent of stores, ——
Hutson, John, clerk, Com. Dept.

Hurdle, James, issuer, Com. Dept.
Hurle, John, labourer, Com. Dept.
Hutton, Joseph, labourer, Com Dept.
Hurton, John, constable, A. C.
Hunter, James, private, Tar. Mil. Settlers
Hursthouse, F., private, Tar. B. Rangers
Hutchings, E., bugler, Col. D. Force
Hunt, Thomas G., corporal, Auck. Mil.
Hurley, John, trooper, Wan. Cav.
Hunter, B. A., corporal, 1st W. Regt.
Hussey, W., captain, Tar. Mil. Settlers
Huckell, Jn., lance-corporal, Tar. Mil. Settlers
Hunt, Henry, private, Tar. Vol.
Hurry, John, R., lance-corporal, Col. D. Force
Hunter, Samuel, private, 3rd W. Regt.
Hurford, William, private, Tar. Vol.
Hunter, Frederick A., private, Auck. Vol.
Humphries, Edward, corporal, Tar. Vol.
Humphries, William, corporal, Tar. Vol.
Humphries, Thomas, ensign, Tar. Vol.
Humphreys, Charles, corporal, Auck. Vol.
Humphreys, William, private, 3rd W. Regt.
Hutchison, David, sub-inspector, A C.
Hutchison, C. J., lieutenant, Tar. Mil. Set.
Hutchison, Alfred, sergeant, Col. D. Force
Hughes, James, trooper, Wan. Y. Cav.
Hughes, George, private, 1st W. Regt.
Hughes, David, sergeant, 1st W. Regt.
Hughes, Thomas, private, 2nd W. Regt.
Hughes, George, private, 3rd W. Regt.
Hughes, W. F., constable, A. C.
Hynes, William, private, 3rd W. Regt.
Hynes, Joseph, constable, A. C.
Hyde, Edward, constable, A. C.
Hyde, Thomas, private, Wan. Vol.

IBBETSON, WILLIAM, private, 1st W. Regt.
Ibbetson, H. J., clerk, Com. Dept.
Ibbetson, Thomas, private, Tar. Vol.
Inglis, Robert, sergeant, 1st W. Regt.
Inglis, James, corporal, M. V.
Inch, Paul, private, Tar. Vol.
Inch, Thomas, private, Tar. Vol.
Ingram, H. S., private, Nap. Mil.
Ingwerson, Marcus, constable, A. C.
Ingram, C. E., constable, A. C.
Irwin, O. O., ensign, 4th W. Regt.
Irwin, Daniel, sergeant, 1st W. Regt.
Irvine, James, corporal, M. V.
Irvine, Daniel, private, 1st W. Regt.
Isaacson, Charles, corporal, Auck. Mil.
Isgard, H. E., constable, A. C.
Isherwood, J. C. R., ensign, Patea Vol.
Ives, William private, 3rd W. Regt.
Iverson, P., boatman, Transpt. Corps.

JACK, JAMES, private, Tar. Mil. Settlers
Jackson, William, major, Forest Ran.
Jackson, J. H., private, Auck. Engineers
Jackson, Charles, private, 3rd W. Regt.
Jackson, Fred., private, 2nd W. Regt.
Jackson, E. H., private, 3st W. Regt.
Jackson, H. B., constable, A. C.
James, George, private, 1st W. Regt.

James, Peter, private, 2nd W. Regt.
James, Alfred, corporal, 3rd W. Regt.
James, J., boatman, Transpt. Corps
James, Robert, labourer, Com. Dept.
Jamieson, James, constable, A. C.
Jamieson, John C., issuer, Com. Dept.
Jamieson, J., bullock driver, Transpt. Corps
Jamieson, J., bullock driver, Transpt. Corps
Jamieson, William, private, 2nd W. Regt.
Jarvis, George, private, 2nd W. Regt.
Jacks, William, private, 3rd W. Regt.
Jarman, Sydney, private, Tar. Mil. Settlers
Jane, J. H., private, 1st W. Regt.
Jeffs, C. K., ensign, 1st W. Regt.
Jennings, James, private, Forest Ran.
Jenkins, W., sergeant, Wairoa Rifles
Jervois, John, corporal, 1st W. Regt.
Jennings, James, private, 2nd W. Regt.
Jess, William, private, 3rd W. Regt.
Jennings, Sergt. A., issuer, Com. Dept.
Jeffares, Isaac, private, Nap. Rifles
Jeffares, Richard, sergeant, Clive Mil.
Jeffs, Henry, private, 1st W. Regt.
Jefferies, Walter, constable, A. C.
Jenkinson, Samuel, corporal, Wairoa Vol.
Jefferies, A fred, private, Hawke's B. Vol.
Jonas, M. J., sergeant, Tar. Vol.
Jordan, Israel, private, Tar. Vol.
Joyce, W. G., private, M. Vol.
Jordan, R. C., private, Auck. Eng.
Joyce, William, private, 1st W. Regt.
Joyce, William, corporal, 3rd W. Regt.
Joyce, James, private, 3rd W. Regt.
Joiner, Henry, private, 3rd W. Regt.
Jowkers, Henry, private, 3rd W. Regt.
John, William, butcher, Com. Dept.
Jordan, Robert, constable, A. C.
Jordan, Thomas Edward, constable, A. C.
Joll, Samuel, private, Tar. Vol.
Johns, William, corporal, Forest Ran.
Jordan, William, private, 1st W. Regt.
Johnstone, James, private, Nap. Mil.
Johnstone, Peter, private, Nap. Mil.
Johnstone, John, private, Nap. Mil.
Johnstone, William, ensign, Well. Vol.
Johnstone, Thomas, private, Nap. Mil.
Johnstone, James, private, M. Vol.
Johnstone, Charles, private, 1st W. Regt.
Johnstone, George, trooper, Kai Iwi Cav.
Johnstone, James, private, Wairoa R.
Johnstone, J. F., sergeant, 1st W. Regt.
Johnstone, Henry, private, 1st W. Regt.
Johnstone, Joseph, private, 2nd W. Regt.
Johnstone, C. J., private, 3rd W. Regt.
Johnstone, Wm, bullock driver, Tr. Corps
Johnstone, John, bullock driver, Tr. Corps
Johnstone, Cosslett, sergeant, Tar. Mil. Set.
Johnstone, Henry, private, 3rd W. Regt.
Johnson, W., ensign, Tar. Cav. Vol.
Johnson, Alexander, constable, A. C.
Johnson, George, private, 1st W. Regt.
Johnson, Samuel, private, 2nd W. Regt.
Johnson, Peter, private, 3rd W. Regt.
Johnson, Edward, private, 3rd W. Regt.

Johnsone, R. B., trooper, Col. D. Force
Johnson, Alexander, constable, A. C.
Johnson, Jas. W., private, Pov. Bay Vol.
Johnson, Thomas, private, Wan. Bush Ran.
Johnson, Edward, private, Wan. Rifles
Johnson, William, private, Wan. Rifles
Jones, M. J., sergeant, Tar. Vol.
Jones, Timothy, private, Tar. Vol.
Jones, John, corporal, Kai-Iwi Vol.
Jones, William, private, 1st W. Regt.
Jones, Thomas, private, 1st W. Regt.
Jones, John, private, 1st W. Regt.
Jones, sen., Thomas, private, 3rd W. Regt.
Jones, jun., Thomas, private, 3rd W. Regt.
Jones, William, private, 3rd W. Regt.
Jones, George, private, 3rd W. Regt.
Jones, Evans, private, 3rd W. Regt.
Jones, Thos., bullock-driver, Transpt. Corps
Jones, H. J., clerk, Com. Dep.
Jones, William, labourer, Com. Dep.
Jones, Henry Ireson, capt., Wan. Vol.
Jones, Edward, bugler, Patea Rifles
Jones, Lloyd, private, Wan. Mil.
Jones, Richard, private, Tar. Mil. Settlers
Jones, Frederick, 1st W. Regt.
Jones, John P., lieut.-colonel, 2nd W. Regt.
Julian, Henry, bullock-driver, Transpt. Corps
Jury, John, bullock-driver, Transpt. Corps
Jury, Henry, private, Tar. Mil Settlers
Judd, Henry, lance-corporal, Tar. Vol.
Jupp, George, sergeant, Tar. Vol.

KATES, GEORGE, private, 2nd W. Regt.
Keefe, Nathan, sergeant, 1st W. Regt.
Kelcher, Jeremiah, private, Wn. Vol.
Kelsey, John, private, 2nd W. Regt.
Kempthorne, Arthur, trooper, P. B. Vol.
Kenah, J. W., private, Tar. Vol.
Kenrich, Rich., sergeant-major, Col. D. Force
Kershaw, Philip, constable, A. C.
Kells, G., captain, Auck. Mil.
Kenny, John, private, 1st W. Regt.
Kerr, James, private, 1st W. Regt.
Keefe, Matthew, private, 1st W. Regt.
Keelan, Thomas, private, 1st W. Regt.
Keeley, Thomas, corporal, 2nd W. Regt.
Keating, James, private, 2nd W. Regt.
Kemen, William, private, 2nd W. Regt.
Kerr, Charles, private, 2nd W. Regt.
Keenan, John, private, 2nd W. Regt.
Keele, Theodore, private, 3rd W. Regt.
Kerr, William, private, 3rd W. Regt.
Kemmisson, William, private, 3rd W. Regt.
Keeley, Patrick, private, 3rd W. Regt.
Keefe, James, private, 3rd W. Regt.
Kells, J. F., clerk, Com. Dept.
Kensington, Sergeant W. C., storekeeper, Com. Dept.
Kelton, Sergeant-issuer, Com. Dept.
Keeling, Robert N., private, Tar. Vol.
Kemp, Henry, private, Tar. Vol.
Kerr, Thomas, private, Wan. Rifles
Kearney, Henry R., sergeant, Patea Rifles
Kernaghan, James, constable, A. C.

Kells, William, ensign, Wan. Vol.
Keene, Laurence, constable, A. C.
Kelsall, William, constable, A. C.
Kells, Thomas, bugler, 1st W. Regt.
Kent, Isaac, corporal, Hawke's B. Vol.
Keelan, Thomas, private, Nap. Mil.
Kenrick, O. L., sergeant, Col. D. Force
Kegs, George, constable, A. C.
Keen, Constantine, private, Tar. Mil. Settlers
Keayon, John, private, Tar. Mil. Settlers
Keeyam, James, private, Tar. Mil. Settlers
Kemp, John, trooper, Col. D. Force
Kerr, Thomas, private, 1st W. Regt.
Keir, Frederick, sergeant, Wan. Rifles
Kenny, Martin, sergeant, Tar. Mil. Settlers
Kennedy, Alexander, captain, Nap. Vol.
Kennedy, Alexander, private, 1st W. Regt.
Kennedy, Denis, sergeant, 1st W. Regt.
Kennedy, James, private, 1st W. Regt.
Kennedy, Thomas, private, 3rd W. Regt.
Kennedy, Thomas, private, 1st W. Regt.
Kennedy, Alexander, constable, A. C.
Kelly, P. J. sergeant, 1st W. Regt.
Kelly, Peter, private, 1st W. Regt.
Kelly, William, private, 2nd W. Regt.
Kelly, James, corporal, 3rd W. Regt.
Kelly, James, private, 3rd W. Regt.
Kelly, John, private, 3rd W. Regt.
Kelly, ——, butcher, Com. Dept.
Kelly, James, baker, Com. Dept.
Kelly, Thomas, private, A. C.
Kelly, John, lieutenant, Tar. Mil. Settlers
Kelly, Michael, sergeant, Tar. Mil. Settlers
Kelly, Thomas, private, Tar. Mil. Settlers
Kelly, William, private, Auck. Mil.
Kelly, Richard, private, Tar. Mil. Settlers
Kirk, Robert, trooper, Kai-Iwi Vol.
Kirkpatrick, Duncan, private, Napier Vol.
Kirwin, W. T., private, 1st W. Regt.
Kiernan, F. W., sergeant, Auck. Mil.
Kirwin, Patrick, private, 1st W. Regt.
Killen, Henry, private, 1st W. Regt.
Kirke, A. W., private, 1st W. Regt.
Kingsley, Joseph, private, 1st W. Regt.
Kirwin, Benjamin, private, 1st W. Regt.
Kirwin, William, private, 2nd W. Regt.
Kirkland, James, private, 3rd W. Regt.
Kirke, Thomas, private, 3rd W. Regt.
Kidd, William, private, 3rd W. Regt.
Kill, T., butcher, Com. Dept.
Kinsby, Joseph, private, 1st W. Regt.
Kinross, John G., private, Napier Mil.
Kindon, Courtney M., lieut., Tar. Mil.
Kirkpatrick, Robt., private, Napier Mil.
Kinniburgh, D. F., private, Well. Rifles
Kingdon, Adolphus, private, Tar. Vol.
Kingdon, Augustus, private, Tar. Vol.
King, Robert, corporal, 1st W. Regt.
King, John, private, 1st W. Regt.
King, William, private, Wan. Rifles.
King, Richard, private, 1st W. Regt.
King, William, private, 1st W. Regt.
King, Edward, private, 1st W. Regt.
King, Richard, private, 1st W. Regt.

King, Thomas, private, 3rd W. Regt.
King, Thomas, private, Tar. Vol.
King, Robert J., constable, A. C.
King, James, corporal, Well. Rifles.
King, Thomas, constable, A. C.
King, William, private, 1st W. Regt.
King, Edward W., private, 2nd W. Regt.
Klauss, August, private, 1st W. Regt.
Knight, Henry, corporal, 2nd W. Regt.
Knaggs, George, private, 2nd W. Regt.
Knapp, Samuel, private, 2nd W. Regt.
Knuckey, Samuel, bullock driver, Tran. Corps
Knuckey, Oliver, bullock d iver, Tran. Corps
Knox, James, issuer, Com. Dept.
Knight, James, private, Tar. Mil. Settlers
Koch, August, col.-sergeant, Napier Vol.
Krimble, William, private, 3rd W. Regt.
Kraeft, Henry, private, Napier Mil.

LAMBERT, C., lieut.-colouel, N. Z. Mil.
Lamont, J. H., corporal, Nap. Mil.
Lane, James, constable, A. C.
Langley, John, private, Nap. Mil.
Langman, Richard, private, Tar. Mil.
Large, J. S., corporal, Nap. Mil.
Lander, Charles, private, Tar. Vol.
Laurence, B. C., sergeant, Tar. Vol.
Lawson, J. R., ensign, Tar. Vol.
Lake, Thomas, private, Poverty Bay Mil.
Laccorrence, E., ensign, 1st W. Regt.
Lammie, George, private, 1st W. Regt.
Lawton, Thomas, private, 1st W. Regt.
Langhorne, Samuel, private, 1st W. Regt.
Latimer, Frederick, private, 1st W. Regt.
Lake, Francis, private, 1st W. Regt.
Lacey, Edward, private, 1st W. Regt.
Lamb, Frederick, private, 1st W. Regt.
Lambert, Edward, private, 2nd W. Regt.
Langshaw, Frederick, private, 2nd W. Regt.
Lang, Hugh, private, 2nd W. Regt.
Lane, John, private, 2nd W. Regt.
Lake, Warwick, private, 2nd W. Regt.
Law, Thomas, private, 3rd W. Regt.
Lamont, John, private, 3rd W. Regt.
Lake, Charles, private, 3rd W. Regt.
Lang, Hugh, private, 3rd W. Regt.
Lamb, Edward, private, 3rd W. Regt.
Lawrence, James, private, 3rd W. Regt.
Lane, George, private, 3rd W. Regt.
Langman, T., bullock-driver, Transpt. Corps
Lambert, Edward, clerk, Com. Dept.
Langdon, F., sergeant, issuer, Com. Dept.
Launcy, Charles, issuer, Com. Dept.
Lawe, W. F., baker, Com. Dept.
Lane, William, baker, Com. Dept.
Ladley, Albert, private, Tar. Mil. Settlers
Laird, James, sergeant, Tar. Mil. Settlers
Lakin, John, private, 1st W. Regt.
Lander, John, corporal, Tar. Vol.
Langdale, Frederick, trooper, Wan. Y. Cav.
Laing, Edward B., private, Tar. Vol.
Lane, James, private, 2nd W. Regt.
Lanauze, H. W. C., constable, A. C.
Lawson, John, sergeant, Napier Vol.

Lacey, Garrett, constable, A.C.
Ladley, Albert, private, Napier Vol.
Langfred, James, constable, A.C.
LaLerre, C. W. R., captain, Col. D. Force
Lawson, Ernest, ensign, 1st W. Regt.
Lamb, James, corporal, 3rd W. Regt.
Lander, Richard, private, Tar. Mil.
Langridge, Matthew, constable, A.C.
Largo, John, lieutenant, Native Com.
Larrett, Philip, corporal, A.C.
Land, J., constable, A.C.
Laurence, James F., private, Tar. Mil.
Lander, George, private, Tar. Mil.
Lanauze, George, constable, A.C.
Leslie, David, private, Napier Mil.
Le Quesne, Joseph, sergeant, Nap. Mil.
Levy, L. L., trooper, Wan. Cav.
Leary, Robt., private, 1st W. Regt.
Leary, Samuel, private, 1st W. Regt.
Lewis, John, private, 1st W. Regt.
Lent, Wm., private, 1st W. Regt.
Lee, Chas., private, 1st W. Regt.
Lees, William, private, 1st W. Regt.
Lempriere, F.C., sergeant, 2nd W. Regt.
Lee, Chas., artificer, Com. Dept.
Leon, Richard, artificer, Com. Dept.
Leo, Wm., private, 3rd W. Regt.
Lewis, John, private, 3rd W. Regt.
Lewis, Matthew, private, 3rd W. Regt.
Lee, John, private, 3rd W. Regt.
Leslie, John, private, 3rd W. Regt.
Leslie, Thomas, private, 3rd W. Regt.
Lee, William, private, 3rd W. Regt.
Lewis, Henry, private, 3rd W. Regt.
Leitze, George, bullock-driver, Transpt. Corps
Lempriere, T. R., clerk, Com. Dept.
Lethbridge, Richard, private, Tar. Mil.
Lea, Edwin, private, 1st W. Regt.
Lemon, George, bugler, 1st W. Regt.
Leslie, A. J., assist. surgeon, A.C.
Leatham, R. B., captain, Well. Cav.
Lenord, John, trooper, Wan. Y. Cav.
Leslie, Jas. L. C., private, Wan. Mil.
Lewis, E. S., private, 4th W. Regt.
LeMasurier, Philip, constable, A. C.
Lewis, John, private, 1st W. Regt.
Lethbridge, Charles, private, Tar. Vol.
Leslie, Charles, private, Well. Rifles
Lethbridge, Thomas, private, Tar. Mil.
Leonard, Wm. Henry, private, Patea Rifles
Leinara, W. H., private, Patea Rifles
Lingard, William, trooper, Wan. Y. Cav.
Litchfield, Charles, sergt.-major, Bay P. Cav.
Littlewood, William, trooper, Kai Iwi Cav.
Livingstone, Saml., private, 1st W. Regt.
Ling, Frank, corporal, 1st W. Regt.
Littlewood, Thomas, private, 1st W. Regt.
Little, George, private, 2nd W. Regt.
Linford, William, private, 2nd W. Regt.
Lingbia, Levin, sergeant, 3rd W. Regt.
Lindsay, William, baker, Com. Dept.
Liebig, Carl, corporal, 2nd W. Regt.
Little, Henry J., private, Wan. Mil.
Liverton, John, private, Taita Mil.

Littledale, William, sergeant, Col. D. Force
Little, Thomas, corporal, Col. D. Force
Linton, William, private, Well. Rifles
Lloyd, Frank, private, 1st W. Regt.
Lloyd, Thomas, corporal, Well. Rifles
Llewellyn, George, sergeant, 1st W. Regt
Lloyd, Henry, private, 1st W. Regt.
Lloyd, Isaac, private, 1st W. Regt.
Lloyd, James, private, 3rd W. Regt.
Llewellyn, Trevor, clerk, Com. Dept.
Locke, Samuel, in command of Natives
Lockie, G. S., quartermaster, Transpt. Corps
Lodder, William, engineer, s.s. Sturt
Long, Joseph, private, 1st W. Regt.
Lockett, E. C., sergt.-major, Wan. Y. Cav.
Lomax, H. A., lieutenant, Well. Mil.
Long, James, constable, A.C.
Lound, Chas., lance-corporal, A.C.
Lovell, George, sergeant, Auck. Mil.
Lomax, H. B., lieutenant, 1st W. Regt.
Lord, Samuel, private, 1st W. Regt.
Lovette, George, private, 1st W. Regt.
Lough, Henry, private, 1st W. Regt.
Logam, M. D., sergeant, 2nd W. Regt.
Lovett, Edward, private, 2nd W. Regt.
Locker, William, private, 2nd W. Regt.
Loveday, Lambert, sergeant, 3rd W. Regt.
Lock, John, private, 3rd W. Regt.
Loner, James, private, 3rd W. Regt.
Loombs, William, private, 3rd W. Regt.
Lockwood, Alfred, private, 3rd W. Regt.
Lock, Albert, private, 3rd W. Regt.
Lowes, Thomas, private, 3rd W. Regt.
Lockie, Geo. S., private, 3rd W. Regt.
Logan, Jas., bullock-driver, Transpt. Corps
Lowe, James, bullock-driver, Transpt. Corps
Loveridge, S., bullock-driver, Transpt. Corps
Lomery, T., boatman, Transpt. Corps
Longbottom, James, clerk, Com, Dept.
Long, Charles, labourer, Com. Dept.
Longbred, ——, labourer, Com. Dept.
Long, Joseph, private, Wan. Ran.
Louis, Edward, private, 1st W. Regt.
Long, Charles, private, 1st W. Regt.
Loveridge, Samuel, private, Tar Mil.
Lowes, William, private, Nap. Vol.
Lockwood, Thomas, private, 1st W. Regt.
Love, Robert, constable, A. C.
Long, Henry, sergeant, Forest Ran.
Lord, R. H., trooper, Nap. Mil.
Lockyer, Charles, private, Well. Rifles
Loxton, William, private, 2nd W. Regt.
Lupton, Isaac, private, Wairoa Vol.
Luff, Joseph, private, Nap. Mil.
Luke, William, private, Tar. Mil. Settlers.
Lush, D. H., major, M. Vol.
Lucas, Charles, private, 1st W. Regt.
Lutterill, Robert, private, 1st W. Regt.
Lundy, A., private, 1st W. Regt.
Luther, Moses, private, 3rd W. Regt.
Lydon, George, constable, A. C.
Lynch, T. D. L., private, Auck. Vol.
Lynch, Edward, private, 1st W. Regt.
Lynch, John, private, 2nd W. Regt.

Lynch, Peter, private, 2nd W. Regt.
Lynch, James, private, 2nd W. Regt.
Lynch, Christopher, private, 2nd W. Regt.
Lyon, W. C., lieut.-colonel, Auck. Mil.
Lyden, John, private, 1st W. Regt.
Lyall, Patrick, private, 1st W. Regt.
Lyons, Robt., private, 1st W. Regt.
Lyden, Christopher, private, 3rd W. Regt.
Lyford, Absalom, private, 3rd W. Regt.
Lyons, Patrick, private, 3rd W. Regt.
Lynas, Fred., private, Wan. Ran.
Lyttelton, E., private, Tar. Mil. Settlers

MADIGAN, PATRICK, private, For. Ran.
Mahoney, Daniel, private, 1st W. Regt.
Mair, W. Gilbert, major, Auck. Mil.
Manly, G. Kent, sergeant, M. Vol.
Mann, Richard, private, Auck. Vol.
Mann, Thomas, private, Auck. Vol.
Mainwaring, R. C., interpreter, Col. Force
Marks, Hannibal, bugler, Auck. Vol.
Marsh, H. T., corporal, Nap. Mil.
Master, J. S., sergeant, Auck. Cav.
Maxfield, Harry, private, Auck. Vol.
Mair, Gilbert, lieutenant, Auck. Vol.
Mangnus, Andrew, private, 1st W. Regt.
Manning, W. B., private, 1st W. Regt.
Mathieson, G. S., constable, A.C.
Malvern, Chas., sergant, Auck. Mil.
Malone, G. D., lieutenant, 2nd W. Regt.
Malton, George, private, 1st W. Regt.
May, John, private, 1st W. Regt.
May, Thomas, private, 1st W. Regt.
Magill, John, sergeant, 1st W. Regt.
Mann, George, private, 1st W. Regt.
Markham, John, private, 1st W. Regt.
Maller, Henry, private, 1st W. Regt.
Malibond, John, corporal, 2nd W. Regt.
Madigan, John, private, 2nd W. Regt.
Malone, William, private, 2nd W. Regt.
Maynes, George, private, 2nd W. Regt.
Mahoney, Patrick, private, 2nd W. Regt.
Mahoney, Simeon, private, 2nd W. Regt.
Makings, John, private, 2nd W. Regt.
Mackie, James, private, 2nd W. Regt.
Mansfield, Mark, private, 3rd W. Regt.
Mahon, Charles, private, 3rd W. Regt.
Mahon, Patrick, private, 3rd W. Regt.
Mander, William, private, 3rd W. Regt.
Major, Isaac, private, 3rd W. Regt.
Mayne, John, private, 3rd W. Regt.
Mallet, Richard, private, 3rd W. Regt.
Marks, Hugh, private, 3rd W. Regt.
Malone, W., bullock-driver, Transpt. Corps.
May, William, bullock driver, Transpt. Corps
Machad, Alx., bullock driver, Transp. Corps
Margron, J., baker, Com. Dept.
Madden, John, private, 1st W. Regt.
May, William, private, Nap. Mil.
Maskery, Stephen, constable, A.C.
Mace, F., captain, Tar. Cav.
Mace, Thomas W., private, Tar. Cav.
Mackie, George, private, Wan. Rangers
Mahoney, Stephen, private, Forest Rangers
Malcombe, Peter, private, H. B. Mil.

Massey John, private, Nap. Mil.
Maher, Patrick, constable, A.C.
Mair, Henry, captain, Opotiki Mil.
Malony, Christopher, sergeant, Guide
Mancy, R. D., trooper, Nap. Cav.
Maynard, H. L., private, 1st W. Regt.
Maycock, Richard, constable, A.C.
Mafers, Henry, private, Well. Rifles
Mayne, Henry, private, Tar. Mil. Settlers
Manley, John, trooper, Wan. Cav.
Marr, Alexander, private, Tar. Vol.
Mac, Owen, private, Well. Rifles
Maxwell, George, sergeant, Kai Iwi Cav.
Maxwell, James, private, 2nd W. Regt.
Maxwell, William, private, Tar. B. Rangers
Maction, Anthony, private, Waiuku Mil.
Maisey, William, private, Nap. Mil.
Mann, Daniel, private, Wan. Rangers
Mawe, W. F., private, H. B. Vol.
May, James M., private, Wan. Mil.
Mackay, James, trooper, Opotiki Cav.
Maslin, George F., private, C. Vol.
Mahoney, William, private, Tar. Mil.
Madden, Richard, private, 1st W. Regt.
Mackintosh, J. M. G., private, Tar. Mil. Set.
Mather, John, private, Tar. Mil. Settlers
Macbeth, Francis, private, 2nd W. Regt.
Macdonald, J. S., trooper, Wan. Y. Cav.
Macpherson, A., lieutenant, Auck. Mil.
Macpherson, James, captain, 4th W. Regt.
Macdonald, Angus A. K., private, Auck. Mil.
Mason, Geo. H., private, 1st W. Regt.
Mason, G. H., corporal, 1st W. Regt.
Mason, Francis, private, 1st W. Regt.
Mason, G. H., private, 1st W. Regt.
Mason, W. G., sergeant, A.C.
Mason, George, private, 1st W. Regt.
Mason, William, private, 1st W. Regt.
Matthews, Henry, private, 1st W. Reg.
Matthews, George, private, 3rd W. Regt.
Matthews, N., bullock-driver, Transpt. Corps
Matthews, A. C., constable, A.C.
Matthews, H. S., private, Tar. Vol.
Martin, John, private, Nap. Vol.
Martin, Bernard, private, 1st W. Regt.
Martin, Patrick, private, 1st W. Regt.
Martin, C., private, 1st W. Regt.
Martin, John, private, 1st W. Regt.
Martin, James, private, 3rd W. Regt.
Martin, Sergt. Denis, butcher, Com. Dept.
Martin, Peter, private, Tar. Vol.
Martin, W. P., private, Tar. Vol.
Martin, J. W., private, Forest Ran.
Marshall, W., constable, A.C.
Marshall, R. A., boatman, Transpt. Corps
Marshall, James, private, Petane Mil.
Marshall, John, private, Nap. Mil.
Marshall, R. W., private, Nap. Mil.
Marshall, W., sergeant, Tar. Vol.
Marshall, James, constable, A.C.
Meard, James, private, Tar. Bush Ran.
Mellsop, C. W., private, M. Vol.
Mellsop, J. T., lieutenant, M. Vol.
Mellsop, James, ensign, Forest Ran.

Meredith, E. C., sergeant, Nap. Cav.
Messenger, W. B., captain, Tar. Mil.
Messenger, C. J., lieutenant, Tar. Mil.
Messenger, William, private, Tar. Vol.
Menzies, James, private, Auck. Vol.
Meade, George, private, 1st W. Regt.
Medine, Thomas, private, 1st W. Regt.
Meikle, Alexander, corporal, 3rd W. Regt.
Mead, Edwin, private, 3rd W. Regt.
Melrose, Alexander, private, 3rd W. Regt.
Melville, J., bullock-driver, Transpt. Corps
Melvin, A., clerk, Com. Dept.
Mete Kingi, asst. superintendent of Transpt.
Meedrum, D., boatman, Transpt. Corps
Mellon, Edward, trooper, Auck. Cav.
Meagher, Patrick, private, 1st W. Regt.
Meredith, James, sergeant, 1st W. Regt.
Merryless, C. J., constable, A.C.
Meadowcroft, Thos., private, Tar. Mil. Set.
Messenger, E. F., private, Tar. Mil. Set.
Metua, ——, constable, A.C.
Meach, J. F., private, 2nd W. Regt.
Miller, William, sergeant, Nap. Vol.
Middlemas, Andrew, ensign, N. Z. Mil.
Miller, Robert, private, 1st W. Regt.
Milne, John, artificer, Com. Dept.
Mills, Hubert, private, 1st W. Regt.
Miller, Alfred, private, 1st W. Regt.
Millichamp, Francis, private, 1st W. Regt.
Mitchell, Edgar, private, 1st W. Regt.
Mitchell, Alexander, trooper, Wan. Cav.
Mitchell, Charles, constable, A.C.
Mitchell, John, private, Auck. Engineers
Mitchell, R., clerk, Com. Dept.
Milligan, John, bullock driver, Trans. Corps
Mitchell, R. M., issuer, Com. Dept.
Mills, H. W., private, 1st W. Regt.
Millar, Thos., private, Napier Mil.
Milne, W. S., private, Wellington Rifles
Milner, William, private, Hawke's B. Mil.
Milner, James, corporal, 1st W. Regt.
Mills, Wm., sergeant, A.C.
Mitchell, Alfred, private, Hawke's Bay Mil.
Milmoe, Laurence, constable, A.C.
Milne, John, constable, A.C.
Minter, Wm., trooper, Col. D. Force
Mitchell, Alex., private, 2nd W. Regt.
Miller, J. H., private, 2nd W. Regt.
Moginie, J. C., private, Auck. Vol.
Mogridge, Chas., sergeant, Napier Mil.
Moir, Wm., captain, 1st W. Regt.
Moody, T. V., sergeant, 2nd W. Regt.
Moore, P. C., private, Tar. Mil.
Morrison, Walter J., captain, Tar. Mil.
Morrison, Thos., private, Napier Mil.
Morrow, Richard, private, Auck. Vol.
Morrow, Arthur, private, Auck. Vol.
Monck, Jas. B., constable, A.C.
Moody, Samuel, private, 1st W. Regt.
Moore, John, constable, A.C.
Morgan, Alfred, trooper, Kai-Iwi Cav.
Morgan, E. J., sergeant, Kai-Iwi Cav.
Morgan, E. R., sergeant, Kai-Iwi Cav.
Morgan, Tom, trooper, Kai-Iwi Cav.

Morrison, Edward, private, Wairoa Vol.
Morton, John, corporal Wairoa Vol.
Moore, Wm., private, 1st W. Regt.
Moore, Wm., corporal, 1st W. Regt.
Morgan, sen., Robert, private, 1st W. Regt.
Morgan, jun., Robert, private, 1st W. Regt.
Moeiller, Chas., private, 1st W. Regt.
Morrison, E. J., private, 1st W. Regt.
Moller, Claus, private, 1st W. Regt.
Monaghan, Michael, private, 1st W. Regt.
Moyle, W. M., private, 1st W. Regt.
Morris, James, private, 1st W. Regt.
Moon, William, private, 1st W. Regt.
Montague, William, private, 1st W. Regt.
Moore, Walter, corporal, 2nd W. Regt.
Morgan, William, artificer, 2nd W. Regt.
Morton, Henry, private, 2nd W. Regt.
Monaghan, John, private, 2nd W. Regt.
Morgan, James, sergeant, 3rd W. Regt.
Molloy, Joseph, sergeant, 3rd W. Regt.
Moore, William, sergeant, 3rd W. Regt.
Morrison, William, sergeant, 3rd W. Regt.
Morton, George, sergeant, 3rd W. Regt.
Morris, James, sergeant, 3rd W. Regt.
Moore, James, sergeant, 3rd W. Regt.
Moore, Gus., sergeant, 3rd W. Regt.
Morgan, James, sergeant, 3rd W. Regt.
Moroney, Francis, sergeant, 3rd W. Regt.
Moore, Walter, sergeant, 3rd W. Regt.
Morrell, J., bullock driver, Transpt Corps
Moore, H., bullock driver, Transpt. Corps
Mowance, W. L., bulck. driver, Trans. Corps
Moir, G., bullock driver, Transpt. Corps
Moyle, W., bullock driver, Transpt. Corps
Monatt, J., boatman, Transpt. Corps
Morton, Sergt. J., issuer, Com. Dept.
Morgan, sen., R., baker, Com. Dept.
Morgan, R., baker, Com. Dept.
Morgan, William, labourer, Com. Dept.
Morpeth, J. B., private, Auck. Vol.
Morrison, Thomas, private, 1st W. Regt.
Monahan, John, trooper, Wan. Cav.
Molloy, W., private, 2nd W. Regt.
Morley, G., private, Tar. Bush Ran.
Morrison, G. T., private, 2nd W. Regt.
Morrison, H. C., sub-inspector, A.C.
Moverley, H. J., private, Tar. Mil. Settlers
Morley, G., private, Tar. Mil. Settlers
Moynahan, Patrick, constable, A.C.
Morsheads, E. F., private, Tar. Bush Ran.
Moore, Henry, private, Tar. Bush Ran.
Morelli, Joseph, private, 2nd W. Regt.
Moiarty, Tim., private, Tar. Mil. Settlers
Morrison, Henry, private, Nap. Vol.
Moyle, Edward, sergeant, Tar. Mil.
Morecroft, Henry G., ensign, Nap. Vol.
Mountgarrett, John, private, M.R.R.
Moon, A. M., sergeant, A.C.
Morgan, William, trooper, Col. D. Force
Money, Charles L., trooper, Wan. Cav.
Morrison, Thomas, private, Nap. Vol.
Mohr, John, private, Forest Ran.
Munn, Daniel, private, Nap. Vol.
Murray, James, private, Wairoa Rifles.

Murray, David, constable, A.C.
Murray, William, baker, Com. Dept.
Murray John, baker, Com. Dept.
Murray, Andrew, sergeant, Wan. Vol.
Murray, Andrew, private, 1st W. Regt.
Murray, William, private, 2nd W. Regt.
Murray, Alexander, private, 2nd W. Regt.
Murray, James, private, 3rd W. Regt.
Muir, James, sergeant, 1st W. Regt.
Mussen, H. G., trooper, Kai-Iwi Vol.
Mussen, Philip, hon. surgeon, Wan. Y. Cav.
Muller, H., ensign, 1st W. Regt.
Murphy, Patrick, sergeant, 1st W. Regt.
Murphy, William, private, 1st W. Regt.
Murphy, Thomas, private, 2nd W. Regt.
Murphy, W. H., private, 3rd W. Regt.
Murphy, Denis, private, 3rd W. Regt.
Murphy, W., bullock-driver, Transp. Corps
Murphy, Owen, private, Hawke's B. Mil.
Murphy, James, sergeant, Well. Rifles
Murphy, R. T., constable, A.C.
Murphy, B. C., trooper, Col. D. Force
Mungeam, Thos., private, Tar. Mil. Settlers
Murant, Henry, private, Col. D. Force
Mundell, David, private, Tar. Mil. Settlers
Mullins, J. H., sergeant, Auck. Vol.
Munday, Walter, private, Auck. Vol.
Munday, William Jas., private, Auck. Vol.
Musgrove, W., baker, Com. Dept.
Munro, William, labourer, Com. Dept.
Munro, Daniel, private, Auck. Mil.
Munro, Cattell, private, 3rd W. Regt.
Mulrenan, Thos., private, 3rd W. Regt.
Myles, Edmond, private, 2nd W. Regt.
Myhea, William, constable, A.C.
Myers, George, private, 3rd W. Regt.
Myles, Robert, private, 1st W. Regt.
McAnliff, James, private, 2nd W. Regt.
McAten, Michael, private, 2nd W. Regt.
McArthur, James, private, 1st W. Regt.
McAdams, W., coxswain, Transpt. Corps
McArthur, David, constable, A. C.
McBride, John, private, 1st W. Regt.
McBean, T. J., clerk, Com. Dept.
McCormick, Patrick, private, Napier Mil.
McCoy, John, constable, A. C.
McCanley, William, constable, A. C.
McCanley, Thomas, private, Well. Rifles
McCanley, William, private, 1st W. Regt.
McCarthy, John, trooper, Col. D. Force.
McClelland, Thomas, sergeant, 2nd W. Regt.
McCann, Lawrence, private, Col. D. Force
McCarthy, Patrick, private, M. Vol.
McCallum, J. M., private, Wairoa Vol.
McCarthy, Timothy, constable, A. C.
McConochie, John, private, Napier Mil.
McConnell, John, private, Auck. Vol.
McConnell, Alexander, private, Auck. Vol.
McCormich, Thos. J., trooper, Col. D. Force
McCullock, George, private, Wan. Mil.
McCollogh, Thos., corporal, Auck. Mil.
McCleary, William, private, 1st W. Regt.
McCormick, Robert, private, 2nd W. Regt.
McCready, Andrew, private, 2nd W. Regt.

McCormick, Michael, private, 2nd W. Regt.
McCready, Maxwell, private, 3rd W. Regt.
McCowat, William, private, 3rd W. Regt.
McConnell, Thomas, private, 3rd W. Regt.
McCrystal, Charles, private, 3rd W. Regt.
McCann, Lawrence, private, 3rd W. Regt.
McCann, Francis, private, 3rd W. Regt.
McClive, Francis, private, 3rd W. Regt.
McCaushie, Thos., bllk. driver, Transpt. Corps
McCormack, R., baker, Com. Dept.
McClinnan, James, baker, Com. Dept.
McCusker, Peter, labourer, Com, Dept.
McCleary, T., labourer, Com. Dept.
McCabe, Charles, boatman, Transpt. Corps
McCashion, P., private, Hawke's B. Vol.
McCarr, John H., private, 1st W. Regt.
McCrovy, Patrick, constable, A.C.
McCauley, James, private, Patea Rifles
McCleary, David, private, Napier Mil.
McClymont, A.G., private, Forest Rangers
McCrea, James, private, Tar. Mil. Settlers
McCartney, Arthur, sergeant, A.C.
McCarthy, Maurice, private, 1st W. Regt.
McConochie, Joseph, private, Napier Mil.
McCarthy, Felix, corporal, Tar. Mil. Settlers
McDonald, James, constable, A.C.
McDonald, William, private, 1st W. Regt.
McDonald, John, private, Tar. Vol.
McDonald, J. K., private, Tar. Vol.
McDonald, D. B., private, Tar. Vol.
McDonald, William, private, 3rd W. Regt.
McDonald, J., bullock driver, Transpt. Corps
McDonald, Wm., bullock driver, Tran. Corps
McDonald, J., butcher, Com. Dept.
McDonald, Charles, private, Wairoa Rifles
McDonald, Wm. H. E., private, Wan. Mil.
McDonald, Alexander, constable, A.C.
McDonald, Norman, constable, A.C.
McDonald, Peter, constable, A.C.
McDonald, Donald, private, 1st W. Mil.
McDonald, Geo. R., private, 2nd W. Mil.
McDonald, D., constable, A.C.
McDonnell, Thomas, lieut. colonel, N.Z. Mil.
McDonnell, Wm., captain, Native Contingent
McDonnell, Geo., sub-inspector, A.C.
McDonnell, Patrick, private, st W. Regt.
McDonnell, Edward, ensign, N.Z. Mil.
McDonell, C , sub-inspector, A.C.
McDaniels, Alex., private, 1st W. Regt.
McDermott, Thos., private, 1st W. Regt.
McDowell, John, private, 2nd W. Regt.
McDermott, Owen, private, 2nd W. Regt.
McDermott, N., baker, Com. Dept.
McDougall, James, private, 1st W. Regt.
McDowall, John, trooper, A.C.
McEnany, James, baker, Com. Dept.
McEvoy, James, private, Tar. Mil. Settlers
McFarland, P., constable, A. C.
McGillivray, S., private, Auck Mil.
McGruther, Robert, private, 2nd W. Regt.
McGahey, John, corporal, 1st W. Regt.
McGuire, Felix, corporal, 1st W. Regt.
McGuire, James, lance-corporal, Auck. Mil.
McGuiness, Thomas, lieutenant, Tar. Vol.

McGahey, C., sergt.-major, Tar. Vol.
McGuire, Henry, private, M. Vol.
McGuirk, James, corporal, F. Rangers
McGloin, Thaddeus, private, 1st W. Regt.
McGwern, George, private, 1st W. Regt.
McGhee, James, private, 1st W. Regt.
McGrath, Patrick, private, 2nd W. Regt.
McGinlay, James, private, 2nd W. Regt.
McGuire, James, sergeant, 3rd W. Regt.
McGillvrey, James, sergeant, 3rd W. Regt.
McGill, Charles, private, 3rd W. Regt.
McGee, James, private, 3rd W. Regt.
McGan, Francis, private, 3rd W. Regt.
McGregor, Hugh, private, 3rd W. Regt.
McGinley, John, bullock driver, Transpt. Corps
McGrath, Ed., bullock-driver, Transpt. Corps
McGeevie, T., boatman, Transpt. Corps
McGuire, H., baker, Com. Dept.
McGibbon, Corporal, boatman, Transpt, Corps
McGhur, T., boatman, Transpt. Corps
McGregor, John, guide, Wanganui
McGoldrick, Henry, corporal, A. C.
McGonagh, Robert, private, Auck. Mil.
McHugh, Patrick, constable, A.C.
McHardie, David, private, N.Z. Mil.
McHewer, William, private, 2nd W. Regt.
McIntyre, Wm., private, M. Vol.
McIldowie, Daniel, private, Wairoa Rifles
McIvor, Wm., private, 3rd W. Regt.
McIntyre, J., butcher, Com. Dept.
McIntyre, Charles, private, Tar. Mil. Settlers
McInness, Thos., trooper, Vol. Cav.
McKearney, Hugh, constable, A.C.
McKain, J. S. corporal, Petone Mil.
McKnight, John, private, Napier Mil.
McKoy, Patrick, private, Tar. Mil. Settlers
McKenzie, Peter, private, Tar. Mil. Settlers
McKenzie, George, private, 1st W. Regt.
McKellar, A. A. M., lieutenant, Tar. Mil.
McKellar, James S., captain, Tar. Mil.
McKenzie, Daniel, private, 2nd W. Regt.
McKay, Andrew, private, 1st W. Regt.
McKenna, Edward, private, 1st W. Regt.
McKennis, Fred., private, 1st W. Regt.
McKaye, John, private, 2nd W. Regt.
McKaye, Alexander, private, 2nd W. Regt.
McKean, John, private, 2nd W. Regt.
McKenzie, John, corporal, 3rd W. Regt.
McKaye, sen., Robert, private, 3rd W. Regt.
McKaye, jun., Robert, private, 3rd W. Regt.
McKenna, Robert, private, 3rd W. Regt.
McKinnon, Alex., private, 3rd W. Regt.
McKenna, Daniel, private, 3rd W. Regt.
McKaye, Thomas, private, 3rd W. Regt.
McKee, Wm., bullock driver, Tran. Corps.
McKee, David, boatman, Tran. Corps
McKenna, Wm., clerk, Com. Dept.
McKenna, Sergeant A., issuer, Com. Dept.
McKaye, T., labourer, Com. Dept.
McKenzie, Daniel, private, 2nd W. Regt.
McKenna, James, private, Tar. Mil. Settlers
McLaughlin, Thomas, private, 1st W. Regt.
McLaughlin, John, private, 2nd W. Regt.
McLeod, Gordon, private, 2nd W. Regt.

McLoughlin, Thomas, private, 3rd W. Regt.
McLaren, Thomas, private, 3rd W. Regt.
McLean, Lachlan, private, 3rd W. Regt.
McLeod, M., bullock-driver, Transpt. Corps
McLean, James, private, 1st W. Regt.
McLeod, John, private, Bay of Islands Mil.
McLachlan, Patrick, constable, A. C.
McLauchlin, Dugald, constable, A. C.
McLean, Henry, constable, A. C.
McManus, Michael, private, Patea Vol.
McMahon, Patrick, private, 1st W. Regt.
McMaster, John, private, 1st W. Regt.
McManus, John, private, 2nd W. Regt.
McMillan, Alexander, sergeant, 3rd W. Regt.
McMillan, Charles, private, 3rd W. Regt.
McMahon, Charles, constable, A.C.
McManus, Bernard, private, Tar. Vol.
McMahon, Thomas, private, 1st W. Regt.
McMahon, Martin, constable, A. C.
McNamara, Michael, private, 1st W. Regt.
McNeil, Alexander, private, 1st W. Regt.
McNeale, John, private, 3rd W. Regt.
McNichol, William, labourer, Com. Dept.
McNulty, J., boatman, Transpt. Corps
Mc Neill, William, constable, A.C.
McNair, Samuel, private, 1st W. Regt.
McPhee, Neil, bullock-driver, Transpt. Corps
McPike, ——, labourer, Com. Dept.
McPherson, James, private, 4th W. Regt
McPherson, James, sergeant, 1st W. Regt.
McQuatters, Edward, private, 1st W. Regt.
McQuarrie, Hugh, corporal, 3rd W. Regt.
McQuarrie, Alexander, private, 3rd W. Regt.
McSweeney, Eugene, corporal, 3rd W. Regt.
McSpadden, Michael, private, 2nd W. Regt.
McShane, James, private, 2nd W. Regt.
McTavish, Thomas, private, 2nd W. Regt.
McWha, William, private, Wan. Rifles

NATHAN, ANTHONY, corporal, Wan. Vol.
Nathan, J. C., trooper, Wan. Cav.
Nash, John, private, 1st W. Regt.
Nankeville, William, private, 1st W. Regt.
Nankeville, Thomas, private, 1st W. Regt.
Nabbs, William, sergeant, 2nd W. Regt.
Naylor, Joseph, private, 3rd W. Regt.
Naylor, William, private, 3rd W. Regt.
Nash, William, private, 3rd W. Regt.
Naylor, John, private, 3rd W. Regt.
Nash, Stephen, corporal, Tar. Mil. Settlers
Nancarrow, Joseph, private, Tar. Mil.
Nash, James, private, Tar. Mil.
Neil, Samuel, qr.-master- sergt., Wan. Mil.
Nelly, M. L., sergt.-major, 2nd W. Regt.
Newall, Stuart, sub-inspector, A.C.
Newland, John, priv te, Tar. Mil.
Newland, Henry, sergeant, Tar. Mil.
Neary, Stephen, trooper, Wan. Cav.
Newby, Francis, private, 1st W. Regt.
Newman, Benjamin, private, 1st. W. Regt.
Nelson, Peter, private, 1st W. Regt.
Neil, Daniel, private, 2nd W. Regt.
Newnol, Loftus, corporal, 3rd W. Regt.
Newburn, Henry, private, 3rd W. Regt.

Neill, James, private, 3rd W. Regt.
Nelson, Charles, private, 3rd W. Regt.
Newton, A., private, 3rd W. Regt.
Nelson, P., boatman, Col. T. Corps
Neil, Robert, private, Forest Ran.
Newland, Geo. S., private, Tar. Vol.
Newland, William, sub-inspector, A.C.
Neale, George, constable, A.C.
Neil, George, private, Tar. Mil. Settlers
Newman, John L., private, Tar. Bush Ran.
Neary, William, constable, A.C.
Newton, W. T., private, 2nd W. Regt.
Newman, William J., private, Forest Ran.
Neville, Robert C., private, Well. Rifles
Nicholson, J. C., corporal, Wan. Y. Cav.
Nixon, John, major, Wan. Mil.
Nicholls, G. W., lieutenant, Well.' Rifles
Nicholls, William, corporal, Kai Iwi Vol.
Nichol, George, ensign, 3rd W. Regt.
Nichols, Richard, private, 1st W. Regt.
Nicholson, Andrew, private, 1st W. Regt.
Nicholson, James, private, 2nd W. Regt.
Nichol, T. B., private, 2nd W. Regt.
Nixon, William, private, 3rd W. Regt.
Nichol, Hugh, private, 3rd W. Regt.
Nicholson, M., bullock-driver, Transpt. Corps
Nicholas, Constantine, constable, A.C.
Nixon, Marmaduke G., colonel, Auck. Mil.
Nichols, David, sergeant, Tar. Mil.
Nodder, John, sergeant, Tar. Vol.
Nolan, John, private, Forest Rangers
Nolan, Martin, private, Forest Rangers
Northe, W. H., private, Napier Mil.
Noake, Maillard, major, N.Z. Mil.
Nolan, Michael, private, 1st W. Regt.
Northcote, J., bullock-driver, Transpt. Corps
Northcroft, H. W., sub-inspector, A.C.
Norris, C. Goddard, private, Tar. Mil.
Nolan, M chael, constable, A.C.
North, Thomas, pr.vate, Patea Mil.
Northcote, John, private, Tar. Mil.
Norton, John, private, 2nd W. Regt.
Nowlan, G. D. B., ensign, Wan. Ran.
Nunn, Edwin, private, 2nd W. Regt.
Nutt, Samuel J., private, 2nd W. Regt.
Nugent, Michael, private, 2nd W. Regt.
Nugent, John, private, 3rd W. Regt.

OAKLEY, WILLIAM, private, 3rd W. Regt.
Oakes, John, sergeant, 2nd W. Regt.
O'Brien, Martin, sergeant, A. C.
O'Brien, Laurence, sergeant, 3rd W. Regt.
O'Brien, Daniel, private, 3rd W. Regt.
O'Brien, William, constable, A. C.
O'Brien, James, constable, A. C.
O'Brien, W., colour-sergeant, 3rd W. Regt.
O'Callaghan, W. J. P., lieutenant, Tar. Mil. Set.
O'Carroll, P. J., assist. surgeon, 3rd W. Regt.
O'Connor, John, private, Tar. Bush Ran.
O'Connor, John, private, 2nd W. Regt.
O'Connell, Thomas, private, 3rd W. Regt.
O'Connor, John, baker, Com. Dept.
O'Connell, George, sergeant, A. C.
O'Donnell, Charles, private, Nap. Mil.

O'Donoghue, Michael, private, 3rd W. Regt.
O'Donnell, B., bullock driver, Transpt. Corps
O'Dell, E., boa'man, Transpt. Corps
O'Dee, K. J., sergeant, Nap. Mil.
O'Donnell, John, private, 2nd W. Regt.
O'Farrell, R. H., clerk, Com. Dept.
O'Grady, John, private, 1st W. Regt.
Ogden, John, private, 1st W. Regt.
O'Halloran, G. L., sub-inspector, A. C.
O'Hanlon, C. P., trooper, Wan. Cav.
O'Halloran, G., clerk, Com. Dept.
O'Hanlon, Peter, constable, A. C.
O'Kearney, Francis J., private, 2nd W. Regt.
Olliver, Frank, trooper, Auck. Cav.
Olliver, Charles, corporal, Tar. Vol.
Olliver, Francis, sergeant, Tar. Vol.
Olson, Edward, trooper, Tar. Cav.
Oldfield, Thomas, sergeant A. C.
Oldfield, James, private, 1st W. Regt.
Olier, James, private, 1st W. Regt.
Oldham, Henry, superintendent of hulks
O'Loghlin, John, labourer, Com. Dept.
Olliver, William, private, Tar. Vol.
O'Meara, Edward, private, Auck. Vol.
O'Neill, Patrick, private, 1st W. Regt.
O'Neil, Patrick, sergeant, 3rd W. Regt.
O'Neill, William, clerk, Com. Dept.
O'Neill, James, private, H. B. Vol.
Ormond, F. F., asst.-surgeon, Nap. Mil.
Orbell, G. G., sergeant, A. C.
O'Rafferty, John, private, 3rd W. Regt.
Ord, William, bullock driver, Transpt. Corps
Orr, James, private, Nap. Mil.
Orr, John, private, Nap. Mil.
Orr, William, constable, A. C.
Osborne, James, private, Forest Rangers
O'Sullivan, John, private, 3rd W. Regt.
Osborne, W., clerk, Com. Dept.
O'Shannessy, Peter, private, 1st W. Regt.
Outon, William, constable, A. C.
Owen, F., ensign, 3rd W. Regt.
Owen, James, corporal, 2nd W. Regt.
Oxenham, John, trooper, Tar. Vol.
Oxenham, William T., trooper, Tar. Vol.
Oxenham, Oliver, private, Tar. Vol.

PAGE, A. M. A., captain, Tar. Mil. Settlers
Pain, John, trooper, Col. Defence Force
Palethorpe, Thos., col.-sergeant, 1st W. Regt.
Palmer, Chas., private, Auck. Vol.
Pakenham, Joshua, assist.-surgeon, Wel. Vol.
Parkes, Charles, trooper, Wan. Cav.
Payne, F. C., constable, A.C.
Patterton, A. de Courcy, private, Auck. Eng.
Patterson, Andrew, private, 1st W. Regt.
Palmer, Benjamin, corporal, 1st W. Regt.
Patton, Robert, private, 1st W. Regt.
Parker, John, private, 1st W. Regt.
Patterson, John, private, 2nd W. Regt.
Painter, John, private, 2nd W. Regt.
Parkhouse, Richard, private, 3rd W. Regt.
Paterson, Matthew, private, 3rd W. Regt.
Parsons, William, private, 3rd W. Regt.
Panton, Robert, private, 3rd W. Regt.

Palmley, Jas., bullock driver, Transpt. Corps
Pattymore, Jacob, bullock driver, Tran. Corps
Palmer, Alfred, clerk, Com. Dept.
Page, Sergt. James, issuer, Com. Dept.
Palmer, James, baker, Com. Dept.
Paviour, E. P., boatman, Tran. Corps.
Palmer, Chas., private, Nap. Mil.
Paul, William, private, Tar. Vol.
Palmer, Alfred, constable, A.C.
Parkinson, Thos., trooper, Opotiki Cav.
Pattimore, Joseph, private, Tar. Vol.
Patten, John, private, Tar. Mil. Settlers
Parkinson, Arthur, private, 1st W. Regt.
Parker, Henry, private, Auck. Naval Vol.
Payne, John J., private, Auck. Vol.
Paynter, William, private, Tar. Vol.
Parker, Henry, private, Nap. Mil.
Patterson, B., private, 1st W. Regt.
Paul, Nicholas, private, Napier Mil.
Paynter, John, private, Tar. Mil.
Pearce, Alfred, private, Tar. Vol.
Percy, John A., captain, Wan. Y. Cav.
Perry, F. F., corporal, Tar. Mil. Settlers
Perry, C. L., ensign, 2nd W. Regt.
Peake, George, trooper, Kai-Iwi Cav.
Peake, H. L., trooper, Kai-Iwi Cav.
Peake, John, trooper, Kai-Iwi Cav.
Pearce, David, private, Well. Ran.
Pearce, Henry, constable, A.C.
Penfold, Edward, trooper, Wan. Cav.
Peacock, Wm., artificer, Auck. Mil.
Percival, W., lieutenant, 3rd W. Regt.
Perry, C. L., ensign, 3rd W. Regt.
Peacock, William, private, 1st W. Regt.
Pearse, Edward, private, 1st W. Regt.
Pearman, J. W., corporal, 1st W. Regt.
Peck, Thomas, artificer, 1st W. Regt.
Peel, Thomas, private, 1st W. Regt.
Pensall, Daniel, private, 1st W. Regt.
Perkins, Fred., private, 2nd W. Regt.
Peat, Wellington, private, 2nd W. Regt.
Pearson, J. F., private, 2nd W. Regt.
Penny, John, private, 2nd W. Regt.
Petty, Wm., private, 3rd W. Regt.
Peacock, John, private, 3rd W. Regt.
Peacock, Wm., private, 3rd W. Regt.
Petit, Gable, private, 3rd W. Regt.
Pellicot, Gabriel, private, 3rd W. Regt.
Perkins, Chas., private, 3rd W. Regt.
Preston, sen., Joseph, private, 3rd W. Regt.
Preston, jun., Joseph, private, 3rd W. Regt.
Percival, Michael, private, 3rd W. Regt.
Percival, James, private, 3rd W. Regt.
Peden, Joseph, private, 3rd W. Regt.
Pearson, Wm., private, 3rd W. Regt.
Peet, Wm., bullock-driver, Tran. Corps
Penny, John, bullock-driver, Tran. Corps
Peter, Alex., bullock-driver, Tran. Corps
Pearne, James, bullock-driver, Trans. Corps
Pemberton, Corporal T. M., issuer, Com. Dept
Pentonny, A., baker, Com. Dept.
Perks, John, labourer, Com. Dept.
Pepperall, John, private, Tar. Vol.
Pearse, Thos. A., private, Hawke's B. Vol.

Peacock, David, private, Napier Mil.
Peacock, Hector S., private, Napier Mil.
Pegley, Roland, constable, A.C.
Perry, F. T., private, Tar. Mil. Settlers
Peet, George, private, 1st W. Regt.
Pearson, Alfred, lance-corporal, A.C.
Pearson, H.M.D., trooper, Col. D. Force
Perkins, Job, private, 1st W. Regt.
Pennefather, Daniel, captain, Tar. Mil. Set.
Pellew, Israel, private, Tar. Mil.
Pearn, W. H., private, Tar. Mil.
Pellen, Edwd. T., private. Tar. Bush Ran.
Peevor, Hy. Edwd., private, Auck. Vol.
Pearson, Robert, sergeant, Col. D. Force
Peevor, T. G., constable, A.C.
Penwarden, Thos. B., private, Tar. Mil.
Perry, William, private, Tar. Mil.
Phillips, Abraham, private, Well. Ran.
Phillips, John, private, Tar. Mil.
Phillips, C. P., sergeant, Auck. Vol.
Phillips, Wyndham, private, 1st W. Regt.
Phillips, Richard, private, 3rd W. Regt.
Phillips, Windham F., private, 1st W. Reg'.
Phillips, George, private, Hutt Mil.
Phillips, George S., private, Well. D. Force
Phillips, George, private, 1st W. Regt.
Phillips, Henry, constable, A.C.
Philpot, George, private, 2nd W. Regt.
Pierse, A., trooper, Wan. Cav.
Pilbrow, John, private, Poverty Bay Vol.
Pilmer, A. A. G., lieutenant, Forest Ran.
Pitt, C. Dean, lieutenant, 1st W. Regt.
Piercy, Francis, sergeant, Auck. Mil.
Pitt, G. D., lieutenant, 1st W. Regt.
Pitt, Henry, private, 1st W. Regt.
Pickett, James, private, 1st W. Regt.
Pierce, Martin, private, 1st. W. Regt.
Piggot, James, private, 2nd W. Regt.
Pilkington, Henry, private, 2nd W. Regt.
Pilkington, Edward, private, 2nd W. Regt.
Piddle, Daniel, private, 3rd W. Regt.
Pile, H., butcher, Com. Dept.
Pierce, Octavius, private, Forest Rangers
Pillatt, David, sergeant, Wan. Rifles
Pilkington, Hamlet, constable, A. C.
Pitcairn, Robt. H., col.-serg ant, Auck. Eng.
Pini, —, sergeant, Native Cont.
Plumber, C., butcher, Com. Dept.
Plummer, Albert, private, H. B. Mil.
Pope, John N., private, Tar. Mil. Settlers
Pohlen, Heinrich, private, Forest Rangers
Porter, Thomas W., sub-inspector, A. C.
Powell, William T., sergeant, A. C.
Powell, Wilmot, captain, Wan. Mil.
Poynter, Jam s B., trooper, P. B. Cav.
Powell, Charles, private, 1st W. Regt.
Potts, John, private, 1st W. Regt.
Porter, James, private, 1st W. Regt.
Pogson, Joseph, private, 1st W. Regt.
Potter, John, private, 1st W. Regt.
Powell, Samuel, private, 1st W. Regt.
Polliski, Henry, private, 2nd W. Regt.
Potter, John, private, 2nd W. Regt.
Polwart, John, private, 2nd W. Regt.

Power, P., bullock driver, Transpt. Corps
Poyser, Otto, conductor, Com. Dept.
Poulter, William, baker, Com. Dept.
Power, John, constable, A. C.
Pope, Charles A., private, Tar. Vol.
Pope, Frederick S. W., sergeant, A. C.
Powell, Hy. Chas., guide to Col. Forces
Powell, Giles, private, Tar. Mil. Settlers
Powell, John H., trooper, Col. D. Force
Powell, W. H., private, Tar. Mil. Settlers
Preece, George, captain, N. Z. Mil.
Prosser, Henry, private, 1st W. Regt.
Pring, F., artificer, Auck. Mil.
Provost, Bartlett, private, 1st W. Regt
Prior, J. H., private, 1st W. Regt.
Price, Charles, private, 2nd W. Regt.
Pratt, Thomas, private, 2nd W. Regt.
Pratt, George, private, 2nd W. Regt.
Pretty, Joseph, butcher, Com. Dept.
Price, Samuel, private, 2nd W. Regt.
Price, I. G., private, 1st W. Regt.
Prowse, C. W., private, Tar. Mil. Settlers
Pritchard, W. S. G., private, 3rd W. Regt.
Pulford, Edward, private, Nap. Rifles
Pull, John, private, 2nd W. Regt.
Pulling, William, 2nd W. Regt.
Purcell, William, private, 2nd W. Regt.
Puck, Hans, private, 3rd W. Regt.
Putnam, P., sergeant-major, Nap. Cav.
Purnell, James, corporal, Tar. Vol.
Purdey, G. B., corporal, Tar. Vol.
Pugh, James, private, Tar. Vol.
Pycroft, Henry, constable, A. C.
Pyke, Vincent A., private, Wan. Mil.
Pye, Henry, private, 1st W. Regt.
Pye, Charles, captain, Col. D. Force

QUAIN, RICHARD, sergeant, 2nd W. Regt.
Quinn, Henry, private, 2nd W. Regt.
Quinlan, Thomas, private, 2nd W. Regt.
Quirke, Felman, private, 3rd W. Regt.
Quinn, Michael, private, 3rd W. Regt.
Quinlan, Andrew, private, 3rd W. Regt.
Quilty, Andrew, private, 3rd W. Regt.
Quint, Henry, private, 3rd W. Regt.
Quick, Edwin, private, 3rd W. Regt.
Quatborough, Richard, constable, A. C.

RAWSON, F. G., private, Tar. Mil.
Rabbits, Edward, Constable, A. C.
Randell, William, sergeant, Auck. Mil.
Raynor, George, lieutenant, 2nd W. Regt.
Ratcliffe, William, private, 1st W. Regt.
Randall, Edward, private, 1st W. Regt.
Randall, John, corporal, 1st W. Regt.
Rattegan, W. H. J., private, 2nd W. Regt.
Raynor, James, private, 2nd W. Regt.
Rawkin, William, private, 3rd W. Regt.
Rafferty, John, bullock driver, Trans. Corps
Rattenbury, J., bullock driver, Trans. Corps
Raynor, Sergeant J., storekeepe , Com. Dept.
Rainor, Sergeant John, issuer, Com. Dept.
Raines, J., issuer, Com. Dept.
Ramsey, J., boatman, Transpt. Corps

Ranford, J., boatman, Transpt. Corps
Ramsay, M. F., corporal, 1st W. Regt.
Ransley, Joseph, private, 1st W. Regt.
Rassman, Charles, private, Tar. Vol.
Raynor, John, private, Auck. Vol.
Raynor, Alfred, private, Auck. Vol.
Rawson, Charles Edward, private, Tar. Vol.
Rawson, Thos. Edward, surgeon, Tar. Vol.
Rawson, Henry Freer, sergeant, Tar. Vol.
Rae, L. H., private, 1st W. Regt.
Rabone, Edward, private, Nap. Mil.
Raithby, R. W., corporal, Col. D. Force
Raven, W. J., private, Forest Ran.
Reed, William, private, Nap. Vol.
Rees, George, sergeant, Tar. Mil. Settlers
Reid, David, private, Nap. Mil.
Reilly, J. G., private, Tar. Mil. Settlers
Revell, F. H., sergeant-major, Col. D. Force
Reynold, H. H., colour-sergeant, 2nd W. Regt.
Resticaux, Walter, private, E. C.
Reilly, Hamilton, private, 1st W. Regt.
Reynolds, George, private, 1st W. Regt.
Reid, William, private, 1st W. Regt.
Reeves, Samuel, private, 1st W. Regt.
Reid, George, private, 1st W. Regt.
Reilly, Peter, private, 1st W. Regt.
Reid, Henry, private, 1st W. Regt.
Reilly, Eugene, sergeant, 2nd W. Regt.
Revell, William, private, 2nd W. Regt.
Reardon, Timothy, private, 2nd W. Regt.
Reid, Cavendish, sergeant, 3rd W. Regt.
Reilly, Cornelius, corporal, 3rd W. Regt.
Reilly, Thomas, private, 3rd W. Regt.
Reilly, Charles, private, 3rd W. Regt.
Reid, Thomas, bullock-driver, Transpt. Corps
Resdale, A., boatman, Transpt. Corps
Redmond, J. J., colour-sergeant, 1st W. Regt.
Reede, C. H., private, 3rd W. Regt.
Reid, William, private, Hawke's B. Vol.
Redfern, George, private, 1st W. Regt.
Rehbork, Christian, constable, A. C.
Reilly, Michael, private, 1st W. Regt.
Reid, John, private, Wan. Mil.
Renouf, John, private, Nap. Mil.
Reynolds, James, private, Tar. Vol.
Reynolds, J. C., private, Tar. Vol.
Reed, F. B., sergeant, A. C.
Reed, Bernard, corporal, A. C.
Redding, John, private, 1st W. Regt.
Redgrave, John, private, 3rd W. Regt.
Reed, H. J., private, Nap. Mil.
Read, John, private, Auck. Vol.
Reid, Archibald, private, Col. D. Force
Reynolds, E., constable, A. C.
Reynolds, T. G., sergeant, Tar. Mil. Settlers
Ready, Patrick, trooper, M. A. C.
Reddy, John, private, Tar. Mil.
Reynolds, Thomas, private, 3rd W. Regt.
Read, Richard, private, 2nd W. Regt.
Rhodes, Thomas, private, 3rd W. Regt.
Rhodes, Joseph, captain, Nap. Mil.
Rhind, James, private, Well. Rifles.
Richards, William, private, Tar. Mil.
Richards, Josiah, trooper, Wan. Cav.

Richard, Loftus, colour sergeant, 1st W. Regt.
Richards, Chas., private, 1st W. Regt.
Richards, Thomas, private, 3rd W. Regt.
Richards, Wm., bullock driver, Tran. Corps
Richards, John, private, Tar. Vol.
Richards, William, constable, A.C.
Richardson, W. A., sub-inspector, A.C.
Richardson, George, trooper, Wan. Cav.
Richardson, Geo. B., trooper, Hawke's B. Cav.
Richardson, Walter, private, 1st W. Regt.
Richardson, Henry, private, 3rd W. Regt.
Richardson, T., bullock driver, Tran. Corps
Riches, Alex., private, Tar. Mil. Settlers
Ritchie, William, private, 1st W. Regt.
Rimnon, John, private, 1st W. Regt.
Rigall, William, private, 2nd W. Regt.
Rigall, William, private, 3rd W. Regt.
Ritchie, William, private, 3rd W. Regt.
Richmond, Thomas, private, 3rd W. Regt.
Ridge, C., boatman, Transpt. Corps
Rigby, John, private, Tar. Mil. Settlers
Rickards, Thos. E., trooper, Well. Cav.
Rivers, Edward, private, Forest Rangers
Roberts, William H., private, Tar. Mil.
Roberts, Thos., private, 1st W. Regt.
Roberts, Thos., private, 3rd W. Regt.
Roberts, Henry, private, 3rd W. Regt.
Roberts, Daniel, baker, Com. Dept.
Roberts, John, private, 1st W. Regt.
Roberts, J. M., inspector, A.C.
Roberts, David, private, Mil. Settlers
Roberts, William H., private, Tar. Mil.
Roberts, John, corporal, Tar. Mil.
Robertson, William, private, Napier Mil.
Robertson, Wm. Edwd., volunteer, Tar. Rifles
Robertson, Robert, corporal, 2nd W. Regt.
Robertson, Robert, private, 2nd W. Regt.
Robertson, Alexander, private, 3rd W. Regt.
Robinson, G., issuer, Com. Dept.
Robinson, John, private, Wan. Rifles
Robinson, John, private, 3rd W. Regt.
Robinson, Wm. R., sergeant, Napier Vol.
Robinson, Charles, trooper, Wan. Vol.
Robinson, Charles, engineer, Govt. Vessel
Robinson, Geo. F., private, Tar. Mil. Settlers
Robinson, Richard, constable, A. C.
Robinson, W. G., trooper, Wairoa Cav.
Robinson, Marshall, private, 3rd W. Regt.
Robson, T. John, private, Napier Mil.
Roche, Parker, private, Tar. Mil. Settlers
Roche, Thomas, private, Tar. Mil. Settlers
Rodriguez, Antonio, trooper, Tar. Cav.
Ross, Alfred, captain, Wan. Mil.
Routledge, William, ensign, Napier Vol.
Roche, Henry, constable, A. C.
Rolfe, Frederick, trooper, Wan. Cav.
Rolls, Mark, constable, A. C.
Ross, George, trooper, Wan. Cav.
Ross, Hugh, private, Wan. Mil.
Rowland, Anthony, sergeant, Kai Iwi Mil.
Rowe, H. F., sergeant, Auck. Eng.
Rowe, Thomas, trooper, Wan. Cav.
Robson, James, private, 1st W. Regt.
Rowe, G. W., private, 1st W. Regt.

Rowley, George, private, 1st W. Regt.
Rogers, Peter, private, 1st W. Regt.
Rooney, Abraham, private, 1st W. Regt.
Rose, W. A., private, 1st W. Regt.
Rolph, Charles, private, 1st W. Regt.
Rogers, Job, private, 1st W. Regt.
Roach, James, private, 2nd W. Regt.
Rodda, William, private, 3rd W. Regt.
Rose, W. H., private, 3rd W. Regt.
Rowe, George, private, 3rd W. Regt.
Rooney, James, private, 3rd W. Regt.
Rodgers, Josiah, bullock-driver, Tran. Corps
Rowe, Wm., bullock-driver, Tran. Corps
Rorrison, G., storekeeper, Com. Dept.
Roy, Corporal Chas., issuer, Com. Dept.
Rose, Edwin, baker, Com. Dept.
Rose, A., boatman, Tran. Corps
Rookes, Chas. Cecil, lieut.-colonel, Wan. Mil.
Rolfe, Chas. W., private, 1st W. Regt.
Rose, Hemming L., constable, A.C.
Ross, James, private, Napier M.l.
Rouse, W. H., private, Tar. Mil. Settlers
Rowan, Fred. C., lieutenant, Tar. Vol.
Ross, Donald, private, Hawke's Bay Vol.
Ross, Fred., captain, A.C.
Rogers, Wm., private, Tar. Mil.
Roose, Elijah, private, Patea Vol.
Ronalds, Jas. A., sergeant, Tar. Vol.
Ronalds, Francis, corporal, Tar. Vol.
Ronalds, Hugh, sergeant, Tar. Vol.
Rogers, Job, private, 1st W. Regt.
Russell, F. N., private, Forest Ran.
Rudd, Wm., constable, A.C.
Rutledge, Johnston, constable, A.C.
Rundell, Richard, trooper, Tar. Vol.
Rutherford, Walter, constable, A.C.
Rundle, Samuel, private, Tar. Vol.
Rush, John, private, Hutt Mil.
Russell, A. H., captain, Napier Mil.
Rudman, Henry, private, Napier Mil.
Rushton, J. Richard, ensign, Opotiki Ran.
Russell, A. H., trooper, Auck. Cav.
Russell, W. Fairweather, sergeant, Wan. Vol.
Russell, John, trooper, Wan. Cav.
Ruck, F. W., captain, 3rd W. Regt.
Rudding, John, private, 1st W. Regt.
Rusden, Samuel, private, 1st W. Regt.
Rudd, William, private, 1st W. Regt.
Rushforth, Thomas, private, 2nd W. Regt.
Russell, Denis, sergeant, 3rd W. Regt.
Ruddock, Daniel, sergeant, 3rd W. Regt.
Russimar, William, private, 3rd W. Regt.
Russell, James, private, 3rd W. Regt.
Russell, George, private, 3rd W. Regt.
Ruthven, Gilbert, bullock driver, Tran. Corps
Russell, John, bullock driver, Transpt. Corps
Rundle, Richard, bullock driver, Tran. Corps
Rundle, Robert, bullock driver, Tran. Carps
Rye, Lewis, lieutenant, Com. T. Corps
Ryan, George, private, Tar. Mil.
Ryan, John, private, 1st W. Regt.
Ryan, Patrick, private, 3rd W. Regt.
Ryan, William, trooper, Wan. Cav.
Ryan, Daniel, constable, A. C.

Ryan, James, private, Forest Rangers
Ryan, John M., constable, A. C.
Rykers, William, private, 1st W. Regt.

SANDES, T. GOODMAN, sergeant, A.C.
Sault, William, private, 1st W. Regt.
Sage, Jesse, sergeant, 2nd W. Regt.
Saunders, Joseph, private, 2nd W. Regt.
Sanders, Thomas, private, 3rd W. Regt.
Sanderson, William, private, 3rd W. Regt.
Saunders, E., bullock driver, Transpt. Corps
Satchell, William, clerk, Com. Dept.
Saunders, Thomas, issuer, Com. Dept.
Sanders, James, issuer, Com. Dept.
Sampson, Gerald, constable, A.C.
Sargent, Henry, private, Nap. Mil.
Sanderson, John, private, 3rd W. Regt.
Savage, James, trooper, A.C.
Saunders, Frank, private, Patea Rangers
Sacker, W. A., private, 2nd W. Regt.
Sampson, George, private, Tar. Vol.
Sands, William, private, Tar. Mil.
Savage, Richard, private, 2nd W. Regt.
Saurie, Thomas, sergeant, 2nd W. Regt.
Schmidt, A., baker, Com. Dept.
Scheckenberg, J., labourer, Com. Dept.
Scarr, J., labourer, Com. Dept.
Scammell, C. George, private, Tar. Vol.
Scholes, John, constable, A.C.
Scower, William, private, Wan. Mil.
Scotter, William, private, Auck. Vol.
Schuckmacker, Julius, private, 1st W. Regt.
Scottie, Nicholas, private, 2nd W. Regt.
Schofield, Samuel, sergeant, 3rd W. Regt.
Scatchard, James, private, 3rd W. Regt.
Scatchard, William, private, 3rd W. Regt.
Scanlan, Wm., bullock driver, Trans. Corps
Schlinker, Albert, bullock driver, Trans. Corps
Scandlyn, Thomas, private, Tar. Mil.
Scanlan, Michael, private, Nap. Mil.
Scantling, Richard, private, Tar. Mil.
Scholes, J., labourer, Com. Dept.
Scott, W. G., private Auck. Mil.
Scott, Herbert, quarter-master sergeant, A.C.
Scott, Matthew, assist.-surgeon, Col. Forces
Scott, Joseph, private, Patea Vol.
Scott, W. H., trumpeter, Wan. Cav.
Scott, G. L., private, 1st W. Regt.
Scott, John, corporal, Wan. Mil.
Scott, Nixon, constable, A.C.
Scott, John, serg ant, 2nd W. Regt.
Scott, John, private, 3rd W. Regt.
Scott, Thomas, private, 3rd W. Regt.
Scott, Chas., bullock-driver, Transpt. Corps
Scott, Henry, labourer, Transpt. Corps
Scott, George, private, Petane Mil.
Scott, James, constable, A.C.
Scott, George J., sergeant, Wan. Mil.
Scott, Dun an, sergeant, Tar. Mil. Settlers
Scott, Joseph, private, Com. Dept.
Scott, Thomas, constable, A.C.
Seedy, James, baker, Com. Dept.
Selby, William, private, Forest Rangers
Sellars, Thomas, private, 1st W. Regt.

Seymour, D. W., private, 1st W. Regt.
Seaton, Richard, private, 2nd W. Regt.
Sevan, Patrick, private, 3rd W. Regt.
Secombe, W. H., trooper, Tar. Vol.
Sedgwick, Henry, private, Well. Mil.
Seymour, George, private, 1st W. Regt.
Shanaghan, James, constable, A.C.
Sheehy, Patrick, sergeant, Tar. Mil. Settlers
Sheppard, George, private, Auck. Vol.
Sheppee, J. Wray, private, Tar. Vol.
Sherret, A. Stephen, lieutenant., Forest Ran.
Shirley, Thos., private, Napier Vol.
Shepherd, Richard, private, 1st W. Regt.
Sherwood, G. F., trooper, Wan. Cav.
Short, John, corporal, A.C.
Short, F. J., trooper, A.C.
Sharman, Thomas, private, 1st W. Regt.
Shaw, Reginald, private, 1st W. Regt.
Shields, William, private, 1st W. Regt.
Sheedon, Elijah, private, 1st W. Regt.
Sherlock, John, private, 2nd W. Regt.
Sharp, David, private, 2nd W. Regt.
Showers, Rufus, private, 2nd W. Regt.
Sharlock, John, private, 2nd W. Regt.
Shennan, Thomas, private, 3rd W. Regt.
Shuten, John, private, 3rd W. Regt.
Short, Edward, clerk, Com. Dept.
Shields, James, baker, Com. Dept.
Sharley, Joseph, private, Nap. Mil.
Sheriff, Bedford, trumpeter, Wan. Cav.
Shirley, Benjamin, private, Nap. Mil.
Shuker, William, private, F. Rangers
Shiley, Henry, trooper, Hawke's B. Cav.
Sherson, William, corporal, Auck. Vol
Shields, James, private, Tar. Mil. Settlers
Shepperd, Henry, sergeant, 1st W. Regt.
Shaw, Reginald, constable, A.C.
Sherges, Louis, private, Col. D. Force
Shawe, John, corporal, Tar. Mil.
Shanaghan, W., sergeant, Auck. Mil.
Shaw, Thomas W., private, 3rd W. Regt.
Shields, James, sergeant, Well. Mil.
Sinclair, A., butcher, Com. Dept.
Sidey, ——, baker, Com. Dept.
Sissons, Charles, private, M.S.
Sibley, Henry Thomas, constable, A.C.
Siddons, James, constable, A.C.
Sivret, F., trooper, Opotiki Cav.
Sirc, Francis, private, Tar. Mil. Settlers
Simpson, Leonard, captain, 2nd W. Regt.
Siddons, James, private, 1st W. Regt.
Simpson, Edward, private, 1st W. Regt.
Sinclair, John, private, 1st W. Regt.
Simpson, John, private, 3rd W. Regt.
Sims, George, private, 3rd W. Regt.
Simpson, Gerald, private, 3rd W. Regt.
Skeet, H. C., captain, Auck. Eng.
Skene, James, captain, 2nd W. Regt.
Skelley, John, private, 2nd W. Regt.
Skinner, W. A., constable, A.C.
Skinner, W. Henry, private, Tar. Vol.
Skene, George, sergeant, A.C.
Skipworth, F. G., lieutenant, Poverty B. Vol.
Skinner, Wm. Henry, private, Forest Ran.

Slator, Walter, private, Napier Mil.
Slator, Francis, colour sergeant, Napier Mil.
Slack, J., butcher, Com. Dept.
Slack, John, baker, Com. Dept.
Sloane, John A., private, Patea Vol.
Smart, Wm., private, Tar. Mil. Settlers
Small, James, sergeant, 1st W. Regt.
Small, Chas., private, E.C.
Smaller, Wm., private, Tar. Mil. Settlers
Small, George F., trooper, Wan. Cav.
Small, James, corporal, 1st W. Regt.
Small, Jabez W., sergeant, 1st W. Regt.
Smith, Wm. A., captain, 1st W. Regt.
Smith, Ezra, private, Forest Ran.
Smith, Peter J., private, Forest Ran.
Smith, Wm., trooper, Poverty Bay Cav.
Smith, A. Randolph, private Tar. Mil.
Smith, Alfred, private, 1st W. Regt.
Smith, James, trooper, Well. D. Force
Smith, Robert, lieut.-sergeant, Nap. Vol.
Smith, William, private, Nap. Vol.
Smith, Gough, sergeant, Auck. Mil.
Smith, George, corporal, Auck. Mil.
Smith, H. G., captain, 1st W. Regt.
Smith, Robert, private, 1st W. Regt.
Smith, W. J , private, 1st W. Regt.
Smith, James, private, 1st W. Regt.
Smith, George, sergeant, 1st W. Regt.
Smith, William, private, 1st W. Regt.
Smith, John, private, 2nd W. Regt.
Smith, George, private, 2nd W. Regt.
Smith, Charles, private, 2nd W. Regt.
Smith, Edward, private, 2nd W. Regt.
Smith, John, private, 2nd W. Regt.
Smith, James, private, 3rd W. Regt.
Smith, sen., Wm., private, 3rd W. Regt.
Smith, jun., Wm., private, 3rd W. Regt.
Smith, Patrick, private, 3rd W. Regt.
Smith, Robert, private, 3rd W. Regt.
Smith, W., boatman, Transpt. Corps
Smith, B., boatman, Transpt. Corps
Smith, Richard, clerk, Com. Dept.
Smith, P. F., butcher, Com. Dept.
Smith, William, private, Auck. Mil.
Smith, A. E., private, Auck. Mil.
Smith, F. S., private, Parnell Ran.
Smith, George, S., sergeant, 1st W. Regt.
Smith, Alfred, private, 3rd W. Regt.
Smith, A. B., captain, N.Z. Vol.
Smith, Stephen, constable, A.C.
Smith, John, sergeant, Forest Rangers
Smith, John Wm., private, Well. Rifles
Smith, Alex., sergeant, A.C.
Smith, W. C., private, 1st W. Regt,
Smith, Thomas, private, Tar. Mil.
Smith, James, corporal, Tar. Mil. Settlers
Smith, Joseph A., private, Wairoa Vol.
Snowden, Thomas, private, 1st W. Regt.
Snape, J., assistant surgeon, 2nd W. Regt.
Southcombe, James, trooper, Wan. Y. Cav.
Somerville, Rich., lieutenant, Auck. Vol.
Solomon, William, constable, A. C.
Spurling, John, private, 1st W. Regt.
Spiering, Andrew, private, 1st W. Regt.

Spring, Francis, constable, A. C.
Speedy, Alfred, private, M. Vol.
Spitter, Harvey, sub-inspector, A. C.
Spurdle, W. A., sergeant, Tar. Vol.
Spittard, James, private, 1st W. Regt.
Spink, James, artificer, Auck. Mil.
Springford, Alfred, private, 1st W. Regt.
Sprennett, Thomas, private, 3rd W. Regt.
Spreddon, Joseph, private, 3rd W. Regt.
Spruce, James, private, 3rd W. Regt.
Spain, Denis, private, Tar. Mil. Settlers
Spence, George, private, Nap. Mil.
Spencer, T. H., interpreter, Col. Forces
Spencer, Gray, volunteer, Wan. N. C.
Spencer, George, trooper, Col. D. Force
Squib, George, private, 2nd W. Regt.
Squibb, George, constable, A. C.
Styack, William, ensign, Transpt. Corps
Stack, W. G., captain, 1st W. Regt.
Standish, Frank, lieutenant, Tar. Mil.
Stapp, C., brevet major, N.Z. Mil.
Stevens, Henry, private, Nap. Mil.
Stevens, Francis, sergeant, Tar. Vol.
Stewart, Thomas, trooper, Auck. Vol.
Stewart, William, corporal, Nap. Mil. Settlers
Stewart, W. C., private, 1st W. Regt.
St. John, J. H. Herbert, lieut.-colonel, N.Z. Mil.
Stratford, John Hugh, ensign, 3rd W. Regt.
Strong, Howard, trooper, Wan. Y. Cav.
Sturmer, Edward, constable, A. C.
Stevenson, John, private, Wan. Mil.
Stewart, Robert, trooper, Wan. Cav.
Stidolph, Sydney, constable, A. C.
Stower, Samuel, trooper, Wan. Cav.
Stevenson, James, corporal, Auck. Mil.
Styak, F. J., ensign, 4th W. Regt.
Stuart, William, private, 1st W. Regt.
Staunton, Robert, private, 1st W. Regt.
Stewart, Robert, private, 1st W. Regt.
Struthers, John, private, 1st W. Regt.
Stubbs, Walter, private, 1st W. Regt.
Stevenson, Malcombe, private, 1st W. Regt.
Steney, James, private, 1st W. Regt.
Starke, James, private, 1st W. Regt.
Stannett, Edward, private, 1st W. Regt.
Stubbings, Benj., private, 2nd W. Regt.
Stapleton, E., private, 2nd W. Regt.
Stevenson, James, private, 2nd W. Regt.
Stevenson, W. D., private, 2nd W. Regt.
Stubbs, Walter, private, 2nd W. Regt.
Stevenson, Matthew, private 2nd W. Regt.
Stevens, James, private, 3rd W. Regt.
Stallard, Francis, private, 3rd W. Regt.
Stewart, Robert, private, 3rd W. Regt.
Streeter, William, private, 3rd W. Regt.
Stewart, James, private, 3rd W. Regt.
Stevenson, George, private, 3rd W. Regt.
Staight, A. A., private, 3rd W. Regt.
Stewart, Robert, bullk. driver, Transpt. Corps.
Stevenson, James, bllk. driver, Transpt. Corps
Stroud, A., boatman, Transpt. Corps.
Stackpole, Sergeant, issuer, Com. Dept.
Stroud, C. A., issuer, Com. Dept.
Staunton, Thos., butcher, Com. Dept.

Stone, Sergeant Chas., baker, Com. Dept.
Stevenson, Wm., baker, Com. Dept.
Stuart, John, private, 1st W. Regt.
Strauchan, T. H., sergeant, A. C.
Stark, Winslow, sergeant, M. S.
Steven, John, private, Nap. Mil.
Stevens, George, private, Nap. Mil.
Strong, George, petty-officer, Auck. Navals
Stone, Charles, private, 1st W. Regt.
Stalker, M. L., captain, s. s. *Huntress*
Stockman, Edward, interpreter, Nap. Vol.
Stockman, George, private, Tar. Vol.
Stott, Abraham, sergeant, A. C.
Stapleton, Herman, private, Patea Mil.
Stribling, Joseph, private, Tar. Mil. Settlers
Stephenson, William, private, Forest Ran.
Stewart, Arthur, private, Wairoa Rifles
Stewart, M. G., private, Tar. Mil. Settlers
Sturm, Charles, private, Hawke's B. Vol.
Street, Sydney, private, 1st W. Regt.
Stark, James, corporal, Well. Rifles
Stewart, Henry, private, Tar. Mil. Settlers
Stewart, James, trooper, Wan. Cav.
St. Clair, John, trooper, Col. D. Force
Steed, John, private, Nap. Mil.
Strode, Alfred C., sub-inspector, A. C.
Standish Arthur, ensign, Tar. Mil.
Stevens, Walter V., private, Auck. Vol.
St. George, Edwin, private, Tar. Mil.
Stuart, William, private, Tar. Mil.
Sutherland, David, private, 1st W. Regt.
Summers, Henry, private, 1st W. Regt.
Sutton, William, private, 1st W. Regt.
Sullivan, Patrick, private, 1st W. Regt.
Summerway, Robert, corporal, 2nd W. Regt.
Sutherland, James, private, 2nd W. Regt.
Sutherland, Alex., private, 3rd W. Regt.
Sutton, Thomas, private, 3rd W. Regt.
Sullivan, James, private, 3rd W. Regt.
Sugar, Lockwood, private, 3rd W. Regt.
Sullivan, John, private, 3rd W. Regt.
Sullivan, Jeremiah, sergeant, 2nd W. Regt.
Sutherland, D., bullock-driver, Transpt. Corps
Sutherland, James G., private, Tar. Vol.
Sumsion, Charles, private, Forest Ran.
Sutherland, Donald, constable, A.C.
Sullivan, John, private, Tar. Mil. Settlers
Summers, Fred., private, 1st W. Regt.
Swainson, H. Gabriel, private, Hutt Mil.
Swainson, W. J., interpreter, Col. Forces
Swanson, William, private, 2nd W. Regt.
Sweeney, James, private, 3rd W. Regt.
Swakwassar, William, private, 3rd W. Regt.
Swan, John, private, 1st W. Regt.
Swan, William, constable, A.C.
Sweyne, William, private, 3rd W. Regt.
Swan, John, private, Tar. Mil. Settlers
Swindley, Fred., sub-inspector
Swan, George H., private, Napier Mil.
Sykes, John, private, 1st W. Regt.
Sylvester, James, private, 3rd W. Regt.

Tatton, W. G., private, Tar. Vol.
Tatton, William, private, Tar. Mil.

Vance, Robert, constable, A. C.
Vandersen, Alex., private, Tar. Mil. Settlers
Vaughan, Matthew, private, Forest Rangers
Veickman, Henry, private, 3rd W. Regt.
Veckness, —, issuer, Com. Dept.
Veal, Thomas, sergeant, Tar. Vol.
Vercoe, William, private, Tar. Vol.
Villers, Joseph, trooper, Wan. Cav.
Vining, James, private, Nap. Mil.
Vivian, William, trooper, Wan. Cav.
Vickers, E. C., ensign, 3rd W. Regt.
Vincent, Richard B., constable, A. C.
Vickers, William, private, Nap. Mil.
Viliars, Edmond, constable, A. C.
Villers, Charles, private, Volunteer
Vivian, Charles, trooper, Col. D. Force
Von Sturmer, Fredk. J., private, Auck. Vol.
Von Rotter, Louis, ensign, Tar. Mil. Settlers
Von Tempsky, G. F., major, N. Z. Mil.
Vragnizan, Peter, private, Auck. Mil.
Vyse, Euclid, private, 1st W. Regt.

WALLIS, HENRY, private, Tar. Vol.
Wall, Silas, trooper, Wan. Cav.
Wallace, John, trumpeter, Kai Iwi Cav.
Warne, G. M., constable, A. C.
Watson, Wm., private, 1st W. Regt.
Watt, A., trooper, Kai Iwi Cav.
Watts, J. R., sub-inspector, A. C.
Walton, George, artificer, Auck. Mil.
Way, H. F., lieutenant, 2nd W. Regt.
Wardell, F. G., ensign, 3rd W. Regt.
Watson, John, private, 1st W. Regt.
Walsh, Patrick, private, 1st W. Regt.
Waterson, George, artificer, 1st W. Regt.
Watt, Robert, private, 1st W. Regt.
Walton, James, private, 1st W. Regt.
Way, Francis, artificer, 2nd W. Regt.
Walters, George, private, 2nd W. Regt.
Warden, John, private, 2nd W. Regt.
Warmington, Ernest, private, 2nd W. Regt.
Wainwright, Chas., corporal, 3rd W. Regt.
Wall, James, private, 3rd W. Regt.
Waring, Charles, private, 3rd W. Regt.
Wall, William, private, 3rd W. Regt.
Waters, George, private, 3rd W. Regt.
Waters, Thos., private, 3rd W. Regt.
Waddington, Henry, private, 3rd W. Regt.
Walters, John, private, 3rd W. Regt.
Warner, Richard, private, 3rd W. Regt.
Waterton, R., bullock-driver, Transpt. Corps
Waters, Edward, clerk, Com. Dept.
Watson, Sergt. Henry, issuer, Com. Dept.
Watson, Sergt. Wm., issuer, Com. Dept.
Way, T., baker, Com. Dept.
Wade, T., boatman, Transpt. Corps
Walmsley, William, private, 1st W. Regt.
Watts, W. J., private, Auck. D. Force
Way, Thomas, private, 1st W. Regt.
Wadsworth, John, private, 1st W. Regt.
Washy, E. Oliver, private, 2nd W. Regt.
Watt, Robert, private, 1st W. Regt.
Waldon, Otto, constable, A.C.
Wadman, George, trooper, Col. D. Force

Watkins, William, sergeant, Tar. Vol.
Watts, W. T., trooper, Col. D. Force
Watson, W. F., private, Tar. Mil. Settlers
Walters, Richard, constable, A.C.
Watt, Isaac N., captain, N. Z. Mil.
Wakeford, Alfred, constable, A.C.
Walton, T. F., constable, A.C.
Waite, William, private, Nap. Mil.
Walsh, William, private, H. B. Mil.
Washington, William, constable, A.C.
Walden, James, corporal, Well. Rifles
Warhurst, Sol., lance-corporal, Tar. Vol.
Waters, George, constable, A.C.
Waters, Thomas, sergeant, Wan. Mil.
Waite, Thomas, private, Tar. Mil.
Watson, William, corporal, H. B. Mil
Wallace, William, sergeant, A.C.
Wallace, Richard, private, Well. Ran.
Waters, John, private, 1st W. Regt.
Wakefield, Alfred, constable, A.C.
Walter, James, sergeant, F. Rangers
Walker, Samuel, assist.-surgeon, N. Z. Mil.
Walker, G. P., captain, 1st W. Regt.
Walker, Daniel, private, 2nd W. Regt.
Walker, James K., private, 1st W. Regt
Walker, Robert, private, 3rd W. Regt.
Walker, Wm. Baker, corporal, Tar. Mil.
Walker, Alex. N., private, Tar. Mil.
Walker, Daniel, private, 2nd W. Regt.
Walker, Isaac, private, Col. D. Force
Walker, Benjamin, private, Tar. Mil. Settlers
Walker, John, private, Well. Rifles
Walker, Thos. Henry, private, Col. D. Force
Walker, Charles, private, Tar. Vol.
Ward, James, private, Tar. Mil. Settlers
Ward, Joe, private, Tar. Mil. Settlers
Ward, John, sergeant, Forest Rangers
Ward, C. E., private, Tar. Bush Rangers
Ward, Fred. W., private, Tar. Bush Rangers
Ward, Patrick, sergeant, Tar. Mil. Settlers
Ward, George, private, Forest Rangers
Ward, John, private, Tar. Vol.
Ward, Daniel, private, 3rd W. Regt.
Ward, John, private, 3rd W. Regt.
Ward, W., labourer, Com. Dept.
Weeks, Henry, surgeon, Auck. Mil.
Webster, William Dawson, private, Tar. Vol.
Webster, F. Lewis, captain, Tar. Vol.
Weston, Warwick, corporal, Tar. Vol.
Webb, James, constable, A.C.
Weston, Henry, private, 1st W. Regt.
Wellesley, Arthur, private, 1st W. Regt.
Webb, Joseph, corporal, 2nd W. Regt.
Weston, N., artificer, 2nd W. Regt.
Webb, Joseph, private, 2nd W. Regt.
West, William, private, 2nd W. Regt.
Weild, John, private, 3rd W. Regt.
Wells, William, private, 3rd W. Regt.
Webb, Edward, private, 3rd W. Regt.
Westbrook, J., blck. driver, Transpt. Corps
Wells, R., bullock driver, Transpt. Corps
Webber, B., clerk, Com. Dept.
Wells, Robert, sergeant, Tar. Vol.
Welch, M. P., private, 1st W. Regt.

Welsman, J. S., private, Auck. Vol.
West, James, corporal, 1st W. Regt.
Webb, H. E., ensign, Nap. Vol.
Wells, R., petty officer, Auck. Navals
Weatherley, James, constable, A. C.
Westrupp, Charles, major, Forest Rangers
Wellsted, G. G., trooper, Wan. Cav.
West, Henry, trooper, P. L. Cav,
Webster, Edward, private, 2nd W. Regt.
Weston, W. J., private, Tar. Vol.
Wheeler, Allen, private, Mauku Vol.
Whiteside, Samuel, private, 2nd W. Regt.
Whitson, Thomas, private, Auck. Vol.
Whitney, Robert, corporal, Auck. Mil.
Whitlow, W. E., corporal, 1st W. Regt.
Whelan Patrick, private, 2nd W. Regt.
Wheeler, Walter, private, 2nd W. Regt.
Wheeler, John, pr vate, 3rd W. Regt.
Whittle, John, bullock driver, Transpt. Corps
Whitaker, Thos., conductor, Transpt. Corps
Wharton, Charles B., A.D.C. Staff
Whitewell, Thomas, private, Tar. Mil.
Whitehead, Joseph, constable, A. C.
Wheeler, Thomas, private, Tar. Mil.
Whitcombe, W. E., private, Tar. Mil. Settlers
Whiting, John, private, E. C.
Whelan, Thomas, constable, A. C.
Whatmore, Edw., private, Tar. Mil. Settlers
Whitelock, George, private, Patea Rifles
Whelan, William, private, Patea Rifles
Wheeler, John, private, M. Vol.
Whitfield, Robert, ensign, Forest Ran.
Whiteman, George, private, Well. Mil.
White, John, private, 1st W. Regt.
White, John, native commissioner, F. Force
White, W. Bertram, ensign, Well. Mil.
White, John, private, 1st W. Regt.
White, Adair, private, 3rd W. Regt.
White, Alfred, constable, A. C.
White, George, private, Wan. Mil.
Wilkes, J. Collins, private, Auck. Vol.
Wilkinson, George T., private, Vol. Engineers
Wilcocks, E. Smyth, bugler, Tar. Vol.
Wills, Thomas, private, Tar. Vol.
Winchcombe, W., sergeant, Tar. Mil. Settlers
Wicksteed, Arthur, trooper, Kai Iwi Cav.
Wilkie, John, private, Wairoa Vol.
Williamson, Francis, private, Guide
Witchell, H. W., ensign, Wan. Mil.
Winter, Jeremiah, sergeant, Auck. Mil.
Wildrow, Joseph, private, 1st W. Regt.
Wigney, Frederick, private, 1st W. Regt.
Wilkinson, Benjamin, private, 1st W. Regt.
Willis, Philip, private, 1st W. Regt.
Wiseman, John, private, 1st W. Regt.
Winter, William, artificer, 2nd W. Regt.
Winepress, William, private, 2nd W. Regt.
Williamson, William, private, 2nd W. Regt.
Williamson, Henry, private, 2nd W. Regt.
Wick, John, private, 2nd W. Regt.
Wiesbadin, William, sergeant, 3rd W. Regt.
Wigmore, Joseph, sergeant, 3rd W. Regt.
Williamson, James, corporal, 3rd W. Regt.
Wilkinson, Alfred, private, 3rd W. Regt.

Wilkinson, Samuel, private, 3rd W. Regt.
Wighton, Charles, private, 3rd W. Regt.
Wight, Thomas, private, 3rd W. Regt.
Wild, Samuel, private, 3rd W. Regt.
Will, Wm., bullock driver, Transpt. Corps.
Wilkinson, John W., private, Tar. Mil.
Winslow, Wm., constable, A. C.
Willison, George, sergeant, A. C.
Windsor, Fredk., private, Tar. Vol.
Withers, Thos., sub-inspector, A. C,
Witty, J. W., lieutenant, N. Z. Mil.
Williamson, George, private, Pov. Bay Mil.
Wilks, John, private, 1st W. Regt.
Williamson, John, private, 3rd W. Regt.
Windsor, Henry, private, Tar. Vol.
Witherley, Chas. H., private, 1st W. Regt.
Wilks, Henry, private, Wan. Ran.
Wixey, Thomas, private, H. B. Mil.
Williamson, Charles, constable, A.C.
Wilkinson, J. F., private, Tar. Mil. Settlers
Williamson, William, private, 1st W. Regt.
Williams, Isaac, private, Nap. Mil.
Williams, James, sergeant, F. Rangers
Williams, Richard, private, Nap. Mil.
Williams, John, private, 1st W. Regt.
Williams, Thomas, private, 2nd W. Regt.
Williams, Henry, private, 3rd W. Regt.
Williams, Francis, private, 3rd W. Regt.
Williams, John, private, 3rd W. Regt.
Williams, R., butcher, Com. Dept.
Williams, George, private, Tar. Mil.
Williams, G. W., lieutenant, N.Z. Mil
Williams, H. J., sergeant, Tar. Mil. Settlers
Williams, Thomas, private, Tar. Mil. Settlers
Williams, H. L., captain, 2nd W. Regt.
Williams, Saml. J., lieutenant, Auck. N. Vol.
Wilson, Thomas, private, Tar. Mil. Settlers
Wilson, John, captain, Nap. Mil.
Wilson, Chas. James, sub-inspector, A. C.
Wilson, P. G., captain, Tar. Vol.
Wilson, Stewart, private, 1st W. Regt.
Wilson, Peter, private, 1st W. Regt.
Wilson, John, private, 1st W. Regt.
Wilson, William, private, 1st W. Regt.
Wilson, James, private, 1st W. Regt.
Wilson, Frederick, private, 2nd W. Regt.
Wilson, J. R. S., private, 2nd W. Regt.
Wilson, Charles, corporal, 3rd W. Regt.
Wilson, Joseph, private, 3rd W. Regt.
Wilson, James, private, 3rd W. Regt.
Wilson, John, private, 3rd W. Regt.
Wilson, Thos., boatman, Com. T. Corps
Wilson, B., boatman, Com. T. Corps
Wilson, T., baker, Com. Dept.
Wilson, J. E., private, Wan. Mil.
Wilson, Peter, private, Nap. Mil.
Wilson, William, private, Tar. Vol.
Wilson, Edward, private, 1st W. Regt.
Wilson, P. C., constable, A. C.
Wilson, J., lieutenant, P. B. Mil. Settlers
Wood, J. M., serjeant, Nap. Mil.
Wood, Reader G., lieutenant, Auck. Mil.
Woolfield, T. R., trooper, Auck. Cav.
Worgan, G., interpreter to forces

Wooley, James, private, Auck. Engineers
Wood, Wm., private, 1st W. Regt.
Worthington, H. C., sergeant, 1st W. Regt.
Woodcock, Thomas, private, 2nd W. Regt.
Woodcock, Alfred, private, 2nd W. Regt.
Worseman, Edward, private, 2nd W. Regt.
Woods, Charles, private, 2nd W. Regt.
Woods, Albert, private, 3rd W. Regt.
Wooliscroft, Henry, private, 3rd W. Regt.
Woodlock, John, private, 3rd W. Regt.
Woolley, William, private, 3rd W. Regt.
Worthington, George, private, 3rd W. Regt.
Wooliscroft, Edward, private, 3rd W. Regt.
Woods, Robt., bullock-driver, Transpt. Corps
Wood, A., coxswain, Transpt. Corps
Wormington, George, clerk, Com. Dept.
Woodward, John, issuer, Com. Dept.
Wooster, Thos., labourer, Com. Dept.
Woon, Garland W., private, Tar. Mil.
Woodruffe, H. S., sergeant, A.C.
Worthington, A., sergeant, A.C.
Wood, Edwd. L., private, 1st W. Regt.
Wolf, Thomas, private, Tar. Mil. Settlers
Woodward, James, private, Hawke's B. Mil.
Worms, Joseph, private, Auck, Mil.
Woods, Henry, private, Well. Rifles
Woouldom, Henry, private, Well. Rifles
Wreford, Chas. R., sergeant, Nap. D. Force
Wrigg, Harry C. W., private, Auck. Mil.
Wray, C. A., lieutenant, E. C.
Wright, Edward, private, Tar. Vol.
Wright, G. S., trooper, Kai Iwi Cav.
Wright, Henry, trooper, Wan. Cav.
Wright, Thomas, private, 1st W. Regt.

Wright, William, sergeant, 2nd W. Regt.
Wright, John, private, 3rd W. Regt.
Wright, Thomas, boatman, Transpt. Corps
Wright, H., boatman, Transpt. Corps
Wright, Samuel, constable, A. C.
Wright, Thomas, private, Tar. Mil. Settlers
Wright, David, trooper, Tar. Cav.
Wroth, Digory, private, 1st W. Regt.
Wren, Thomas, sergeant, 3rd W. Regt.
Wyatt, Edward, private, 2nd W. Regt.
Wyon, James, constable, A. C.
Wylass, James, private, 1st W. Regt.
Wyllie, James, interpreter, Col. D. Force

YATES, G. W., lieutenant, 2nd W. Regt.
Yates, W. W., private, Nap. Mil.
Yeates, G. W., captain, 2nd W. Regt.
Yondan, W. A., corporal, Tar. Mil. Settlers
Young, John, trooper, Wan. Cav.
Young, James, sergeant, Auck. Mil.
Young, John, private, 1st W. Regt.
Young, George, private, 1st W. Regt.
Young, W. J., private, 2nd W. Regt.
Young, Daniel, private, 2nd W. Regt.
Young, W., bullock driver, Transp. Corps
Young, Corporal T., boatman, Trans. Corps
Young, John, private, 1st W. Regt.
Young, David, private, 1st W. Regt.
Young, James, private, Tar. Mil. Settlers
Young, George, private, 1st W. Regt.
Young, Thomas, constable, A. C.
Young, John, private, Nap. Mil.

ZIELESTIERE, SAMUEL, private, 3rd W. Regt.
Zornig, Henry, constable, A. C.

NOMINAL RETURN

Of Officers and Men of the Colonial Force who were Killed by the Natives in Action.—1860—70.

Name.	Rank.	Corps.	Date of Death.
Alexander, H...	Corporal	Colonial Defence Force	Feb. 21, 1864
Appleby, James	Sergeant	Taranaki Military Settlers	March 25, '64
Armstrong, John Alexander	Corporal	3rd Waikato Regiment	April 2, '64
Banks, John	Corporal	Taranaki Military Settlers	April 6, '64
Banks, James	Constable	Armed Constabulary	Feb. 18, '69
Barris, Abel	Constable	Armed Constabulary	Feb. 18, '69
Barth, Robert	Constable	Armed Constabulary	Feb. 18, '69
Beysick, W.	Private	1st Waikato Regiment	October 23, '63
Best, Francis Eldred	Private	Forest Rangers	May 14, '65
Bedois, Joseph	Trooper	Tauranga Cavalry	June 8, '69
Beamish, Allen	Constable	Armed Constabulary	July 12, '68
Biggs, Reginald	Major	New Zealand Militia	Nov. 10, '68
Borthwick, Christopher	Private	Hawke's Bay Mil. Settlers	October 4, '65
Borthwick, David	Private	Hawke's Bay Mil. Settlers	Nov. 18, '65
Bonaparte, —.	Constable	Armed Constabulary	March 13, '69
Boyle, Connell	Constable	Armed Constabulary	Feb. 18, '69
Blake, John	Corporal	Armed Constabulary	July 12, '68
Brewer, S.	Private	Patea Rifle Volunteers	Nov. 7, '68
Brown, Francis	Private	Taranaki Militia	Nov. 6, '60
Brown, Thomas Melville	Private	4th Waikato Regiment	October 5, '65
Brown, Duncan Michie	Sub-inspector	Armed Constabulary	January '69
Brown, Samuel	Private	Patea Rifle Volunteers	Nov. 9, '68
Brown, Samuel	Constable	Armed Constabulary	Nov. 9, '68
Buck, George	Captain	Wellington Rifles	Sept. 7, '68
Byrne, P.	Constable	Armed Constabulary	August 8, '68
Cahill, David	Sergeant	Wanganui Militia	June 9, '68
Cadle, John	Trooper	Mounted Rifles	Nov. 10, '68
Carr, Oswald	Captain	Royal Artillery	August 8, '68
Canning, James Davis	Settler	Volunteer	August 8, '68
Chislett, James	Constable	Armed Constabulary	January 3, '69
Clark, William	Private	Wanganui Militia	June 9, '68
Clarendon, Alfred Henry	Private	Wanganui Militia	June 9, '68
Clowen, Matthew	Private	Wanganui Militia	Feb. 18, '69
Coates, W.	Private	Wanganui Militia	August 8, '68
Coghlan, Charles	Private	Forest Rangers	April 2, '64
Cole, George	Constable	Armed Constabulary	Nov. 7, '68
Cooper, John	Private	Wairoa Volunteers	April 10, '69
Collins, T.	Lance-corporal	Patea Yeomanry Cavalry	October 16, '68
Condon, P.	Constable	Armed Constabulary	August 8, '68
Cook, John	Trooper	Poverty Bay Cavalry	June 8, '69
Cummings, Thomas	Constable	Armed Constabulary	Jan. 26, '69
Darlington, Robert Francis	Constable	Armed Constabulary	Sept. 7, '68
Davis, Israel	Constable	Armed Constabulary	Sept. 7, '68
Davis, Robert	Constable	Armed Constabulary	May 7, '69
Deeks, John Hicks	Private	Taranaki Military Settlers	Sept. 7, '68
Devon, J.	Private	Patea Yeomanry Cavalry	Sept. 7, '68
Deerlove, —.	Lance-corporal	Hawke's Bay Mil. Settlers	October 11, '65
Dodd, G. N.	Lieutenant	New Zealand Militia	Nov. 10, '68
Doonan, William	Sergeant	Hawke's Bay Mil. Settlers	Nov. 18, '65
Downs, William Henry	Constable	Armed Constabulary	Sept. 7, '68
Donald, Donald	Trooper	Bay of Plenty Cavalry	June 6, '68
Duff, Francis DeCourcy	Sergeant	Wanganui Yeo. Cavalry	October 2, '66
Dwyer, James	Constable	Armed Constabulary	August 21, '68
Eastwood, Charles	Constable	Armed Constabulary	Sept. 7, '68
Economedes, Hercules	Private	Wanganui Rangers	Nov. 3, '66
Edgecombe, Henry	Private	Taranaki Militia	Nov 6, '60

Name.	Rank.	Corps.	Date of Death.
Elkin, Alexander	Constable	Armed Constabulary	Sept. 7, '68
Emus, Henry	Sergeant-major	1st Waikato Regiment	Jan. 18, '67
Edwards, Richard	Lieutenant	Taranaki Militia	Feb. 14, '69
Fahey, —.	Sergeant	Taranaki Militia	March 28, '60
Farrand, Edward George	Constable	Armed Constabulary	Sept. 7, '68
Fennessy, Richard	Constable	Armed Constabulary	Sept. 7, '68
Fergusson, Finlay	Trooper	Poverty Bay Cavalry	Dec. 12, '68
Fleurs, Thomas	Guide	New Zealand Militia	March 13, '69
Gascoigne, B.	Lieutenant	Taranaki Militia	Feb. 14, '69
Gallagher, John	Private	Taranaki Military Settlers	April 6, '64
Gaynor, William	Constable	Armed Constabulary	July 12, '68
Gearey, Joseph	Private	Wellington Rifles	August 21, '68
Gilgan, Joseph	Constable	Armed Constabulary	Sept. 7, '68
Gill, Frederick	Trooper	Tauranga Cavalry	June 8, '69
Glennon, Martin	Constable	Armed Constabulary	Nov. 30, '68
Greaves, Chas. Marmaduke	Private	Hawke's Bay Mil. Settlers	October 3, '65
Green, —.	Private	Wanganui Rangers	October 2, '66
Grant, Thomas	Private	Wellington Rifles	Sept. 7, '68
Gundry, Frederick	Corporal	Armed Constabulary	March 13, '69
Guerin, Jean	Civilian	Whakatane	March 9, '69
Hanly, C.	Trooper	Wanganui Yeo. Cavalry	Nov. '66
Hartley, Charles	Private	Taranaki Military Settlers	April 6, '64
Hart, Richard	Constable	Armed Constabulary	Sept. 7, '68
Hastings, Hy. Chas. Holland	Lieutenant	Wellington Rangers	Sept. 7, '68
Hegarty, M.	Trooper	Wanganui Yeo. Cavalry	Sept. '66
Herford, Walter Vernon	Major	3rd Waikato Regiment	April 2, '64
Holden, George	Constable	Armed Constabulary	July 12, '68
Horspool, George	Lance-corporal	Armed Constabulary	Feb. 18, '69
Howe, John	Constable	Armed Constabulary	Feb. 18, '69
Hunter, Henry	Lieutenant	Wellington Rangers	Sept. 7, '68
Hughes, George	Private	Wellington Rangers	Sept. 7, '68
Hunter, William Magee	Inspector	Armed Constabulary	Nov. 7, '68
Hussey, William Augustus	Captain	Taranaki Military Settlers	Dec. 25, '65
Hunter, B.	Constable	Armed Constabulary	January '70
Jeffs, Henry	Volunteer	1st Waikato Regiment	Feb. 15, '67
Johnston, Charles	Trooper	Tauranga Cavalry	June 8, '69
Jordan, Thomas Edward	Private	Engineers	Feb. 15, '67
Kelly, James	Constable	Armed Constabulary	Nov. 7, '68
Kelty, Edward	Lance-corporal	Armed Constabulary	May 8, '69
Keneally, William	Private	Patea Rifle Volunteers	Nov. 7, '68
Kerr, William A.	Private	Wellington Rangers	August 21, '68
Kerwin, Edwin	Sergeant	Armed Constabulary	Nov. 7, '68
Lavin, J. P. M.	Lieutenant	Wairoa Volunteers	March 13, '69
Lawson, Ernest	Ensign	Auckland Militia	June 8, '69
Lees, William	Constable	Armed Constabulary	Nov. 7, '68
Lemon, Richard	Civilian	Storekeeper	July 18, '68
Leckey, John	Private	2nd Waikato Regiment	May 31, '64
Little, Thomas	Corporal	Colonial Defence Force	Feb. 21, '64
Lumsden, George	Lance-corporal	Wellington Rifles	Sept. 7, '68
Mann, John	Trooper	Mounted Rifles	Nov. 10, '68
Martin, Robert	Private	Hawke's Bay Mil. Settlers	Nov. 18, '65
Mackie, John	Constable	Armed Constabulary	August 21, '68
Maxwell, George	Sergeant	Kai Iwi Cavalry	Dec. 28, '68
Menzies, George	Sergeant	Armed Constabulary	Feb. 18, '69
Melvin, John	Volunteer	Taranaki	Sept. 7, '68
Morrison, Henry	Private	Napier Rifle Volunteers	October 26, '66
Moran, John	Private	New Zealand Militia	Nov. 10, '68
Milne, John	Private	Taranaki Militia	Feb. 14, '69
McBean, John	Private	Forest Rangers	May 13, '65
McCulloch, John	Trooper	Mounted Rifles	Nov. 10, '68
McEwen, John	Constable	Armed Constabulary	January 3, '69
McDonald, Donald	Trooper	Bay of Plenty Cavalry	June 6, '69
McFadden, John	Sergeant	Armed Constabulary	July 12, '68
McGillavray, Farquhar	Private	1st Waikato Regiment	October 23, '63
McGiven, —.	Constable	Armed Constabulary	January 1, '69
McHale, Edward	Constable	Colonial Defence Force	Feb. 21, '64
McKenzie, Thomas	Constable	Armed Constabulary	Jan. 26, '69
Newenham, A.,	Trooper	Poverty Bay Mounted Rifles	Nov. 10, '68
Neagle, James	Private	Taranaki Military Settlers	April 6, '64
Newman, —.	Sergeant	Armed Constabulary	June 10, '69
Nixon, Marmaduke George	Colonel	Auckland Militia	Feb. 21, '64
Nicholls, William	Constable	Armed Constabulary	Nov. 7, '68
Nogus, —.	Constable	Armed Constabulary	Nov. 7, '68
Norman, Peter	Constable	Armed Constabulary	Nov. 7, '68
Norman, Thomas	Lieutenant	Auckland Militia	October 23, '63
Noonan, —.	Trooper	Armed Constabulary	June 10, '69
O'Born, George	Private	1st Waikato Regiment	Oct. 23, '63
O'Connor, John	Constable	Armed Constabulary	Sept. 7, '68
Padbury, James	Sergeant	Mounted Rifles	
Parsons, Patrick	Private	Expeditionary Force	October 5, '65

Name.	Rank.	Corps.	Date of Death.
Palmer, Alfred Picking	Captain	Patea Rifle Volunteers	Sept. 7, '68
Path, James	Constable	Armed Constabulary	Nov. 7, '68
Parkinson, John	Constable	Armed Constabulary	May 8, '69
Peppard, Richard	Trooper	Mounted Rifles	Nov. 10, '68
Perceval, John Spencer	Lieutenant	Auckland Militia	October 23, '63
Pierson, William	Lance-corporal	Hawke's Bay Mil. Settlers	Nov. 18, '65
Pitcairn, Robert	Surveyor	Whakatane	March 3, '69
Poictiers, Charles	Trooper	Tauranga Cavalry	June 8, '69
Power, M.	Corporal	1st Waikato Regiment	October 23, '63
Poole, G.	Constable	Armed Constabulary	Nov. 7, '68
Pearson, —.	Constable	Armed Constabulary	May 7, '69
Rathbone, C.	Trooper	Mounted Rifles	Nov. 10, '68
Ratsey, Charles	Private	Expeditionary Force	October 5, 65
Reed, Samuel	Sergeant	Armed Constabulary	Dec. 13, '68
Ross, Gillian Hector	Lieutenant	Auckland Militia	June 8, '69
Ross, Frederick	Sub-inspector	Armed Constabulary	July 12, '68
Ross, Ralph	Constable	Armed Constabulary	July 12, '68
Rogers, Frederick Samuel	Constable	Armed Constabulary	Nov. 7, '68
Russell, James	Corporal	Armed Constabulary	Sept. 7, '68
Sarten, John Edmonds	Private	Taranaki Militia	March 26, '60
Salter, George	Constable	Armed Constabulary	Nov. 7, '68
Savage, Joseph	Constable	Armed Constabulary	Nov. 7, '68
Sawyer, Charles	Constable	Armed Constabulary	January 2, '69
Shields, Patrick	Constable	Armed Constabulary	July 12, '68
Smith, —.	Constable	Armed Constabulary	Sept. 30, '68
Smith, James	Constable	Armed Constabulary	March 13, '69
Smith, Thomas	Constable	Armed Constabulary	June 12, '68
Spain, Denis	Private	Taranaki Military Settlers	August 2, '66
Stevenson, William	Private	1st Waikato Regiment	Jan. 23, '69
Stevenson, James	Constable	Armed Constabulary	March 13, '69
Swords, Edward	Private	Hawke's Bay Militia	Nov. 18, '65
Swords, Peter	Constable	Armed Constabulary	July 12, '68
Stockfish, Charles Newman	Corporal	Patea Rifle Volunteers	Nov. 7, '68
Slattery, Michael	Sergeant	Tauranga Cavalry	June 8, '69
St. George, John Chapman	Captain	Napier Militia	October 4, '69
Squires, Thomas	Private	Wanganui Militia	June 9, '68
Taylor, William	Sergeant	Forest Rangers	April 2, '64
Thompson, Richard	Constable	Armed Constabulary	Nov. 7, '68
Travers, Henry Boyle	Sub-inspector	Armed Constabulary	May 8, '69
Urquhart, Douglas	Constable	Armed Constabulary	Nov. 7, '68
Vance, William	Constable	Armed Constabulary	Nov. 7, '68
Von Tempsky, Gustavus F.	Inspector	Armed Constabulary	Sept. 7, '68
Walsh, R.	Constable	Armed Constabulary	Sept. 7, '68
Walsh, James	Lieutenant	Mounted Rifles	Nov. 10, '68
Ward, Denis Augustus	Private	1st Waikato Regiment	Jan. 23, '67
Wallace, Richard	Private	Wellington Rangers	August 21, '68
Watt, Charles	Corporal	Armed Constabulary	March 13, '69
White, David	Lieutenant	Opotiki Volunteers	May 7, '69
Whitley, Thomas	Constable	Armed Constabulary	Feb. 3, '70
Wells, George	Private	Taranaki Rifle Volunteers	Sept. 7, '68
Whitfield, Robert	Ensign	2nd Waikato Regiment	March 13, '65
Wilkie, James	Private	Hawke's Bay Mil. Settlers	Nov. 18, '65
Williamson W.	Private	1st Waikato Regiment	October 23, '63
Wilson, James	Captain	New Zealand Militia	Nov. 10, '68
Worthington, William	Private	Mauku Volunteers	October 23, '68
Wright, William	Volunteer		October 2, '66
Wilkinson, Richard	Private	Wairoa Volunteers	April 10, '69